THE ROUTLEDGE HANDBOOK OF POPULISM IN THE ASIA PACIFIC

This handbook brings national and thematic case studies together to examine a variety of populist politics from local and comparative perspectives in the Asia Pacific. The chapters consider key and cross cutting themes such as populism and nationalism, religion, ethnicity and gender, as well as authoritarianism. They show how populist politics alters the way governments mediate state-society relations.

The essays in this volume consider:

- diverse approaches in populist politics, for example, post-colonial, strategic vs ideational, growth and redistribution, leadership styles, and in what ways they are similar to, or different from, populist discourses in Europe and the United States;
- under what social, political, economic and structural conditions populist politics has emerged in the Asia-Pacific region;
- national case studies drawn from South, East and Southeast Asia as well as the Pacific analyzing themes such as media, religion, gender, medical populism, corruption and cronyism, and inclusive vs exclusive forms of populist politics;
- modes and techniques of social and political mobilization that populist politicians employ to influence people and their impact on the way democracy is conceived and practiced in the Asia Pacific.

As a systematic account of populist ideologies, strategies, leaders and trends in the Asia Pacific, this handbook is essential reading for scholars of area studies, especially in the Asia Pacific, politics and international relations, and political and social theory.

D. B. Subedi is Lecturer in Peace and Conflict Studies in the School of Political Science and International Studies at the University of Queensland, Australia.

Howard Brasted is Emeritus Professor of History specializing in Islamic history at the School of Humanities, Arts and Social Sciences at the University of New England, Australia.

Karin von Strokirch is Adjunct Senior Lecturer in Politics and International Relations at the University of New England, Australia.

Alan Scott is Professor in the Department of Social and Philosophical Inquiry, University of New England, Australia, and Professor of Sociology (i.R.) at the University of Innsbruck, Austria.

INDO-PACIFIC IN CONTEXT

This series brings together topical research on contemporary and long-standing issues encompassing the Asia-Pacific region.

With countries steeped in history, communities diverse in cultures, developing economies and emerging markets, the Asia Pacific has emerged as the key stakeholder in a world order in flux. The region has solidified its presence in the global political discourse through multilateral initiatives, defence agreements, and strategic partnerships. It has emerged as a zone of contestations, conflict, and cooperation.

The works published in this series showcase interdisciplinary research in the arts, the humanities, and the social sciences, including a range of subject areas such as politics and international relations, international economy, sociology and social anthropology, women, gender and sexuality studies, history, geo-politics, military studies, area studies, cultural studies, environment and sustainability, development studies, migration studies, urban development, digital humanities, and science and technology studies.

Works in the series are published simultaneously in UK/US and South Asia editions, as well as in e-book format. We welcome a range of books aimed at furthering scholarship and understanding of the Asia-Pacific region. Authors and researchers interested in contributing to this series may get in touch with rioeditorial@tandfindia.com

HANDBOOK OF INDO-PACIFIC STUDIES
Edited by Barbara Kratiuk, Jeroen J. J. Van den Bosch, Aleksandra Jaskólska and Yoichiro Sato

JAPAN AND ITS PARTNERS IN THE INDO-PACIFIC
Engagements and Alignment
Edited by Srabani Roy Choudhury

For more information about this series, please visit: www.routledge.com/Indo-Pacific-in-Context/book-series/IPC

THE ROUTLEDGE HANDBOOK OF POPULISM IN THE ASIA PACIFIC

Edited by
D. B. Subedi, Howard Brasted,
Karin von Strokirch, and Alan Scott

LONDON AND NEW YORK

Designed cover image: © Getty Images

First published 2024
by Routledge
4 Park Square, Milton Park, Abingdon, Oxon OX14 4RN

and by Routledge
605 Third Avenue, New York, NY 10158

Routledge is an imprint of the Taylor & Francis Group, an informa business

© 2024 selection and editorial matter, D. B. Subedi, Howard Brasted, Karin von Strokirch, and Alan Scott; individual chapters, the contributors

The right of D. B. Subedi, Howard Brasted, Karin von Strokirch, and Alan Scott to be identified as the authors of the editorial material, and of the authors for their individual chapters, has been asserted in accordance with sections 77 and 78 of the Copyright, Designs and Patents Act 1988.

All rights reserved. No part of this book may be reprinted or reproduced or utilised in any form or by any electronic, mechanical, or other means, now known or hereafter invented, including photocopying and recording, or in any information storage or retrieval system, without permission in writing from the publishers.

The views and opinions expressed in this book are those of author and do not necessarily reflect the views and opinions of Routledge.

Trademark notice: Product or corporate names may be trademarks or registered trademarks, and are used only for identification and explanation without intent to infringe.

British Library Cataloguing-in-Publication Data
A catalogue record for this book is available from the British Library

ISBN: 978-0-367-70185-7 (hbk)
ISBN: 978-0-367-74877-7 (pbk)
ISBN: 978-1-003-16001-4 (ebk)

DOI: 10.4324/9781003160014

Typeset in Sabon
by Apex CoVantage, LLC

CONTENTS

List of contributors ix
List of tables xv
List of figures xvi
List of graphs xvii
Acknowledgements xviii

PART I
Introduction 1

1 Populism's shifting meanings and geographical diffusion 3
  Alan Scott, D. B. Subedi, Howard Brasted,
  and Karin von Strokirch

PART II
Approaches and key issues 19

2 Populism, nationalism, and national identity in Asia 21
  Howard Brasted and Imran Ahmed

3 The strategic approach to populism 37
  Paul D. Kenny

4 Between people power and state power: The ambivalence
  of populism in international relations 49
  Angelos Chryssogelos

5 Growth, redistribution, and populism in Asia   65
   Ming-Chang Tsai and Hsin-Hsin Pan

6 The populist radical right, gendered enemy, and religion:
   Perspectives from South Asia since 2014   77
   Shweta Singh

7 Charismatic leadership, leader democracy, and populism in Asia   89
   D. B. Subedi and Alan Scott

PART III
Cross-cutting themes   **105**

8 Populism, media, and communication in the Asia Pacific: A case
   study of Rodrigo Duterte and Pauline Hanson   107
   Kurt Sengul

9 Religion, secularism and populism in contemporary Asia   120
   D. B. Subedi and Francis K. G. Lim

10 Islam and populism in the Asia Pacific   134
   Ihsan Yilmaz and Syaza Shukri

11 Medical populism in the Asia Pacific   149
   Gideon Lasco and Vincen Gregory Yu

PART IV
National cases   **161**

12 'Inclusionary' populism and democracy in India   163
   Paul D. Kenny

13 From Zulfiqar Ali Bhutto to Imran Khan: A comparative analysis
   of populist leaders in Pakistan   176
   Zahid Shahab Ahmed

14 Variants of populism in Bangladesh: Implications of charisma,
   clientelism, cronyism, and corruption   190
   Habib Zafarullah

15 Gender, populism, and collective identity: A feminist analysis
    of the Maoist movement in Nepal   207
    Heidi Riley, Hanna Ketola, and Punam Yadav

16 Contemporary Sri Lanka: Nationalism meets 'soft populism'   223
    D. B. Subedi and Siri Hettige

17 Islamic nationalism, populism, and democratization in the Maldives   240
    Mosmi Bhim

18 Democracy icon or demagogue? Aung San Suu Kyi and
    authoritarian populism in Myanmar (Burma)   255
    Johanna Garnett

19 The Duterte phenomenon as authoritarian populism in the Philippines   270
    Bonn Juego

20 Gender, media, and populism: The vilification of first lady Ani
    Yudhoyono in the Indonesian online news media   288
    Jane Ahlstrand

21 Weaponizing populism: How Thailand's civil society went from
    anti-populism to anti-democracy campaigns   302
    Janjira Sombatpoonsiri

22 South Korea: Still the 'politics of the vortex'? A historical analysis
    of party solidarities and populism   316
    Kan Kimura

23 Patriotic songs and populism in Chinese politics   330
    Xiang Gao

24 Taiwanese populism in the shadow of China   343
    Guy C. Charlton and Yayut Yi-shiuan Chen

25 Populism in Japan: actors or institutions?   357
    Toru Yoshida

26 From populism to authoritarianism? The contemporary frame of
    politics in Australia   370
    Tim Battin

27 Man alone: Winston Peters and the populist tendency in New Zealand politics 383
    Luke D. Oldfield and Josh van Veen

28 Are Fiji's two military strongmen populists? 396
    Thomas A. J. White

    Index 412

CONTRIBUTORS

Jane Ahlstrand is Lecturer in Indonesian at the University of New England (NSW). Her Ph.D. examines the use of language in the Indonesian online news media to represent female politicians and their dynamic relationship with power. Specializing in critical discourse analysis, her research interests include power relations, political discourse, media discourse, Indonesian studies and gender studies. She is author of *Women, Media, and Power in Indonesia* (Routledge, 2022).

Imran Ahmed writes on religion, law and politics in late-colonial India and contemporary Pakistan. His current research projects focus on religion and politics, constitution-making and blasphemy laws in South Asia. He has published in leading journals of history, politics and law, including *South Asia*, the *Journal of Contemporary Asia*, *Third World Quarterly*, *The Round Table*, *Griffith Law Review* and the *Journal of Law, Religion and State*. He is co-editor of the volume *Religion, Extremism and Violence* (Palgrave, 2022).

Zahid Shahab Ahmed is Research Fellow at the Alfred Deakin Institute for Citizenship and Globalization, Deakin University. He is also Non-Resident Research Fellow at the National University of Singapore's Institute of South Asian Studies. Prior to joining Deakin University in 2016, he was Assistant Professor at the Centre for International Peace and Stability, National University of Sciences and Technology, Pakistan. He is the author of *Regionalism and Regional Security in South Asia: The Role of SAARC* (Routledge, 2013).

Tim Battin is an honorary associate of The Australia Institute, Canberra. His research interests range across contemporary politics, social democracy and labour parties, political disenchantment, neoliberalism and political economy.

Mosmi Bhim teaches the Bachelor of Applied Social Sciences (BASS) programme at the Fiji National University (FNU). For her Ph.D. research, she analyzed authoritarianism in small island states and focused on electoral authoritarianism in three case studies from Fiji, the Maldives, and the Seychelles. Her other research interests include elections, democratization, and civil and political rights.

Contributors

Howard Brasted is Emeritus Professor of History, specializing in Islamic history at the School of Humanities, Arts and Social Sciences at the University of New England (NSW). He is the co-director of the UNE Asia Network and was a long-time editor (1984–2001) of *South Asia: Journal of South Asian Studies*.

Guy C. Charlton is Associate Professor of Law at the University of New England (NSW). He is Adjunct Professor at Auckland University of Technology (New Zealand) and Curtin University. He has a Ph.D. in Law from the University of Auckland, a J.D. from the University of Wisconsin-Madison and an MA in international relations from the University of Toronto.

Angelos Chryssogelos is Senior Lecturer in Politics and International Relations at the School of Social Sciences, London Metropolitan University. He was Fellow at the Global Populism Cluster of the Weatherhead Center at Harvard and Jean Monnet Fellow at the Schuman Centre of the European University Institute. He is the co-editor (with Vedi Hadiz) of the 2017 special issue 'Populism in World Politics' in the *International Political Science Review* and author of *Party Systems and Foreign Policy Change in Liberal Democracies* (Routledge, 2021).

Xiang Gao is Senior Lecturer in Politics and International Relations at the University of New England (NSW). She has a Ph.D. in politics and international relations from the University of Auckland and an MA in international relations from the Johns Hopkins University School of Advanced International Studies and Nanjing University. Her research interests include China's international relations and comparative politics in the Asia Pacific.

Johanna Garnett is Senior Lecturer in Sociology and Peace Studies at the University of New England (NSW) and is a member of The Australian Sociological Association and the Australian Political Studies Association. Her research foci include social movements, everyday politics, and social and environmental justice, with a particular interest in youth as agents of social change. She has been engaged with Myanmar politics and activism since 2012, conducting extensive fieldwork and longitudinal research into a number of grassroots development initiatives in the country.

Siri Hettige is Emeritus Professor of Sociology at the University of Colombo in Sri Lanka. He held the position of Chair of Sociology at the same university from 1992 to 2016. He is also an adjunct professor at Royal Melbourne Institute of Technology (RMIT), Melbourne. He has published extensive research on such themes as youth, education, social and political conflict, social policy and governance and development. He has also held visiting faculty/researcher positions at a number of overseas universities and held the founding Sri Lanka chair position at the University of Heidelberg (2017).

Bonn Juego teaches on sustainability in the School of Business and Economics, University of Jyväskylä, Finland. Previously, he was Lecturer in World Politics at the University of Helsinki. He has also held visiting research fellowships at the Nordic Institute of Asian Studies, University of Copenhagen, and in the Southeast Asia Research Centre, City University of Hong Kong. He has written and published extensively, including recently on authoritarian populism, the concept of authoritarian neoliberalism and the political economy of Southeast Asia.

Contributors

Paul D. Kenny is Professor in the Institute for Humanities and Social Sciences at the Australian Catholic University. His research on populism, corruption and institutions has been published in journals including *The Journal of Politics* and the *British Journal of Political Science*. He is the award-winning author of three books, *Populism and Patronage: Why Populists Win Elections in India, Asia, and Beyond* (OUP, 2017), *Populism in Southeast Asia* (CUP, 2018), and *Why Populism? Political Strategy from Ancient Greece to the Present* (CUP, 2023).

Hanna Ketola is Postdoctoral Fellow at the University of York (UK). Her research explores war and peacebuilding with a particular focus on feminist understandings of agency and embodiment. She is currently a member of the UK Research and Innovation (UKRI)-funded 'Civil War Paths' project, where she works on feminist approaches to civil wars, focusing on Nepal. Hanna's research has been published in *Security Dialogue* and *International Political Sociology*.

Kan Kimura is Professor in the Graduate School of International Cooperation Studies at Kobe University, Japan. He has previously been a visiting scholar at Harvard University, Korea University, Australia National University, the Sejong Institute, and the University of Washington. He has published more than 17 books and numerous articles, and is an expert on the relationship between Korea and Japan.

Gideon Lasco is a physician, medical anthropologist and writer. He is Senior Lecturer at the University of the Philippines Diliman's Department of Anthropology, Research Fellow at Ateneo de Manila University's Development Studies Program, and Honorary Fellow at Hong Kong University's Centre for Criminology. He is currently doing comparative research on COVID-19 responses and pursuing language studies at the Universidad Nacional Autónoma de México.

Francis K. G. Lim is Associate Professor in the School of Social Sciences, Nanyang Technological University (NTU). His research interests revolve around religion and tourism in various Asian cultures and societies. He has conducted research in Nepal, Singapore, Tibet and various sites in China. His latest monograph is *Christianity and Social Engagement in China* (Routledge, 2021). He is the author of *Imagining the Good Life: Negotiating Culture and Development in Nepal Himalaya* (Brill, 2008) and the editor of *Christianity in Contemporary China: Socio-cultural Perspectives* (Routledge, 2013).

Luke D. Oldfield is Doctoral Scholar at the School of Social Sciences, Waipapa Taumata Rau, University of Auckland. He was Senior Research Assistant for the 2020 New Zealand Election Study and the 2017 iteration of Vote Compass. His research interests are interdisciplinary, contributing to the fields of political science, sociology and critical higher education.

Hsin-Hsin Pan is Assistant Professor of Sociology at Soochow University in Taiwan. She received her Ph.D. in political science from Michigan State University. Her research interests include political sociology, social psychology, survey methods and social foundation for political transformation in contemporary China. Her publications appear in the *Journal of Asian and African Studies*, *Journal of Contemporary China*, *International Relations of the Asia-Pacific*, *Democratization*, and *Global Asia*.

Contributors

Heidi Riley is Research Fellow in the School of Politics and International Relations, University College Dublin. Her research straddles multiple areas of peace and conflict scholarship, including work into insurgency and ideology, gender and masculinities, peace mediation and conflict-related trauma. She is the author of the *Rethinking Masculinities: Ideology, Identity and Change in the People's War in Nepal and its Aftermath* (Rowman and Littlefield, 2022). She is currently Co-Principal Investigator for the Talk4Peace project, which examines 'transformative mediation' as a mechanism for inclusive dialogue in peacebuilding.

Alan Scott is Professor in the Department of Social and Philosophical Inquiry, University of New England (NSW), and Professor of sociology (i.R.) at the University of Innsbruck, Austria. He has held visiting positions at CRASSH (University of Cambridge); Sciences Po, Paris (Vincent Wright Chair); and the Institute for Social Anthropology, Vienna. He is currently working on leadership and populism, and on political and intellectual debates in Vienna in the 1920s and 1930s. He is co-author (with Antonino Palumbo) of *Remaking Market Society* (Routledge, 2018).

Kurt Sengul is currently a sessional academic in the Department of Media and Communication at the University of Sydney. His research centres on the communicative strategies and discourses of the contemporary populist far-right in Australia.

Syaza Shukri is Assistant Professor at the Department of Political Science, Kulliyyah of Islamic Revealed Knowledge and Human Sciences, International Islamic University, Malaysia. Her area of specialization is in comparative politics, specifically in democratization and politics in the Middle East and Southeast Asia. Her current research interests include populism, identity politics, inter-ethnic relations, political Islam, geopolitics and gender studies, specifically in Muslim-majority contexts.

Shweta Singh is Senior Assistant Professor of International Relations at the South Asian University in New Delhi. She was recently appointed as the UN Women's International Expert on populism, nationalism and gender (Regional Office for Asia and the Pacific). She is co-editor (with Tiina Vaittinen and Catia Confortini) of a Rowman and Littlefield book series entitled *Feminist Studies on Peace, Justice and Violence*. Her primary areas of research are feminist international relations, the women, peace and security agenda (South Asia) and the contemporary politics of Afghanistan, Sri Lanka and Kashmir.

Janjira Sombatpoonsiri is Assistant Professor at the Institute of Asian Studies, Chulalongkorn University; Visiting Fellow at the ISEAS Yusof-Ishak Institute in Singapore; and Associate at the German Institute for Global and Area Studies, Hamburg. Her research focuses on nonviolent protests, social movements, civil society space and autocratic-digital repression. She is the author of *Humor and Nonviolent Struggle in Serbia* (Syracuse University Press, 2015). She is a member of the Carnegie Endowment for International Peace's Civic Research Network and Digital Democracy Network.

D. B. Subedi is a Lecturer in Peace and Conflict Studies in the School of Political Science and International Studies at the University of Queensland, Australia. His research interests include religion and politics, right-wing extremism, countering violent extremism, populism and nationalism, and conflict transformation and peacebuilding. He is the author of *Combatants to Civilians: Rehabilitation and Reintegration of Maoist Fighters in Nepal's Peace Process* (Palgrave, 2018) and co-editor of *Reconciliation in Conflict-Affected Communities* (Springer, 2018).

Ming-Chang Tsai (Ph.D., Stony Brook University) is Research Fellow and Deputy Director of the Research Center for Humanities and Social Sciences (RCHSS), Academia Sinica, Taiwan. He was President of the International Society for Quality of Life Studies, the Taiwanese Sociological Association, and the Research Committee of Social Indicators (RC55) of the International Sociological Association. His current research project focuses on growth, distribution and equality in East Asia. Recent books include *Global Exposure in East Asia* (Routledge, 2015) and *Family, Work, and Wellbeing in Asia* (co-editor, Springer, 2017).

Josh van Veen is Research Associate with the Public Policy Institute at the University of Auckland. His research interests include electoral politics and policy, voter behaviour and attitudes to social policy. He was Associate Investigator with the 2020 New Zealand Election Study team, and his co-authored chapter on the 2020 election is forthcoming with ANU Press in 2022.

Karin von Strokirch is Adjunct Senior Lecturer in Politics and International Relations at the University of New England (NSW). Her research interests include Australian foreign and security policy, Pacific island politics and regionalism, with a focus on environmental issues.

Thomas A. J. White is Senior Research Fellow in Leipzig University's Kolleg-Forschungsgruppe 'Multiple Secularities—Beyond the West, Beyond Modernities'. His research focuses on the histories, politics and effects of secular modes of law and governance as applied in the Pacific Islands. Before his doctoral and postdoctoral posts at Otago University (2016–2021), he was a lecturer in the Ethics and Governance Department at Fiji National University (2012–2015).

Punam Yadav is Associate Professor of Humanitarian Studies and Co-Director of the Centre for Gender and Disaster at the Institute for Risk and Disaster Reduction. She is also a Co-Investigator of the GRRIPP (Gender Responsive Resilience in Policy and Practice) Network Plus project (2019–2023). Recent publications include 'Can women benefit from war? Women's agency in conflict and post-conflict contexts' in the *Journal of Peace Research* (2021) and *Social Transformation in Post-conflict Nepal: A Gender Perspective* (Routledge, 2016), which has also been translated into Chinese.

Ihsan Yilmaz is Professor and Research Chair of Islamic Studies at the Alfred Deakin Institute for Citizenship and Globalisation, Deakin University, Melbourne. He is the author of *Creating the Desired Citizen: Ideology, State and Islam in Turkey* (Cambridge University Press, 2021). He is the academic editor of the book series *Palgrave Studies in Populisms*. He has conducted mixed-method research on Islam-state-law relations in majority and minority contexts; Islamism; populism; securitization; authoritarianism; nation-building; citizenship; ethnic, religious and political minorities; intergroup relations; and transnationalism.

Yayut Yi-shiuan Chen is Assistant Professor at the Master's Programme of Land Policy and Environmental Planning for Indigenous Peoples, National Chengchi University (NCCU),

Taipei, Taiwan. She obtained her Ph.D. degree from the Department of Geography and Planning at Macquarie University, Sydney, in 2019. She has been working with the Tayal people, an Indigenous group in northern Taiwan, since 2009. Her previous research focused on Tayal women's ecological knowledge.

Toru Yoshida is Professor at the Department of Policy Studies at Doshisha University, Japan, and Research Associate at L'École des hautes études en sciences sociales, Paris. He has been a visiting professor at Sciences Po, Paris, and a visiting scholar at New York University. Specialized in comparative politics, his interests cover party politics, party organization and political leadership in Japan and European countries. Recent publications include 'Parliaments in an age of populism' in *Handbook of Parliamentary Studies* by C. Benoit and O. Rozenberg (Eds.) (Edward Elgar, 2020).

Vincen Gregory Yu is a health researcher in the Development Studies Program at Ateneo de Manila University, Philippines. He obtained his Doctor of Medicine degree from the University of the Philippines Manila and is pursuing his M.Sc. in medical anthropology at the same institution. His research interests include drug policy, epidemics, vaccination and the politics of health. His short fiction, poetry and art criticism pieces have been published and anthologized in print and online platforms in the United States, the United Kingdom, Singapore, Hong Kong, and the Philippines.

Habib Zafarullah is Adjunct Associate Professor in the Department of Social and Philosophical Inquiry, University of New England (NSW). His areas of academic interest are democratic governance, comparative bureaucracy, public policy and administration, and international development, and he has published extensively in these areas. His authored/edited books include: *Handbook of Development Policy* (Edward Elgar, 2021) and *Managing Development in a Globalized World* (Routledge, 2012). Currently, he is Chair of the South Asian Network for Public Administration.

TABLES

1.1　The Contemporary Populist Repertoire　　　　　　　　　　　　　9
7.1　Characteristics of Charismatic-Plebiscitary Leadership　　　　93

FIGURES

5.1 Variation of Populism in Southeast Asia   66

GRAPHS

22.1 Approval Rates of Political Leaders 326
24.1 Changes in the Taiwanese/Chinese Identity of Taiwanese 347

ACKNOWLEDGEMENTS

We would like to thank our authors, not merely for their contributions but also for their patience. Editing, particularly during a pandemic, proved a more challenging task than the editors had anticipated. Thanks are also due to Richard Benjamin for his diligent work in proofreading and checking the manuscript.

PART I

Introduction

PART I

Introduction

1
POPULISM'S SHIFTING MEANINGS AND GEOGRAPHICAL DIFFUSION

Alan Scott, D. B. Subedi, Howard Brasted, and Karin von Strokirch

The current state of play for populist politics in the Asia Pacific

This handbook sets out to extend the investigative focus on populism to the Asia-Pacific region,[1] which until very recently, has barely figured at all. For several decades, and with growing intensity, a vast and still-expanding body of literature has largely confined its study of populism to Europe, Latin America, and, since Trump's election in 2016, the United States, analyzing it from myriad angles within these geographic regions. While a considerable body of knowledge and analysis has been produced, we still lack consensus about what populism is (Mudde, 2007, pp. 16–24), and some doubt remains that there is anything that can be identified as being uniquely and characteristically populist.

The search not only for a settled definition of populism but also for a framework of analysis that best conceptualizes it as a political movement continues to underpin debate. Scholars still tend to part company over the essence of populism and its underlying causes, the beliefs and convictions its adherents ostensibly subscribe to, and the reasons it can manifest in different forms and be mobilized for different objectives. That populism can unfold in a predominantly leftist form in Latin America and a predominantly rightist form in Europe further complicates the search for conceptual precision.

Whether turning the spotlight on the Asia Pacific will provide the degree of clarity that is currently missing is unclear, but doing so will certainly redress the Eurocentric imbalance that characterizes the scholarly treatment of populism to date, provide a larger base from which to seek answers, and hold out the prospect of delivering fresh insights into what has clearly become a global phenomenon. A start in this direction was made by the encyclopaedic *Oxford Handbook of Populism* (Rovira Kaltwasser et al., 2017) and the *Routledge Handbook of Global Populism* (de la Torre, 2019), although the coverage of the former only included chapters on India and East Asia, and the 'regional trajectory' of the latter provided a single chapter with snapshots of populism in India, Indonesia, Thailand, and the Philippines. More substantial studies of the latter three countries by Case (2017) and Kenny (2018) and a string of research papers touching on other parts of Asia and the Pacific region would indicate that a correction is underway.

This trend was confirmed when *Populism in Asian Democracies* appeared in 2021 (Lee et al., 2021b). Although the most Asia-inclusive study to date, it specifically narrows its investigation to the impact of populism on the 'quality' of democracy in 11 of Asia's democracies. While it proceeds to identify four broad 'subtypes' or 'patterns' of Asian populism in the process, the conclusions its editors advance are that the concept of populism is no easier to grasp in Asia than in Europe, and that 'no single definition of populism' readily springs out of the Asian context either, because Asia is essentially too heterogeneous (Lee et al., 2021a, pp. 16–18; Wu et al., 2021, p. 222 and p. 225).

Combining not only a more thematic but also a more comparative approach, this handbook—*The Routledge Handbook of Populism in the Asia Pacific*—extends the dimension of populist politics to the Pacific and provides a larger sample of case studies from Asia. What informs its investigation are questions that prompt contributors to probe the distinctive features of Asian populism:

- Under what social, political, economic, and structural conditions has populism emerged in the Asia Pacific?
- What forms, modes, and techniques of social and political mobilization have Asian populists employed to influence people and access power?
- To what extent does Asian populism have different roots from European populism and differently affect the way government is being conducted across the region?

Anti-globalization, anti-elitism, anti-pluralism, and ultra-nationalism, for example, are as intrinsic to the populist discourse in the Asia Pacific as they are in Europe and the Americas, but as this edited handbook reveals, these beliefs can manifest in ways that seem purpose built not so much to buttress primordial national identities as to stir the pot of religious antipathies and bring them to the brim of cultural war (Kingston, 2019).

Intriguingly, the year in which we completed the writing of this volume, 2022, proved an inauspicious one for populist leaders around the world, when their number fell to a '20-year low' (Wintour & Elgot, 2023). Following Donald Trump's electoral demise in 2020, Jair Bolsonaro and Boris Johnston were removed from office as well, and some of their Asian and Pacific counterparts experienced a similar fate. Confronted by massive street protests in Sri Lanka, Gotabaya Rajapaksa fled to Singapore; Imran Khan was toppled by the Pakistan establishment he undertook to disempower; Rodrigo Duterte was constitutionally barred from seeking a second term as President of the Philippines; and Scott Morrison lost the 2022 Australian general election. India's Narendra Modi, however, seems in no immediate danger of losing his political ascendancy, but the longevity of his Bharatiya Janata Party (BJP) government may ultimately work against him. Indonesian President Joko Widodo will see out his second and final term in 2024 unless the law is changed to allow a third term.

On this evidence, populist leaders are not immune to experiencing popular swings against them and are vulnerable to the kind of cycles that most political movements go through. Whether the current 21st century wave of populism in Asia and the Pacific, which this volume charts, will at some point simply peter out, as previous waves of populism have done, is certainly something to keep a watchful eye on. Our starting point, however, is not to double guess what the future of populism in the Asia Pacific might hold. Rather, in this chapter, we wish to give a general overview of populism, its geographical dissemination, and the conceptual shifts that have accompanied its expansion. We will then pick out the major themes that run through this volume.

Understanding contemporary populism: shifting meanings and geographical diffusion

> Now we must address ourselves to the biting of the sour apple . . . which is the attempt to formulate some kind of model or definition or formula into which we can fit all the various types and nuances of populism.
>
> *(Berlin, 1967, p. 4)*

Analysts of populism have been biting into Isaiah Berlin's sour apple ever since. Indeed, Berlin's own observations on populism, in his role as Session Chair at the conference To Define Populism organized by Ghiţă Ionescu and Ernest Gellner and held at the London School of Economics (LSE) in May 1967, illustrate a problem that is still with us. On the one hand, he warns of the trap of imagining that there is a Platonic form of populism to which some existing case must correspond and against which all others can be measured, a Cinderella's slipper 'for which somewhere there must exist a foot' (Berlin, 1967, p. 6). On the other hand, he distinguishes between true and false (or pseudo-) populisms: those that embody genuine populist principles, and those that simply seek to mobilize populist sentiments for political ambitions of their own, usually for acquiring and/or retaining power.[2] A similar distinction was drawn by Margaret Canovan (1984, p. 314) between 'substantial populism' and 'politicians' populism', the latter being 'a matter of style rather than of substance' (see also Chapter 26).

Such distinctions assume there are some commonalities between all those phenomena that may be legitimately gathered under the heading of 'populism'. Berlin's catalogue of these common features is long. True populism is egalitarian, speaks for those who have in some sense been 'left out', is backward- rather than forward-looking, elevates the 'free, spontaneous natural behaviour of uncorrupted men' (Berlin, 1967, p. 9) over that of cosmopolitan elites, identifies a specific enemy of the people, and so forth. Its 'essential elements' are 'fraternity, freedom from imposed authority, above all equality' (Berlin, 1967, p. 11). On the basis of this list of essential characteristics, Berlin proposed a sociological hypothesis, again one applicable to all true populism: 'in some sense it would be just to say that it occurs in societies standing on the edge of modernisation—that is to say, threatened by it, or hoping for it' (Berlin, 1967, p. 10).

Most, or all, of the items on this list would be familiar to anyone acquainted with the contemporary academic literature on populism. Berlin's 'left out', for example, reappeared in the guise of the 'left behind' in media and academic debates surrounding Brexit in the UK. Nevertheless, few current analysts of populism would risk a list of defining characteristics that is as comprehensive as Berlin's, let alone seek to identify *essential* elements. There are two reasons for this reticence, the second of which is particularly relevant to this collection.

The first factor is the influence of Cas Mudde's well-known claim, referred to in almost all conceptual discussions, that populism is a 'thin-centred ideology' consisting merely of the antagonistic juxtaposition of the 'pure people' and the 'corrupt elite' plus the claim to speak in the name of the former's 'general will' (Mudde, 2004, p. 543). Mudde's intentionally minimalist definition aimed to bypass conceptual problems and acknowledge populism's plasticity without emptying the concept of all content. As a thin-centred ideology, populism can, indeed must, piggyback on more substantial, philosophically richer, ideologies such as nationalism or socialism, hence its flexibility and adaptability. Mudde's argument has given rise to what claims to be the most influential school of analysis, the 'ideational' approach.

But even this partial conceptual evacuation has not been enough for some, namely for advocates of the rival 'strategic' approach for whom, in the words of one of its main proponents, populist politicians 'lack firm commitment to ideologies and principles and concentrate on the quest for personal power' (Weyland, 2013, p. 31).[3] Populism, in this view, is nothing more than the attempt to attain, retain, or increase power through strategies of, for example, voter maximization via polarization (Pappas, 2012; see also Chapter 3).

Populist politicians, by this account, are entrepreneurs for whom politics is reduced to its technical aspects and any political cause is an irrelevancy unless it is a means to the end: garnering votes and gaining power. Here, political power becomes either an end in itself or a means to access other social resources, such as prestige, celebrity, or wealth. The implication is that populism is immanent within democracy rather than an exogenous disruptive force. The logic of contemporary politics presents instrumentally rational and self-regarding actors with opportunities that they are able to utilize and manipulate for self-serving ends.

Both the ideational and strategic approaches have stripped populism of much or all of what, for Berlin, were its essential elements: fraternity, freedom, anti-authority, and equality. In this sense, the difference between the two approaches seems to be more one of degree than kind. By taking this development to its logical conclusion, the strategic approach has reduced all populism to Berlin's false or Canovan's politicians' populism, or, amounting to the same thing, has elided the distinction between true and false forms. Even in Mudde's influential and somewhat thicker definition, anti-authority, now in the form of anti-elitism, remains, but what of fraternity and equality? This shift from a substantive to a formal conceptualization of populism is reinforced by a second factor: its many changes of geographical location and its global dissemination, which have further diluted its substantive content.

In characterizing populism's essential ideas as fraternity, hostility to external authority, and equality, Berlin was in part looking back to its original historical manifestations, populism's original form: agrarian, progressive movements in the United States—the People's Party—in the 1890s and, to a degree, similar movements—the Narodniks—in Russia a couple of decades earlier. By the time of the To Define Populism conference in 1967, the term had become most closely associated with Latin America, where it described both left- and right-wing regimes with a strong tendency towards charismatic-plebiscitary leadership (see Chapter 7). The impulse for much of the recent debate, which coincides with an exponential increase in use of the term in both the media and social sciences, was the rise and electoral success of far-right populist parties in Western Europe from the late 1980s, such as the Front National in France (founded in 1972) and the Haider-FPÖ in Austria (from 1986), followed by the emergence of forms of authoritarian populism in Eastern Europe and Trump's election victory in 2016. Thus, the geographical migration of populism has been accompanied by various migrations in its meaning. This volume arguably exacerbates this problem further by extending the term's usage to yet another geographical region. In this sense, time has only amplified the problem that animated the LSE conference: is populism merely a homonym—a single word with a variety of distinct meanings—or can we discern sufficient commonalities, or at least family resemblances, to justify such a seemingly expansive usage?

The extent of the problem becomes clear when we note how little the contemporary usage of the term, whether in the ideational or strategic literature, corresponds to the populism of the 1890s in the United States. What once described a bottom-up, left-wing movement with, for a brief period, broad support among both farmers and industrial workers now describes movements, parties, and regimes that are generally top-down, right-wing, nationalist, authoritarian, and, in many cases, inclined to attack the institutional pillars of liberal democracy: the judiciary, the rule of law, the constitution, the independent media—all those bodies, including universities, that enjoy a degree of autonomy and are, as yet, not under direct political control.

What are the main options available to analysts in face of this conceptual drift? One of the oldest responses is that of the American historian Richard Hofstadter (1955), for whom the original populists contributed to an atmosphere—a 'paranoid style' of politics—that would soon mutate into populism's default position: xenophobic, authoritarian, and conspiratorial. Few, if any, contemporary analysts would accept this simple equation of right and left populism, though Postel (2019) argues that traces of it can still be found in the ideational approach.[4] One possible reaction against Hofstadter's (in)famous analysis is to contend that the only legitimate use of the term is with reference to its progressive and egalitarian original form and like-minded movements (see Frank, 2016). Neither of these polar positions is particularly helpful for analyzing contemporary developments. The former does indeed tar left and right with the same brush, while the latter suffers from the Cinderella complex, the belief that there is one, and only one, foot that fits the shoe—i.e., that the original form and the Platonic form of populism are one and the same.

This volume adopts a more pragmatic response. First, we accept that there has been a gradual but radical shift in the meaning and referent of the term.[5] Secondly, this conceptual drift is in part a response to 'real world' developments: most of the phenomena we now characterize as populist are right-wing, nationalistic, sovereigntist, xenophobic, and, potentially or actually, anti-pluralist to authoritarian. This becomes even more evident if we distinguish between populism as campaign strategy and populism as a mode of governing. Beyond Latin America, where left-wing politicians continued to pursue populist strategies in government (see Weyland, 2013), while there are left-wing movements and parties that draw on populist language, sometimes inspired by the post-Marxist analyses of Ernesto Laclau, Chantal Mouffe, and Étienne Balibar, notably Podemos in Spain and SYRIZA in Greece, once in power, they tend to govern conventionally and 'responsibly'. They mobilize and campaign but do not *govern* as full-blown populists, for whom being in power is no excuse for ceasing campaigning, polarizing, and mobilizing the base.[6] In the contemporary world, this has largely been the prerogative of the right. So, rather than equate right and left populism, we might plausibly argue that there is no consistent left populism outside the 'pink wave' in Latin America.[7] Thirdly, the populisms we now have, including those examined in this collection, resemble Berlin's false or Canovan's politicians' populism: top-down and leader-centred. In sum, it would seem that original, genuine populist sentiments have provided a resource that has been tapped most effectively by would-be charismatic leaders of the right who then govern as false populists via policies that combine authoritarianism with anti-pluralism and, not infrequently, neo-liberalism—a flexible 'repertoire' that can be borrowed and adapted (Brubaker, 2017).

Arguably, one of the limitations of contemporary analysis—whether ideational, strategic, or socio-cultural—is that it has relatively little to say about the *specific* conditions that facilitate populism, and correspondingly tends to view it as democracy's permanent shadow (e.g., Müller, 2016) thus obscuring 'differences along the dimension of substance' (Tushnet,

2019, p. 383). However, some recent literature seeks to address this by pointing to two primary factors: (i) growth in inequality combined with a decline of social, economic and welfare protection; (ii) depoliticization as the outcome of (a) the increasing convergence of political parties of the left and right on a common programme and the resultant tendency towards the formation of cartel parties, and (b) the increasing outsourcing of government capacities and reliance on policy instruments, plus a degree of redistribution of power from representative to 'non-majoritarian' institutions such as regulatory agencies.

In this spirit, Zürn offers a more *political* explanation of the rise and spread of populism. The growing power of non-majoritarian institutions and the corresponding decline of power of majoritarian institutions (NMIs and MIs respectively) combined with the cartelization of political parties means that 'the silent majority consider themselves as suppressed or at least forgotten by a political class controlling the parliament and by liberal cosmopolitan experts controlling NMIs' (Zürn, 2021, p. 789). The relationship between rulers and ruled has been altered in a way that enables authoritarian populists to exploit the new political cleavage emerging between cosmopolitan elites (UK Prime Minister Teresa May's 'citizens of nowhere') and those more firmly ensconced in the container of the nation-state. Where populists have been able to take advantage of these new opportunities, 'the *volonté générale* plays out as a pre-political and de-proceduralized will that is embodied in the leaders of the populist party' (Zürn, 2021, p. 789).

The changing ruler-ruled relationship and the growing irresponsiveness of the political system to popular demands, including those concerning the effects of economic globalization, austerity, and the deterioration of welfare provision, reinforce economic inequality. The mutually supportive mechanisms of growing political irresponsiveness, the cosmopolitanization of elites, and growing economic inequality have been neatly summarized by Tushnet (2019, p. 348): 'As political elites became more cosmopolitan, self-reproducing, insulated from economic stress, and self-satisfied, they became increasingly indifferent to fulfilling the social welfare promises they had made'.

Populism here is understood as a response to demands for greater protection against the impacts of unfettered markets *and* as re-politicization. While these demands can be voiced by either the left or right, existing populisms, including those discussed in this volume, are generally sourced from the latter. Furthermore, as Zürn notes (2021, p. 802), the 'reactive sequence'[8] that has facilitated populism within consolidated democracies is a characteristic they increasingly share with precarious democracies. Thus, rather than making a case for any form of exceptionalism for the Asia-Pacific region, what we may be witnessing is a growing convergence across regional contexts as populism takes on broader regional and international relations significance (see Chapter 4).

Populism in the Asia Pacific: this collection

If we adopt a pragmatic view of populism's contemporary usage, we can cull recent literature to draw up an inventory of the typical—or ideal-typical—'repertoire' imputed to it.[9] We seek to do this in Table 1.1 under two headings: (i) discursive and strategic repertoires; (ii) action repertoires. The distinction is a little artificial, and certainly not as clear-cut as its tabular representation suggests. We use it to approximately distinguish how contemporary social scientists characterize, on the one hand, populist language and strategy, and, on the other, what populists typically do in power. Such an inventory is by no means as minimal as Mudde's definition.

Table 1.1 The Contemporary Populist Repertoire

Discursive and strategic repertoires	Action repertoires
'Antagonistic re-politicization': raising levels of conflict, both 'vertical (people vs. elite) and 'horizontal' (ethnic, linguistic, or religious 'others') (Brubaker, 2017, pp. 362–364).	Adopting plebiscitary instruments of democracy (referenda, petitions, etc.) that reinforce the yes/no logic of polarization; engage in so-called 'culture wars'.
Asserting the 'interests, rights, and will of the majority against those of minorities' (Brubaker, 2017, p. 365).[10] This majority is taken—*pars pro toto*—to stand for 'the people' (Müller, 2016).	Anti-pluralism and the politics of identity (Müller, 2016): 'the people' are imagined not simply as a homogenous unit (Mudde, 2004) but as a community of fate rather than as a political community.
Anti-institutionalist and anti-systemic: opposition to existing institutions (Brubaker, 2017, p. 365), often on the grounds that these are corrupt, and to the "establishment" and "elites"—the populist politician as outsider/of the people, not the elite.	(i) Populists 'colonialize or "occupy" the state', creating a state 'to their own political liking and image' (Müller, 2016, pp. 44–45) via attacks on institutions that enjoyed a degree of autonomy from and/or constrained political will, and on civil society.
	(ii) Increasingly hybrid regime forms in which aspects of liberal democracy are retained but weakened, and which display a growing tendency towards authoritarianism (see, for example, Halmai, 2019).
Economic, securitarian, and cultural protectionism (Brubaker, 2017, p. 366) or, in an overlapping list, economic and symbolic nativism and welfare chauvinism (Betz, 2019). Symbolic nativism includes the protection of local, particularistic cultures against values 'imposed' by a secular cosmopolitan elite; foreign, 'colonial' powers (Korolczuk & Graff, 2018); or immigrants.	Border protection and sovereigntism increasingly becoming the *raison d'être* of government (Kallis, 2018): (i) "Economic sovereigntism"—e.g., protectionism (Ivaldi and Mazzoleni 2020).[11] (ii) Pushback not merely against economic but also cultural globalization —e.g., defence of the putative traditional family form and gender roles, opposition to LGBTQ+ rights, etc. (Inglehart & Norris, 2016). (iii) Postsecularism: the preservation of the majority religion (Stoeckl, 2016).
A 'low' style (crude, vulgar, plain speaking) (Brubaker, 2017, p. 366). Populist appeals are 'transgressive, improper, and antagonistic, in that they are intended to "shock" or provoke' (Ostiguy, 2020, pp. 33–34).	The permanent campaign, carried over into government, in which the majority, or simply the political base, is continuously mobilized, occasionally to the point of 'calculated ambivalence' (Wodak, 2013), including towards the use of political violence.
A 'moralistic imagination of politics' (Müller, 2016, p. 19) in which politics is envisaged as a Manichean struggle between good (the people) and evil (the elite), and thus operates with a logic of 'friend and foe'.	Politics increasingly follows a Schmittian logic of friend and foe. This encourages 'mass clientelism' (Müller, 2016, p. 46), cronyism, and, not infrequently, graft and corruption, the latter further facilitated by the breakdown of the boundaries between state and economy brought about by policies of privatization, marketization, and selective deregulation.

(*Continued*)

Table 1.1 (Continued)

Discursive and strategic repertoires	Action repertoires
Plebiscitary leadership: only the (putatively charismatic) leader can drain the swamp and give voice to the 'will of the people' with whom he/she enters in unmediated communication (Körösényi et al., 2020).	Elections increasingly take on a plebiscitary quality—acclamation of the leader—and parties are increasingly transformed into leader parties, while leadership itself is performative—a 'symbolically mediated performance' (Moffitt, 2020, Ch.4) in terms of style, and autocratic in terms of substance.

If Table 1.1 presents the ideal type of contemporary populism that has emerged out of the term's various conceptual and geographical migrations, to what extent can it be applied to yet another geographical region, the Asia Pacific? What, if any, changes or additions have to be made to this inherited model?

As this volume shows, the Asia-Pacific region manifests varieties of populism and cycles of populist movements. Given the heterogeneity of populism in the Asia Pacific, viewing it through a singular conceptual lens—whether ideational, strategic, or socio-cultural—proves insufficient. We also see that the binary of exclusionary and inclusionary populism becomes fluid and shifts when populists accede to power. In contrasting Indira Gandhi's populism in India in the 1970s with the contemporary populism of Narendra Modi, Paul D. Kenny (Chapter 12) argues that populist movements are characterized by considerable political flexibility rather than ideological rigidity. Comparative evidence in this volume further suggests that the form taken by the institutionalization of populist politics at the national level provides a better guide to understand how populist leaders perform when they are in power than does populist discourse.

Cycles of populism across the Asia Pacific do not follow a universal pathway or *modus operandi*. Rather, they vary according to new and old social cleavages, the effects of neo-liberalization and globalization, and how politicians have manipulated these conditions to advance their self-serving agendas. Many of the examples and much of the analysis that follows suggest that the cycles of populism in the Asia Pacific have followed the path of Canovan's (1984, p. 314) politicians', rather than substantial, populism.

Here, we shall briefly seek to draw out the main themes to emerge from the contributions to this collection, focusing specifically on the similarities and differences between populism in the Asia-Pacific region and those more familiar cases elsewhere.

The fragility of politicians' populism

A number of case studies point to the ephemeral nature of populism in the region. From Imran Khan in Pakistan to Rodrigo Duterte in the Philippines, and from the Rajapaksa brothers in Sri Lanka to Aung San Suu Kyi in Myanmar (Chapters 13, 19, 16, and 18 respectively), all of these leaders faced a similar fate of populist decline and were either forced to step down or defeated in the elections (with the exception of Suu Kyi, who was ousted in the 2021 military coup). Despite their initial popularity and dominance in national politics, populist leaders faced bureaucratic and legal hurdles in implementing populist governance amidst rising economic inequalities, increasing cost-of-living pressures, and poor management of the COVID-19 pandemic (see Chapter 11), leading to growing anti-government protests. Moreover, public demand and aspiration for democratic governance and freedom means that populists seem to do well in leading populist opposition but are vulnerable once in power (see Chapters 13, 16, 18, and 23). To borrow a concept from social movement analysis, what we see are high (strong) and low (weak) *cycles* of populism.

Populists in the region face typical economic constraints (see Chapter 5 on growth and redistribution), social pressure (see Chapter 21 on Thailand) and political opposition (see Chapters 13 on Pakistan and 22 on South Korea). This has two potential consequences. First, these constraints force shifts in ideological positioning and political strategies as conditions alter. Modi, for example, vacillates between populist nationalism and neo-liberal internationalism. Duterte was authoritarian and illiberal but likewise adopted neo-liberal economic development policies (see Chapter 19). These ideological and strategic shifts make populists appear inconsistent, opportunistic, and 'chameleon'. It also makes them vulnerable in power.

Second, to avoid such pressure, many leaders resort to ruling through coercion (see Chapters 12 on India, 16 on Sri Lanka, 23 on China, and 28 on Fiji). The authoritarian strategies they adopt pose a threat to democracy itself, as has been the case in Bangladesh (Chapter 14), the Maldives (Chapter 17), and the Philippines (Chapter 19). With some exceptions, for example in India and Indonesia (Chapters 11 and 20), politicians' populism in the contemporary Asia Pacific has proved a risky and insecure undertaking.

Post-colonial cleavages and the ambiguity of nationalism and national identity

As elsewhere, populists in the region benefit from and manipulate what Brubaker (2017, pp. 362–364) calls the 'antagonistic re-politicization of the masses'. This re-politicization, commonly fuelled by enduring social and political cleavages, results in the scapegoating of ethnic, linguistic, or religious minorities and the intensification of anti-elite politics. In this respect, populism in the Asia Pacific displays similar traits to populism elsewhere.

On the other hand, populism in the region has been shaped by the specific form of colonial and post-colonial state formation. The popular aspiration for an independent nation-state and the way states have been formed and imagined in the post-colonial period has politicized the meaning of nation, national identity, natives (or the 'pure' people), and 'others'. The social and ethnic cleavages that continued through the post-colonial period in countries like Sri Lanka, Myanmar, Indonesia, Thailand, and India display the logic of friend and foe that the radical conservative political and legal theorist Carl Schmitt thought common to all politics.[12] This has had two effects on the way contemporary populism has emerged.

First, as Brasted and Ahmed show in Chapter 2, the question of national identity in South Asia especially has become an issue fraught with complexity, contradictions, and contestation, but it has also provided fertile ground for xenophobic identity politics, mass clientelism, and exclusionary ethnic and cultural nationalism. While ethnic, cultural, and religious nationalism provided an impetus to nationalist movements in, for example, colonial Bangladesh, Pakistan, Sri Lanka, Myanmar, Indonesia, and the Maldives, once independence had been achieved, nationalist leaders and elites came to replace the former imperial rulers as the enemies. The result has been social unrest and occasionally civil war in newly independent states. Both populists and nationalists have exploited this friend-foe logic as a template through which populism and nationalism have emerged and evolved.

Nationalism and populism have travelled together and have often overlapped in this region. The close affinity explains why both have been elite-driven and have an exclusionary character, frequently conflating *demos* and *ethnos* (Mann, 2005, see also Chapter 16). These developments are traced in Chapters 12 (on India), 16 (on Sri Lanka), 17 (on the Maldives), 18 (on Myanmar), and 28 (on Fiji).

Second, populist action repertoires converge on the single issue of national identity, leading to the clashes or 'culture wars' we are currently witnessing between majorities and minorities based on ethnic and religious differences. In these conflicts, the minorities in question are 'insiders' rather than 'outsiders', yet they are *in* but not *of* the national community. The majority-minority divide and the related cultural conflicts that fuel populist movements draw international attention only after they generate massive anti-minority violence (see the analysis of Sri Lanka—Chapter 16, Myanmar—Chapter 18, and Fiji—Chapter 28). The cultural war, however, was not a significant force for social polarization and conflict in countries which have homogeneous national and ethnic identity, such as the Maldives (Chapter 17), South Korea (Chapter 22), and Japan (Chapter 25).

Like violent and divisive nationalism, populism in religiously and culturally diverse countries in the Asia Pacific justifies, normalizes, and even defends violence against religious and cultural minorities, particularly where democracy is unconsolidated and fragile. For this reason, populism in the Asia Pacific must be seen as part of enduring identity politics. While these dynamics are not absent in 'consolidated democracies'; they take a different, and typically less violent, form.

Globalization, neo-liberalization, and de/re-politicization of economic inequalities

The Asia-Pacific region has seen rapid economic growth and poverty reduction in recent decades, but also has simultaneously experienced increasing income and wealth inequality and the rise of an ultrarich class (Zhuang, 2023). Discontent over rising socio-economic inequality has fuelled cultural and religious conflicts encouraging populism, authoritarianism, far-right politics, and atavistic nationalism in Asia (Chapter 5; see also Clements, 2018; Chacko & Jayasuriya, 2018). Several case studies in this volume provide evidence of this and further highlight that a number of populist leaders have used development and inequality issues to *re-politicize* the masses. Claiming to give voice to the people left behind by political elites, populist nationalists in, for example, Sri Lanka, India, Bangladesh, and Thailand, have used a rhetoric of development and good government as a trope to garner popular support from below. What we see is that income and wealth inequality fuel social tensions and cultural wars as well as provoke anti-globalization, anti-elitist, and anti-Western sentiments, except in Asia-Pacific settler states considered 'Western', such as Australia and New Zealand (see Chapters 26 and 27). Populists have been effectively using these divisions as part of an action repertoire to raise political, gender, and class consciousness (see Chapter 15).

Income and wealth inequality, however, play out rather differently when a movement leader becomes head of government. Once in power, populist leaders come face-to-face with the difficulty of delivering on their radical promises, the implementation of which is often impeded by bureaucratic hurdles and limited economic and financial resources. In the resulting balancing act, they tend to *depoliticize* economic inequality by focusing on cultural and personality issues that deflect attention from their own underperformance. Not only can they resort to 'personality driven politics', as in Bangladesh (Chapter 14), but also they invariably attribute their nation's ills to an admixture of globalization, neo-colonialism, and elite skulduggery (see Chapters 12, 13, 16, and 21).

This does not mean that populist governments necessarily proceed to cut ties with business elites and neo-liberal market forces. Indeed, they are perfectly prepared to enter into collaborative, if collusive, arrangements with these very forces by reorienting their growth and redistribution policies. In analyzing the growth and redistribution policies of populist governments in Asia, Ming-Chang Tsai and Hsin-Hsin Pan (Chapter 5) distinguish four types of populism: *developmental*, *pro-business*, *degenerative*, and *redistributive* populism. All of these forms disappoint the expectations that they may have inspired and favour the interests of some clients/supporters over those of others.

Centrality of leadership and the necessity of minimal electoral democracy

With respect to questions of leadership and democracy, the contributions to this collection suggest three broad conclusions. First, populist movements across the Asia Pacific are leader-centric, converging on the dominance of powerful leaders at the national or subnational level. From Frank Bainimarama in Fiji to Imran Khan in Pakistan to Duterte in the Philippines to Hun Sen in Cambodia, the political parties they represent are transformed into leader parties. While leaders exercise the power to control their parties, the party network enhances the leader's mobilizing capabilities, leading to a 'strongman' political culture throughout the region (see Chapters 12 and 25 on India and Japan, respectively). The strongman phenomenon sees parties lose their ideological cohesion and increasingly rely on the leader's dramatic and performative actions. For example, Cambodia's governing party heavily relies on Hun Sen's electoral abilities and fund-raising capacity to stay in power. In Pakistan, Imran Khan always cut an imposing figure as the former captain of its World Cup-winning cricket team, although his politics was a mixed and contradictory bag of Islamism, nationalism, and elements of liberal internationalism (see Chapter 13).

Secondly, unlike past populists in Asia, who were quite prepared to use authoritarian methods, contemporary populists tend to compete with mainstream political leaders and use the democratic system of government to come to power (see Mietzner, 2018, and Chapters 13, 22, 24, 27, 28). Although populism in general, and right-wing populism in particular, threatens the core principles and ideals of democracy—pluralism, multiculturalism, freedom, and equality—our case studies show that all types of leaders, whether populist, nationalist, or authoritarian, require the plebiscitarian elements of electoral democracy.[13] While democratic institutions and practice have been seriously weakened under populist governments, populists seek to maintain a minimal democracy to accord them some semblance of legitimacy (Chapters 22, 24 and 26).

Finally, the patron-client relationship has been a dominant mode of political engagement across the Asia Pacific and has historically shaped the relationship between people and political parties; between rulers and ruled. Populists demand the dismantling of the traditional patron-client relationship and 'old system' by demonizing mainstream political elites whom they hold responsible for injustice against, and the misery of, the masses (Chapters 13, 22, and 27). Once in power, they seek to de-traditionalize and revolutionize the political arena, thus creating new clientelist relations more closely aligned with their own interests (see Chapter 16). In most cases, new forms of patronage are distributed primarily at the discretion of the leader, and the leader party becomes a vehicle to facilitate the leader's relationship with the followers (see Chapters 14, 15, and 17).

Significance of secularism and the religious culture of fear and emotion

In the Asia Pacific, faith and culture can potentially create a political site in which religion and populism converge, producing a right-wing populist discourse not so different from the xenophobic and exclusionary right-wing populism found in Europe and the United States. However, unlike in Western Europe, where populists are more interested in the strategic use of religion than in defending faith and theology—and are therefore likely be in conflict with faith leaders (Roy, 2016)—in the Asia Pacific, populists and nationalist leaders manipulate religion strategically and in some cases, for example, India, Sri Lanka, Bangladesh, and Indonesia, they also defend faith and culture as an ideological plank of their politics. As a result, they do not so much fall out with religious leaders as recruit them as needed. What all these cases, however, have in common is that they engender collective 'we' identities—the 'pure people' ranged against some 'other', however defined (see Chapters 6, 16, and 18).

As Subedi and Lim show in Chapter 9, what facilitates or hinders the rise of religious populism in many parts of Asia depends on the level of commitment by political leaders to secular practice. The secularization of government and society in South, East, and Southeast Asia, although originally imposed by the colonial rulers, was in no small part maintained by nationalist political elites (Dean & van der Veer, 2019, p. 2). In non-secular or semi-secular states, however, secularism was considered an alien legacy which had no place in determining how the state should function. By contrast, in strongly secular states such as Singapore, Australia (Chapter 26), and New Zealand (Chapter 27), and in an officially atheist state like China, the constitutional separation of faith and state renders religious populism less tenable. In these countries, populists are likely to turn to culture and tradition rather than religion and faith as an ideological and strategic resource to advance populism (Chapter 24).

The politics of fear central to populism in general and to religious populism in particular (Palaver, 2019) plays a key role in the manipulation of faith by populist leaders. So engrained are religious and ethnic identities in Asian societies (Chapters 9, 16, and 18) that populists readily play on fear of other minority religious groups, thus outmanoeuvring their secular opponents in the process. But they have also found that appealing to religious emotions works as effectively as fear in galvanizing populist support (Chapters 9 and 10). Similar to the 'politics of fear', the 'politics of (religious) emotion' is a populist instrument used selectively to construct an emotional and moral bonding of religiously defined in-groups opposed to some outgroup, usually ethnic and religious minorities, Western governments, and corporations.

Manipulation of online media, gender, and anti-science discourse

With over 2.6 billion users in the Asia Pacific in 2022, the reach and influence of online media and communication platforms in contemporary populism cannot be emphasized enough. This phenomenon is familiar in Europe, the United States, and Latin America;[14] however, the populist relationship with the online world is somewhat ambivalent in the Asia Pacific. While there is growing affinity between social media and populist politics, at the same time, there is also a growing hostility between populist leaders and those critical media organizations that favour pluralism, good governance, and liberal democracy.

As Jane Ahlstrand shows in Chapter 20, the gender impacts of online media in populism are distinct and often ignored. While online news media outlets give momentum to the populist movement, they can simultaneously divide it through their vilification of female political figures. In the Asia-Pacific region, where gender-based discrimination and injustice are prevalent, female populist leaders easily get more media attention than their male counterparts, but are just as likely to be on the receiving end of online vilification and character assassination.

Finally, one common thread running through populist discourse is the distrust of expert systems and science in particular, whether with respect to climate change and the environment or the COVID-19 pandemic. While this is an aspect of populism most commonly associated with Trump and Bolsonaro, Chapter 11 examines the impact of 'medical populism' in the region covered in this volume. By ruling as populists, as we noted at the start, a number of politicians have recently paid a price for the consequent reduction of state capacity in the face of crisis.

The aim of this volume, then, is not simply to supply national case studies, but to draw out the differences and similarities across contemporary politics in the Asia Pacific. As elsewhere, there is considerable heterogeneity in forms and themes, but there are also shared elements and clear, or at least 'elective', affinities. In this way, we hope to have widened the focus of debates on a phenomenon that, unless or until a better successor term is coined, we must call populism.

Notes

1 Definitions of the Asia-Pacific region vary. Some are very broad, including Russia and Turkey (i.e., the whole of Asia) and those countries in the Americas that have a Pacific coastline. Others are narrower, excluding the aforementioned countries, but including China. Here, we understand Asia-Pacific region in the selective and narrower sense, focusing mostly on South, East and Southeast Asia and the South Pacific region, including New Zealand and Australia.
2 For a useful, recent discussion of this distinction, see Halmai, 2019.
3 The ideational and strategic approaches do not exhaust current perspectives on populism. However, other contemporary approaches are likewise inclined to reduce the substantive content of populism to something close to a minimum. Thus, for example, in Laclau's discursive approach (2005), populism is largely an empty signifier, while for those who view populism as a question of style (e.g., Moffitt & Tormey, 2014) or socio-cultural approaches emphasizing its 'low' language (e.g., Ostiguy, 2020), populism becomes a matter of *performativity*—of *form* rather than *substance*.
4 Even where contemporary analysts identify commonalities between right and left populism, as de la Torre (2017) did in comparing Latin American left populism and Trump, they are keen to stress that the underlying conception of 'the people' is quite different in the two cases. The former rejects the exclusivist view of the people as a religious, ethnic, or linguistic community of fate by making 'inclusive ethnopopulist appeals' (la Torre, 2017, p. 191) or by rejecting the idea that 'the people' constitute a unity.
5 Müller (2016, p. 90) has acknowledged this by suggesting that the original populists are *not* populists in the contemporary sense of the term; 'they rarely if ever claimed to be the people as such'.
6 As Marlière (2022) has noted in the case of the Nouvelle union populaire écologique et sociale (Nupes)—the coalition of left parties formed to fight the French legislative election of 2022—this shift from left populism to a more reformist, or social democratic, position can also occur during an electoral campaign.
7 It is telling that only one chapter in the volume (Chapter 15) discusses a case of left-wing populism.
8 By 'reactive sequence', Zürn means the stages that have, since the Second World War, led from 'historic compromise' (embedded liberalism) to authoritarian populism.
9 The terms 'repertoire' and 'action repertoire' are borrowings from the American historical sociologist Charles Tilly, and originally applied by him to social movements. The appeal of these terms here is that rather than treating ideational, strategic, discursive, or stylistic aspects of populism

as though each were the exclusive property of distinct schools or approaches, repertoires imply that these are facets of populism that can be combined and recombined flexibly across time and space—i.e., that they are, to borrow another term from Tilly, 'shifting repertoires' with no immutable core or essence.

10 Brubaker calls this "majoriterianism". The term is a little confusing as, in its more usual political sense, majoritarian is precisely what populists are not.
11 Ivaldi and Mazzoleni (2020, p. 213) argue that the political economy of radical right-wing populist parties (RRPPs) 'is characterized primarily by economic populism and economic sovereigntism', which are linked to their core ideology. However, in many cases, populist parties (e.g., the BJP under Modi) have pursued neo-liberal policies that appear consistent with neither their proclaimed economic populism nor the interests of their base. Here, as in the case of Trump, who 'has continued to present himself in populist garb, but it has rarely carried over to policy' (Pierson, 2017, p. 106), we may simply be dealing with the gap between what is proclaimed and what is implemented, or with what Kallis (2018, p. 292) calls the 'performance of sovereignty' and 'performances of a re-empowered demos'.
12 For a useful brief discussion and contextualization of this Schmittian distinction, see Neocleous, 1996.
13 Whether populism exacerbates or ameliorates constitutional democracy is a point of debate. One line of argument suggests that, depending on the host ideologies, the examples of democratic, liberal, and socially inclusive forms of populism show that authoritarianism and anti-pluralism are not necessarily the key elements of populism (Bugaric, 2019). Others contend that populism in opposition can be good for democracy, while populism in power carries considerable risks to the principles and values of liberal democracy (Mansbridge & Macedo, 2019).
14 For the discussion on internet, social media, and populism in Europe and Latin America, see Bennett and Seyis (2021) and Waisbord and Amado (2017), respectively.

References

Bennett, A., & Seyis, D. (2021). The online market's invisible hand: Internet media and rising populism. *Political Studies*, 1–21. https://doi.org/10.1177/00323217211033230
Berlin, I. (1967). To define populism (from the transcript of the conference to define populism, London School of Economics and Political Science, 20–21 May 1967). *The Isaiah Berlin Virtual Library*. http://berlin.wolf.ox.ac.uk/lists/bibliography/bib111bLSE.pdf
Betz, H. G. (2019). Facets of nativism: A heuristic exploration. *Patterns of Prejudice*, 53(2), 111–135. https://doi.org/10.1080/0031322X.2019.1572276
Brubaker, R. (2017). Why populism? *Theory and Society*, 46, 357–385. https://doi.org/10.1007/s11186-017-9301-7
Bugaric, B. (2019). Could populism be good for constitutional democracy? *Annual Review of Law and Social Science*, 15, 41–58. https://doi.org/10.1146/annurev-lawsocsci-101518-042927
Canovan, M. (1984). 'People', politicians and populism. *Government and Opposition*, 19(3), 312–327. www.jstor.org/stable/44484266
Case, W. (2017). *Populist threats and democracy's fate in Southeast Asia. Thailand, the Philippines, and Indonesia*. Routledge.
Chacko, P., & Jayasuriya, K. (2018). Asia's conservative moment: Understanding the rise of the right. *Journal of Contemporary Asia*, 48(4), 529–540. https://doi.org/10.1080/00472336.2018.1448108
de la Torre, C. (2017). Trump's populism: Lessons from Latin America. *Postcolonial Studies*, 20(2), 187–198. https://doi.org/10.1080/13688790.2017.1363846
de la Torre, C. (Ed.) (2019). *Routledge handbook of global populism* (pp. 44–56). Routledge.
Dean, K., & van der Veer, P. (2019). Introduction. In K. Dean, & P. van der Veer (Eds.), *The secular in South, East, Southeast Asia* (pp. 1–12). Palgrave Macmillan.
Frank, T. (2016). *Listen, liberal or what ever happened to the party of the people?* Metropolitan Books.
Halmai, G. (2019). Populism, authoritarianism and constitutionalism. *German Law Journal*, 20, 296–313. https://doi.org/10.1017/glj.2019.23

Hofstadter, R. (1955). *The age of reform*. Vintage.
Inglehart, R. F., & Norris, P. (2016). *Trump, Brexit, and the rise of populism: Economic have-nots and cultural backlash* (HKS Working Paper RWP16-026). http://dx.doi.org/10.2139/ssrn.2818659
Ivaldi, G., & Mazzoleni, O. (2020). Economic populism and sovereigntism: The economic supply of European radical right-wing populist parties. *European Politics and Society*, 21(2), 202–218. https://doi.org/10.1080/23745118.2019.1632583
Kallis, A. (2018). Populism, sovereigntism, and the unlikely re-emergence of the territorial nation-state. *Fudan Journal of the Humanities and Social Sciences*, 11, 285–302. https://doi.org/10.1007/s40647-018-0233-z
Kenny, P. D. (2018). *Populism in Southeast Asia*. Cambridge University Press.
Kingston, J. (2019). *The politics of religion, nationalism, and identity in Asia*. Rowan & Littlefield.
Korolczuk, E., & Graff, A. (2018). Gender as 'Ebola from Brussels': The anti-colonial frame and the rise of illiberal populism. *Signs*, 43(3), 797–821. https://doi.org/10.1086/696691
Körösényi, A., Illés, G., & Gyulai, A. (2020). *The Orbán regime: Plebiscitary leader democracy in the making*. Routledge.
Laclau, E. (2005). *On populist reason*. Verso.
Lee, S. J., Wu, C., & Bandyopadhyay, K. K. (2021a). Introduction: Democracy in Asian. In S. J. Lee, C. Wu, & K. K. Bandyopadhyay (Eds.), *Populism in Asian democracies. Features, structures, and impacts*. Brill.
Lee, S. J., Wu, C., & Bandyopadhyay, K. K. (Eds.) (2021b). *Populism in Asian democracies. Features, structures, and impacts*. Brill.
Mann, M. (2005). *The dark side of democracy: Explaining ethnic cleansing*. Cambridge University Press.
Mansbridge, J., & Macedo, S. (2019). Populism and democratic theory. *Annual Review of Law and Social Science*, 15, 59–77. https://doi.org/10.1146/annurev-lawsocsci-101518-042843
Marlière. P. (2022, May 30). Can the 'Nupes' revive the French left's fortunes? *Brave New Europe*. https://braveneweurope.com/philippe-marliere-can-the-nupes-revive-the-french-lefts-fortunes
Mietzner, M. (2018). Movement leaders, oligarchs, technocrats and autocratic mavericks: Populists in contemporary Asia. In C. de la Torre (Ed.), *Routledge handbook of global populism* (pp. 370–384). Routledge.
Moffitt, B., & Tormey, S. (2020). Rethinking populism: Politics, mediatisation and political style. *Political Studies*, 62(2), 381–397. https://doi.org/10.1111/1467-9248.12032
Mudde, C. (2004). The populist Zeitgeist. *Government and Opposition*, 39(4), 541–563. https://doi.org/10.1111/j.1477-7053.2004.00135.x
Mudde, C. (2007). *Populist radical right parties in Europe*. Cambridge University Press.
Müller, J.-W. (2016). *What is populism?* University of Pennsylvania Press.
Neocleous, M. (1996). Friend or enemy? Reading Schmitt politically. *Radical Philosophy*, 79, 13–23.
Ostiguy, P. (2020). The socio-cultural, relational approach to populism. *Partecipazione e Conflecto*, 13(1), 29–58. https://doi.org/10.1285/i20356609v13i1p29
Palaver, W. (2019). Populism and religion: On the politics of fear. *Dialog*, 58(1), 22–29. https://doi.org/10.1111/dial.12450
Pappas, T. S. (2012). *Populism emergent: A framework for analysing its context, mechanisms, and outcomes* (EUI Working Paper RSCAS 2012/01). European University Institute. http://cadmus.eui.eu/handle/1814/20114
Postel, C. (2019). Populism as a concept and the challenge of U.S. history. *IdeAs* [Online], 14, 1–17. https://doi.org/10.4000/ideas.6472
Rovira Kaltwasser, C., Taggart, P., Ochoa Espejo, P., & Ostiguy, P. (Eds.) (2017). *The Oxford handbook of populism*. Oxford University Press.
Roy, O. (2016). Beyond populism: The conservative right, the courts, the churches and the concept of a Christian Europe. In N. Marzouki, D. McDonnell, & O. Roy (Eds.), *Saving the people: How populists hijack religion* (pp. 185–202). Hurst.
Stoeckl, K. (2016). Political liberalism and religious claims: Four blind spots. *Philosophy & Social Criticism*, 43(1), 34–50. https://doi.org/10.1177/0191453716651665
Tushnet, M. (2019). Varieties of populism. *German Law Review*, 20(3), 382–389. https://doi.org/10.1017/glj.2019.27

Waisbord, S., & Amado, A. (2017). Populist communication by digital means: Presidential Twitter in Latin America. *Information, Communication & Society*, *20*(9), 1330–1346.

Weyland, K. (2013). Latin Americas authoritarian drift: The threat from the populist left. *Journal of Democracy*, *24*(3), 18–32. https://doi.org/10.1353/jod.2013.0045

Wintour, P., & Elgot, J. (2023, January 5). Number of populist leaders at 20-year low. *The Guardian*. www.theguardian.com/world/2023/jan/05/number-of-populist-world-leaders-at-20-year-low

Wodak, R. (2013). 'Anything goes!'–The Haiderization of Europe. In R. Wodak, N. Khosrivi, & B. Mral (Eds.), *Right-wing populism in Europe: Politics and discourse* (pp. 23–38). Bloomsbury Academic.

Wu, C., Lee, S. J., & Bandyopadhyay, K. K. (2021). Conclusion: Sources and features of Asian democracy. In J. J. Lee, C. Wu, & K. K. Bandyopadhyay (Eds.), *Populism in Asian democracies. Features, structures, and impacts*. Brill.

Zhuang, J. (2023). Income and wealth inequality in Asia and the Pacific: Trends, causes, and policy remedies. *Asian Economic Policy Review*, *18*, 15–41. https://doi.org/10.1111/aepr.12399

Zürn, M. (2021). How non-majoritarian institutions make silent majorities vocal: A political explanation of authoritarian populism. *Perspectives on Politics*, *20*(3), 788–809. https://doi.org/10.7910/DVN/7BCD4I

PART II

Approaches and key issues

2
POPULISM, NATIONALISM, AND NATIONAL IDENTITY IN ASIA

Howard Brasted and Imran Ahmed

The scholarly debate

Populist nationalism

Central to the phenomenon of populism, the study of which has focussed primarily on Europe and Latin America and been explained predominantly within these geographic contexts, is the debate on the relation between populism and nationalism. Some 50 years ago, populism and nationalism were intricately linked as congruent, one dealing with 'the people', and the other with 'the people as the nation'. Indeed, populism was characterized as 'a kind of nationalism', and since they appeared so much alike on occasion, they were virtually treated as interchangeable movements (Bonikowski et al., 2018; Brubaker, 2020).

In more recent times, this has continued to be the case. Scholars predominantly use the hybrid or composite term *populist nationalism* to describe the global rise of 21st century populism and its invocation not only to define *the people*, but also to reconfigure the nation they identify with. That populism is attached to nationalism as an adjective is because, as Miller-Idress explains, it makes 'most sense' of populism—a political philosophy notoriously lacking definitional precision—to pair them in this way. Populism can draw on nationalism, the more established ideology, to provide it with the coherence and 'political meaning' it appears to lack (Miller-Idriss, 2019, p. 19). A recent study has even gone so far as to describe populist nationalism as a 'distinctive' discourse that has merged into something that can stand in its own right (Subedi, 2022). The trouble is that the resulting entity, ostensibly implying that populism exists as a kind or sub-type of nationalism, has not made it any easier to apprehend or to identify the particular impulses that drive it.

That it has become almost commonplace for populism to be cast going hand-in-hand with nationalism has led De Cleen and Stavrakakis to question not only the utility of analytically linking them quite so closely, but also the degree of actual linkage between them (De Cleen & Stavrakakis, 2020). De Cleen (2017) mounts a strong case against any routine coupling or conflation. If populism and nationalism are strictly defined, he argues, they stand intrinsically apart as altogether different concepts dealing with different things. Populism is a vertical 'up-down' appeal to 'the people as the underdog', while nationalism is a horizontal 'in-out' appeal to 'the people as the nation'. Who belongs in each grouping is determined by who is deemed not to belong: the corrupt elites with respect to the people, and foreigners and outsiders with respect to the nation (De Cleen, 2017, pp. 342–343 and 349). Populists and nationalists may share a claim to represent an 'us' by excluding a 'them', but the insiders and outsiders they thereby proceed to identify are not necessarily identical.

Although in sympathy with the attempt to arrive at a stand-alone, 'clear' conceptualization of populism, Brubaker (2020, p. 45) remains sceptical that populism can be 'purified' by removing concepts such as nationalism from the equation altogether. He maintains that in practice, populism and nationalism intersect and overlap in a closely relational way. They may be 'analytically distinct', he concedes, but they are not 'analytically independent'. To separate them completely would obscure populism's interplay with nationalism in upholding the purity of the people on the one hand and the integrity of the nation on the other. As he explains it, the interplay occurs because populism not only has a vertical dimension that pits populists against elites at the top—and often those considered least worthy at the bottom—but also, importantly, a horizontal dimension that puts them in opposition to 'alien' outside forces, such as immigrants, or global organizations run by foreign elites (Brubaker, 2020, p. 60). It is along this horizontal axis that populism and nationalism do intersect, and European right-wing politics is full of such examples where this has occurred.

As the debate currently stands, most scholars proceed to occupy a position somewhere in between. Contributors to an exchange on the subject, for example, agree that populism and nationalism are not necessarily the same, but nonetheless share 'elective affinities' that 'often—but not always—coincide'. Where there is disagreement, it is over how different types of nationalism relate to populism, given that nationalism may be liberationist, secessionist, linguistic, ethnic, or cultural, to name some of the more common forms. It is *ethnonationalism* in exclusionary majoritarian form, Bonikowski points out, that the radical right in Europe especially latches onto in its populist vilification of racial, religious, or cultural minorities (Bonikowski et al., 2018, pp. 60–65). Varshney agrees that when nationalism focusses on attacking minorities, it is most likely to form a 'partnership of convenience' with populism and look 'virtually indistinguishable' from it. But otherwise, populism and nationalism are 'two distinct phenomena' with clearly identifiable differences (Varshney, 2021, pp. 131–132 and 145).

Undoubtedly, one of the roots of the problem of conflation is the fact that populism 'rarely' travels alone. While populism predominantly travels in tandem with nationalism, it also piggybacks on a range of related phenomena with which it tends consequently to be linked with as well (Rovira Kaltwasser et al., 2017, pp. 17–18; Rooduijn in Bonikowski et al., 2018, p. 69). Depending on the context, populists can appear to share many of the political positions associated with, for instance, anti-pluralism, nativism, and authoritarianism. In short, there is no single 'identikit' populism with standard features but rather a variety of populisms that can manifest differently in different situations.

Analytical approaches

Through his definition of populism as a 'thin' ideology, which many scholars have subsequently adopted, Mudde is credited with significantly cutting through the problem that populism as a political philosophy has proven stubbornly difficult to categorize or satisfactorily capture. As a thin rather than fully formulated set of beliefs, Mudde explains, populism is apt to appropriate the more formalized and better-known ideas of 'thicker' host ideologies it may at times run parallel with (Mudde, 2004, p. 543; Mudde, 2017, pp. 27–47). Miller-Idriss goes a step further in suggesting that for populism to 'thrive', it must actually feed off a 'host' ideology parasitically. Removed from its host, it will weaken and likely fall by the wayside (Miller-Idriss, 2019, p. 19; Frank, 2017, pp. 630–32). This is particularly the case with nationalism.

Several alternative approaches to Mudde's *ideational* encapsulation of populism have been ventured to account for its chameleonic propensity to appear in different guises and to advocate different things (Rooduijn in Bonikowski et al., 2018, p. 70). Emphasising the central role of leadership, Weyland (2021) and Kenny (see Chapter 3 in this volume) argue that populism is not the bottom-up movement for empowering the people that the thin ideological approach allows for. Nor is it something that all and sundry can simply invoke. It is ostensibly a 'political strategy' adopted by charismatic leaders to mobilize popular support, not only to achieve power but also to consolidate their rule once in power. Accordingly, the performative side of politics is exploited to mobilize an entrusting, though generally unorganized, mass following, for the most part in a top-down way (Weyland, 2001, p. 14).

A discursive or rhetorical style in politics has accrued some support as an even broader classification of populism. In this form, populism is available to any political actor to use as a means of rhetorical persuasion and not just exclusively to those at the top who seek to reconfigure the nation state along a polarising 'them and us' axis. The virtue of this approach—even if might be seen as casting 'too wide a net' (Weyland, 2001, p. 12)—is that populism can be visualized as a two-way phenomenon that dynamically connects leaders and supporters. What connects them is less a shared world view or ideology than the rough and ready, 'transgressive', rather vulgar way of 'doing' politics that is credited with appealing to the metaphorical 'common man'. This socio-cultural approach involves the political 'spectacle' of leaders and followers harmoniously 'flaunting' a low 'cultural nativism' to mobilize opposition to a high 'cosmopolitan' understanding of the nation state and how it should function (Ostiguy, 2017).

Irrespective of whether populism is construed as a 'thin ideology', a 'political strategy', a 'low brow discourse', a 'style' of leadership, or indeed something else, or whether any of these definitions adequately or completely capture its essence, they are not mutually exclusive (Lee et al., 2021, p. 3). One may simply fit better than another in explaining a particular context or manifestation of populism. Where there is little disagreement is in defining the core attributes of populism. Opposition to elites and the dominance they wield heads the list. But anti-pluralism is not far behind. In fact, populism has come to be characterized almost reductively as a movement of people who see minorities in any form as the true enemies of the people. Against the backdrop of the 'War on Terror' and the stream of refugees from North Africa and war-torn Syria, immigrant minorities have been coming under sustained attack from rank-and-file populists in Europe as not only culturally incompatible outsiders, but also as a distinct threat to national security as potential fifth columnists.

Anti-globalization

Studies show general agreement that the current wave of populism in the West is being fuelled by a growing resentment towards globalization and the world order of neoliberal capitalism that informs it (Lee et al., 2021, p. 1). While globalization may have increased standards of living worldwide, in Europe it is increasingly associated with job insecurity, growing wealth disparity, offshore outsourcing, the decline of skilled labour, and the influence of international bodies such as the World Trade Organization and the International

Monetary Fund (Shopina et al., 2017; Woods, 2001). With the lower and middle classes perceiving themselves to be losing ground not only economically but also in terms of cultural and national identity, there seems little doubt that the way globalization is impacting developed countries is providing a conducive climate for populist views to gain traction.

It is in the way that globalization increasingly invokes the issue and politics of national identity that populism and nationalism can be seen to converge. This is certainly the case in developed Europe. Not only is it experiencing the negative side of neoliberal market forces in its economic dealings with the rest of the world but it is also confronting an unprecedented migratory inflow of Middle Eastern refugees and other non-European peoples seeking refuge and a better life. In such circumstances, it is little wonder that nationalists, like populists, have expressed a marked suspicion of ethnic minorities and the challenge pluralism poses to the concept of nationality as the basis of the nation state. In the European context, there are undoubtedly very strong echoes of anti-globalist nationalism in populist opposition to porous borders and immigrant driven multiculturalism (Müller, 2016, p. 101; Lee et al., 2021, p. 5).

Nationalist variants

While the issue of who is thought to be endangering the nation brings populism and nationalism together, any factors differentiating between them remain ambiguous. As with populism, there is no single or uniform pathology of nationalism, despite a forensic examination of its much thicker ideological underpinnings and the impulses that drive it (Bar-On, 2018, pp. 20–24). A vast literature, for instance, divides over whether the concept of nationhood is primordially derived from a distant past or instrumentally created by nationalists to achieve power in an immediate present (Brasted & Bridge, 1994). There is further disagreement over whether the real agents of political and social change were actually the 'subaltern' classes from below rather than the upper middle-class elites who led the nationalist movements (Ludden et al., 2001). More recently, scholars have come to distinguish between two more types of nationalism: ethnic nationalism, which tends to be exclusivist and intolerant of cultural difference, and civic nationalism, which points up traditional liberal values of tolerance and equality, and is more accepting of cultural diversity (Rooduijn in Bonikowski et al., 2018, p. 72). Not surprisingly, left-wing populists gravitate to the inclusive, civic variant of nationalism and right-wing populists to the exclusionary variant (Halikiopoulou et al., 2012, p. 512).

Whatever the case, as Benedict Anderson persuasively shows in his still seminal work on nationalism, the national 'community', as the basis for constituting the nation and establishing the sovereign state in congruence with it, is largely imagined (Anderson, 1983), though it is imagined in different ways. Nationalism potentially parts company with populism over its perspective of the elites, for instance, as the main enemies of the people. In nationalist histories, elites continue to figure at the forefront of conceptualising the nation, shaping its identity and construction, and leading it on the global stage.

The Asian context

Shifting the focus

By investigating populism within the broad, if still relatively neglected, regional backdrop of Asia, this chapter aims to shed additional light on the populist-nationalist debate and also critically on the key issue of populism in Asia and its relation to populism in Europe and elsewhere. Do these populisms follow the same or similar paths, or do they reveal distinctive twists and turns that need to be taken account of in the literature?

Since space does not allow for blanket coverage of Asia as a whole, this chapter will focus mainly on South Asia (India, Bangladesh, Pakistan, Sri Lanka) and to a lesser extent Southeast Asia (Indonesia, Malaysia, and the Philippines). What case studies of these countries sufficiently reveal is that Asia's experiments with populism are as varied and diverse as elsewhere, and arguably at times more so. Suffice to say, there are differences with the European experience in terms of the interconnectedness of populism and nationalism, the central role religion plays in the Asian context of both movements, the dominance of charismatic leadership, and the more common top-down rather than bottom-up kind of populist mobilization. At the very least, Asia reveals the complexity of the populist phenomenon. While there are commonalities in the way populism impacts different countries, regionally speaking, South Asia's populism follows a different trajectory, for instance, from Southeast Asia's. And East Asia's is different again.

What Asia also potentially brings up is the extent to which populism can emerge in non-democratic, totalitarian states such as Thailand, China, Myanmar, and Cambodia, and the forms this takes in those countries (see Chapters 21, 23, and 18 in this volume). Are there examples of populist activity in Asia that are completely independent of the nationalist connection? If not, is the nexus so close that populism can be said to, for all intents and purposes, constitute a subset of nationalism, or vice versa, as the hybrid composite terms 'populist nationalism' and 'nationalist populism' (Singh, 2021, pp. 250–260) imply?

Is the rise of populism in Asia similarly related not only to a growing disillusionment with globalization, as in Europe and the United States, but also to the exacerbating factor of waves of migrants seeking refuge? Ultimately, can it be said that the term populism in the Asian context usefully explains what is happening in the various political spheres across the region as a whole?

Religious nationalism

The point of departure in this chapter is to suggest that Asia ostensibly provides a more varied, more virulent, and more violent setting than Europe to observe the interplay of populism and nationalist politics. This is not to deny that wherever populist movements emerge, whether in Europe, Latin America, or Asia and the Pacific, they can look very much alike. Regardless of regional location and cultural background, the convictions populists hold, the grievances they express, and the remedies they promote may appear to have considerable similarity. Clearly, as the literature reveals, there are common global factors that encourage the rise of populist movements. The insecurity of employment, the widening gulf between rich and poor, the increasing power of multinational corporations, and the impotence of governments and politicians to bring about meaningful change are among the things that universally feed into a growing populist resentment of the international economic system and the hegemonic, unaccountable way in which it operates.

These factors are very much present in Asia too (Hadiz, 2017, pp. 184–189; Hadiz, 2019; Kingston, 2019, p. 10) and increasingly punctuate populist rhetoric in narratives that directly blame the West and depict globalization as Western imperialism in just another exploitative, if postcolonial, form. If these narratives have yet to translate into the fervent and widespread anti-globalization that is gripping Europe, they are clearly on the path to doing so (Lee et al., 2021, pp. 1–8; Chacko, 2018). Disgruntled young Asians are taking to the streets to attack the secular, capitalist modernity that globalization appears to foist on their countries as not only culturally but also economically alien.

What does seem to be distinctive and to have little or no parallel in Europe and Latin America is that populism and nationalism is Asia are coalescing in an altogether different way. Asia does not face the predicament of high levels of refugees and migrants that constitute a leading focus and trigger of European populism. The forced exodus of Rohingyas from Myanmar to neighbouring Bangladesh and Thailand is ostensibly the exception, providing an isolated case of a large body of people fleeing persecution and physical danger. It is the enemy within rather than the enemy without that is the basis of *otherness* in Asia. Religious and ethnic minorities resident in a country—not foreign outsiders desperately massing on the borders seeking refuge— constitute the perceived threat.

The context in which populism and nationalism are increasingly coming together in Asia is religious culture and the creation of majoritarian national identities based on religion and ethnicity. If in Europe, populist rhetoric has devoted some space to the cause of protecting a 'Judaic-Christian' heritage against an Islamic challenge, it has stopped well short of projecting religion as the core marker of statehood or nationality (Minkenberg, 2018). In Asia, however, whatever the dominant religion in a country or region may be—Buddhism, Hinduism, Islam, Sikhism, Christianity, etc.—political movements have arisen actively promoting national identity in terms essentially of that religion. The resulting exclusivism not only presages an authoritarian brand of governance, but also threatens to deprive minorities of their status as equal nationals, certainly in South and Southeast Asia. Under such a majoritarian prescription of nationhood, there is no place for the multicultural state or for pluralism in any shape or form. Its logic, as Kingston has starkly put it, is ultimately the emergence of monocultural states based on religion. Thus, 'to be Indian is to be Hindu, to be Sri Lankan is to be Sinhalese Buddhist, to be Indonesian is to be Muslim', and so on (Kingston, 2019, p. 10). Should such a conception of nationality come to prevail, either mass conversion or ethnic cleansing on an unprecedented scale would seem to follow.

The unfinished business of national identity

In South Asia specifically, but to a degree in Southeast Asia as well, populist rhetoric is striking a popular chord within the milieu of increasingly activated religious nationalism. While in Europe, the construction of national identities has largely taken place, in much of Asia, this quest has acquired renewed poignancy and fervent contestation at the constitutional, political, and street levels. This can be directly traced back to most Asian countries beginning the transition from colonies to independent states armed with constitutions that failed to provide precise definitions of their nation, who constituted it, and the principles it would operate by. The original designs of nationhood that emerged not only tended to be full of compromises and ambiguities, but they were also largely drafted with little or no grassroots input. Accordingly, they have been looked upon as works in progress rather than sacred documents set in stone, thus leaving the door ajar for different nationalist blueprints to be put forward.

This clearly happened in India. Although its first generation of nationalist leaders, for example, signed off on a constitution that prohibited discrimination on grounds of race, religion, caste or place of birth, a question mark hung over the secular, pluralistic idea of the India they promoted. A different vision of India as a Hindu nation or *Rashtra*, in which religious identity was paramount, existed in more extremist articulations of nationalism, particularly that of V. D. Savarkar, who became leader of the Hindu Nationalist Party from 1938–1948. His ideology of Hindutva, or Hinduness, as the essence of being Indian, which he had developed in the early 1920s, made no headway in the run up to independence, nor during the early decades of Congress party domination after 1947. But Hindu nationalism began to make political inroads with the emergence of the Bharitiya Janata Party (BJP) in the 1990s and the growing popularity of its anti-secular, pro-Hindu pitch to Indian voters. Suffice to say that Hindutva helped bring the BJP to power in 1998, 1999, 2014, and 2019.

Despite its creation in 1947 as an Islamic state, constitutional finality eluded Pakistan as well. After nine years of long, drawn-out discussion, it came up with a constitution that critically failed to define the position Islam would occupy in the new nation. Its first two constitutions circled round the issue, and an amendment to the third and current constitution—the 1973 constitution—to 'impose *Shariah* law as the supreme law of the land' failed to pass on the two occasions it was proposed. Pakistan thus remains 'ambivalent' about the place of religion in the state and the relationship between the executive, legislative, and judicial branches of government (Brasted et al., 2019, pp. 171–170; Zakaria, 1988; Paul, 2014, pp. 72–73 and 136). A constitutionally confused Pakistan has had martial law thrust on it three times—in 1958–1971, 1977–1988, and 1999–2008 (Ahmed, 2013; Shah, 2014)—and continues to confront Islamic demands to fulfil its Islamic destiny. Underpinning what has been called its crisis of identity, the very question that was posed about Pakistan when it separated from India plagues it still (Shaikh, 2009, p. 9; Cohen, 2004, pp. 2–4): should Pakistan function as a secular Muslim state, as its founding father Muhammad Ali Jinnah had intended, or along strictly Islamic lines as Abul A'la Maududi, the foremost spokesperson for Islam, had demanded? (Brasted et al., 2019, pp. 173–174; Ahmed & Brasted, 2021, pp. 356–360). After 75 years, this question has not been answered to the satisfaction of important elements in society.

Both Bangladesh and Indonesia designed constitutions that were intended to depoliticize religion. Bangladesh, in fact, took Islam out of the political equation altogether when, as East Pakistan, it broke away from West Pakistan in 1971 to establish itself as an independent democratic republic. Although language, culture, and a superior demographic trajectory, rather than religion, lay at the heart of the rift between them, Bangladesh proceeded to distance itself even more from Pakistan by immediately constituting itself a secular state. From practically that moment on, however, a secular national identity was something that has not sat comfortably with it. Removed from the constitution in 1977 after a military coup, secularism and religious freedom were 'restored' in 2011 after a Supreme Court ruling, but now exist somewhat ambiguously alongside Islam, which was installed as the official religion in 1988. Despite the incumbent Awami League government continuing to insist that religious minorities have equal rights, it has shown a willingness to afford Muslim hardliners concessions that have proceeded to whittle these rights away. Garnering Islamist support may help offset the democratic legitimacy it has forfeited for stifling dissent and ruling Bangladesh along authoritarian lines (see Chapter 14 in this volume), but it comes at the cost of breaching the 15th amendment's ratification of Bangladesh's secular pluralism.

The salience of identity politics lies similarly at the heart of constitutional building in Sri Lanka, Malaysia, and Indonesia. All three countries, which have the added complicating factor of significant ethnic minorities, devised constitutions that were designed to avoid religious conflict and racial disharmony. Sri Lanka's 1948, Malaysia's 1957, and Indonesia's

1945 constitutions established pluralistic states guaranteeing equal rights of citizenship and freedom of religion to all their inhabitants. Indonesia did this famously by means of the five principles of Pancasila, which was constitutionally enshrined as the ideological foundation of the new nation and embodiment of its national motto: *Bhinneka Tunggal Ika* (unity in diversity). However, through a plethora of constitutional amendments, Sri Lanka, Malaysia, and Indonesia have chipped away at religious minority protections, and all three can be seen moving, though at different speeds, towards more exclusivist iterations of national identity.

The prime example is Sri Lanka, where Sinhalese Buddhist nationalists have proclaimed themselves the pure people and declared Sri Lanka to be a homogeneous ethnoreligious state—Sinhale—with no place for Tamils or Muslims, despite their long-established connection to and inhabitancy of the island (Jayasinghe, 2021, p. 187). Faced with the constant rejection of their claims for equal community status, Sri Lanka's minority Hindu Tamils took the drastic step of fighting for an independent homeland in the northeast, resulting in a bitter three-decade civil war. With this challenge seen off in 2009, a more extreme Buddhist strain of Sinhala nationalism came to the fore in the form of the ultra-nationalist Bodu Bala Sena (BBS) or Army of Buddhist Power in 2012 (Shirley, 2016). Led by militant monks, it began targeting Sri Lanka's Muslims as the 'new social enemy', especially after the Easter attacks on Christians in 2019. Although Buddhism in Sri Lanka has never been in any danger from Islam, with Muslims making up a bare 9% of the population, the BBS's new-found Islamophobia is in line with its goal of creating a Buddhist equivalent of Hindutva and restricting Sri Lankan nationality to Sinhalese Buddhists alone (Holt, 2016, pp. 8–11). Moves to amend Articles 10 and 14(1) of the constitution, which uphold 'freedom of thought, conscience and religion', likely beckon.

With freedom of religion still guaranteed in their respective constitutions, both Malaysia and Indonesia face persistent pressure from Islamic parties to scrap this provision unequivocally. In Malaysia, secularism faces all kinds of restrictions, none more so than Article 160 of the Constitution, which stipulates that all ethnic Malays must be Muslim and remain so since they cannot convert to another religion. The Pan-Malaysian Islamic Party (PAS) in fact demands the death penalty for apostasy. While successive governments appear reluctant to interfere with the religious practices of non-Muslims, they have found the accusation of blasphemy against them a useful weapon for communal control. Courtesy of the *Dakwah* movement and the closeness of the linkage between Islam and the state, 'creeping' Islamization has become the order of the day (Shah, 2017).

Much the same can be said of Indonesia. The secular identity it constitutionally embraced in 1945 has consistently drawn the fire of Islamic parties, such as the Islamic Defenders Front (IDF), a populist organization notorious not only for attacking churches, the ethnic Chinese, and Muslim minorities but also for mobilising mass rallies against a multicultural Indonesia. Banned in December 2020 for undermining Indonesia's national ideology, its most famous protest in 2016 led to the imprisonment of the Chinese Christian governor of Jakarta, Basuki Tyahaja Purnama (better known as Ahok), on the grounds of blasphemy against Islam.

The nationalism that early informed the constitutional histories of all these Asian countries played down ethnicity and religion in the cause of securing self-determination from colonial rule. The resulting constructions of collective national identity generally did this, but the secularism and pluralism they appeared to commend were later subjected to serious challenge for failing to provide appropriate or authentic ideological bases for their nation states. Today, a more exclusivist nationalism not only divides the peoples of Asia according to cultural and 'civilizational' differences (see Chapter 10 in this volume), but also results in widespread attacks on minorities on a scale that is deemed to amount to 'cultural war' (Kingston, 2019, p. 7). Ethnic and religious minorities are reportedly being subjected throughout much of Asia to widespread discrimination, vigilante violence, hate crimes, and even lynching, most of which go unpunished.

Enter top-down populism

What has made the current situation so combustible in South and Southeast Asia is populism, which has been thrust into a context of smouldering religious nationalist sentiment and unfinished constitutionalism with an accelerant effect. Not that populism is a new feature on the Asian political landscape. As the literature attests, Asia has experienced previous waves of populism (Mietzner, 2019, pp. 371–372), and boasts an array of former charismatic leaders such as, for example, Indonesia's Sukarno, Pakistan's Zulfikar Ali Bhutto (see Chapter 13 in this volume), and India's Indira Gandhi (see Chapter 12 in this volume; and Jaffrelot & Tillin, 2017, p. 179ff.), all of whom identified closely with the 'people', in typical populist fashion, as the very embodiments of their respective nations. As 'Mother India' to her supporters—the poor and the peasantry especially—Indira Gandhi came close to acquiring almost God-like status (Chakrabarti & Bandyopadhyay, 2021, p. 101). Because all three committed themselves to 'socialist' projects—Indira to agrarian and social reform, Bhutto to a socialist Islam, and Sukarno to a socialist Indonesia—they have been characterized as 'left-wing' populists.

Today, while no politicians can ignore the phenomenon of religious nationalism, it has been the political 'right wing' who have captured the marketplace of identity politics this involves. As never before, right-wing charismatic leaders are subscribing to national mythologies and models of exclusivist, purified, religious homelands that once only religious zealots dreamed of, bending history and culture to their electoral advantage. The manipulation of populist and nationalist mentalities in creating all kinds of 'anti-other' divides—us vs them, virtuous people vs venal elites, friends vs foes, the pure vs the impure—is classic textbook divide and rule politics. The blatant 'othering' of ethnic and religious minorities throughout Asia, both vertically and horizontally, is in fact ubiquitous. What we are mostly witnessing throughout Asia are political leaders resorting to a vulgar, 'plebian' style language of populism (Ostiguy, 2017, pp. 77–79), not only to seek or exercise power but also to mobilize their followers in the cause of religious nationalism.

No national leader better illustrates this than India's Narendra Modi, who has stood on the BJP platform of 'One Nation, One People and One Culture' throughout his political career, not only as Chief Minister of his home state of Gujarat from 2001 to 2014, but also as India's Prime Minister over the last nine years. As a lifelong member of the Rashtriya Swayamsevak Sangh or RSS—the mother organization of the Hindu nationalist movement—he was exposed to its 'saffronized' ideology of India as a Hindu nation from an early age. According to Jaffrelot and Tillin (2017, pp. 186–189), the pro-Hindu, anti-Muslim political campaign he blatantly pursued in Gujarat and carried over to the national stage embodied the whole 'repertoire of Hindutva populism'. Proclaiming the sacredness of cows and prohibiting their slaughter, canvassing *shuddhi* (reconversion) of Muslims and Christians, and foreshadowing their return to *ghar wapsi* (the Hindu fold) are aspects of a political strategy calculated to whip up Hindu nationalist fervour.

Leading this campaign from the front, Modi spread the message of a polarising religious nationalism, initially through spectacular marches and public rallies, but later and more effectively through the mass media: the internet, the mobile phone, his personal NaMo TV channel, and interactive holographic presentations (Jaffrelot & Tillin, 2017). Hindutva may have taken a back seat when he swept to power as Prime Minister in 2014 on ambitious promises of economic development and a better life for all. But with India's economic record failing to measure up by the time of the 2019 general elections, 'one nation' and 'Hindu-first' politics became front and centre again.

Against a backdrop of renewed tensions with neighbouring Pakistan and Bangladesh, Modi played the 'Hinduism in danger' card, and India's Muslims found themselves once again in the BJP firing line, this time as the traitorous 'them', the potential enemy within. Through changes to the citizenship law in 2020, the 'Indianness' of India's non-Hindu minorities was put under a cloud, and 200 million Muslims came face to face with the prospect of being rendered either second class citizens or even foreigners ('Modi's Dangerous Moment', 2019). Labelled 'India's divider in chief' by Time Magazine in 2019 (Taseer, 2019, p. 21), Modi stands out as the outstanding example of a right-wing populist leader redefining national identity in majoritarian religious terms. But he is certainly not alone in Asia in combining populism, religion, and nationalism in this way.

Former Prime Minister of Pakistan, Imran Khan, has clearly done this too, although the Islamic nationalism he embraced as the defining feature of his government was less exclusivist than Modi's. His Pakistan Tehreek-e-Insaf party came to power in 2018 on a domestic populist platform of battling corrupt elites, uplifting the poor and ending social injustice. While Imran Khan could hardly claim to be one of the people, unlike Modi who frequently proclaimed his OBC (other backward class) roots (Chakrabarti & Bandyopadhyay, 2021, p. 102; Chacko, 2018, p. 555), Khan has always insisted he was different, framing himself as the charismatic outsider who already had attained fame and fortune and had entered politics not for personal gain, but to transform Pakistan itself.

For him, the way ahead lay in establishing *Naya Pakistan* (a new Pakistan) and adopting the Medina Constitution devised by Muhammad fourteen centuries earlier to deliver a just and moral society (Khan, 2022). The more tolerant Pakistan that Imran Khan was convinced would emerge would be one able to negotiate 'the narrow path that lies between all possible extremes' (Khan, 2011, p. 335). This meant a Pakistan that did not slavishly follow in the footsteps of the West and serve its 'materialist' interests. Nor did it mean giving ground to 'myth-making mullahs' (Khan, 2011, pp. 334–338) and Sunni militant groups over their push to distinguish between a 'true' or 'false' Islam and ridding Pakistan of anyone who failed the test they set (Rafiq, 2014, pp. 9, 11, 21, and 29).

In the event, Imran Khan failed to walk the tightrope between a global and an independent economy—having had to go cap-in-hand to the International Monetary Fund in 2019—or to usher in the inclusive religious co-existence of Riyasat-e-Medina (State of Medina). He had to back away, for instance, from supporting the construction of the first Hindu Temple in Islamabad (Abi-Habib, 2020), and was powerless to prevent an ultra-right extremist party like the Tehreek-e-Labbiak from persistently demonising religious minorities or subjecting both Muslims and non-Muslims to accusations of blasphemy. Upon his removal from office in 2022, following a parliamentary vote of no confidence, Khan, in typical populist fashion, angrily accused an outgroup of 'treasonous' politicians of colluding with hostile international forces. Four years after coming to power, with enemies jailed, the media muzzled, and government back in the hands of the establishment Muslim League, Khan's new Pakistan looked pretty much the same as the old Pakistan he had set out to change.

Similar national identity conflicts continue to be ignited in other Muslim majority countries, as much by fundamentalist Islamic groups applying populist pressure on the governments of the day to end pluralism as by their respective presidents or prime ministers. Remarkably forthcoming about the kind of' 'modernist' Islam he wanted Malaysia to embrace, for example, the flamboyant Mohamad Mahathir was consistently at the forefront of de-secularising Malaysia (Kessler, 2004) and making life more difficult for its sizeable plural, non-Muslim communities. While it is not clear whether he did this to appease Islamic opposition or to advance his own vision of a dynamic Islamic state, Mahathir lays claim to being recognized as a populist-nationalist par excellence (Schottman, 2011).

In Bangladesh and Indonesia in recent years, the Arabization of Islam has seen not only money pouring into mosques and madrassas, but also the funding of increasingly anti-secular shows of strength against religious and ethnic minorities. Both Sheikh Hasina Wazed in Bangladesh and Joko Widodo in Indonesia have had to concede some ground to Islamic demands to do away with pluralism altogether to counter claims that their continued support for religious others constitutes an affront to Islam and discounts the primacy of Muslim culture (Kingston, 2019, pp. 97–101).

Like Imran Khan, Sheikh Hasina also invoked the Medina Constitution, though less to propose it as a model to follow than to make the point that, in protecting religious freedom, Bangladesh was already governing in its spirit (Hasan, 2016). However, to judge from the over 3600 attacks on the Hindu minority since 2013, the killing spree against secular bloggers between 2016 and 2018, and hostile anti-blasphemy demonstrations (Mostofa, 2021), conciliation has been one way traffic. While publicly standing firm against the demand for a blasphemy law, for example, her Awami League government has permitted a de facto blasphemy law to operate under the aegis of the Information and Communications Act (Kingston, 2019, p. 102). At no stage a natural populist, Sheikh Hasina has compensated for any presumed Islamic failings by constantly reminding Bangladeshis of her historic connection to the birth of the nation as the daughter of Bangladesh's founding father, Sheikh Mujibur Rahman. Sponsored under her prime ministership in 2011, the 15th amendment to the constitution officially venerated Mujibur Rahman as the architect of independence, and his portrait has hung in every public institution since 2009.

As the standard currency of Indonesian politics, populist appeals to the people have become almost commonplace. Mobilising nationalist and anti-foreign sentiment, Joko Widodo (Jokowi) won the 2014 and 2019 presidencies from the oligarchic Prabowo Subianto on similar if much more polite populist, anti-elite, anti-foreign capitalist, and pro-social justice platforms. But without a party base to provide institutional support, his political authority has lacked leverage (Mietzner, 2019, p. 376). Indeed, as soon as he took office, his promise to begin a new era of popular rule was easily blocked by elite opponents. He also had to retreat in the face of massive Islamist street demonstrations against his Chinese Christian friend and ally, Basuki Tjahaya Purnama, the Governor of Jakarta, who was accused of blasphemy, subsequently found guilty, and jailed for two years (Mietzner, 2019, pp. 375–376). As test cases of Indonesia's religious tolerance, not only was this a notably symbolic setback, but so also was Widodo's choice of Ma'ruf Amin as his presidential running mate in the 2019 election. As the Chairman of the Ulama Council of Indonesia (MUI) who testified against Ahok, Ma'ruf Amin was also the head of its Fatwa Committee when it issued the so-called SIPILIS fatwa against secularism, liberalism and pluralism in 2005 (Kingston, 2019, pp. 195–201).

As an indicator of a growing trend in favour of greater Islamization, a presidential decree in 2017 warning Islamic organizations against challenging Pancasila told much the same story. While Pancasila was not believed to be in any immediate danger, this was attributed to the failure of Islamic nationalism to constitute anything approaching an ideologically cohesive force in Indonesia at that time (Hadiz & Robinson, 2017, pp. 497–500). The picture, which it also conjures up, of the Indonesian people belonging to an international *ummah* (community of believers), and pan-Islamic caliphate beyond that, also constitutes perhaps an overly-transnational perspective to attract street-level support. Nonetheless, the possibility remains that the Islamic demand for *Shariah* law may at some stage gain sufficient momentum to put Indonesia's Pancasila to the absolute test.

In the case of Sri Lanka, what is immediately striking is that the way populist politics has centralized around religious nationalism, particularly following the civil war, closely mirrors the situation in India. Whether Mahinda Rajapaksa, as president from 2005–2015, or his brother, Gotabaya Rajapaksa, who succeeded him in 2019, identify Sri Lanka as a primordial Sinhalese Buddhist nation extending back 25 centuries, they have been supported by Sinhalese Buddhist nationalists who do. Certainly, they have cast themselves as the representatives of the pure people of Sri Lanka—namely Sinhalese Buddhists—and resort to the kind of polarising, civilizational populism that has characterized the politics of the BJP in India.

As the president who secured victory over the Tamil Tigers, Mahinda Rajapaksa cultivated the image that like the mythical Sinhalese hero kings in the Mahavamsa chronicle, he too had successfully liberated his people through conquest. As president, his picture could be seen everywhere—on billboards, on buses, on the currency—and like Modi, he was able to command social media outlets. This did not stop Mahinda from unexpectedly losing the 2015 presidential election to a government strongly supported by 'outsider' Muslims and Tamils. But Gotabaya Rajapaksa's victory in 2019 returned the Rajapaksa family to power, with the backing not only of the Sinhalese majority, but also symbolically the ultra-nationalist BBS army of Buddhist power. While the ideological commitment of the Rajapaksas to a Sinhalese Buddhist Sri Lanka may be questioned, they demonstrate how top-down populism can effectively popularize the cause of majoritarian religious identities.

Where religious nationalism does not seem to have played a seminal role is the Philippines, which has had a long line of populist leaders (Thompson, 2010), Rodrigo Duterte being the latest (until the 2022 election of Ferdinand 'Bong Bong' Marcos). Securing power as a firebrand populist promising to save the people from criminals, murderers, and the dangerous other, Duterte is deemed to have captured the brash chauvinism scholars and observers associate with the populism of the Trump mould. Insofar as he envisaged a different Philippines emerging, his apparent goal was to transform it from a crime and corruption hub into a prosperous economic powerhouse and to make it a more independent player in the realm of foreign politics. But otherwise, its cultural identity was not something he necessarily believed to be at stake. In signing the landmark Bangsamoro Organic Law, giving self-rule to Muslims in the south of the country, Duterte opted to halt four decades of separatist hostilities rather than continuing to treat the issue as the ultimate test of the Philippines' national integrity (Curato, 2017, p. 148). The predicament of Christians in Bangsamoro may continue to remain a concern, but religious majoritarianism in the Philippines has never been in doubt. Duterte's up-front, vulgar populism, which promised to feed criminals to the fishes and by inference anyone else who opposed him, may have earned him the ire of local and international rights organizations, but it sufficed to keep him popular until the last year or so of his tenure as president (Mietzner, 2019, p. 377).

Conclusion

Comparing the European and Asian landscapes of populism and nationalism, several differentiating features stand out. The sheer scale of Asia's diversity constitutes the most obvious. Not only can populists come from such different backgrounds that they appear to be poles apart, but they can also face off against each other as bitter opponents. Indeed, the populisms they espouse can reflect altogether different motivations and objectives. Populism in East Asia, which this chapter has not covered, looks nothing like populism in India, Sri Lanka, or Malaysia. Taiwan even offers an example of populism and nationalism being placed at odds and on opposite sides (see Chapter 24 in this volume). And in Thaksin Shinawatra of Thailand, we encounter a 'reluctant' populist, one who only adopted populist rhetoric on behalf of the poor when he saw how well this had worked to win government in neighbouring countries (Hewison, 2017).

By far the biggest difference with Europe is the way populism and nationalism have combined for mutual reinforcement to posit new national identities based on majoritarian religious affiliation and to persecute their religious and ethnic minorities as aliens and outsiders. The battlegrounds, particularly in those countries that have emerged from colonial rule, are the various constitutional settlements they started out with. These are invariably being contested, either because of the vestiges of secular and plural design they still contain, or because they have not gone far enough in satisfying their respective religious constituencies. While nationalism in religious form has been at the forefront of providing the ideological rationale for constitutional change, populism has been instrumental in seeding a climate of civic and cultural discord that backs this up on the ground. Simmering intercommunal violence seems dangerously poised to boil over throughout Asia.

There is nothing quite like this happening in Europe. Far-right populists and nationalists may claim that refugees and migrants are overrunning their respective countries and may, like Viktor Orbán in Hungary, have defined national identity in terms of a single ethnicity. But no one has gone as far as to seriously propose radical reformulations of their nation states, as certain Asian leaders have done, based on a single religion. Insofar as regime change is sought in Europe, it is to usher in anti-immigration measures and border closures, not to reconfigure existing constitutions.

Finally, what this chapter tends to confirm is that populism, as a category of analysis, emerges in the Asian context more 'usefully' as either a political strategy (Weyland, 2017; Kenny, Chapter 3 in this volume) or a political style (Brubaker, 2020, pp. 60–61; Ostiguy, 2017; Moffitt, 2016, p. 3). Ideologically thin-centred and possessing, as Taggart argues, an 'empty heart' (Taggart, 2004, p. 275), populism tends to play the facilitating role of mobilising support for a variety of religious nationalist causes. In whatever form, nationalism, with its ideological thickness and greater identarian capacity, stands out clearly as the more dominant partner. But what happens when that relationship is strained to breaking point? Although a scenario yet to be played out, a recently bankrupted Sri Lanka may provide some of the clues, particularly if the 'people' follow through on their initial show of unity to hold the Rajapaksas and their populist politics accountable for the country's crippling economic crisis.

References

Abi-Habib, M. (2020, July 8). Islamists block construction of first Hindu temple in Islamabad. *The New Times*. www.nytimes.com/2020/07/08/world/asia/hindu-temple-islamabad-islamists-pakistan.html

Ahmed, I. (2013). *Pakistan the garrison state: Origin, evolution, consequences 1947–2011*. Oxford University Press.

Ahmed, I., & Brasted, H. V. (2021). Recognition and dissent: Constitutional design and religious conflict in Pakistan. *Journal of Contemporary Asia*, 51(2), 351–367. https://doi.org/10.1080/00472336.2020.1719538

Anderson, B. (1983). *Imagined communities: Reflections on the origin and spread of nationalism*. Verso.

Bar-On, T. (2018). The radical right and nationalism. In J. Rydgren (Ed.), *The Oxford handbook of the radical right* (pp. 17–41). Oxford University Press.

Bonikowski, B., Halikiopoulou, D., Kaufmann, E., & Rooduijn. M. (2018). Populism and nationalism in a comparative perspective: A scholarly exchange. *Nations and Nationalism*, 25(1), 58–81. https://doi.org/10.1111/nana.12480

Brasted, H. V., Ahmed, I., & Orakzai, S. (2019). Whither Pakistan: The ambivalence of constitutional road mapping? In J. Lahai, K. von Strokirch, H. V. Brasted & H. Ware (Eds.), *Governance and political adaptation in fragile states* (pp. 167–194). Palgrave Macmillan.

Brasted, H. V., & Bridge, C. (1994). Reappraisals: The transfer of power in South Asia: An historiographical review. *South Asia*, XVII(1), 93–114.

Brubaker, R. (2020). Populism and nationalism. *Nations and Nationalism*, 26(1), 44–66. https://doi.org/10.1111/nana.12522

Chacko, P. (2018). The right turn in India: Authoritarianism, populism and neoliberalisation. *Journal of Contemporary Asia*, 48(4), 541–565.

Chakrabarti, K., & Bandyopadhyay, K. K. (2021). Populism in contemporary Indian politics. In S. J. Lee, C. Wu & K. K. Bandyopadhyay (Eds.), *Populism in Asian democracies* (pp. 97–120). Brill.

Cohen, S. P. (2004). *The idea of Pakistan*. Brookings Institution Press.

Curato, N. (2017). Flirting with authoritarian fantasies? Rodrigo Duterte and the new terms of Philippine populism. *Journal of Contemporary Asia*, 47(1), 142–153. https://content.csbs.utah.edu/~mli/Economies%205430-6430/Curato-Duterte%20and%20Philippine%20Populism.pdf

De Cleen, B. (2017). Populism and nationalism. In C. Rovira Kaltwasser, P. Taggart, P. Ochoa Espejo & P. Ostiguy (Eds.), *The Oxford handbook of populism* (pp. 342–362). Oxford University Press.

De Cleen, B., & Stavrakakis, Y. (2020). How we should analyse the connections between populism and nationalism: A response to Rogers Brubaker. *Nations and Nationalism*, 26(2), 314–322. https://doi.org/10.1111/nana.12575

Frank, J. (2017). Populism and praxis. In C. Rovira Kaltwasser, P. Taggart, P. Ochoa Espejo & P. Ostiguy (Eds.), *Oxford handbook of populism* (pp. 629–643). Oxford University Press.

Hadiz, V. R. (2019, March 11). *Islamic and nationalist populisms*. https://www.youtube.com/watch?v=qUc2PW1mHrA&ab_channel=KanalPengetahuanFakultasFilsafatUGM

Hadiz, V. R., & Robinson, R. (2017). Competing populisms in post-authoritarian Indonesia. *International Political Science Review*, 38(4), 488–502. https://doi.org/10.1177/0192512117697475

Halikiopoulou, D., Nanou, K., & Vasilopoulou, S. (2012). The paradox of nationalism: The common denominator of radical right and radical left Euroscepticism. *European Journal of Political Research*, 51(4), 504–539. https://doi.org/10.1111/j.1475-6765.2011.02050.x

Hasan, M. (2016, June 13). Religious freedom with an Islamic twist: How the Medina Charter is used to frame secularism in Bangladesh. *South Asia @ LSE blog*. https://blogs.lse.ac.uk/southasia/2016/06/13/religious-freedom-with-an-islamic-twist-how-the-medina-charter-is-used-to-frame-secularism-in-bangladesh/

Hewison, K. (2017). Reluctant populists: Learning populism in Thailand. *International Political Science Review*, 38(4), 426–440. https://doi.org/10.1177/0192512117692801

Holt, J. C. (2016). Introduction. In J. C. Holt (Ed.), *Buddhist extremists and Muslim minorities: Religious conflict in contemporary Sri Lanka* (pp. 18–53). Oxford University Press.

Jaffrelot, C., & Tillin, L. (2017). Populism in India. In C. Rovira Kaltwasser, P. Taggart, P. Ochoa Espejo & P. Ostiguy (Eds.), *The Oxford handbook of populism* (pp. 179–194). Oxford University Press.

Jayasinghe, P. (2021). Hegemonic populism: Sinhalese buddhist nationalist populism in contemporary Sri Lanka. In S. J. Lee, C. Wu & K. K. Bandyopadhyay (Eds.), *Populism in Asian democracies* (pp. 176–196). Brill.

Kessler, C. (2004). The mark of the man: Mahathir's Malaysia after Mahathir. In B. Welsh (Ed.), *Reflections: The Mahathir years* (pp. 179–194). John Hopkins University Press.

Khan, I. (2011). *Pakistan*. Bantam Press.

Khan, I. (2022, January 17). Spirit of Riyasat-i-Madina: Transforming Pakistan. *Express Tribune.* https://tribune.com.pk/story/2339025/spirit-of-riyasat-i-madina-transforming-pakistan.

Kingston, J. (2019). *The politics of religion, nationalism, and identity in Asia*. Rowan & Littlefield.

Lee, S. J., Wu, C., & Bandyopadhyay, K. K. (2021). 1ntroduction. In S. J. Lee, C. Wu & K. K. Bandyopadhyay (Eds.), *Populism in Asian democracies* (pp. 1–18). Brill.

Ludden, D. (Ed) (2001). *Reading subaltern studies: Critical history, contested meaning and the globalization of South Asia*. Permanent Black.

Mietzner, N. (2019). Movement leaders, oligarchs, technocrats and autocratic mavericks: Populists in contemporary Asia. In C. de la Torre (Ed.), *Routledge handbook of global populism* (pp. 370–384). Routledge.

Miller-Idriss, C. (2019). The global dimensions of populist nationalism. *The International Spectator*, 54(2), 17–34. https://doi.org/10.1080/03932729.2019.1592870

Minkenberg, M. (2018). Religion and the radical right. In J. Rydgren (Ed.), *The Oxford of the radical right* (pp. 523–560). Oxford University Press.

Modi's dangerous moment. (2019, March 2). *The Economist.* https://www.economist.com/weeklyedition/2019-03-02

Moffitt, B. (2016). *The global rise of populism: Performance, political style, and representation*. Stanford University Press.

Mostofa, S. M. (2021, December 6). Bangladesh's identity crisis: To be or not to be secular. *The Diplomat.* https://thediplomat.com/2021/12/bangladeshs-identity-crisis-to-be-or-not-to-be-secular/

Mudde, C. (2004). The populist zeitgeist. *Government and Opposition*, 39(4), 541–563. https://doi.org/10.1111/j.1477-7053.2004.00135.x

Mudde, C. (2017). Populism. An ideational approach. In C. Rovira Kaltwasser, P. Taggart, P. Ochoa Espejo & P. Ostiguy (Eds.), *The Oxford handbook of populism* (pp. 27–47). Oxford University Press.

Müller, J.-W. (2016). *What is populism?* University of Pennsylvania Press.

Ostiguy, P. (2017). Populism: A socio-cultural approach. In C. Rovira Kaltwasser, P. Taggart, P. Ochoa Espejo & P. Ostiguy (Eds.), *The Oxford handbook of populism* (pp. 73–97). Oxford University Press.

Paul, L. V. (2014). *The warrior state: Pakistan in the contemporary world*. Oxford University Press.

Rafiq, A. (2014). *Sunni Deobandi-Shi'i sectarian violence in Pakistan. Explaining the resurgence since 2007*. Middle East Institute. https://education.mei.edu/files/publications/Arif%20Rafiq%20report.pdf

Rovira Kaltwasser, C., Taggart, P., Esperjo, P. O., & Ostiguy, P. (2017). Populism: An overview of the concept and the state of the art. In C. Rovira Kaltwasser, P. Taggart, P. Ochoa Espejo & P. Ostiguy (Eds.), *The Oxford handbook of populism* (pp. 1–24). Oxford University Press.

Schottman, S. A. (2011). The pillars of 'Mahathir's Islam': Mahathir Mohamad on being-Muslim in the modern world. *Asian Studies Review*, 35(3), 355–372. https://doi.org/10.1080/10357823.2011.602663

Shah, A. (2014). *The army and democracy*. Harvard University Press.

Shah, D. A. H. (2017). *Constitutions, religion and politics in Asia: Indonesia, Malaysia and Sri Lanka*. Cambridge University Press.

Shaikh, F. (2009). *Making sense of Pakistan*. Columbia University Press.

Shirley, B. M. (2016, April 12). The Bodu Bala Sena: Sinhalatva origins and international influences. *South Asia Journal*, 16. http://southasiajournal.net/the-bodu-bala-sena-sinhalatva-origins-and-international-influences/

Shopina, I., Oliinyk O., & Finaheiev, V. (2017). Globalization and its negative impact on the global economy. *Baltic Journal of Economic Studies, 3*(5), 457–461. http://dx.doi.org/10.30525/2256-0742/2017-3-5-457-461

Singh, P. (2021). Populism, nationalism, and nationalist populism. *Studies in Comparative International Development, 56*, 250–269. https://doi.org/10.1007/s12116-021-09337-6

Subedi, D. B. (2022). The emergence of populist nationalism and 'illiberal' peacebuilding in Sri Lanka. *Asian Studies Review, 46*(2), 272–292. https://doi.org/10.1080/10357823.2021.1983519

Taggart, P. (2004). Populism and representative politics in contemporary Europe. *Journal of Political Ideologies, 9*(3), 269–288. https://doi.org/10.1080/1356931042000263528

Taseer, A. (2019, May 20). India's divider in chief. *Time, 193*(19).

Thompson, M. R. (2010). Reformism vs. populism in the Philippines. *Journal of Democracy, 21*(4), 154–168

Varshney, A. (2021). Populism and nationalism: An overview of similarities and differences. *Studies in Comparative International Development, 56*(2), 131–147. https://doi.org/10.1007/s12116-021-09332-x

Weyland, K. (2001). Clarifying a contested concept: Populism in the study of Latin American politics. *Comparative Politics, 34*(1), 1–22. https://doi.org/10.2307/422412

Weyland, K. (2017). Populism: A political-strategic approach. In C. Rovira Kaltwasser, P. Taggart, P. Ochoa Espejo & P. Ostiguy (Eds.), *The Oxford handbook of populism* (pp. 48–72). Oxford University Press.

Weyland, K. (2021). Populism as a political strategy: An approach's enduring—and increasing—advantages. *Political Studies, 69*(2), 185–189.

Woods, N. (2001). Making the IMF and the World Bank more accountable. *International Affairs, 77*(1), 83–100. Oxford University Press. https://www.jstor.org/stable/2626555

Zakaria, R. (1988). *The struggle within Islam: The conflict between religion and politics*. Penguin.

3
THE STRATEGIC APPROACH TO POPULISM

Paul D. Kenny

Populism can be conceptualized in a number of ways, but it is most usefully understood as a political strategy. Populists, according to the *strategic approach*, are charismatic leaders who seek to establish direct links with unattached mass constituencies in their quest to gain and retain power. Populism in this sense is less a matter of what people supposedly *believe* than of what they, or rather their leaders, in fact *do*. This strategic approach has its origins in the writings of Max Weber and, prior to the development of the *ideational approach* (Hawkins et al., 2019), was the predominant way of understanding populism (Barr, 2018). By returning directly to the insights of Weber, this chapter outlines the rationale for the strategic definition of populism.

The chapter also shows that the strategic understanding makes sense of two features of populism that are frequently noted by scholars who have viewed the concept through an ideational lens. First, the absence of institutionalized ties to supporters allows, if it does not compel, populists to appeal to a vaguely defined *people* rather than to specific interest groups. Drawing capacious and fuzzy boundaries around their potential constituency makes good strategic sense for political outsiders with a relatively disorganized support base. Second, without a deeply institutionalized party that has a strong corporate existence independent of its leader, populists are both motivated and permitted to weaken checks on their authority. Thus, the erosion of democracy under populism is not necessarily a matter of ideology. Rather, the illiberal tendencies of populism are built into how populists organize the pursuit and retention of power.

The origins of the strategic approach

Although populism has become a popular analytical concept through which to explain politics in the consolidated democracies of the West (e.g., Mounk, 2018; Mudde, 2007), for a long time, populism was understood to apply primarily to young and weakly institutionalized democracies, including that of nineteenth century America (Goodwyn, 1976; Hofstadter, 1964; Ionescu & Gellner, 1969). Populism was something that occurred in the context of social disruption and political realignment, processes that for early writers were frequently the result of economic changes such as industrialization. Populism gained the most traction as a sociological concept when applied to the study of a number of iconic political figures in mid-twentieth century Latin American history—Getúlio Vargas, Juan Perón, and José Maria Velasco Ibarra being the most prominent of them (Di Tella, 1965; Germani, 1978; Mouzelis, 1985; Van Niekerk, 1974). These movements were generally anti-oligarchic and highly nationalistic, but beyond that, they were ideologically heterogeneous, combining traditionally left- and right-leaning policies. The feature that united these contemporaneous movements, and concomitantly differentiated them from others, therefore, was not ideology, but the organizational form that they took on. Focusing in particular on Argentina, Gino Germani (1978) argued that populist movements comprised masses of previously marginalized citizens, especially rural migrants, who were mobilized by charismatic leaders to outflank establishment parties. Populism for these leaders was a way of directly connecting with a sociologically diverse base of support over the heads of a political establishment that was struggling to maintain control in an era of rapid structural change.

Critics of the strategic approach argue that it is too restrictive and that it describes only a few instances in mid-twentieth century Latin America, in which there was a sudden influx of masses of new urban voters (or potential voters) who lacked ties to established parties (Mudde & Rovira Kaltwasser, 2017; Pappas, 2019). It could only, it seemed, be the product of late industrialization and the rapid urbanization and social disruption that it caused. However, this line of critique takes the first proponents of the strategic approach too literally. The early structuralists' major breakthrough was in developing a sociological framework for explaining populism's success, not their specific focus on class conflict or demography. Echoing explanations then being made for the rise of fascism in Europe, structuralists like Germani (1978) essentially argued that the disruption of old social networks and the moderate political parties they sustained was central to the flourishing of populism in mid-century Latin America (on fascism, see Arendt, 2017 [1951]; Kornhauser, 1959). There is no reason that other social or economic shocks could not have similar effects, as subsequent students of Latin American politics would demonstrate (Barr, 2009; Roberts, 1995; Weyland, 1999). Understood more broadly, the populist strategy can be successful in a range of contexts that make other forms of political mobilization—namely programmatic or clientelistic mobilization—more challenging or more costly (Kenny, 2023), with Latin America, Asia, and Africa providing especially fertile territory (Kenny, 2019; Resnick, 2015).

Though strong on the sociological roots of populism, the first structuralists left the actual processes of political organization and mobilization underdeveloped. The value of this conceptual approach would thus not become clear until the comparative work of Nicos Mouzelis (1985) was published some decades later. Mouzelis (1985) conceived of populism as a general form of linkage, or what he called a 'mode of incorporation', between parties (or leaders) and voters. Mouzelis argued that political leaders purposively incorporate or mobilize the public into the political system. Political mobilization, in other words, is active, not passive. Drawing on Weber's (1978 [1922]) celebrated distinction between bureaucratic, patrimonial, and charismatic forms of authority, Mouzelis (1985) maintained that political incorporation or linkage tends to occur in one of three ways: through programmatic incorporation, clientelistic incorporation, or populist incorporation. Populists, in short, organize the pursuit of power differently from the leaders of other types of political movements, most notably, those of programmatic (or bureaucratic) and clientelistic (or patrimonial) parties (Kenny, 2017, 2023; Kitschelt, 2000).

As the pre-eminent theorist of modernization, Weber himself was mostly concerned with how the modern bureaucratic form of authority, the legal-rational state or *Rechtsstaat*, emerged from the patrimonial or traditional form. Modern political parties, for Weber (1958), fit this bureaucratic form of authority. Bureaucratic parties are characterized by rules and procedures governing the distribution of authority within the organization and a range of institutionalized relationships with supporters externally. Civil society organizations like unions, churches, and nationalist associations provide an enduring link between programmatic parties and voters (Mair, 2013; Panebianco, 1988). In contrast, clientelistic parties engage in a quid pro quo with supporters in which support is exchanged for particularistic material benefits. Such parties are governed internally according to factional strength, itself determined by which groups can mobilize the most resources and blocs of clients (voters) (Hicken, 2011; Stokes, 2007).

Focusing especially on populism in his native Greece and in Latin America, where clientelistic parties had long predominated, Mouzelis (1985, p. 334) writes that under populism, 'it is plebiscitarian leadership rather than intricate patronage networks that provides the basic framework for political incorporation'. For Mouzelis, while populist supporters are not tied to establishment parties through clientelistic or bureaucratic linkages, no other assumptions about their social class or political ideas were necessary. He writes:

> As a rule, populist leaders are hostile to strongly institutionalized intermediary levels, whether clientelist or bureaucratic. The emphasis on the leader's charisma, on the necessity for direct, nonmediated rapport between the leader and 'his people' as well as the relatively sudden process of political incorporation all lead to a fluidity of organizational forms.
>
> *(p. 334)*

This organizational approach implies a preference for a certain kind of political technology. In contrast to programmatic or clientelistic parties, as Herbert Kitschelt (2000) describes, populist movements or parties rely heavily on the charisma—or personalized authority—of the party leader to establish such linkages through the mass media and mass rallies. Populist leaders aim to establish unhindered ties with voters. Or as Kurt Weyland (2001, p. 14) puts it, populism is 'a political strategy through which a personalistic leader seeks or exercises government power based on direct, unmediated, and uninstitutionalized support from large numbers of mostly unorganized followers'.

Populism and charismatic leadership

Mouzelis's conceptualization implies that populism rests on the third of Weber's forms of authority: *charisma*. Charisma is often thought of as a personality trait, as some quality that an individual possesses (e.g., House & Howell, 1992; Simonton, 1984). This interpretation is given weight by the fact that in its original Greek, charisma signified that an individual had divine grace or favour. In everyday usage, charisma also refers to something like personal charm or magnetism. Weber's (1978 [1922], p. 241) own definition adds somewhat to the confusion, as he states that charisma refers to 'a certain quality of an individual personality by which he is set apart and treated as endowed with supernatural, superhuman, or . . . exceptional powers or qualities'. Management studies have often operationalized charisma as a set of personality traits that leaders are believed to possess. These include having vision, pride, selflessness, optimism, enthusiasm, confidence, respect, power, morals, values and beliefs, and a sense of purpose or mission (Antonakis et al., 2003).

However, even though charismatic leaders may be confident, passionate, magnetic, and persuasive speakers who are at ease with crowds, charisma is ultimately not simply a trait or characteristic; it is not something that an individual possesses in isolation. Rather, reading Weber more closely, it becomes clear that charisma describes a relationship. An individual is charismatic only to the extent that his followers *treat him as endowed* as such. Weber (1978 [1922], p. 242) contended, 'It is recognition on the part of those subject to authority which is decisive for the validity of charisma'. Charismatic leadership, by definition, requires a people to lead, even if any such popular movement is relatively fluid and temporary. Charismatic leadership, and hence populism, is not a performance put on by some individual but a collective process in which both leader and supporters play their part (Davies, 1954; Willner, 1984, pp. 14–17). Arguably, it is the followers, not the leader, who play the primary role. To quote Weber (1978 [1922], pp. 1112–1113) again, 'What is alone important is how the individual is actually regarded by those subject to charismatic authority, by his "followers" or "disciples"'. According to two later Weberian scholars, charisma is 'an attribute of the belief of the followers and not of the quality of the leader' (Bensman & Givant, 1975, p. 578). It is the 'emergent following which sets the charismatic figure apart from ordinary mortals' (Madsen & Snow, 1991, p. 2).

Charisma, as Weber understood it, forms an entirely distinct basis on which to construct political authority. It is a non-routinized or non-institutionalized form of politics and is thus categorically separate from bureaucratized or patrimonial forms of political mobilization. A charismatic leader is made so by popular acclaim rather than by rules, tradition, or personal favour. Charismatic leadership is thus in a sense *extraordinary*. A number of contemporary writers have taken this extraordinary characteristic to mean that Weber understood charismatic authority as something 'radical' (Pappas, 2016b) or 'revolutionary' (Bensman & Givant, 1975). This approach, however, represents a significant departure from Weber. Charismatic authority is antithetical to the two most common institutionalized forms of authority, the bureaucratic and the patrimonial. Charismatic leaders oppose the parties and institutions that undergird these other forms of authority, but it would be a mistake to interpret charismatic authority as being antithetical to conservatism in general. Charismatic leaders may invoke an idealized past as much as they do a utopian future. Donald Trump's main campaign slogan was to 'Make America Great *Again*' (although he never clearly specified when that period of greatness was). In any case, for Weber, it was the manner of followers' devotion, rather than 'the aims of rule' (Pappas, 2016b, p. 379) that were determinative of charismatic authority. By virtue only of the special personal qualities with which their followers believe them to be endowed, it seemed to Weber, charismatic leaders can rally their followers behind them in a challenge to more institutionalized bureaucratic or patrimonial forms of power (Weber, 1978 [1922], pp. 244–250, 1116).

Charismatic leadership is distinctive in terms of 'the absence of significant mediation of the relationship [between leader and follower], either by formal structures or informal networks' (Madsen & Snow, 1991, p. 5). This absence of intermediation is at the heart of populism as a political strategy (Kenny, 2017, 2019, 2023; Urbinati, 2015, 2019; Weyland, 2001, 2017). Weyland (2001), for instance, writes that charismatic populist leaders often establish a 'direct, quasi-personal relationship [between them and supporters that] bypasses established intermediary organizations' such as parties.

A common critique of the strategic approach is that politicians like France's Marine Le Pen and Austria's Jörg Haider cannot be classified as populists due to the presumed institutionalization of their parties. However, both the Front National (FN) (renamed the National Rally or RN) and the Freedom Party of Austria (FPÖ) may be less institutionalized than they first appear. The FN was established as the personal vehicle of Jean-Marie Le Pen; although the RN has expanded its local footprint in recent years, the party remains personally led and controlled by his daughter, Marine. The FPÖ was traditionally a clientelistic party, but Haider transformed it into a 'leader party'. As recent experience has demonstrated, even well-established parties, like the Republican Party in the United States, can be subject to 'hostile takeover' by populist leaders. In general terms, Weyland (2001, p. 14) notes that populists can deinstitutionalize parties and subordinate them to 'the leader's personal will'. That is, the degree to which any given party is populist can vary over time.

In any case, the distinctive characteristic of the populist strategy is not the absence of organization, but its personalistic structure. As Weber (1978 [1922], p. 1119) himself wrote, 'charismatic authority does not imply an amorphous condition; it indicates rather a definite social structure with a staff and an apparatus of services and material means that is adapted to the mission of the leader'. Charismatic authority entails the personalization of political authority; no rules, whether bureaucratic or traditional, constrain the leader's will. Just as Messiahs have disciples, charismatic leaders have *followers*. In other words, charismatic leaders can rule over organizations with varying degrees of sophistication, or as Mouzelis (1985, p. 334) put it, a 'fluidity of organizational forms'. They may be elaborate formal organizations like the Nazi Party or transitory movements like Peruvian president Alberto Fujimori's *Cambio 90* election vehicle. What distinguishes charismatic leaders from others is that they can rewrite the rules of their organizations or movements as and when they see fit. Of course, it is not that procedures and positions in a charismatically led organization are altogether absent, rather it is that the *charisma* of populist leaders allows them to redefine those procedures and positions *arbitrarily*. In this sense, populist movements or organizations can exist but are *uninstitutionalized* in the sense of not being based on the application of formal rules.

Charismatic leaders aim to build (or take over) a movement and to personalize their authority over it. Whatever its relationship to the broader populace or masses, where a political organization has multiple centres of power, collective leadership, and ready procedures for removing the leadership, and so on, it is not based on charismatic authority and, hence, is not populist. Charismatic leadership requires a near singular identification of leader and party; consequently, Perónismo, Chávismo, Dutertismo, or more contentiously, Trumpism. Not only does this fact characterize leaders like Hitler as charismatic, it also precludes merely independent or personalistic leaders from being categorized as such. Crucially, independents can be constrained by forces other than the people's collective ascent. Independent leaders often strike agreements with various factions to gain and retain power. Charismatic leadership is something out of the ordinary. It entails a measure of authority over people that is not bound by rules or traditions. This *internal* feature of populist organizations is just as crucial as the *external* one, and we will see the important effects this has on the relationship between populism and democracy.

Researching populist leadership

So dependent on an individualistic leader is charismatic authority that it tends to be limited in duration. As Weber (1978 [1922], p. 1120) so eloquently posited, 'Every charisma is on the road from a turbulently emotional life that knows no economic rationality to a slow death by suffocation under the weight of material interests: every hour of its existence brings it nearer to this end'. Thus, even for the pioneer of the subject, charismatic authority was of less significance than the bureaucratic and patrimonial forms of authority that lasted for whole eras, not merely the lifetimes of particular rulers. In turn, the necessary attention to extraordinary individual leadership that is part of any understanding of charismatic authority has kept it at the margins of political science ever since (but see Davies, 1954; Kenny & Holmes, 2020; Madsen & Snow, 1991; Merolla et al., 2007; Spinrad, 1991; Willner, 1984). Properly understood, however, an analysis of charismatic leadership means an examination of the social, economic, and political conditions that make this extraordinary, or uninstitutionalized, form of authority possible. Charismatic leadership, and in turn populism, are thus less matters of individual psychology than they are of context. As Weber's (1978 [1922]) original work indicated, charismatic leadership is associated with periods in which other more regularized forms of authority—bureaucracy and patronage—are absent or in crisis. Social science can productively direct attention towards understanding how, when, and why such periods of transition or crisis are causally related to the emergence of populism (Kenny, 2023).

To do so, however, requires that we distinguish populists from non-populists empirically. To accomplish this, we do not necessarily need to know what people or leaders *believe*. We just need to know what they *do* (Urbinati, 2019). If leaders come to office through rule-based party mechanisms and the support of people that are incorporated through party and civil society networks, we can identify them as the leaders of bureaucratic mass parties. If leaders mobilize support through the patron-client networks of parties or factions, we can call them clientelistic. For our purposes, the determinant of whether a given figure is populist is the degree to which they possess those two features of charismatic leadership of the masses in the pursuit of political power: first, do they rely *primarily* on the direct mobilization of a mass of people unattached to a party by personalistic appeals through mass rallies, and more recently the mass media, rather than through institutional or clientelistic linkages? And second, are they the unequivocal leader of a mass movement or party whose authority within that organization is absolute and arbitrary?

Of course, as Weber repeatedly stressed, charismatic, bureaucratic, and patrimonial forms of authority are ideal types. Delineating clear boundaries between populist and non-populist leaders has a heuristic attractiveness (Pappas, 2016a). In previous research, drawing on both primary and secondary sources, I developed a binary measurement to distinguish populists from non-populists in this way (Kenny, 2017). This approach greatly simplifies empirical analysis and makes any conclusions that much starker: populists erode press freedom more than non-populists (Kenny, 2020); populists undermine the rule of law (Houle & Kenny, 2018); populists obtain a greater share of votes when clientelistic ties between parties and voters break down (Kenny, 2017). All of these criteria are by necessity *relative*. Few politicians are unambiguously populist in the sense that they depend *exclusively* on charismatic leadership of the masses in the pursuit or exercise of power. In practice, no modern leader can function without some measure of bureaucratic organization. In a more general sense, populism is not strictly a categorical description but a trait every political leader must possess to a degree: the more reliant the leader is on charismatic linkages with supporters, the greater the extent to which they lead the movement or organization, and the more encompassing their arbitrary personal authority over it, the more populist they are. The more institutionalized a party leader's support, and the more constrained they are by party rules and factions, the less populist they are. Indeed, even though

Weyland (1999, 2001) conceived of his approach in categorical terms initially, in his most recent writing on the subject, he too has come to the conclusion that populism is a quantitative concept (Weyland, 2017).

As of yet, we have no stipulated set of criteria by which to measure a leader's reliance on unmediated linkages with supporters and command of unfettered authority within the movement. There continues to be legitimate disagreement on these counts, even in the best-studied cases of charismatic leadership. However, there is nothing inherently unquantifiable about these strategic elements of populist mobilization (Barr, 2018; Kitschelt, 2013). Measures of party membership, party institutionalization (e.g., age, nationalization), civil society endorsements, management structure, and leadership succession practice and policy can all be codified. Surveys could also be used to gather information on supporters and the degree to which they view leaders as charismatic (Kenny & Holmes, 2020). Are they members of any party or caucus? What sources of information do they use to make their political choices? What motivates them to support a particular leader? These remain potentially fertile areas of future research.

Strategy and discourse

The most common alternative to the strategic approach is to conceive of populism as a kind of political ideology according to which the people, not the elite, should rule (Galston, 2018; Hawkins & Rovira Kaltwasser, 2019; Mounk, 2018, p. 8; Mudde, 2004; Müller, 2016). People who adhere to a populist ideology are said to agree with statements such as 'the people, not the politicians, should make our most important policy decisions' (Akkerman et al., 2014). This approach is based, in part, on the observation that many aspiring political leaders use some variant of anti-establishment or people-centric rhetoric. Populists are anti-political politicians. Donald Trump, for instance, stated on the campaign trail in April 2016: 'On every major issue affecting this country, the *people* are right and the governing *elite* are wrong,' (Wilkin, 2018, p. 17) and in May of that year, 'The only important thing is the unification of the [real] people . . . the other people don't mean anything' (Galston, 2018, p. 37). Others have argued that populism reflects an earthy, folksy style that goes beyond rhetoric (Moffitt, 2016, 2020; Ostiguy, 2009). Not only do populists appeal to the people but they supposedly speak (simply) like them, dress like them, and so on. Populism in this sense is a kind of rhetorical and visual performance.

The strategic approach is consistent with populists' use of this kind of language or style. Indeed, the nature of charismatic leadership is such that we would in fact predict that such leaders would adopt these forms to varying degrees. Rational politicians use the rhetoric and ideas that are best suited to gaining and retaining power given the context. Language and style are side-effects of populists' overall political strategy. Appealing to a vaguely defined people makes good sense for a politician without strong institutionalized links to a body of supporters. Almost anyone, indeed almost *everyone*, can envisage themselves as a constituent of *the people* (Ochoa Espejo, 2015). This broadens the populist's potential support base in a way that leaders of parties with institutional ties to labour unions or farmers associations cannot contemplate. Programmatic party leaders have to speak in terms that appeal to the interests of far narrower sections of the population. As a result, despite their differing conceptual origins, there is considerable empirical overlap between those leaders and parties classified as populist in both the ideational and organizational approaches (Kenny, 2020; Ruth, 2018). Ultimately, though, to rely on the outward (rhetorical or stylistic) manifestations of populist strategies to define the concept itself is, we might say, to be drawn to the superstructure rather than the base, *power*. Speech and style are prominent features of populism, just not the central ones, at least for understanding populism's causes and consequences.

Moreover, contrary to the proposition that populist supporters are not motivated by policy, while those of bureaucratic parties are, the strategic framework posits that policy appeals may be highly relevant to populist voters. As populists are not institutionally tied to clearly bounded interest groups, it is often the case that their messaging is vague on policy specifics, especially in the economic realm. Thus, Thaksin Shinawatra, Thailand's populist prime minister, articulated his contradictory economic policy: 'I'm applying socialism in the lower economy and capitalism in the upper economy' (Wilkin, 2018, pp. 27–28). However, on certain issues, populists look to draw cleavages through appeals to the greater majority. They oppose crime, corruption, immigration, religious minorities, and sometimes the oligarchy, thus drawing very large boundaries around their potential support group (Kenny, 2019). A firm stance on illegal immigration and crime in general constitutes a natural populist policy; the potential constituency in favour of illegal immigrants or criminals (neither of which are themselves usually able to vote) is politically marginal. Such broad appeals make enormous sense as low-cost electoral tactics compared with the investment in time and money required to build up bureaucratic or clientelistic party organization and management. We should note, however, that at the micro-level, even though populist supporters may be attracted by such policy appeals, this does not make populist movements 'bureaucratic' (or 'programmatic' in the Weberian sense). Ironically, given the enduring nature of their party loyalties, it may be that supporters of bureaucratic parties are less motivated by policy than the supporters of populists (Green et al., 2002). It is not policy that divides populist and non-populist candidates or parties but their organization and management. Policy, like rhetoric and style, is part of the strategic arsenal used by populists to gain and retain power by appealing directly to relatively unattached constituencies through the use of mass communication.

Populism and illiberalism

A further advantage of the strategic approach vis-à-vis the ideological is the clear hypotheses that it generates with respect to the effects of populist government. Populism as an ideology is indeterminate when it comes to its relationship with democracy (Abts & Rummens, 2007; Canovan, 1999, 2004; Rovira Kaltwasser, 2012). Scholars working in the ideational tradition have thus tended to parse populism into democratic and illiberal sub-types (Mudde & Rovira Kaltwasser, 2013). This approach, however, has an unsatisfactory, ad hoc quality to it (Kenny, this volume), not least because the classification operates on two different dimensions, the economic and the cultural, at once (Norris & Inglehart, 2019). Empirical research on the effect of populist rule on democracy has, however, been much less equivocal. Relying on a strategic conceptualization, previous research shows that populist rule is associated with a decline in: judicial autonomy and the rule of law (Kenny, 2017); legislative checks on executive authority (Houle & Kenny, 2018); respect for international treaties (Voeten, 2020); freedom of speech (Kenny, 2020); and democratic quality (Diamond, 2021). Why does populism in the strategic sense have this antipathetic relationship with democracy?

As noted above, understood as a form of political strategy or organization, populism is highly personalistic. This fact alone generates distinct expectations about how populists will behave in office when compared to leaders of programmatic or clientelistic parties (Kenny, 2020). Programmatic and clientelistic parties have corporate life expectancies that extend beyond any particular leader or period of government. This gives organized political parties a markedly longer time horizon, which in turn affects their propensity to maintain or undermine institutions that protect the interests of minorities (i.e., the opposition). Although no party leadership wants to be out of government, it acknowledges that this is a possibility as long as the playing field is somewhat open. Any stifling of political liberties while in power could lead to reciprocal repression if they themselves lose power. Perhaps more importantly, there is also the possibility that the means of coercion could be turned on a leader's own party rivals. The institutional constraints on leaders that exist within both programmatic parties (e.g., confidence votes) and clientelistic parties (e.g., factional competition) mean that the behaviour of leaders adheres more closely to the interests of the party elite (if not its full membership), and hence restrains the erosion of democratic checks on the executive. In contrast, populist leaders are interested in their own survival rather than in the continued prosperity of a party per se, thus curtailing their time horizon. Therefore, once a populist has gained power, they have a greater interest in suppressing any opposition in order to retain power for as long as possible, as the long-term consequences for political competition are of little importance to them.

Without deeply institutionalized bases of support, populists must cultivate popular support. Thus, even though charismatic leadership is far from incompatible with dictatorship, we should be careful not to simply equate the two. Populists are not totalitarians. Indeed, charismatic leaders may depend on popular support to a greater degree than other types of leaders who can draw on tradition and law to legitimate their rule. The 'genuinely charismatic ruler' is 'responsible to the ruled—responsible, that is, to prove that he himself is indeed the master willed by God . . . If the people withdraw their recognition, the master becomes a mere private person' (Weber, 1978 [1922], pp. 1114–1115). The authority of the charismatic leader derives from popular adoration alone in contrast to other merely personalist rulers. Charismatic leadership 'rests on the faith of the ruled' (Weber, 1978 [1922], p. 1125). As Weber understood it, charismatic leadership tended to be transitional. Either it becomes institutionalized through the adoption of patronage or programmatic organizational linkages, or it must resort to some sort of demobilization or even repression. As a result, although we would expect populists to erode some liberal constraints on executive authority, we would also expect that they maintain a measure of popular participation that would not be observed in military, monarchical, or merely personalist dictatorships.

Conclusion

In summary, populist movements or parties can be distinguished from both bureaucratic and clientelistic organizations based on how they are structured internally and how they mobilize support externally. The exercise of authority within bureaucratic parties is bound by rules and procedures, while externally they are founded on stable institutionalized relationships with supporters. Analogously, in patrimonial organizations, authority is both traditional and transactional. Leadership is often inherited, and privileges are distributed accordingly to clients in return for their loyalty. Externally, such patronage-based parties engage in a quid pro quo with supporters in which votes are exchanged for particularistic material benefits. Charismatic authority is instead characterized by a concentration of arbitrary control in the person of a popularly acclaimed leader. Populism refers to the charismatic mobilization of the masses in pursuit of power. This strategic conceptualization is compatible with various manifestations of populism, being restricted neither to right-wing (xenophobic) nor left-wing (economic) populism. It is also consistent with various political styles but tends towards a vague *popularist* framing of the political space and towards policies that promote wide boundaries around their potential support base (e.g., law-abiding, native, middle-class, etc.). In power, populists are likely to erode checks on their authority.

References

Abts, K., & Rummens, S. (2007). Populism versus democracy. *Political Studies*, 55(2), 405–424. https://doi.org/10.1111/j.1467-9248.2007.00657.x

Akkerman, A., Mudde, C., & Zaslove, A. (2014). How populist are the people? Measuring populist attitudes in voters. *Comparative Political Studies*, 47(9), 1324–1353. https://doi.org/10.1177/0010414013512600

Antonakis, J., Avolio, B. J., & Sivasubramaniam, N. (2003). Context and leadership: An examination of the nine-factor full-range leadership theory using the Multifactor Leadership Questionnaire. *The Leadership Quarterly*, 14(3), 261–295. https://doi.org/10.1016/S1048-9843(03)00030-4

Arendt, H. (2017 [1951]). *The origins of totalitarianism*. Penguin.

Barr, R. R. (2009). Populists, outsiders and anti-establishment politics. *Party Politics*, 15(1), 29–48. https://doi.org/10.1177/1354068808097890

Barr, R. R. (2018). Populism as a political strategy. In C. de la Torre (Ed.), *Routledge handbook of global populism* (pp. 44–56). Routledge.

Bensman, J., & Givant, M. (1975). Charisma and modernity: The use and abuse of a concept. *Social Research*, 570–614. www.jstor.org/stable/41582855

Canovan, M. (1999). Trust the people! Populism and the two faces of democracy. *Political Studies*, 47(1), 2–16. https://doi.org/10.1111/1467-9248.00184

Canovan, M. (2004). Populism for political theorists? *Journal of Political Ideologies*, 9(3), 241–252. https://doi.org/10.1080/1356931042000263500

Davies, J. C. (1954). Charisma in the 1952 campaign. *American Political Science Review*, 48(4), 1083–1102. https://doi.org/10.1146/annurev-orgpsych-041015-062305

Di Tella, T. (1965). Populism and reform in Latin America. In C. Veliz (Ed.), *Obstacles to change in Latin America*. Oxford University Press.

Diamond, L. (2021). Democratic regression in comparative perspective: Scope, methods, and causes. *Democratization*, 28(1), 22–42. https://doi.org/10.1080/13510347.2020.1807517

Galston, W. (2018). *Anti-pluralism: The populist threat to liberal democracy*. Yale University Press.

Germani, G. (1978). *Authoritarianism, fascism, and national populism*. Transaction Books.

Goodwyn, L. (1976). *Democratic promise: The populist moment in America*. Oxford University Press.

Green, D. P., Palmquist, B., & Schickler, E. (2002). *Partisan hearts and minds: Political parties and the social identities of voters*. Yale University Press.

Hawkins, K. A., & Rovira Kaltwasser, C. (2019). Introduction: The ideational approach. In K. A. Hawkins, R. E. Carlin, L. Littvay & C. Rovira Kaltwasser (Eds.), *The ideational approach to populism: Concept, theory, and analysis*. Routledge.

Hicken, A. (2011). Clientelism. *Annual Review of Political Science*, 14, 289–310. https://doi.org/10.1146/annurev.polisci.031908.220508

Hofstadter, R. (1964, November). The paranoid style in American politics. *Harper's Magazine*. https://harpers.org/archive/1964/11/the-paranoid-style-in-american-politics/

Houle, C., & Kenny, P. D. (2018). The political and economic consequences of populist rule in Latin America. *Government and Opposition*, 53(2), 256–287. https://doi.org/https://doi.org/10.1017/gov.2016.25

House, R. J., & Howell, J. M. (1992). Personality and charismatic leadership. *The Leadership Quarterly*, 3(2), 81–108. https://doi.org/10.1016/1048-9843(92)90028-E

Ionescu, G., & Gellner, E. (Eds.). (1969). *Populism: Its meaning and national characteristics*. Macmillan.

Kenny, P. D. (2017). *Populism and patronage: Why populists win elections in India, Asia, and beyond*. Oxford University Press.
Kenny, P. D. (2019). *Populism in Southeast Asia*. Cambridge University Press.
Kenny, P. D. (2020). 'The enemy of the people': Populists and press freedom. *Political Research Quarterly*, 73(2), 261–275. https://doi.org/10.1177/1065912918824038
Kenny, P. D. (2023). *Why populism? Political strategy from ancient Greece to the present*. Cambridge University Press.
Kenny, P. D., & Holmes, R. (2020). A new penal populism? Rodrigo Duterte, public opinion, and the war on drugs in the Philippines. *Journal of East Asian Studies*, 20(2), 187–205. https://doi.org/10.1017/jea.2020.8
Kitschelt, H. (2000). Linkages between citizens and politicians in democratic politics. *Comparative Political Studies*, 33(6–7), 845–879.
Kitschelt, H. (2013). *Dataset of the democratic accountability and linkages project (DALP)*. Duke University. https://web.duke.edu/democracy/index.html
Kornhauser, W. (1959). *The politics of mass society*. Free Press.
Madsen, D., & Snow, P. G. (1991). *The charismatic bond: Political behavior in time of crisis*. Harvard University Press.
Mair, P. (2013). *Ruling the void: The hollowing of Western democracy*. Verso.
Merolla, J. L., Ramos, J. M., & Zechmeister, E. J. (2007). Crisis, charisma, and consequences: Evidence from the 2004 U.S. presidential election. *The Journal of Politics*, 69(1), 30–42. https://doi.org/10.1111/j.1468-2508.2007.00492.x
Moffitt, B. (2016). *The global rise of populism: Performance, political style, and representation*. Stanford University Press.
Moffitt, B. (2020). *Populism*. Polity.
Mounk, Y. (2018). *The people vs. democracy: Why our freedom is in danger and how to save it*. Harvard University Press.
Mouzelis, N. (1985, September 1). On the concept of populism: Populist and clientelist modes of incorporation in semiperipheral polities. *Politics & Society*, 14(3), 329–348. https://doi.org/10.1177/003232928501400303
Mudde, C. (2004). The populist zeitgeist. *Government and Opposition*, 39(4), 542–563. https://doi.org/10.1111/j.1477-7053.2004.00135.x
Mudde, C. (2007). *Populist radical right parties in Europe*. Cambridge University Press.
Mudde, C., & Rovira Kaltwasser, C. (2013). Populism and (liberal) democracy: A framework for analysis. In C. Mudde & C. Rovira Kaltwasser (Eds.), *Populism in Europe and the Americas: Threat or corrective for democracy?* Cambridge University Press.
Mudde, C., & Rovira Kaltwasser, C. (2017). *Populism: A very short introduction*. Oxford University Press.
Müller, J.-W. (2016). *What is populism?* University of Pennsylvania Press.
Norris, P., & Inglehart, R. (2019). *Cultural backlash: Trump, Brexit, and the rise of authoritarian-populism*. Cambridge University Press.
Ochoa Espejo, P. (2015). Power to whom? The people between procedure and populism. In C. de la Torre (Ed.), *The promise and perils of populism: Global perspectives* (pp. 59–90). University Press of Kentucky.
Ostiguy, P. (2009). *The high and the low in politics: A two-dimensional political space for comparative analysis and electoral studies* (p. 360). University of Notre Dame.
Panebianco, A. (1988). *Political parties: Organization and power*. Cambridge University Press.
Pappas, T. S. (2016a). Modern populism: Research advances, conceptual and methodological pitfalls, and the minimal definition. In *Oxford research encyclopedia of politics*. Oxford University Press. https://doi.org/10.1093/acrefore/9780190228637.013.17
Pappas, T. S. (2016b). Are populist leaders 'charismatic'? The evidence from Europe. *Constellations*, 23(3), 378–390. https://doi.org/10.1111/1467-8675.12233
Pappas, T. S. (2019). *Populism and liberal democracy: A comparative and theoretical analysis*. Oxford University Press. https://doi.org/10.1093/oso/9780198837886.001.0001
Resnick, D. (2015). Varieties of African populism in comparative perspective. In C. de la Torre (Ed.), *The promise and perils of populism: Global perspectives* (pp. 317–348). University Press of Kentucky.

Roberts, K. M. (1995). Neoliberalism and the transformation of populism in Latin America: The Peruvian case. *World Politics*, *48*(1), 82–116. https://doi.org/10.1353/wp.1995.0004

Rovira Kaltwasser, C. (2012). The ambivalence of populism: Threat and corrective for democracy. *Democratization*, *19*(2), 184–208. https://doi.org/10.1080/13510347.2011.572619

Ruth, S. P. (2018). Populism and the erosion of horizontal accountability in Latin America. *Political Studies*, *66*(2), 356–375. https://doi.org/10.1177/0032321717723511

Simonton, D. K. (1984). *Genius, creativity and leadership: Historiometric inquiries*. Harvard University Press.

Spinrad, W. (1991). Charisma: A blighted concept and an alternative formula. *Political Science Quarterly*, *106*(2), 295–311. https://doi.org/10.2307/2152231

Stokes, S. C. (2007). Political clientelism. In C. Boix & S. C. Stokes (Eds.), *The Oxford handbook of comparative politics* (pp. 604–627). Oxford University Press.

Urbinati, N. (2015). A revolt against intermediary bodies. *Constellations*, *22*(4), 477–486. https://doi.org/10.1111/1467-8675.12188

Urbinati, N. (2019). *Me the people: How populism transforms democracy*. Harvard University Press.

Van Niekerk, A. E. (1974). *Populism and political development in Latin America*. Rotterdam University Press.

Voeten, E. (2020). Populism and backlashes against international courts. *Perspectives on Politics*, *18*(2), 407–422. https://doi.org/10.1017/S1537592719000975

Weber, M. (1958). Politics as vocation. In H. H. Gerth & C. Wright Mills (Eds.), *From Max Weber: Essays in sociology*. Oxford University Press.

Weber, M. (1978 [1922]). *Economy and society: An outline of interpretive sociology* (Vol. 2). University of California Press.

Weyland, K. (1999). Neoliberal populism in Latin America and Eastern Europe. *Comparative Politics*, *31*(4), 379–401. https://doi.org/10.2307/422236

Weyland, K. (2001). Clarifying a contested concept: Populism in the study of Latin American politics. *Comparative Politics*, *34*(1), 1–22. https://doi.org/10.2307/422412

Weyland, K. (2017). Populism: A political-strategic approach. In C. Rovira Kaltwasser, P. Taggart, P. Ochoa Espejo & P. Ostiguy (Eds.), *The Oxford handbook of populism*. Oxford University Press.

Wilkin, S. (2018). *History repeating: Why populists rise and governments fall*. Profile Books.

Willner, A. R. (1984). *The spellbinders: Charismatic political leadership*. Yale University Press.

4
BETWEEN PEOPLE POWER AND STATE POWER

The ambivalence of populism in international relations

Angelos Chryssogelos

Introduction

Populism in recent years has become a major topic of debate in the study of international relations. While long a phenomenon and concept confined to domestic politics, in the last decade, its relevance to international order has become evident. In Western liberal democracies, populism has been associated with major developments like: the election of Donald Trump as President of the United States and all the consequences this entailed for transatlantic relations, multilateralism, and the global trade regime; the Brexit victory in the 2016 British referendum that led to the United Kingdom exiting the European Union; and the near-fracturing of the European Union by the Eurozone and refugee crises. In the Global South, populism has been ascendant in powers like India, Brazil, and in a different context, perhaps even China, as well as regional players like Venezuela, Thailand, and the Philippines.

This chapter explores the theoretical implications of the international rise of populism. The main argument is that, while the study of populism in world politics still draws heavily on important insights from comparative politics and political theory, viewing it as a distinct concept and phenomenon of international relations yields novel and more pervasive perspectives on its nature and consequences. If the conventional view of populism, especially among Western political, academic, and lay audiences, is one of disruption to democracy and the international order, appreciating populism's position on the interface of state power, domestic society, and the international system provides a more nuanced picture. Although populism indeed challenges entrenched elites, in the context of economic globalization and internationalization of political rule, its main role has evolved to accommodate and incorporate popular demands in a new equilibrium between international and domestic politics that shelters political power from societal demands.

The chapter begins by presenting the principal directions in the literature on populism, international relations, and foreign policy, before discussing how populism can be conceptualized as a phenomenon of international relations. On this basis, I will put forward a strategic-discursive perspective that I think is the most appropriate to capture populism's rise, presence, and effect on international politics today. I will then summarize the implications of this perspective for how we can understand a range of international phenomena and populism's role in them, including the politicization of foreign policy, regional integration and its contestation, and the fragmentation of the international multilateral order.

The effects of populism will be demonstrated on the basis of a cross-regional comparison that also places developments in the Asia Pacific in a global context. The idea is not only to apply the insights of the existing literature on populism, international relations, and foreign policy to Asian cases but also to use developments there, which are rarely used for comparative analysis in this literature, to challenge and refine dominant theoretical assumptions. Cases from the Asia Pacific offer opportunities to explore three of the major unknowns regarding populism and international relations: the structural effect of international developments on the domestic rise of populism (e.g., Thailand), populists' relations with regional institutions (e.g., Duterte's and Jokowi's relations with the Association of Southeast Asian Nations [ASEAN]), and populism's role in a major state's foreign policy (e.g., Modi's India). As I will show, Asian cases justify the more nuanced perspective about populism's origins and impact on the international system as captured by the strategic-discursive perspective I develop here.

Populism, international relations, and foreign policy: the state of the art

Although often unacknowledged, the international-structural dimension has been present in the evaluation of the rise of populism since early on (Ionescu & Gellner, 1969). The agrarian populism of the U.S. People's Party was a response to the unequal integration of a peripheral economy in international capitalism in the 1890s (Goodwyn, 1978). A comparable dynamic was observed in the post-colonial populism of newly independent states in the 1970s (Johnson, 1983). The voluminous literature on Latin American populism has accounted for the different geopolitical and structural economic conditions impinging on Latin America over time (for an overview, see Grigera, 2017). Finally, the end of the Cold War has been indirectly acknowledged as a factor influencing the shape of populism in Latin America as well as Europe (Weyland, 1999).

Populism was long a predominant feature of politics in the Global South, especially in Latin America, but also in Africa and Asia. In this sense, it is both ironic and telling that the academic literature's preoccupation with it increased only when populism started making its appearance in Western democracies. When it comes to populism in the West, the debate in recent years over the reasons behind its rise can be understood as one between cultural factors like immigration and economic/material factors like trade exposure, although both draw on the notion of globalization as the structural process affecting democracy at the national level.

The cultural perspective sees globalization as affecting a cultural anxiety about ethnic and national sovereignty, induced by the rise of immigration and multiculturalism. The effect of immigration as a major policy issue in Western democracies has led to the emergence of radical right-wing populist parties (Kriesi et al., 2008). Populism in this sense is operating in conjunction with nationalist, and particularly nativist, sentiments (Brubaker, 2020, pp. 55–57). The economic perspective sees populism as a reaction to economic crises and material dislocation. This economic perspective was common in analyses of populism in the Global South but was relatively novel for Western democracies, where the focus was hitherto on the populist radical right. Yet phenomena like the Eurozone crisis and the emergence of left-wing populism in the European Union's southern periphery have brought economic factors to the forefront (Stavrakakis & Katsambekis, 2014).

Donald Trump's polarizing discourse on trade and protectionism also pointed to economic factors behind populism, particularly in the post-industrial heartlands of the U.S. Midwest and northern England that heavily supported Trump and Brexit in 2016, respectively. For this reason, rather than immigration or the crisis of neoliberalism, some scholars attributed populism's rise to exposure to free trade (Rodrik, 2017). Although the economy vs. culture debate has often been conducted in binary terms, more nuanced accounts have attempted to combine them, seeing populism as an expression of compounding feelings of economic, cultural, and political peripheralization (Gidron & Hall, 2020).

The study of populism and foreign policy has also expanded substantially in recent years. Here as well, works on populism and foreign policy already existed (e.g., Mead, 2011; Liang, 2007), but it was in the mid-2010s that foreign policy analysis (FPA) undertook a more systematic analysis of patterns and effects of populism in this area. This increase in interest was again concentrated on Western democracies, but has spread to populism in the Global South (e.g., Latin America: Ellis, 2014; Wajner, 2021).

Most works on populism and foreign policy embark from the ideational perspective, viewing it as a thin-centred ideology and examining whether its ideological tenets are translated into foreign policy implementation (Verbeek & Zaslove, 2017, pp. 392–393). Populism's anti-elitism is considered antithetical to major international or regional institutions (Zürn et al., 2012), as well as established powers like the United States, as these are seen as the 'elites' of international relations (Dodson & Dorraj, 2008). Its exaltation of the 'people', on the other hand, drives a focus on, ostensibly, popular sovereignty that often morphs into an emphasis on national sovereignty and independence (Chryssogelos, 2020, pp. 30–33). The anti-pluralism of populism primarily impacts the functioning and modes of foreign policy making (Destradi & Plagemann, 2019). Given populism's antipathy towards technocratic elites and experts, we can expect populist governments to be detrimental to the functioning of foreign policy bureaucracies and the independence of the diplomatic corps (Lequesne, 2021).

While these considerations stemming from the mainstream ideational perspective of populism yield interesting first-cut hypotheses about its impact on foreign policy, recent works undertake a more sophisticated assessment of the influence of populism. For instance, the ideological impact of populism must be separated from that of the thicker ideologies with which populism co-exists (Chryssogelos, 2017a, p. 11). Populists perhaps tend to mistrust international organizations, though this may not be due to populism as such but rather to the influence of their core ideologies; for example, far-right nativists distrust the dilution of national sovereignty, while radical leftists oppose neoliberal economic institutions.

A second source of ambiguity is the differences and similarities with the foreign policies of non-populists. While in some cases populists indeed bring about a fundamental reorientation in areas of foreign policy, the exact impact of populism on foreign policy changes is actually more unclear (Chryssogelos, 2021). In other cases, the changes by populists are not reversed by their opponents when they return to power, as has been the case with Joe Biden and U.S. trade policy, raising the possibility that these changes were not really due to populism but rather a response to new international conditions that populists simply expedited or were better placed to 'sell' to domestic audiences.

In light of the above, populism on its own may not bring about changes, but rather intensify pre-existing trends in world politics. Populism is often seen as the reason behind the increasing personalization of foreign policy and international politics, the proliferation of new methods of direct transborder communication (e.g., through social media), and the strengthening of executives over foreign policy bureaucracies. In reality, these trends have been evident for some time now and populism just intensifies them. Populism, in this sense, is less a cause than a symptom of underlying changes in international politics (Destradi & Plagemann, 2019).

At the same time, even populism's association with sovereignty can be qualified. First, populism may not always have a nationalist character because it can speak for and represent a transnational 'people'—an anti-imperialist Latin America, the Muslim ummah, the European Union, Global South, etc. (De Cleen, 2017, pp. 355–358). This demonstrates the analytical difference between populism and nationalism, although the two are often conflated (Brubaker, 2020). Populism mobilizes the 'people' against the 'elites' in an antagonistic vertical dimension of politics, while nationalism differentiates nations along a horizontal inside/outside dimension. In this sense, popular sovereignty may often co-exist with, overlap, or intensify nationalist attitudes, but the two are analytically distinct (De Cleen & Stavrakakis, 2017, pp. 310–312).

Thus, populism is not always a driver of nationalist and anti-institutionalist foreign policies. Many populists actually want their state to become more involved with at least some international institutions. For such populists, the representation of *the people* necessitates its recognition in the international system, symbolized by their state's prominent position in processes of negotiation, treaty-making, summitry, etc. This is one of the main differences between populists in the West and the Global South. As their states are deeply enmeshed in dense webs of regional and international governance that impinge on sovereignty, populists in the West seek their emancipation from these institutions. Populists in the Global South, on the other hand, view international institutions from the vantage point of the outsider, perceiving them as unfair and unrepresentative. For them, differently than for Western populists, the representation of the people means not retreating from international institutions, but rather engaging with them so they become more representative, and through them, asserting their state's hard-won independence in the international system (Chryssogelos, 2017a, pp. 13–14; Plagemann & Destradi, 2019).

Thinking about populism as a concept of international relations

Despite the increase in the number of works studying populism in international relations and FPA, there is still a lack in the theorization of populism as a concept and phenomenon of international relations. International relations and FPA scholars engage with conceptualizations of populism from comparative politics (e.g., populism as a thin-centred ideology), but essentially import those into the international relations field rather than match them to concepts and debates in international relations or FPA literature. Having said this, there are some efforts to understand populism as a concept of international relations, especially in light of the complex and ambiguous picture concerning populism's policy influence painted earlier in this chapter.

Efforts to conceptualize populism in international relations have taken place primarily from a critical and discursive perspective. One way to understand populism is as an antagonistic mode of politics that emerges in reaction to the dislocations of neoliberal globalization (Hadiz & Chryssogelos, 2017). We drew on Laclau's (2005) discursive approach but combined it with a materialist ontology that took seriously class struggles and elite strategies in the face of popular frustrations with globalization. In this way, populism can, in certain cases, be a potent tool to challenge the hold of traditional elites through the construction of heterogeneous and fluid class coalitions, as well as a strategy to restructure from above the power relations in states embedded in globalization. This political economy approach builds on a cross-regional comparative methodology, similarly to works that also see populism at the interface of state power, neoliberal economics, and international structure (Aytaç & Öniş, 2014).

Closer to more typical international relations considerations, I have conceptualized populism as a distinct discourse of international relations. At issue here is the transformation of the role, capacities, and relationship of the state with its domestic society as its functions become transposed and diluted in a web of supranational institutions and global governance processes. Populist discourse juxtaposes the demand of the rooted and territorialized political community for representation against the legitimating discourse of global governance focusing on efficiency, flexibility, and expertise. As a result, populism results in foreign policies that, irrespective of their policy content, aim at the re-territorialization of the functions of the state and their realignment with popular representation at the national level. Crucially, however, the focus on the representation and dignity of the people need not result in fundamentally new, genuinely pro-popular foreign policies; rather, it can act as a novel, more effective legitimating discourse of state power operating in a modified and updated equilibrium between domestic societal demands and the exigencies of the international system (Chryssogelos, 2020).

An alternative way of viewing populism within international relations theory is provided by Cadier, who understands it as a set of practices (Adler & Pouliot, 2011). Here, populism in foreign policy is understood as a practice that embodies and perpetuates a specific understanding of the political community, its relationship with power, and the state's relationship with important international *others*: other states, international or regional organizations, the state's own history, etc. This approach eschews the problem of the policy indeterminacy of populism, as its importance lies more in allowing leaders to present the political community as a downtrodden people in the international system (Cadier, 2021; Cadier & Szulecki, 2020). In a similar vein, Wojczewski (2020) uses another concept from international studies—security/securitization—to showcase how populist discourses perform a similar function of *securitizing* (presenting as threats) opponents of the *people*.

This emerging agenda of engagement with populism from the perspective of international relations highlights three issues. First, any work that discusses populism in international relations must take seriously the state as an actor and the arena in which populist ideas play out. Second, an account of populism in the international system must incorporate the international-structural/systemic dimension, especially the shifts in the international structure that impinge on the state and complicate its relationship with domestic society. Third, such analysis can benefit from engaging with the still underdeveloped debate in comparative politics over populism's dual nature: as a genuinely emancipatory phenomenon rising from below to challenge elites, and as a political strategy from above used to occupy state power.

Populism from above and from below

Starting with the third question, leadership indeed has often been identified as a core feature of populism, especially since populism's loose ideological character and espousal of frequently contradictory positions can be resolved by being embodied in a strong, usually male, leader (Eksi & Wood, 2019). But developments like the channelling of populism in long-standing political parties over the last four decades in Europe (Heinisch & Mazzoleni, 2016) and the entry of populists into power for long periods of time across the world also belie the idea of populism as a genuinely emancipatory phenomenon, as opposed to a political and mobilizational strategy used by outsiders or peripheral members of the elite (Barr, 2009, p. 38). This perspective is mostly associated with Kurt Weyland, whose work on Latin American populism led him to argue in no uncertain terms that populism is a political strategy devoid of any other ideational content (Weyland, 2001; 2017).

And yet for another set of scholars, the concept of populism describes primarily the mass anti-establishment mobilization of inclusive and ideologically empty popular identities (Laclau, 2005). These mobilizations, whether they develop from specific occupational groups like peasants and farmers (Goodwyn, 1978) or engulf the whole society, often acquire a movement-like character, without clear leadership. Anti-austerity mobilizations in the southern countries of the Eurozone in 2011–12 (Greece, Spain, Italy) fulfil many of the criteria for this genuine, emancipatory grassroots populism (Aslanidis, 2017, pp. 311–312). The question is: can this bottom-up perspective of populism be reconciled with the top-down, leader-driven one?

Despite their opposing conceptualizations, the discursive and the strategic perspectives overlap in a limited definition of populism on the basis of its ideologically empty appeal to a broad and heterogeneous *people* in opposition to the *system*. The presence of other, thicker ideological traits in a populist discourse—nationalist, socialist, religious, etc.—dilute its genuinely populist character, and it then becomes crucial to examine to what extent the core ideals of populism are not displaced as central nodes of discourse by these other ideological traits (Stavrakakis et al., 2017, p. 425; Weyland, 2017, pp. 61–67). This definition of populism has an advantage, in that it translates more easily to political contexts where well-developed, thick ideologies, like those that exist in the West and largely provide the precise policy content of different populisms, are lacking. In Latin America, Africa, and Asia, on the other hand, this empty perspective of populism may be a more realistic way to understand this phenomenon.

The second area of overlap between the two perspectives is their focus on agency, contrary to the ideational perspective, which sees populist ideas as ontologically objective and existent irrespective of who holds them (Hawkins et al., 2018). Political agency picks up available dimensions of popular frustration and grievances, choosing how to combine them in an overwhelming popular identity mobilized against the system. Whether from below by street activists and movement entrepreneurs or from above by maverick or anti-system politicians (Barr, 2009, p. 32), populist discourses construct and articulate the political identity of the people, united by their demand for recognition, representation, and the intention to construct an alternative hegemony to that of entrenched elites (De Cleen & Stavrakakis, 2017, pp. 306–307).

In this sense, the bottom-up and the top-down nature of populism can be seen as two sides of the same coin, i.e., as different expressions of a phenomenon distinguished by its constructed and discursive nature, politicizing the relationship between the people and political system (Aslanidis, 2017, p. 307; see Lee et al., 2021, for an Asian application). The bottom-up and top-down faces of populism are parts of the same cycle, especially in societies without strongly and independently organized societal interests, where successive waves of popular mobilization against the elites of the time are picked up by leaders aiming to occupy power, usually relying on unmediated appeals to the people rather than permanent party structures (Weyland, 2001).

Populism and the state

If populism seeks primarily to politicize the relationship between the state and the political community, this on its own is an important departure from most IR works that see state-society relations as relatively stable background conditions or, at most, intermediate variables of the impact of international factors on domestic politics (Checkel, 1999; Risse-Kappen, 1995). Populism, however, forces us to view the state as an active player in its own right, aiming to maintain its domestic legitimacy and ability to extract resources from society in the light of international geopolitical, economic, and ideological pressures. Viewed this way, populism forces international relations scholars to problematize the state's ability to control domestic society and to enquire about the conditions under which this relationship breaks down and society reconstitutes itself as a people mobilized against authority (Chryssogelos, 2017b).

Populism's role can be better understood if we turn to the notion of *incorporation*, used by Mouzelis in an older, though no less relevant today, strand of post-Marxist literature on populism. For Mouzelis, populism can incorporate, in a top-down, paternalistic fashion, popular masses that remain politically disenfranchised, even though economic modernization has created new demands and political awareness among them. Incorporation by populism differs from horizontal sectional and occupational mobilization of self-aware social classes, like the labour unions and parties in Western Europe in the 19th century. Rather, populist incorporation mobilizes the masses from the top, using anti-elite discourses and the promise of popular empowerment to satisfy the demand of political participation; yet, all the while, populist leaders remain sheltered from genuine societal interest-formation (Mouzelis, 1985).

The point here is that populism, especially in its top-down, leader-driven variant, is a distinct form of linking the state to its domestic society based on anti-establishment appeals and a discourse that articulates, constructs, and mobilizes a political identity of the *people* against the *elites*, understood usually as the dominant groups of previous, unresponsive regimes. This form of mass incorporation becomes catalyzed by a disruption or breakdown of state-society relations when a political regime's traditional modes of incorporation and suppression of societal demands fail. In this sense, populism is just a different iteration of state power, updating the link between domestic society and the state and using the promise of enfranchisement, representation, and recognition of the people to neutralize deeper and more far-reaching material demands.

The international dimension

Finally, an international perspective of populism needs to account for why state-society relations enter a condition of rupture in the first place. Every political system has different representational deficits that create pressures on state-society relations and hurt the legitimacy of the elites. But international change—geopolitical pressures, economic competition, and changes in the values, norms, and rules of appropriate statehood in the international system—can accentuate them, generating costs for groups exposed to these pressures (Rodrik, 2017) or hampering the ability of the state to satisfy them. The state is caught in the double pressure of incorporating domestic society and adapting to these international pressures for the sake of its survival, integrity, or reproduction in the international system (Chryssogelos, 2017b). As satisfying both the conditions of domestic and international legitimacy becomes untenable, states face generalized discontent as well as the need to devise new ways to absorb it. In its bottom-up and top-down forms, populism performs both these functions.

International change can have a more indirect, but no less important, role in the breakdown of state-society relations and the emergence of populism: it can be an argumentative resource for discursively weaving together a variety of frustrated demands—political, economic, ideational—as an overarching call of the people to fight back against the elites. Even if state-society gaps and ruptures are endogenous, the international system may generate suitable *others* for the people to mobilize against: geopolitical foes, historical enemies, intrusive supranational organizations (Cadier, 2021), new values and norms that challenge a domestic society's traditions and mores, structures of global inequality that populists can attack as systemic impediments to the people's representational equality and recognition, etc. In all these ways, the international system allows populists to bring together multiple disenfranchised groups and articulate their common frustration as an overarching condition of *peripheralization*, akin to the state's own (perceived or actual) international peripherality (Johnson, 1983; Zarycki, 2000).

Populism as a concept of international relations

Based on the above, we can now outline a conceptualization of populism as a phenomenon of international relations. Populism is understood as a discourse of international relations; i.e., it reflects the agency of leaders, entrepreneurs, or actors who articulate politics as a binary struggle between the people and the elites, seeking to galvanize a broad (and floating) popular identity on the basis of the frustrated demands of multiple groups. These frustrated demands intensify or catalyze a sense of representational exclusion from the political system; a rupture in state-society relations that combines political, material, and ideational disenchantment. These facets of disenchantment create a compound sense of the peripheralization of parts of society.

Domestic peripheralization is a function of the state's inability to satisfy domestic demands under pressing international conditions, understood in terms of geopolitical pressure, economic competition, or international normative and value changes. In trying to reproduce internationally, the state loses sight of domestic societal demands and is faced with a generalized call for the removal of the elites by the people. However, populism is not an automatic consequence of objective material dislocation brought about by the state's effort to adapt to international conditions. Rather, successful populist mobilization only takes place when frustrated societal demands are articulated in terms of the moral call for representation of the people against the dominant ideas and norms of the international system underpinning notions of appropriate statehood. In other words, populism can be understood as a *counter-normative discourse of world politics*, challenging international orthodoxy with a rival call for restitution of popular sovereignty.

This discourse can be expressed from below, by leaderless social movements and mobilized groups, or from above by leaders of parties and, eventually, governments. When it acquires power, however, populism's importance for international politics lies in its ability to act as a new mode of top-down incorporation of society by the state. Populists may seek to redefine the terms of the state's incorporation in the international system, which in effect deflects domestic societal demands to an open-ended and elusive quest for representation, recognition, and sovereignty in the international system. Populist foreign policy can appear more disruptive than its predecessors, though it ultimately creates a new equilibrium between a state's relationship with its domestic society and its adaptation to the international system. Populism thus ends up being an updated way to incorporate domestic societies into the functioning of the international system, at the price of heightened demands for sovereignty, inter-state tensions, and fragmentation and politicization of global and regional governance institutions.

How populism matters for international relations: a cross-regional perspective

Cross-regional comparison is an essential methodological tool for assessing the relationship of populism with international relations and foreign policy (Mudde & Rovira Kaltwasser, 2011). This is especially important today, when there is a heightened interest in populism in Western liberal democracies and their foreign policies, though the centrality of Western thought and priorities tends to colour global assessments of populism. As hinted at earlier, many assumptions about Western populism's approach to international relations—its focus on national sovereignty, opposition to international and regional institutions, anti-Americanism, belligerent foreign policy posture—are not always applicable to the actions of populists in other world regions, including Asia.

One area where such a nuanced perspective would have been in order is the relationship and response of populism to economic crisis. In the past decade, two such populist explosions in Western democracies lent credence to the idea of populism as a reaction to external economic shocks and, consequently, a phenomenon challenging the international liberal order: the emergence of left-wing populism in the European Union's southern periphery in response to the Eurozone crisis of 2010 to 2015 (Stavrakakis & Katsambekis, 2014), and that of right-wing populism in Anglo-Saxon democracies in 2016, when Trump and Brexit attributed to the nativist turn of the *peripheralized, left-behind* post-industrial working class (Gest, 2016). These two populist waves seemed to translate in the West into patterns already experienced in other regions, especially Latin America, where International Monetary Fund (IMF)-imposed neoliberalism in the 1990s is seen as the main incubator of the leftist *pink wave* populism of the 2000s (Grigera, 2017). A cross-regional comparison between Turkey and Argentina (Aytaç & Öniş, 2014) also traced the rise of populism as a reaction to the consequences of IMF restructuring programs at the turn of the century.

But on closer inspection, these populist waves have had, in practice, far less radical effects on world politics than what their emancipatory discourse would suggest. In reality, populism was much more consequential in reconstituting relations between state power and domestic society at home than it was in fundamentally altering the course of international affairs.

In the most impressive example of populist reversal, Greece's populist coalition led by Alexis Tsipras succumbed to European Union pressure in 2015, signed a new bailout agreement, and implemented the same austerity for which it had once castigated others to secure another four years in power until 2019. In that period, its foreign policy was a paradoxical mix of populist proclamations and increasing alignment with the priorities of the United States and the European Union (Chryssogelos, 2021). In Italy, the two populist forces that formed a *Eurosceptic* coalition in 2018—the ideologically heterogeneous Five Star Movement and the far-right Lega—eventually joined an all-party technocratic government led by their old nemesis, ex-European Central Bank chief Mario Draghi.

Right-wing populism in Anglo-Saxon democracies in the second half of the 2010s arguably had a more tangible effect, with Great Britain leaving the European Union in 2020 and the United States, under Donald Trump, severely disrupting, among others, the international trade regime, climate change cooperation, and relations with Western allies. Here as well, there have been developments that create a more complex picture. In the United States, the Biden administration may have reversed Trump's policies on climate but has largely kept in place protectionist measures and suspicion towards trade multilateralism, shedding doubt on the idea that such stances are distinct definitional characteristics of populism while exhibiting similar unilateral instincts towards Europeans (e.g., during the Afghanistan withdrawal and in vaccine policy and travel bans). In the United Kingdom, Brexit has gone hand-in-hand with an over-compensatory internationalist posture captured by the term *Global Britain*, expressed in a flurry of new trade deals, engagement with Asia, and activist diplomacy on global issues like climate.

In summary, structural crisis does foster the rise of populism as a reaction, though this populism does not appear to lead to a consistent change across all areas of foreign policy either, whether in relation to what a state was doing before or in comparison to the policies of non-populists. Rather, populism fosters international disruption due to a more selective politicized and ideological engagement with the international order. This engagement reflects populists' domestic strategies of follower mobilization, antagonism towards foes, and efforts to control institutions. What emerges is a new equilibrium, where new types of links between states and domestic societies end up underpinning a transformed, fragmented, more politicized international order that, nonetheless, retains many of its liberal institutional characteristics.

Western observers could perhaps have anticipated that populism is the *midwife* of a new equilibrium between structural crises, reconstituted state power, and a transformed but not wholly undone international order if they had paid closer attention to the trajectories of populism in other world regions. As a paradigmatic leftist populist who rose on an anti-neoliberal wave, Evo Morales of Bolivia is a good example of how populism in power ultimately results in the incorporation and neutralization of popular movements through technocratic governance and strategic co-optation (McNelly, 2020). Similar trends were also visible in Brazil under Luiz Inacio Lula da Silva. Viewed this way, the co-optation of southern European populism by European Union power structures was not a surprise, just as the shifts in U.S. and U.K. foreign policy after 2016 towards protectionism and Eurosceptic internationalism, respectively, have had little practical impact (especially for the material grievances that fed right-wing populism) than to act as legitimators of a more *people-minded* state power.

In Asia, the best example of this ambivalent nexus of structural crisis, populism, state power, and the international order is Thailand under Thaksin. At first sight, the rise of populism in a royalist-authoritarian setting appears related to the Asian financial crisis of 1997 and the IMF-driven response, analogous to the rise of Erdogan in Turkey and of left-wing populists in Latin America in the same period. The dislocation of the crisis generated various populist streams from below (McCargo, 2001) that were harnessed by Thaksin upon his electoral victory in 2001. Leaving aside the conceptual question of whether Thaksin was initially a populist (Hewison, 2017; Phongpaichit & Baker, 2008), the effect of his tenure was less to undo Thailand's economic development model than to restructure and re-legitimize it along popular-participatory lines, which themselves were not necessarily at odds with the diktats of international technocracy at the time (Jayasuriya & Hewison,

2006). Even this was, of course, too much for Thailand's traditional elites, who repeatedly sought to unseat Thaksin. It is interesting, however, that the deep polarization left the main tenets of Thai foreign policy untouched (a pragmatic alignment with the United States, engagement with regional institutions, and equivocal relations with China), or at least has not affected them in clear, politicized patterns (Pongsudhirak, 2016). As expected by the latest works in the literature on populism and foreign policy, the impact of Thaksin was seen primarily in the procedure and personalization of foreign policy conduct, rather than its content (Chachavalpongun, 2010).

Another alleged feature of populist foreign policy that observers of Western politics have detected is its problematic relationship with international and regional institutions. In Europe, Euroscepticism is a defining feature of populism, as the European Union is seen by populists of the left and right as quintessentially *elite*—undemocratic, aloof, technocratic. In the United States, Trumpist populism is extremely hostile towards all kinds of international institutions, even long-standing U.S.-led alliances like NATO. An antagonistic posture towards some or all institutions of the post-war liberal international order is also evident in various populisms beyond the United States and Europe, including Latin American left-wing populism's opposition to the IMF or Erdogan's combative stance towards NATO and the European Union.

Here, as well, the picture is more mixed. While it is true that Western populists are preoccupied with the threats to their sovereignty from intrusive international institutions, they still remain members of them, seeking to steer them from the inside while accruing political capital domestically by posing as their foes. The nationalist-populist governments of Hungary and Poland, which constantly castigate Brussels while receiving big sums of European Union money, are typical examples. Similarly, Trump never acted upon his threat to leave NATO. If anything, the U.S. withdrawal from, or complex relationship with, various institutions of the international order—the World Trade Organization Appellate Body, UNESCO, the United Nations Human Rights Council, and the International Criminal Court—both preceded Trump's populism and will persist after his departure.

At the same time, regional integration is not always inimical to populism. Populists may dislike highly institutionalized, technocratic, and supranational structures of regional governance, although they see value in intergovernmental regional or subregional groupings that legitimize their model of sovereignty-minded engagement between strong leaders. Latin American populists, for example, have sought to create alternative structures of ideological regional integration (Wajner, 2021), while the governments of Poland and Hungary have cultivated the Visegrád Four sub-grouping as an alternative paradigm of regional integration influencing European Union policies.

Asia presents an interesting case in this sense due to the presence of ASEAN, arguably the most advanced experiment of regional cooperation in the world after the European Union. Following a Western-influenced view of populism, one would expect ASEAN to be a ripe target for Asian populists. From a critical perspective, one can see ASEAN as the regional projection of authoritarian regime legacies in Asia, against which populists have historically emerged. However, at the same time, ASEAN's operation in many ways agrees with populist priorities on the international stage, such as enabling performances of sovereign equality (Nair, 2019). In this sense, ASEAN reminds us that any assessment of the relationship between populism and regionalism needs always to consider the specific nature of the institutions and their rooting in distinct regional patterns of state-society relations.

Two contemporary examples of Asian populists and their foreign policy showcase the ambiguous relationship between populism and regional cooperation. Joko Widodo (Jokowi), Indonesia's president since 2014, signalled at the beginning of his presidency a more transactional, sovereigntist and unilateral approach to foreign policy and relations with ASEAN, in what he touted as 'pro-people diplomacy'. As such, Jokowi fits the model of populist foreign policy that is inward-looking and pursues a narrower definition of the national interest. A changing tone of foreign policy, however, has not meant substantially new content in Indonesia's foreign policy, nor in engagement with ASEAN, which continued essentially unchanged from previous administrations (Andika, 2016; Lundry, 2018). Once again, the main effect of Jokowi's foreign policy is in the domestic arena, using a personalization of diplomatic practices to foster communication with his followers (Wicaksana & Wardhana, 2021). This underpins Indonesian populism's role in updating state power without fundamentally altering class relations (Hadiz & Robison, 2017).

A better-known example to international observers of Asian populism is the president of the Philippines, Rodrigo Duterte (succeeded by another populist Ferdinand 'Bong Bong' Marcos in 2022), who owes his notoriety as much to his outspoken style and violent policies as to the coincidence of his election in 2016 with Trump's presidential victory. The first years of Duterte's presidency exhibited foreign policy features familiar to scholars of Western populism. An attempted realignment away from the United States and towards China fitted the model of populist foreign policy as guided by anti-elitism, anti-Americanism, and orientation towards the emerging powers of a multipolar world, particularly authoritarian ones. The pro-China turn also was perceived as going against the Philippines' role in ASEAN, a regional bulwark against Chinese expansionism, in favour of a unilateral approach of securing gains at the expense of partners (Magcamit, 2020; Sevilla, 2018). These initial moves, however, were followed by a more sanguine perspective on China's role, as well as a return to the multilateral framework by Duterte, who after 2018 tried to re-engage the United States, fostered a security partnership with Japan, and promoted an ASEAN-China code of conduct in the South China Sea (De Castro, 2020).

Thus, regional institutions make a convenient target for populist rhetoric on independence and sovereignty, though they also remain an important resource for asserting populist leaders' international status. In this sense, given ASEAN's origins in authoritarian modes of state-society relations and its identification with an elite-driven, technocratic conception of democracy, populism's accommodation with it should cause a more critical assessment of both its democratic and emancipatory proclamations and of liberal regional institutions' self-avowed role as guardians of democracy in the region. If anything, populism and regionalism can always settle in a pragmatic and eclectic cohabitation, with populists gaining legitimacy from their participation in regional institutions while they update the terms of incorporation of domestic societies by the same state power that underpins the structures of regionalism. ASEAN, after all, contains several authoritarian, undemocratic states that have very poor human rights records, notably Myanmar and Cambodia. The overtly idealistic view of European Union values and membership as inherently inconsistent with populist and illiberal modes of state power (as practised in Hungary and Poland) may then need to be reassessed in the light of the Asian experience.

Finally, Asia is home to one of the most prominent populist leaders on the world stage, Narendra Modi of India. That the world's largest democracy is led by a populist is indeed proof of the global relevance of this phenomenon. Modi is seen as part of the populist wave of the 2010s, particularly its right-wing, nativist variant. Indeed, the combination of populism with the thick ideology of Hindu nationalism makes Modi comparable with the European populist radical right as well as with Trump and Bolsonaro, with whom he shares similarities in his exclusionary racial and religious conception of the *real people*. Of course, the prominence of nativism in Modi's ideology also raises the question of whether populism is the primary frame in which to analyze him or is even relevant at all. As noted above, scholars embarking from different methodological and theoretical assumptions agree that genuine empty populism must be devoid of highly ideological conceptions of the people (Stavrakakis et al., 2017; Weyland, 2017).

When it comes to his foreign policy, scholars converge on the view that Modi's actions are primarily dictated by his thick ideology of Hindu nationalism rather than populism's thin tenets. The populist impact is seen primarily in the procedural aspects of his foreign policy, with increased personalization, the sidelining of the diplomatic bureaucracy, and the use of new media technologies to directly contact his followers. Modi's example, however, also belies the Western-informed view of populism as irreconcilable with the international order and preoccupied with state sovereignty. Modi certainly showcases the potential of populism to reach out to *a people* extending beyond state borders (De Cleen, 2017), in his case the Indian diaspora, as well as the ability to remain engaged in international multilateralism (Plagemann & Destradi, 2019). Modi is indeed the strongest demonstration of how populism's dispositions differ between the West and the Global South (Chryssogelos, 2017a). But his example also gives credence to a more critical perspective of its relationship with state power and domestic society, with foreign policy serving as a *boundary-drawing practice* that reproduces specific understandings of the people and their identity with the populist leader domestically (Wojczewski, 2019).

Conclusion

The study of populism is a growing area in international relations and FPA literature. This does not mean, however, that scholarship has made use of the whole arsenal provided by the populism literature in comparative politics, or of all relevant concepts from international relations that could help paint a more nuanced picture of populism's effects on global politics. By engaging with critical perspectives in the populism literature and international relations, this chapter has tried to show that the relationship of populism with international relations is more complex than the simplistic accounts predominant in Western public, policy, and even scholarly debate. Through developing a strategic-discursive conceptualization, I argued that populism in international relations is best understood as a counter-normative discourse, which articulates a new relationship between the state and the international system in a way that updates and reproduces the terms of incorporation of domestic society by state power under changing international conditions. This implies a more critical assessment both of populists' democratic and pro-people proclamations and of the alleged liberal democratic character of global and regional institutionalism. As both of these views predominate in Western discourse (albeit emanating from different quarters of the public debate), the chapter has shown how cross-regional comparison, bringing in cases from the Global South including Asia, is essential for understanding populism's role in international relations.

References

Adler, E. L., & Pouliot, V. (2011). *International practices*. Cambridge University Press.

Andika, M. T. (2016). An analysis of Indonesia foreign policy under Jokowi's pro-people diplomacy. *Indonesian Perspective*, 1(2), 93–105. https://doi.org/10.14710/ip.v1i2.14284

Aslanidis, P. (2017). Populism and social movements. In C. Rovira Kaltwasser, P. Taggart, P. Ochoa Espejo & P. Ostiguy (Eds.), *Oxford handbook of populism* (pp. 305–325). Oxford University Press. https://doi.org/10.1093/oxfordhb/9780198803560.013.22

Aytaç, S. E., & Öniş, Z. (2014). Varieties of populism in a changing global context: The divergent paths of Erdoğan and Kirchnerismo. *Comparative Politics*, 47(1), 41–59. www.jstor.org/stable/43664342

Barr, R. R. (2009). Populists, outsiders and anti-establishment politics. *Party Politics*, 15(1), 29–48. https://doi.org/10.1177/1354068808097890

Brubaker, R. (2020). Populism and nationalism. *Nations and Nationalism*, 26(1), 44–66. https://doi.org/10.1111/nana.12522

Cadier, D. (2021). Populist politics of representation and foreign policy: Evidence from Poland. *Comparative European Politics*, 19, 703–721. https://doi.org/10.1057/s41295-021-00257-2

Cadier, D., & Szulecki, K. (2020). Populism, historical discourse and foreign policy: The case of Poland's law and justice government. *International Politics*, 57(6), 990–1011. https://doi.org/0.1057/s41311-020-00252-6

Chachavalpongun, P. (2010). *Reinventing Thailand: Thaksin and his foreign policy*. Institute of Southeast Asian Studies.

Checkel, J. T. (1999). Norms, institutions and national identity in contemporary Europe. *International Studies Quarterly*, 43, 83–114. www.jstor.org/stable/2600966

Chryssogelos, A. (2017a). Populism in foreign policy. In *Oxford research encyclopedia of politics*. Oxford University Press. http://politics.oxfordre.com/view/10.1093/acrefore/9780190228637.001.0001/acrefore-9780190228637-e-467

Chryssogelos, A. (2017b). The People in the 'here and now': Populism, modernization and the state in Greece. *International Political Science Review*, 38(4), 473–487. https://doi.org/10.1177%2F0192512117702524

Chryssogelos, A. (2020). State transformation and populism: From the internationalized to the neo-sovereign state? *Politics*, 40(1), 22–37. https://doi.org/10.1177/0192512117702524

Chryssogelos, A. (2021). The dog that barked but did not bite: Greek foreign policy under the populist coalition of SYRIZA-Independent Greeks, 2015–2019. *Comparative European Politics*, 19, 722–738. https://doi.org/10.1057/s41295-021-00258-1

De Castro, R. C. (2020). From appeasement to soft balancing: The Duterte administration's shifting policy on the South China Sea imbroglio. *Asian Affairs: An American Review*. https://doi.org/10.1080/00927678.2020.1818910

De Cleen, B. (2017). Populism and nationalism. In C. Rovira Kaltwasser, P. Taggart, P. Ochoa Espejo & P. Ostiguy (Eds.), *The Oxford handbook of populism* (pp. 342–362). Oxford University Press.

De Cleen, B., & Stavrakakis, Y. (2017). Distinctions and articulations: A discourse theoretical framework for the study of populism and nationalism. *Javnost*, 24(4), 301–19. https://doi.org/10.1080/13183222.2017.1330083

Destradi, S., & Plagemann, J. (2019). Populism and international relations: (Un)predictability, personalisation, and the reinforcement of existing trends in world politics. *Review of International Studies*, 45(5), 711–730. https://doi.org10.1017/S0260210519000184

Dodson, M., & Dorraj, M. (2008). Populism and foreign policy in Venezuela and Iran. *Whitehead Journal of Diplomacy and International Relations*, 9, 71–87. https://ciaotest.cc.columbia.edu/journals/shjdir/v9i1/f_0016623_14365.pdf

Eksi, B., & Wood, E. A. (2019). Right-wing populism as gendered performance: Janus-faced masculinity in the leadership of Vladimir Putin and Recep T. Erdogan. *Theory and Society*, 48, 733–751. https://doi.org10.1007/s11186-019-09363-3

Ellis, R. E. (2014). Latin America's foreign policy as the region engages China. *Security and Defense Studies Review*, 15(1), 41–59.

Gest, J. (2016). *The new minority: White working class politics in an age of immigration and inequality*. Oxford University Press.

Gidron, N., & Hall, P. A. (2020). Populism as a problem of social integration. *Comparative Political Studies*, 53(7), 1027–1059. https://doi.org10.1177/0010414019879947

Goodwyn, L. E (1978). *The populist moment: A short history of the agrarian revolt in America*. Oxford University Press.

Grigera, J. (2017). Populism in Latin America: Old and new populisms in Argentina and Brazil. *International Political Science Review*, 38(4), 441–455. https://doi.org 10.1177/0192512117701510

Hadiz, V. R., & Chryssogelos, A. (2017). Populism in world politics: A comparative cross-regional perspective. *International Political Science Review*, 38(4), 399–411. https://doi.org10.1177/0192512117693908

Hadiz, V. R., & Robison, R. (2017). Competing populisms in post-authoritarian Indonesia. *International Political Science Review*, 38(4), 488–502. https://doi.org 10.1177/0192512117697475

Hawkins, K. A., Carlin, R. E., Littvay, L., & Rovira Kaltwasser, C. (Eds.) (2018). *The ideational approach to populism: Concept, theory, and analysis*. Routledge.

Heinisch, R., & Mazzoleni, O. (Eds.) (2016). *Understanding populist party organisation: The radical right in Western Europe*. Palgrave Macmillan.

Hewison, K. (2017). Reluctant populists: Learning populism in Thailand. *International Political Science Review*, 38(4), 426–440. https://doi.org/10.1177/0192512117692801

Ionescu, G., & Gellner, E. (Eds.) (1969). *Populism: Its meanings and national characteristics*. Macmillan.

Jayasuriya, K., & Hewison, K. (2006). The antipolitics of good governance: From global social policy to a global populism? *Critical Asian Studies*, 36(4), 571–590. https://doi.org/10.1080/14672710420000273257

Johnson, R. H (1983). The new populism and the old: Demands for a new international economic order and American agrarian protest. *International Organization*, 37(1), 41–72. https://doi.org/10.1017/S0020818300004197.

Kriesi, H., Grande, E., Lachat, R., Dolezal, M., Bornschier, S., & Frey, T. (2008). *West European politics in the age of globalization*. Oxford University Press.

Laclau, E. (2005). *On populist reason*. Verso.

Lee, S. J., Wu, C.-E., & Bandyopadhyay, K. K. (2021). *Populism in Asian democracies: Features, structures, and impacts*. Brill.

Lequesne, C. (2021). Populist governments and career diplomats in the European Union: The challenge of political capture. *Comparative European Politics*, 19(1–2), 1–17. https://doi.org/10.1057/s41295-021-00261-6

Liang, C. S. (Ed.) (2007). *Europe for the Europeans. The foreign and security policy of the populist radical right*. Routledge.

Lundry, C. (2018). Assessing Indonesia's foreign policy under Jokowi. *Asia Policy*, 13(4), 30–35. www.jstor.org/stable/26533123

Magcamit, M. (2020). The Duterte method: A neoclassical realist guide to understanding a small power's foreign policy and strategic behaviour in the Asia-Pacific. *Asian Journal of Comparative Politics*, 5(4), 416–436. https://doi.org/10.1177/2057891119882769

McCargo, D. (2001). Populism and reformism in contemporary Thailand. *South East Asia Research*, 9(1), 89–107. www.jstor.org/stable/23747114

McNelly, A. (2020). The incorporation of social organizations under the MAS in Bolivia. *Latin American Perspectives*, 47(4), 76–95. https://doi.org/10.1177/0094582X20918556

Mead, W. R. (2011). The Tea Party and American foreign policy: What populism means for globalism. *Foreign Affairs*, 90(2), 28–44.

Mouzelis, N. (1985). On the concept of populism: Populist and clientelist modes of incorporation in semiperipheral polities. *Politics and Society*, 14(3), 329–348. https://doi.org/0.1177/003232928501400303

Mudde, C., & Rovira Kaltwasser, C. (2011). *Voices of the peoples: Populism in Europe and Latin America compared* (WP #378). Kellogg Institute for International Studies.

Nair, D. K. (2019). Saving face in diplomacy: A political sociology of face-to-face interactions in the Association of Southeast Asian Nations. *European Journal of International Relations*, 25(3), 672–697. https://doi.org/10.1177/1354066118822117

Phongpaichit, P., & Baker, C. (2008). Thaksin's populism. *Journal of Contemporary Asia*, 38(1), 62–83. https://doi.org/10.1080/00472330701651960

Plagemann, J., & Destradi, S. (2019). Populism and foreign policy: The case of India. *Foreign Policy Analysis*, *15*(2), 283–301. https://doi.org/10.1093/fpa/ory010

Pongsudhirak, T. (2016). An unaligned alliance: Thailand-U.S. relations in the early 21st Century. *Asian Politics and Policy*, *8*(1), 63–74. https://doi.org/10.1111/aspp.12233

Risse-Kappen, T. (Ed.) (1995). *Bringing transnational relations back in: Non-state actors, domestic structures and international institutions.* Cambridge University Press.

Rodrik, D. (2017). *Populism and the economics of globalization* (NBER Working Paper No. 23559). National Bureau of Economic Research.

Sevilla, H. A. (2018). The Philippines' foreign policy direction: An assessment of the first year of President Duterte. *Journal of South Asian Studies*, *6*(3), 165–173. https://doi.org/10.33687/jsas.006.03.2558

Stavrakakis, Y., & Katsambekis, G. (2014). Left-wing populism in the European periphery: The case of SYRIZA. *Journal of Political Ideologies*, *19*(2), 119–142. https://doi.org/10.1080/13569317.2014.909266

Stavrakakis, Y., Katsampekis, G., Nikisianis, N., Kioupkiolis, A., & Siomos, T. (2017). Extreme right-wing populism in Europe: Revisiting a reified association. *Critical Discourse Studies*, *14*(4), 420–439. https://doi.org/10.1080/17405904.2017.1309325

Verbeek, B., & Zaslove, A. (2017). Populism and foreign policy. In C. Rovira Kaltwasser, P. Taggart, P. Ochoa Espejo & P. Ostiguy (Eds.), *Oxford handbook of populism* (pp. 384–405). Oxford University Press.

Wajner, D. F. (2021). Exploring the foreign policies of populist governments: (Latin) America First. *Journal of International Relations and Development*, *24*, 651–680. https://doi.org/10.1057/s41268-020-00206-8

Weyland, K. (1999). Neoliberal populism in Latin America and Eastern Europe. *Comparative Politics*, *31*(4), 379–401. https://doi.org/10.2307/422236.

Weyland, K. (2001). Clarifying a contested concept: Populism in the study of Latin American politics. *Comparative Politics*, *34*(1), 1–22. https://doi.org/10.2307/422412

Weyland, K. (2017). Populism: A political-strategic approach. In C. Rovira Kaltwasser, P. A. Taggart, P. Ochoa Espejo & P. Ostiguy (Eds.), *Oxford handbook of populism* (pp. 48–72). Oxford University Press.

Wicaksana, I. G. W., & Wardhana, A. (2021). Populism and foreign policy: The Indonesian case. *Asian Politics and Policy*, *13*(3), 408–425. https://doi.org/10.1111/aspp.12594

Wojczewski, T. (2019). Populism, Hindu nationalism, and foreign policy in India: The politics of representing 'the People'. *International Studies Review*, *22*(3), 396–422.

Wojczewski, T. (2020). 'Enemies of the people': Populism and the politics of (in)security. *European Journal of International Security*, *5*(1), 5–24. https://doi.org/10.1017/eis.2019.23

Zarycki, T. (2000). Politics in the periphery: Political cleavages in Poland interpreted in their historical and international context. *Europe-Asia Studies*, *52*(5), 851–873. www.jstor.org/stable/153522

Zürn, M., Binder, M., & Ecker-Ehrhardt, M. (2012). International authority and its politicization. *International Theory*, *4*(1), 69–106. https://doi.org/10.1017/S1752971912000012

5
GROWTH, REDISTRIBUTION, AND POPULISM IN ASIA

Ming-Chang Tsai and Hsin-Hsin Pan

Many populist parties, long crouched on the fringes, have become high-profile, dominant forces on the mainstream political stage. Crosscutting the conventional left-right divide, many populist leaders successfully seize power by professedly appealing to the *general will* of the voters. The populist leadership boldly erodes social support for democratic norms and governance. Such shocking waves of populism have prevailed in wealthy Western societies, such as the Trump administration in the United States, the Brexit campaign in the United Kingdom, and the Rassemblement National (National Rally), previously the Front National, in France (Herman & Muldoon, 2018). However, the ways in which populism influences economic policymaking and even commandeers the market system remain understudied. Conceptually, populism as a political regime tends to override institutional regulations and defy rational and scientific procedures in policymaking, exuding an anti-establishment spirit. For this reason, populism has been criticized for lacking a comprehensive and coherent program for solving policy issues (Stanley, 2008). In this sense, populism has been critiqued as a *thin ideology*, often conveying preliminary information on critical public policies. In contrast to full-fledged ideologies such as liberalism or socialism, populism is more likely to rely on an ontologically simplified zeitgeist to define and differentiate the good and the bad groups, ideas, interests, and policies (Mudde, 2004). More often than not, policy choices appear to be vacillating rather than steadfast—neoliberal austerity is promoted one day but a pro-distributive agenda the next. Such inconsistency in adopting economic ideas and policy tools might be viewed as incoherent and chaotic by traditional camps. Equally essential for research on populist governments is to understand the choice of specific economic policies and evaluate their consequences for the well-being of the citizenry who have supported or rejected them in elections.

This chapter concentrates on the growth and distribution policies generated by prominent populist governments in Asia. This distinct contribution deepens our understanding of populism's influence on national development and improvement of the general public's well-being. Typically, academic studies focus on the socio-political evolution that preceded populist government control in Thailand, the Philippines, and Indonesia (Hellmann, 2017; Mietzner, 2018). The policy outcomes of populist regimes are all the more intriguing because populism has been criticized for its inability to build a political structure with a justifiable complete ideology (or at least a series of coherent and sensible guiding ideas for actions) for the matter of governance (Stanley, 2008). This does not mean that populist parties have failed in framing inspiring ideas to succeed in policy debates.

On the contrary, as the case of the Brexit campaign indicates, the populist *leave* camp effectively projected a conception of negative identity in the form of xenophobic emphasis, along with arousing fears or anger about remaining in the European Union due to inter alia expensive membership, loss of sovereignty, and social vulnerability due to a lack of border protection (Harrison, 2019). Nevertheless, when populist parties or politicians come to power, they may immediately find it awkward to continue using anti-elite discourse to bolster their popularity. From this viewpoint, we evaluate examples of proposed policies and their outcomes—in particular, those policies to sustain growth and redistribute a large pie.

We first propose a typology of populist governments based on policy outcomes in terms of growth and distribution. The former is expressed graphically with economic growth and economic stagnation as the two extremes of the X-axis and the latter as redistribution and inequality on the extremes of the Y-axis. Together, they constitute four quadrants representing developmental, pro-business, degenerative, and redistributive populism, as shown in Figure 5.1.

The upper-right (x, y) quadrant represents *developmental populism*, in which developmental policies achieve economic growth and broader redistribution. Populist leaders are not only applauded by the working class and the poor but also acclaimed by the corporate sector and the wealthy. The lower-right $(x, -y)$ quadrant represents *pro-business populism*, where economic policies support corporate interests rather than redistribution favouring the disadvantaged. The lion's share of profits often goes to tycoon firms, property owners, or the upper class. Reduction of poverty is not a policy priority. Inequality is likely to be exacerbated irrespective of economic growth going up. The lower-left $(-x, -y)$ quadrant represents *degenerative populism*. It refers to a populist regime that neither promotes economic growth nor alleviates economic inequality, the worst outcome scenario, leading

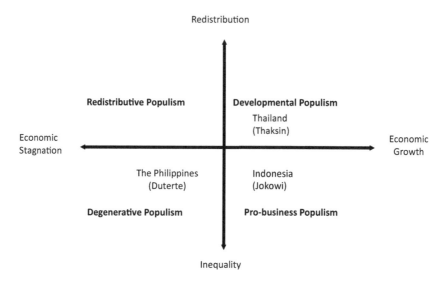

Figure 5.1 Variation of Populism in Southeast Asia

to national economic shrinkage after the populist government assumes power. The upper-left (-x, y) quadrant represents *redistributive populism*, in which economic stagnation and social redistribution co-exist. Ideologically, it is likely to be anti-elitist, instituting full-scale social structural adjustments to reduce poverty and give the poor a larger proportionate share of the minimal economic growth.

The four theoretical prototypes of populism provide a relational means of referencing through which to explain and evaluate the divergent evolutionary pathways progressing into the quadrants, mapping out governmental performance relative to economic growth and redistribution in the nations under study. In the following sections, we provide evidence explaining how case studies of three Southeast Asian populist regimes fit into this analytical scheme, identifying Thaksin in Thailand for achieving developmental populism, Jokowi in Indonesia for pro-business populism, and Duterte in the Philippines for degenerative populism. An appropriate case that fits comfortably into the redistributive populism prototype is not available in Asia. In the concluding section, we also briefly discuss an interesting, recent case from Taiwan, where a populist who promised to deliver an income increase from a growth model with a pro-China strategy failed to mobilize sufficient support in a national election due to widespread opposition from below. The cross-country typology and comparison enhance a deeper understanding of populism's growth and distributive outcomes in contemporary Asia.

Developmental populism: Thaksin in Thailand

Thaksin Shinawatra, with his Thai Rat Thai Party (TRT), has been deemed the most well-known example of populism in Southeast Asia and the whole Asian region (Hellmann, 2017; Mietzner, 2018). The conditions facilitating his ascent to power, the tactics he employed, and to what extent Thaksin represents a populist regime are questions that have triggered a series of intense debates. There was a long-evolving trend toward parliamentary democracy that slowly replaced military dictatorship after the King of Thailand intervened by appointing a new prime minister in the wake of the nationwide student uprising of 1973. Alongside Thailand's subsequent rapid economic growth, wealthier and more ambitious business elites emerged, who saw parliamentary rule as a means to curb the military regime's taxing of profits and role in national policymaking (Phongpaichit & Baker, 2005).

This interest, or intention, was all the more observable in the wake of the 1997 Asian financial crisis. Thaksin, a multi-billionaire tycoon controlling a large conglomerate marketing computer rentals, telecommunications, and cable television, represents an ideal example of a wealthy business community's political influence. Hewison (2017) describes Thaksin as a 'reluctant populist' because his primary concern was the macro-level economic infrastructure and business interests of Bangkok while doling out some minor benefits to his electoral base in the poor rural villages (Schmidt, 2007). It was when he ran for his second term as prime minister that he undertook his first major populist foray by mingling with the rural poor, speaking strategic, people-centred rhetoric with a heavier grassroots accent, and targeting the oligarchy of the military, monarchy, and urban bourgeoisie (Hewison, 2017).

After Thaksin's TRT won the 2001 election, he implemented several pro-poor policies, constituting an essential element of *Thaksinomics*. This wide-ranging package of policies attempted to accomplish two goals. The first was to create high-paying jobs and earn foreign exchange to reduce dependency on the international market and avoid future external shocks. These policy tools were not particularly innovative, but they addressed the problem of Thailand's slow growth after the 1997 financial crisis. The second was to increase domestic consumption through increased government expenditure in the short run and strengthen local industries and diversify production to move up the value chain in the long run. The first goal was to promote local industries through specialty products for each district (the One Tambon Project), small enterprise initiatives, and the Capital Creation Scheme (to redefine dead capital in terms of attaining legal rights and the documentation necessary for collateralized bank loans), and larger projects designed to create new regional centres of economic activity, including an aviation hub in Chiang Mai and a high-tech lab in Phuket (Chambers, 2013).

While there is a concern that economic nationalism seemed to loom large in response to slow growth in the post-crisis years and some painful remedies in the International Monetary Fund's structural adjustment policies, an inward-looking development model was not really what Thaksin pursued in practice. Some critical industries were chosen to promote a model *pilot cluster*: the automotive and parts, fashion and textile, and electronic and electrical appliance industries in 2003. The ceramics and digital industries were later added to this list. Growth strategies in Thaksinomics resembled neo-mercantilism, in which the state cooperated with Thai economic elites in a joint effort to reconstruct their ventures and increase global competitiveness (Glassman, 2004).

However, the achievement, while not negligible in terms of growth records, was limited. Thaksin's chief concern seems to have been stimulating entrepreneurship. At the same time, technological innovation and industrial upgrading were constrained by ad hoc decisions derived from highly personalized, discretionary power with insufficient administrative capacity. Steering public policy was a business coalition more interested in reaping quick profits from service sectors like telecoms, real estate, entertainment, media, and banking (Lauridsen, 2009). The linkages between firms and research institutes in the government and universities were weak. Financial intermediaries were hardly existent, through which the banking system could have played a critical role in generating a capital market for longer-term support (Intarakumnerd & Chaminade, 2011).

In contrast to the constraints and limitations of Thaksin's growth policies, his redistributive efforts have received a great deal of attention, leading to many regarding Thaksin as a typical populist. The Thaksin government was financially generous to some of his support groupings. For instance, farm assistance was aided by a three-year moratorium on farmers' debt payments. Small loans were made available to pavement vendors. The Village and Urban Revolving Fund and other financial credit agencies were established to assist small enterprises. Civil servants were offered novel, more generous retirement plans. Thaksin's economic policies were considered proto-populist and intended to attract support from the poor. He personalized compensation despite a potential threat from Bangkok's established oligarchy. Thaksin once portrayed himself as a man of the people under threat from dinosaurs (Phongpaichit & Baker, 2005).

Thaksin's universal health coverage policy probably attracted the most attention. It should be noted that this policy was first discussed in 1999 and was not originally his idea but resulted from a meeting with preeminent members of the Rural Doctors Society, a prominent advocacy group for enhancing health and care facilities in rural areas, from whom Thaksin sought advice for TRT social policy formulation. Thaksin immediately recognized the policy's appeal to the general public and branded it the 20-Baht Health Care Scheme (approximately U.S. $0.50), providing health care at this negligible cost per visit, irrespective of the severity of the disease. Although the fee was lifted to 30 baht, this policy was successfully institutionalized, with the poor and medically uninsured benefitting greatly from this flagship initiative. This generous new health care policy was alternatively understood as a *developmental* capture (Harris, 2015); a state-led agenda initiated by a network of action within the state apparatus to leverage necessary resources and realize inclusive policies that serve a broader range of society. This is in contrast to a *regulatory* capture, which tends to steer the direction of policy away from public interest to benefit organized private enterprise. While it is debatable whether this was merely a populist measure shrewd enough to gain more comprehensive support from voters regardless of hospital capacities or financial impacts (Phongpaichit & Baker, 2005), this universal care scheme continues to be of prime importance for the well-being of the poor in Thai society, which has long been characterized by extreme inequality between rich and poor (Hewison, 2014).

Thaksin appears to have prompted a series of populist regimes in Thailand. The Democratic Party, which led the government after the coup in 2006, came up with the *Wara Prachchachon* (People's Agenda), introducing expanded welfare policies, guaranteed income for farmers, an old-age pension fund, and other redistributive measures. Consequently, Thaksin's successor—his younger sister, Yingluck Shinawatra—won the general election of 2011 under the banner of the Pheu Thai Party (For Thais Party).[1] She revived inter alia the 30-Baht Health Care Scheme, raised the minimum wage, and executed a rice-pledging policy. In another coup, a military junta led by General Prayut Chan-o-cha took over the government in 2014. He introduced a welfare card system for the 14 million Thai citizens, making a monthly 600-baht credit per card available. This was deemed another pro-poor sweetener to win votes. Indeed, redistributive populism appears to have become a necessary political game in a highly unequal society, particularly when the junta faced an election, together with the adoption of a pro-royalist stance, irrespective of the use of repression and institutional violence to maintain order whenever considered necessary (Chambers & Waitoolkiat, 2016).

Pro-business populism: Jokowi in Indonesia

When President Joko Widodo, popularly known as Jokowi, came to power in 2014, he presented an alternative form of populism. Populism in Indonesia relied on two ideological mobilization strategies: Indonesia vs. foreign powers, and the people vs. the ruling elite. Populist ideas and policies along these two lines had been vehicles for the old and new players in the struggle for power within a self-sustained oligarchy comprising powerful families, patronage-based parties, security forces, and a vast corps of public officials (Hadiz & Robison, 2017). Jokowi did not pursue confrontational politics with the old order. However, he claimed, 'the very, very rich do not understand you as well as I do' (Mietzner, 2015, p. 26), which seems to have been one of his most provocative campaign statements. He could have pursued populist nationalism, which would have targeted giant foreign companies that had extracted rich natural resources for decades, some even for centuries. However, he did not harbour an anti-foreign sentiment.

In contrast to the strong accent on anti-colonialism and anti-imperialism adopted by prominent national leaders, he was moderate in using populist rhetoric and ideas (Mietzner, 2015). Jokowi differed in style by stressing a keen interest in serving the underprivileged, expressed by frequently chatting with ordinary people. He proposed technocratic improvements and solutions, avoiding impractical theorizing and promises. Academics have described his regime as *technocratic* populism (Mietzner, 2015). This term, however, is vague on specific measures supportive of growth and redistribution.

Jokowi successfully took advantage of a time of adversity in Indonesia. Despite a resource boom in the early 2010s, widespread public discontent had emerged regarding the Yudhoyono government's disappointing economic record and failure to deal with corruption. Notwithstanding an average solid economic growth rate of nearly 5% between 2004 and 2014, slightly exceeding the global average,[2] development was limited to selling natural resources, low-added-value manufacturing, and agricultural products. It could not absorb the millions of young people entering the labour market annually (Mietzner, 2015). A capital-intensive foreign investment concentrated narrowly on natural resource extraction and offered insufficient job opportunities. Poverty outside Jakarta remained widespread, with the World Bank estimating in 2018 that 30% of the population was either poor or vulnerable to a regression into poverty.[3]

The main thrust of Jokowi's growth strategy is his infrastructure agenda. Acknowledging that the state's principal task is to be an excellent service deliverer, his administration has focused exclusively on a series of infrastructure building projects, including 5,000 km of railways, 2,600 km of roads, 49 dams, 24 seaports, and several large power plants (Salim & Negara, 2018). It was hoped that poverty could be reduced, as these new infrastructures were expected to trigger rapid economic growth that would substantially benefit the poor. It can be argued that this new developmental policy, more aggressive in spending than Yudhoyono's government, was too restrictive in vision and conservative in ideology, with politically sensitive problems such as land reform, corruption, bureaucratic incapability, and civil rights and justice issues being subordinated for the sake of preserving the stability of hard-won power (Warburton, 2016).

Indonesia is a resource-rich country with a legacy of solid economic nationalism, which originated with the nationalization by Soekarno, the country's first president, of hundreds of Dutch banks and mining and plantation companies. It continued under successive governments, regardless of whether they were populist or not. Jokowi is no exception. After his inauguration, he instituted many new nationalist measures—mostly non-tariff barriers such as quotas, import licenses, and export bans (Patunru, 2018). After taking office, he banned rice imports, promising to achieve self-sufficiency in food. However, two years later, this ban was lifted because the national stocks were running low as the consumption demand of the world's fourth most populous nation continued to rise.

The previous president, Yudhoyono, had imposed controls on foreign ownership of mineral rights in response to widespread domestic anger over foreign exploitation of natural resources. The 2009 Mining Law aiming to achieve economic sovereignty was based on a concern that Indonesia's finite resources were being shipped overseas too quickly and cheaply, mainly due to China's huge demand. This law mandated that foreign companies divest 51% of assets to a state or domestic company after the tenth year of production (Warburton, 2016). While Jokowi strongly supported this law when he came to power, in early 2017 his government reversed the course to ban raw mineral exports. This change should not be interpreted as a move away from statist developmentalism toward deeper marketization. A primary motivation was to save the state-owned nickel company Antam from huge revenue loss under the ban and to support its acquisition of foreign-owned companies such as U.S.-owned Freeport Indonesia (Gellert, 2019; Warburton, 2017). In 2020, Jokowi introduced another mining law that raised the maximum size of traditional mining zones to 100 hectares and allowed mining activities in rivers and offshore. Another controversial step was the automatic renewal of mining contracts for over 20 years, overturning the requirement that the government could 'not immediately extend' expired mining contracts without first offering them to state-owned firms (Ballesteros, 2020). However, nationalist in economic ideology, policy innovations under Jokowi showed greater flexibility than determination.

Paralleling the strong resource nationalism are various redistribution policies to narrow the income gap between rich and poor. Two cards were issued by Jokowi, exemplifying his concern for the poor. First, the *Kartu Indonesia Pinta* (KIP), Indonesian Smart Card, provides scholarships of Rp450,000 (approximately U.S. $32) per annum for primary school children, 750,000 (U.S. $53) for junior high students, and 1,000,000 (U.S. $70.9) for senior high students. The coverage has increased from 11.2 million to 19.7 million students (Suryahadi & Al Izzati, 2018). Second is the *Kartu Indonesia Sehat* (KIS), Indonesian Health Card for the poor. Jokowi increased the premium assistance to Rp23,000 (U.S. $1.6) per recipient in 2017 from the Rp19,225 (U.S. $1.4) under the previous government, and the number of beneficiaries was significantly expanded. At the community level since 2015, a village fund, *Dana Sesa*, has been disbursed, with each village receiving an average of Rp280 million (U.S. $19,861). Most villages allocate the fund's proceeds to infrastructure development (roads) or community empowerment. Further, recommended increases in the national minimum wage by 11.5% in 2016, 8.3% in 2017, and 8.7% in 2018—all essential—were ratified (Manning & Pratomo, 2018). These increases should have reduced income disparities at the district level had all local governors complied, which was not the case, as only those of a few provinces did. All in all, these new social programmes helped sustain positive growth in consumption among the poor and the near-poor. Notwithstanding, rural communities and the urban poor remained disconnected from real economic growth while the middle class and the rich benefited substantially (Suryahadi & Al Izzati, 2018; Yusuf & Sumner, 2015).

Jokowi's government shows that a populist government can be highly attentive to allocating public resources for distribution—it is a necessity for his political survival. However, Jokowi appears to fall short of effective developmental policies. Indonesia's economy and society under this populist regime remain very much constrained, just as they were under the powerful oligarchs. Populism, rather than an agency of the people, seems to be a reactionary force that functions to keep the status quo—business interests and oligarchies—intact, thus constituting a subtype of pro-business populism.

Degenerative populism: Duterte in the Philippines

The Philippines has been hampered by a languishing economy and gigantic income gap since the late 20th century. Throughout its recent history, the country has been fertile ground for populism and populist leaders who have vowed to tackle the malaise of economic stagnation and inequality but have ultimately failed (Thompson, 2010). After President Rodrigo (Rody) Roa Duterte vowed to institute all means necessary to deal with both problems, he took his people by surprise when he showed that he meant it literally. However, as extra-judicial killing and extra-congressional policies were pushed to the extreme, he opened a new chapter on populism in terms of bloodbath and death toll (Arguelles, 2019; Coronel, 2019).

Like his populist counterparts in Thailand and Indonesia, Duterte proposed a developmental scheme named after himself, *Dutertenomics*. Although Dutertenomics aimed simultaneously to attain economic growth and poverty reduction, it barely succeeded (Capuno,

2020). Duterte proposed a battery of policy initiatives, mindful that restoring social order is essential to economic growth. The first policy was the War on Drugs in 2016. Duterte publicly endorsed the extra-judicial killing of drug dealers and drug addicts (Johnson & Fernquest, 2018). The following year, the opposition party in the House of Representatives impeached Duterte for violating human rights. However, his impeachment was quickly overturned—despite nearly 12,000 people having been executed without due process—when his allies in the House formed a supermajority (Dressel, 2011). A Social Weather Station poll in 2016 indicated that most Filipinos were satisfied with Duterte's policy to combat illegal drugs, even though 71% and 94% preferred arresting rather than killing drug suspects (Juego, 2017). For most Filipinos, a drug-free environment was essential for the public good and economic growth.

Duterte's administration increased state investment in public infrastructure and championed industry, initially proposing the five-year Build, Build, Build project between 2017 and 2022 (Arguelles, 2019; Capuno, 2020; Coronel, 2019). The government further proposed to invest between U.S. $160 and 180 billion—projected to account for 7.3% of the GDP in 2022—in basic infrastructure for inter alia public transportation, agriculture, and mining. This project had been expected to create 1.2 billion jobs and benefit the working class. However, elite-owned companies took the lion's share of profits by securing government contracts and obtaining public-private partnerships (PPP). The Duterte government also campaigned to promote the Davao Model of an iron-fisted drug control policy and generously funded industrial development, deriving from Duterte's legacy of enacting public policies that pleased the people yet violated judicial procedures for criminal prosecutions during his service as Mayor of Davao City.

In the interest of industrial transformation, the Comprehensive National Industrial Strategy (CNIS) targeted five core national industries: agriculture, manufacturing, tourism, logistics, and information technology. (Rosellon & Medalla, 2017). Additionally, after requesting a judicial review of the Constitution, he removed policy constraints on foreign investment (Capuno, 2020). Despite these constructive economic policies, increased government spending, and relaxing regulations on foreign direct investment, which promised economic growth, the GDP growth rate for the Philippines dropped from 7% in 2016 to 6% in 2019.[4]

In addition to economic growth, poverty reduction was championed as a core element of Dutertenomics, yet 16.6% of the population still lives below the poverty line.[5] To reduce poverty, the Duterte government enacted a series of policy changes. First, tax reforms set the portion of income tax allocated to social welfare to 30%. Moreover, the income tax was reduced to less than 20,000 pesos (about U.S. $110) annually for 99% of all labourers (Capuno, 2020; Coronel, 2019; Dressel, 2011), while the threshold for tax deduction exceeded the minimum wage.

Duterte committed government resources to a raft of social welfare policies, which included spending on labour, health, and education. Although he promised to end contract labour, he only banned subcontracting and legalized the notorious contract labour and fixed-term employment in 2018, disappointing labour activists (Capuno, 2020). Duterte also vowed to improve the health care system, particularly the coverage of PhilHealth, the public health programme (Arguelles, 2019; Picazo et al., 2016), as well as pledging to extend mandatory education to grade 12 (Capuno, 2020). Critics noted that the public education system mainly trains low-end labourers and that scholarship programmes focused conspicuously on private and profit-seeking schools.

Overall, Duterte has failed to deliver on his promises to the people. The economy has not grown, nor has the working class benefited from a substantial redistribution of funding. Ironically, in the sluggish Philippine economy, Duterte has been feted for his authoritarian approach to maintaining social order at the expense of human rights, which manifests a degenerative form of populism. At the cost of a deterioration in democracy, his populist regime seems to have brought greater economic dismay rather than the promised improvements in living conditions.

Conclusion

Economic stagnation and income inequality jointly breed economic grievances that fuel the rise of populism worldwide (Inglehart & Norris, 2016). Asia is no exception. New and partial democracies are particularly vulnerable to the appeal of populist leaders, who promise their supporters a rosy future to the detriment of democracy. Given that Asia is home to many nascent democracies where a range of populisms have been largely ignored, greater attention must be paid to the region by academics. Asia is significant to our theoretical understanding of populism, particularly in a context where a left-right ideological cleavage barely exists.

In this chapter, we proposed a typology of populism to explore the varieties of populism, focusing on growth and redistribution outcomes. Thailand under Thaksin represents a model of developmental populism: growth and redistribution were not substantial, although they were observable. This is the reason Thailand's developmental populism is positioned closer to the origin of the coordinates in Figure 5.1. Indonesia has pro-business populism, while the Philippines show degenerative populism. We reviewed the prominent cases of populist leaders in Asia, showing how those such as Thaksin in Thailand, Jokowi in Indonesia, and Duterte in the Philippines have exploited their faltering national economies and widening income gaps to their political advantage in electoral campaigns, ironically sowing the seeds of democratic decay.

One significant debate about populism concerns its thin ideology, which often is attached to specific policy values, powers, or interests. This is how various subtypes emerge in the analysis (Mudde & Rovira Kaltwasser, 2018). Also, the absence of populism can be an equally intriguing situation. Precisely what makes populism take root in some countries but not others? For instance, what makes Singapore and Vietnam seemingly immune to populism when they also hold regular elections like the Philippines, Indonesia, and Thailand?

Furthermore, what makes populism quickly fade away in some countries, though it can last for quite a long while elsewhere? A short-lived populism in Taiwan is worth mentioning here for a comparative perspective. From 2019 to 2020, a populist regime appeared whose birth and death came at a shockingly swift pace. The significance of this case is that it is one of the few stories in which a populist politician has been prevented from seizing power over the government. As a candidate for the presidency in 2020, Han Kuo-Yu from the Kuomintang Party proposed the idea of a 'people's economy' to rescue a stagnant economy and reduce income inequality in Taiwan. In the spectrum of political ideology, Han is more pro-China. He believes that the large market of China can be accessed if Taiwan is willing to acknowledge the One-China policy. Like prominent populist politicians in Southeast Asia, he claimed he would deliver growth policies that people needed (Bailey, 2020). He ended up falling in the 2020 presidential election. He also lost his position as Mayor of Kaohsiung in June 2020 in a recall election, mainly because of the effective mobilization of grassroots movements and pro-independence organizations. His failure offers a lesson that strong civic organizations can resist the threat of populists, who would otherwise veer quickly toward authoritarian rule once they come into power. In comparison, such resistance from below seems less likely in Southeast Asia. Populism in Asia appears to have flourished in poorer economies but effectively prevented political participation and redistribution movements in the poor's favour.

Research into populism currently focuses more on its causes rather than its effects. Hopefully, this chapter will motivate future studies of populism concerned with its consequences for development. More investigation is needed into how and why the commitments of populist leaders to their supporters are so often not delivered and the long-term impact this has on growth and redistribution.

Notes

1 The Pheu Thai Party was the third version of a political party founded and controlled by Thaksin in 2008. Thaksin founded the Thai Rak Thai Party (TRT) in 2007 and the People's Power Party (PPP) in 2008. Both were short-lived and constitutionally dissolved due to electoral fraud.
2 The GDP growth rates for Indonesia from the World Bank: https://data.worldbank.org/indicator/NY.GDP.MKTP.KD.ZG?locations=ID. The annual GDP growth rates worldwide are from the website of the World Bank: https://data.worldbank.org/indicator/NY.GDP.MKTP.KD.ZG.
3 Please refer to the website of the World Bank for the poverty rate in Indonesia: www.worldbank.org/en/country/indonesia/overview.
4 The GDP growth rates for the Philippines from the World Bank: https://data.worldbank.org/indicator/NY.GDP.MKTP.KD.ZG?locations=PH.
5 The poverty data for the Philippines from the Asian Development Bank: https://www.adb.org/countries/philippines/poverty.

References

Arguelles, C. V. (2019). 'We are Rodrigo Duterte': Dimensions of the Philippine populist publics' vote. *Asian Politics & Policy*, 11(3), 417–437. https://doi.org/10.1111/aspp.12472
Bailey, K. C. (2020). Maintaining Taiwan's democracy. *Comparative Strategy*, 39(3), 223–238. https://doi.org/10.1080/01495933.2020.1740568
Ballesteros, A. (2020, June 21). Indonesia passes new mining law 'marred by controversy.' *Asean Economist*. www.aseaneconomist.com/indonesia-passes-new-mining-law-marred-by-controversy/
Capuno, J. J. (2020). Dutertenomics: Populism, progress, and prospects. *Asian Economic Policy Review*, 15(2), 262–279. https://doi.org/10.1111/aepr.12296
Chambers, P. (2013). Military 'shadows' in Thailand since the 2006 coup. *Asian Affairs: An American Review*, 40(2), 67–82. www.jstor.org/stable/23527229
Chambers, P., & Waitoolkiat, N. (2016). The Resilience of monarchised military in Thailand. *Journal of Contemporary Asia*, 46(3), 425–444. https://doi.org/10.13140/RG.2.2.34032.69126
Coronel, S. S. (2019). The vigilante president: How Duterte's brutal populism conquered the Philippines autocracy now. *Foreign Affairs*, 98(5), 36–43. www.foreignaffairs.com/articles/philippines/2019-08-12/vigilante-president.
Dressel, B. (2011). The Philippines: How much real democracy? *International Political Science Review*, 32(5), 529–545. https://doi.org/10.1177/0192512111417912
Gellert, P. K. (2019). Neoliberalism and altered state developmentalism in the twenty-first century extractive regime of Indonesia. *Globalizations*, 16(6), 894–918. https://doi.org/10.1080/14747731.2018.1560189
Glassman, J. (2004). Economic 'nationalism' in a post-nationalist era. *Critical Asian Studies*, 36(1), 37–64. https://doi.org/10.1080/1467271042000184571

Hadiz, V. R., & Robison, R. (2017). Competing populisms in post-authoritarian Indonesia. *International Political Science Review*, *38*(4), 488–502. https://doi.org/10.1177/0192512117697475

Harris, J. (2015). 'Developmental capture' of the state: Explaining Thailand's universal coverage policy. *Journal of Health Politics, Policy and Law*, *40*(1), 165–193. https://doi.org/10.1215/03616878-2854689

Harrison, S. (2019). The weight of negativity: The impact of immigration perceptions on the Brexit vote. In L. Herman & J. Muldoon (Eds.), *Trumping the mainstream: The conquest of mainstream democratic politics by far-right populism* (pp. 185–203). Routledge.

Hellmann, O. (2017). Populism in East Asia. In C. Rovira Kaltwasser, P. Taggart, P. Ochoa Espejo & P. Ostiguy (Eds.), *The Oxford handbook of populism* (pp. 161–178). Oxford University Press. https://doi.org/10.1093/oxfordhb/9780198803560.001.0001

Herman, L. E., & Muldoon, J. (2018). Populism in the twenty-first century: From the fringe to the mainstream. In *Trumping the mainstream: The conquest of democratic politics by the populist radical right* (pp. 1–20). Routledge. https://doi.org/10.4324/9781315144993

Hewison, K. (2014). Considerations on inequality and politics in Thailand. *Democratization*, *21*(5), 846–866. https://doi.org/10.1080/13510347.2014.882910

Hewison, K. (2017). Reluctant populists: Learning populism in Thailand. *International Political Science Review*, *38*(4), 426–440. https://doi.org/10.1177/0192512117692801

Inglehart, R. F., & Norris, P. (2016). *Trump, Brexit, and the rise of populism: Economic have-nots and cultural backlash* (HKS Faculty Research Working Paper Series RWP16-026). Harvard Kennedy School. https://www.hks.harvard.edu/publications/trump-brexit-and-rise-populism-economic-have-nots-and-cultural-backlash

Intarakumnerd, P., & Chaminade, C. (2011). Innovation policies in Thailand: Towards a system of innovation approach? *Asia Pacific Business Review*, *17*(2), 241–256. https://doi.org/10.1080/13602381.2011.533504

Johnson, D. T., & Fernquest, J. (2018). Governing through killing: The war on drugs in the Philippines. *Asian Journal of Law and Society*, *5*(2), 359–390. https://doi.org/10.1017/als.2018.12

Juego, B. (2017). Demystifying Duterte's populism in the Philippines. *IAPS Dialogue*. https://iapsdialogue.org/2017/02/22/demystifying-dutertes-populism-in-the-philippines

Lauridsen, L. S. (2009). The policies and politics of industrial upgrading in Thailand during the Thaksin era (2001–2006). *Asian Politics & Policy*, *1*(3), 409–434. https://doi.org/10.1111/j.1943-0787.2009.01133.x

Manning, C., & Pratomo, D. (2018). Labour market developments in the Jokowi years. *Journal of Southeast Asian Economies*, *35*(2), 165–184. www.jstor.org/stable/26539212

Mietzner, M. (2015). *Reinventing Asian populism: Jokowi's rise, democracy, and political contestation in Indonesia* (Policy Studies 72). East-West Center. www.eastwestcenter.org/system/tdf/private/ps072.pdf?file=1&type=node&id=35018

Mietzner, M. (2018). Movement leaders, oligarchs, technocrats, and autocratic mavericks: Populism in contemporary Asia. In C. de la Torre (Ed.), *Routledge handbook of global populism* (pp. 370–384). Routledge.

Mudde, C. (2004). The populist zeitgeist. *Government and Opposition*, *39*(4), 542–563. https://doi.org/10.1111/j.1477-7053.2004.00135.x

Mudde, C., & Rovira Kaltwasser, C. (2018). Studying populism in comparative perspective: Reflections on the contemporary and future research agenda. *Comparative Political Studies*, *51*(13), 1667–1693. https://doi.org/10.1177/0010414018789490

Patunru, A. A. (2018). Rising economic nationalism in Indonesia. *Journal of Southeast Asian Economies*, *35*(3), 335–354. www.jstor.org/stable/10.2307/26545317.

Phongpaichit, P., & Baker, C. (2005). Challenge and change in East Asia: 'Business populism' in Thailand. *Journal of Democracy*, *16*(2), 58–72.

Picazo, O. F., Ulep, V. G. T., Pantig, I. M., & Ho, B. L. (2016). A critical analysis of purchasing of health services in the Philippines: A case study of PhilHealth. In A. Honda, D. McIntyre, K. Hanson & V. Tangcharoensathien (Eds.), *Strategic purchasing in China, Indonesia and the Philippines* (pp. 152–218). World Health Organization. http://www.jstor.org/stable/resrep28440.6

Rosellon, M. A., & Medalla, E. M. (2017). *Macroeconomic overview of the Philippines and the new industrial policy*. Philippine Institute for Development Studies. https://pidswebs.pids.gov.ph/CDN/PUBLICATIONS/pidsdps1748.pdf

Salim, W., & Negara, S. D. (2018). Infrastructure development under the Jokowi administration: Progress, challenges and policies. *Journal of Southeast Asian Economies, 35*(3), 386–401. www.jstor.org/stable/10.2307/26545320

Schmidt, J. D. (2007, Feburary 19–21). From Thaksin's social capitalism to self-sufficiency economics in Thailand. *Paper Presented at the Autochthoneity or Development? Asian 'Tigers' in the World: Ten Years After the Crisis Conference*. Austrian Foundation for Development Research (Österreichische Forschungsstiftung für Entwicklungshilfe—OFSE). https://vbn.aau.dk/ws/files/13639418/From_Thaksin_s_Social_Capitalism_to_Self-sufficiency_Economics_in_Thailand

Stanley, B. (2008). The thin ideology of populism. *Journal of Political Ideologies, 13*(1), 95–110. https://doi.org/10.1080/13569310701822289

Suryahadi, A., & Al Izzati, R. (2018). Cards for the poor and funds for villages: Jokowi's initiatives to reduce poverty and inequality. *Journal of Southeast Asian Economies, 35*(2), 200–222. www.jstor.org/stable/26539214

Thompson, M. R. (2010). Reformism vs. Populism in the Philippines. *Journal of Democracy, 21*(4), 154–168. https://doi.org/10.1353/jod.2010.0002

Warburton, E. (2016). Jokowi and the new developmentalism. *Bulletin of Indonesian Economic Studies, 52*(3), 297–320. https://doi.org/10.1080/00074918.2016.1249262

Warburton, E. (2017). Resource nationalism in Indonesia: Ownership structures and sectoral variation in mining and palm oil. *Journal of East Asian Studies, 17*(3), 285–312. https://doi.org/10.1017/jea.2017.13.

Yusuf, A. A., & Sumner, A. (2015). Growth, poverty, and inequality under Jokowi. *Bulletin of Indonesian Economic Studies, 51*(3), 323–348. https://doi.org/10.1080/00074918.2015.1110685

6
THE POPULIST RADICAL RIGHT, GENDERED ENEMY, AND RELIGION

Perspectives from South Asia since 2014

Shweta Singh

Introduction

Giorgia Meloni was sworn in as Italy's first woman prime minister in October 2022 and heads the country's first far-right government since World War II. Her Brothers of Italy party won approximately 25% of the vote. Meloni has a history of extremist rhetoric and has embraced the Great Replacement white supremacy narrative. Regarding gender and the populist radical right (henceforth PRR), it is noteworthy that Meloni's success has been partly attributed to her campaign narratives, which used sexual violence against women for racist and xenophobic purposes.

In France, the far right made steady progress over the last decade to become the major opposition in 2022, and in Spain it has likewise gained ground. A Swedish political party founded by neo-Nazis and other right-wing extremists is now the second-largest faction in the Riksdag, while in both Hungary and Poland, the far right has been in power for more than a decade. In South Asia, populism drives Hindu nationalist and chauvinism projects in India, Islamist popular movements in Bangladesh and Pakistan, and Sinhala Buddhist nationalism in Sri Lanka (Jaffrelot & Tillin, 2017; Chacko, 2018; Singh, 2021). However, while there has been an increase in research into both left- and right-wing populism, it remains understudied from a gender perspective.

This chapter is intended to fill this gap in populism research by presenting a gender perspective on PRR, drawing on insights from South Asia and particularly India since 2014. By focusing on the Bharatiya Janata Party (BJP) and its affiliate organizations, such as Rashtriya Swayamsevak Sangh (RSS) and Vishva Hindu Parishad (VHP), the chapter aims to analyze the factors leading to the rise of PRR and how, with its salient nationalist ethnoreligious character, it intersects with the social construction of gender in India. The analysis presented in this chapter supports Laclau's argument that 'populism is not constitutive of a type of movement or special social base or a particular ideological orientation but is identifiable with structuring political logic—to be precise, the logic of "the people"—rather than an ideology' (2005, p. 117). This analysis is significant in considering gender and populism in India and in South Asia more broadly. Laclau's most important insights in *On Populist Reason* are, foremost, that 'the people' is inherently an empty signifier, and thus a discursive construct that can be filled with any given content, in most cases stemming from the structuring political logic that attaches itself to different historical moments, contexts, crises, and ideologies. Furthermore, as a floating or empty signifier, the concept of *the people* is articulated in conjunction with one or more of a range of identity categories, such as gender, class, or religion, and as such requires an intersectional analysis (Kovala et al., 2018). Building on my previous research (Singh & Féron, 2021), I argue in this chapter that the lens of intersectionality offers critical insights into the study of gender and PRR both at a national level and across South Asia.

This chapter presents three key arguments from the standpoint of gender concerning radical-right populism in South Asia with implications for further research from a comparative perspective. First, the universal ideational template that views populism as a 'thin-centred ideology' that separates society into two homogeneous and antagonistic groups, the 'pure people' and 'corrupt elite' (Mudde, 2004, p. 543), while relevant, does not fully capture the complexity of gender and PRR discourses in South Asia. This is because neither of the analytical tropes, 'the people' and 'gender', can be forced into constricting monolithic templates but instead need to be situated in varied and intersecting identity matrices of class, caste, age, religion, etc. Returning to Laclau, I am persuaded that there is a need to understand populism not as a thin-centred ideology but as a 'structuring political logic'. Second, I underline the importance of applying an intersectional approach to the study of populism and gender (see Singh & Féron, 2021) with a specific focus on religion. The point of emphasis is that PRR discourse employs exclusionary tropes that are used to construct not just the people and the elite, but also the people and 'non-people', more commonly referred to as 'the other'. The construction of this subject category of people and non-people, I would argue, is gendered and draws heavily on religious or secular references reassembled as civilizational frameworks (for details, see Öztürk et al., 2022) such as *Hindutva*[1] in the BJP narratives of India.[2] Third, most writings on gender and PRR that stem from Europe tend to focus on the 'neoliberal crisis of governability' (Yuval-Davis, 2019), which 'provokes new forms of governing through gendering and religiosization' (Sauer, 2022, p. 451). In postcolonial states like India, these new forms of governing are marked less by a neoliberal crisis of governability than by 'necropolitics' (See Mbembe, 2003)[3] and stem from postcolonial anxieties, postcolonial secularization projects, and the fractured histories of the region.

This chapter proceeds in three steps. First, it provides a broad overview of debates on PRR and gender. Second, it provides the conceptual nuts and bolts and empirical evidence from analysis of the BJP and its affiliate organizations in India (after 2014) to elaborate on the three key arguments made above. Third, it discusses how this analysis is relevant from the standpoint of comparative research on gender and populism in South Asia and beyond. For instance, it raises question marks over universal narrow analyses of both gender and populism in South Asia and argues that there is a need to pay attention to identity categories such as religion, race, class, and caste.

Gender and the populist radical right: an overview

PRR politics has taken centre stage in the changing political narrative of global politics, and a gender lens offers a distinctive political framing in terms of content and articulation. So, what is *populism*? How does gender intersect with its contentions, characterization, and articulation? Historically, the term 'populism' was originally applied to the politics of such

19th century political movements as the U.S. Democratic Party forerunner, the People's Party, also known as the Populist Party; the Russian socialist Narodniks (populists); and the nationalist Boulangists, intent on avenging France's defeat in the Franco-Prussian War (Rovira Kaltwasser et al., 2017). Recently, the term has gained traction when applied to the wave of radical-right politics around the globe (see Chapter 1 in this volume). While there is broad agreement that populism thrives on the elite-people divide, its intersection with gender has not clearly emerged in academic writing and policy debates. This is because most writings on gender and populism view its intersections through the left-right ideological axis.

Expanding on the intersectional approach intrinsic to my earlier feminist and populist studies (Singh & Féron, 2021; Singh, 2021), the focus on PRR politics in India in this chapter calls for an analysis that transcends the left-right axis. That is to say, this is a context which demands an approach sensitive to the complex and multifaceted dimensions of identity inequalities—in terms of gender, class, sexual orientation, ethnicity, etc.—and how these overlap, interact, and are mutually reinforcing. In applying this matrix to contemporary India, a primary focus on the interrelationships of PRR politics, gender, and religion is paramount. Before moving on to specific themes, the most relevant strands of debate on populism are examined, noting which conceptualizations of populism include or exclude gender, which have relevance, and which are similar or dissimilar to those framing gender and PRR debates in the Global North and Global South.

In terms of conceptualization, two schools of thought are relevant. The first, posited by Mudde, approaches populism as a thin-centred ideology (Mudde, 2004). In Mudde's early writings, gender is subsumed under the idea of the people. In later writings, while maintaining his earlier line of argument, he acknowledges that although conceptually, populism makes no reference to gender, as a thin-centred ideology, it seldom exists alone. Thus, in most cases, populist actors combine their populism with ideologies such as nationalism, socialism, or communism. It follows that the 'gender politics of populist actors are influenced by a combination of the national culture and accompanying ideology rather than by populist ideology itself' (Mudde & Rovira Kaltwasser, 2015, p. 17).

Extensive scholarship on gender and populism has employed Mudde's ideational approach to reveal how gender shapes populist right politics. For instance, PRR discourse tends to construct antagonisms like the identity of the pure people (we) in opposition to the 'other' (they)—not necessarily the elite, but any entity excluded from the category of pure people (Mudde, 2007; Aslanidis, 2016; Brubaker, 2020). Among the significant exclusions supporting PRR antagonisms is 'anti-gender discourse' and evocation of the 'crisis of masculinity' (Graff et al., 2019, p. 548).

The second approach, of which Laclau is a key proponent, focuses on populism as a political logic, an argument he first expounded in *Politics and Ideology in Marxist Theory* (1977). Laclau, whose work continues to influence many studies on populism (see, for example, Azzarello, 2011; Stavrakakis, 2004), held, as noted above, that populism is a 'structuring political logic' rather than a specific ideology, movement, or social base (Laclau, 2005).

In his analysis, there is a strong emphasis first on 'the people' as an 'empty signifier', and second on the need to determine the discursive sequences through which a social force or movement carries out its overall political performance. Developing this line of analysis, Eklundh and Knott (2020, p. 3) highlight that 'populism is akin to a form or logic, and hence has the ability to attach itself to different historical moments, contexts, crisis or ideologies'. This analysis is significant in its articulation of the concept of people, where differing identities such as gender, class, or religion matter and are given a specific content or political logic (see, for example, Kovala et al., 2018).

While the relationship between gender and populism is receiving increasing attention within these two broad strands of literature, there is a growing recognition that a universal template cannot fully capture the complexity of their intersections. Hence, scholars such as Dietze and Roth (2020, pp. 8–9) refer to a right-wing populist complex and call for an analysis of intersectional constellations as this complex intersects with identity categories such as race, class, religion, and ethnicity. Singh and Féron (2021) note the significance of an intersectional approach as populists tend to construct the 'other' through discursive gendered sequences rather than solely through nationalist or socioeconomic tropes. Here, we draw attention to the entanglement of gender and populism with religion, specifically in PRR discourse in India. Another approach has been to systematize scholarship on gender, PRR, and religion, for example, by highlighting the role of cultural Christianity in populist discourse, particularly in Northern Europe. Norocel and Giorgi (2022), for example, seek to bridge the gap between the writings on radical-right populism and gender on the one hand, and radical-right populism and religion on the other. They examined how 'cultural Christianity'—Christian religious symbols, heritage, or roots—has been discursively mobilized 'to differentiate "natives" from "immigrants" in a national, European, or Western perspective' (2022, p. 422).

This kind of analysis is not confined to Northern Europe, but resonates across the continent, for example in Hungary and Poland, where questions of gender and sexuality are not sub-themes of populism but core elements. In Poland, anti-genderism, as a discursive structure, feeds into the anticolonial framework and provides an ideological glue to an otherwise loose coalition of religious and national players in PRR discourse (Korolczuk & Graff, 2018). In most instances, religion, race, and class play intersecting roles in the discursive constellations that are employed to construct the 'other'. The 'other' in Europe can be the Muslim or black man threatening 'the people's' women. Further, Donà (2020, p. 290) argues that right populists 'invoke women's rights and gender equality to stigmatize Muslim men'. In the construction of the 'other', and who is portrayed as the enemy, a sense of fear is evoked (Wodak, 2015) and moral panic induced (Betz, 2017). Norocel (2013) and Wodak (2015) argue that the politics of fear, to which PRR resorts, has a clear gendered aspect, which manifests itself in two interconnected processes.

> On the one hand, they are scapegoating foreign 'others', accused of being a source of fear themselves as potential rapists of 'people's women', or endangering people's moral unity. On the other hand, they exacerbate the fear of potential extinction, by stoking fears of a 'demographic race' resulting in the replacement of the native ethnic and religious majority.
>
> *(Norocel & Giorgi, 2022, p. 423)*

Here, it is noteworthy how religion—both Islam and Christianity—is deployed in PRR narratives and how women's bodies become the boundary markers in terms of the distinction between 'us' and the 'other'.

Research on veils and Muslim body coverings, for example, clearly demonstrates how veiled Muslim women, as objects of PRR discourse, are evoked in a language of visible 'othering'—as needing to be saved not just from violent Muslim men but also from the patriarchy embedded within the Islamic tradition itself (see El-Tayeb, 2011; Meer et al., 2010; Hadj-Abdou, 2019; Wodak, 2015; Sauer, 2022). While this gendered populist right discourse is often couched in the language of liberation and emancipation (Betz, 2017, p. 383; Rosenberger & Sauer, 2011), its underlying import is anti-Islamic. These dynamics have been variously labelled. Sauer describes this framing as 'racist bordering in the radical right populist necropolitical project' (2022, p. 458). She further notes that Farris (2017) 'labels these frames "femonationalism", while Hadj-Abdou (2019) uses the term "gender nationalism"'. In these kinds of approaches, 'the objective of unveiling becomes a marker of a Western, national identity' (2020, p. 450). For Brubaker (2017), this strategy, which is frequently deployed by right-wing parties in Western Europe, is a form of 'civilizationalism' (see Sauer, 2022, p. 451).

Further, a defining characteristic of the intersection of PRR politics, gender, and religion is that religion is both instrumentalized and mobilized to construct a politics of fear (Wodak, 2015 and Chapter 9 in this volume), in which women's bodies become contested sites for moral panic (Betz, 2017, p. 326). In right-wing discourse, religion has become a 'racialized boundary' (Marzouki & Mc Donnell, 2016, p. 6; Fekete, 2009), and what follows are discursive constellations of enemy images where both religion and gender intersect along with identities such as caste, class, religion, and race.

The following section provides the conceptual nuts and bolts of radical-right populism, gender, and religion based on empirical evidence from India covering the period 2014 to 2021 to illustrate the three key arguments made at the outset of this chapter.

The populist radical right, gender, and religion: perspectives on gendered enemy and the 'other' from India (2014–2021)

In 2014, a watershed year in India, the BJP won 282 parliamentary seats and 31.3% of the vote, which increased to 37.4% in the 2019 parliamentary (Lok Sabha) elections. The BJP has been characterized as a PRR party based on its conceptions of 'the people', 'elites', and 'others' (Basu, 1993; McDonnell & Cabrera, 2018). What gives BJP populist radical politics its distinctive character? How does its politics intersect with gender and religion? And how does it resemble or differ from PRR political parties in Europe and other parts of Asia?

The BJP, under Prime Minister Narendra Modi (2014–), repackaged PRR politics with a novel mix of developmental narrative, nationalism, nativism, religion, and national security (Subedi & Scott, 2021). The party combined political Hinduism, or Hindutva, with populist discourses to construct a narrative of a civilizational state in crisis requiring a strongman to lead the people back to the glorious *Hindu Rashtra* (Hindu Kingdom) (Lefèvre, 2020). It would be misleading to characterize PRR in India as ideologically thin-centred because of its emphasis on the separation of two homogeneous and antagonistic groups, namely, the people and the elite. While this distinction is fundamental to BJP radical-right populism, the party departs from the default (ideational) conception and construes 'the people' to comprise distinct identity constellations such as class, religion, caste, and age (for details, see Singh & Féron, 2021). It is here that Laclau's explanation of 'the people' as an empty signifier translates into practical terms and can be filled with a specific content, which may or may not, in the Indian context, align with the political logic of Hindutva.

What is paramount here is where gender interposes in the populist discursive constellation of 'the people' and 'the othered'. Gender impinges on PRR politics and is integral to the political logic (in this case Hindutva) that is used to construct not just the people and the elite but also the people and the enemy. It is important to stress here that this structuring political logic hinges both on gender and the intersecting identity of religion, and that the case of India is useful in understanding the intersecting mesh of PRR politics, gender, and religion. So, what is Hindutva, and why is its structuring political logic employed to give people a discursive characterization pertinent from a feminist standpoint? These questions are addressed through a brief comparison of the framing of Hindu and Muslim women in PRR discourse in India.

The discourse of the BJP, which rests on the ideology of Hindutva, promotes the idea that Hindus are not members of disparate religious sects but rather comprise a single distinct people who have fallen victim to powerful foreign elites in the form of Muslim and later British conquering forces (Jaffrelot, 2007). Emphasizing an organic (maternal) conception of citizenship, Hindutva rests on the notion that Hindus were the original, and thus the most legitimate, inhabitants of India (Basu, 1993). The ideology of Hindutva is also shared by affiliate organizations, referred to as the *Sangh Parivar* (Family of the Rashtriya Swayamsevak Sangh). These include professional associations; economic, educational, and religious organizations; and think tanks, which support, complement, and mobilize BJP Hindu ideology at the local level (Andersen & Damle, 2018). Many groups in the *Sangh Parivar*, like RSS (founded in 1925), VHP (founded in 1964), and Bajrang Dal (founded in 1984) articulate a far more radical-right discourse, and also have affiliated women's wings such as Rashtriya Sevika Samiti (in the RSS) and Durga Vahini (in the VHP).

A close examination of these two women's wings indicates that certain women are recognized as the cultural repository of Hindutva, serving *Hindu Rashtra* (the Hindu nation), and bringing *paramvaibhav* (utmost honour) to the nation. These women symbolize Hindu womanhood. Thus, women's bodies and sexuality become the sites for control and protection as they are essential to maintain the purity of the Hindu nation against the 'other', in this case the Muslim man. This supports the assertion that the structuring political logic of Hindutva hinges both on gender and the intersecting identity of religion. Within this gendered narrative, the concepts of honour, motherhood, and familial ties are predominant. The aims and objectives of the Rashtriya Sevika Samiti,[4] along with the publicly available newsletters, describe how women's roles are essentialized within the boundaries of the family—as mother, wife, daughter—with the primary aim of protection and safeguarding the honour, *sanskar* (lit. to improve, purify, refine) and *dharma* (religion) of the community and nation. The Samiti regularly organizes nearly 4350 *shakhas* (branches) with a focus on practical *sanskar*, the process of adherents developing their potential in every aspect of human life and preserving and purifying moral and cultural values in Hindu society as a whole.

These insights clarify how patriarchy and religion are privileged in the framing of rights and freedom, and that both are framed within the categories of family, community, and religion and nation, all of which are gendered. Politically, the analysis is significant as it reveals how gender and religion intersect in the BJP's PRR discourse and how the Hindu woman is framed in the discourse. Further, it challenges the constricting analysis that views Hindu women only as a boundary marker in the service of the community and nation, and as lacking agency. Many Hindu women argue that the discourse of Hindutva gives them the space to reclaim both their political identity and agency within the patriarchal setup of the family and the community (see Bedi, 2006).

Furthermore, the analysis calls for attention on how the PRR conceptualization of women as boundary markers of the community and nation legitimizes militant vigilantism and gives rise to the politics of fear and of moral panic. Yuval-Davis (2003) makes the case that there are three major dimensions of nationalist projects that relate in somewhat different ways to gender. First, there is the genealogical dimension with a focus on the origin of the people (race); second is the cultural dimension that imbues an 'essence' to the character of the nation drawing on language, religion, and other customs and traditions. This 'essence' enables people to be classified into us and them categories and allows for a discursive construction of the 'other' as the enemy. The third dimension concerns citizenship as determining the boundaries of the nation, as well as notions of state sovereignty and territoriality. In the process, as Yuval-Davis shows, gendered bodies and sexuality play pivotal roles as the boundary markers of the nation (Yuval-Davis, 1980). As noted earlier, right-wing discourse has developed religion into a 'racialized boundary' (Marzouki & Mc Donnell, 2016, p. 6; Fekete, 2009, p. 47), with discursive constellations of enemy images based on religion, gender, class, and race emerging. The case of India illustrates the point that women's bodies become contested sites for moral panic, a point that will be developed through a discussion on the politics of 'Love Jihad' and the conception of a 'gendered enemy'.

The so-called Love Jihad, also known as Romeo Jihad, is the alleged practice by young Muslim men who are said to target Hindu and Christian women through trickery and expressions of false love to convert them to Islam (see Gupta, 1998; Holzberg & Raghavan, 2020). In the discourse of the Love Jihad (reflected mostly in social media posts, visual images, pictures, and videos), the Hindu woman needs to be protected from the enemy. We can see how, between 2014 and 2019, the concept of Love Jihad was propagated through discursive symbols, pamphlets, and images, instilling a sense of fear among the people mobilized to 'protecting' Hindu women (Wilson et al., 2018, p. 119). The RSS, VHP, and affiliate organizations organized a systematic campaign against Love Jihad in which Muslim men were construed as the enemy, destined, unless something was done, to bring dishonour and shame to Hindu communities and the nation (*rashtra*) through sexual control, progeny, conversion, and marriage. The President of the VHP, Alok Kumar, alleged that there were systematic attempts by Muslim forces to entice Hindu girls into converting to Islam: 'When one Hindu girl is converted, whole generations are converted. We do advise the Hindu girls to not fall [into] the trap and marry within the community' (quoted in 'Offer Bike Rides', 2018).

The Vishwa Hindu Parishad organized systematic campaigns in schools and colleges in West Bengal to disseminate details of the alleged Love Jihad committed by Muslim men against Hindu women. These campaigns aimed to recruit vigilantes called *Dharma Yoddhas* (religious fighters) to monitor instances of Love Jihad and cow slaughter and to protect Hindu sacred places.[5] As the *Times of India* reported, a VHP spokesperson stated that 'the idea is to cultivate a cadre which is fully dedicated to protection and preservation of our culture. It is rather a way to inoculate the feeling of nationalism among our youth' (Shah, 2018). *Dharma Yoddhas* exemplify the patriarchal values of control, protection, and militant vigilantism. Wilson et al. (2018) encapsulate the retribution for the alleged Love Jihad as 'moral policing, targeting women's sexual autonomy, blackmailing Hindu women who are in [a] consensual relationship with Muslim men, through far-right militias, vigilante groups and mobs are promoted and legitimized by the state, in which gender violence is central' (2018, p. 2).

The sense of fear and moral panic is further enhanced using images from popular culture, which are then circulated either through pamphlets or social media. For instance, as reported by news media a manipulated image (half face covered with Burqa) of a popular Bollywood actor Kareena Kapoor was used as the cover photo of the issue of *Himalaya Dhwani*, a magazine brought out by the women's wing of VHP, Durga Vahini (Gera, 2015). The cover carried the headline *dharmantaran se rashtraantaran* (conversion of nationality through religious conversion), underlining how women's bodies—while symbolizing the cultural repository of the nation and citizenship—are discursively constructed, deploying religious tropes to create a sense of anxiety and fear. Furthermore, there has been a recent backlash against popular Hindi films such as *Padmavat, Jodha Akbar*, and *Kedarnath*, where it was argued by Hindu vigilante groups that popular media, by showcasing Hindu-Muslim love stories, were aiding Love Jihad. It was thus incumbent on a righteous Hindu man to protect his Hindu woman against such influence. This speaks directly to both fear and moral panic narratives in which women's bodies are constructed as being under existential threat.

Just as Hindu women's bodies serve as the boundary marker of the nation, so Muslim women's bodies provide a site for counterposing populist strategies. At one level, Muslim women's bodies are framed as threatened by the patriarchal practices of the religious community to which she belongs; at another they are framed as the 'other', or enemy women. What requires emphasizing here is that in PRR discourse, neither Hindu nor Muslim women can be fitted into a uniform template which ignores or fails to discern the paradoxes in its framing. For instance, in the case of BJP discourse on the Triple Talaq Bill (The Muslim Women [Protection of Rights on Marriage] Bill, 2019),[6] it was surmised that Muslim women needed protection from the regressive practices of Islam and from a patriarchal Islam. The same argument was, however, not applied to Hindutva. While the question of Muslim women's agency was revived in the context of the Triple Talaq Bill, it did not figure in an ongoing controversy in the state of Karnataka over the banning of the Hijab. The Hijab ban in Karnataka classrooms effectively denies Muslim women not just the right to an education but also subjects them to the dehumanizing politics of othering. Scholars such as Sauer (2022) rightly argue that Muslim women's body coverings offer insights into 'new forms of governing that uses the gendering of race, and "racialization of religion"'(Anthias, 2020, p, 148, as cited in Sauer, 2022, p. 459). Sauer further highlights that this new form of governing constitutes a form of *necropower* and states that 'the concept of necropower does not only refer to the physical death of a person, but also to social and political death, that is, discrimination, exclusion or erasure through the processes of de-humanization' (2020, p. 452). In the case of India, it can be said that while Hindu women are elevated to a sacred pedestal in the discourse of Hindutva; Muslim women, in contrast, are being subjected to necropolitics.

There is substantial historical evidence indicating that Hindu masculinity was constructed in opposition to the sexually charged Muslim male, against whom the Hindu people, and particularly Hindu women, had to be defended and protected (Gupta, 1998, p. 738). Gupta emphasizes that 'women were both active and passive markers of communal difference. They were not simply by products of history. They acted and were acted upon' (1998, p. 733). The relevant point here is that the roots of the enemy image of the 'other', in this case the Muslim man, and consequent necropolitics that characterized various articulations of Hindu movements can be found even during colonial times. All this goes beyond a 'neoliberal crisis of governability', on which writings on the political right lay stress.

The populist radical right, gender, and religion: directions for future research

While PRR and gender have received increasing attention, the relevance of gender and religion is still marginal in academic and policy perspectives. Most research has centred around the right-left axis, and despite the broad potential that the lens of intersectionality offers to research on populism, it has had minimal application. This chapter contended that there is a need to question the narrow analysis of populism as a 'thin-centred ideology'. Alternately, as has been argued, PRR ideologies across different cultural contexts centre around the idea of 'the people' as an 'empty signifier'. Within this conceptualization, gender and religion play an important role, not just in the construction and articulation of populist subject categories but also in their mobilization.

This template of analysis, I argue, has a significant potential for cross-cutting research in both South and Southeast Asia, and indeed beyond. For instance, it has relevance for authoritarian populism, such as the Rajapaksa regime in Sri Lanka (see Chapter 17 in this volume), particularly with reference to the idea of Muslim men as the gendered enemy, or in the case of the Philippines under the former president Duterte (see Chapter 20 in this volume) in shaping discourse on hypermasculinity. Beyond that, an intersectional approach allows us to explore how gender and populism intersect, not just with religion, but also with race, class, caste, ethnicity, and age. Similarly, in the Global North, an understanding of populism as a structuring political logic in terms of how 'the people' is defined provides a multi-layered entry point into the politics of race and immigration, both of which are relevant from a feminist perspective. Similar patterns of political logic and the construction of a gendered enemy also resonate with developments in Scandinavia. This suggests the need for comparative research that cuts across regions to examine patterns of PRR more closely, along with its intersections with gender and religion.

Notes

1 The discourse of the BJP rests on the ideology of Hindutva, which promotes the idea that Hindus are not members of disparate religious sects but instead comprise a single distinct people—one which has been the victim of powerful foreign elites in the form of Muslims, and then British conquering forces (Jaffrelot, 2007).
2 The point on gendering on horizontal and vertical axes draws from Öztürk et al., 2022.
3 'Necropolitics' and 'necropower' refer to socio-political death arising from discrimination and exclusion; on forms of 'erasure' (cf. Sauer, 2022, p. 452).
4 Keshav Baliram Hedgewar formed the RSS in 1925; Laxmibai Kelkar (Mausiji) carried out Golvarkar's request that she form an exclusively women's organization on the ideological lines of the RSS and his promised support. The first *shakha* (branch) of the *Samiti* (committee) was held at Wardha in 1936.
5 For examples of such campaigns, see *Offer Bike Rides*, 2018 and Shah, 2018.
6 The Muslim Women (Protection of Rights on Marriage) Act, 2019, is an Act of the Parliament of India criminalizing triple talaq (instant divorce). It underlines that any pronouncement of talaq (divorce) by a Muslim husband upon his wife by words, either spoken, written, in electronic form, or in any other manner whatsoever, shall be void and illegal. https://www.indiacode.nic.in/handle/123456789/11564?sam_handle=123456789/1362.

References

Andersen, W., & Damle, S. (2018). *The RSS: A view to the inside*. Penguin.
Anthias, F. (2020). *Translocational belongings: Intersectional dilemmas and social inequality*. Routledge.
Aslanidis, P. (2016). Is populism an ideology? A refutation and a new perspective. *Political Studies*, 64(1), 88–104. https://doi.org/10.1111/1467-9248.12224
Azzarello, S. (2011). *'Populist masculinities': Power and sexuality in the Italian populist imaginary* (Master's thesis, Utrecht University). https://studenttheses.uu.nl/handle/20.500.12932/6758
Basu, A. (1993). Feminism inverted: The real women and gendered imagery of Hindu nationalism. *Bulletin of Concerned Asian Scholars*, 25(4), 25–37. https://doi.org/10.1080/14672715.1993.10416136

Bedi, T. (2006). Feminist theory and the right-wing: Shiv Sena women mobilize Mumbai, *Journal of International Women's Studies*, 7(4), 51–68. https://vc.bridgew.edu/jiws/vol7/iss4/4

Betz, H.-G. (2017). Populism and Islamophobia. In R. C. Heinisch, C. Holtz-Bacha & O. Mazzoleni (Eds.), *Political populism* (pp. 373–389). Nomos.

Brubaker, R. (2017). Between nationalism and civilizationism: The European populist moment in comparative perspective. *Ethnic and Racial Studies*, 40(8), 1191–1226. https://doi.org/10.1080/01419870.2017.1294700

Brubaker, R. (2020). Populism and nationalism. *Nation and Nationalism*, 26(1), 44–66. https://doi.org/10.1111/nana.12522

Chacko, P. (2018). The right turn in India: Authoritarianism, populism and neoliberalisation. *Journal of Contemporary Asia*, 48(4), 541–565. https://doi.org/10.1080/00472336.2018.1446546

Dietze, G., & Roth, J. (2020). *Right-wing populism and gender. European perspectives and beyond.* Transcript Verlag.

Donà, A. (2020). What's gender got to do with populism? *European Journal of Women's Studies*, 27(3), 285–292. https://doi.org/10.1177/1350506820929222

Eklundh, E., & Knott, A. (2020). *The populist manifesto: Understanding the spectre of populism.* Rowman & Littlefield.

El-Tayeb, F. (2011). *European others: Queering ethnicity in postnational Europe.* University of Minnesota Press.

Farris, S. (2017). *In the name of women's rights. The rise of femonationalism.* Duke University Press.

Fekete, L. (2009). *A suitable enemy: Racism, migration and islamophobia in Europe.* Pluto Press.

Gera, S. (2015, January 9). Kareena Kapoor's morphed picture used as warning against 'Love Jihad', VHP says actress is free to sue them. *indianexpress.com*. https://indianexpress.com/article/entertainment/entertainment-others/kareena-kapoors-morphed-picture-used-as-a-warning-against-love-jihad-vhp-says-actress-can-sue-them-if-she-wants/

Graff, A., Kapur, R., & Walters, S. D. (2019). Introduction: Gender and the rise of the global right. *Signs: Journal of Women in Culture and Society*, 44(3), 541–560. https://doi.org/10.1086/701152

Gupta, C. (1998). Articulating Hindu masculinity and Femininity 'Shuddhi' and 'Sangathan' movements in United Provinces in the 1920s. *Economic and Political Weekly*, 33(13), 727–735. www.jstor.org/stable/4406586

Hadj-Abdou, L. (2019). Gender(ed) nationalism of the populist radical right. In G. Fitzl, J. Mackert & B. S. Turner (Eds.), *Populism and the crisis of democracy. Vol. 3: Migration, gender and religion* (pp. 94–104). Routledge.

Holzberg, B., & Raghavan, P. (2020). Securing the nation through the politics of sexual violence: Tracing resonances between Delhi and Cologne. *International Affairs*, 96(5), 1189–1208. https://doi.org/10.1093/ia/iiaa099

Jaffrelot, C. (2007). Introduction. In C. Jaffrelot (Ed.), *Hindu nationalism a reader*. Princeton University Press.

Jaffrelot, C., & Tillin, L. (2017). Populism in India. In C. Rovira Kaltwasser, P. Taggart, P. Ochoa Espejo & P. Ostiguy (Eds.), *The Oxford handbook of populism* (pp. 179–193). Oxford University Press.

Korolczuk, E., & Graff, A. (2018). Gender as 'Ebola from Brussels': The anticolonial frame and the rise of illiberal populism. *Signs: Journal of Women in Culture and Society*, 43(4), 797–821. https://doi.org/10.1086/696691

Kovala, U., Palonen, E., Ruotsalainen, M., & Saresma, T. (Eds.) (2018). *Populism on the loose.* University of Jyvaskyla.

Laclau, E. (1977). *Politics and ideology in Marxist theory: Capitalism, fascism, populism.* New Left Books.

Laclau, E. (2005). *On populist reason.* Verso.

Lefèvre, C. (2020). Heritage politics and policies in Hindu Rashtra. In A. Mohammad-Arif, J. Naudet & N. Jaoul (Eds.), *The Hindutva turn: Authoritarianism and resistance in India*. https://doi.org/10.4000/samaj.6728

Marzouki, N., & McDonnell, D. (2016). Introduction: Populism and religion. In N. Marzouki, D. McDonnell & O. Roy (Eds.), *Saving the people. How populists hijack religion* (pp. 1–11). Hurst & Company.

Mbembe, A. (2003). Necropolitics. *Public Culture*, *15*(1), 11–40. https://doi.org/10.1215/08992363-15-1-11

McDonnell, D., & Cabrera, L. (2018). The right-wing populism of India's Bharatiya Janata Party (and why comparativists should care). *Democratization*, *26*(3), 484–501. https://doi.org/10.1080/13510347.2018.1551885

Meer, N., Dwyer, C., & Modood, T. (2010). Embodying nationhood? Conceptions of British national identity, citizenship, and gender in the 'veil affair'. *The Sociological Review*, *58*(1), 84–111. http://dx.doi.org/10.1111/j.1467-954X.2009.01877.x

Mudde, C. (2004). The populist Zeitgeist. *Government and Opposition*, *39*(4), 541–563. https://doi.org/10.1111/j.1477-7053.2004.00135.x

Mudde, C. (2007). *Populist radical right parties in Europe*. Cambridge University Press.

Mudde, C., & Rovira Kaltwasser, C. (2015). Vox populi or vox masculini? Populism and gender in Northern Europe and South America. *Patterns of Prejudice*, *49*(1–2), 16–36. https://doi.org/10.1080/0031322X.2015.1014197

Norocel, O. C. (2013). *Our people—A tight-knit family under the same protective roof: A critical study of gendered conceptual metaphors at work in radical right populism*. Unigrafia.

Norocel O. C., & Giorgi, A. (2022), Disentangling radical right populism, gender, and religion: An introduction. *Identities*, *29*(4), 417–428. https://doi.org/10.1080/1070289X.2022.2079307

'Offer bike rides, give gifts': VHP's 'love jihad' brochure in WB lists 10 ways how Muslims 'lure' Hindu girls. (2018, September 5). *Timesnownews.com*. www.timesnownews.com/india/article/vishwa-hindu-parishad-west-bengal-love-jehad-jihad-hindu-women-muslim-men-brochures-communal-politics-trinamool-congress-bharataiya-janata-party/280260

Öztürk, E., Serdar, A., & Nygren, K. G. (2022). The veil as an object of right-wing populist politics: A comparative perspective of Turkey, Sweden, and France. *Identities*, *29*(4), 538–555. https://doi.org/10.1080/1070289X.2022.2029067

Rosenberger, S., & Sauer, B. (Eds.) (2011). *Politics, religion and gender. Framing and regulating the veil*. Routledge.

Rovira Kaltwasser, C., Taggart, P., Espejo, P. O., & Ostiguy, P. (2017). Populism: An overview of the concept and the state of the art. In C. Rovira Kaltwasser, P. Taggart, P. O. Espejo & P. Ostiguy (Eds), *The Oxford handbook of populism* (pp. 1–24). Oxford University Press.

Sauer, B. (2022). Radical right populist debates on female Muslim body-coverings in Austria. Between biopolitics and necropolitics. *Identities*, *29*(4), 447–465. https://doi.org/10.1080/1070289X.2022.2071515

Shah, P. (2018, September 29). Recruitment from October: VHP's Dharma Yoddhas to check love jihad, cow slaughter. *Times of India*. https://timesofindia.indiatimes.com/city/lucknow/dharma-yoddhas-to-check-love-jihad-cow-slaughter/articleshow/66001798.cms

Singh, S. (2021). The security mom, and 'America first': A feminist intersectional gaze from India (In M. A. Boyer, C. G. Thies, L. W. Pauly, C-Y. Shih, J. De Alba-Ulloa, S. Singh, . . ., & E. Parajon (Eds.), Forum: Did 'America first' construct America irrelevant?). *International Studies Perspectives*, *22*(4), 458–494. https://doi.org/10.1093/isp/ekab013

Singh, S., & Féron, E. (2021). Towards an intersectional approach to populism: Comparative perspectives from Finland and India, *Contemporary Politics*, *27*(5), 528–549, https://doi.org/10.1080/13569775.2021.1917164

Stavrakakis, Y. (2004). Antinomies of formalism: Laclau's theory of populism and the lessons from religious populism in Greece. *Journal of Political Ideologies*, *9*(3): 253–267. https://doi.org/10.1080/1356931042000263519

Subedi, D. B., & Scott, A. (2021). Populism, authoritarianism, and charismatic-plebiscitary leadership in contemporary Asia: A comparative perspective from India and Myanmar. *Contemporary Politics*, *27*(5), 487–507. https://doi.org/10.1080/13569775.2021.1917162

Wilson, K., Ung Loh, J., & Purewal, N. (2018). Gender, violence and the neoliberal state in India. *Feminist Review*, *119*(1), 1–6. https://doi.org/10.1057/s41305-018-0109-8

Wodak, R. (2015). *The politics of fear: What right-wing discourse means*. Sage. https://dx.doi.org/10.4135/9781446270073

Yuval-Davis, N. (1980). The bearers of the collective: Women and religious legislation in Israel. *Feminist Review*, 4(1), 15–27. https://doi.org/10.1057/fr.1980.4

Yuval-Davis, N. (2003). Nationalist projects and gender relations. *Narodna umjetnost: Croatian Journal of Ethnology and Folklore Research*, 40(1), 9–35. https://hrcak.srce.hr/33084

Yuval-Davis, N. (2019). Autochthonic populism, everyday bordering and the construction of 'the migrant'. In G. Fitzl, J. Mackert & B. S. Turner (Eds.), *Populism and the crisis of democracy, vol. 3: Migration, gender and religion* (pp. 69–77). Routledge.

7
CHARISMATIC LEADERSHIP, LEADER DEMOCRACY, AND POPULISM IN ASIA[1]

D. B. Subedi and Alan Scott

Introduction

The historical discussion of authoritarian leadership and the more recent revival of interest in populist and authoritarian rule are both closely, but not exclusively, bound up with European trends: the rise of fascism in the 1920s and 1930s and, much more recently, the re-emergence of 'strong' or 'illiberal' leaders, particularly in countries that were previously part of the Soviet Bloc—e.g., Hungary's Viktor Orbán (Fabry, 2021) or Jarosław and Lech Kaczyński in Poland (Smiecinska, 2021).

In this chapter, we apply the concepts of charisma and plebiscitary leader democracy (PLD), largely emerging out of this European context, to contemporary leadership in South and Southeast Asia to better understand Asia's 'conservative moment' (Chacko & Jayasuriya, 2018). While several scholars have studied Asia's charismatic leaders (Bendix, 1967; Tan & Wee, 2002), the concept of charisma has not been sufficiently explored in the context of the recent resurgence of populism and authoritarianism within the region. We aim to address this gap by comparing and contrasting the charismatic leadership of Narendra Modi in India with that of Aung San Suu Kyi in Myanmar prior to the military coup in February 2021.

Our argument unfolds in two stages. First, we argue that charisma is not an inherent personal quality; it is socially and politically constructed and conditioned by the *relationship* between leaders and their followers. In its top-down form, it requires a leader to *claim* charisma and demonstrate an ability to attract followers. In this sense, charisma is a kind of political *performance* in which the leader articulates and claims to represent the 'will' of the people. Viewed from the bottom up, followers must come to *accept* the leader's claim to exceptional qualities. It is the interplay of these two dimensions—rather than any intrinsic quality of the leader—that constitutes charisma. Such a relational or interactive view of charismatic leadership ascribes followers (and followership) an equal standing to leaders (and leadership).

Second, we show that charismatic-plebiscitary leaders mobilize cultural resources and deploy cultural divisions to sustain and, where possible, 'expand their power and attack enemies' (Weyland, 2019, p. 326), according to the 'inner logic' of populism. To support this argument, we propose a catalogue of the criteria of charismatic-plebiscitary leadership, both from the perspective of the leader and followers, and use the criteria to analyze our case studies from India and Myanmar. While socio-political contexts in the two countries vary, they share strikingly similar recent political developments: charismatic leaders have been in power, adopting a populist, nationalist, and authoritarian style of politics and using the plebiscitary elements of modern democracy (Subedi & Scott, 2021). There is also a striking difference: while Narendra Modi remains in power in India, in Myanmar, the military seized power on February 1, 2021, and Aung San Suu Kyi, along with several other political leaders, human rights activists, and pro-democracy civil society leaders have been detained ever since (see Chapter 18 in this volume). Our analysis focuses exclusively on Suu Kyi's time in power between 2012 and 2021 in order to delineate the rise and fall of her leadership in Myanmar's competitive political arena. Thus, the two case studies allow us to compare and contrast how charismatic leadership emerges and declines, and what it means for the rise and fall of a populist style of politics in Asia's hybrid democracies.

Charisma, acclamatory politics, and leader democracy

The aim of this section is to identify a set of criteria that will be applied in the two case studies. To this end, we draw on Weber's classical analysis of charisma and one of its forms—plebiscitary leadership—to unpack an interactive component of the leader-follower relationship. This leader-follower dialectic is a key characteristic of contemporary populist politics. Contemporary populist leaders—both right and left—seek to foster institutionally unmediated relationships with their followers, bypassing democratic institutions and undermining the checks and balances these institutions impose on democratically elected leaders.

Before delving into the leader-follower dialectic in contemporary populism, we start with the *locus classicus* of leadership analysis, written shortly before the rise of European fascism: Max Weber's account of charismatic domination and authority. This account is sufficiently well and widely known, so we shall selectively mention only those aspects that are relevant to the analysis developed herein. In particular, we want to draw attention to the following aspects of Weber's account of charisma as a specific form of rule and legitimation of that rule:

First, the charismatic rule is *relational*: it involves both the claims of those who assert their charismatic—i.e., extraordinary—qualities and authority *and* the degree of acceptance of those claims among a broader public—among those who are thus ruled. This relational aspect is clear in Weber's definition of the term, which concludes: 'what matters is how this quality is **actually** judged by those who are ruled charismatically: how "**followers**" see things' (Weber, 2019 [1922], p. 374, original emphasis). Charismatic authority has to be *recognized*, and charismatic leadership popularly *acclaimed*.

Second, in its pure form, charisma is '**disconnected from the economy**' (Weber, 2019 [1922], p. 377, original emphasis) and from all considerations of an everyday, rational, economic kind, even as it remains dependent upon economic resources (e.g., gifts, donations, extortion, patronage, etc.). Charisma is not strictly *instrumentally* rational and is guided by an ethic not of responsibility but of conviction.

Third, charisma (like bureaucracy) is a *revolutionary force* against tradition. As Weber famously noted, it is governed by the principle: 'It is written . . . but I say unto you'

(Weber, 2019 [1922], p. 376). Unlike bureaucracy, which seeks to change the conduct of life externally by setting rational goals that ultimately alter behaviour, charisma seeks direct, immediate change by altering the subject's basic orientation to the world through conversion. Its course is thus unpredictable, even arbitrary, since it is not merely disconnected from the economy (*wirtschaftsfremd*) but also from existing institutions, procedures, and practices. These are trumped by the will of the leader. Charismatic authority is the triumph of political will over due process and a rejection of the conventional restraints that embody the spirit and, not infrequently, the letter of the law.

Fourth, and following the previous point, the relationship between leader and follower is not mediated by institutions; it is direct and immediate. It is a 'social relationship in which the realization of charisma depends on personal qualities and their personal **proof**' (Weber, 2019 [1922], pp. 378–79, original emphasis). It thus has a clear *affective* component, at least on the side of the followers.

Finally, charisma has to be routinized if it is to be more than ephemeral. It is a highly unstable form of rule and authority.

This ideal type covers a wide variety of specific leadership forms, from shamans to leaders of religious cults, revolutionary leaders, etc. But there is one specific form of charismatic leadership that is central to Weber and much of the contemporary analysis, namely *plebiscitary leadership*. This is the specific form with which we are concerned here. The centrality of this leadership type is due to its political character and, despite all the differences between Weber's context and ours, its contemporary relevance.

Plebiscitary leadership has the general qualities of charismatic rule, of which it is a subtype, but these are manifested in specific ways. In its exceptional and temporary form, the plebiscitary leader is freely elected, rules by the 'grace of those who follow him' (Weber, 2019 [1922], p. 406), and can be rescinded at will. Such leaders are thus obliged to constantly provide proof of their worth to retain the 'devotion and trust' (p. 407) upon which their authority rests. So long as it is maintained, this devotion and trust give the leader power outside—and frequently against—institutions, potentially including parliaments, laws, and the courts. While initially anti-authoritarian and often revolutionary, like all forms of charisma, plebiscitary leadership can be routinized and institutionalized, in this case as PLD. Nevertheless, it involves a special relationship between leader and followers, one which rests upon the latter's emotion and on their devotion or dedication (*Hingabe*).

It is not difficult to see the relevance of Weber's account of plebiscitary-charismatic leadership and leader democracy for contemporary debates on populism; indeed, Weber comes close to making the link for us:

Leadership democracy is therefore generally characterized by a naturally emotional dedication to and trust in the leader, which tends to result in an inclination to follow the most extraordinary, most promising leader who deploys the most attractive means of persuasion.

Weber, 2019 (1922), p. 408

Weber treats all forms of charismatic authority as temporary, not least because, as forms of *personal* power, they are affixed to a mere mortal. For personal authority to survive in any form, it must be, at least partially, transformed into or supplemented by another type of authority and legitimacy: traditional or bureaucratic. Thus, Weber's account is a form of punctuated equilibrium theory: it starts with an event—the appearance of the charismatic figure—which disrupts path-dependent behaviour and self-reproducing institutions before these reconsolidate in a new constellation.

Plebiscitary leadership is a particularly unstable form of charismatic authority and is generally associated with sharp transitions or interregnums—e.g., the revolutionary tribunal. Freely elected authority, which is at the grace of the followers and which can be rescinded at their will, is especially ephemeral. The question is, what will it transform into? If the criteria of the followers have been in accord with the qualities Weber lists in the previous quotation, there will be a strong pull for this anti-hierarchical form of power to morph into its opposite: authoritarianism. In other words, it can easily revert to what Weber identifies as charisma's default position: 'the principle of charisma is authoritarian' (Weber, 2019 [1922], p. 405). Its anti-hierarchical form is a temporary exception.

The fragility of charismatic-plebiscitary leadership has recently been illustrated by the fate of that archetypical strongman, Philippine President (2016–2022) Rodrigo Duterte (see Chapter 19 in this volume). Based on expert interviews, one researcher reports that 'all interviewees forecasted that Duterte will stay in power until the end of his term' (Czech, 2022, p. 219). While this turned out to be the case, by the time of his State of the Nation Address on July 26, 2021, his mishandling of the COVID pandemic (see Chapter 11 in this volume) plus corruption scandals had weakened his position (Teehankee, 2022). That analysts have spent so much effort explaining Duterte's popularity is less evidence of the fallibility of expert judgement than of the volatility of such charismatic rule, which, in promising simple solutions to complex problems, has a built-in capacity to disappoint. As Czech (2022, p. 216) notes, Duterte's legitimacy took the form of 'more of an acceptance or even a wait-and-see attitude than the unconditional support of the masses'.[2] Devotion and trust are fickle emotions (as Machiavelli warned princes), and thus unstable foundations for rule.[3] Even authoritarian populists are to a degree reliant on the conditional grace of their followers. Such grace appears a solid and stable ground for power until it is withdrawn and/or such leaders can no longer demonstrate their worth and/or the performance palls. Duterte's ultimate failure, however, illustrates a further weakness of charismatic-plebiscitary rule: failure to secure succession. As a result, in the Philippines, authoritarian-charismatic rule has given way to, or paved the way for, quasi-dynastic rule.

It should finally be noted that while Weber sees a natural affinity between charismatic rule and authoritarianism, except in its temporary democratic form, this does not imply there is a necessary or sufficient relationship between charisma and populism, as the latter is now understood. Rather, populism represents one possible path that charismatic leadership can take.

What we find in much current literature is essentially an elaboration of the analysis of charisma and plebiscitary leadership that still takes its cue from and builds on Weber's account. Takis Pappas, for example, defines charisma as a 'distinct type of legitimate leadership that is personal and aims at the radical transformation of an established institutional order' (2016, p. 380)[4] while, from a different corner of political studies, for the political theorist Jeffery Green (2009), plebiscitary leadership is a direct, unmediated relationship between leaders and their followers in which the former must constantly demonstrate they are not bound by customary rules and can to go 'off script' in order to engage directly with and sustain the attention of the audience. This suggests that the very characteristics that strike non-followers as evidence of lack of leadership quality—e.g., unpredictability, erratic behaviour, making extravagant promises, or appealing to magical solutions—are, for followers, evidence of the leader's exceptional and revolutionary qualities. In this sense, charismatic leadership polarizes at a very basic level, that of the perception and interpretation of facts. Followers and non-followers 'see things' differently.

Much of the immediate stimulus for the revival of interest in populist, charismatic, plebiscitary, and authoritarian leadership was the emergence in Europe of what appeared to be a new style of leadership of which Hungary under Viktor Orbán is perhaps the most prominent case (see, for example, Körösényi, 2019; Fabry, 2021). This interest was then, of course, reinforced and geographically extended by the election of Trump in 2016.

This discussion has been selective, but it has a limited aim: to identify criteria for defining charismatic-plebiscitary leadership, which we shall apply as set out in the following table:

Table 7.1 Characteristics of Charismatic-Plebiscitary Leadership

From the perspective of the leader	*From the perspective of the followers*
1a) The leader claims to possess extraordinary qualities that justify bypassing existing institutions and breaking with customary political practices.	1b) This claim is accepted by followers on the basis of trust in and devotion to the leader. The experience of personal connections to leaders is grounded in processes of social identification and self-categorization
2a) The justification for leadership is grounded in a holistic and organicist conception of the community, and 'the will of the people' is conceived as its unified expression but is empirically bounded and exclusionary.	2b) New 'we-identities' (Steffens et al., 2014, p. 303) are formed in which followers arrive and are encouraged to think of themselves as part of a bounded and organic community of fate and as embodying the whole, or that part of it that genuinely belongs.
3a) The leader has acquired sufficient control over the party and elections have taken on a sufficiently plebiscitary character to lend the leader the necessary authority to follow through with the transformative/revolutionary project associated with charismatic authority.	3b) In this, the leader is able to retain the support of followers and of the party itself, which thus comes to resemble a 'leader party'.

Central and Eastern Europe provide a template or benchmark for our two national cases. Moving on now to these cases, we shall seek to apply and refine this framework. The underlying question we consider is to what extent these types of analysis can be applied to and adapted for hybrid democracies in a non-European context.

Narendra Modi, *Hindutva*, and populist leadership in India

Narendra Modi is the leader of the Hindu nationalist Bhartiya Janata Party (BJP) and Prime Minister of India, serving two consecutive terms since 2014. Between 2001 and 2013, he had been elected as the Chief Minister of the State of Gujarat for three consecutive terms. In the public images in India and beyond, Modi has been portrayed variously. Some see him as a staunch Hindu nationalist (Kaur, 2015), a populist (Sundar, 2020), a 'strongman', and a charismatic leader capable of leading contemporary India. Others portray him as an emerging authoritarian leader, intolerant of religious minorities, especially Muslims, and an advocate of anti-immigrant policies, threatening the secular and multicultural foundation of democracy in India (Chacko, 2020). Modi himself associates his identity with India's ordinary citizens, the underdogs, by proudly claiming his often-controversial past as a *chaiwala* (tea vendor). The questions that arise here are what made Modi successful in claiming extraordinary leadership and why the people support his claim. Who are the people who have accepted his claim of charismatic leadership, and how did Modi succeed in constructing his political community of followers in a vastly multicultural country? To address these questions, we analyze how Modi combined Hindu nationalist narratives with his populist political style and policies and examine the perception of existential crisis and threat as a strategy to legitimate his charismatic leadership, define his followship, and appeal to large sections of India's population who have come to support his authoritarian populist politics.

As the Chief Minister of the state, Modi's leadership in Gujrat has left both positive and negative marks in the public memory. On the positive side, he is remembered for his economic vision—the 'Gujarat model' (Jaffrelot, 2015)—which combined Hindu sub-nationalism and economic neoliberalism to accelerate private and foreign direct investments (Chhaya & Ambedkar, 2018). Under his leadership, the state's per capita income and economic growth increased significantly, placing Gujrat in fifth place in terms of economic growth among India's 28 states. However, as Jaffrelot (2015) argues, Gujrat still lagged in human development indicators, particularly in areas of health, education, and social justice. Ghatak and Roy (2014) have contended that Gujrat already had a high economic growth rate before Modi came to power due to the implementation of neoliberal policies in the early 1990s. Hence, ascribing the economic growth exclusively to Modi's leadership is overstated. Irrespective, the blending of Hindu sub-nationalism in the state policy resulted in exclusionary political and policy discourse in Gujrat, which deepened social polarization between the Hindu majority and Muslim minorities and precipitated in Gujarat one of India's worst Hindu-Muslim riots in 2002 (Patil, 2017).

Although the courts did not find Modi guilty of inciting the Gujarat riots, his ascent into national politics engendered great anxiety and fear among India's Muslims, secularists, and liberals (Varshney, 2014, p. 35). The personalization of the Gujarat model in public and political discourses, however, was instrumental in forging his strong influence and relation with his followers and supporters. This was evident in the 2014 general election, which the BJP and its National Democratic Alliance (NDA) contested under Modi's leadership. The Gujarat model—albeit a contested idea—underpinned the vision for radical socio-economic transformation and good governance in India (Jaffrelot, 2015). Even the election was idiomized and personalized as the 'Modi wave' (Rai, 2019, p. 253). The BJP and its coalition won the election, and Modi became the prime minister in 2014. Since then, the personalization of elections has continued in some form or other. The subsequent general election in 2019 was considered a 'referendum on Modi's leadership' (Kumar, 2019), which indicates how his influence in navigating the BJP's Hindu right-wing politics at the centre impacts his claims for extraordinary, charismatic leadership—one which his followers have accepted, as demonstrated by his successive election victories in 2014 and 2019.

The social and political base of this claim to charisma, however, must be traced to the BJP's Hindu nationalist ideology or *Hindutva*, and the way in which Modi mobilized this ideology to construct an organicist and bounded political community of Hindu believers and followers. In other words, Modi's leadership style has benefitted from Hindu ideology and political structures. *Hindutva* emphasizes that India is a Hindu nation and refers to virtually everyone who has ancestral roots in India and accepts the sacredness of India as part of his cultural and political identity. As such, India collectively constitutes a (Hindu) nation. This definition includes the Hindu majority as well as religious minorities—Sikhs, Jains, and Buddhists—who consider India their Holy Land.

Despite the BJP's claim since its formation to represent the voices of the extended community of Hindus, the Hindu community in India has historically been fractured along caste hierarchies and class divisions. The majority of voters in the past supported secular politics, mainly represented by the founders and successive leaders of the secularist Indian National Congress (INC), as well as the socialist and Marxist parties. Jawaharlal Nehru, the first Prime Minister of post-colonial India, championed a secular ideology and vision that shaped the social compact based on cultural pluralism and liberal values in post-independence state formation. However, unlike the Western manifestation of secularism characterized by strict church-state separation, India's post-colonial secular constitution favoured a 'principled distance' between religion and the state, meaning that religious ideologies and practices continued to shape the political arena and the state-society relationship (Vaishnav, 2019, p. 6). *Hindutva* as an alternative state concept was unpopular in the past, partly due to its history of violent political action; for example, the assassination of Mahatma Gandhi by a Hindu nationalist in 1948. However, when the leading Muslim political parties disappeared from the national polity after the formation of Pakistan in 1947 and Marxist political parties fragmented in the 1970s, the community of Hindu nationalists has emerged as the main opposition to secular political forces. The BJP's predecessors, including the *Sangha Pariwar* (the Sangha family), embraced Hindu ideology and culture to define India and its 'pure' people—the extended Hindu community—and restructure religiously defined modes of political mobilization.

The right-wing Hindu nationalist government under Modi's leadership follows the path of the BJP's predecessors, embracing the idea of *Hindutva* as its political ideology. However, the difference is that Modi revolutionized the ideology of *Hindutva* to support his charismatic leadership by promoting religious and cultural protectionism and articulating transformative economic agendas such as the Gujrat Model, which combined Hindu nationalism and economic neoliberalism. While Hindu nationalism as a political ideology appeals to Hindu supporters and voters, economic neoliberalism appeals to the business class. It is notable that India's burgeoning corporate sector has largely benefitted from business opportunities created by Hindu religious revivalism and the complex interplay of state, temple governance, and corporatism (Nanda, 2011). India's rapid economic growth is attributable to a special 'Hindu mindset'. As a result, Hindu institutions are replacing public ones and the Hindu 'revival' itself has become a major source of capital formation and accumulation (Nanda, 2011). This nexus between religion and business works in favour of *Hindutva* and those who advocate for it in the political arena. This complex interaction of religion and religious mindset with market and economic neoliberalism has supported not only Modi's claim to charismatic leadership but also combines neoliberal economic policy with Hindu ideologies, or what Priya Chacko (2020, p. 205) calls the 'political project of marketized *Hindutva*'. To a degree, this view of marketized *Hindutva* was personalized in the Gujrat model, also called *Moditva*, which loosely translates to 'the way of Modi' (Mehta, 2010, p. 578), to echo the language of the 'third way' found elsewhere. This view not only captured the economic and political imagination and aspirations of ordinary Indians but also personifies the BJP's electoral politics, with Modi as its living embodiment.

Modi and the BJP have popularized the marketized *Hindutva* in populist electoral slogans such as '*Achhe din aane waale hain*' (Good days lie ahead) and 'minimum government, maximum governance', although these slogans seem more moderate than the radical slogans of the past such as '*Garv se kaho hum Hindu hai*' (Say with pride that we are Hindus), which the BJP and its sister organizations had used to appeal to Hindus in the 1980s.

For the purpose of mass mobilization, these slogans and similar narratives are broadly disseminated via what Siddhartha Bhatia (2020) calls an 'ecosystem of *Hindutva*', which includes the community of learned and devoted supporters comprising the mainstream media, intellectuals, think tanks, and the members and affiliates of the *Sangha Pariwar*,[5] of which the BJP is a member. As such, the *Hindutva* ecosystem provides Modi with both resources and leverage to define his culturally bounded political community and to construct the narratives of charisma to garner the bottom-up support of his followers.

In the 2019 election, the BJP's transformational logic shifted from a focus on governance and socioeconomic development to national security as a national priority, primarily triggered by a suicide bomber attack on the Indian paramilitary Central Reserve Police Force (CRPF) in the Pulwama district in Kashmir (Hall, 2019). This was a game changer in national electoral politics in that it allowed Modi and the BJP to shift the election debate away from economic issues to national security. Islamist terrorism in particular and Pakistan in general were portrayed as the primary threats to the survival of Hindus. In electoral politics, this event was instrumental not only in invoking a national security crisis but also in reinforcing Modi's image as a strongman capable of protecting India and Indians from external national security threats (Hall, 2019). Modi cast himself as a humble *Chowkidar* (watchman) of India. He renamed his Twitter account as '*Chowkidar Narendra Modi*' and urged his followers to do the same, using the hashtag #*MainBhiChowkidar* (I am a watchman too). The shift of Modi's image from a *vikas purus* (development man, in the 2014 election) to a *Chowkidar* in 2019 represented the personalization of BJP electoral politics and—in line with PLD—its increasingly acclamatory nature. On one hand, as noted, this shifted the political agenda from *vikas* (development) to national security. On the other hand, the shift also points to the fact that development and national security as the will of the Indian people were largely constructed by Modi himself (and his party, the BJP). This further points to his similarity with populist and authoritarian leaders who form the popular will themselves from 'above' (see Pappas, 2016; Kenny, 2018). The outcome of this type of personalized populist politics has threatened pluralism, marginalized Muslim minorities, and endangered the secular foundation of India's democracy (see Anand, 2016).

In summary, Modi mobilized *Hindutva* as a cultural resource to define a bounded 'organic' political community—a community of fate from which, in a typically populist fashion, he drew his support. This facilitated Modi's direct and institutionally unmediated relationship with his followers within an increasingly plebiscitary form of democracy. Both strategies have further polarized India. While Modi's charismatic authority has benefitted from this social polarization, democracy in India is descending into populist authoritarian rule, which has increasingly taken on a plebiscitary and acclamatory quality.

Aung San Suu Kyi in Myanmar

Aung San Suu Kyi is a co-founder of the National League for Democracy (NLD), the largest political party in Myanmar, which emerged from the pro-democracy revolution against the military dictatorship in 1988, known in Myanmar as the '8888 Uprising' (Steinberg, 2013).

Myanmar acceded to independence in 1948, but persistent political turmoil, faltering post-colonial state formation, and growing ethnic resentment towards the state led to the military coup of 1962 (Callahan, 2004). Military dictators ruled the country between 1962 and 2010. In 2011, the military regime handed over power nominally to the pro-military government of President Thein Sein and the fragile political transition continued until February 2021, when the military once again dissolved the elected government of Aung San Suu Kyi and reimposed military dictatorship. Even between 2011 and 2021, the military wielded significant power in government and in parliament under the provisions of the 2008 constitution (see Subedi, 2017).

As the 8888 Uprising created a political platform seeking freedom and democracy, Aung San Suu Kyi emerged as a charismatic leader whose popularity grew exponentially, both nationally and internationally. This was partly due to her victim status, not to say martyrdom, upon her house arrest in July 1989, which continued intermittently until November 2010. Moreover, her enduring commitment to the struggle for democracy, freedom, and justice for all nationalities and religions (Fisher, 2017) earned immense respect and the trust of the majority ethnic group, the Bamar Burmese, as well as various ethnic minorities. The respect accorded Suu Kyi as an icon of democracy provided a vital basis for her *ascribed* charisma, which the international community consolidated by awarding her Norway's Professor Thorolf Rafto Memorial Prize for Human Rights in 1990, the European Parliament's Sakharov Prize for Freedom of Thought the same year, and the Nobel Peace Prize in 1991.

Suu Kyi's leadership, however, also benefitted from an *inherited* charisma. Many female leaders of Asia in the past consolidated their inherited charisma in the context of hierarchical dynastic political systems. Derichs and Thompson (2013) have shown that 'female leaders more easily acquire "inherited charisma" . . . because the charisma of the martyred father/husband could shine through a female leader who was not expected to match his accomplishments' (pp. 15–16). Although the context in which she rose to power cannot be described as a typical example of dynastic politics common elsewhere in Asia, Suu Kyi inherited the charisma of her late father, General Aung San.

General Aung San, the principal architect of the independence movement in what was then Burma, was revered by his people for his ability to mobilize both ethnic minorities and Bamar Burmese constituencies for independence and state building. His aspiration for building an ethnically and democratically plural Burma/Myanmar, however, remained incomplete due to his assassination in July 1947. The heroic image of General Aung San still shapes the way a future inclusive nation-state is imagined in Myanmar. Suu Kyi herself claims that she inherited a 'moral sense of duty and responsibility' as the political legacy of her father, 'a man who put the interests of the country before his own needs' (Kyi & Aris, 2010, p. 37). Morality and ethics are often at stake in inherited charisma formations. This is more so for female leaders because by 'inheriting the charisma of a "martyred" father or husband . . . female dynastic leaders can more easily claim allegiance to high ethical principles than can their male counterparts' (Derichs & Thompson, 2013, p. 16).

Nonetheless, Suu Kyi differed in one fundamental respect from her father in her handling of religion and politics. Initially, Aung San was a Marxist who became the first Secretary General of the Communist Party of Burma (CPB), but subsequently abandoned revolutionary Marxist ideology and promoted social-democratic values characterized by multiculturalism and secularism (Smith, 1991). Consequently, Aung Sun became a charismatic leader, popular among both the Burmese majority and ethnic minorities, with social democracy and secularism being his political aspiration for post-independence Burma. Aung Sun's case implies that there can be forms of charismatic authority that are not populist.

In contrast, Suu Kyi's position on the relationship of religion to politics was ambiguous. To appeal to Bamar/Buddhist followers, she initially infused her political messages with her own brand of modern Buddhism, known as *socially engaged* Buddhism (McCarthy, 2004), which advocates mediation, individual empowerment, and social ethics to resist spiritual and material exploitation by the state (Schober, 2005, pp. 113–114). This version of Buddhism differs from the nationalist, centralized, and ritualistic patronage of Buddhism by the military regime (Schober, 2005), although both visions of political Buddhism provide interpretations of power and authority justified by the philosophy of *Theravada* tradition. But the political outcomes have been different. The state patronage of Buddhism and its manipulation for exclusionary state formation and military regime survival have led to the rise of Buddhist extremism and religious revivalism, most recently expressed in the movements of radical Buddhist organizations such as the *Ma Ba Tha* (Patriotic Association of Myanmar) and the 969 movement (Subedi & Garnett, 2020). In contrast, social activism and non-violence embraced by the idea of socially engaged Buddhism have often manifested themselves in non-violent resistance to the state power, as was the case in the 2008 Saffron Revolution.

While Suu Kyi claimed allegiance to Western liberal democratic values and practice, religion in general, and socially engaged Buddhism in particular, was central to how she combined religion and politics to define the national community. This was not so different from the military government's approach in the past, which identified Myanmar's national races—*taing-yin-tha*—according to narrow conceptions of religion and race. Suu Kyi defended the view that socially engaged Buddhism is compatible with the idea of liberalism and freedom, as articulated in Western liberal democracy (McCarthy, 2004). Like democracy, she argued, socially engaged Buddhism is concerned with justice and liberation, and actively and non-violently engages with social, economic, political, and ecological problems (King, 2009). While this kind of interpretation enabled her to be seen as an icon of liberal democracy, it also helped her to establish an institutionally unmediated relationship with her followers through the appeal to Buddhism as a bounded national community. Such a direct relationship with followers earned widespread support for her leadership, as evidenced in the NLD's election victories in 1990, 2015 (see Myat, 2019), and most recently in 2020, when the general election was seen as a 'litmus test' of her popularity (Subedi, 2020).

As noted earlier, on February 1, 2021, the Myanmar military seized power and detained Aung San Suu Kyi, several other NLD leaders, and hundreds of human rights activists. In the highly competitive political space of the political transition prior to the 2021 coup d'état, maintaining the balance between socially engaged Buddhism and liberal democracy seemed difficult, if not impossible. After decades of military rule and sustained isolation from the rest of the world, a large proportion of her Bamar Buddhist majority followers and supporters had minimal exposure to the Western version of democracy and how this might be applied to an ethnically and religiously hierarchical society like Myanmar. With its non-secular foundation, the conceptual core elements of liberal democracy—multiculturalism and pluralism—have long been ambiguous concepts in Myanmar. Moreover, socially engaged Buddhism forms the main opposition to the religiously inspired Buddhist nationalism favoured by the military as its political as well as state ideology. As a result, Myanmar has continued to experience political crisis and economic inequalities, leading to ethnic and cultural conflicts. Under these conditions, the Bamar Buddhist majority have understood their national and racial identity to be threatened by 'others', especially Muslims and secularists. This, in turn, led them to favour Buddhist nationalism to safeguard their race, religion, and culture (Subedi & Garnett, 2020), although this form of Buddhist nationalist sentiment fragmented Suu Kyi's political support base in ethnic majority areas. She was therefore left with the challenge of re-navigating her political and ideological path in ways that neither antagonized the Bamar Buddhist majority *nor* the ethnic minorities.

The 2021 military coup was partly a result of the above-mentioned impossible balancing act Suu Kyi attempted between 2012 and 2020. In this venture, she did not entirely give up the idea of combining socially engaged Buddhism and liberal democracy in principle, but at the same time, she was inclined to favour a non-secular nationalist manifestation of political Buddhism to retain the support of hardline Buddhist followers. In doing so, she expected that she would forge cooperation and collaboration rather than conflict with the nationalist military through classical power sharing between a civilian government and the armed forces (see Bünte, 2014). Power sharing necessitated Suu Kyi to establish civilian control over the military to initiate political reforms, but her government also required the support of the military to contain the ongoing ethnic armed conflicts and, more importantly, to change the constitution that barred her from becoming President (Barany, 2018). Suu Kyi's efforts to change the constitution and bring about political reforms were frequently blocked by the military. Paradoxically, her attempt to survive via power sharing weakened her popularity as a charismatic-plebiscitary leader.

As her charismatic leadership became challenged by both liberals and minority rights activists, her government resorted to ever more authoritarian rule by adopting stringent social control mechanisms and centralizing power (Bünte et al., 2019). To many, her increasingly coercive rule was reminiscent of the military regime, while for others, it greatly reduced the space for dissenting voices from civil society, minority groups, and human rights activists (see Forum-Asia, 2018). One recent study found that the NLD government prosecuted more civilians, journalists, and activists between 2015 and 2020 than the previous government of Thein Sein (Athan Myanmar, 2020).

The 2021 military coup has, for the moment, put an end to this hybrid regime—formally democratic but with growing authoritarian tendencies—and seeks to restore the pre-2010 status quo ante: authoritarianism in its pure form. While nationwide protests and resistance are mounting against the military takeover, Suu Kyi is also receiving growing moral, emotional, and political support from her followers and from the people of Myanmar in general. Although her political future remains uncertain in the face of the military coup, her detention will likely extend her popularity—at a national if not international level—and thus sustain her charisma. Nonetheless, Suu Kyi's case presents an example of an unstable charismatic leadership that changed and became more autocratic once she was in power, in the face of pressures from the military as well as ethnic minorities. Her case also points to the fragility of charismatic-plebiscitary leadership, the fate of which rests on the support of followers on the one hand and highly hostile political opposition on the other.

Suu Kyi took an authoritarian and nationalist path after forming the government in 2015. But this was bound to have deleterious effects on her political power because her political actions undermined the very concept of democracy on which her charismatic leadership was initially formed and consolidated. The hybrid nature of the regime has not, in this case, necessarily been advantageous to the leader.

In summary, in an attempt to maintain her charismatic authority, Suu Kyi focused on her core followers, the Bamar Buddhists. This resulted in dwindling support for liberal values and minority rights, which in turn alienated non-Bamar and non-Buddhist followers who increasingly withdrew their trust in and support for her leadership. In this respect, the period between 2015 and 2021 appears to follow a logic that Michael Mann (2004) has identified: ethnic cleansing is rarely an initial aim, but the outcome of a step-by-step process in which the failure of one policy (plan A) is followed by ever more repressive measures (plan B to plan *n*) that need not, but *may*, lead to ethnic cleansing. In Suu Kyi's case, plan A appears to have been the mobilization of socially engaged Buddhism as a cultural resource for partial democratization, proposed as a culturally enriched and culturally specific version of liberalism. But this gave way to a narrower and organicist view of the people as a religious/ethnic community of fate in response to pressures emanating both from the military and from 'charismatic monks', for whom Therāvada Buddhism 'should be protected and promoted by the government to serve as a unifying force' (MacLean, 2019, p. 93). The Rohingya crisis in 2015 was in part the result of that shift.

Conclusion

Our initial question was whether the framework developed in Europe to study styles of leadership, which we would now associate with authoritarian populism from the early part of the 20th century onwards, is of use in understanding contemporary populist leadership in South and Southeast Asia. To this end, we suggested a catalogue of criteria of charismatic-plebiscitary leadership, from the perspectives of both leaders and followers (see Table 7.1). The two cases we have discussed cannot provide a definitive answer to that question, but they do offer initial support for the applicability and utility of this framework for understanding political developments beyond Europe.

Our catalogue is an ideal type. It is unlikely that factual examples of charismatic-plebiscitary leadership will conform to all the criteria set out. Bearing that caveat in mind, two broad conclusions may be drawn from our case studies:

1) Modi and Suu Kyi have distinct leadership styles, reflecting the diverse socio-political contexts of the two nations, but both are recognizably charismatic-plebiscitary leaders based on some of the criteria we have set out.
2) India and Myanmar (prior to the 2021 coup) can both be characterized as hybrid regime types—part democratic, part authoritarian—like those that have been noted in Eastern European cases, and which facilitate the emergence of charismatic-plebiscitary leadership.

The cases of Myanmar and the Philippines also suggest that, as in many European countries, charismatic-plebiscitary leadership in some of Asia's hybrid democracies is fragile and unstable, with a strong likelihood of descending into failure rather than the opposite, thereby morphing into permanent authoritarian rule.

More specifically, our analysis and discussion suggest the following:

First, the leader claims extraordinary qualities that legitimize bypassing existing institutions and breaking with customary political practices. Both Modi and Suu Kyi have deployed religious narratives and ideologies to connect them directly with the people and establish institutionally unmediated relationships with their followers. As our cases reveal, several elements, such as election slogans and the social and political framing of a national crisis, are expressions of radical worldviews and articulations of transformative political and socioeconomic agendas, while symbolic and emotive politics are crucial to how charismatic leaders perform politics utilizing plebiscitary forms of democracy.

Second, the legitimizing ideology assumes an organic community defined as 'the people' that includes certain cultural characteristics but excludes others. The re-articulation of *Hindutva* ideology in India and socially engaged Buddhism in Myanmar are central to how a politically bounded and organicist political community is defined, and how it excludes othered ethnic and religious minorities. We also find that cultural and social networks (in the case of Modi), kinship and familiar connections (in the case of Suu Kyi), and political-institutional settings (in the case of both), further determine how and when charismatic leadership is formed, consolidated, validated, or impaired. Modi and Suu Kyi have not only used cultural identities and narratives to construct organicist political communities but have mobilized such identities to form and represent the 'popular will' from above.

Finally, leaders achieve their levels of success by imposing their will on the party to the degree that the party has taken on the character of a 'leader party' and has successfully challenged existing political arrangements and the constitution. The constitutional and legal changes introduced by the Modi and Suu Kyi governments illustrate how the mainstream political landscape in India and Myanmar has, or in the latter case had, become leader-centric and authoritarian while remaining formally democratic—hence, these too are hybrid regime types in which elections have taken on an increasingly plebiscitary character.

Notes

1 This chapter is a slight reworking and updating of earlier article published in *Contemporary Politics* (Subedi & Scott, 2021). Its republication here is permitted under the copyright agreement.
2 The question of the degree of Duterte's popular support is a matter of debate. While data (e.g., from *Pulse Asia*) indicate higher than usual and sustained popularity, some of these results have been ascribed to the 'fear factor' or 'social desirability bias' (Teehankee, 2022, p. 130). Czech (2022, p. 221) doubts that the poll results provide evidence of depth of support: 'Duterte is popular in surveys, but he does not have fascist-like true believers behind him'.
3 The fall of Imran Khan's power in Pakistan (see Chapter 13 in this volume) and the ousting of Sri Lanka's President Gotabaya Rajapaksa in July 2022 (see Chapter 16 in this volume) are further examples of the fragility of charismatic-plebiscitary leadership in hybrid democracies in Asia.
4 Pappas (2016) concludes that the European case does not support the view that a new form of charismatic leader has emerged. His model, however, is a top-down one focusing on the leader rather than on the relationship between leader and followers.
5 The Sangha Parivar, the family of Rastriya Swayamsevak Sangh (RSS), is an umbrella term referring to the constellation of Hindu nationalist religious, political, and social organizations.

References

Anand, D. (2016). *Hindu nationalism in India and the politics of fear*. Springer. www.bol.com/nl/nl/p/hindu-nationalism-in-india-and-the-politics-of-fear/9200000000968142/
Athan Myanmar (2020). Analysis on freedom of expression situation in four years under the current regime. *Athan Myanmar.* www.athanmyanmar.org/analysis-on-freedom-of-expression-situation-in-four-years-under-the-current-regime/
Barany, Z. (2018). Burma: Suu Kyi's missteps. *Journal of Democracy*, 29(1), 5–19. https://doi.org/10.1353/jod.2018.0000
Bendix, R. (1967). Reflections on charismatic leadership. *Asian Survey*, 7(6), 341–352. https://doi.org/10.2307/2642609

Bhatia, S. (2020, July 31). Why the Hindutva right is better at propaganda than its opponents. *The Wire*. https://thewire.in/politics/hindutva-right-propaganda

Bünte, M. (2014). Burma's transition to quasi-military rule: From rulers to guardians? *Armed Forces & Society*, 40(4), 742–764. https://doi.org/10.1177/0095327X13492943

Bünte, M., Köllner, P., & Roewer, R. (2019). Taking stock of Myanmar's political transformation since 2011. *Journal of Current Southeast Asian Affairs*, 38(3), 249–264. https://doi.org/10.1177/1868103420905140

Callahan, M. P. (2004). *Making enemies: War and state building in Burma*. National University of Singapore Press.

Chacko, P. (2020). Gender and authoritarian populism: Empowerment, protection, and the politics of resentful aspiration in India. *Critical Asian Studies*, 52(2), 204–225. https://doi.org/10.1080/14672715.2020.1711789

Chacko, P., & Jayasuriya, K. (2018). Asia's conservative moment: Understanding the rise of the right. *Journal of Contemporary Asia*, 48(4), 529–540. https://doi.org/10.1080/00472336.2018.1448108

Chhaya, K., & Ambedkar, B. (2018). Economic growth: Story of Gujarat since 1960, What next? *Paper Presented at the Pace and Pattern of Economic Development of Gujarat*. https://papers.ssrn.com/sol3/papers.cfm?abstract_id=3273786

Czech, F. (2022). Between legitimation and support of Rodrigo Duterte. Understanding enduring popularity of the President of the Philippines. *Polish Sociological Review*, 2(218), 207–223. https://doi.org/10.26412/psr218.04

Derichs, C., & Thompson, M. R. (2013). Introduction. In C. Derichs & M. R. Thompson (Eds.), *Dynasties and female political leaders in Asia: Gender, power and pedigree* (pp. 11–26). LIT Verlag.

Fabry, A. (2021). Neoliberalism, crisis and authoritarian-ethnicist politics: The consolidation of the Orbán regime in Hungary. In B. Berberoglu (Ed.), *The global rise of authoritarianism in the 21st century: Crisis of neoliberal globalization and the nationalist response* (pp. 221–250). Routledge. https://doi.org/10.4324/9780367854379

Fisher, M. (2017, October 19). Myanmar, once a hope for democracy, is now a study in how it fails. *The New York Times*. www.nytimes.com/2017/10/19/world/asia/myanmar-democracy-rohingya.html

Forum-Asia (2018, March 21). *Myanmar: Lower House should reject proposed amendments to Peaceful Assembly Law*. Asian Forum for Human Rights and Development. www.forum-asia.org/uploads/wp/2018/03/Statement-on-amednment-of-law-on-peaceful-assembly-Ver.2.pdf

Ghatak, M., & Roy, S. (2014). Did Gujarat's growth rate accelerate under Modi? *Economic and Political Weekly, xlix*(15), 12–15. https://econ.lse.ac.uk/staff/mghatak/EPWModi.pdf

Green, J. E. (2009). *The eyes of the people: Democracy in an age of spectatorship*. Oxford University Press.

Hall, I. (2019). India's 2019 general election: National security and the rise of the watchmen. *The Round Table*, 108(5), 507–519. https://doi.org/10.1080/00358533.2019.1658360

Jaffrelot, C. (2015). What 'Gujarat Model'?—Growth without development—and with socio-political polarization. *South Asia: Journal of South Asian Studies*, 38(4), 820–838. https://doi.org/10.1080/00856401.2015.1087456

Kaur, R. (2015). Good times, brought to you by brand Modi. *Television & New Media*, 16(4), 323–330. https://doi.org/10.1177/1527476415575492

Kenny, P. (2018). *Populism in Southeast Asia*. Cambridge University Press.

King, S. B. (2009). *Socially engaged Buddhism*. University of Hawaii Press.

Körösényi, A. (2019). The theory and practice of plebiscitary leadership: Weber and the Orbán regime. *East European Politics and Cultures*, 33(2), 280–301. https://doi.org/10.1177/1527476415575492

Kumar, N. (2019, May 24). India's Modi made the election a referendum on his leadership -and it paid off. *CNN*. https://edition.cnn.com/2019/05/23/asia/india-modi-referendum-leadership-intl/index.html

Kyi, A. S. S., & Aris, M. (2010). *Freedom from fear: And other writings*. Penguin.

MacLean, K. (2019). The Rohingya crisis and the practice of erasure. *Journal of Genocide Research*, 21(1), 83–95. https://doi.org/10.1080/14623528.2018.1506628

Mann, M. (2004). *The dark side of democracy. Explaining ethnic cleansing*. Cambridge University Press.

McCarthy, S. (2004). The Buddhist political rhetoric of Aung San Suu Kyi. *Contemporary Buddhism*, 5(2), 67–81. https://doi.org/10.1080/1463994042000291556

Mehta, N. (2010). Ashis Nandy vs. the state of Gujarat: Authoritarian developmentalism, democracy and the politics of Narendra Modi. *South Asian History and Culture*, 1(4), 577–96. https://doi.org/10.1080/19472498.2010.507028

Myat, M. M. (2019). Is politics Aung San Suu Kyi's vocation? *Palgrave Communications*, 5(1), 1–8. https://doi.org/10.1057/s41599-019-0258-1

Nanda, M. (2011). *The god market: How globalization is making India more Hindu* (2nd ed.). Monthly Review Press.

Pappas, T. S. (2016). Are populist leaders 'charismatic'? The evidence from Europe. *Constellations*, 23(3), 378–390. https://doi.org/10.1111/1467-8675.12233

Patil, T. (2017). The politics of race, nationhood and Hindu nationalism: The case of Gujarat riots of 2002. *Asian Journal of Social Science*, 45(1–2), 27–54. https://doi.org/10.1163/15685314-04501002

Rai, P. (2019). 'Wave elections', charisma and transformational governance in India. *South Asia Research*, 39(3), 253–269. https://doi.org/10.1177/0262728019861763

Schober, J. (2005). Buddhist visions of moral authority and modernity in Burma. In M. Skidmore (Ed.), *Burma at the turn of the 21st century* (pp. 113–132). University of Hawaii Press.

Smiecinska, N. (2021). Crisis of neoliberalism and the rise of authoritarianism in Poland. In B. Berberoglu (Ed.), *The global rise of authoritarianism in the 21st century: Crisis of neoliberal globalization and the nationalist response* (pp. 251–274). Routledge. https://doi.org/10.4324/9780367854379

Smith, M. (1991). *Burma: Insurgency and the politics of ethnicity*. Zed Books.

Steffens, N. K., Haslam, S. A., & Reicher, S. D. (2014). Up close and personal: Evidence that shared social identity is a basis for the 'special' relationship that binds followers to leaders. *The Leadership Quarterly*, 25(2), 296–313. https://psycnet.apa.org/doi/10.1016/j.leaqua.2013.08.008

Steinberg, D. (2013). *Burma/Myanmar: What everyone needs to know* (2nd ed.). Oxford University Press.

Subedi, D. B. (2017). Managing armed groups in Myanmar's peace process: Security sector governance as a way forward. *CSG Papers* No. 18. Centre for Security Governance. www.academia.edu/34716904/Managing_Armed_Groups_in_Myanmar_s_Peace_Process_Security_Sector_Governance_as_a_Way_Forward

Subedi, D. B. (2020, November 6). Why Myanmar's election is unlikely to herald major political reform or support transition to democracy. *The Conversation*. https://theconversation.com/why-myanmars-election-is-unlikely-to-herald-major-political-reform-or-support-transition-to-democracy-146021

Subedi, D. B., & Garnett, J. (2020). De-mystifying Buddhist religious extremism in Myanmar: Confrontation and contestation around religion, development and state-building. *Conflict, Security & Development*, 20(2), 223–246. https://doi.org/10.1080/14678802.2020.1739859

Subedi, D. B., & Scott, A. (2021). Populism, authoritarianism, and charismatic-plebiscitary leadership in contemporary Asia: A comparative perspective from India and Myanmar. *Contemporary Politics*. https://doi.org/10.1080/13569775.2021.1917162

Sundar, N. (2020). India's unofficial emergency. In B. Vormann and M. D. Weinman (Eds.), *The emergence of illiberalism: Understanding a global phenomenon*. Routledge.

Tan, H. H., & Wee, G. (2002). The role of rhetoric content in charismatic leadership: A content analysis of a Singaporean leader's speeches. *International Journal Organization Theory and Behavior*, 5(3–4), 317–342. https://doi.org/10.1081/OTB-120014894

Teehankee, J. C. (2022). The Philippines in 2021: Twilight of the Duterte presidency. *Asian Survey*, 62(1), 126–136. https://doi.org/10.1525/as.2022.62.1.12

Vaishnav, M. (2019). Religious Nationalism and India's future. In M. Vaishnav (Ed.), *The BJP in power: Indian democracy and religious nationalism* (pp. 5–21). Carnegie Endowment for International Peace. https://carnegieendowment.org/files/BJP_In_Power_final.pdf

Varshney, A. (2014). India's watershed vote: Hindu nationalism in power? *Journal of Democracy*, 25(4), 34–45. https://doi.org/10.1353/jod.2014.0071

Weber, M. (2019). *Economy and society: A new translation* (K. Tribe, Editor-Translator). Harvard University Press (Original work published 1922).

Weyland, K. (2019). Populism and authoritarianism. In C. de la Torre (Ed.), *Routledge handbook of global populism* (pp. 319–333). Routledge. https://doi.org/10.4324/9781315226446

PART III
Cross-cutting themes

8
POPULISM, MEDIA, AND COMMUNICATION IN THE ASIA PACIFIC

A case study of Rodrigo Duterte and Pauline Hanson

Kurt Sengul

Introduction

The purpose of this chapter is to critically analyze the complex relationship between populism and media and communication. The central role of media and communication in the populist phenomenon has received far more scholarly attention over the last decade, but this has frequently been European and North American in scope. Moffitt (2015, p. 294) refers to this as the *Atlantic Bias* in research into populism. This chapter seeks to redress this bias by exploring the relationship between media, communication, and populism through case studies of two prominent populist actors in the Asia Pacific: the former president of the Philippines, Rodrigo Duterte, and Australia's most prominent populist politician, Pauline Hanson. Both leaders were elected in 2016[1] alongside a number of notable populist actors and movements that included Donald Trump and the Brexit referendum. The chapter introduces key concepts such as *mediatization* and *media populism* and interrogates the so-called *affinity* between social media and populist politics. In particular, this chapter examines the communicative styles and strategies of the respective political leaders, their relationships to the media, and the role of social media in their rise and success. It is argued that both Hanson and Duterte employ a communication style characterized by 'bad behaviour' (Moffitt, 2016) and 'shamelessness' (Wodak, 2021). It is further argued that both leaders have been effective at exploiting the mediatized political landscapes in their respective countries, which privilege conflict, scandal, and spectacle. Yet, typical of populist politicians, both Duterte and Hanson have maintained an antagonistic and frequently hostile relationship with critical media organizations. The aim of this chapter is to introduce readers to the key concepts and debates in relation to populism, media, and communication, and to further our understanding of the communicative aspects of populism in the Asia Pacific.

The study of populist communication

While the role that media and communication have played in the 'global rise of populism' (Moffitt, 2016) has received extensive attention over the last five years, scholars have been making these connections for decades. Indeed, as Mazzoleni argued, 'a full understanding of the populist phenomenon cannot be achieved without studying mass communication perspectives and media-related dynamics' (2003, p. 2). The 2016 election of Donald Trump, the Brexit referendum, and a host of populist successes globally, including those of Pauline Hanson and Rodrigo Duterte, have sharpened our focus to the communicative aspects of this rise. Yet as late as 2017, scholars were lamenting the lack of scholarly attention given to the role of media and communication in the populist phenomenon (Stanyer et al., 2017). As Aalberg and de Vreese (2017) noted, the communicative aspects of populism have largely been underexplored or ignored, which is disconcerting given its key role in populist politics. They further argue that 'in light of the current large-scale social, political, and economic turmoil of recent populist backlashes against governments, and of the changing media environment—the study of populist political communication has never been more important' (Aalberg & de Vreese, 2017, p. 3). While undoubtedly true, it would be difficult to maintain this argument in 2023 given the volume of sophisticated scholarship that has been published over the last five years interrogating various aspects of populist communication, including the role of digital and social media (Sengul, 2019a). A recent and important development within populism scholarship has not only been the increasing recognition of the role of media and communication in the populist phenomenon but also a number of scholars suggesting that the communicative, discursive, and stylistic aspects of populism are, in fact, its defining characteristics. For example, Jagers and Walgrave's (2007) influential work defines populism as a *political communication style* that refers to *the people*. More recently, populism has been referred to as a *communication phenomenon* (de Vreese et al., 2018), a *communicative strategy* (Waisbord, 2019), a *communication logic* (Engesser et al., 2017b), and a *political style* (Moffitt, 2016). Waisbord (2019, p. 223) suggests that populism is a communicative strategy 'that articulates political actors and defines politics as a matter of irreconcilable interests between two actors'. In defining populism as a communication phenomenon, de Vreese et al. (2018) acknowledged that

> populist ideas must be communicated discursively to achieve the communicator's goals and the intended effects on the audience . . . [and that] the communicative tools used for spreading populist ideas are just as central as the populist ideas themselves.
>
> *p. 425*

Moffitt's (2016) *political style* approach is a valuable contribution for understanding populism in the contemporary media setting. Moffitt defines populism as 'a political style that features an appeal to "the people" versus "the elite", "bad manners" and the performance of "crisis, breakdown or threat"' (2016, p. 45). There is no doubt that communicative-centred approaches to populism have become more sophisticated, multidisciplinary, and holistic in scope.

As noted, much of the literature on populist communication has been centred on European and North American case studies. For example, such excellent volumes as *Communicating Populism: Comparing Actor Perceptions, Media Coverage, and Effects on Citizens in Europe*, by C. Reinemann et al. (2019) and *Populist Political Communication in Europe* by T. Aalberg et al. (2017) have been invaluable in furthering our empirical and theoretical understanding of populist communication, but they are entirely European in scope. Similarly, we have seen an explosion in communication-centred research examining the Trump phenomenon in the United States, including his prolific use of social media (see Ross & Caldwell, 2019). As such, it may be more accurate to argue that populist communication *outside* Europe and North America is still very much under-researched.

Of recent interest to communication scholars is how populists are interacting with traditional and online forms of media. Chadwick (2017, p. 4) anticipates that 'the rapid diffusion of new communication technologies creates a pressing need to rethink the complex and multifaceted forces that are reshaping the political communication environments of the Western democracies'. Chadwick's *hybrid media system* involves the complex interaction between 'older and newer media logics' (p. 5). It has been argued that populists are savvy users of both traditional and online forms of communication (Mazzoleni, 2008).

Mediatization and media populism

In attempting to understand the central role of media and communication in the populist phenomenon, the interrelated concepts of *mediatization* and *media populism* are particularly useful. Mazzoleni (2008) observed that the media play a significant role in the rise, success, and fall of populist movements. The media, which refers to the 'organizations, technologies, and platforms that produce and distribute content to large publics, including news, information, fiction, entertainment, and personal' (Waisbord, 2019, p. 221), should be seen as one of the 'central stages on which contemporary populism plays out' (Moffitt, 2016, p. 70). This is particularly the case in the contemporary mediatized landscape. The concept of *mediatization* refers to the long-term process of increasing the influence, pervasiveness, and importance of media in political and social life (Strömbäck & Esser, 2014; Waisbord, 2019). As Strömbäck and Esser note, 'as the importance of the media has increased, and the media have become more embedded and integrated in all key aspects of social and political life, so has the influence of the media' (2014, pp. 8–9). The concept of mediatization has utility in explaining the transformative implications of media in Western democracies. The mediatization of politics has meant that it is increasingly important for politicians to engage with the media to reach a diverse range of voters. In light of this, Mazzoleni (2008) suggests that political actors are employing a range of communicative and performative strategies to adapt to the conditions of mediatization. In this context, it is argued that populists in particular have been adept at adapting to—and exploiting—the contemporary mediatized environment (Waisbord, 2019). In other words, the media is said to have a particular *logic* that aligns with the logic of populism.

Understanding the media logic is valuable because it helps us to understand why populists thrive under the conditions of mediatization. The media logic is characterized by commercialization, spectacularization, personalization, tabloidization, conflict-centred discourse, and simplified rhetoric (Mazzoleni, 2008), and these are said to converge in the populist style of communication. As Manucci (2017, p. 468) notes, populism is argued to 'fit the media-logic by providing controversial and newsworthy content' to media outlets who 'privilege conflict and negativity, which, in turn, foster political alienation and cynicism, thus, providing a fertile ground for populist messages'. Alarmingly, one of the manifestations of the *media logic-populist logic* nexus has been the mainstreaming and normalization of far-right ideas and actors who are said to fit perfectly within the logic of the media. Indeed, the media are said to constitute one of the most powerful forces in the mainstreaming of the far-right in the 21st century (Mudde, 2019). As Cas Mudde notes, the commercial imperatives of the media have resulted in *mediagenic* far-right actors being given disproportionate coverage and platforms because the media know they will provide controversy and spectacle. Of course, Donald Trump is an oft-cited recent example, but the media's role in popularizing, mainstreaming, and normalizing right-wing populist actors in particular certainly preceded the rise of Trump. Here, it is appropriate to introduce the idea of *media populism*, which Krämer defines as:

> The use of stylistic and ideological elements [defined as populist] by some media . . . [including] the construction and favouritism of in-groups, hostility toward, and circumvention of the elites and institutions of representative democracy, reliance on charisma and (group-related) common-sense, and appeal to moral sentiments (thus on an emotionalizing, personalizing, and ostentatiously plain-spoken discourse).
>
> *Krämer, 2014, p. 48*

In this sense, certain media organizations are 'actively engaging in their own kind of populism' (Esser et al., 2017, p. 367). Tabloid media, talkback radio, and conservative cable news outlets can be thought of as prominent sites of media populism. The relationship between populist actors and media outlets has been referred to as a 'convergence of goals' (Mazzoleni, 2008) that is mutually beneficial for both parties. Despite frequently targeting the media as being part of the *corrupt elite*, and most recently *fake news*, the reality is that many populist actors benefit from the media. The convergence of the populist and media logic has significantly boosted populists in the contemporary mediatized landscape. To draw on Hatakka (2019, p. 37), we can 'regard the media environment as the engine of populist communication . . . [in that] it keeps populist ideas churning'. However, early discussions of mediatization and media populism occurred in the absence of social media. The following section discusses the implications of social and digital media in the populist phenomenon.

Populism and social media

The role of social media in the rise and success of populism has exploded over the last five years as a focus of scholarly inquiry. This is partly attributable to the prolific use of social media by high profile populist actors and, more broadly, its increasing role in political communication. However, despite the proliferation of scholarship, Jacobs et al. (2020) contend that 'the study of populism and online media is still in its infancy' (p. 12). It has been suggested that populists are adept at exploiting the affordances of social media and disproportionately benefit from this form of communication (Gerbaudo, 2018; Hopster, 2021). Contemporary populists are said to be savvy social media users. Engesser et al. (2017a), for example, describe social media as 'particularly well-suited to meet the communicative preferences of populist actors' (p. 1123). Similarly, Gerbaudo (2018, p. 746) declares 'the populist logic seems to have found a propitious space on social media'. Arguing that an *elective affinity* exists between social media and populism, Gerbaudo (2018, p. 746) suggests that social media platforms favour populist communication 'because of the aggregation logic embedded in its algorithms and the way it can focus attention of an otherwise dispersed people'. This point is echoed by Hopster (2021), who argues that the affective nature of the populist style of communication is rewarded by social media algorithms. He further argues that a mutually beneficial relationship exists between populist leaders and social media platforms who 'contribute to the popularity of the platforms' (p. 9). Social media is said to provide populists with a *direct* channel to supporters, thus avoiding traditional media who are seen as hostile to populist actors. Engesser et al. (2017a, p. 1113) describe the added value of this form of connectivity succinctly:

> Populists may turn toward social media in order to circumvent the media institutions and journalistic gatekeepers. In this way, the populist messages do not have to follow the news values and are frequently more personal and sensationalistic in nature.

While social media may allow populists to circumvent traditional media channels and speak directly to voters, we should not view this in isolation. The integrated nature of the *hybrid media system* (Chadwick, 2017) means that populist messages on social media are often picked up by traditional media outlets (Hopster, 2021). In this context, we need to remember that populists pursue a hybrid media strategy that involves the integration of online communication with traditional media (Engesser et al., 2017a). In this sense, the view that populists are particularly well suited to the contemporary hybrid media system is convincing and supported by recent examples.

However, the so-called elective affinity between populism and social media has also been met with caution by scholars, who suggest that we should treat this relationship critically. One of the simplest but most compelling of these arguments is that non-populist leaders have also proven to be very skilled at social media communication (Postill, 2018). Politicians such as Barack Obama, Alexandria Ocasio-Cortez, Jacinda Ardern, Justin Trudeau, and Kevin Rudd have all proven to be *savvy* social media users without displaying the antagonistic style that supposedly benefits populists on these platforms. As Moffitt (2018, p. 38) puts it, we need to be careful in 'assuming that social media is a godsend for all populist actors, or that all populists . . . are social media wizards'. Moreover, the idea that social media provides populists with a direct, unmediated line to their supporters has also been questioned. Moffitt (2018), for example, cautions us not to overstate the 'directness' of social media communication. Social platforms such as Twitter and Facebook, which are favoured by populists, 'are still intermediaries . . . and are not actually "direct" or "unmediated" forms of communication' (Moffitt, 2018, p. 35). As we interrogate populism in the hybrid media system, we should also heed the call of Jacobs et al. (2020) to avoid 'lumping' different platforms together under the banner of 'social media', arguing that 'the differences in user base and architecture matter empirically' (2020, p. 28). In the context of these welcome calls for circumspection when it comes to the alleged affinity between social media and populism, following Hatakka (2019), rather than simply saying that populists are savvy social media users, we should continue to investigate whether the 'architecture of social media works especially well with the underlying logic of populism' (p. 45). The following sections analyze the communication of Rodrigo Duterte and Pauline Hanson.

Rodrigo Duterte

Described as a foul-mouthed, populist, autocratic strongman, Rodrigo Duterte served as President of the Philippines from 2016–2022. Typical of populist politicians, the former mayor of Davao City showed little regard for institutional checks and balances or separation of powers and immediately launched a campaign of extra-judicial killings against drug dealers (Heydarian, 2018). The timing of Duterte's election and his rhetoric, tactics, and style of communication led to comparisons with other populist actors, most notably Donald Trump. Duterte's communication style has been variously referred to as crass, offensive, rough, irreverent, sexist, rambling, vulgar, sensual, and theatrical (Thompson, 2016; Casiple, 2016; Webb & Curato, 2019). Heydarian (2018) follows Moffitt's (2016) perception of coarse and non-conventional populist leader characteristics in his assessment that Duterte employs a populist political style that appeals to the people, invokes crises, and exhibits bad behaviour. This has been echoed by Webb and Curato (2019), who argue that Duterte performs a political style that is sensitive to the demands of the contemporary mediatized landscape in the Philippines. During his 2016 election campaign, Curato suggests that Duterte 'put on a spectacle that pushed the boundaries of traditional political practice' (2017, p. 147). His utilization of media, communication, and spectacle has been viewed as a factor contributing to his rise and success (Heydarian, 2018). Duterte has been described as an expert at 'attention hacking' (Webb & Curato, 2019, p. 59), known to deliver televised speeches lasting hours. In 2016, he infamously referred to then U.S. President Barack Obama as a 'son of a whore', has a litany of rape jokes including one about the rape and murder of an Australian missionary worker, and provoked international outrage with a tasteless reference to Adolf Hitler (McKirdy, 2016). He launched a profanity-filled tirade against the European Union and gave it the 'middle finger', and he has directed curse words at the Pope and Catholic bishops. Yet, in spite of the appalling jokes and outbursts, Duterte maintained a consistently high approval rating throughout his tenure, which may be the key to understanding his popularity. As Casiple puts it, while his comments and actions may have drawn international outrage, 'his supporters loved it' (2016, p. 181). Underlying Duterte's offensive comments and stunts, he is said to be an effective communicator. Heydarian (2018) likens Duterte to Donald Trump in being 'unusually media savvy' (p. 34) and being remarkably successful in generating earned media. Heydarian (2018) continues, asserting that the more controversial Duterte is, the greater media attention he enjoys. In government, Duterte was effective at promoting his government's achievements due to what Heydarian calls a 'well-oiled communications machine' (2018, p. 101). The success of Duterte in generating media attention through controversy, spectacle, and stunt was facilitated by the 'highly sensationalist media industry' of the Philippines, which was keenly exploited by Duterte and his team (p. 101).

Yet, despite benefiting from and skilfully exploiting the media logic of the Philippines, Duterte's relationship with the media was often hostile, authoritarian, and dangerous. Duterte's presidency was characterized by rhetorical attacks on critical media outlets and the undermining of media freedom. The media was one of a number of democratic institutions targeted by Duterte. His attacks on the Fourth Estate were consistent with the 'broader pattern of the Duterte administration's strategy of injuring institutions that scrutinize state power' (Curato, 2019, p. 264). Key examples of Duterte's hostile relationship with critical media include his long-running attacks on the media outlets Rappler and ABS-CBN. He attacked the Rappler online news website, alleging it constituted fake news due to its critical coverage of his war on drugs (Ragragio, 2020). As Curato explained, 'the harassment of Rappler has had a chilling effect on media organizations in the Philippines' (2019, p. 264). More broadly, Duterte's feuds with the media led to the imposition of a 'no press conference policy' which lasted for weeks (Webb & Curato, 2019) and included reporters being labelled 'vultures' and 'sons of bitches' (Placido, 2016). Similarly, the Duterte administration's war with the influential ABS-CBN broadcast network resulted in the network being ordered by the government's telecommunication agency to cease operations in May 2020 when its 25-year franchise license expired. The effect of this was a serious undermining of journalistic freedom and the democratic watchdog role of the media. As noted by Curato (2019) and Ragragio (2020), the Philippines is a dangerous place to practice journalism, and ranked 136th in the Reporters Without Borders 2020 World Press Freedom Index. Duterte was said to be a key player in cultivating this dangerous climate for reporters.

A particular area of interest for scholars since Duterte's 2016 election win has been the role that social media has played in his rise and success. The 2016 presidential election was referred to as the country's *first social media election* (Arguelles, 2019), and represented a 'watershed' moment in social media campaigning in the Philippines (Tapsell, 2020). Heydarian (2018) suggests that Duterte's electoral success was, in part, due to the strength of his social media strategy. Similarly, Sinpeng (2016) contends that 'Duterte did not just win the election at the ballot. He also won it on Facebook'. With 4.5 million followers, Duterte's presence on Facebook was significant, particularly given the prevalence of the Facebook platform in the Philippines with close to 75 million users. Tapsell argues that Facebook was not only employed in winning the election, but also in 'maintaining the legitimacy of [the Duterte] administration' (2020, p. 7). This is supported by empirical research. A study of the 2016 campaign by Sinpeng et al. (2020) found that Duterte's social media campaign was 'the best performing and unmatched by his rivals' (p. 8). Moreover, the authors cite Facebook statistics which showed that Duterte dominated 71% of conversations about the Philippine election. Given this, it may be tempting to argue that Duterte's success on Facebook is another example of populist savvy social media usage. However, a critical examination reveals a more complex picture. While acknowledging Duterte's success on Facebook, Sinpeng et al. (2020) found that this occurred in *spite* of him rather than *due* to his social media genius. They argue that Duterte's Facebook communication was 'a textbook example of "how-not-to-do" online campaigning' (p. 3). His Facebook messaging was found to be lacklustre, uninspiring, unresponsive, and lacked the flair of his offline communication. Rather, the authors attribute Duterte's online success to his committed social media base, which was described as 'uniquely zealous, aggressive, and unrelenting in their support for Duterte' (Sinpeng et al., 2020, p. 2). This characterization of Duterte's Facebook followers is consistent with the accounts of others who noted the toxic nature of their engagement with critical media and opposition parties (Curato, 2019; Tapsell, 2020). Based on this engagement with the literature, it is clear that Duterte was largely successful in exploiting a media environment that privileges conflict, scandal, and controversy. However, it is also evident that a strong critical media also exists in the Philippines, whose mission of holding power accountable has come into conflict with Duterte's illiberal tendencies. Moreover, like many populist leaders, social media has been a powerful tool for Duterte, but we should be careful in labelling him a savvy social media user given the empirical evidence cited here.

Pauline Hanson

The year 2016 marked the return of Australia's most prominent populist radical right actor, Pauline Hanson, to the federal parliament after an 18-year absence. Described as the archetypal populist radical right politician (Betz, 2019), a resurgent Hanson warned Australia of the risk of being 'swamped by Muslims', 20 years after her similar warning about Asian immigration. Hanson's right-wing populist style of politics first emerged in Australia in 1996 when she was elected as the federal member for Oxley. Originally preselected to represent the Liberal Party at the 1996 federal election, Hanson was disendorsed by the party after making racist comments directed at First Nations peoples to a Queensland newspaper (Curran, 2004).

It is argued that the media are both *friend* and *foe* of the far-right (and the populist radical right in particular) and this is certainly the case with Pauline Hanson (Mudde, 2019). Indeed, this is how Hanson herself views her relationship with the media, which can be characterized as antagonistic, transactional, paradoxical, and mutually beneficial (Sengul, 2021b). Hanson has benefited enormously from media attention throughout her political career, to the extent that some scholars have directly attributed her rise to this. Deutchman and Ellison (1999), for example, suggest that Hanson would not have become as important as she did without the media, and that 'the media have made Hanson a star' (p. 48). Moreover, Hanson and her party One Nation have been described as a *media-fuelled phenomenon* whose political success was tied to media coverage (Curran, 2004). As Curran noted of Hanson in the 1990s, 'when media attention declined, so too did Hanson's political profile' (2004, pp. 41–42). However, despite the unquestionable role that the media have played in Hanson's rise and success, Hanson has largely been hostile to the media who, as with most populists, she views as part of the 'corrupt elite'. Hanson believes that the media played a central role in her downfall in the late 1990s and in subsequent legal issues, which led to her conviction for electoral fraud (Broinowski, 2017). Hanson's relationship with critical media in Australia has been hostile, underpinned by the belief that the media are 'out to get her and One Nation'. In conversation with Broinowski, Hanson remarked, 'Why the hell doesn't the media just report facts and let the public judge us? You're all so opinionated . . . this is what pisses me off about the media' (2017, p. 299). Furthermore, in the wake of the 2019 National Rifle Association (NRA) scandal, Hanson suggested, 'Media across Australia have been blinded by their hate and bias toward One Nation and myself' ('Pauline Hanson Says', 2019). Hanson has also imported the Trumpian *fake news* rhetoric to describe media reports that she has disapproved of. Hanson has remained perpetually suspicious of journalists and has periodically announced boycotts of certain outlets and advocated for the privatization of the multicultural Special Broadcasting Service (SBS) and for funding cuts to the Australian Broadcasting Corporation (ABC) (Sengul, 2019b).

Not only were the media vital in her first political stint in the 1990s but they also played a key role in rehabilitating Hanson after her party's implosion and subsequent legal issues. In the 18 years between her political iterations, Hanson successfully transitioned from politician to celebrity, which kept her in the public consciousness. This laid the groundwork for her successful return to Australian politics in 2016. By the time of the 2016 election, Hanson was a 'polished media performer . . . [and] a rolled-gold celebrity' (Jose, 2019, p. 176). Throughout this period, Hanson maintained a consistent media presence that included appearances on 'The Sunrise Program', 'The Today Show', 'Celebrity Apprentice', 'Dancing with the Stars', and 'Who Wants to Be a Millionaire?'. Indeed, breakfast television has been particularly important in keeping Hanson's name alive and exposing her to large national audiences. Hanson, who at various times has been a paid contributor on 'Sunrise', is often pitted against a sparring partner on these programs to encourage debate and controversy. Here we can see Hanson's controversial nature aligning with the commercial media logic in Australia. However, it would be wrong to think that Hanson's disproportionate presence in the media is solely driven by commercial interests.

There is also an ideological dimension to Hanson's increasing presence in the media, particularly in the context of her contemporary iteration. The hegemony of conservative media in Australia has provided Hanson with numerous favourable platforms across radio, print, and television. Indeed, a strong case could be made that the Australian media has shifted considerably to the *right* since Hanson's first stint in politics in the 1990s. Hanson and *Hansonism* are warmly received on the Murdoch-owned Sky News Australia, which can be considered a cousin of the Fox News network in the United States, within the conservative tabloid media, and on talkback radio, which has always been a sympathetic medium and asset for Hanson (Goot, 2000). This should not suggest that the media has always been favourable to Hanson. Indeed, there has been a strong critical section of the media who scrutinize Hanson and hold her accountable. Similarly, Hanson's media appearances have not always gone well. In April 2020, Hanson was dropped from her regular spot on the 'Today Show' after making racist and classist comments about people living in social housing during the COVID-19 crisis in the state of Victoria. This greatly diminished Hanson's national media presence. Hanson and her staff even blamed One Nation's poor result in the 2020 Queensland state election on the consequential reduction in media coverage. This highlights that both Hanson and her team are acutely aware of the vital role of media exposure in the continued success of One Nation.

Hanson employs a combative, 'us/them' style of communication that is designed to construct fear and pit a homogenous people against a corrupt, illegitimate elite (Sengul, 2020). Hanson has increasingly employed political stunts in order to generate media attention and controversy in the modern media landscape. The 2017 stunt when she wore a burqa in the Senate and the 2018 'It's OK to be White' motion were noteworthy examples of Hanson's successful use of a political stunt to gain traction in the media. Often dismissed as inarticulate and unsophisticated in her communication, these critiques belie the fact that Hanson is an effective political communicator (Fenton-Smith, 2020). This point recognizes that Hanson has been remarkably successful in exploiting the media and generating coverage attention in spite of her party's relatively small electoral impact with only two federal senators. Hanson, aided by Australia's contemporary mediatized landscape, has consistently maintained a disproportionately strong presence in the media. In both of her political iterations, Hanson has been far more successful with new forms of media than traditional outlets such as print. In the 1990s, it was said that 'New Media', comprising talkback radio, commercial television, and tabloid media were particularly favourable channels for Hanson (Lewis, 1997). In her contemporary resurgence, social media has proven to be a useful tool for the One Nation leader.

In his analysis of populist leaders' social media use, Moffitt (2018) categorizes Hanson as having a *strong social media presence*. Despite being active on Twitter and YouTube, Facebook is by far Pauline Hanson's most important social media platform. Indeed, the *Pauline Hanson's Please Explain* Facebook page can be described as very active, frequently updated, and often including dialogic engagement with her followers (Sengul, 2021a). With 445,000 followers, Hanson has one of the largest online followings of any federal political leader in Australia. This following is prolific given One Nation's status as a minor party which has consistently polled under 5% for most of Hanson's time in the senate. Coghlan (2019, p. 194) suggests that Facebook 'provides a vehicle for Hanson to talk directly to her supporters. No journalists asking questions. One-way communication from Hanson to Hanson voters'. Hanson herself appears to understand the power of her social media page, commenting to Broinowski regarding an anti-Islam post, 'nearly 72,000 people reached already. . . . I did a post on this in May: we reached 4 million' (Broinowski, 2017, p. 269). Like talkback radio, social media does provide Hanson with a more, if not completely, direct platform to communicate with her followers. Like her experience in the 1990s with emerging media, Hanson's contemporary social media use does indicate that she is a savvy adopter of new media and has used these platforms effectively. While some accounts of the role of the media in the Hanson phenomenon have perhaps been too deterministic, it is clear from this discussion that the media has played a key role in the rise, success, fall, and resurgence of Pauline Hanson in Australia.

Discussion and conclusion

The analysis of Pauline Hanson and Rodrigo Duterte reveals the central role of the media in both the rise and success of these respective populist actors. This chapter demonstrates that despite important ideological differences between the two, Hanson and Duterte share similarities in terms of their communication styles, antagonistic relationships with the media, and their use of social media. In this way, both Hanson and Duterte can be said to employ a conventional populist style which is characterized by an appeal to the people versus the elite, bad manners, and the invocation of crisis and threat (Moffitt, 2016). Yet, there are also subtleties that distinguish Hanson and Duterte's political communication styles. Whereas Duterte is liberal in his use of profanities and crass statements designed to shock, Hanson typically engenders controversy through the contents of her rhetoric and strategic use of political stunts. Both populist actors can be argued to exhibit the 'bad manners' typical of the populist style, which represents a 'coarsening of political rhetoric, and a disregard for "appropriate" modes of acting in the political realm' (Moffitt, 2016, p. 44). It is important to note, as Moffitt (2016) points out, that bad manners are necessarily subjective and determined by the cultural practices of a particular country. However, it is particularly the case with Rodrigo Duterte that these actions and rhetoric go beyond bad manners and fall under what Ruth Wodak refers to as 'shamelessness' (Wodak, 2021). Wodak suggests that 'the boundaries of the "sayable" are being shifted, and "anything goes"'. Traditional norms and rules of political culture, of negotiation and deliberation, are 'transcended by continuous provocations [and] disseminated via the media' (Wodak, 2021, p. 6). It is clear that both leaders have benefited from, and have skilfully exploited, the mediatized landscapes of Australia and the Philippines, which privilege spectacularization, scandal, stunt, and controversy. The argument that we are witnessing a convergence of the media logic and populist logic appears to hold when examining Duterte and Hanson. The concepts of *mediatization* and *media populism* have utility in helping to explain how and why Duterte and Hanson have managed to receive disproportionate media coverage and attention during their time in office. Both have skilfully exploited a media that craves controversy and conflict, while at the same time relentlessly attacking critical media outlets. At the heart of populism is the antagonistic pitting of a *morally pure* people against an *irredeemable* elite (Sengul, 2022a). And, like all populists, Duterte and Hanson have tended to view the media as a central part of the corrupt elite. In Hanson's case, this has primarily manifested in a rhetorical critique of critical media outlets. In Duterte's case, this resulted in deteriorating press freedom and an increasingly dangerous environment for journalists. This speaks to the fact that Duterte was a *populist in power*, whereas Hanson has limited capacity in her role as a minor party senator. However, it must also be noted that not all populist critiques of the media are invalid. For example, left-populist criticisms of concentrated media ownership and a tendency to protect elite interests are well-founded. In the case of Australia, it is clear that the media has largely been responsible for the mainstreaming and normalization of Hanson and her ideas (Sengul, 2022b). For both political actors, Facebook has been a vital platform in mobilizing their supporters and speaking directly to them with minimal journalistic intervention and mediation. The experience of Duterte and Hanson on social media is consistent with recent arguments which propose an *affinity* between social media and populist actors. However, as the case of Duterte shows, this phenomenon is more complex. As demonstrated by Sinpeng et al. (2020), Duterte's success on Facebook occurred in spite of his communicative strategy. As such, Moffitt's (2018) point that we should not automatically assume populists are savvy users of social media appears to be correct. The relationship between populists and social media is more complex and requires further scholarly examination. What has been clear is that both Hanson and Duterte have pursued an effective *hybrid media strategy*, with both traditional and digital media playing key roles in their success. This supports the argument that one cannot have a holistic understanding of contemporary populism without centring media and communication in this phenomenon.

Note

1 Pauline Hanson was elected to the Australian Senate in 2016 as leader of Pauline Hanson's One Nation (PHON), along with three PHON senators. Since the 2022 election, they hold only two seats in the federal Senate.

References

Aalberg, T., & de Vreese, C. (2017). Introduction: Comprehending populist political communication. In T. Aalberg, F. Esser, C. Reinemann, J. Strömbäck & C. de Vreese (Eds.), *Populist political communication in Europe* (pp. 3–11). Routledge.

Aalberg, T., Esser, F., Reinemann, C., Strömbäck, J., & de Vreese, C. (2017). *Populist political communication in Europe*. Routledge.

Arguelles, C. V. (2019). 'We are Rodrigo Duterte': Dimensions of the Philippine populist publics' vote. *Asian Politics & Policy*, 11(3), 417–437. http://dx.doi.org/10.1111/aspp.12472

Betz, H. G. (2019). Australia's own brand of radical populism. *Centre for Analysis of the Radical Right*. www.radicalrightanalysis.com/2019/06/22/australias-own-brand-of-radical-populism

Broinowski, A. (2017). *Please explain: The rise, fall and rise again of Pauline Hanson*. Penguin.

Casiple, R. C. (2016). The Duterte presidency as a phenomenon. *Contemporary Southeast Asia: A Journal of International and Strategic Affairs*, 38(2), 179–184. www.muse.jhu.edu/article/628453

Chadwick, A. (2017). *The hybrid media system: Politics and power* (2nd ed.). Oxford University Press.

Coghlan, J. (2019). Rebranded Pauline Hanson: A party of policy or protest? In B. Grant, T. Moore & T. Lynch (Eds.), *The rise of right-populism: Pauline hanson's one nation and Australian politics* (pp. 179–199). Springer. https://doi.org/10.1007/978-981-13-2670-7

Curato, N. (2017). Flirting with authoritarian fantasies? Rodrigo Duterte and the new terms of Philippine populism. *Journal of Contemporary Asia*, 47(1), 142–153. http://dx.doi.org/10.1080/00472 336.2016.1239751

Curato, N. (2019). Toxic democracy? The Philippines in 2018. In D. Singh & M. Cook (Eds.), *Southeast Asian affairs 2019* (pp. 261–274). ISEAS—Yusof Ishak Institute.

Curran, G. (2004). Mainstreaming populist discourse: The race-conscious legacy of neo-populist parties in Australia and Italy. *Patterns of Prejudice*, 38(1), 37–55. http://dx.doi.org/10.1080/0031322032000185578

de Vreese, C. H., Esser, F., Aalberg, T., Reinemann, C., & Stanyer, J. (2018). Populism as an expression of political communication content and style: A new perspective. *The International Journal of Press/Politics*, 23(4), 423–438. http://dx.doi.org/10.1177/1940161218790035

Deutchman, I. E., & Ellison, A. (1999). A star is born: The roller coaster ride of Pauline Hanson in the news. *Media, Culture & Society*, 21(1), 33–50. http://dx.doi.org/10.1177/016344399021001002

Engesser, S., Ernst, N., Esser, F., & Büchel, F. (2017a). Populism and social media: How politicians spread a fragmented ideology. *Information, Communication & Society*, 20(8), 1109–1126. http://dx.doi.org/10.1080/1369118X.2016.1207697

Engesser, S., Fawzi, N., & Larsson, A. O. (2017b). Populist online communication: Introduction to the special issue. *Information, Communication & Society*, 20(9), 1279–1292. http://dx.doi.org/10.1080/1369118X.2017.1328525

Esser, F., Stępińska, A., & Hopmann, D. (2017). Populism and the media: Cross-national findings and perspectives. In T. Aalberg, F. Esser, C. Reinemann, J. Strömbäck & C. H. de Vreese (Eds.), *Populist political communication in Europe* (pp. 365–80). Routledge.

Fenton-Smith, B. (2020). The (re)birth of far-right populism in Australia: The appeal of Pauline Hanson's persuasive definitions. In M. Kranert (Ed.), *Discursive approaches to populism across disciplines* (pp. 339–365). Springer.

Gerbaudo, P. (2018). Social media and populism: An elective affinity? *Media, Culture & Society*, 40(5), 745–753. http://dx.doi.org/10.1177/0163443718772192

Goot, M. (2000). Pauline Hanson and the power of the media. In M. Leach, G. Stokes & I. Ward (Eds.), *The rise and fall of one nation* (pp. 115–135). University of Queensland Press.

Hatakka, N. (2019). *Populism in the hybrid media system: Populist radical right online counterpublics interacting with journalism, Party politics and citizen activism*. University of Turku.

Heydarian, R. J. (2018). *The rise of Duterte: A populist revolt against elite democracy*. Palgrave.

Hopster, J. (2021). Mutual affordances: The dynamics between social media and populism. *Media, Culture & Society*, 43(3), 551–560. http://dx.doi.org/10.1177/0163443720957889

Jacobs, K., Sandberg, L., & Spierings, N. (2020). Twitter and Facebook: Populists' double-barreled gun? *New Media & Society*, 22(4), 611–633. http://dx.doi.org/10.1177/1461444819893991

Jagers, J., & Walgrave, S. (2007). Populism as political communication style: An empirical study of political parties' discourse in Belgium. *European Journal of Political Research*, 46(3), 319–345. http://dx.doi.org/10.1111/j.1475-6765.2006.00690.x

Jose, J. (2019). 'Manning up' with Pauline Hanson: Playing the gender card, again. In B. Grant, T. Moore & T. Lynch (Eds.), *The rise of right-populism: Pauline Hanson's one nation and Australian politics* (pp. 167–178). Springer.

Krämer, B. (2014). Media populism: A conceptual clarification and some theses on its effects. *Communication Theory*, 24(1), 42–60. http://dx.doi.org/10.1111/comt.12029

Lewis. G. (1997). The media and the Pauline Hanson debate: Cheap talk or free speech? *Australian Journal of Communication*, 24(1), 9–41.

Manucci, L. (2017). Populism and the media. In C. Rovira Kaltwasser, P. Taggart, P. Ochoa Espejo & P. Ostiguy (Eds.), *The Oxford handbook of populism* (pp. 467–492). Oxford University Press.

Mazzoleni, G. (2003). The media and the growth of neo-populism in contemporary democracies. In G. Mazzoleni, J. Stewart & B. Horsfield (Eds.), *The media and neo-populism: A contemporary comparative analysis* (pp. 1–20). Praeger.

Mazzoleni, G. (2008). Populism and the media. In D. Albertazzi & D. McDonnell (Eds.), *Twenty-first century populism: The spectre of Western European democracy* (pp. 49–64). Palgrave Macmillan.

McKirdy, E. (2016, September 30). Philippines president likens himself to Hitler. *CNN*. https://edition.cnn.com/2016/09/30/asia/duterte-hitler-comparison/index.html

Moffitt, B. (2015). Contemporary populism and 'the people' in the Asia-Pacific region: Thaksin Shinawatra and Pauline Hanson. In C. de la Torre (Ed.), *The promise and perils of populism: Global perspectives* (pp. 293–316). University Press of Kentucky.

Moffitt, B. (2016). *The global rise of populism: Performance, political style, and representation*. Stanford University Press.

Moffitt, B. (2018). Populism 2.0: Social media and the false allure of 'unmediated' representation. In G. Fitzi, J. Mackert & B. S. Turner (Eds.), *Populism and the crisis of democracy: Politics, social movements and extremism* (Vol. 2, pp. 30–46). Routledge.

Mudde, C. (2019). *The far right today*. Polity.

Pauline Hanson says media was blinded by hate for one nation in reporting NRA sting. (2019, March 28). *ABC News*. www.youtube.com/watch?v=LvL72OXbXwc&t=19s

Placido, D. (2016). Duterte blasts 'vultures pretending to be journalists'. *ABS-CBN News*. https://news.abs-cbn.com/nation/06/02/16/duterte-blasts-vultures-pretending-to-be-journalists

Postill, J. (2018). Populism and social media: A global perspective. *Media, Culture & Society*, *40*(5), 754–765. http://dx.doi.org/10.1177/0163443718772186

Ragragio, J. L. D. (2020). Framing media populism: The political role of news media editorials in Duterte's Philippines. *Journalism*, *23*(6), 1301–1318. http://dx.doi.org/10.1177/1464884920959505

Reinemann, C., Stanyer, J., Aalberg, T., Esser, F., & de Vreese, C. H. (Eds.) (2019). *Communicating populism: Comparing actor perceptions, media coverage, and effects on citizens in Europe*. Routledge.

Ross, A. S., & Caldwell, D. (2020). 'Going negative': An APPRAISAL analysis of the rhetoric of Donald Trump on Twitter. *Language & Communication*, *70*, 13–27. http://dx.doi.org/10.1016/j.langcom.2019.09.003

Sengul, K. (2019a). Populism, democracy, political style and post-truth: Issues for communication research. *Communication Research and Practice*, *5*(1), 88–101. http://dx.doi.org/10.1080/22041451.2019.1561399

Sengul, K. (2019b). Critical discourse analysis in political communication research: A case study of right-wing populist discourse in Australia. *Communication Research and Practice*, *5*(4), 376–392. https://doi.org/10.1080/22041451.2019.1695082

Sengul, K. (2020). 'Swamped': The populist construction of fear, crisis and dangerous others in Pauline Hanson's senate speeches. *Communication Research and Practice*, *6*(1), 20–37. http://dx.doi.org/10.1080/22041451.2020.1729970

Sengul, K. (2021a). Never let a good crisis go to waste: Pauline Hanson's exploitation of COVID-19 on Facebook. *Media International Australia*, *178*(1), 101–105. http://dx.doi.org/10.1177/1329878X20953521

Sengul, K. (2021b). 'It's OK to be white': The discursive construction of victimhood, 'anti-white racism' and calculated ambivalence in Australia. *Critical Discourse Studies*, 1–17. http://dx.doi.org/10.1080/17405904.2021.1921818

Sengul, K. (2022a). Performing islamophobia in the Australian parliament: The role of populism and performance in Pauline Hanson's 'burqa stunt'. *Media International Australia*, *184*(1), 49–62. https://doi.org/10.1177/1329878X221087733

Sengul, K. (2022b). The role of political interviews in mainstreaming and normalizing the far-right: A view from Australia. In O. Feldman (Ed.), *Adversarial political interviewing* (pp. 357–375). Springer.

Sinpeng, A. (2016, May 12). How Duterte won the election on Facebook. *New Mandala*. www.newmandala.org/how-duterte-won-the-election-on-facebook/

Sinpeng, A., Gueorguiev, D., & Arugay, A. A. (2020). Strong fans, weak campaigns: Social media and duterte in the 2016 Philippine election. *Journal of East Asian Studies*, *20*(3), 353–374. http://dx.doi.org/10.1017/jea.2020.11

Stanyer, J., Salgado, S., & Strömbäck, J. (2017). Populist actors as communicators or political actors as populist communicators: Cross-national findings and perspectives. In T. Aalberg, F. Esser, C. Reinemann, J. Strömbäck & C. de Vreese (Eds.), *Populist political communication in Europe* (pp. 353–361). Routledge.

Strömbäck, J., & Esser, F. (2014). Mediatization of politics: Towards a theoretical framework. In F. Esser & J. Strömbäck (Eds.), *Mediatization of politics: Understanding the transformation of western democracies* (pp. 3–28). Palgrave.

Tapsell, R. (2021). Social media and elections in Southeast Asia: The emergence of subversive, underground campaigning. *Asian Studies Review*, *45*(1), 117–134. http://dx.doi.org/10.1080/10357823.2020.1841093

Thompson, M. R. (2016). The early Duterte presidency in the Philippines. *Journal of Current Southeast Asian Affairs*, *35*(3), 3–14. http://dx.doi.org/10.1177/186810341603500301

Waisbord, S. (2019). Populism as media and communication phenomenon. In C. de la Torre (Ed.), *Routledge handbook of global populism* (pp. 221–234). Routledge.

Webb, A., & Curato, N. (2019). Populism in the Philippines. In D. Stockemer (Ed.), *Populism around the world: A comparative perspective* (pp. 49–65). Springer.

Wodak R. (2021). *The politics of fear. The shameless normalization of far-right discourse* (2nd rev. ext. ed.). Sage.

9
RELIGION, SECULARISM AND POPULISM IN CONTEMPORARY ASIA

D. B. Subedi and Francis K. G. Lim

The garb of religion is the best cloak for power.

William Hazlitt (1819, p. 302)

Introduction

Recent studies on religion and populism mostly focus on Western secular liberal democracies, with Christianity being a principal analytical focal point while non-Christian religions are excluded (Yilmaz & Morieson, 2022). In this chapter, we adopt a pan-Asian perspective to explicate the relationship between religion and populism by expanding the analytical lens to Hinduism, Buddhism and Islam in South, East and Southeast Asia.

We show that the current wave of right-wing populism in Asia, commencing around the new millennium, reflects a global trend in which populists hijack religion as a readily available resource for constructing social cleavages between the natives or 'good people' and the 'others' and between 'people' versus 'bad elites' (see Roy, 2016). Further, we demonstrate that what typifies many cases in Asia is the populists' desire and ability to mobilize the emotional and moral *content* of religion and religious culture to establish a direct relationship with their followers. This content, broadly defined, includes religious narratives, symbols, values, faith, practice, identity and rituals.[1] These elements when considered in a populist political discourse can bind people together, inculcating in them the sense of 'we-ness' reified by common religious emotion, morality and the sense of cultural belonging. In this process, a faith-based collective identity and the role it plays in social polarization become driving forces of populist politics. Importantly, we argue that what facilitates or hinders the rise of religious populism in many parts of Asia is dependent on the ideological practice of secularism (or lack thereof) in these places. Given the centrality of collective identity and polarization, religious populism in Asia shares characteristics of religiously-driven traditional identity politics. As such, religious populism in Asia is an extension of unresolved traditional identity politics, reliant on contentions around race, religion and nation-building.

This trend is markedly different from populism in the post-independence period, roughly from the 1950s to 1970s, when religion still functioned as a marker of collective national identity. However, with some exceptions such as Sri Lanka and Pakistan, it played an insignificant role in shaping populist discourses. This may be attributed partly to the fear that exploiting religious identity would divide populist support bases in newly independent nation-states, and partly to the dominance of class-based, rather than cultural identity-based, mobilization in left-wing political movements, which exploded across Asia as an effect of the global ideological divide of the Cold War (see Hansson et al., 2020).

Using examples from India, Sri Lanka, Bangladesh, Myanmar, Singapore, Indonesia and China, we show that populists in Asia are increasingly turning to religious content to redefine their populist political ideologies as well as actions. However, their ability to mobilize the emotional and moral content of religion is determined by a key structural condition: the degree of secularization and its discontents. To expand our argument, we analyze the relationship between religion and populism in three types of states: semi/non-secular, strongly secular and atheist. The religion-populism interface is stronger in non-secular or semi-secular states, whereas in strongly secular or atheist states, populists turn to cultural rather than religious content as an ideological and strategic resource to advance populism.

Religion and populism in Asia

The literature shows that the construction of a collective identity along religious lines provides a foundation for cross-class populist mobilizations of people; vertically against 'political elites' and horizontally against outsiders (Roy, 2016). This form of social polarization is a precondition for exclusionary right populism, in which religion is discursively framed as an instrument of social polarization between the good ('us') and bad ('others').

Recent studies from Western Europe and the United States reveal that right-wing populists are not primarily interested in ideological and theological aspects of religion but exploit the strategic use of religion for populist purposes (see Roy, 2016). Such manipulations of religion mean that religious populism in Europe claims to protect common identity and culture, rather than faith or belief (Marzouki, 2022). Given that secularism is the principal framework of statehood and citizenship in Western Europe, the populist ambition to defend identity and culture rather than faith can be an attractive populist project that potentially averts backlash from liberal-minded leaders and institutions. However, in the civil society domain, this increases the risk of backlash populists may face from religious and theological leaders and institutions that would oppose the manipulation of faith and belief.

In contrast, populist leaders in Asia have increasingly relied on and benefited from formal and informal alliances with religious leaders and institutions, not only to avoid their opposition from below but also to augment their mobilizing capabilities. In doing so, religion becomes as much a source of populist ideology as an enabler of populist action. For example, in India, the right-wing populist politics of Narendra Modi and his Hindu nationalist Bharatiya Janata Party (BJP) share the ideology of *Hindutva*—the Hindu nationalist ideology—with various Hindu organizations that include the Vishwa Hindu Parishad (World Hindu Council), Hindu Swayamsevak Sangh (Hindu Volunteer Association), Bajrang Dal and Vivekanada Kendra (Vivekanada Centre), to name a few. The networks of these Hindu organizations are part of what Bhatia (2020) calls an 'ecosystem of *Hindutva*'. They play crucial roles in disseminating populist narratives and Hindu ideology at the grassroot levels, assisting Modi to leverage political outreach (Subedi & Scott, 2021 and Chapter 7 in this volume). Likewise, the support of radical Buddhist monks and their institutions augmented the populist and nationalist activities of the Rajapaksa brothers in Sri Lanka between 2010 and 2022 (see Chapter 16 in this volume). The symbiosis between right-wing populists and religious institutions, defined by their cultural affinity and historical ties, has made religious populism a viable project in Myanmar, Bangladesh and Indonesia, among others. What is equally remarkable is that right-wing populists in Asia tend to defend collective identity and culture as well as faith and belief, ostensibly avoiding confrontations with faith leaders and institutions. This creates a nexus of religion and politics that favours populism.

The literature shows that both religion and populism are strongly related to fear and the associated notion of crisis. Palaver (2019, p. 22) argues that 'the more our contemporary societies have turned into societies of fear, the more we also can observe populist developments in the realm of politics'. Throughout history, religion has provided a crucial social mechanism to respond to threats and fears and to maintain social control. Religion broadly provides a cultural framework for friend-enemy patterns, in which fear galvanizes solidarity among those who feel threatened by outsiders. In populist political discourses, the effects of fear are diverse. As Zulehner (2016, cited in Palaver, 2019) elaborates, fear leads to populist activities and action which can have various political results: border controls, Islamophobia, fights for cultural purity and specialized provisions for social welfare to a selected group of people.

In Asian societies, the social effects of religion are deep-rooted, influencing identity, culture, morality, rituals and the belief system. Religion serves as a mechanism not only to address fears of earthly matters and material conditions, but also to legitimize and respond to the fear of supernatural forces and monstrosities. Faith provides the moral courage to engage with fears arising from the enemy, both known and unknown (Beggiora et al., 2018). While the perception of fear continues to shape populist agendas and narratives in Asian societies, what is typically different is the friend-enemy logic within which the perception of fear, often from a known enemy, is mobilized. The scapegoating of the Rohingya Muslims in Myanmar and the Muslim minority in Sri Lanka, along with associated religious and political violence, operated in the religious and social framework of friend and enemy. Such a framework provides an ideological platform in which populism and nationalism have converged (see Chapter 2 in this volume).

What is clear is that unlike Western European nations and the United States, where immigrants and cultural minorities in general and Muslims in particular are projected as enemies of the native-born inhabitants (Marzouki, 2022), in Asia, the enemies are cultural and religious minorities from within the nation-state or region, which may well include members of the native population (we will return to this point later). At the societal level, fear and the perceived risk of existential threats of race and religion from 'others' enhances solidarity within the majority. At the political level, the fear of 'religious others' has resulted in several types of populist action repertoire: securitization of minority identity and tightening of national security agendas, for example, in India and Sri Lanka. As in Europe and the United States, populism intensifies and benefits from the politicization of fear mostly in semi-secular states, but as we will show later, this is not so much the case in a strongly secular or atheist state. The implication is that secularism is a significant independent variable that determines the presence or absence of religious populism.

Religion and populism in South/Southeast Asia: evolution and diffusion

Populism is not an alien concept in Asia, although its use in politics seems relatively new compared to that in Europe and Latin America.[2] Though not defined exclusively as populist, some of the first-generation leaders who fought for the independence of their nation-states were charismatic and nationalist. The political style of these charismatic leaders may occasionally have seemed to reflect populist rhetoric, especially in their claims to represent the 'native population' and the nation, and in their desire to connect directly with the people, often bypassing formal institutional processes. For example, the 'national hero' often denotes the popularity of an independence leader enjoying a direct relationship and connection with the masses—a political style which is common among contemporary populists around the world. Meanwhile, these leaders often centralize power, claiming to be the true leader of the people and promising to bring about radical socioeconomic transformation in the newly born nation-state. The populist elements found in the political styles of nationalist leaders (or heroes) such as Jawaharlal Nehru in India and Prince Norodom Sihanouk in Cambodia were invisible for a particular reason: the common aim of the early waves of populist movements in Asia was to mobilize the masses for independence, and the populist discourse that emerged roughly between the 1940s and 1970s painted colonial rulers as political elites and 'outsiders' or 'enemies' of the people. As these populist movements gravitated around the demand for total independence from colonial powers, they were underpinned by the ideology of state formation often subsumed within nationalist movements.

The role of religion did not feature prominently in the early waves of populism, primarily because mobilizing people along religious and cultural lines could divide politics and even threaten the existence of a nation-state. Where religion was mobilized to construct a bounded national political community, state formation was a violent process. The separation of India and Pakistan and the birth of Bangladesh (previously East Pakistan) from West Pakistan (now Pakistan) are examples of how religion-based nationalist politics can engender sectarian violence and potentially disintegrate a nation-state.

The newly formed independent states, however, suddenly found themselves entangled in a messy politics of state formation that led to enduring social tensions, elite fragmentation, and a lack of constitutional consensus on the distribution of power and resources. As Brasted and Ahmed show in Chapter 2 of this volume, even the founding father of the newly formed Pakistan, Muhammad Ali Jinnah and his Muslim League party, failed to take a definite position in relation to the role of religion in the state system. In the years that followed independence, some states, such as India, Malaysia and Singapore, however, navigated relatively peacefully through the predicament of state formation and consolidation. Others, such as Sri Lanka, Myanmar and Bangladesh, descended into social and communal conflicts and a dramatic rise in contentious identity politics (De Silva, 2000).

The populist and nationalist leaders, who had enjoyed widespread public support at the time of independence, suddenly found themselves in the ruling position, while the 'enemy' they had been fighting—the colonizers—had disappeared. This dramatic shift in the socio-political context altered the interface of religion, nationalism, and populism, resulting in the decline of populist politics. This was mainly due to the loss of the people's enemy (i.e., the colonizers) as well as the declining people's support for charismatic leaders amidst fragmented politics in the post-independence period.

The difficulties populist leaders faced at this stage brought about a turning point in populism in Asia. It forced populists to redefine the 'enemy', which in many cases was within the nation-state. This accentuated the majority-minority divide and intensified the political struggle to forge a unitary national identity, as was the case in Sri Lanka, Myanmar and Thailand. Ultimately, the defining of an enemy within (and sometimes outside, such as Muslim refugees in India) hindered nation-state building and led to the painting of religious and cultural minorities as the enemy of the majority. Through this post-colonial political manoeuvring, religion, populism, nationalism and identity politics gradually began to blend and produce complex political discourses. As an effect of this historical reality, in contemporary South and Southeast Asia, populism in general and religious populism in particular exist in this political complexity, in which careful attention must be paid to differentiating between religious populism, religious nationalism, and religiously-driven identity politics. In most cases, these phenomena are almost inseparable and overlapped. This is one respect in which the manifestation of religious populism in Asia has differed from elsewhere.

In reference to the enabling factors of populism in a historical context in Asia, the Cold War comes into play. Even though many Asian states, including Indonesia, Nepal and India advocated the non-aligned movement in the 1980s to resist the Cold War's global ideological division, it had discernible effects across Asia. It intensified class consciousness among people and politicians, which led to the dramatic rise of left-wing politics, class conflicts, and revolutions in South and Southeast Asia in the 1970s and 1980s (Goodwin, 2001). Vietnam, Cambodia, India, Nepal and Laos experienced powerful left-wing political and revolutionary movements which amplified class contradictions and shaped much of the debates on political systems. At this juncture, some countries saw the rise of left-wing populism at national and sub-national levels. For example, the rise of agrarian populism in India in the 1970s exposed class contradictions between rural farmers and the national political elites who failed to bring about change and transformation in the lives of the agrarian masses (Dhanagare, 2015; Mehta & Sinha, 2022). In Nepal, a communist political movement emerged out of agrarian revolution in the 1980s. A strand of this movement morphed into radical Maoism, which employed populist strategies to mobilize support from below in the armed conflict from 1996 to 2006 (see Chapter 15 in this volume).

Today, the weakening of left-wing politics in South and Southeast Asia and the rise of an authoritarian style of politics in countries like Cambodia, the Philippines, Myanmar, India and Sri Lanka has not only pushed class-based mobilizations to the margin but has also strengthened cross-class political mobilization bringing religion, culture and the 'people', as natives or insiders, to the centre of politics. In the name of serving the people, populists in Asia have now reinvented the masses, who are defined in cultural and religious terms rather than on the basis of class divide.[3] Expressed differently, populism today involves admixtures of cross-class and cultural mobilization with populist agendas which seek to protect the majority from the existential threat of minorities (we elaborate on this point later). It is the faith of the majority that populists seek to manipulate across South and Southeast Asia.

Religion profoundly matters for this reinvention of the masses, primarily because faith, race and ethnicity are closely intertwined and almost inseparable in Asian societies. Let us consider the case of Sri Lanka, where the Sinhalese majority, who consider themselves a superior race to the Tamil and Muslim minorities, are Buddhists. With some exceptions, the majority of Tamils follow Hinduism. The Bamar majority in Myanmar is predominantly Buddhist, whereas the majority of Muslims in Indonesia, Pakistan and Bangladesh follow different branches of Islam. Even though the Muslim communities are fragmented into distinct branches and schools, religion and race are central to their collective identity. The intertwining of race, religion and national identity means religious populism in Asia shares and extends the exclusionary and reactive characteristics of identity politics that emerged in the post-colonial period.[4]

The inter-connectedness of religion, ethnicity and race also means managing diversity and pluralism is challenging, and has constantly divided the society into ethnic, religious and racial binaries and hierarchies. The pre-existing binaries and hierarchies provide a political template on which contemporary religious populism benefits from the emotional and moral content of religion in Asia. Although there is no Asian exceptionalism regarding how religion constructs social boundaries and hierarchies, what seems typical is that there is a relatively high degree of religious plurality in many Asian societies, unlike the United States and European countries. To understand the nuances of how religious populism manifests amidst religious pluralism, we propose to examine a key enabling condition: secularism and its discontents.

Secularism and religious populism in Asia

Central to the relationship of religion and politics is the contentious issue of secularism. Since the Enlightenment, the principle of secularism has created a public space that separates state, economy and science from religion within 'Western' modernity. Casanova (2013, p. 34) describes this as a decline of religious belief and religion's relegation to the private or personal. A question that arises here is: how do we make sense of religious populism, where religion is formally segregated from the public affairs, but religious belief in society has not necessarily declined? To explain this phenomenon in already secularized societies, Habermas (2006) discusses the idea of a 'post-secular society', in which religion is, under certain circumstances, permitted in the public sphere and the dialogue between secular and religious actors is encouraged. A law that is open to all citizens cannot privilege the secular over the religious or vice versa. Rather, religion plays a substantive role in organizing everyday practices for many people. The split between secular and non-secular can only be addressed through 'dialogue', a key element to maintaining the social order that both secularization and fundamentalism prohibit (Habermas, 2006). While Habermas's post-secular thesis helps to unpack why religion continues to influence the public sphere in Asia, post-secularism hardly becomes an appropriate concept in Asia, where secularism was not consolidated in the first place.

Secularization in South, East and Southeast Asia is an unfinished and contentious political project, originally imposed by the colonial rulers and carried over by nationalist political elites in the post-colonial period (Dean & van der Veer, 2019, p. 2). Although the importation of the Western idea looked promising in theory, it had limitations in clearly separating religion and politics and failed to move religion from the public sphere to the private domain. Even in a constitutionally secular country like India, secularism is contested because of the continuing powerful influence of religion in the political domain—a phenomenon that Laborde (2021) calls 'minimal secularism'.

The historical context, including the nature of pre-colonial states, cannot be ignored in discussing religion and politics in Asia. In the pre-colonial period, the state system was traditionally organized on the basis of power and patronage distributed by kings or the traditional central political authority. Religion was not only a source of faith but also provided ethical and moral guidance to define citizenship and modes of governance. In pre-colonial India, ruled by princes and kings, religion formed the state ideology, moral principles of governance and a force for peaceful social order (Washbrook, 2019). Similar instances can be found in the Sinhalese kingdoms in Sri Lanka, the Buddhist kingdom in Thailand and Muslim states in present day Malaysia and Indonesia. The emotional and moral content of Buddhism and Hinduism such as kindness, empathy, benevolence and duty of care provided normative guidance to kingship. On the one hand, these qualities contributed to making a king a popular leader, a benevolent ruler and a traditional authority in the Weberian sense. On the other hand, the kings and the traditional authorities enjoyed the popular support of their followers and subjects. Thus, religion in pre-modern Asia was a powerful social institution that mediated the direct relationship between leaders and followers. Emotions, values and morality associated with religion played an important role in leader-follower interactions. For example, the Sinhalese kings in Ceylon (now Sri Lanka) had a duty to protect the Sinhalese Buddhist race and religion and, further, a moral duty to protect whoever came under their rule. History shows that most Sinhalese kings welcomed Muslim traders and allowed them to settle and practice their own religion, Islam, from as early as the seventh century BC (Jayawardena, 1985). In short, unlike in contemporary religious populism, in the past, the minorities were generally protected as long as they complied and cooperated with the ruler. Religion was a source of social cooperation rather than conflict.

Although a populist-type leader-follower relationship was found in ancient states and kingdoms, we are not suggesting they were necessarily populist states. Yet, religion still played a central role in shaping the leader-follower relationship. Right-wing populists in Asia seemed to reinvent this trend by exploiting the emotional content of religion to establish a direct relationship with followers, although a key difference has been that religion seemed to facilitate more conflict and violence than fostering inter-group cooperation and cohesion. This explains why religious populism either manifests violently or includes some form of political and religious violence and conflict in contemporary Asia.

The historical context aside, today, secularism in Asia exists in different forms and secularization proceeds in varying degrees. Although there are some states that are constitutionally secular, as noted earlier, religion has not essentially disappeared from the public and political domains of Asia. Vaishnav (2019, p. 6) argues that even in the case of India, unlike secularism in the West characterized by strict church-state separation, the country's secular constitution favoured a 'principled distance' between religion and the state. This means, although post-independence India was born as a constitutionally secular nation-state, religious ideologies and practices continue to shape the political arena and the state-society relationship as well. Apart from Singapore, a strong form of secularism is rare in Asia, and this impacts how religious populism appears in this region. To explain this dynamic in detail, we discuss three types of states which either create an enabling condition or present a barrier to religious populism.

Type 1: the semi-secular state

Typically, a semi-secular state shows some degree of political secularization, but the country as a whole may experience low levels of social secularization. There may be some official acknowledgement of the privileged position of particular religion(s), and religious groups may form political parties and play a legitimate role in political life. This implies that some secular political parties may at times seek to establish alliances with religiously affiliated political parties and institutions for political expediency. The general population may be moderately to highly religious, while religious symbolism and practice is a commonplace in public culture and different domains of everyday life.

In semi-secular states such as Sri Lanka and Bangladesh, religious populism blends with nationalist politics. In these countries, populists not only exploit religion to construct the meaning of the masses but also deploy the emotional and moral content of religious ideology, practice and culture to maintain political order and social control. In Sri Lanka, for example, this form of political and social control can be seen in the moral policing of the Sinhala Buddhist community by radical Buddhist organizations such as the Bodu Bala Sena (BBS). A similar example of moral policing of the believers by radical religious groups is found in Myanmar (see Subedi & Garnett, 2020).

For the BBS, modernization of younger Sinhalese generations threatens to make the Sinhala Buddhist community less religious. This presents an existential threat to Sinhala Buddhism.[5] While BBS's ideology can qualify as a case of religious populism in civil society, their perception of the existential threat was shared by populist-nationalist leaders such as Mahinda Rajapaksa (see Subedi, 2022). The case of Sri Lanka suggests that in a semi-secular state, the political populist and civil society populist may embrace a similar ideology and worldview of religion, society and politics, hence working side by side to manipulate religion as a way of mobilizing their support base. A similar example is found in Bangladesh, where populists benefit from the support of Islamic leaders and institutions and vice versa (see Chapter 15 in this volume).

Also, consider the case of Indonesia. The nation has the world's largest Muslim population, and Islam has been politically significant as both a cultural and ideological resource for populists. It is also a state that maintains a mild version of secularism while acknowledging the cultural and political importance of religion. In 2008, the Indonesian Constitutional Court reiterated the principles of religious pluralism and constitutional sovereignty of the country in a case brought by Islamists urging the application of *shari'a* (Islamic law) throughout the country. The ruling recognized that the Indonesian state has a 'legitimate stake in the promotion of religion and the curbing of orthodoxy' (Hefner, 2018, p. 215). Because the state is secularized politically to some degree, while Islam, the dominant religion, is still deeply embedded in Indonesian social and cultural life, populists often cultivate social alliances by recourse to cultural and ideological resource pools, specifically the idioms and symbolism associated with the Islamic religion (Hadiz, 2016).

In post-independence India, the separation of religion and politics was constitutionally clear but socially ambiguous because of religion's role in political mobilization (van der Veer, 2019, p. 46). Under Nehru, the first prime minister of post-colonial India, secular ideology and vision were promoted to define India's post-independence social compact based on cultural pluralism and liberal values. In contrast, the Muslim League, originally named the All India Muslim League, used Islamic faith and Muslim culture to create a support base to push for a separate Muslim nation. When the Muslim League's political geography shifted to the newly-created Pakistan in 1947, the absence of strong Muslim opposition in India eventually allowed the Bhartiya Janata Party (BJP)—the Hindu nationalist party—to capture the religious nationalist space in the Hindu dominated country. Today, *Hindutva*, the ideology of Hindu nationalism, influences the political ideology and modes of grassroots mobilization, as well as the populist-nationalist politics of the BJP, particularly its leader and current prime minister, Narendra Modi. A strong presence of the ecosystem of *Hindutva*, including political and social organizations that subscribe to the *Hindutva* ideology, created an enabling condition for religious populism to grow despite India being a constitutionally secular state.

The examples of Sri Lanka, Indonesia, Bangladesh and India show that semi-secular states have the majority religion as a readily available precondition of populism: religious polarization and emotional contents of faith that can facilitate a leader's direct and institutionally unmediated relationship with the masses or followers. Growing socioeconomic inequalities and weakening trust in the formal political system and governments are other factors that accentuate the role of religion in populism.

There are multiple consequences of religious populism that affect pluralism and secularism. Religious populists across Asia have sought to re-traditionalize the society by propagating religious revivalism and the narrative of de-secularization. For instance, in the view of liberals and Marxists, the BBS's moral policing campaigns, supported by populist nationalists, are re-traditionalizing Sri Lankan society and its public sphere. The same can be said about religious populism in India, Bangladesh and Indonesia. The rise of Hindu revivalism in India, Buddhist revivalism in Sri Lanka and Myanmar and Islamic revivalism in Bangladesh and Indonesia have another major consequence: the resurrecting of ancient conflicts between religious groups. The conflicts between Hindus and Muslims in India and between Sinhala Buddhists and Muslims in Sri Lanka are new, but their drivers are rooted in historical animosity and clashes between the groups. What this means is that unlike populism in general, which thrives under social polarization, religious populism tends to benefit from social and religious conflicts with historical roots.

Type 2: the (strongly) secular state

Compared with non-secular and semi-secular states, a strongly secular state manifests a higher degree of political secularization when the formal political engagement of religions is strictly curtailed, religious pluralism is safeguarded and constitutional sovereignty is strenuously maintained by political actors and institutions. Religion is not a factor in legitimizing important political institutions, nor is it considered an essential component of national identity and culture. It is discursively constructed, represented by the state to manifest religious pluralism under a secularist constitution and marshalled for a state-promoted agenda. Religious groups may be encouraged to contribute to social welfare and socially desired public goods, but they are not allowed to use religious symbolism, values, or ideals for political ends that challenge the fundamental principles of the secular state.

Singapore is an example of a strongly secular Asian state with a form of secularism that contrasts with the anti-theistic, militant type. It recognizes the importance of religion in people's lives, and in principle accords equal treatment to all religions while promoting dialogue between religious and secular leaders and institutions.

Singaporean secularism involves two essential aspects. First, the state insists on keeping religion out of politics, most notably by prohibiting religious organizations from mobilizing their members for political activism. For the Singaporean government, secularism is considered essential for the peaceful coexistence of the country's diverse religious and ethnic groups. Thus, the institutionalization of the Presidential Council for Minority Rights and the Maintenance of Religious Harmony Act (1991) aims to entrench multiculturalism and peaceful religious coexistence in the country (Lai, 2010).

In a strongly secular state, in theory, there is no legitimate space for religion to be utilized by populists as an ideological or strategic resource to participate in political processes. This does not mean that there is universal support for secularism among its citizens or that there is a common understanding of what the term entails. But it does imply that populists who oppose the prevailing secularist principles or push for a greater political role for religion may attempt to do so through illegitimate or extra-legal means. Alternatively, such social actors can still promote religion's relevance in public life by discursively constructing and mobilizing religion as a cultural, but not ideological, resource. Thus, religion may be discursively constructed as a 'cultural heritage' or 'tradition', to forge communal or national identity. Religiously constituted groups opposing the secularist political elite will be suppressed by the secularist government if they are deemed to be undermining the secularism that underpins the state constitution. Thus, it can be concluded that compared with semi-secular states, religious populism and religious nationalism as political movements are generally absent in a strong secular state.

Given the strong secularism that is practiced in Singapore, populists would not be able to mobilize religion as an ideological, moral or emotional resource without attracting the suppressive mechanisms of the secular state. This is because religious political activism is regarded by the dominant secularist political elite as an anathema to the ideological practice of multiculturalism, and thus undermines a core founding principle of the nation. Relatedly, since no single religion or religious organization was directly involved in the country's struggle for independence, in contrast to, for example, the case of India, Singaporean populists were unable to draw discursively upon the religious ideals and symbolism of a majority or dominant socio-ethnic group or to forge a 'people's identity' as means of populist mobilization. To a certain extent, the presence of strong secularism explains why, unlike other Asian countries, Singapore is an outlier in the study of populism.

Type 3: the atheist state

When examining the relationship between secularism, populism and religion in Asia, we cannot ignore the atheist state. Conceptually the opposite of the non-secular state, its ideal type is the communist state, which is characterized by its ideological opposition to religion. This does not mean that religion has no public function in an atheist state. In the context of what Ngo and Quijada (2015) call atheist secularism, religion can be mobilized or expected by state actors to perform certain social, cultural or political functions, strictly circumscribed within state-demarcated domains. At the ideological level, communist state-sponsored atheism requires an antithesis, namely, religion, in order to define itself and mobilize the population for social transformation. Religion is regarded as a fundamental threat to the political interests of state actors in an atheist state, precisely due to its position as an 'ideological other'. What, then, is the possible relationship between religion and populism in such as state?

Let us examine the case of China. The ruling Chinese Communist Party (CCP) poses religion as its 'other'. The CCP construction of this 'other' forms part of its own political imaginaries and efforts to shore up its legitimacy. Therefore, over several decades, the CCP has constructed various meanings of 'religion' for its own political projects through ideological, legal and administrative means (Yang, 2011; Lim & Sng, 2021). Religion may be used politically, but not as an ideological resource that underpins political authority. On the other hand, any potential populist political challengers to the ruling elites will be severely suppressed, especially if the former seek to mobilize religion in support of their causes. Currently, many faith-based organizations working with local governments on community development projects in China publicly downplay the 'religious' aspects of their work. For example, Master Xing Yun, the founder of Foguang Shan, a prominent Buddhist group from Taiwan, mentions in an interview with the New York Times that the group's activities in China are not meant to spread Buddhism, but 'only to promote Chinese culture to cleanse humanity' (Johnson, 2017). For some Buddhists in China, the endemic social suffering they witness motivates them to actively practice compassion in their daily lives and engage in voluntarism as a form of worldly spiritualism. The Buddhists consider this kind of social engagement *humanistic Buddhism* (*renjian fojiao*).

Typically, religious leaders seeking to play an active public role in China tend to present their activities as part of 'culture' or 'tradition' or align their social engagement efforts with the broader discourse 'development' (Lim & Sng, 2021). In other words, both state and mainstream non-state actors tend not to mobilize religion as an emotional resource that provides an alternative political vision to the prevailing atheist secularism enforced by the ruling Communist Party.

Generally, in the atheist/communist state, populism can emerge—but only from within the ruling party as a form of 'socialist populism'. Populist ruling elites may utilize religion, not to legitimate their political authority in religious terms but as a cultural resource or for social 'othering'. An example of the latter can be found in the way Chinese authorities have 'socially othered' the Uighur Muslims. In an atheist state, populists may alternatively acknowledge or attack religion as part of the people's 'tradition' or 'heritage', as one of the sources of citizens' moral values, according to political expediencies, or as an enemy of the people. Even so, religion will not constitute an essential component of the ruling elite's forging a national identity, since it needs be discursively linked to the ideology of atheist secularism and socialism. Thus, unlike in the non-secular and secular states, religious populism will be absent in atheist secular states.

Conclusion

In this chapter, we examined the relationship between religion and populism in South, East and Southeast Asia. We showed that religion played a somewhat less significant role in the early waves of populism roughly between the 1940s and 1970s, hosted by nationalism and its revolutionary thrust for independence. In the 1970s and 1980s, at the height of the Cold War-driven ideological polarization, many countries in South and Southeast Asia saw left-wing, communist and revolutionary movements. During this period, class contradictions shaped much of the grassroots political mobilization and left-wing agrarian populism in countries like India and Nepal. Still, in this leftist wave of Asian populism, religion was an insignificant factor, partly due to the general leftist view that a religious divide would weaken class-based mobilization.

In the contemporary wave of populism in Asia that started around the new millennium, religion has become a catalytic factor in the enabling of populism. The root of contemporary religious populism in Asia can be traced back to pre-modern days, in which for leaders and kings, religion was a source of traditional authority through which they established a direct relationship with their subjects. Although this happened under entirely different circumstances, such as in the absence of competitive politics, the pattern of leader-follower relationship shared some commonalities with how religious populists engage with the people today. Religious populism appears to reinvent charismatic and traditional authorities in many Asian states.

Highlighting the significance of the socio-cultural and historical contexts, we have shown that right-wing populists in Asia used religious institutions, ideologies and narratives to construct their populist political rhetoric and narratives that enabled the leaders to mobilize the masses against political elites. Asian populists are particularly interested in the moral and emotional content of religion. The moral content of religion, as discussed earlier, makes it easy for populists to exploit people's moral judgement and emotion. This in turn helps to deepen the ties between leaders and followers. However, we need to be cautious not to over-generalize this argument, considering that not all contemporary populist movements in Asia have exploited religion.

An important factor that either enables or hinders the emergence and perpetuation of religious populism in different Asian countries has been the ideological practice of secularism. To elaborate on this argument, we discussed the viability of religious populism in three types of states: semi-secular and/or non-secular (Sri Lanka, India and Indonesia), strongly secular (Singapore) and atheist (China). Our analysis shows that semi-secular or non-secular states have a significantly more conducive environment for the rise of religious populism, precisely because of the deep and persistent influence and dominance of religion in both public and private spheres. Religion, in this instance, fulfils its collective identity-making function, enables populist leaders to define their collectively bounded support base and helps mediate a direct relationship between leaders and followers. Religion becomes an instrument of exclusion—the exclusion of those others who do not fit in the native-born category and/or do not adhere to the majority religion—and the source of deeper social polarization. This type of religious populism shares similarities with right-wing populism found elsewhere. In addition to using religion to forge a collective identity and widening social polarization, populists in semi-secular and/or non-secular states seek to re-traditionalize the society, de-secularize the public space and polity and advocate for religious revivalism, as has been the case in Sri Lanka, India and Myanmar, among others.

In contrast, a strongly secular state provides less incentive for and is not favourable to religious populism. Populists in this type of state are left with one of two choices: either play secular populist politics or find an alternative to religion in populist mobilization. What we have seen in the case of Singapore is that culture replaces religion as a resource for populism.

In an atheist state, religion has no place in either the political or public sphere, and adherence to religious faith and practice is often strongly curtailed. Indeed, religion can become the 'other' against which populists mobilize the people. China provides an example where the populist movement led by the party-state has often identified religion as an 'enemy' of the system and the people. In short, religious populism in an atheist state is almost impossible to materialize. However, political actors in such a state may still exploit culture and national heritage in populist movements. Along this line of analysis, Gao (Chapter 23 in this volume) shows how the authorities have engaged and drawn on nationalist and patriotic songs as a resource for populism in China.

Finally, both strongly secular and atheist states present institutional and ideological barriers to religious populism. But a key difference is that the former allows religious and political leaders to engage in religious and cultural dialogues and encourages the use of such dialogue to foster peaceful social and political order. In contrast, in an atheist state, religious dialogue is strictly prohibited, whereas cultural dialogue may be allowed provided it does not threaten the atheist secularism and, in the case of China, the communist ideology.

Notes

1. Yilmaz and Shukri observed a similar role of religious emotions in Islamic populism in Asia (Chapter 10 in this volume).
2. For a historical overview of the early stages of populism in the USA, Russia, Europe and Latin America, see Canovan (1981) and Edwards (2019).
3. In this regard, Chacko (2018) argues that the negative impacts and inequality produced by neoliberal economic globalization has created an enabling condition for the rise of right-wing nationalist populism in Asia, mainly in India.
4. For more on identity, conflict politics and nation building in Asia, see Liow (2016). See Singh (2006) for an overview of identity politics in South Asia.
5. First author's interview with Buddhist monks in Colombo and Kandy, October 2019. Additionally, radical Buddhist leaders think that the existential threat also comes from religious conversion and the 'invasion' of Islamic religion and Muslim culture.

References

Beggiora, S., Guzy, L., & Skoda, U. (2018). Fear and fright in South Asia. Encounters with ambivalence and alterity in vernacular religion and society. *International Quarterly for Asian Studies*, 49(3–4), 5–18. https://doi.org/10.11588/iqas.2018.3-4.9305

Bhatia, S. (2020, July 31). Why the Hindutva right is better at propaganda than its opponents. *The Wire*. https://thewire.in/politics/hindutva-right-propaganda

Canovan, M. (1981). *Populism*. Harcourt Brace Javonovich.

Casanova, J. (2013). Exploring the postsecular: Three meanings of 'the secular' and their possible transcendence. In C. Calhoun, E. Mendieta, & J. Van Antwerpen (Eds.), *Habermas and religion* (pp. 27–48). Polity.

Chacko, P. (2018). The right turn in India: Authoritarianism, populism and neoliberalisation. *Journal of Contemporary Asia*, 48(4), 541–565. https://doi.org/10.1080/00472336.2018.1446546

De Silva, K. M. (2000). *Reaping the whirlwind: Ethnic conflict, ethnic politics in Sri Lanka*. Penguin.

Dean, K., & van der Veer, P. (2019). Introduction. In K. Dean & P. van der Veer (Eds.), *The secular in South, East, Southeast Asia* (pp. 1–12). Palgrave Macmillan. https://doi.org/10.1007/978-3-319-89369-3_1

Dhanagare, D. N. (2015). *Populism and power: Farmers' movement in western India, 1980–2014*. Routledge.

Edwards, S. (2019). On Latin American populism, and its echoes around the world. *Journal of Economic Perspectives*, 33(4), 76–99. https://doi.org/10.1257/jep.33.4.76

Goodwin, J. (2001). *No other way out: States and revolutionary movements, 1945–1991*. Cambridge University Press.

Habermas, J. (2006). On the relations between the secular liberal state and religion. In H. de Vries & L. E. Sullivan (Eds.), *Political theologies: Public religion in a post-secular world* (pp. 251–260). Fordham University Press.

Hadiz, V. R. (2016). *Islamic populism in Indonesia and the Middle East*. Cambridge University Press.

Hansson, E., Hewison, K., & Glassman, J. (2020). Legacies of the Cold War in East and Southeast Asia: An introduction. *Journal of Contemporary Asia*, 50(4), 493–510. https://doi.org/10.1080/00472336.2020.1758955

Hazlitt, W. (1819). *Political essays, with sketches of public characters*. William Hone.

Hefner, R. W. (2018). The religious field: Plural legacies and contemporary contestations. In R. W. Hefner (Ed.) *Routledge handbook of contemporary Indonesia* (pp. 211–225). Routledge. https://doi.org/10.4324/9781315628837

Jayawardena, K. (1985). *Ethnic and class conflict in Sri Lanka*. Kumaran Publishers.

Johnson, I. (2017). *The souls of China: The return of religion after Mao*. Pantheon Books.

Laborde, C. (2021). Minimal secularism: Lessons for, and from, India. *American Political Science Review*, 115(1), 1–13. https://doi.org/10.1017/S0003055420000775

Lai, A. E. (2010). Religious diversity in Singapore. In T. Chong (Ed.), *Management of success: Singapore revisited* (pp. 309–331). ISEAS.

Lim, F. K. G., & Sng, B. B. (2021). *Christianity and social engagement in China*. Routledge. https://doi.org/10.4324/9781003006503

Liow, J. C. (2016). *Religion and nationalism in Southeast Asia*. Cambridge University Press.

Marzouki, N. (2022). Populism and religion. In L. Manucci (Ed.), *The populism interviews: A dialogue with leading experts* (pp. 152–158). Routledge.

Mehta, S., & Sinha, S. (2022). The rise and fall of agrarian populism in post-colonial India: Farmers' movements and electoral politics at crossroads. *Sociological Bulletin*, 71(4), 601–618. https://doi.org/10.1177/00380229221116944

Ngo, T. T. T., & Quijada, J. B. (2015). Introduction: Atheist secularism and its discontent. In T. T. T. Ngo & J. B. Quijada (Eds.), *Atheist secularism and its discontent: A comparative study of religion and communism in Eurasia* (pp. 1–26). Palgrave Macmillan.

Palaver, W. (2019). Populism and religion: On the politics of fear. *Dialog: A Journal of Theology*, 58(1), 22–29. https://doi.org/10.1111/dial.12450

Roy, O. (2016). Beyond populism: The conservative right, the courts, the churches and the concept of a Christian Europe. In N. Marzouki, D. McDonnell & O. Roy (Eds.), *Saving the people: How populists hijack religion* (pp. 185–202). Hurst.

Singh, B. (2006). Politics of identities: Global, South Asian and Indian perspective. *The Indian Journal of Political Science*, 205–220. https://doi.org/10.2307/41856209

Subedi, D. B. (2022). The emergence of populist nationalism and 'illiberal' peacebuilding in Sri Lanka. *Asian Studies Review*, 46(2), 272–292. https://doi.org/10.1080/10357823.2021.1983519

Subedi, D. B., & Garnett, J. (2020). De-mystifying Buddhist religious extremism in Myanmar: Confrontation and contestation around religion, development and state-building. *Conflict, Security & Development*, 20(2), 223–246. https://doi.org/10.1080/14678802.2020.1739859

Subedi, D. B., & Scott, A. (2021). Populism, authoritarianism, and charismatic-plebiscitary leadership in contemporary Asia: A comparative perspective from India and Myanmar. *Contemporary Politics*, 27(5), 487–507. https://doi.org/10.1080/13569775.2021.1917162

Vaishnav, M. (2019). Religious nationalism and India's future. In M. Vaishnav (Ed.), *The BJP in power: Indian democracy and religious nationalism* (pp. 5–21). Carnegie Endowment for International Peace.

van der Veer, P. (2019). The secular in India and China. In K. Dean & P. van der Veer (Eds.), *The secular in South, East and Southeast Asia* (pp. 37–50). Palgrave Macmillan.

Washbrook, D. (2019). Forms of citizenship in pre-modern South India. *Citizenship Studies*, 23(3), 224–239. https://doi.org/10.1080/13621025.2019.1603270.

Yang, F. (2011). *Religion in China*. Oxford University Press.

Yilmaz, I., & Morieson, N. (2022). Religious populisms in the Asia Pacific. *Religions*, 13(9), 1–18. https://doi.org/10.3390/rel13090802

Zulehner, P. (2016, August 19). Fürchtet Euch nicht! [fear not!] *Zeit Online*. www.zeit.de/2016/35/angst-klima-politik-vertrauen-debatte-glaube

10
ISLAM AND POPULISM IN THE ASIA PACIFIC

Ihsan Yilmaz and Syaza Shukri

Introduction

Adherents of Islam comprise 24% of the global population, making it the world's second most followed religion (Lipka, 2017; Park, 2004). Countries with a Muslim majority have a predominant global coverage from the Middle East and North Africa (MENA) to East Asia, while a significant number of Muslim diasporas have spread throughout the world (Lipka, 2017). Historically, countries with Muslim-majority populations have fared poorly in democratization and in granting their citizens the basic freedoms considered inviolable human rights in Western society. There is no clear evidence that this lack of progress is caused by faith—rather, there are a host of explanations, including socioeconomic circumstances (Pryor, 2007; Şahin, 2006; Kamrava, 2005). Several Muslim-majority countries saw a move towards democratization as part of the global trend in the late 20th century. However, given the weak institutional structures and preliminary phases of democracy, populism may be found within the democratic systems of most Muslim-majority countries (Yilmaz et al., 2021; Shukri & Smajljaj, 2020).

Populism in Muslim-majority countries has flourished in the form of political parties and religious organizations that play a key role in political lobbying. In a more informal space, populist narratives have also been used by fundamentalist Islamist groups (Salazar, 2017; Hadiz, 2014; Jati, 2013). In Indonesia, groups such as *Front Pembela Islam* (Islamic Defenders Front, or FPI) have gathered support with their anti-Western, anti-Sino, and anti-elite rhetoric combined with Salafi-inspired morality (Barton et al., 2021). Terrorist organizations such as al-Qaida and ISIS have also used Islamist populism to weave a narrative of victimhood that motivates 'the people' to participate in *jihad* to safeguard them against 'the others' (Yilmaz et al., 2021). Moreover, in seemingly democratic countries, Islamist populism has become mainstream, as evidenced by the rise of *Adalet ve Kalkınma Partisi* (the Justice and Development Party or AKP) in Turkey in response to Imran Khan's call for the creation of *Riyasat-e-Medina* (State of Medina) in Pakistan (Yilmaz, 2021; Yilmaz et al., 2021; Yilmaz & Shakil, 2021a, 2021b; Hadiz, 2014).

This chapter examines how populism and religion exist in Muslim-majority contexts in electoral democracies, where 'the people' and 'the others' are cast and mobilized with the use of emotions and civilizational divides. We look at the idea of *Islamism*, which is used by populist actors. Islamism offers 'material and cultural understandings of religion' and is 'a multivalent religio-moral populism—a potentially explosive articulation of different class interests and religious cravings' (Tugal, 2002, p. 86). The rise of Islamism in the 20th century was due to the rejection by Muslims of secularism and modernity. As a discourse, Islamism constructs a social reality in religion, and thus creates a dichotomy of 'us' against the non-Islamic 'others', which is widely understood to be the discourse of populist leaders. Similar to other populists, those rooted in Islamism seek to correct the system by forcing upon the nation a true Islamic system that happens to be the supposed will of the people. The framing and use of Islamism as a populist tool allow for an understanding of how Islamic ideas 'of justice, particularly economic justice' are used and positioned as 'notions of elites acting unjustly towards "the people"' (Yilmaz et al., 2021).

Relationship between Islam and populism

Muslim-majority geographies are not witnessing the first wave of populism. Decolonization in the first half of the 20th century paved the way for many freedom movements and post-freedom political scenarios which saw the rise of pan-Islamism. The underlying assumption of pan-Islamism made it a transnational call for unification of the *ummah* under the banner of Islam (Formichi, 2010; Aydın, 2006). The ummah is a body that is united and identified primarily by faith rather than ethnicity or geography (Formichi, 2010; Aydın, 2006).

One of the early examples of populism manifested in the form of the *Khilafat* (Caliphate) Movement in the British-ruled subcontinent (1919–1924). An offshoot of the nationalist movement against colonialism in India, the Khilafat Movement aimed at uniting Muslims to rally support for the Ottoman Empire after it faced a precarious future in the aftermath of World War I (Pernau-Reifeld, 1999). Thousands of kilometres away from Anatolia, the Muslims of India led a zealous movement that aimed to save the 'sacred' leadership of the ummah, which was later dissolved in 1924 (Pernau-Reifeld, 1999; Trivedi, 1981, pp. 458–67).

Another example of pan-Islamism was found in Egypt, where the populism of Gamal Abdel Nasser led to a union of Muslim states. This pan-Islamist union was the manifestation of the *ummah* ideology (Lahouari & Roberts, 2017, p. 210; Crabbs, 1975). He also used populism, nationalism, socialism, and pan-Arabism in his narrative of ushering Egypt into an era of great socioeconomic improvement (Yilmaz, 2020a).

Deep into the Cold War, Islamist populism remained a part of the political discourse (Casanova, 1994). Post-revolutionary Iran is one example of Islamist populism from the 1980s (Zúquete, 2017, p. 449; Dorraj, 2014, pp. 134–140). Most recently, Islamist associations such as al-Qaeda calling for a so-called 'Global Jihad' exhibit populist elements, in which the ummah is supposedly victimized and oppressed by non-Muslims and secular elites (Yilmaz et al., 2021; Zúquete, 2017, p. 449).

Islamic populist framing may appear in the form of nationalism or civilizationism, and they often operate in combination (Yilmaz et al., 2021). Embedded in both are the ideas of material and social injustice that serve the purpose of creating horizontal (anti-others) and vertical (anti-elites) populist divides. Both variations have found electoral success in diverse Muslim-majority countries (Hadiz, 2018, p. 567). Hadiz (2018, p. 567) looks particularly at Indonesia, Egypt, Tunisia, and Turkey with observations about populist usage of Islamism as 'cultural idioms associated with Islam are required . . . for the mobilization of a distinctly ummah-based political identity in contests over power and resources in the present democratic period'.

Like populists around the world, Islamist populist leaders use emotional references to substantiate their rhetoric. Populist leaders tend to 'identify with key religious figures from early Islamic history' (Yilmaz et al., 2021). In a neo-Ottoman fashion, President Erdogan of Turkey likes to display himself as Caliph for the ummah, and Imran Khan of Pakistan draws inspiration from the political and social model of the Prophet and his companions ('My Inspirations Are Prophet Muhammad', 2018; also see Chapter 14 in this volume). Turkey's brand of restorative nationalism under Islamist populism may be more disruptive than other categories of nationalism, according to Ding et al. (2021). Usage of populist religious imagery evokes emotions that create a feeling of 'heartland' and hopes of achieving the utopia that populists paint (Taggart, 2004).

A range of negative emotions is also used by Islamist populists, aimed at exploiting pre-existing vulnerabilities of citizens, aiding in 'public support in contests over power and resources based on an ummah-based political identity' (Hadiz, 2018, p. 567). Yilmaz and Morieson (2021) noted this instrumentalization, remarking:

> Populists can instrumentalize religion in a variety of ways. Religion can help sacralize 'the people' by tying them to an existing religious tradition. Religion can also be used to perpetuate an 'us vs. them' mentality—the religion of 'the people' can be framed positively, while the religion (or lack of religion) of 'others' can be demonized as an existential threat to 'us'.

As part of this process, 'the others' or 'the elite' are highly stigmatized and turned into 'the enemy', and 'the people' are shown to be 'victims' of the antagonists. This supports the populist claim to be the 'saviours'.

Political survey of Muslim-majority countries in the Asia Pacific

Pakistan

Founded in 1947 as the British withdrew from South Asia, Pakistan was created primarily for the Muslim minority of India. The country is densely populated, and more than half of its rapidly expanding population is under the age of 35. Over centuries, the region has blended Hellenistic, Persian, Gandharan, Vedic, Arab, Central Asian, Turkish, and European influences; it is largely a Muslim country, but its cultural values are diverse.

To date, Pakistan has witnessed four military dictatorships, three outright military confrontations with India, and an ethnically driven civil war in 1970 that split the country and granted Bangladesh its independence. The country's first free general elections took place in 1970, following the end of Ayyub Khan's military regime. Populist leader Zulfiqar Ali Bhutto and his Pakistan Peoples Party (PPP) rose to power, with Bhutto assuming leadership until 1977. Unlike Islamist populists today, Bhutto represented left-wing populism pitted against the elite and portrayed himself to be one among the people. Unable to deliver his socialist promises of 'bread, clothing, and shelter,' Bhutto faced growing unrest. As state oppression grew, massive anti-state protests led to political instability, and the country was plunged into its third dictatorship.

Prime Minister Bhutto's daughter galvanized popular support in the 1988 elections based on an anti-establishment narrative against the former regime. Ironically, Benazir Bhutto soon lost her government to Muhammad Nawaz Sharif, as he aroused popular support by positioning himself as a right-wing conservative who did not belong to dynastic politics, as opposed to the 'elite', 'corrupt', and 'Western' Bhutto. As we see the split of populism in Pakistan between those on the left and the right, the versatility of populism becomes obvious as a discursive strategy. After four failed governments, General Pervez Musharraf took power until he was forced to resign in 2008.

In the 21st century, Pakistan has witnessed the widespread prevalence of populism in its many forms. Anti-state narratives have been used by the opposition, ruling governments, and religious factions. Amidst increased instances of domestic terrorism in 2007, Benazir Bhutto was murdered during her election campaign. Before her assassination, Bhutto was able to give the PPP populist momentum by addressing issues close to the people such as terrorism, income inequality, and Afghan immigration. Her death made her a martyr who was 'sacrificed for democracy' ('The Bhutto Populism', 2009).

The 2013 election was won by Sharif and his party, the Pakistan Muslim League-Nawaz (PLM[N]). Returning from self-exile, Sharif was able to appeal to the people as a vanguard of democracy, as opposed to the Zardari-led PPP, which was engulfed in corruption scandals. As a centre-right party, PLM(N) promised a 'stronger economy' for a 'strong Pakistan' and vowed to make neoliberal reforms, solve the country's energy crises, invest in counterterrorism legislation, and create jobs for the youth by supporting investments and infrastructure projects. Positioning himself as a counter to the 'corrupt PPP', Sharif's party was able to win 166 of 342 seats in the National Assembly.

These elections also ushered the populist *Pakistan Tehreek-e-Insaf* (PTI), or Pakistan Movement for Justice, into the limelight. PTI was formed in 1996 by Pakistan's beloved former national cricket captain and philanthropist Imran Khan. Using his public image as the 'captain' who had achieved the impossible for Pakistan, Khan formed the PTI with a manifesto of expanding welfare, fighting corruption, and ending dynastic politics in Pakistan (Paracha, 2020; Findlay & Bokhari, 2019; Mulla, 2017). After boycotting the 2008 elections on grounds of lack of transparency, PTI launched its 2013 campaign through social media and general rallies. To affirm his stance as pro-democracy, Khan held a U.S.-style intra-party election to ensure his voters a fresh alternative to the 'dynastic politics' of the PPP and PML(N).

In 2014, PTI was able to amass support while running on a populist platform. Following the election, Khan led an *Azadi* or Freedom March, dismissing the election results and calling out vote-rigging. PTI's protests were informally synchronized with the *Pakistan Awami Tehreek*'s (PAT), an Islamic party led by cleric Muhammad Tahir-ul-Qadri, aligning Khan with a far-right Islamic party. Although PTI was yet to manipulate civilizational discourse, its affiliation with PAT put it on the track to becoming an Islamist populist movement. Also called the 'tsunami march', it led to the closure of the capital for over two weeks. Police crackdowns in Islamabad dismantled the protests and led to injuries among journalists, women, and children, with mass arrests of PTI workers following. This earned the Sharif government an undemocratic reputation in popular media at home, while the fight for justice by PTI and PAT was reflective of Islamism (Mulla, 2017).

As the opposition leader, Khan's appeal grew and his social media campaigns portrayed him as a contemporary *Jinnah*, a 'just man' who would dedicate his life to the people. He was able to mobilize young voters with the hope of delivering *Naya Pakistan* or 'New

Pakistan' by exploiting emotion and attachment in modelling Pakistan on the idealized and romanticized state of Medina (Bukhari, 2018). His welfare-focused promises appealed to the poor. Instead of being a left-wing populist, Khan's fiery and angry speeches condemning International Monetary Fund (IMF) borrowing and Western interference situated him within the anti-Western rhetoric that is typical of an Islamist populist. He earned further popular support through his 2015 emotional pronouncement, 'I will prefer death over a begging bowl' (A. Hussain, 2019).

In 2018, PTI won a majority of seats in the National Assembly and Khan launched his '100 Day Plan', which promised somewhat exciting and magical antidotes to Pakistan's chronic problems by generating tax revenue, weeding out corruption, supporting industry, bolstering an economic recovery, and improving public trust in government institutions. However, due to the grand nature of these populist promises, PTI was unable to fulfil most of them (Z. Hussain, 2019; Jamal, 2018). Despite promising to return offshore wealth from 'corrupt' leaders, nothing substantive was achieved. He disappointed minorities when he was forced to drop economist Atif Main from his advisory board due to his Ahmadi background amidst pressure from extremist factions. His anti-West and anti-IMF stance was shattered when his government was forced to enter another structural adjustment program with the IMF. However, PTI was able to maintain their anti-West rhetoric such as an excessive emphasis on the politics of fear and conspiracy theories that included the CIA creating the Taliban and the West's Machiavellian intentions towards Pakistan (Abbas, 2012).

As an Islamist populist party, PTI also increased the role of religious teaching in schools under the Single National Curriculum and curbed the freedom of media outlets and social media via the Pakistan Media Regulatory Authority (Haqqani, 2020; Kamran, 2020; Shams, 2019; Chaudhry, 2018). Khan's Islamist populism also has a transnational dimension that is part of the larger Islamic civilizational discourse. His government extensively collaborated with Turkey to introduce and popularize emotional, anti-Western conspiratorial TV serials with exceedingly Islamized content. Pakistan's transmission of the Turkish TV series *Dirilis Etrugul* in Urdu, depicting the heroic war against the Crusades waged by Ertugrul Ghazi (whose son founded the Ottoman empire), is a prime example of transnational Islam-induced civilizationist populism (Yilmaz & Shakil, 2021a, 2021b).

As argued earlier, Islamist populists include in their list of 'enemies' supposed deviant Muslims. Khan has been highly unsympathetic to the plight of factions that fall outside Sunni-Islam or 'the people' (Shams, 2020). When the ethnically and religiously distinct Shia Hazara protestors refused to bury their dead after repeated loss of life due to targeted terrorism, Khan said their right to protest was the victim's way of 'blackmailing' him ('India Backing IS', 2021). The government also washed its hands of assuming responsibility for the attack by conveniently blaming India for sponsoring terrorism in Pakistan. A similar attitude of Khan's Islamist populism surfaced when he called the *Aurat March*'s (Women's March) feminist slogans a 'Western concept' and highly unnecessary in a Muslim society where women are supposedly highly protected and respected—contrary to the statistical evidence on violence against women in Pakistan ('PM Imran Khan', 2020).

The rise of the ultra-right Islamist party *Tehreek-e-Labbaik Pakistan* (TLP) shows a nexus between religious extremism and populism. The party was founded in 2015 and initially led by Khadim Hussain Rizvi (1966–2020), a cleric from the Barelvi school of Islam. Rizvi's anti-establishment rhetoric earned him a strong following among rural and peri-urban voters as well as madrassa schools. The group views the government as 'puppets' installed by Western nations, argues that Pakistan should be a 'true Islamic state,' and wants to curb any form of expression that they deem as 'blasphemous'.

TLP has repeatedly demonstrated its street power by launching mass protests such as the Faizabad Sittings (2017) and the anti-Ahmadi protest, as well as anti-blasphemy activism and protests against any films they deem anti-Islamic. They also incite hate speech through social media, which led to the murder of a schoolteacher by his student (a TLP follower) on the basis of 'perceived blasphemy' (Barker & Iqbal, 2018). The unchecked use of insults and dehumanizing language to incite radical sentiments against the state, minorities, democratic forces, and liberal factions is worrying, as TLP has shown it is able to muster dangerously radical popular support.

Despite having its third consecutive, democratically elected government in power, Pakistan is a fragile democracy. Its people have been economically stretched thin, religious-cultural divides run deep, and the slightest incidents can trigger instability. Surveillance of its people, use of security forces to curb dissent, limitation of freedom of speech, denying political space for civil society, and enforced disappearances of human rights activists continue in 'New Pakistan'. A COVID-19-ravaged economy is likely to lead to further discontent among Pakistanis, and parties such as TLP can potentially widen their populist base under such circumstances, threatening Pakistan's fragile democracy.

Malaysia

Malaysia has a highly diverse population in terms of both religion and ethnicity. By the time the country became independent, in addition to its Malay population, it had a vast number of Chinese and Indian residents who were encouraged by the British to immigrate, increasing the rubber plantation and tin mining workforces (Cavendish, 2007). Malaysia identifies as a Muslim country but allows non-Muslims the freedom to practice their faith. Since independence in 1957, its politics has been dominated by Malay Muslims, making the country fertile ground for Islamist populism. According to the constitution, Malays are automatically Muslims, and in Malaysia, only Sunnis are recognized. This segment of the population, while being the demographic majority, has been historically behind in socio-economic terms. Keeping in line with global trends, religious and nationalist populism has increasingly become a part of politics in Malaysia.

The Second World War had a pronounced impact on the country, as it was occupied by Japan until its surrender in 1945, followed by re-colonization by the British. Post-WWII, the Malay independence movement was primarily led by the Bumiputera (Indigenous) Muslims. From 1957, the year of Malaysian independence, to 2018, the United Malays National Organization (UMNO) held power continuously as the dominant party in various coalitions. Its right-wing ideology combines national and social conservatism founded on ethnic and religious ideals. The UMNO espoused Malay ethnic identity and coupled it with Islam to gain support from the majority. Since the 1970s, a series of affirmative action plans have been introduced to promote the economically disadvantaged Malay-Muslim population (Guan, 2005; Sowell, 2004). The 1970s also marked the formation of *Barisan Nasional* (BN), or National Front, a nationalist conservative pro-Malay-Muslim coalition dominated by the UMNO. In the 1980s, however, the UMNO faced a revitalized Malaysian Islamic Party (*Parti Islam Se-Malaysia*, or PAS), an Islamist party that broke away from the BN coalition in 1977. The contestation for the Malay vote thus forced the government, led by Mahathir Mohamad, to introduce further pro-Islamic policies.

Mahathir has been the longest-serving Malaysian prime minister (1981–2003; 2018–2020). He was able to consolidate power by appealing to both negative and positive emotions of conservative Muslims due to his outright pro-Malay policies that glorified Muslims and marginalized non-Malays. Although it was fundamentally an ethnocentric party, the UMNO under Mahathir justified its pro-Malay policies as a correctional measure in accord with the justice and fairness embedded in the ideas of Islamism. The UMNO successfully cast Malay Muslims as 'the people' on the same religio-cultural lines, while non-Malays and non-Muslims were 'otherized'. This process of otherization extended beyond the rhetoric, taking the form of institutional discrimination (Shah, 2019).

At the same time, Mahathir qualifies as an anti-establishment politician who introduced punch cards and name tags for civil servants to dissipate the 'elitist aura' and enable members of the public to file a complaint should they encounter a 'rude or indolent' official (Shah, 2019). Apart from his anti-elite populism, Mahathir used authoritarianism as a means of entrenching his power; for instance, he was responsible for maintaining the draconian Internal Security Act (ISA), which was used to oppress critics and evade judicial review of his government's actions, as well as to execute pro-Malay social and economic policies (Juego, 2018). In 1987, the torture of activists from a wide spectrum of political viewpoints that included feminists, environmentalists, political opposition, and leftists was also carried out under the ISA (Shah, 2019).

After 2003, the BN introduced a 'softer' version of Islam under Abdullah Badawi, and the coalition stayed in power until its historic defeat by the Pakatan Harapan (Alliance of Hope or PH) coalition in the 2018 elections. Najib Razak's infamous corruption scandal, the prolonged history of human rights violations, and mounting external debt crises had caused the UMNO party to lose its dominance after several decades (Azhari & Halim, 2021).

The 2018 elections saw two populist factions competing for power: the right-wing populism of BN-UMNO and the left-wing populism of Pakatan Harapan. BN-UMNO rallied support from the conservative Malay Muslims on the basis of ethno-religious nationalism (Shah, 2019). While it promised economic reform, its overall oratory for the election campaigns included 'ethno-religious sentiments'. The BN-UMNO successfully exploited civilizational discourse by characterizing Malays and Muslims as the 'sacred people' while the 'others' comprised Christians, Hindus, and liberals such as LGBTQ activists. It is interesting to note that the conservatives made a distinction between the 'good' minority—the Catholics—who supported them on conservative grounds, and 'bad' minorities such as non-Catholic Christians that included anti-BN Evangelicals (Shah, 2019).

The election became a battle between the BN-UMNO casting Malay Muslims as 'the sacred people' and the PH coalition campaigning against an 'out-of-touch elite' and promising to promote multiculturalism and good governance (Zaharia, 2020; Azhari & Halim, 2021). As opposed to Islamist populism, the PH utilized anti-establishment populism since the coalition represented 'the othered', encompassing secular non-Muslims, non-Malays, and soft-line Islamic groups such as the National Trust Party (Amanah), People's Justice Party (PKR), Democratic Action Party (DAP), and Malaysian United Indigenous Party (Bersatu), which was later joined by some former UMNO members (Shah, 2019, p. 57). Their populist rhetoric advocated that victimized 'citizens' reinstate their lost 'pride' and 'honour' that had been taken away by the corrupt, self-serving, and conservative establishment (Shah, 2019).

Mahathir, as the PH leader, reinvented his populist image, becoming the 'bold Mahathir', who in the 1990s was able to keep Malaysia from entering an austere IMF-imposed capital control scheme. In 2018, he pledged to keep Chinese investment loans away during a growing external debt crisis to ward off and protect the country from external influences (Zaharia, 2020), i.e., a civilizational other. He did this because he understood the Malays' emotional distrust of Chinese expatriates. Despite his authoritarian legacy, he was able to connect through praying with the common people, visiting bazaars, and in the company of his wife partaking in meals together with his supporters, thus resonating a sense of 'good family values' (Saat, 2018). By rebranding Mahathir's image, he was re-cast as a 'reformer', and the PH coalition promoted economic nationalism (Juego, 2018). However, his reformist zeal proved to be short-lived due to the growing competition from other Malay-based parties who were more brazen in taking advantage of Islamist sentiments of the populace. During Mahathir's brief second term as prime minister, he reneged on several promises such as the ratification of the International Convention on the Elimination of All Forms of Racial Discrimination (ICERD) because the Malay sector was not prepared to forego their conviction that, as the Indigenous population, they were entitled to preferential rights to land. Mahathir also attended a so-called Muslim dignity congress to appease the negative emotions and insecurities of conservative Malay Muslims. (Shukri & Smajljaj, 2020).

In several by-elections in 2019, UMNO showed signs of regaining its former level of support after entering into an alliance with PAS, a right-wing pan-Islamist party, intent on establishing a Sharia-driven Islamic state in Malaysia. The party is currently led by the conservative Muslim scholar and politician Hadi Awang, a firebrand populist who previously speared divisions in rural Malaysia with the practice of *takfir*, which otherized and hatefully targeted Muslims with alternative political views, labelling them 'infidels'. He has a record of participating in global right-wing conventions, advocating an 'Islamic awakening' (Hussin, 2018). The UMNO-PAS alliance, *Muafakat Nasional*, is preparing to consolidate voters under Islamist populism following the failure of the PH. For example, the new alliance has exploited the politics of fear, claiming that the PH government had been 'selling off' Muslim assets to non-Muslims, specifically targeting the PH's Chinese finance minister, Lim Guan Eng. Thus, the Malay Muslims of Malaysia are depicted as being under threat due to the presence of an ethnically diverse executive (Shukri, 2021).

Despite domestic challenges to its commitment to Islam, in 2019, Malaysia hosted the Kuala Lumpur Summit in close collaboration with Turkey to discuss issues such as the global persecution of Muslims and Islamophobia. The Organization of Islamic Cooperation refused to participate and pressured Pakistan out of the summit ('Muslim Leaders Gather', 2019). Recent Malaysian Islamist populist discourse incorporates a civilizational dimension, in which Malaysian leaders project connecting with the global ummah as part of a larger Islamic civilization. This is not an unprecedented development, as Malaysia has sheltered religious scholars such as Zakir Naik, who fled India after being charged with spreading hate speech and embezzling funds (Rodzi, 2019; Mukhopadhyay, 2020).

Under intense pressure due to its inability to fulfil populist promises such as abolishing tolls and student loans, the PH government collapsed in 2020. Mahathir resigned from office and the coalition's leadership sidelined vocal Malay advocate, Anwar Ibrahim, the presumptive heir to the top post. Based on his activism, Anwar had secured the support of urban Malay Muslims, while his anti-establishment stance resulted in him leading a strong coalition of Chinese and Indian Malaysians. Nonetheless, Muhyiddin Yassin of the Bersatu

Party was appointed as prime minister in 2020 by the monarch. While in power, Muhyiddin used UMNO-established repressive laws to curb the opposition ('Anwar Ibrahim Is in a Familiar Place', 2020). COVID-19 caused further instability, and the prime ministership of the Bersatu leader lasted only 17 months before he was replaced by UMNO's Ismail Sabri Yaakob, further prolonging Malaysia's lengthy experience of Islamist populism.

Indonesia

Indonesia is mainly situated in Southeast Asia, although several of its islands are located within Oceania. It is a collection of islands, the biggest island country in the world, with Java representing the largest and most populous of its landmasses. Over the centuries, the islands have been influenced by Hinduism, Buddhism, Islam, and Christianity, giving it a diverse culture, despite its current demographic status as a Muslim-majority nation. The first Europeans to arrive in the region were the Portuguese in 1512, followed by the British and the Dutch. During the 17th century, the Dutch East India Company established a stronghold following the formal colonization of the territory under its former name, the Dutch East Indies, in 1800.

The national ideology of Indonesia is *Pancasila*, or the Five Principles (nationalism, internationalism, democracy, social prosperity, and belief in God). After a turbulent political beginning, the country was governed by means of 'guided democracy' which was an autocratic rule supported and justified by the cause of political stability (Palmier, 1957). During the 1960s, the Sukarno regime supported the Communist Party of Indonesia (PKI); however, this move alienated two powerful stakeholders—the military and Islamic factions. In 1967, with the people's support, the armed forces and Islamist political groups were able to force Sukarno to resign.

The appointment of Suharto as the second president did little to change the political structure of the country, as his rule also developed into a dictatorship. Under his 'New Order', the country was ruled by a centralized military-led government until Suharto's forced resignation in 1998 (Sub, 2016). Understanding the importance of the Islamic factions, Suharto did not oppose them. A general renewal of a more conservative Islamic popular identification became prominent in the early 1970s, and there were calls for the institutionalization of 'political Islam'. This was tied to the emergence of a Muslim middle class that had remained secondary to the successful quasi-secular business class of predominately Chinese ethnicity (Sidel, 2008). However, the 1997 Asian financial crisis promoted a wave of dissatisfaction among the masses. Corruption led to an outbreak of ethnic riots targeting Chinese Indonesians that developed into nationwide unrest. Police brutality turned peaceful protests into riots that paralyzed the country's capital, Jakarta. Thousands of university students demanded Suharto's resignation and all attempts to delay his resignation were rejected (Sub, 2016).

The impact of two successive dictatorships is integral to the contemporary socio-political dynamics of the country. Firstly, the fall of Suharto led to greater political freedoms, which had been curtailed for decades. This created an opportunity for the emergence of Islamic political parties and liberal groups, dividing the political spectrum (Zarkasyi, 2008). Historically, most religious parties in Indonesia have been unable to make an impact alone and have formed alliances with the government or opposition (Barton et al., 2021). Secondly, post-Suharto, the complete 'consolidation' of democratic forces did not take place. Instead, years of wealth generation among a handful of elites ushered in an era of oligarchic rule

(Fukuoka, 2013). This allowed for the rise of Megawati Sukarnoputri, who has been described as an anti-elite populist despite being the daughter of the first president (Ziv, 2001).

The 2014 Indonesian presidential election brought two faces of populism into the country: the traditional anti-elite populist Prabowo Subianto of the Great Indonesia Movement Party (Gerindra), and Joko Widodo—popularly known as Jokowi and described as a polite populist—representing the Indonesian Democratic Party of Struggle (PDI-P) (Mietzner, 2014, 2015). Subianto, a former general of the army and former son-in-law of Suharto, left his Golkar Party to form the Gerindra, a right-wing populist party. With loyal supporters mainly among the rural population and the working-class, he promised to revamp the corrupt government and tackle the people's problems with his military-style efficiency. This placed him in the role of a classic third-world populist leader—a member of the elite who claims to empathize with the suffering of the masses. However, this comes with an authoritarian overtone centred around the personality of the leader (Mietzner, 2015).

Opposing Subianto was Jokowi, a self-made man who introduced a milder and more pragmatic brand of populism in Indonesia. From a humble, often indigent family background, he rose to become the mayor of his hometown Surakarta and later governor of Jakarta. His unassuming origins and grassroots linkages provided Jokowi with the credentials to challenge the arrogant and hostile political status quo (Mietzner, 2015). Rather than promising the voters a 'grand clean up' of the political system, his campaign focused on a promise to provide people with improved services, akin to the left-wing populists of Latin America. His record of having improved health services and education in the constituencies he had represented established his credibility in the eyes of voters (Mietzner, 2015).

During his first term, Widodo faced many challenges, but his non-confrontational style aided him in dealing with the oligarchy and military. However, increasing pro-Islamic sentiment severely threatened his position. Early in his presidency, the Front Pembela Islam (FPI) reacted in outrage to an alleged blasphemy that disrespected the Quran, uttered by Jakarta's governor, a Christian of Chinese ethnicity known as Ahok. While the FPI had been formed in 1998 by the Salafi-inspired cleric Muhammad Rizieq Shihab, it opportunistically claimed the moral high ground in the Ahok affair (Maulia, 2020; Nuryanti, 2021; Adiwilaga et al., 2019). When a video of Ahok discussing Quranic verses surfaced, it was elevated by right-wing factions to the level of a national scandal and used to curtail Ahok's political future and further stir the negative emotions of the Islamic masses (Nuryanti, 2021). *Majlis Ulama Indonesia* (Indonesian Ulama Council or MUI) issued a *fatwa* (ruling) claiming that Ahok had indeed committed blasphemy and hurt the sentiments of Indonesian Muslims (Nuryanti, 2021; Mietzner, 2018). The next few months saw a mass wave of angry anti-Ahok protests which led to the former governor being tried and jailed with his political career destroyed (Nuryanti, 2021).

With over one million Muslims who felt their religion was under attack participating in rallies across the country in 2016 and 2017, Islamist populism was ripe for the picking. Jokowi's hard stance against radical Islamic groups and his counter-terrorism policies also earned him the disfavour of moderate religious organizations such as the Islamic Community Forum (*Forum Umat Islam* or FUI). Even before the protest, FPI's Rizieq had labelled Jokowi a 'troublemaker' and 'bringer of disasters' who had opened the 'Golden Entry Gate for non-Muslims to dominate and control the system' (Aspinall & Mietzner, 2019). In other words, Jokowi is guilty by his association with 'the others' being non-Muslim Chinese. Thus, the Ahok protests were not random or isolated. The political opportunity was taken up by Prabowo Subianto, who was closely allied with FPI and the anti-Ahok momentum.

During one of his speeches, Subianto took an apologist approach towards Islamist terrorists by blaming poverty on foreign forces exploiting vulnerable Indonesians, implying that the West is the enemy of mostly Muslim Indonesians in an attempt to stir anti-Western emotions (Kennedy, 2019). While Subinato lost the elections, the Ahok events made a dent in Indonesian politics. To offset the accusation that he lacked 'strong Islamic credentials', Jokowi picked an Islamic cleric, Ma'ruf Amin, formerly president of Nahdlatul Ulama, the nation's largest Muslim organization, as his running mate and current vice-president (Yilmaz, 2020b).

The FPI promotes the implementation of sharia in Indonesia, which it views as the perfect 'divine law', espousing justice and fairness, and thus fit to replace the anthropogenic constitution (Barton, 2021; Mietzner, 2018; Hadiz, 2016, p. 112). This belief is central to FPI Salafi-inspired civilizationism that seeks to 'purify' Indonesia, as reflected in Rizieq's tweets that merge Islamism, nationalism, and the politics of fear: 'Do you want NKRI [Indonesia] to be Syariah [sharia]? Do you want Indonesia to be blessed? Do you want the State and Nation to be safe?' ('Dukung Prabowo', 2018). A highly alarming aspect of FPI civilizationism has manifested in various members joining *jihad* via terrorist organizations such as al-Qaeda and ISIS through their local chapters ('Jihadi Recruitment', 2021; Idris, 2018, p. 9l).

Conclusion

The Islam and populism nexus is closely related to the political form of Islam—Islamism. Islamism is deeply wedded to Islamic ideas of justice and can easily be attached to populism, which is itself based on notions of elites acting unjustly towards 'the people'.

Islamist populist framing may take on nationalist forms or civilizationist forms, though often these are found in combination. In Islamist populist discourse, the vertical and horizontal dimensions of populism emphasize civilizational and theological differences between groups. Civilizationism is, thus, a common feature of Islamist populism in the Asia Pacific. Indeed, most often, Islamist populists couch their nationalism within a wider civilizationist frame, informed by Islamist notions of a cosmic battle between 'good' Muslims and 'evil' non-Muslims.

Islamist populists resort to the politics of fear in warning Muslims that their religion is under attack, aiming to mobilize and rally the Islamic masses under the banner of their religion. They elicit public emotions which produce the demand for civilizationism—anger towards the secular ruling class, fear of non-Muslims, a belief in a divine right to exclusive ownership of their homeland, and a desire to protect Islam from its non-Muslim internal and external enemies.

Islamist populists take advantage of the transnational nature of the Muslim community to construct a civilizational populist rhetoric in which Islamist populism transcends national boundaries. The ummah became the basis for Islamist populists to situate one nation's crisis within a global narrative of Muslim civilization.

Islamist populism takes diverse forms, which can manifest as political parties, religious groups, and political lobbyists. While differing in position and strategies, they share a common sense of populist divisions cast on religious lines that take a civilizational form. The demand in the political status quo for this populism is created by the extensive use of feel-good and feel-bad emotional appeals attached to the duality of 'the people' and 'the others'.

A populist leader acting out a 'symbolically mediated performance' claims to represent the people against an enemy embedded in the current system (Moffitt, 2016). In today's Europe, populists are typically anti-liberal, anti-elite, and anti-immigrant, on the right of the political spectrum, but in Venezuela, President Chavez represents left-wing populism supportive of socialist patriotism against neoliberal capitalism. Among Muslim countries in Asia, populist leaders such as Imran Khan and Mahathir Mohamad conform to Europe's current right-wing populism in their reliance on exclusivist rhetoric, but differ from their European counterparts in their otherizing of religious deviants and non-Muslims among their citizenries. Similar to a populist narrative of a constant state of crisis, populists such as Rizieq Shihab preferred a direct link to the people, bypassing the purportedly corrupt state institutions to enumerate the ills of the system and the need for change. In the case of these Islamist populists, that change is understood through discourse on Islamism. While the recent rise of populism in Europe can be traced to the 2008–2011 global financial crisis, the rise of Islamist populism has followed mass protests over government incompetence, such as the 2014 Azadi March in Pakistan, the 2017 anti-Ahok rallies in Indonesia, and the general protest against the Pakatan Harapan government in Malaysia.

References

Abbas, A. (2012, November 2). Khan, Taliban and the Crackpot Science. *Dawn*. www.dawn.com/news/760981/khan-taliban-and-the-crackpot-science

Adiwilaga, R., Mustofa, M. U., & Rahman, M. R. T. (2019). Quo vadis Islamic populism? An electoral strategy. *Central European Journal of International and Security Studies*, 13(4), 432–453. https://cejiss.org/images/issue_articles/2019-volume-13-issue-4/26-quo-vadis-islamic-populism-an-electoral-strategy.pdf

Anwar Ibrahim is in a familiar place, close to leading Malaysia. (2020, October 3). *The Economist*. https://www.economist.com/asia/2020/10/03/anwar-ibrahim-is-in-a-familiar-place-close-to-leading-malaysia

Aspinall, E., & Mietzner, M. (2019). Indonesia's democratic paradox: Competitive elections amidst rising illiberalism. *Bulletin of Indonesian Economic Studies*, 55(3), 295–317. https://doi.org/10.1080/00074918.2019.1690412

Aydın, C. (2006). Beyond civilization: Pan-Islamism, Pan-Asianism and the Revolt against the West. *Journal of Modern European History/Zeitschrift Für Moderne Europäische Geschichte/Revue D'histoire Européenne Contemporaine*, 4(2), 204–223. www.jstor.org/stable/26265834

Azhari, A., & Halim, F. A. (2021). The changing nature of populism in Malaysia. In S. J. Lee, C. Wu & K. K. Bandyopadhyay (Eds.), *Populism in Asian democracies* (pp. 147–162). Brill.

Barker, M., & Iqbal, A. (2018, November 2). Asia-Bibi: Anti-blasphemy protests spread across Pakistan. *The Guardian*. https://www.theguardian.com/world/2018/nov/01/asia-bibi-anti-blasphemy-protests-spread-across-pakistan

Barton, G. (2021). Contesting Indonesia's democratic transition: Laskar Jihad, the Islamic Defenders Front (FPI) and Civil Society. In A. Vandenberg & N. Zuryani (Eds.), *Security, democracy, and society in Bali* (pp. 305–331). Palgrave Macmillan.

Barton, G., Yilmaz, I., & Morieson, N. (2021). Religious and pro-violence populism in Indonesia: The rise and fall of a far-right Islamist civilisationist movement. *Religions*, 12, 397. https://doi.org/10.3390/rel12060397

The Bhutto populism. (2009, November 22). *The Nation*. https://nation.com.pk/22-Nov-2009/the-bhutto-populism

Bukhari, G. (2018, August 25). Imran Khan wants to create a Medina-like Pakistan but he is no sentinel of human rights. *In Print*. https://theprint.in/opinion/imran-khan-wants-to-create-a-medina-like-pakistan-but-he-is-no-sentinel-of-human-rights/104903/

Casanova, J. (1994). *Public religions in the modern world*. University of Chicago.

Cavendish, R. (2007, August). Malayan Independence. *History Today*, 57(8). www.historytoday.com/archive-independence
Chaudhry, F. (2018, September 8). Under pressure govt backtracks on Atif Mian's appointment; Removes economist from advisory council. *Dawn*. www.dawn.com/news/1431495
Crabbs, J. (1975). Politics, history, and culture in Nasser's Egypt. *International Journal of Middle East Studies*, 6(4), 386–420. https://www.jstor.org/stable/162751
Ding, I., Slater, D., & Zengin, H. (2021). Populism and the past: Restoring, retaining, and redeeming the nation. *Studies in Comparative International Development*, 56, 148–1469. https://doi.org/10.1007/s12116-021-09333-w
Dorraj, M. (2014). Iranian populism: Its vicissitudes and political impact. In D. Woods & B. Wejnert (Eds.), *The many faces of populism: Current perspectives* (pp. 127–42). Emerald Books.
Dukung Prabowo, Rizieq Shihab lempar isu NKRI Bersyariah [Support Prabowo, Rizieq Shihab throws the issue of the unitary Republic of Indonesia]. (2018, September 17). *CNN Indonesia*. www.cnnindonesia.com/nasional/20180917142559-32-330808/dukung-prabowo-rizieq-shihab-lempar-isunkri-bersyariah#
Findlay, S., & Bokhari, F. (2019, May 16). Imran Khan swallows pride to clinch toughest IMF bailout yet. *Financial Times*. www.ft.com/content/10318f10-7677-11e9-bbad-7c18c0ea0201
Formichi, C. (2010). Pan-Islam and religious nationalism: The case of Kartosuwiryo and Negara Islam Indonesia. *Indonesia*, 90, 125–146. http://www.jstor.org/stable/20798235
Fukuoka, Y. (2013). Oligarchy and democracy in post-Suharto Indonesia. *Political Studies Review*, 11(1), 52–64. https://doi.org/10.1111/j.1478-9302.2012.00286.x
Guan, L. H. (2005). Affirmative action in Malaysia. In C. K. Wah & D. Singh (Eds.), *Southeast Asian Affairs 2005* (pp. 211–228). ISEAS Publishing.
Hadiz, V. R. (2014). A new Islamic populism and the contradictions of development. *Journal of Contemporary Asia*, 44(1), 125–143. https://doi.org/10.1080/00472336.2013.832790
Hadiz, V. R. (2016). *Islamic populism in Indonesia and the Middle East*. Cambridge University Press.
Hadiz, V. R. (2018). Imagine all the people? Mobilising Islamic populism for right-wing politics in Indonesia. *Journal of Contemporary Asia*, 48(4), 566–83. https://doi.org/10.1080/00472336.2018.1433225
Haqqani, H. (2020, August 11). Imran Khan's populism clashes with Pakistan's economic realities. *The Diplomat*. https://thediplomat.com/2020/08/imran-khans-populism-clashes-with-pakistans-economic-realities/
Hussain, A. (2019, August 25). Imran Khan: A year facing Pakistan's harsh realities. *BBC*. www.bbc.com/news/world-asia-49450145
Hussain, Z. (2019, April 10). PTI in la-la land. *Dawn*. www.dawn.com/news/1475122/pti-in-la-la-land
Hussin, R. (2018, January 21). Unmasking the recalcitrant Hadi. *MalaysiaKini*. www.malaysiakini.com/news/409460
Idris, I. (2018, September). Youth vulnerability to violent extremist groups in the Indo-Pacific. *GSDRC*. https://gsdrc.org/publications/youth-vulnerability-to-violent-extremist-groups-in-the-indo-pacific/
India backing IS to spread unrest in Pakistan: PM Imran on Hazara killings. (2021, January 10). *Dawn*. www.dawn.com/news/1600800
Jamal, N. (2018, November 29). 100 day roundup. *Dawn*. www.dawn.com/news/1447754/100-day-roundup-has-the-pti-government-delivered-on-its-promises
Jati, W. R. (2013). Radicalism in the perspective of Islamic-populism: Trajectory of political Islam in Indonesia. *Journal of Indonesian Islam*, 7(2), 268–287. https://doi.org/10.15642/JIIS.2013.7.2.268-287
Jihadi recruitment and return: Asian threat and response. (2021, September 21). *MEI@75*. www.mei.edu/publications/jihadi-recruitment-and-return-asian-threat-and-response
Juego, B. (2018). *Human rights against populism: A progressive response to the politics of Duterte and Mahathir*. Heinrich Böll Stiftung. https://th.boell.org/en/2018/12/28/human-rights-against-populism-progressive-response-politics-duterte-and-mahathir
Kamran, T. (2020, August 23). The single national curriculum and the problems of education. *The News on Sunday*. www.thenews.com.pk/tns/detail/704311-the-single-national-curriculum-and-the-problems-of-education

Kamrava, M. (2005). Development and democracy: The Muslim world in a comparative perspective. In S. Hunter & H. Malik (Eds.), *Modernization, democracy, and Islam* (pp. 52–64). Praeger Publishers.

Kennedy, E. S. (2019). Presidential debate: How can Prabowo call terrorists sent by foreign countries? *Tirto*. https://tirto.id/debat-capres-kok-bisa-prabowo-sebut-teroris-dikirim-negara-asing-deEH

Lahouari, A., & Roberts, A. (2017). *Radical Arab nationalism and political Islam*. Georgetown University Press.

Lipka, M. (2017, August 9). *Muslims and Islam: Key findings in the U.S. and around the world*. Pew Research Centre. www.pewresearch.org/fact-tank/2017/08/09/muslims-and-islam-key-findings-in-the-u-s-and-around-the-world/

Maulia, E. (2020, December 11). Indonesian firebrand cleric Habib Rizieq faces arrest in Jakarta. *Nikkei Asia*. https://asia.nikkei.com/Spotlight/Islam-in-Asia/Indonesian-firebrand-cleric-Habib-Rizieq-faces-arrest-in-Jakarta

Mietzner, M. (2014, April 27). Jokowi: Rise of a polite populist. *Inside Indonesia*. www.insideindonesia.org/jokowi-rise-of-a-polite-populist

Mietzner, M. (2015). *Reinventing Asian populism: Jokowi's rise, democracy, and political contestation in Indonesia*. East-West Center.

Mietzner, M. (2018). Fighting illiberalism with illiberalism: Islamist populism and democratic deconsolidation in Indonesia. *Pacific Affairs*, 91, 261–82. https://doi.org/10.5509/2018912261

Moffitt, B. (2016). *The global rise of populism: Performance, political style, and representation*. Stanford University Press.

Mukhopadhyay, A. (2020, June 17). Zakir Naik: India seeks to extradite Islamic preacher in Malaysia. *DW*. www.dw.com/en/zakir-naik-india-seeks-to-extradite-islamic-preacher-in-malaysia/a-53845156

Mulla, A. (2017, October 17). Mediatized populisms| Broadcasting the dharna: Mediating "contained" populism in contemporary Pakistan. *International Journal of Communication*, 11, 16. https://ijoc.org/index.php/ijoc/article/view/6735

Muslim leaders gather in Malaysia for summit shunned by Saudi. (2019, December 18). *Dawn*. www.dawn.com/news/1522976

My inspirations are Prophet Muhammad, the city of Medina that he founded: Imran Khan. (2018, July 26). *ummid.com News Network*. www.ummid.com/news/2018/July/26.07.2018/imran-khan-in-first-speech-my-inspiration-is-prophet-muhammed-and-ideal-state-madinah-munawwera.html

Nuryanti, S. (2021). Populism in Indonesia: Learning from the 212 movement in response to the blasphemy case against Ahok in Jakarta. In S. J. Lee, C. Wu & K. K. Bandyopadhyay (Eds.), *Populism in Asian democracies* (pp. 165–175). Brill.

Palmier, L. H. (1957). Sukarno, the nationalist. *Pacific Affairs*, 30(2), 101–119. https://doi.org/10.2307/2752683

Paracha, N. F. (2020, June 14). Is Imran Khan a Populist? *Dawn*. www.dawn.com/news/1563414

Park, C. (2004). Religion and geography. In J. Hinnells (Ed.), *The Routledge companion to the study of religion* (Chap. 25). Routledge. https://doi.org/10.4324/9780203412695.

Pernau-Reifeld, M. (1999). Reaping the whirlwind: Nizam and the Khilafat movement. *Economic and Political Weekly*, 34(38), 2745–2751. https://www.jstor.org/stable/4408427

PM Imran Khan says aurat march is a result of cultural differences like it's a bad thing. (2020, March 14). *Dawn*. https://images.dawn.com/news/1184828

Pryor, F. L. (2007). Are Muslim countries less democratic? *Middle East Quarterly*, 14(4), 53–58.

Rodzi, N. H. (2019, March 11). Kuala Lumpur says foreign militants eyeing Malaysia as safe haven. *Straits Times*. www.straitstimes.com/asia/se-asia/kl-says-foreign-militants-eyeing-malaysia-as-safe-haven

Saat, N. (2018, June 20). Mahathir's 'reinvented' populism has weakened ideological barriers, but what next? *Today*. www.todayonline.com/commentary/mahathirs-reinvented-populism-has-weakened-ideological-barriers-what-next

Şahin, B. (2006). Is Islam an obstacle to democratization? The debate of the compatibility of Islam and democracy revisited. *bilig*, 37, 189–206. https://dergipark.org.tr/tr/download/article-file/234384

Salazar, P.-J. (2017). *Words are weapons: Inside ISIS's rhetoric of terror*. Yale University Press.

Shah, S. (2019). Populist politics in the new Malaysia. *New Diversities*, 21(2), 53–67.

Shams, S. (2019, July 14). Pakistani PM Imran Khan draws ire over taxes, rising inflation. *DW*. www.dw.com/en/pakistani-pm-imran-khan-draws-ire-over-taxes-rising-inflation/a-49585589

Shams, S. (2020, October 27). Opinion: Erdogan and Khan are hypocritical about Macron's France. *DW*. www.dw.com/en/opinion-erdogan-and-khan-are-hypocritical-about-macrons-france/a-55408436

Shukri, S. (2021, July 5). Malay political polarization and Islamic populism in Malaysia. *Stratsea*. https://stratsea.com/malay-political-polarization-and-islamic-populism-in-malaysia/

Shukri, S. F. M., & Smajljaj, A. (2020). Populism and Muslim democracies. *Asian Politics & Policy*, *12*(4), 575–591. https://doi.org/10.1111/aspp.12553

Sidel, J. (2008). The social origins of democracy revisited: Colonial state and Chinese immigrant in the making of modern Southeast Asia. *Comparative Politics*, *40*(2), 127–47. https://doi.org/10.5129/001041508X12911362382670

Sowell, T. (2004). *Affirmative action around the world: An empirical study*. Yale University Press.

Sub, J. (2016). The Suharto case. *Asian Journal of Social Science*, *44*(12), 214–245. https://10.1163/15685314-04401009

Taggart, P. (2004). Populism and representative politics in contemporary Europe. *Journal of Political Ideologies*, *9*(3), 269–88. https://doi.org/10.1080/1356931042000263528

Trivedi, R. K. (1981). Mustafa Kemal and the Indian Khilafat movement (to 1924). *Proceedings of the Indian History Congress*, *42*, 458–467. https://www.jstor.org/stable/44141163

Tugal, C. (2002). Islamism in Turkey: Beyond instrument and meaning. *Economy and Society*, *31*(1), 85–111. https://doi.org/10.1080/03085140120109268

Yilmaz, I. (2020a). *Egypt*. European Center for Populism Studies. www.populismstudies.org/tag/egypt/

Yilmaz, I. (2020b, 21 October). *Indonesia*. European Center for Populism Studies. www.populismstudies.org/tag/indonesia/

Yilmaz, I. (2021). *Creating the desired citizen: Ideology, state and Islam in Turkey*. Cambridge University Press.

Yilmaz, I., & Morieson, N. (2021, May 18). *How are religious emotions instrumentalized in the supply of and demand for populism?* European Center for Populism Studies. www.populismstudies.org/how-are-religious-emotions-instrumentalized-in-the-supply-of-and-demand-for-populism/

Yilmaz, I., Morieson, N., & Demir, M. (2021). Exploring religions in relation to populism: A tour around the world. *Religions*, *12*(5), 301. https://doi.org/10.3390/rel12050301

Yilmaz, I., & Shakil, K. (2021a). *Pakistan Tehreek-e-Insaf: Pakistan's iconic populist movement*. European Center for Populism Studies. www.populismstudies.org/pakistan-tehreek-e-insaf-pakistans-iconic-populist-movement/

Yilmaz, I., & Shakil, K. (2021b, February 10). *Imran Khan: From cricket batsman to populist captain Tabdeli of Pakistan*. European Center for Populism Studies. www.populismstudies.org/imran-khan-from-cricket-batsman-to-populist-captain-tabdeli-of-pakistan/

Zaharia, M. (2020, May 10). Mahathir's shock Malaysian election win raises populist economics specter. *Reuters*. https://jp.reuters.com/article/instant-article/idUSKBN1IB12N

Zarkasyi, H. F. (2008). The rise of Islamic religious-political movements in Indonesia: The background, present situation and future. *Journal of Indonesian Islam*, *2*(2), 336. https://doi.org/10.15642/JIIS.2008.2.2.336-378

Ziv, D. (2001). Populist perceptions and perceptions of populism in Indonesia: The case of Megawati Soekarnoputri. *South East Asia Research*, *9*(1), 73–88. https://doi.org/10.5367/000000001101297324

Zúquete, J. P. (2017). Populism and religion. In C. Rovira Kaltwasser, P. Taggart, P. Ochoa Espejo & P. Ostiguy (Eds.), *The Oxford handbook of populism* (pp. 445–266). Oxford University Press.

11
MEDICAL POPULISM IN THE ASIA PACIFIC

Gideon Lasco and Vincen Gregory Yu

Introduction

Public health crises have been a recurring feature of 21st century politics in Asia and the Pacific. From the drug wars of Thailand and Indonesia (Lasco, 2020a) to infectious disease outbreaks across the region (Lasco & Yu, 2021a), these crises have repeatedly affirmed that health is, and will always be, a political matter (Oliver, 2006). The inextricability of health and politics has been further amplified by the rise of populism in the region (Mietzner, 2015; Moffitt, 2014) and by the many ways in which populist politics has shaped public health policy and decision-making around the world (Speed & Mannion, 2017).

This chapter approaches the convergence of health and politics, nominally *medical populism*, in the Asia Pacific (Lasco & Curato, 2019). Rooted primarily in understanding populism as a political *style* (Moffitt, 2016)—rather than a political *phenomenon* (Müller, 2014)—medical populism encapsulates the performative repertoire commonly employed by politicians during health crises. The cardinal tenets enacted are 'the politicization of a health-related issue', and its portrayal as 'a public emergency that demands immediate response' (Lasco & Curato, 2019, p. 2). As exigencies of profound public anxiety and uncertainty, health crises enable medical populists to exhibit the fastest possible responses, 'creatively performed to evoke reactions from a targeted, yet fragmented and globalized audience', instead of those that 'emphasize certainty and stability' (Lasco & Curato, 2019, p. 3).

Medical populism has four core dimensions. The first is *dramatization*, whereby medical populists, who are usually influential individuals like politicians, *spectacularize* their responses to a health crisis through tangible action and colourful rhetoric. Second, parallel to the dramatization, is the *forging of divisions* between the people and either an existing establishment such as government, the academic elite, or dangerous others. Third, the divisions, in turn, become part of a *simplification*, referring not only to the reduction of complicated crisis discourse to an *us-versus-them* dichotomy, but also to the tendency of medical populists to offer quick and easy fixes to the multifactorial problem at hand. Lastly, the fourth dimension is the *invocation of knowledge claims*, which may not necessarily be evidence-based but nonetheless can lay the foundations for the aforementioned dramatization of crisis, forging of divisions, and simplification of the discourse (Lasco & Curato, 2019; Lasco & Yu, 2021a).

In this chapter, we apply the concept of medical populism to examine the political construction of three contemporary public health crises in the region. The first example focuses on the drug war initiated by Prime Minister Thaksin Shinawatra in Thailand in 2003. The second considers the controversy surrounding a mass immunization programme against dengue fever in the Philippines in late 2017, and the third centres on the first 16 months of the COVID-19 pandemic in India under the leadership of Prime Minister Narendra Modi. These narrative reconstructions are intended to highlight the instantiations of medical populism in these crises, rather than to capture their full course. Following Lasco and Curato (2019), we apply a descriptive perspective to the concept rather than a normative one; that is to say, 'we offer a vocabulary to describe a response to contemporary medical crises without necessarily making judgments on its ethical value' (p. 1). As empirical material, we have utilized academic sources, journalistic reportage, and government documents in both print and online forms, with a particular focus on material originating from the relevant country or written by local authors. We conclude with a brief reflection on the unifying elements of, as well as the lessons imparted by, these case studies in regard to public health, crisis communications, and the politics of health.

Case study 1: the drug war in Thailand, 2003

Coming to power at the start of the new millennium, Prime Minister Thaksin quickly adopted a populist playbook that advocated for health and rural reform while framing himself as a fresh and desirable alternative to traditional Thai political leadership (Phongpaichit & Baker, 2008). Part of this supposed socio-political rejuvenation—and what would become one of his most consequential policies—was an anti-drug campaign launched in February 2003, which aimed to eradicate illegal drugs in the country within three months (Petsuksiri, 2008). This war on drugs, which claimed close to 3,000 lives in its first seven weeks and racked up countless human rights violations, came in the aftermath of the 1997 Asian financial crisis, the repercussions of which included an inadvertent boom in the country's drug trade as more people turned to selling drugs for a living or using them to cope with economic hardship (Phongpaichit, 2003). During the 1990s, the use of methamphetamine, which became colloquially known as *ya ba* (mad drug), had already become widespread—not only among blue-collar workers who used it to stay awake but also among the youth who used it recreationally—to the point of becoming an epidemic (Cohen, 2014; Poshyachinda et al., 2005). In the latter part of the decade, students were 'the most prominent users', and 'schools, vocational colleges and universities became a prime target for traffickers and dealers' (Cohen, 2014, p. 777). When the drug war commenced, Thailand had gone through severe economic contraction, while its prisons had become among the world's most overcrowded, with an estimated 100,000 inmates being held on drug-related charges (Kazmin, 2007; Petsuksiri, 2008).

From the outset, Thaksin used imagistic language and evocative rhetoric in referring to *his war*. The youth, in particular, figured prominently in his speeches. 'Our country will have no future if our children are addicted to drugs', he proclaimed early on (cited in Dabhoiwala, n.d., para. 1). Then, justifying the use of violent measures for the war, he stated separately: 'Because drug traders are ruthless to our children . . . being ruthless back to them [should not be] a big thing' (cited in Chouvy, 2013, p. 46). Apart from such rhetoric, the Thaksin administration also relied on exaggerated statistics (e.g., the alleged presence of six million drug addicts in the country) as grounds for its drastic policies. As the war and extrajudicial killings unfolded, the government ensured public awareness of its fatal outcomes by reporting them constantly, often in gory detail, in print and broadcast media (Phongpaichit, 2003).

Even so, the drug war enjoyed a considerable degree of public support. A poll conducted by Bangkok University within the war's first month found that 90% of the population believed in the campaign's necessity (Montlake, 2003), while another poll conducted the following month by Suan Dusit College found that '75 percent of Thai people in all seventy-six provinces throughout the country fully supported Thaksin's hard line stand on the drug war, and 12 percent were particularly satisfied that drug dealers had been killed by law enforcement officials' (Human Rights Watch, 2004, p. 8). What could have accounted for this sweeping public approval?

Besides the widely held opinion at the time that drugs had become a serious national concern (Petsuksiri, 2008), one could point to the discourse propagated by Thaksin's government that thrived on the forging of divisions. For instance, Thaksin constantly dehumanized people involved in drugs as dangerous *others*, labelling them the scum of society, threats to security, traitors, and wicked people (Human Rights Watch, 2004, p. 50; Petsuksiri, 2008, p. 125). In this way, the war tapped into the fears of middle- and upper-class citizens whose children had started taking *ya ba*, which was ostensibly associated with the poor (Lasco, 2020a). But Thaksin also appealed to the masses with his anti-establishment—and therefore, of-the-people—posturing. Apart from entering the political scene set up as 'a national saviour ready to lead the country' out of the shadow of the financial crisis (Kazmin, 2007, p. 1), he had also fashioned himself as a challenger of the cosmopolitan elite and, in vague terms, a supposed anti-corruption crusader with the interests of the poor at heart (Hawkins & Selway, 2017; Kazmin, 2007). Besides the anti-establishment projection, Thaksin also cast himself in a nationalist light. Part of the justification for his drug war was to curb the 'continuous flood of amphetamines' coming into the country from neighbouring Myanmar, whose drug factories he had publicly condemned ('Burma–Thailand Relations', 2009), thereby fuelling his image as the 'defender of national sovereignty' (Phongpaichit, 2004, p. 7). In all, drugs—and the people associated with them—were portrayed as dangerous, anti-nationalist, undesirable, and therefore deserving of elimination through extreme means. Thus, even as the drug war came under criticism from international bodies like the United Nations, it was also praised by influential figures, including the nation's king at the time, who called the death toll 'a small price to pay' compared to the failure to suppress the so-called drug problem ('Royal Speech', 2003).

The drug war evidently failed to meet its three-month target; the official legislation was extended to last through the rest of 2003, and the war's victims overwhelmingly consisted of poor, small-time, unorganized dealers and users (Dabhoiwala, n.d.). Nevertheless, the popularity achieved by Thaksin through this war was apparently partly responsible for his landslide re-election for a second term, though he would eventually be ousted from office in 2006 (Aglionby, 2003; Kuhonta & Mutebi, 2006).

As this case study illustrates, Thaksin's drug war became an instrument of medical populism in the sense that it was used to forge a division between the *virtuous* public and dangerous *others* to justify the inherent violence; in its execution as a spectacularized response to a perceived social emergency; and in the 'very use of the language of war [as] an invocation of crisis' (Lasco, 2020a, p. 2).

Case study 2: the dengue vaccine controversy in the Philippines, 2017

In 2016, the Philippines launched a mass vaccination program to combat dengue fever, which cost the country some U.S. $345 million annually in state-funded hospitalizations from 2008 to 2012 (Edillo et al., 2015). The programme utilized the French pharmaceutical Sanofi Pasteur's Dengvaxia, making the Philippines the first Asian country to approve the novel vaccine for commercial use. Yu et al. (2021) listed the significant historical markers of the immunization campaign.

> [It] unfolded at a transitional time in Philippine politics: It was approved and begun during the term of the late President Benigno Aquino III, pilot-tested in three regions during the weeks surrounding the 2016 national elections, and continued by the new administration of President Rodrigo Duterte.
>
> *p. 4964*

In December 2017, nearly two years after the programme started, Sanofi announced that Dengvaxia could actually result in a more severe course of disease among the *dengue-naïve*, i.e., those not previously infected. By this time, some 800,000 Filipino schoolchildren had been given at least one dose of the vaccine (Lardizabal, 2017).

The program was immediately suspended. Within days of this suspension, a single talking point dominated the media coverage—the cases of vaccinated children who had allegedly died from, or suffered a severe bout of, dengue during the past year (e.g., Lardizabal, 2017). An independent expert panel from the Philippine General Hospital (PGH), the National Referral Centre, was swiftly convened to investigate a cohort of 14 such deaths. The panel eventually concluded that only three of the deaths were actually because of dengue—and even then, they could not be directly attributed to the Dengvaxia inoculation (Cepeda, 2018).

This expert decision was overshadowed, however, by the Duterte administration's medical populism. Although Duterte himself has been recognized as a medical populist (Lasco, 2020b), it is more insightful to analyze the controversy in terms of how his government as a whole framed it primarily as the fault of the preceding administration. For instance, numerous state-affiliated factions called for criminal investigations against the political actors involved in the vaccination programme's inception, including former President Aquino, with one such complaint filed by a known political rival of Aquino's health secretary based on accusations of *mass murder* (Buan, 2017). On social media, one of the most popular pro-Duterte bloggers accused Sanofi and the Aquino administration of treating Filipino children as 'disposable money machines', and plunging the country into a 'healthcare disaster of intercontinental proportions' (Thinking Pinoy, 2018, paras. 51–52).

At the forefront of this national scandal was Persida Acosta and the Public Attorney's Office (PAO) of which she was chief. Acosta's highly dramatized responses centred on a bond constructed between the present government and the bereaved families on whose behalf she now claimed to speak. Her narratives also created an antagonism pitting the two aforementioned camps against an ostensible *elite establishment* represented by top-ranking politicians of the Aquino administration, and, to some extent, expert institutions like the PGH (Lasco & Curato, 2019). At the height of the controversy, the PAO conducted its own, highly publicized autopsies, the press conferences for which sometimes involved the victims' families, with Acosta appearing beside them in a show of solidarity as she hurled accusations of negligence and cover-ups against the perceived establishment figures (Lopez, 2017). At the time of the crisis, Lasco and Curato (2019) described the PAO chief's style of discourse.

> Acosta's discursive style uses enough legalese to establish professional credibility (e.g., citing forensic investigation evidence, identifying the conflict of interest of the Health Department and medical experts in leading the investigation) but melodramatic enough to respond to the demands of televisual cultures. This dramatized strategy allows her to claim to speak for aggrieved people in a crisis, much unlike the dispassionate, technical, and perhaps callous language of the medical establishment that sought to diffuse the crisis.
>
> p. 5

Such efforts to portray herself and her office as an ally of the people evidently bore fruit, as she gained the sympathy and support of organizations like United Parents Against Dengvaxia Philippines, whose members went so far as to personally confront Aquino's health secretary after a congressional hearing (Roxas, 2018). Acosta also sought to cast doubt on the scientific institutions that contradicted her office, especially after the release of the PGH expert panel findings. In one media interview, Acosta openly questioned the integrity of the Health Department and the country's leading forensic pathologists, asking, 'Whose interests do they protect?' to justify her office's refusal to cooperate with the national agency (Cabico, 2018, para. 8)—in effect discrediting the intellectual authority of these institutions.

Almost a year after the controversy erupted, the Philippines experienced a resurgence of measles. Expert analyses and qualitative research pointed to the Dengvaxia controversy—specifically, to the alleged link between vaccination and the deaths of those children that Acosta and her office propagated as the inciting phenomenon that led many Filipinos to become fearful or hesitant of having their children undergo any form of immunization, including that for measles, thereby precipitating the outbreak (e.g., Yu et al., 2021).

As this case study demonstrates, medical populism as a style of governance can enable politicians to capitalize on public health controversies to further their political agenda. By allowing Acosta and other state-affiliated individuals to continue blaming the previous administration for the vaccine controversy, the Duterte administration was able to partly deflect attention from its culpability in the resulting measles outbreak while preserving its preferred narrative of institutional change in comparison to the previous administration—a narrative best captured by the signature Duterte catchphrase 'change is coming'. Consequently, as the aforementioned measles outbreak demonstrates, medical populism can directly affect not only public policy, but also the health of individuals and communities.

Case study 3: COVID-19 pandemic in India, 2020–2021

At the time of writing, the COVID-19 pandemic in India had unfolded in two distinct phases: a first wave that transpired through much of 2020, and a second, far deadlier wave that started during the first quarter of 2021, which has been attributed not only to the spread of the highly infectious Delta variant but also to a failure of national leadership and public health policy (Chandra, 2021). At the helm during the pandemic was Prime Minister Narendra Modi, a staunch Hindu nationalist and tech-savvy populist under whose leadership India has witnessed worrying democratic backsliding (Rai, 2019; Sud, 2020) and who, throughout the pandemic, has been criticized for '[privileging] image over substance and accountability' (Kaul, 2021, para. 3). It is through this recognition of the socio-political climate engendered by Modi's leadership that elements of medical populism in the ongoing Indian experience of the pandemic are rendered most coherent.

Like many populist leaders, Modi also framed his country's potential success against the pandemic as dependent mainly on the cooperation of ordinary citizens. The centrepiece of his initial interventions in 2020, announced with only four hours' notice for the entire country, was a *Janata* lockdown—literally, a lockdown for the *people*, the nomenclature betraying its intended appeal to the masses. Speaking to the press in highly evocative terms, he called upon citizens to draw a *Laxman Rekha* line on their doorsteps and not to venture beyond that line during this 'decisive battle against coronavirus'; sans lockdown, he proclaimed, 'India will go back 21 years' (Hebbar, 2020, para. 8). His later pandemic responses were also similarly dramatized in keeping with his PR-conscious branding: an economic relief fund, for example, was named, quite tellingly, 'PM Cares', the website bearing his likeness in full (Hollingsworth, 2021), while vaccinations were promoted by Modi himself as the path to becoming *Baahubali*, or *one with strong arms*, in reference to the protagonist of a popular fantasy-action movie ('Those Who Get Jabbed', 2021).

To be clear, unlike many populist leaders, Modi was no pandemic denier; in fact, throughout much of 2020, he encouraged science-based interventions like mask-wearing and social distancing ('India's Modi Slammed', 2021). Instead, ever conscious of projecting an image of success and control, Modi and his government engaged in downplaying the magnitude of the crisis. During the country's first wave, this was evident in the government's persistent denials of community transmission, despite cases already surpassing the one-million mark (Shetty, 2020), and, more significantly, in the rampant repression of criticism from the medical sector and free press (Chakma, 2020; Kalra & Ghoshal, 2020), who were sounding the alarm over the rapidly mounting cases and the government's inadequate responses. True to medical-populist style, Modi declared in his 2021 Independence Day speech that the country's health workers, whom his administration had attempted to censor repeatedly, 'all deserve to be worshipped' 'Doctors, Scientists', 2021, para. 2).

At the World Economic Forum in January 2021, Modi prematurely proclaimed victory over COVID-19: 'Today, India . . . has saved the world from disaster by bringing the situation under control,' he said (cited in Mishra, 2021, para. 5). Then, the second wave erupted. With it, the Modi administration intensified efforts to downplay the pandemic's consequences and to stifle its critics (Choudhury, 2021) while framing the worsening situation as simply the discrete failures of ill-prepared local governments ('Won't Say Anything', 2021). For their part, Modi's supporters, especially his Cabinet ministers, lavished the government with praises across social media and sparred publicly with those who dared say otherwise (Bedi & Khan, 2021; Tribune News Service, 2021). On a day in March 2021 that tallied over 81,000 new cases, the country's health minister, Vardan, went on record insisting, 'The situation is under control' (Hollingsworth, 2021, para. 14).

Modi's political party, the *Bharatiya Janata Party* (BJP), has been notorious for propagating unfounded knowledge claims throughout the pandemic, especially those that appealed to their Hindu base. In March 2020, the BJP's head of foreign affairs accused experts who predicted severe outcomes for the pandemic of belonging to an 'anti-Modi lobby', while highlighting the need for traditional Indian medicine to combat COVID-19 (Chauthaiwale,

2020). Some influential BJP figures advocated the use of cow urine as an immunity booster (Singh, 2020). With the second wave already underway, one minister famously pushed for devotees to still attend religious festivals in person, calling the pandemic restrictions unnecessary and telling the devotees that *faith* was enough to overcome the virus ('Devotees' Faith', 2021).

Meanwhile, the divisions encouraged by Modi and his government manifested in scapegoating the country's Muslim minority, a visible continuation of Modi's legacy of Islamophobia (Waikar, 2018). The notable inciting incident of March 2020 concerned an international gathering organized by the Islamic missionary reformist group, Tablighi Jamaat, in Delhi, which produced some 4,000 COVID-19 cases and not only qualified as a super-spreading event but became a convenient justification for Hindu nationalist fronts to scapegoat the larger Muslim community for the worsening pandemic scenario. As detailed in a report by the Centre for Study of Society and Secularism (2020), Modi's followers denounced the incident immediately, with vulgar condemnations of Muslims as 'human bombs' and perpetrators of 'corona jihad' who were intentionally spreading the virus to undermine the state emanating from government ministers, celebrities, and television news anchors (p. 29). The report further chronicles how several prominent media outlets amplified the Islamophobic rhetoric, even extending the conversations far beyond the realm of health care to the point of accusing the Muslims of attempting *jihad* across the many other sectors of daily life in India, including the economy and education. Overt discrimination also transpired within the health sector itself: one hospital issued a ban against COVID-positive Muslim patients, claiming—incorrectly—that most of those patients could be traced to the aforementioned gathering, while another started segregating Muslim patients from Hindus, allegedly under local government orders (Centre for Study of Society and Secularism, 2020). This was in stark contrast to the Modi administration's leniency toward predominantly Hindu mass gatherings during that time (The Wire Staff, 2020); leniency extended to the political rallies and religious festivals since identified as *superspreader* events of the second wave ('Rallies, Religious Gatherings', 2021). Presumably, to quell the spate of Muslim hate following the Delhi gathering, Modi offered vague, generic responses appended to an essay that mainly tackled the digital transitions imposed by the pandemic: 'COVID does not see race, religion, colour, caste, creed, language or border before striking' (Modi, 2020, para. 35).

As shown by this case study, disease outbreaks, particularly those of novel infections, are ideal settings for medical populism. The fearful atmosphere they beget provides apparent justification for drastic, spectacularized responses (Lasco & Yu, 2021a) and, amid this epistemic uncertainty, foment the proliferation of unfounded factual claims (Lasco & Yu, 2021b). Moreover, they can also aggravate pre-existing social prejudices as medical populists forge divisions in a facile search for culpability (Lasco, 2020b).

Discussion and conclusion

Our three case studies demonstrate how medical populism is a recognizable pattern of governance and 'a familiar response to medical emergencies' (Lasco & Curato, 2019, p. 6). The element of simplification, for example, was evident in each populist regime's framing of its respective crisis: a drug war to solve the drug problem; a vaccination programme gone awry because of the preceding government's ineptitude and malevolent design; a disease outbreak that could be solved easily if only ordinary citizens did their part. Dramatization was evident in both the language employed by the prominent political actors of each crisis and in the responses enacted by each government. Divisions were forged between the virtuous public and dangerous drug addicts in Thailand; conniving elite institutions in the Philippines; and Muslims who were COVID-19 superspreaders in India. Finally, factual claims propped up many populist contentions, from the exaggerated statistics on Thai drug addicts as justification for a drug war to the unfounded insistence on Dengvaxia as the cause of death of those Filipino schoolchildren and the labelling of government critics in India as anti-Modi agitators.

The glaring danger of medical populism, then, lies in its propensity to obscure the systemic nature of a health crisis. Through rhetoric that taps into people's extant fears, promises of quick solutions, and the convenient scapegoating of the *minoritized other*, medical populists can sustain the illusion of addressing the root causes of a crisis without actually doing so (Jay et al., 2019). Thaksin's drug war, for instance, conveniently masked the historical and socioeconomic contexts that advanced drug use and trafficking in the first place (Chouvy, 2013), while Modi's medical populism overshadowed the already troubled and exclusionary state of India's public health infrastructure (Rahman, 2020). Moreover, as 'another piece in the enduring puzzle of health inequity' (Lasco & Yu, 2021a, p. 10), medical populism can in fact exacerbate the crisis at hand by breeding novel and equally consequential problems.

The political narrative of the dengue vaccine controversy in the Philippines starkly illustrates how the theatrics of state actors circuitously gave rise to a full-blown disease outbreak only a year later. And as the Thai drug war and the COVID-19 pandemic in India demonstrate, the authoritarian proclivities of medical populists can lead to rampant violations of human rights, which become treated as 'an impediment to their conception of the majority will, a needless obstacle to defending the nation from perceived threats and evils' (Roth, 2017, p. 79). While the outcomes of medical populism may emulate those of populism itself in the way they both undermine institutional checks and balances and strip the state of accountability, medical populism would conceivably more likely flourish in contexts where such institutional safeguards are weak to begin with (Lasco & Yu, 2021a).

Fortunately, the recurring nature of medical populism means that essential interventions against it can and should be anticipated (Lasco & Yu, 2021a). That this phenomenon thrives on the proliferation of knowledge-based claims and watered-down discourses emphasizes 'biomedicine's imperative to manage people's trust in public health institutions', and the role of these institutions in addressing the knowledge and communication gaps laid bare by such claims and discourses (Lasco & Curato, 2019, p. 6). The rise of vaccine hesitancy following the Dengvaxia controversy in the Philippines best exemplifies this, as does the popularity of unproven cures and the disregard for mass-gathering restrictions that took root in India with the endorsement of medical populists. More significantly, these case studies highlight the urgency to 'demand accountability from powerful actors from the establishment', whether they be entire political blocs or individual officials (Lasco & Curato, 2019, p. 11). Conversely, they also reveal the vulnerability of the predominantly scientific institutions that may find themselves delegitimized and on the receiving end of the politicization of health crises (Lasco, 2020b), and the critical need to support these institutions as they counter the streams of disinformation. In the end, medical populism is a political style in need of traction, and how this traction builds depends on the levels of trust between the public and government, the communicative architecture already in place at the time the crisis hits, and the pre-existing contexts that provide fertile ground for this phenomenon to prosper (Lasco & Curato, 2019).

References

Aglionby, J. (2003, December 4). The war on yaa-baa. *The Guardian*. www.theguardian.com/world/2003/dec/04/drugstrade

Bedi, A., & Khan, F. (2021, May 5). Indians scramble for help but Modi's ministers busy thanking his 'leadership' for O2, ration. *ThePrint*. https://theprint.in/politics/indians-scramble-for-help-but-modis-ministers-busy-thanking-his-leadership-for-o2-ration/652571/

Buan, L. (2017, December 3). To depict 'mass murder' Syjuco uses clip art in dengue vaccine complaint vs Aquino. *Rappler*. www.rappler.com/nation/noynoy-aquino-janette-garin-dengvaxia-syjuco-complaint

Burma–Thailand relations strained over drug traffic—2003-08-22. (2009, October 30). *Voice of America*. www.voanews.com/a/a-13-a-2003-08-22-24-burma-thailand/393919.html

Cabico, G. K. (2018, February 9). PAO chief Acosta cries 'conflict of interest' Dengvaxia probe. *The Philippine Star*. www.philstar.com/headlines/2018/02/09/1786163/pao-chief-acosta-cries-conflict-interest-dengvaxia-probe

Centre for Study of Society and Secularism. (2020). *The Covid pandemic: A report on the scapegoating of minorities in India*. https://cjp.org.in/wp-content/uploads/2021/04/The-Covid-Scapegoatig-Report-by-CSSS.pdf

Cepeda, M. (2018, February 2). DOH considers UP-PGH findings as primary 'evidence' on Dengvaxia. *Rappler*. www.rappler.com/nation/doh-pgh-findings-primary-evidence-dengvaxia

Chakma, S. (2020, June 15). *India: Media's crackdown during COVID-19 lockdown*. Rights & Risks Analysis Group. www.rightsrisks.org/banner/india-medias-crackdown-during-covid-19-lockdown-2/

Chandra, S. (2021, June 9). Why India's second COVID surge is so much worse than the first. *Scientific American*. www.scientificamerican.com/article/why-indias-second-covid-surge-is-so-much-worse-than-the-first/

Chauthaiwale, V. (2020, March 24). Anti-Modi lobby quotes voodoo COVID-19 math of US economist, forgets to verify the numbers. *ThePrint*. https://theprint.in/opinion/anti-modi-lobby-quotes-voodoo-covid-19-math-of-us-economist-but-mocks-turmeric-on-immunity/386759/

Choudhury, C. (2021, May 24). Modi is worsening the suffering from India's pandemic. *Scientific American*. www.scientificamerican.com/article/modi-is-worsening-the-suffering-from-indias-pandemic/

Chouvy, P.-A. (2013). Drug trafficking in and out of the Golden Triangle. In P.-A. Chouvy (Ed.), *An atlas of trafficking in Southeast Asia: The illegal trade in arms, drugs, people, counterfeit goods and natural resources in mainland Southeast Asia* (pp. 29–52). Bloomsbury.

Cohen, A. (2014). Crazy for Ya Ba: Methamphetamine use among northern Thai youth. *International Journal of Drug Policy*, 25(4), 776–782. http://dx.doi.org/10.1016/j.drugpo.2014.06.005

Dabhoiwala, M. (n.d.). *A chronology of Thailand's 'war on drugs'*. Asian Human Rights Commission. www.humanrights.asia/resources/journals-magazines/article2/special-report-extrajudicial-killings-of-alleged-drug-dealers-in-thailand/a-chronology-of-thailands-war-on-drugs/

Devotees' Faith Will Overcome fear of Covid-19 in Mahakumbh: CM Rawat. (2021, March 20). *Hindustan Times*. www.hindustantimes.com/cities/others/devotees-faith-will-overcome-fear-of-covid-19-in-mahakumbh-cm-rawat-101616253395877.html

Doctors, scientists, paramedics must be worshipped for their work during Covid-19 pandemic. (2021, August 15). *Deccan Herald*. www.deccanherald.com/national/doctors-scientists-paramedics-must-be-worshipped-for-their-work-during-covid-19-pandemic-1019919.html

Edillo, F. E., Halasa, Y. A., Largo, F. M., Erasmo, J. N. V., Amoin, N. B., Alera, M. T. P., Yoon, I.-K., Alcantara, A. C., & Shepard, D. S. (2015). Economic cost and burden of dengue in the Philippines. *The American Journal of Tropical Medicine and Hygiene*, 92(2), 360–366. http://dx.doi.org/10.4269/ajtmh.14-0139

Hawkins, K., & Selway, J. (2017). Thaksin the populist? *Chinese Political Science Review*, 2, 372–394. http://dx.doi.org/10.1007/s41111-017-0073-z

Hebbar, N. (2020, March 25). PM Modi announces 21-day lockdown as COVID-19 toll touches 12. *The Hindu*. www.thehindu.com/news/national/pm-announces-21-day-lockdown-as-covid-19-toll-touches-10/article31156691.ece

Hollingsworth, J. (2021, May 1). Prime Minister Narendra Modi could have prevented India's devastating Covid-19 crisis, critics say. He didn't. *CNN*. https://edition.cnn.com/2021/04/30/india/covid-second-wave-narendra-modi-intl-hnk-dst/index.html

Human Rights Watch. (2004). *Not enough graves: The war on drugs, HIV/AIDS, and violations of human rights*. www.hrw.org/reports/2004/thailand0704/thailand0704.pdf

India's Modi slammed for COVID handling amid spiralling crisis. (2021, May 5). *Al Jazeera*. www.aljazeera.com/news/2021/5/5/crime-against-humanity-indias-modi-slammed-for-covid-handling

Jay, S., Batruch, A., Jetten, J., McGarty, C., & Muldoon, O. T. (2019). Economic inequality and the rise of far-right populism: A social psychological analysis. *Journal of Community & Applied Social Psychology*, 29(5), 418–428. http://dx.doi.org/10.1002/casp.2409

Kalra, A., & Ghoshal, D. (2020, April 6). 'Don't target doctors': Indian medics say coronavirus critics being muzzled. *Reuters*. www.reuters.com/article/health-coronavirus-india-doctors/dont-target-doctors-indian-medics-say-coronavirus-critics-being-muzzled-idINKBN21O1YL?edition-redirect=in

Kaul, N. (2021, May 12). COVID in India: A tragedy with its roots in Narendra Modi's leadership style. *The Conversation*. https://theconversation.com/covid-in-india-a-tragedy-with-its-roots-in-narendra-modis-leadership-style-160552

Kazmin, A. (2007). A setback for Thai democracy: The rise, rule and overthrow of Thaksin Shinawatra. *Asian Affairs*, 38(2), 211–224. http://dx.doi.org/10.1080/03068370701349284

Kuhonta, E. M., & Mutebi, A. M. (2006). Thaksin triumphant: The implications of one-party dominance in Thailand. *Asian Affairs: An American Review*, 33(1), 39–51. http://dx.doi.org/10.3200/AAFS.33.1.39-51

Lardizabal, C. (2017, December 8). DOH: More than 800,000 children vaccinated with Dengvaxia. *CNN Philippines*. https://cnnphilippines.com/news/2017/12/06/DOH-more-than-800000-children-vaccinated-with-dengvaxia.html

Lasco, G. (2020a). Drugs and drug wars as populist tropes in Asia: Illustrative examples and implications for drug policy. *International Journal of Drug Policy*, 77, 102668. http://dx.doi.org/10.1016/j.drugpo.2020.102668

Lasco, G. (2020b). Medical populism and the COVID-19 pandemic. *Global Public Health*, 15(10), 1417–1429. http://dx.doi.org/10.1080/17441692.2020.1807581

Lasco, G., & Curato, N. (2019). Medical populism. *Social Science & Medicine*, 221, 1–8. http://dx.doi.org/10.1016/j.socscimed.2018.12.006

Lasco, G., & Yu, V. G. (2021a). Medical populism and the politics of dengue epidemics in the Global South. *Global Public Health*, 17(9). http://dx.doi.org/10.1080/17441692.2021.1965181

Lasco, G., & Yu, V. G. (2021b). Pharmaceutical messianism and the COVID-19 pandemic. *Social Science & Medicine*, 292, 114567. http://dx.doi.org/10.1016/j.socscimed.2021.114567

Lopez, V. (2017, December 19). PAO chief Acosta: Claims of no deaths related to Dengvaxia are lies. *GMA News Online*. www.gmanetwork.com/news/news/nation/637016/pao-chief-acosta-claims-of-no-deaths-related-to-dengvaxia-are-lies/story/

Mietzner, M. (2015). *Reinventing Asian populism: Jokowi's rise, democracy, and political contestation in Indonesia*. Policy Studies 72. East-West Center. https://www.eastwestcenter.org/publications/reinventing-asian-populism-jokowis-rise-democracy-and-political-contestation-in

Mishra, H. S. (2021, January 28). India beat all odds in coronavirus fight, says PM Modi. *NDTV.com*. www.ndtv.com/india-news/there-will-be-more-made-in-india-vaccines-soon-says-pm-modi-2359470

Modi, N. (2020, April 19). *Life in the era of COVID-19*. LinkedIn. www.linkedin.com/pulse/life-era-covid-19-narendra-modi?articleId=6657590574998228992#comments-6657590574998228992&trk=public_profile_article_view

Moffitt, B. (2014). Contemporary populism and 'the people' in the Asia-Pacific region. In C. de la Torre (Ed.), *The promise and perils of populism: Global perspectives* (pp. 293–316). University Press of Kentucky.

Moffitt, B. (2016). *The global rise of populism: Performance, political style, and representation*. Stanford University Press.

Montlake, S. (2003, February 25). Thai drug war yields killing spree. *The Christian Science Monitor*. www.csmonitor.com/2003/0225/p10s01-woap.html

Müller, J.-W. (2014). 'The people must be extracted from within the people': Reflections on populism. *Constellations*, 21(4), 483–493. http://dx.doi.org/10.1111/1467-8675.12126

Oliver, T. R. (2006). The politics of public health policy. *Annual Review of Public Health*, 27, 195–233. http://dx.doi.org/10.1146/annurev.publhealth.25.101802.123126

Petsuksiri, P. (2008). The war on drugs—2003–2006: Tackling a tough social issue . . . , but at what cost? *NIDA Case Research Journal*, *1*(1), 117–148. https://so04.tci-thaijo.org/index.php/NCRJ/article/view/25022/21298

Phongpaichit, P. (2003, October 23–25). Drug policy in Thailand [Paper presentation]. *Senlis Council International Symposium on Global Drug Policy*. http://pioneer.netserv.chula.ac.th/~ppasuk/papers.htm

Phongpaichit, P. (2004). *Thailand under Thaksin: Another Malaysia?* (Working Paper No. 109). Asia Research Centre, Murdoch University. https://citeseerx.ist.psu.edu/viewdoc/download?doi=10.1.1.477.2271&rep=rep1&type=pdf

Phongpaichit, P., & Baker, C. (2008). Thaksin's populism. *Journal of Contemporary Asia*, *38*(1), 62–83. http://dx.doi.org/10.1080/00472330701651960

Poshyachinda, V., Na Ayudhya, A. S., Aramrattana, A., Kanato, M., Assanangkornchai, S., & Jitpiromsri, S. (2005). Illicit substance supply and abuse in 2000–2004: An approach to assess the outcome of the war on drug operation. *Drug and Alcohol Review*, *24*(5), 461–466. http://dx.doi.org/10.1080/09595230500285999

Rahman, S. Y. (2020). 'Social distancing' during COVID-19: The metaphors and politics of pandemic response in India. *Health Sociology Review*, *29*(2), 131–139. http://dx.doi.org/10.1080/14461242.2020.1790404

Rai, S. (2019). 'May the force be with you': Narendra Modi and the celebritization of Indian politics. *Communication, Culture & Critique*, *12*(3), 323–339. http://dx.doi.org/10.1093/ccc/tcz013

Rallies, religious gatherings aggravate India's worst COVID surge. (2021, April 9). *Al Jazeera*. www.aljazeera.com/news/2021/4/9/rallies-religious-gatherings-aggravate-indias-worst-covid-surge

Roth, K. (2017). The dangerous rise of populism: Global attacks on human rights values. *Journal of International Affairs*, 79–84. www.jstor.org/stable/44842604

Roxas, P. A. V. (2018, February 5). Furious mothers confront Garin over Dengvaxia. *Philippine Daily Inquirer*. https://newsinfo.inquirer.net/966304/emotional-mothers-confront-garin-over-dengvaxia

Royal speech given to a group of people who attended to pay tribute to the auspicious occasion of his majesty the king's birthday at Dusidalai Hall, Chitralada Park, Dusit Palace. (2003, December 4). *The Golden Jubilee Network*. http://kanchanapisek.or.th/speeches/2003/1204.th.html

Shetty, D. (2020, July 21). How denying community transmission is hampering India's COVID-19 response. *IndiaSpend*. www.indiaspend.com/how-denying-community-transmission-is-hampering-indias-covid-19-response/

Singh, S. S. (2020, July 18). Drink cow urine to fight virus: Bengal BJP chief. *The Hindu*. www.thehindu.com/news/cities/kolkata/drink-cow-urine-to-fight-virus-bengal-bjp-chief/article32119516.ece

Speed, E., & Mannion, R. (2017). The rise of post-truth populism in pluralist liberal democracies: Challenges for health policy. *International Journal of Health Policy and Management*, *6*(5), 249–251. http://dx.doi.org/10.15171/ijhpm.2017.19

Sud, N. (2020). The actual Gujarat model: Authoritarianism, capitalism, Hindu nationalism and populism in the time of Modi. *Journal of Contemporary Asia*, *52*(1). http://dx.doi.org/10.1080/00472336.2020.1846205

Thinking Pinoy. (2018, February 20). *#DengGate: Sanofi, DoH turned Pinoy kids into guinea pigs? No, a lot worse than that*. www.thinkingpinoy.net/2018/02/denggate-sanofi-doh-turned-pinoy-kids.html

The Wire Staff. (2020, April 17). Karnataka: Chariot pulling ritual held in violation of lockdown, police register case. *The Wire*. https://thewire.in/government/kalaburagi-chariot-pulling-covid-19-lockdown-violation

Those who get jabbed become 'Baahubali'; Over 40 crore people vaccinated against Covid: PM Narendra Modi. (2021, July 19). *The EconomicTimes*. https://economictimes.indiatimes.com/news/politics-and-nation/those-who-get-jabbed-become-baahubali-over-40-crore-people-vaccinated-against-covid-pm-narendra-modi/articleshow/84549310.cms

Tribune News Service. (2021, May 3). Jaishankar-Jairam spat over oxygen shortage in embassies. *The Tribune*. www.tribuneindia.com/news/nation/jaishankar-jairam-spat-over-oxygen-shortage-in-embassies-247247

Waikar, P. (2018). Reading Islamophobia in Hindutva: An analysis of Narendra Modi's political discourse. *Islamophobia Studies Journal*, 4(2), 161–180. http://dx.doi.org/10.13169/islastudj.4.2.0161

'Won't say anything': PM Modi's veiled dig at Covid-19 vaccine 'politics'. (2021, April 9). *Hindustan times*. www.hindustantimes.com/india-news/wont-say-anything-pm-modi-s-veiled-dig-at-covid-19-vaccine-politics-101617938263856.html

Yu, V. G., Lasco, G., & David, C. C. (2021). Fear, mistrust, and vaccine hesitancy: Narratives of the dengue vaccine controversy in the Philippines. *Vaccine*, 39(35), 4964–4972. https://doi.org/10.1016/j.vaccine.2021.07.051

PART IV

National cases

12
'INCLUSIONARY' POPULISM AND DEMOCRACY IN INDIA

Paul D. Kenny

Introduction

Populism is a deeply contested concept (Moffitt, 2020). Although early studies tended to conceive of populism as a type of political strategy or organization (see Chapter 3 in this volume), in the last decade or so, many scholars have preferred the idea that populism is a 'thin ideology', in which society is considered 'to be ultimately separated into two homogeneous and antagonistic groups, "the pure people" versus "the corrupt elite", and which argues that politics should be an expression of the *volonté générale* (general will) of the people' (Mudde, 2004, p. 543). Recasting populism as a *thin ideology* seemed to address the need for a concept that could adequately capture the diverse group of movements, parties, and regimes commonly termed *populist*, while still distinguishing populists from their non-populist counterparts (Crick, 2005; Mudde, 2004; Stanley, 2008). Problematically, however, this definition created a conceptual container that was so broad that it could say little about whether populism, as a people-centric and anti-elite form of politics, is threatening or corrective to democracy; theory and evidence have suggested that it could be both (Canovan, 1999; Rovira Kaltwasser, 2012).

To resolve this ambiguity, there have been several efforts to develop a taxonomy of populisms, the most concise and ambitious being the differentiation between *inclusionary* and *exclusionary* populism (Mudde & Rovira Kaltwasser, 2013). Exclusionary or right-wing populism is almost universally viewed as a threat to democracy, as it seeks to exclude immigrants, minorities, and other *non-people* and to prioritize order over the rule of law or liberties such as press freedom. Inclusionary or left-wing populism poses much greater analytical problems, with scholarship divided on whether it represents a similar danger to democracy and its associated political and civil liberties. Although some observers view inclusionary populist movements as authentically democratic, identifying rather than masking the cleavages around which emancipatory political projects can be made (Laclau & Mouffe, 2014), others suggest that nominally inclusionary populist movements are also likely to engage in the centralization of power, the delegitimization of political opposition, and the erosion of press freedom and other individual liberties at the core of democracy (Houle & Kenny, 2018; Kenny, 2020; Mainwaring, 2012; Mudde, 2015; Weyland, 2013).

Through an examination of the Indian experience of the late 1960s and 1970s, this chapter critiques the notion of inclusionary populism and the *ideational approach* to understanding the relationship between populism and democracy more generally. The imagery, discourse, and practice of Indira Gandhi's populism was consistently inclusionary, pitting ordinary, poor people against a corrupt political elite. Her administration pushed through seminal progressive economic and social legislation in the late 1960s, including bank nationalization and the revocation of the privileges of India's aristocracy. However, through the late 1960s and early 1970s, her government also eroded judicial independence, concentrated power in the executive, and suppressed the political opposition. In 1975, democracy was prorogued entirely. The Emergency period from 1975 to 1977 was accompanied by a total clampdown on press freedom, arbitrary detentions, and a litany of other human rights abuses, including forced sterilizations and even the torture of suspects by police. Notably, many of the victims of these policies were from the same underprivileged groups to whom Mrs. Gandhi had appealed at the height of her populist election campaigning in the early 1970s.

The Indian case suggests that the characterization of populist movements according to a single master *inclusionary-exclusionary* cleavage is deeply problematic. That division is almost impossible to sustain in practice, most actual populist movements or parties having features that are both inclusionary and exclusionary. The Indian case shows that although populist movements are distinctive in the unmediated way in which they organize the pursuit of political power, beyond this, they are characterized by tremendous political adaptivity, not ideological rigidity (Rooduijn et al., 2014). Consequently, this chapter argues that populist ideology or discourse, whether relatively more inclusionary or exclusionary, economic or nativist, is a poor guide as to how populist movements are likely to behave in power. Rather, of more consequence is the way in which populist movements like Mrs. Gandhi's are necessarily structured. Populists are charismatic leaders who appeal directly to the people to gain and retain power. The unmediated nature of this relationship frees populists from the informal constraints of party discipline that tend to check arbitrary power (Kenny, 2020; Urbinati, 2019). These pressures and incentives towards the personalization of power apply whether populist leaders hew to a supposed inclusionary or exclusionary conception of their support base among the people. Populism undermines democracy by the very nature of its organization—irrespective of ideology.

India's turn to populism

For the 20 or so years after independence in 1947, the Jawaharlal Nehru-led Congress party engineered a state of democratic stability in India through the distribution of patronage to its political supporters. However, within a few years of Nehru's death in 1964, this patronage-based one-party system descended into crisis. Nehru's daughter, Indira Gandhi, was installed as the head of the Indian National Congress party and Indian prime minister in 1966, but following a series of electoral reversals at the state level in 1967, the party split in 1969, with the majority following Mrs. Gandhi into the Congress (I)—'I' for Indira—and the conservative rump remaining in the Congress (O)—'O' for organization. Indira Gandhi refashioned herself as a radical populist, seeking to legitimize her leadership by going over the heads of the conservative party elites and appealing directly to the people (Kenny, 2017; Chapter 7 in this volume). Mrs. Gandhi felt that she could, in P. N. Haksar's description, 'project herself as a national figure who needs the Congress less than it needs her' (as cited in Guha, 2007, p. 438). She could, as another contemporary observed, simply 'appeal to the people over the heads of party bosses' (Mother India, 1971).

Moving against the old guard of the Congress, many of whom elected to remain in the Congress (O) after 1969, meant a shift towards the left (Carras, 1979). Leftists within the Congress, known collectively as the Congress Forum for Socialist Action (CFSA), interpreted the electoral losses of 1967 as a signal that the poor were being neglected by the Congress. The CFSA advocated a new 10-point programme at the All India Congress Committee (AICC) meeting in June 1967 (Hewitt, 2008, p. 82). Many of these programmes were in turn advocated by Mrs. Gandhi in an ostensible shift to the inclusionary populist left, a shift that would 'open the way for direct mediation between New Delhi and the Indian electorate' (Hewitt, 2008, p. 85). Mrs. Gandhi referred to this rationale in a speech in late 1969: 'We started losing in State after State and I saw no way in which I would bridge the gap except by going once more direct to the people'.[1]

The first policy plank in Mrs. Gandhi's populist turn was the nationalization of the banks, which P. N. Dhar, a senior advisor to Mrs. Gandhi, believed was 'a powerful weapon in the factional fight against the Syndicate' (Dhar, 2000, p. 114). Given the economic hardship faced by ordinary citizens, the perceived wealth of India's private banks was an understandable source of contention. On 20 July 1969, Mrs. Gandhi nationalized 14 commercial banks by presidential ordinance. This procedure—rather than the alternative legislative approach—emphasized that the measure was Mrs. Gandhi's decision alone. This served not only to gain her great credit with the people, but to cast her conservative opponents as acting contradictory to the interests of the common man. As a sympathetic biographer summarizes, 'Bank nationalization was a populist move and predictably it was greeted with public euphoria' (Frank, 2001, p. 315).

The second inclusionary populist policy pushed through by Mrs. Gandhi was the termination of the special privileges accorded to the Indian aristocracy. At the time of independence, only about 60 percent of India's territory was ruled directly by the British, the remainder being governed by subsidiary native princes. Partly to entice the princes into the Union of India when the British left, they were allowed to keep their royal titles and received substantial allowances, called privy purses, from the government. In September 1970, Indira Gandhi placed a bill that would rescind the privy purses before the Lok Sabha (lower house). Although the Lok Sabha approved the bill by 339 to 154 votes, the conservative Rajya Sabha (upper house) subsequently rejected it by one vote. Mrs. Gandhi, nonetheless, overrode the prerogatives of the upper house and had President V. V. Giri *derecognize* the princes (Frank, 2001, p. 323).

As was the case with the nationalization of the banks, the abolition of princely purses was opposed by conservatives within the Congress. When the Supreme Court ruled against the derecognition of the princes and against aspects of bank nationalization, Mrs. Gandhi and her allies portrayed it as a 'conflict between the established and entrenched bosses and the progressive forces'.[2] She claimed that she only sought to 'ensure a better life to the majority of our people and satisfy their aspiration for a just social order... [while] reactionary forces have not hesitated to obstruct [this] in every possible way' (as cited in Guha, 2007, p. 442). Presenting herself as an outsider to the conservative institutions of the Rajya Sabha and the Supreme Court, Mrs. Gandhi's platform fell comfortably within the inclusionary populist paradigm as it is commonly understood.

Mrs. Gandhi's rhetoric reinforced these inclusionary populist policies. She called national elections in 1971, a year earlier than scheduled, declaring (quoted in Frank, 2001, p. 324):

> Time will not wait for us. . . . The millions who demand food, shelter and jobs are pressing for action. Power in a democracy resides with the people. That is why I have decided to go to our people and seek a fresh mandate from them.

The decision to call early elections was strategic and reflected Mrs. Gandhi's newfound populist approach. By separating the national elections from the state elections (still scheduled for 1972), she was able to ask voters to put local issues aside and 'bypass the intermediary structures—the village notables and vote banks—that had been the base of the Congress machine' (Hardgrave & Kochanek, 1993, pp. 237–238). Mrs. Gandhi sought to use her celebrity and her recent record of popular pro-poor measures to appeal to the people in a way no other candidates could. She launched her campaign at a mass rally at the Ramlila grounds in New Delhi, which a journalist for *The Guardian* newspaper described as 'a textbook example of how to mount a broad-based appeal' (Keatley, 1971, p. 10), and railed against the establishment, declaring:

> For us, fundamental rights are not the princes, exemption from water taxes, 12-gun salutes, or privy purses; but education for all and the right to make a living. The (new) Congress is committed to enlarge the economic base, until every man gets his full needs and we have a truly free India—free from economic, social and political exploitation.

She repeatedly sought to make the elections about the preferences of the common man, not the elites. Building on the outpouring of public support following the nationalization of the major banks, she stated (quoted in Vasudev, 1974, p. 509):

> Many people say that the rickshaw pullers, cobblers, and others who came to my residence do not know anything about banks or nationalization. What I would like to know is that when I go out and seek their votes do I say that they do not know anything about democracy?

Adoring crowds attended her rallies with chants of 'Indira Gandhi—win!' and 'Indira Gandhi will come to remove poverty!' (Adeney, 1971, p. 4). Mrs. Gandhi herself described the campaign as (as quoted in Frank, 2001, p. 326):

> exhilarating . . . a sort of movement—a people's movement. It is true that I like being with the people. I shed my fatigue when I am with them . . . I don't see the people as a mass, I see them as so many individuals . . . Each person feels that I am communicating with him.

Indira Gandhi's Congress (I) won the elections in a landslide, garnering a critical two-thirds majority in the Lok Sabha. Mrs. Gandhi had dramatically reshaped the nature of Indian politics, making the national arena independent of the local.

Through to the early 1970s, the label of inclusionary populism seemed a good fit for Mrs. Gandhi. Pundits and academics have spent a great deal of time agonizing over whether she was truly socialist by inclination or whether her embrace of leftist policies was merely a political tactic to bolster her populist image. However, her *true* intentions seem beside the point here. Both in policy and rhetoric, she had clearly moved to the interests of ordinary people defined by class rather than by national identity, even if her own motivation was more strategic than ideological (Vasudev, 1974, p. 521). Holding a majority in parliament after 1971, Mrs. Gandhi set about fulfilling her inclusionary populist manifesto. Yet despite her supermajority in the Lok Sabha, her legislative agenda quickly brought her into conflict with a series of deeply embedded institutional checks on the executive. She interpreted this resistance as a direct contravention of the 1971 popular mandate and she set about overriding institutional checks on her personal authority. Her previous circumventions of the Rajya Sabha and the Supreme Court through executive action were just a precursor of what was to come.

Eroding checks and balances

Following English common law precedent, the framers of the Indian constitution conceived of the judiciary's role as one of benighted liberality. Mostly lawyers themselves, the framers imagined that the judiciary would be politically independent and that its autonomy would be inviolable (Austin, 1999, ch. 5). In the early decades after independence, the selection of Chief Justice was a largely apolitical process. The principle of seniority was strictly followed for appointments throughout the Nehru era (1947–1963). This is not to say that relations between the executive, legislative, and judicial branches were unproblematic. Following legal challenges to land reform, the judiciary prioritized the fundamental right to property in the Constitution over its more progressive directive principles. In response, however, Nehru worked within the law, seeking to make the question of compensation non-justiciable. As Jacob (1977, p. 178) concludes, when faced with conflicting political and legal imperatives, 'Nehru proceeded constitutionally and got the Constitution amended'.

Conflicts between the executive and judicial branches escalated under Indira Gandhi, especially after the 1971 election. With both signature pieces of her legislation, nationalization of the banks and revocation of the privy purses, rejected by the courts, the Lok Sabha enacted the Twenty-Fifth Amendment (1971), which dramatically curtailed the scope of judicial review. In 1973, Mrs. Gandhi then made a more substantial change in direction, departing from the practice of seniority and installing A. N. Ray as Chief Justice, even though there were three more senior justices on the court, on account of his perceived sympathies with her agenda (Guha, 2007, p. 472). Mrs. Gandhi's critics quickly accused her of making the court into a 'mouthpiece of the Government' (Frankel, 2005, p. 488).

The relationship between the government and its executing agents—the bureaucracy—is theoretically more problematic. On the one hand, the bureaucracy is simply an extension of the elected executive; it should do exactly as instructed by the government. On the other, it is argued that civil servants have a right, if not a duty, to disobey illegal orders. In this sense, as its agent, the bureaucracy may be understood as an additional check on executive overreach (Deb, 1978). In this context, Mrs. Gandhi's politicization of what was already an increasingly corrupt bureaucracy was another element in her personalization of power (Corbridge & Harriss, 2000; Joshi & Little, 1994). She called for greater commitment from civil servants, arguing that 'the so-called neutral administrative machinery is a hindrance, not a help' and 'is hardly relevant to Indian conditions' (as cited in Potter, 1994, p. 87). With loyalty to Mrs. Gandhi taking precedence in promotion prospects, personal connections were more important than merit. As with the upper levels of the judiciary, senior administrators would not be able to offer any concerted resistance to Mrs. Gandhi in the years that followed.

In a parliamentary democracy, political parties also function as an additional institutional check on the personal authority of the executive. Strict party whips and leaders with strong coattails can mitigate this function, but even within consolidated party systems like that of the United Kingdom, members of the party of government will vote against the government on particularly contentious issues, the Brexit campaign being an outstanding example. Thus, in a functioning party-based democracy, the party and government leadership must take at least some account of the preferences of its members. Indira Gandhi seriously eroded this institutional check on her authority. Following her election victory in 1971, the Congress party became increasingly subordinate to the personal preferences of its leader. Many members of Mrs. Gandhi's 1972 parliamentary party were freshmen, elected only by the strength of her coattails. In addition, Mrs. Gandhi used her network of political clients to build up a massive war chest of what were essentially illicit electoral funds, which she used in turn to discipline her party (Hewitt, 2008, pp. 94–95; Verghese, 2010, p. 185). While members of a functioning programmatic party can constrain its leadership through the threat of a spill motion or leadership challenge, Mrs. Gandhi's personalization of the party meant that no such disciplinary mechanism could operate.

The Emergency

Mrs. Gandhi eventually became trapped by the logic of her populist strategic shift. Pulled to the left by her backers within the Congress but at the same time lacking the organizational basis in civil society for a sustained reorganization of the economy, Mrs. Gandhi was driven towards a more authoritarian means of governance. Although there was some dissatisfaction with her government from within her leftist coalition (Guha, 2007, p. 476), the most vocal criticism came from students with the backing of the rural middle class (Frankel, 2005, p. 492). In 1972, students in Gujarat protested the state of the educational system and accused the Indira Gandhi-backed Congress government of gross corruption. The leader of this movement, a Gandhian by the name of Jayaprakash Narayan took the campaign nationwide in 1974, attempting to force the resignation of Indira Gandhi. He addressed gatherings of up to 200,000 people in Rajasthan, Punjab, and Delhi through October and November (Chandra, 2003; Kenny, 2017, pp. 117–118). Looting and rioting occurred in cities across the state of Gujarat, where much of the resistance was concentrated. Strikes followed in a concerted attempt to precipitate the fall of the government.

In response, the government deployed troops and reserve police to monitor and restrain the agitation in Gujarat, Bihar, and other states (Kenny, 2017, p. 117). Police were ordered onto university campuses and several students were beaten and arrested. One contemporary described Bihar as a war zone (Wood, 1975). Mrs. Gandhi dissolved the Gujarat legislative assembly and consolidated her control over the country's security forces and intelligence community, bringing them under her 'direct control' (Kenny, 2017, p. 117). By early 1975, the demonstrations had spread to New Delhi, with a permanent body of demonstrators encamped outside Mrs. Gandhi's residence in the capital. The situation was pushed closer to the brink by a national railway strike. Although the strike was swiftly broken by the government and its leaders arrested under the Maintenance of Internal Security Act (MISA) provisions, the government railway minister, L. N. Mishra, was assassinated in retaliation (Frankel, 2005, pp. 529–530). The prospect of a violent overthrow of the government had become realistic.

Mrs. Gandhi's efforts to contain the growing unrest within constitutional parameters were dealt a blow in early June 1975. Since her electoral victory in 1971, her opponent in the Rae Bareli Constituency, Raj Narain, had sought to have the result overturned. Narain accused Mrs. Gandhi of a number of campaign law infringements, which gradually made their way through courts via several rounds of appeals. The Allahabad High Court gave its ruling on 12 June 1975. Although the court exonerated Mrs. Gandhi of the most serious charges, it found that Mrs. Gandhi had inappropriately used government resources in her electoral campaign. Even though the abuse was only a minor technicality, the court ruled that Mrs. Gandhi would be 'disqualified for a period of six years' from holding office (Shah, 1978a, p. 17). Mrs. Gandhi stood firm, however, accusing her political enemies of attempting to remove her undemocratically. Mass protests—both for and against Mrs. Gandhi—followed.

Just before midnight on 25 June 1975, the President of India, Fakhruddin Ali Ahmed, instructed by Indira Gandhi, declared a state of national emergency under Article 352 of the Constitution. Two days later, the president issued a proclamation under Article 359 of the Constitution suspending the right to motion any court for the enforcement of any of the fundamental rights of the Constitution. The Emergency declaration empowered state governments and their security forces to make 'all necessary arrangements to prevent formation of crowds or processions or any form of agitation likely to lead to violence'. It also allowed for preventive detention, pre-censorship of news, confiscation of pamphlets or other news sources, and the blocking of any international news by wire, fax, or other means. There would, in short, be a total shutdown of the public sphere while order was restored. Democracy in any effective sense had been prorogued (Jaffrelot & Anil, 2021).

The Ministry of Home Affairs quickly released a document entitled 'Why Emergency?', which purported to explain and justify the suspension of democracy as a result of the declining state of law and order and the agitations of the opposition. Mrs. Gandhi repeatedly accused organizations on the Hindu nationalist right, especially the Rashtriya Swayamsevak Sangh (RSS), of being fascists bent on creating the very disorder they used to justify their protests against her government. Of the 26 organizations banned at the outset of the Emergency, most of these were from the communal far right with a few coming from the non-democratic left (e.g., the Naxalites). Mrs. Gandhi also used the provisions of MISA to imprison leading figures from within her own party, including Chandra Shekhar, Mohan Dharia, Krishan Kant, Ram Dhan, and P. N. Singh (Vasudev, 1977, p. 2). Eventually, about 110,000 people were detained under MISA and Defence of India Rules (DIR) during the Emergency. The Supreme Court ruled that the power of any court to issue a writ for *habeus corpus* was suspended for the duration of the Emergency. At least one instance of the torture and death of a detainee in custody was documented (Shah, 1978b, pp. 1–12),[3] while many thousands of prisoners were kept in appalling conditions without trial for extended durations (Shah, 1978b, pp. 135–152). Strict censorship laws enacted under Rule 48 of the Defence and Internal Security of India Rules and the Prohibition of Objectionable Matter Act of 1976 (in force as an ordinance since December 1975) prevented the media from investigating and reporting on these abuses.

Although Mrs. Gandhi upheld the pretence of operating within the law, this could only be achieved by frequent, wholesale, and arbitrary amendments to the Constitution. There were even rumours that Mrs. Gandhi planned to convene a constituent assembly to write a new constitution with a stronger executive, following the French and U.S. examples. Her law minister, H. R. Gokhale, stated in parliament on 6 August 1975 that the government would take a second look at the 'whole process of the constitution as early as possible' (Kenny, 2017, p. 120). The following day, he continued to argue in parliament that the Indian constitution was no longer relevant to the times. Uma Shankar Dikshit, the union minister for transport and shipping, similarly argued in November 1975 that 'if the Supreme Court debarred the government from making changes in the constitution, a constituent assembly might be called to frame a new constitution guaranteeing social and economic justice' (Kenny, 2017, p. 120). While Mrs. Gandhi eschewed a full rewrite of the Constitution, she radically shifted the balance of power in favour of the executive branch. The Thirty-Eighth Amendment to the Constitution safeguarded the Emergency and put presidential rule in the states and the promulgation of ordinances beyond the purview of the courts, allowing recalcitrant state governments to be dismissed. The Thirty-Ninth Amendment absolved Mrs. Gandhi of any wrongdoing regarding the election. The Forty-First Amendment gave complete immunity to the prime minister for any actions done in an official capacity. The controversial Forty-Second Amendment gave parliament the unrestricted right to make future amendments to the Constitution. It also massively strengthened the executive at the expensive the legislature and the judiciary. Fundamental rights (such as those to property) were subordinated to the Directive Principles (which concerned issues of social justice and development). The amendment also reduced the powers of the states vis-à-vis the centre. Of course, Mrs. Gandhi sought to portray her suspension of democracy as a defence of democracy and declared,[4]

> It is malicious slander to say that the amendments to the Constitution have debased it. On the contrary, they have removed obstacles to the fulfillment of the ideals enshrined and openly proclaimed in the Constitution and thus have given strength to it.

Given the fragmentation of the opposition, security was restored relatively quickly. The streets were cleared, businesses were reopened, and trains ran on schedule for the first time in years. In fact, so smooth and relatively peaceful was the reestablishment of order that some of Mrs. Gandhi's advisors encouraged her to use the opportunity to push through modernizing reforms. On 1 July 1975, Mrs. Gandhi put out a 20-point programme designed to appeal to the rural and urban poor. The programme promised to eliminate rural indebtedness, abolish bonded labour, and provide credit to small farmers. It would redistribute land, enhance worker participation in enterprises, subsidize vital goods like cloth, and provide cheap or free educational materials to children. The programme was ambitious and appeared progressive and well-intentioned. Its implementation was, however, accompanied by some serious violations of civil liberties and human rights, the most egregious excesses being the forced sterilization and compulsory removal of slum residents.

Observers have had great difficulty in explaining Mrs. Gandhi's authoritarian reversal. Mrs. Gandhi portrayed the imposition of Emergency rule in *inclusionary* populist terms. She justified the Emergency as an appropriate response to a minority that was 'attempting to submerge the voice of the majority' (as cited in Chandra, 2003, p. 78). She decried 'The deep-seated and widespread conspiracy which has been brewing ever since I began to introduce certain progressive measures of benefit to the common man and woman in India' (as cited in Frankel, 2005, p. 546). In reality, however, many Emergency era provisions were improvised rather than planned. Family planning was an arguably sensible end goal in a poor and populous country with high birth rates, but the pressures placed on civil servants and health officials led to massive numbers of coerced sterilizations (Shah, 1978b, pp. 153–207). The multipoint economic programme was drawn up only after the Emergency had been declared. It was a retroactive legitimation of her self-coup rather than a proactive justification for it. We should, therefore, be careful in attributing her motivations for declaring the Emergency to her actions during the Emergency itself.

My view is that the erosion of democracy, including the so-called excesses of the Emergency, was less the product of a particular ideological framework than the result of unchecked executive power. The erosion of respect for laws and procedures in favour of results spread throughout the system. Many of the systematic abuses, from arbitrary arrests to forced sterilizations, were not deliberately conceived or executed by the central government. However, that state and local governments engaged in this kind of behaviour should not come as a great surprise. Since 1971, Mrs. Gandhi's government had systematically circumvented institutional checks and balances when it suited her purposes. Constitutional and legislative provisions were interpreted in whatever way proved most expedient. The leaders of state governments simply reproduced this behaviour, knowing that results were what counted and that they could be arbitrarily removed should they fail to achieve them. At the same time, the Emergency provided a means of disciplining rebels within her own party as well as controlling the opposition. With the threat of detention or other disciplinary procedures hanging over their heads, members of the parliament could offer no resistance to Mrs. Gandhi. The Lok Sabha was effectively made a rubber stamp, while state governments were removed and states administrated by centrally appointed governors. Any semblance of internal democracy within Mrs. Gandhi's party was stamped out. Thus, although not all explicitly intended, the abuses of the Emergency were an outgrowth of Mrs. Gandhi's *populist* strategy for winning and keeping power. The erosion of checks and balances on the executive branch was justified by Mrs. Gandhi's claim to represent the popular will. The outcome, unfortunately, was the widespread violation of individual rights, not so much of the upper classes whose property was threatened but, ironically, of the poor who stood in the way of modernization (Jaffrelot & Anil, 2021).

Is populism ideological or instrumental?

When we consider the relationship between populism and the erosion of democracy in India, discussion inevitably turns to the Hindu nationalist Bharatiya Janata Party (BJP) government of Narendra Modi. Modi's government does appear to have eroded freedom of expression and, more debatably, to have taken measures to tame the political opposition (Ganguly, 2020). What this chapter has shown is that the erosion of democracy is not the preserve of exclusionary or right-wing populism. In fact, the evidence from India renders any neat bifurcation of inclusionary and exclusionary populism problematic. Many populist movements seem to necessarily draw elements from each. The evidence presented here also challenges the dominant ideational conceptualization of populism itself. So capacious is this definition that it provides very little guidance as to what populists actually do. The key component of the ideational conceptualization of populism is the invocation of the idea of popular sovereignty (Mudde, 2004, p. 543; Panizza, 2005). Put most simply, populism is based on the idea that the people should rule (Crick, 2005; Stanley, 2008). By itself, of course, this risks replicating the very etymology of democracy. Populism then loses its force as a social scientific construct. Paying attention to what populists *do*, rather than to what they *say*, helps to resolve some of these conceptual difficulties, providing a simpler rationalist explanation for the inimical relationship between populism and democracy.

What distinguishes populism from democracy more generally is the way in which it relates the people with the instruments of rule, i.e., the state. Populism demands the closest possible identification of the people and the state and thus inherently opposes those formal and informal institutions that intermediate between the two (Crick, 2005; Laclau, 2005; Panizza, 2005; Stanley, 2008; Urbinati, 2015, 2019; Worsley, 1969). In short, there should be no obstacles between the people and the state; indeed, in populist rhetoric the two are often coeval: the people *are* the state and the people's will is the law (Riker, 1982, p. 238). We can find references to the antipathy to intermediation embedded in nearly all of the most influential analyses of populism. Crick (2005, p. 626) writes:

> The populist leader usually blames intermediary institutions for frustrating the will of the people. At various times, and, in various places, these intermediary and divisive institutions have appeared as the landlords, the bankers, the bureaucrats, the priests, the elite, the immigrants and, most popular of all for populists to denounce, the politicians.

Urbinati (1998, p. 119) notes that the aim of populism is 'that of blurring any mediation between leadership and the people so as to bypass indirect forms of politics'. This opposition to intermediation goes as far as an opposition to political parties themselves. Mudde (2004, p. 546) writes that 'populists argue that political parties corrupt the link between leaders and supporters'. Urbinati (2019) writes that populism is simply *antipartyism*. For many theorists, this feature does not in itself make populism inimical to democracy. For many writers, democracy in the sense of rule by the people is possible without liberalism, or the set of values and institutions that constrain the majority.

However, this parsing of liberalism and democracy is inappropriate. Democracy is just not possible without some degree of institutional protection for minorities. In fact, while it might seem like institutions such as supreme courts are undemocratic to the extent that they can make decisions that run against majority views, as the primary author of the United States Constitution, James Madison, argued, without these kinds of institutions, 'it would be the interest of the majority in every community to despoil and enslave the minority'.[5] Without such protections, the minority could never become the majority and the criterion of free and fair competition for power, necessary to any minimal definition of democracy, would not be met. Populism, to the extent that it threatens these intermediary institutions, not least parties, is inherently menacing to democracy.

Critically, moreover, the opposition to institutional intermediation results from how populist movements are organized. Considering it as a form of political mobilization, Roberts (2007, p. 5) writes that populism refers to 'the top-down political mobilization of mass constituencies by personalistic leaders who challenge elite groups on behalf of an ill-defined pueblo, or "the people"'. Populists aim to mobilize the masses directly with a minimal degree of organization (Weyland, 2001). As I have written elsewhere, including in this volume (see Chapter 3), populism describes the charismatic mobilization of the masses in pursuit of political power (Kenny, 2017, 2023). Public rallies, television appearances, and even social media are used to communicate directly with actual and potential supporters. While populists clearly employ pro-people rhetoric, populist movements go further and actually structure their political machines in a way that reflects the ambition to bring follower and leader, people and the state, closer (Mouzelis, 1985). Rule-based parties with procedures for selection and succession are hostile to the populist project (Weyland, 2001).

This in turn implies that populist movements in power will centralize power, erode checks and balances on executive authority, and attempt to engineer permanent majorities. All of these processes feature in the Indian case, in spite of Mrs. Gandhi's professed progressive or inclusionary goals (Kenny, 2017). In the Indian case, as in others, the erosion of institutional checks and balances on arbitrary rule was made possible by Mrs. Gandhi's prior personalization of the Congress party machine. Notwithstanding the low regard that most of the public holds for political parties, these organizations play a critical role in maintaining democracy. To understand this relationship, we need not imagine that populists are devils while partymen are angels. Rather, we can assume that all politicians have the same ultimate goal of gaining and retaining power, and still arrive at the same conclusion.

If the leader of a bureaucratically organized party can be removed by some institutional procedure, such as a vote of no confidence, she is constrained to follow the interests of her party membership (or at least the part of the membership that decides her fate). That is, she can retain her leadership role only by best ensuring that her co-partisans also retain their own positions. She must avoid measures that will harm their electability. Any such leader who undermines the accepted democratic rules of the game poses a direct threat to her party members, who face punishment by association in future elections. A populist faces no such concerns. A populist does not have to attend to the future viability of a party. Mrs. Gandhi had only to secure her own political survival, or perhaps that of her family. If that survival is procured by eroding democracy, then, as Indira Gandhi demonstrated, this is the rational strategy.

Notes

1 'Can India Survive?' Speech at the Indo-French Colloquium, New Delhi, 13 December 1969, in Gandhi, 1975, p. 88.
2 Fakhruddin Ali Ahmed from a speech to the AICC in 1969, quoted in Frankel, 2005, p. 431
3 For more on other rumoured instances, see 'Current Political Situation', Diplomatic cable New Delhi to Kabul etc., 14 July 1975, no: 1975NEWDE09442_b
4 Interview to *Socialist India*, New Delhi, 26 Jan 1975, in Gandhi, 1984, p. 111
5 'From James Madison to James Monroe, 5 October 1786', Founders Online, National Archives, https://founders.archives.gov/documents/Madison/01-09-02-0054. [Original source: The Papers of James Madison, vol. 9, 9 April 1786—24 May 1787 and supplement 1781–1784, ed. Robert A. Rutland and William M. E. Rachal. Chicago: The University of Chicago Press, 1975, pp. 140–142.]

References

Adeney, M. (1971, February 26). A head start for Mrs Gandhi. *The Guardian*.
Austin, G. (1999). *The Indian constitution: Cornerstone of a nation*. Oxford University Press.
Canovan, M. (1999). Trust the people! Populism and the two faces of democracy. *Political Studies*, 47(1), 2–16. https://doi.org/10.1111/1467-9248.00184
Carras, M. C. (1979). *Indira Gandhi: In the crucible of leadership: A political biography*. Beacon Press.

Chandra, B. (2003). *In the name of democracy: JP movement and the emergency*. Penguin.
Corbridge, S., & Harriss, J. (2000). *Reinventing India: Liberalization, Hindu nationalism, and popular democracy*. Polity.
Crick, B. (2005). Populism, politics and democracy. *Democratisation, 12*(5), 625–632. https://doi.org/10.1080/13510340500321985
Deb, R. (1978). Public services under the rule of law—Right to disobey illegal orders. *Journal of the Indian Law Institute, 20*(4), 574–583. www.jstor.org/stable/43950554
Dhar, P. N. (2000). *Indira Gandhi, the 'Emergency', and Indian democracy*. Oxford University Press.
Frank, K. (2001). *Indira: The life of Indira Nehru Gandhi*. Harper Collins.
Frankel, F. R. (2005). *India's political economy, 1947–2004: The gradual revolution* (2nd ed.). Oxford University Press.
Gandhi, I. (1975). *Indira Gandhi: Speeches and writings*. Harper & Row.
Gandhi, I. (1984). *Selected speeches and writings of Indira Gandhi* (Vol. III). Government of India.
Ganguly, S. (2020, September 18). India's democracy is under threat. *Foreign Policy*. https://foreignpolicy.com/2020/09/18/indias-democracy-is-under-threat/
Guha, R. (2007). *India after Gandhi: The history of the world's largest democracy*. Ecco.
Hardgrave, R. L., & Kochanek, S. A. (1993). *India: Government and politics in a developing nation* (5th ed.). Harcourt Brace Jovanovich.
Hewitt, V. M. (2008). *Political mobilisation and democracy in India: States of emergency*. Routledge.
Houle, C., & Kenny, P. D. (2018). The political and economic consequences of populist rule in Latin America. *Government and Opposition, 53*(2), 256–287 https://doi.org/https://doi.org/10.1017/gov.2016.25
Jacob, A. (1977). Nehru and the judiciary. *Journal of the Indian Law Institute, 19*(2), 169–181. www.jstor.org/stable/43950472
Jaffrelot, C., & Anil, P. (2021). *India's first dictatorship: The Emergency, 1975–1977*. Oxford University Press.
Joshi, V., & Little, I. M. D. (1994). *India: Macroeconomics and political economy 1964–1991*. World Bank. https://elibrary.worldbank.org/doi/abs/10.1596/0-8213-2652-X
Keatley, P. (1971, February 10). Rendevous with destiny. *The Guardian*.
Kenny, P. D. (2017). *Populism and patronage: Why populists win elections in India, Asia, and beyond*. Oxford University Press.
Kenny, P. D. (2020). 'The enemy of the people': Populists and press freedom. *Political Research Quarterly, 73*(2), 261–275. https://doi.org/10.1177/1065912918824038
Kenny, P. D. (2023). *Why populism? Political strategy from Ancient Greece to the present*. Cambridge University Press.
Laclau, E. (2005). *On populist reason*. Verso.
Laclau, E., & Mouffe, C. (2014). *Hegemony and socialist strategy: Towards a radical democratic politics* (2nd ed.). Verso.
Mainwaring, S. (2012). From representative democracy to participatory competitive authoritarianism: Hugo Chávez and Venezuelan politics. *Perspectives on Politics, 10*(4), 955–967. https://doi.org/10.1017/S1537592712002629
Moffitt, B. (2020). *Populism*. Polity.
Mother India (1971, March 12). *The Guardian*, p. 11.
Mouzelis, N. (1985). On the concept of populism: Populist and clientelist modes of incorporation in semiperipheral polities. *Politics and Society, 14*(3), 329–348. https://doi.org/10.1177/003232928501400303
Mudde, C. (2004). The populist zeitgeist. *Government and Opposition, 39*(4), 542–563. https://doi.org/10.1111/j.1477-7053.2004.00135.x
Mudde, C. (2015, February 17). The problem with populism. *The Guardian*. www.theguardian.com/commentisfree/2015/feb/17/problem-populism-syriza-podemos-dark-side-europe
Mudde, C., & Rovira Kaltwasser, C. (2013). Exclusionary vs. inclusionary populism: Comparing contemporary Europe and Latin America. *Government and Opposition, 48*(2), 147–174. https://doi.org/10.1017/gov.2012.11
Panizza, F. (2005). Introduction: Populism and the mirror of democracy. In F. Panizza (Ed.), *Populism and the mirror of democracy* (pp. 1–31). Verso.

Potter, D. (1994). The prime minister and the bureaucracy. In J. Manor (Ed.), *Nehru to the nineties: The changing office of prime minister in India*. University of British Columbia Press.

Riker, W. H. (1982). *Liberalism against populism: A confrontation between the theory of democracy and the theory of social choice*. W.H. Freeman.

Roberts, K. M. (2007). Latin America's populist revival. *SAIS Review*, 27(1), 3–15.

Rooduijn, M., de Lange, S. L., & van der Brug, W. (2014). A populist zeitgeist? Programmatic contagion by populist parties in Western Europe. *Party Politics*, 20(4), 563–575. https://doi.org/10.1177/1354068811436065

Rovira Kaltwasser, C. (2012). The ambivalence of populism: Threat and corrective for democracy. *Democratization*, 19(2), 184–208. https://doi.org/10.1080/13510347.2011.572619

Shah, J. C. (1978a). *Shah commission of inquiry: Interim report I*. Government of India. http://library.bjp.org/jspui/handle/123456789/741

Shah, J. C. (1978b). *Shah commission of inquiry third and final report*. Government of India. http://library.bjp.org/jspui/handle/123456789/743

Stanley, B. (2008). The thin ideology of populism. *Journal of Political Ideologies*, 13(1), 95–110. https://doi.org/10.1080/13569310701822289

Urbinati, N. (1998). Democracy and populism. *Constellations*, 5(1), 110–124. https://doi.org/10.1111/1467-8675.00080

Urbinati, N. (2015). A revolt against intermediary bodies. *Constellations*, 22(4), 477–486. https://doi.org/10.1111/1467-8675.12188

Urbinati, N. (2019). *Me the people: How populism transforms democracy*. Harvard University Press.

Vasudev, U. (1974). *Indira Gandhi: Revolution in restraint*. Vikas Publishing House.

Vasudev, U. (1977). *Two faces of Indira Gandhi*. Vikas Publishing House.

Verghese, B. G. (2010). *First draft: Witness to the making of modern India*. Tranquebar Press.

Weyland, K. (2001). Clarifying a contested concept: Populism in the study of Latin American politics. *Comparative Politics*, 34(1), 1–22. https://doi.org/10.2307/422412

Weyland, K. (2013). The threat from the populist left. *Journal of Democracy*, 24(3), 18–32.

Wood, J. R. (1975). Extra-parliamentary opposition in India: An analysis of populist agitations in Gujarat and Bihar. *Pacific Affairs*, 48(3), 313–334. https://doi.org/10.2307/2756412

Worsley, P. (1969). The concept of populism. In G. Ionescu & E. Gellner (Eds.), *Populism: Its meaning and national characteristics* (pp. 212–250). Macmillan.

13
FROM ZULFIQAR ALI BHUTTO TO IMRAN KHAN

A comparative analysis of populist leaders in Pakistan

Zahid Shahab Ahmed

The rise of right-wing populism has culminated in political successes in many parts of the world, most notably among the major nations in the electoral triumphs of Modi in India and Trump in the United States.

Historically, populism in Pakistan has appeared in different forms. Zulfiqar Ali Bhutto, founder of the Pakistan People's Party (PPP), is considered the country's first populist leader. A prominent factor in Bhutto's populist appeal was that he projected himself as the people's leader, completely accessible on all social levels. Through regular appearances among the masses, he was bestowed with the title *Quaid-i-Awam*, the great leader of the people (Zaidi, 2019), eventually serving as the ninth prime minister of Pakistan between 1973 and 1977. In recent times, Pakistan witnessed the rise of another socialist leader, Imran Khan, whose populist politics was founded on his national popularity gained through a high-profile career as an international cricketer. Khan's socialist revolution targeting corruption led to his success in the 2018 general elections and his appointment as the 22nd prime minister of Pakistan. In April 2022, Imran Khan was removed from his position after being defeated in a no-confidence motion in parliament, the first Pakistani prime minister to be removed in this manner, as others such as Benazir Bhutto and Shaukat Aziz had survived similar motions. While there is an abundance of studies devoted to the individual careers of Bhutto and Khan as populist leaders, no comparative analysis has yet been undertaken, particularly with reference to their populist narrative. This chapter aims to address this gap.

Studies that have partially shared the focus of this research have revolved around challenges to democratization in Pakistan. Imran Khan's government was criticized for its ties with the armed forces (Afzal, 2019; A. Shah, 2019). The military has sustained its influence in Pakistani politics through long periods of martial law that have contributed to the deterioration of political institutions, undermining democracy (Ganguly, 2008). A comprehensive study concludes that Pakistani 'political leaders continue to reveal lack of commitment to the principles of democracy' (Shafqat, 1998, p. 295). Correspondingly, former Information Minister Fawad Chaudhry claimed recently: 'All Pakistani political parties are standing on an undemocratic system' ('Basic Democratic "Skeleton"', 2021). This may well be ascribed to the fact that the leadership of several parties, including the prominent PPP and Pakistan Muslim League (PML), is controlled by traditional political families.

Many scholars note that Islam has been integral to the political development of Pakistan, a factor that strongly motivated Imran Khan's political ingenuity (Fatima, 2013). It has been asserted that Khan 'rose to power on a classic populist platform', presenting his party, the Pakistan Tehreek-e-Insaf (PTI), as a non-corruptible alternative to the two largest political parties of the day, namely the Pakistan Muslim League-Nawaz (PML-N) and the PPP (Afzal, 2019, p. 1). Khan's populism, promoted by his anti-Western, pro-Taliban rhetoric, may be classified as pandering to both left and right wings. His pro-poor social welfare policies were drawn from the left, as was his foreign policy, intended to reduce dependence on the West through a 'leftist brand of nationalism' (Afzal, 2019, p. 1). Based on an assessment of the 2018 elections that carried Khan to power, A. Shah described Pakistan's system of governance as a 'pseudo-democratic façade covering the reality of continued military tutelage' (2019, p. 128).

It has been contended that Imran Khan and Zulfiqar Ali Bhutto exhibited similar populist traits. After Pakistan's disintegration in 1971, Bhutto began promoting Islamic socialism through anti-Western rhetoric. Jafferlot rightly describes Bhutto 'as less a democrat than a populist, more an authoritarian than a parliamentarian, more a centralizer than a federalist, and as much a socialist as a product of his social background' (2015, p. 10). After placing restrictions on the media, Bhutto denied Pakistan free and fair elections in 1977, unwittingly preparing the ground for another military coup d'état in July of that year. Similarly, Khan used anti-Western rhetoric to promote his party through the promise of a corruption-free Pakistan, idealistically modelled on the first Islamic State of Madinah under Prophet Muhammad. Khan was criticized for reneging on his promises and attacking opposition parties, the media, and human rights activists under the guise of accountability (Siddiqui, 2019), while his dodging a no-confidence vote early in 2022 was also interpreted as undemocratic (Averre, 2022).

The recent sharp increase in research on populism reflects the rapid emergence of populist leaders worldwide. A study found that populist leaders are not fundamentally different from other categories of political leaders, 'who apart from gaining power seek to implement certain policies and normalize certain ideologically informed discourses' (Rueda, 2021, p. 180). However, specialized research on personality types and character traits has revealed that populist leaders are commonly charismatic but ill-mannered. A comparative analysis of politician types found that populists scored lower on 'agreeableness, emotional stability and conscientiousness' and higher on 'extraversion, narcissism, psychopathy and Machiavellianism' (Nai & Coma, 2019, p. 1337). By virtue of their political success and significance as populist figures, decision-making in populist ruling parties is dominated by individual leaders, with lesser members of the inner circle playing supporting roles. Barber argues,

> It is the leader who has the direct connection with the people; others in government are tasked with carrying out the leader's commands or communicating her decisions; it is not their job to express dissent or to seek to alter the leader's mind.
>
> *(2019, p. 129)*

The analysis focuses on similarities in the populist discourse of the two former prime ministers, the one anti-Western, the other anti-Indian. Further, the two leaders shared several personality traits and a similar political background. While Bhutto belonged to a feudal family, Khan descended from a highly qualified professional line on both sides. Both studied at Oxford, and in their political ascents to premiership, both collaborated with their contemporary military dictators. Bhutto served as Minister of Foreign Affairs under the military regime of Ayub Khan from 1963 to 1966 and, thereafter, under Yahya Khan until 1977. Khan achieved the highest level of recognition and respect throughout the cricket world, leading his country to victory in the 1992 World Cup, after which he retired. He supported Pervez Musharraf's coup and backed him during the 2002 referendum. A thorough examination of their relatively similar backgrounds and personalities is fundamental to a comparison of their individual populist narratives.

The populist discourses of Bhutto and Khan compared

The populist discourses of the two former Pakistani leaders are categorized thematically according to anti-Westernism, anti-Indianism, and the tenets of Islam as topics of political discourse in Pakistan.

Anti-Westernism

A key aspect of Imran Khan's populism was his expression of antagonism towards the global powers and the West, especially the United States. Bhutto's disapproval of the West and the United States was inherently linked to the developments leading up to the disintegration of Pakistan in 1971.[1] At this point, Pakistan faced an embarrassing defeat at the hands of India, but more shocking for Bhutto was the revelation that his country's security alliances with the West, such as the Southeast Asian Treaty Organization (SEATO), proved useless in terms of Pakistan's security. He thus withdrew Pakistan's membership of SEATO in 1973.[2] Faced with anti-government protests at home and in the wake of the U.S. evacuation of Saigon in 1975, Bhutto upscaled his anti-American rhetoric by delivering an anti-American speech to Pakistan's parliament in 1977. In the speech, he blamed the United States for conspiring against his government and bankrolling the local demonstrations (Kugelman, 2013).[3]

After parting ways with the West, Bhutto looked towards the *ummah*, or greater Islamic community, to achieve Pakistan's national objectives, i.e., economic development and security. Naturally, this revived Pakistan's interest in pan-Islamism, and Bhutto followed a pan-Islamic path, forging closer relations with other Muslim countries, and visiting Afghanistan, Algeria, Egypt, Iran, Libya, Morocco, Syria, Tunisia, and Turkey in January 1972 (Rizvi, 1993, p. 74). This foreign policy aimed to reduce economic dependence on the United States through financial support from wealthier Muslim countries such as Libya and Saudi Arabia (Delvoie, 1995). He further successfully strengthened relations with key Muslim states, for example, by organizing the second summit of the Organisation of Islamic Cooperation (OIC)[4] in 1974 in Lahore at which Colonel Gaddafi dubbed Pakistan 'the citadel of Islam in Asia', a moral tribute to and boost for the young nation (Bhutto, 2010, p. 111).

Not unlike Bhutto's anti-imperialist form of populist discourse, Imran Khan consistently emphasized an anti-imperialist line in his speeches and statements. Pakistan, according to Khan, has always been subservient to foreigners; first the British and then the Americans. At the heart of Khan's rhetoric was an emphasis on Pakistan's sovereignty—the idea that Pakistan should be an independent nation, free from foreign influence (Aslam, 2015, p. 79). It is within this context that his anti-United States discourse emerged. The American war on terror was, according to Khan, 'the most insane and immoral war of all time' (Jeffries, 2011). He likened the 'War on Terror' to the United States' involvement in Vietnam, both of which led to their military failure in two other global regions (Jeffries, 2011). This brings Khan closer to Bhutto, who regarded the Vietnamese resistance against the United States military as a heroic victory. United States foreign policy in the contemporary era, according to Khan, represents an 'era of neocolonialism', an era 'in which Pakistan's people seem destined to suffer as much as, if not more, than they did during British colonial rule' (Jeffries, 2011). Khan called for 'the end of American hegemony' (Judah, 2018) and his anti-American rhetoric reached its apex when stated, 'We will not allow the United States to conduct its drone attacks in Pakistan. If the United States continues its attacks, then we will shoot down their drones, and we will protest in the United Nations' (Aslam, 2015, p. 87). Khan used his anti-American discourse to gain legitimacy in the eyes of the populace, according to the principle that 'anti-American rhetoric has long been a populist vote winner' in Pakistan, as a journalist noted (Campbell, 2018). As he faced the no-confidence motion at the beginning of 2022, Khan blamed the United States for plotting the downfall of his government (Averre, 2022).

Anti-elitism has been central to populist movements around the world. In the case of Brexit in the United Kingdom, it was found that 'nativist sentiment and anti-elitist attitudes, the cocktail of right-wing populism, led to widespread support for Brexit' (Lakhnis et al., 2018, p. 1). The term *elite* does not refer exclusively to political elites and may include leaders of other institutions, such as the military in the case of Pakistan. A visible compromise in Khan's administration was the clear neglect of human development in the 2020 budget notwithstanding his anti-military elite position before becoming prime minister. As a populist leader, Khan often linked his anti-American discourse to his criticism of former Pakistani political leaders, increasing his legitimacy via delegitimization of the former political leaders. His discourse conformed to general populist discourse in being directed at enmity and distrust towards political elites. He referred to former presidents of Pakistan, especially Pervez Musharraf and Asif Zardari, as 'American stooges' (Aslam, 2015, p. 79). As noted by Aslam, 'A consistent theme in Khan's political rhetoric is that current Pakistani leaders have brought shame to the country's name by not taking a stance against the use of drones by the United States' (Aslam, 2015, p. 79). For Imran Khan, 'puppet government' in Pakistan referred to the receipt of American aid which inversely destroyed the country. Accordingly, he claimed that the Pakistani military killed 'our own people with American money. We have to separate from the United States' (Jeffries, 2011). Thus, his populist discourse was not only directed at American foreign policy with regard to the Middle East, but also at successive Pakistani governments for entrapping their country in a dismal cycle of mass deaths by supporting the war on terror in return for U.S. financial aid (Jeffries, 2011). His grandstanding on the anger that the Pakistani electorate had shown toward the war on terror enhanced his support, which he further broadened with the promise to pull Pakistan out of the global anti-terrorist campaign. Interviewed by Stuart Jeffries of *The Guardian* in 2011

> According to the government economic survey in Pakistan, $70bn has been lost to the economy because of this war. Total aid has been barely $20bn. Aid has gone to the ruling elite, while the people have lost $70bn. We have lost 35,000 lives and as many maimed—and then to be said to be complicit. The shame of it!
>
> *(Jeffries, 2011).*

Both Eastern and Western studies conclude that populist leaders use religion in ideational, performative, and strategic political approaches (Peker & Laxer, 2021). Khan's early anti-Western rhetoric turned the focus onto Islamophobia and showed how, in the West, it has arisen through a failure to understand Islam. As prime minister, he used the stage of the United Nations General Assembly in 2019 to talk about these issues:

> Millions of Muslims are living in the United States and European countries as minorities. Islamophobia, since 9/11 has grown at an alarming pace. Human communities are supposed to live together with understanding among each other. But Islamophobia is creating a division.
>
> ('Takeaways from Imran', 2019)

Khan repeatedly referred to the oppressed globally. His government compared the Indian government security restrictions in the union territory of Jammu and Kashmir with Israeli atrocities against Palestinians ('Pakistan Hits Back', 2019). While Khan has spoken for the ummah, including Muslims in majority-Muslim and other states, it came as a surprise that he completely avoided the issue of Uighur Muslims in Xinjiang, China. In a televised interview, as the prime minister of Pakistan, he was caught off guard on the issue and responded to a question on the detention of two million Muslims in Xinjiang, 'Frankly, I don't know much about that' (Westcott, 2019). This reaction from a Pakistani leader is not surprising considering China's promise to invest US$62 billion in Pakistan supporting the China-Pakistan Economic Corridor project. Realistically, that qualifies as another compromise made by Khan for his survival, going to the extreme of applauding China's poverty alleviation program as an exemplary lesson for Pakistan (' Pakistani PM Praises', 2019). The compromise made him a clear target of criticism in the West. In his bi-weekly *Wall Street Journal* column on Indian and South Asian regional politics, Sadanand Dhume jibed,

> Imran Khan's foreign-policy agenda carries a contradiction at its heart. Mr Khan seeks to project himself as a global defender of Islam, but he wouldn't utter a peep about one of the most egregious persecutions of Muslims: China's repression of Xinjiang's Uighur and its project to Sinicize Islam.
>
> (Dhume, 2019)

Aligned to the PTI's anti-Western/American agenda was the promise to the masses that it would not approach the International Monetary Fund (IMF) for loans. The realities of government, however, were tougher than Khan may have envisaged, especially the financial circumstances of his country, and the Khan government was obliged to return to the IMF for further loans to address the emerging balance of payments challenge. According to the *Telegraph*, 'Mr Khan appeared to have bowed to IMF demands for sweeping reforms to the economy, despite only months ago saying he refused to bend to the lender' (Farmer, 2019). This has been a serious blow to his populism that had clear anti-Western/American rhetoric. The country's poor economy pushed him towards a comprise in the shape of a bailout package worth US$6 billion from the IMF, which is dominated by the US (Landler, 2009). Another key ingredient of Khan's populist rhetoric was to tax the rich to give concessions to the lower classes, and the IMF deal basically meant more taxes for whoever pays tax. Deputy Director and Senior Associate for South Asia at the Wilson Centre, Michael Kugelman, commented, 'The IMF package will make it quite tough for Khan to achieve his economic promises and therefore undercut the populist image that he has sought to showcase to the electorate' (Janjua, 2019). His government was under pressure from the IMF to achieve a new target PKR 5,100 billion in tax revenue for the fiscal year 2020–21. Additionally, the IMF deal was blamed for a sudden hike in the interest rate to 12.5 percent (Bokhari, 2019). The IMF-led economic reforms led to mass discontentment with a government that continually increased taxes. The tax reforms showed that the rich perpetually circumvent greater taxation by finding new methods to obtain tax relief, which has traditionally widened the rich-poor gap in Pakistan (Tavernise, 2010). The situation under Imran Khan—following the IMF deal—was no different with the middle-class mainly funding taxation reforms (S. Shah, 2019) and local businesses protesting against the increased sales taxes (Shams, 2019).

Bhutto and Khan thus relied upon and used favourably under local and external circumstances several notions of anti-Western/American expression. While the 1971 disintegration of Pakistan provided Bhutto a background to appeal to the masses using anti-American and pan-Islamic narratives, Khan's populism was facilitated by the post-9/11 dynamics under which Pakistan became a U.S. partner in the global war on terror. Local Pakistani dynamics suited a display of anti-Western sentiment when Western allies, especially the United States, failed to rescue Pakistan in the 1971 India-Pakistan War. A similar set of external and local circumstances arose from Pakistani participation in the war on terror that cost the nation 80,000 lives and economic losses estimated at US$102.5 billion (Mirza, 2021).

The failure of the West to provide support for the Pakistani government in the war against India in 1971 provided an impetus for the populist discourse of Bhutto; alternatively, for Khan, the impetus was the high cost for the nation of the post-2001 global war on terror alliance with the West. Here, it seems clear that anti-Westernism provides a valuable inflammatory narrative for drawing support for a Pakistani populist leader, whichever way the wind blows.

Anti-India

In terms of external factors that shaped Bhutto's rhetoric, it is important to notice that India was central. The anti-Indian narrative came naturally to Bhutto, who had held the post of Foreign Minister from 1963 to 1966, during which time Pakistan lost the 1965 war against India. Further, he was a popular political figure at the time of the country's disintegration in 1971. As Foreign Minister, he was openly aggressive in international forums in speaking against India. In 1965 at the United Nations Security Council, he declared a thousand-year war against India (Shaikh, 2019). Later, in December 1971 at a session of the UN Security Council, Bhutto expressed his displeasure at the Soviet Union's veto to block any action against India's involvement in East Pakistan, stating theatrically, 'I hate this body. I don't want to see their faces again. I'd rather go back to a destroyed Pakistan' (Tanner, 1971). It is therefore no surprise, considering the historical context of successive wars against their neighbour, that 'Bhutto's populism was characterized by a heavy dose of anti-India rhetoric' (Akhtar, 2010, p. 110), and as Noor (2017) contends, Bhutto played 'the anti-India card for all it was worth'.

The PTI also targeted other political parties/leadership as friends of India. Leading up to the 2018 general elections, a noticeable change in Khan's targeting of opposition parties was the fact that he blamed the leader of the PML-N for maintaining a friendship with Indian Prime Minister Narendra Modi. Khan tweeted, 'Beginning to wonder why whenever

Nawaz Sharif is in trouble, there is increasing tension along Pakistan's borders and a rise in terrorist acts? Is it a mere coincidence?' (Ali, 2018). It is important to note that Modi is not just seen in Pakistan as leader of an enemy state but further as anti-Muslim. This aspect of Islamophobia may be discerned in the way the PTI government imposed restrictions on social movements, civil society organizations, and the media, expanding these to target members of the Pashtun Tahafuz Movement (PTM), a civil movement critical of the military's role in the war on terror. A case was lodged by the Federal Investigation Authority against Gulalai Ismail, a prominent member of a local NGO, Aware Girls, for allegedly receiving millions from India and for her organization's involvement in suspicious activities ('Transfer of Millions', 2019). In July 2019, at the height of Pakistani-Indian tensions, the PTI official Twitter account was used to attack the media, sending a clear message that recent criticism of the government could well be construed as treason: 'Freedom of expression is beauty [sic] of democracy, expressing enemy's stance is not freedom of speech but treason against its people' ('PTI Says', 2019).

Bhutto was a key figure during two of Pakistan's biggest wars with India, in 1965 and 1971, at a time when anti-India sentiments were running high. This was purely a political strategy of Bhutto, as he did not allow the Awami League, which had gained a majority in the 1970 elections, to lead the government. Hence, the first session of the new National Assembly was postponed in February 1971, an event considered a trigger of the subsequent insurgency led by the Awami League in East Pakistan (Ahmer, 2018).

Focusing on India was also a key feature of Khan's political ascent. Here again, the context played a key role because Modi was elected as Indian Prime Minister in 2014, after which Hindutva, a form of right-wing Hindu nationalism, became more visible in India through widespread campaigns such as *Ghar Wapsi*[5] (homecoming) and cow protection. As the Hindu nationalists gained more confidence after Modi's victory, they began attacking non-Hindus, especially Muslims, in India, and Khan used this in his discourse. Even after becoming prime minister of Pakistan, Khan spoke aggressively when referring to India and the Modi administration, going as far as to label India a fascist state inspired by Nazis (' Modi-led Govt', 2021). This level of antagonism sets the PTI leadership apart from that of other prominent politicians, who historically refrained from aggressive language against India and its leaders. This typifies the discourse of populists in general. As a broad study concluded, populists 'rely on provocation and a more aggressive rhetoric that sets them apart from other mainstream candidates' (Nai & Coma, 2019, p. 1337). In the case of both Khan and Modi, their aggressive rhetoric is very different from their predecessors.

The use of Islam

Since the founding of Pakistan, Islam has been at its core. It became an Islamic Republic in 1956, with its constitution subscribing 'to a diluted form of pluralism' (Hoodbhoy, 2016, p. 36). The blueprint 'Objective Resolution' for the Islamic republic was prepared during the era of Liaqat Ali Khan, Pakistan's first prime minister. While the Objective Resolution provided hints to the religious (Islamic) alignment of the government, there was no mention of *sharia* in the document (Zaidi, 2003, p. 102). Zulfiqar Ali Bhutto, however, initiated the process of Islamization in the 1970s. It was also an era in which Pakistan first experienced the initial wave of populist politics under a socialist party, the PPP. Akhtar (2010, p. 106), like many other scholars, has called Bhutto 'the symbol of Pakistani populism', and in this section, the author aims to dissect the multidimensional populist movement of Bhutto.

PPP populism has unique features with its roots in external and internal issues, an example of the latter being the mass movement against the dictatorship of Field Marshal Ayub Khan, who had come to power after imposing martial law in 1958. Bhutto was one of only two civilians in the military-led government, and at the time of the war against India in 1965, he was Ayub's Minister of Defence. Following the military defeat at the hands of India, public sentiment shifted against the government. Bhutto discerned the shift in public sentiment and cleverly opted out of the government to lead the mass public rallies against Ayub Khan. This popular resistance was not completely successful as General Yahya Khan replaced Ayub Khan in 1969, leaving the country still under military rule. The era of Yahya Khan witnessed one of the most traumatic episodes in the history of Pakistan, the breakup of East Pakistan (Bangladesh) in 1971. This further fuelled the fire in the form of public anger toward the army and paved the way for a civilian government (Milam & Nelson, 2013). Thus, began Bhutto's era, first as a President from 20 December 1971 to 13 August 1973, and as prime minister from 14 August 1973 to 5 July 1977. With his foreign education that included a degree from Oxford, Bhutto was charismatic and emerged at a time when the Pakistan populace had had their fill of military rulers. As prominent Pakistani journalist, Ayaz Amir, was quoted in *Pakistan Today*:

> In the aftermath of the strict, almost suffocating military rule that Ayub Khan's time is often referred to by the left, Bhutto must have been quite a breath of fresh air. He was seasoned, he was educated. He was well-spoken and a powerful orator. And of course, his greatest appeal: he connected with the people.
>
> *(Noor, 2017).*

It is noteworthy that Bhutto's populist rhetoric was wide-ranging and not limited to a pro-democracy or anti-dictatorship mandate. Bhutto's populism also brought together masses against the 22 privileged families who controlled the country at the time (Rehman, 2014). This dimension demanded structural reforms in Pakistan, which Bhutto repeatedly referred to as part of the PPP manifesto. After coming to power at the end of General Yahya Khan's tenure in December 1971, Bhutto rushed to announce agrarian reforms, abolishing feudalism and modernizing agriculture, which he claimed would uplift the lives of millions of rural Pakistanis (Herring, 2009, p. 519). This naturally resonated across a country with an agriculture-based economy, but constituted empty promises as Bhutto, a feudal lord himself, could hardly introduce reforms reducing the rich-poor gap in Pakistan. As Herring noted, 'Bhutto himself came from a background which could only be called 'feudal' in the terms of Pakistani political discourse, and surrounded himself politically with scions of similar families' (Herring, 2009, p. 519).

Islam was central to Imran Khan's populism.[6] Khan had a public record of charitable activities and securing donations, which included funding the construction of a cancer hospital. This proved to be a catalyst for his political career (Jeffries, 2011). In his political rhetoric, Khan has frequently referred to Islam, using certain principles of Islamic teachings to emphasize the importance of promoting democracy and economic justice in society. Interviewed live on Saudi Arabian *Al-Arabiya* News Channel in September 2018 and asked why he had chosen Saudi Arabia as his first international call after taking office as Pakistani prime minister, he replied: 'I wanted to go to Mecca and Medina and get the blessings of Almighty Allah, and I wanted to pay respect to our holy Prophet Muhammad' (Aldakhil, 2018). Like Bhutto's populism, Khan's emphasizes the notion of ummah and its place in the national narrative. Indeed, as a prime minister, Imran Khan sought to refashion the country's foreign policy to forge closer ties with other Muslim nations and considered that Pakistan should play a significant role in unifying the ummah. In the interview, he indicated that 'Pakistan would play a role of getting Muslim countries together. I really see that as the big role of Pakistan' (Aldakhil, 2018). Just as Islamic populism in Turkey had emphasized the revival of the glorious days of Muslims through unity among majority Muslim states, Khan consistently focused on the 'Golden Age of Islam', and was determined to revive major principles of the golden age in the contemporary Muslim world (Khan, 2011, p. 43). As he asserted in his autobiography, 'We were a free people, free to rediscover an Islamic culture that had once towered over the subcontinent. Free to implement the ideals of Islam based on equality, and social and economic justice' (Khan, 2011, p. 12).

As other Muslim populist politicians such as Erdogan of Turkey had done, Khan emphasized the notion of a *true Islam*—there is but one valid interpretation—to criticize the policies of former Pakistani leaders. He accused other Pakistani politicians and previous governments of using Islam as a tool to increase their legitimacy and strengthen their power. In particular, he pointed out that General Zia-ul-Haq 'failed to introduce true Islamic social justice', and that his regime 'promoted inequality and corruption. His political use of Islam was aimed more at capturing the mood of the time'. (Khan, 2011, p. 39). For Khan, Zia-ul-Haq used Islam merely for political purposes and his policies went against the essence of the religion (Khan, 2011, p. 43), notwithstanding that Khan as prime minister would do same to appease the right-wing elements in the country.

Imran Khan's populist rhetoric also sought a pro-democracy or anti-dictatorship endorsement, and he consistently emphasized that promoting democracy was fundamental to Islamic teachings, in this regard resembling Bhutto's populism that represented a balance of Islam and democracy. Steeped in the ideas of many 20th century Muslim thinkers, notably Jamal al-Din Afghani, Muhammad Abduh, and Rashid Rida, who sought to bridge the gap between the content of Islamic revelation and modern Western socio-political ideas and institutions, Khan believes that democratic principles are an inherent part of an Islamic society, and that after the fourth caliph (Ali ibn Abi Talib), democracy had disappeared from the Muslim world (Khan, 2011, p. 43). On the relationship of Islamic principles and Western human rights, he wrote:

> Islamic legal discourse covers both spiritual matters and the rights of an individual in everyday life . . . it protects the most basic human needs and rights expected under civil law in the West—the rights to life, religion, family, freedom of thought and wealth. An Islamic state also guards against the executive accumulating too much power by emphasizing that even a ruler is not above the law.
>
> *(Khan, 2011, p. 44)*

Similar to Bhutto's notion that 'Islam is our faith and socialism is our economy', Imran Khan employed the notion of *Islamic socialism* (Islamic welfare state) in his political discourse (Judah, 2018). Bhutto's Islamic socialism aimed to eliminate feudalism and uncontrolled capitalism, although his party also 'denounced the conservative religious parties and clergy as representatives of monopolist capitalist, feudal lords, military dictators, "the imperialist forces of capitalism," and being agents of backwardness and social and spiritual stagnation' (Paracha, 2013). This naturally led the PPP towards a conflict with religious parties as the Jamaat-e-Islami managed to get hundreds of Islamic scholars (ulema) to declare PPP 'atheistic' and 'anti-Islam' (Paracha, 2013).

Islamic socialism as employed by Imran Khan revolves around one central concept: promoting socialism based on Islamic norms and values; at the heart of an Islamic state is an emphasis on the people's welfare. Following Muhammad Iqbal, Khan consistently emphasizes that the rules of Islam 'would tend naturally towards social justice, tolerance, peace and equality' (Khan, 2011, p. 16). To support this belief, he regularly focused on the prophetic sayings in which *taqwa* (righteousness) is highlighted (Khan, 2011, p. 16), intent on reviving the 'true principles' of Islam in the contemporary Muslim world: '[We] believe in Islam's potential for creating a just society as had been seen during what is known as the Golden Age of Islam in the first five hundred years after the Prophet's (PBUH) death' (Khan, 2011, p. 53).

Khan used the concept of 'Islamic socialism' to put forward the idea that the status of the poor, including their health and education, should be improved in Pakistan. As already noted, a populist discourse frequently emphasizes uplifting the socioeconomic conditions of the poor. In contemporary Pakistan, according to Khan, the poor 'cannot afford education, health or justice . . . Almost two-thirds of the country lives on less than U.S.$2 a day and about 40 per cent of Pakistani children suffer from chronic malnutrition' (Khan, 2011, p. 44). He asked rhetorically: 'How can Pakistan be called an Islamic society under such circumstances?' (Khan, 2011, p. 44). In the *Al-Arabiya* television interview (Aldakhil, 2018), he stressed: 'In Pakistan, we have not spent money on human development, which means developing human resources, spending money on education, on health, on providing them with justice. [In this condition] the rich get richer and the poor get poorer'. He went on to reveal his economic plan: 'We completely reverse the situation, trying to raise the standard of living of people . . . [We] make the rich make taxes and [we] spend it on the poor people' (Aldakhil, 2018). Accordingly, he said: 'We will cut down expenditure, tax the rich and fight corruption' (Jeffries, 2011).

Khan used 'Islamic socialism' to gain legitimacy among Pakistani Muslims and as his discourse intended 'the most fervent new supporters were the poor and working class of Karachi' (Judah, 2018). His brand of Islamic socialism was also used to dismiss the policies implemented by former Pakistani politicians and elites. Pakistan, he asserted, had never been a truly Islamic state because the poor had 'no safety other than their own families or tribes'. For Khan, 'the corrupt political elite is trying to protect itself. We have hit rock bottom. The poor are getting poorer, and a tiny number of people are getting richer' (Campbell, 2018).

From a comparative perspective, Khan's and Bhutto's populisms share several common principles. Their rhetoric was oriented around uplifting the country's position in regional and global politics. They both highlighted the importance of 'Islamic socialism' rhetoric and initiated anti-Western policies in Pakistan. Their populist discourse stressed improving the status of the poor, with particular attention to income, health and education. However, it should be noted that Bhutto engaged in the process of Islamization in the 1970s, whereas Khan had been influenced primarily by the Sufi branch of Islam and, accordingly as prime minister, he did not aim to establish a theocratic state but criticized the mullahs, traditional religious scholars, and fiqh-oriented interpretations of the religion (Campbell, 2018). Muhammad Iqbal was his source of inspiration, as he was quick to point out: 'Iqbal, who is my great inspiration, clashes with the mullahs . . . The message of all religions is to be just and humane but it is often distorted by the clergy' (Jeffries, 2011). In addition to Iqbal, Khan had been influenced by Rumi, the renowned Persian mystic and poet of the 13th century (Khan, 2011, p. 53). Khan insisted in his book that Pakistan could be 'the shining example' in the Muslim world of what is based on Islamic principles but that a theocracy is not an ideal form of government for the country (Khan, 2011, p. 53).

As already noted, a populist discourse often involves an emphasis upon lifting the position of the poor in the socioeconomic structure of the society. Khan once elaborated on the social welfare aspect by stating that the major focus of his government would 'be to address the plight of the oppressed and weakest segments of the society' (Hussain, 2018). During the COVID-19 crisis, it was to be expected that the health sector would be a top priority in the government's 2019–20 budget. That did not turn out to be the case and the government allocated PKR 25 billion for the health sector, PKR 82 billion for education, and PKR 1.29 trillion for defence (Zafar, 2020).

Conclusion

In this chapter, the author compared the two noted Pakistani populist leaders in the light of their narratives. Both leaders emerged within a historical context of heightened anti-Western sentiment in the country. While Bhutto used anti-Americanism to counter domestic opposition to his government's alleged fraud in the 1977 elections, Khan accused the previous government of bringing shame and misery to Pakistan by partnering with the United States in the war on terror. Leading up to the 2018 general elections in Pakistan, Khan had spoken vehemently against U.S. drone strikes on the country, and it was seen that the anti-Americanism of both men was inherently bound with contemporaneous public sentiment.

The two leaders' use of anti-Indian sentiment for their political gains exhibited some significant differences. Unlike Khan, Bhutto did not accuse Pakistani opposition parties and their leaders of being friends of India. The dynamics were different, as Bhutto, unlike Khan, was not facing a populist regime in neighbouring India. For Khan, it became increasingly difficult to deal with an antagonistic regime in India that denied any reproach by Pakistan. During Khan's period as prime minister, Hindu nationalism reached new heights in India, demonstrated through an escalation of attacks on minority Muslims. Hence, Khan and members of his cabinet labelled the Modi regime fascist.

The anti-Western and anti-Indian sentiments of both Pakistani populists were intricately interwoven with Islam and the overwhelmingly Muslim identity of the Pakistani nation. In Bhutto's case, Pakistan was reeling following its defeat in the 1971 India-Pakistan War, and he began promoting pan-Islamism to gain the support of wealthier Muslim countries for Pakistan's nuclear program. Khan's foreign policy carried Muslim identity at its heart as he slammed increasing Islamophobia in the West and India. In the realm of domestic politics and the promise of upliftment for the Pakistani masses, Bhutto's Islamic socialism and Khan's ideal of a Muslim welfare state were very similar. Khan's Muslim welfare state, like the first Islamic State of Madinah, promised improved education, health, and justice. Bhutto's Islamic socialism focused on the rich-poor divide by eliminating feudalism and uncontrolled capitalism. Within their Islamic rhetoric, they both targeted opposition parties: the PPP under Bhutto labelled conservative religious parties representative of civil and military elites or imperialist forces of capitalism, while Khan's opposition was characterized as friends of Modi.

As this comparative analysis demonstrated, Bhutto and Khan's populist rhetoric is similar to that of populists globally, who use a variety of strategies to target opponents internally and externally.

Funding: *This work was supported by the Australian Research Council [ARC] under Discovery Grant [DP220100829], Religious Populism, Emotions and Political Mobilisation.*

Notes

1. As a result of the insurgency in East Pakistan and the 1971 India-Pakistan War, Pakistan disintegrated, while Bangladesh was created in former East Pakistan.
2. The Central Treaty Organisation was disbanded after the 1979 Islamic Revolution in Iran.
3. The Bhutto government faced demonstrations from a coalition of nine political parties which accused Bhutto of fraud in the March 7 elections.
4. The OIC was then known as the Organisation of Islamic Conference and was renamed the Organisation of Islamic Cooperation in 2011.
5. *Ghar Wapsi* is a joint campaign of Hindu nationalist groups, such as Vishva Hindu Parishad, Rashtriya Swayamsevak Sangh, and Hindu Makkla Katchi to facilitate the conversion of Christians and Muslims to Hinduism and Sikhism.
6. Imran Khan's focus on 'faith came following his mother's illness and a profound personal interrogation . . . prompted . . . after the publication of Salman Rushdie's *Satanic Verses*. Wanting to defend Islam from what he saw as ignorant attacks, Khan began to read more widely about the religion' (Burke, 2012).

References

Afzal, M. (2019). *An inflection point for Pakistan's democracy*. Brookings.

Ahmed, Z. S., & Zahoor, M. (2020). Impacts of the 'war on terror' on the de-humanization of Christians in Pakistan: A critical discourse analysis of media reporting. *Islam and Christian—Muslim Relations*, 31(1), 85–103. http://dx.doi.org/10.1080/09596410.2020.1713569

Ahmer, M. (2018, March 4). History: Bhutto, Mujib and the generals. *Dawn*. www.dawn.com/news/1392750

Akhtar, A. S. (2010, February 1). Pakistan: Crisis of a frontline state. *Journal of Contemporary Asia*, 40(1), 105–122. http://dx.doi.org/10.1080/00472330903270742

Aldakhil, T. (2018, December 6). Pakistani PM Imran Khan's sit-down interview with Al Arabiya News Channel on his visit to Saudi Arabia. *Al Arabiya*. www.youtube.com/watch?v=od8iJL9PC2A

Ali, K. (2018, July 14). Imran taunts Nawaz over his 'friendship' with Modi. *Dawn*. www.dawn.com/news/1419959

Aslam, W. (2015). The political appropriation of casualties in threat construction: The case of U.S. drone strikes in Pakistan. In M. Aaronson, W. Aslam, T. Dyson & R. Rauxloh (Eds.), *Precision strike warfare and international intervention: Strategic, ethico-legal and decisional implications* (pp. 73–92). Routledge.

Averre, D. (2022, April 4). Imran Khan is accused of 'burning down democratic order' as the Pakistan PM dissolves parliament to avoid vote of no confidence which he claims is a U.S.-backed bid to remove him. *Daily Mail*. www.dailymail.co.uk/news/article-10683325/Imran-Khan-accused-burning-democratic-order-Pakistan-PM-dissolves-parliament.html

Basic democratic 'skeleton' exists in country and its principles are being fulfilled: Asad Umar. (2021, September 15). *Dawn*. www.dawn.com/news/1646551

Bhutto, F. (2010). *Songs of blood and sord: A daughter's memoir*. Penguin.

Bokhari, F. (2019, May 21). Pakistan hikes interest rates to 5-year high after IMF deal. *Nikkei Asian Review*. https://asia.nikkei.com/Economy/Pakistan-hikes-interest-rates-to-5-year-high-after-IMF-deal

Burke, J. (2012, March 4). Imran Khan: The man who would be Pakistan's next prime minister. *The Guardian*. www.theguardian.com/world/2012/mar/04/imran-khan-pakistan-cricketer-politician

Campbell, C. (2018, July 9). Cricket hero Imran Khan led Pakistan's team to victory. As a politician, he's riding a populist wave. *Time*. http://time.com/5324713/imran-khan-pakistan-prime-minister/

Delvoie, L. A. (1995). The Islamization of Pakistan's foreign policy. *International Journal*, 51(1), 126–147. www.jstor.org/stable/40203754

Dhume, S. (2019, October 3). Pakistan gives a pass to China's oppression of Muslims. *The Wall Street Journal*. www.wsj.com/articles/pakistan-gives-a-pass-to-chinas-oppression-of-muslims-11570142866

Farmer, B. (2019, May 13). Imran Khan's Pakistan forced to swallow IMF medicine in return for $6bn bailout. *The Telegraph*. www.telegraph.co.uk/business/2019/05/13/imran-khans-pakistan-forced-swallow-imf-medicine-return-6bn/

Fatima, N. (2013). Impediments to democracy in Pakistan. *Pakistan Journal of History and Culture*, 34(1), 115–134.

Ganguly, S. (2008). Pakistan after Musharraf: The burden of history. *Journal of Democracy*, 19(4), 26–31. http://dx.doi.org/10.1353/jod.0.0036

Herring, R. J. (2009). Zulfikar Ali Bhutto and the 'eradication of feudalism' in Pakistan. *Comparative Studies in Society and History*, 21(4), 519–557. https://doi.org/10.1017/S0010417500013165

Hoodbhoy, P. (2016). Could Pakistan have remained pluralistic? In J. Syed, E. Pio, T. Kamran & A. Zaidi (Eds.), *Faith-Based violence and deobandi militancy in Pakistan* (pp. 35–64). Macmillan.

Hussain, Z. (2018, July 27). Imran Khan vows to help Pakistan's weakest, oppressed. *UCA News*. www.ucanews.com/news/imran-khan-vows-to-help-pakistans-weakest-oppressed/82940

Iakhnis, E., Rathbun, B., Reifler, J., & Scotto, T. J. (2018). Populist referendum: Was 'Brexit' an expression of nativist and anti-elitist sentiment? *Research & Politics*, 5(2), 1–7. http://dx.doi.org/10.1177/2053168018773964

Janjua, H. (2019, May 13). Fresh IMF deal a 'political blow' to Pakistan PM Imran Khan. *DW*. www.dw.com/en/fresh-imf-deal-a-political-blow-to-pakistan-pm-imran-khan/a-48719858

Jeffries, S. (2011, September 19). Imran Khan: America is destroying Pakistan. We're using our army to kill our own people with their money. *The Guardian*. www.theguardian.com/global/2011/sep/18/imran-khan-america-destroying-pakistan

Judah, B. (2018, October 19). Pakistan's pivot to Asia. *The Atlantic*. www.theatlantic.com/ideas/archive/2018/10/imran-khans-pakistan-foreshadows-globalism/573316/

Khan, I. (2011). *Pakistan: A personal history*. Bantam.

Kugelman, M. (2013, December 23). The most magnificent delusion. *Foreign Policy*. https://foreignpolicy.com/2013/12/23/the-most-magnificent-delusion/

Landler, M. (2009, March 29). Rising powers challenge U.S. on role in I.M.F. *The New York Times*. www.nytimes.com/2009/03/30/world/30fund.html

Milam, W. B., & Nelson, M. J. (2013). Pakistan's populist foreign policy. *Survival*, 55(1), 121–134. http://dx.doi.org/10.1080/00396338.2013.767409

Mirza, A. M. (2021, January 8). Pakistan has contributed significantly to the fight against terrorism. *The Diplomat*. https://thediplomat.com/2021/01/pakistan-has-contributed-significantly-to-the-fight-against-terrorism/

Modi-led govt inspired by Nazi ideology: PM. (2021, September 5). *The Express Tribune*. https://tribune.com.pk/story/2318729/modi-led-govt-inspired-by-nazi-ideology-pm

Nai, A., & Coma, F. M. (2019). The personality of populists: Provocateurs, charismatic leaders, or drunken dinner guests? *West European Politics*, 42(7), 1337–1367. http://dx.doi.org/10.1080/01402382.2019.1599570

Noor, R. K. (2017, April 9). The politics of populism and the idea of the great Bhutto legacy. *Pakistan Today*. https://archive.pakistantoday.com.pk/2017/04/09/the-politics-of-populism-and-the-idea-of-the-great-bhutto-legacy/

Pakistan hits back at Indian diplomat's 'Israel model' for Kashmir remark. (2019, November 27). *TRT world*. www.trtworld.com/magazine/pakistan-hits-back-at-indian-diplomat-s-israel-model-for-kashmir-remark-31730

Pakistani PM praises China's achievement in poverty alleviation. (2019, September 24). *Xinhua news*. www.xinhuanet.com/english/2019-09/24/c_138417578.htm

Paracha, N. F. (2013, February 21). Islamic socialism: A history from left to right. *Dawn*. www.dawn.com/news/787645/islamic-socialism-a-history-from-left-to-right

Peker, E., & Laxer, E. (2021). Populism and religion: Toward a global comparative agenda. *Comparative Sociology*, 20(3), 317–343. https://doi.org/10.1163/15691330-bja10037

PTI says critical media coverage may be 'treason'. (2019, July 17). *Dawn*. www.dawn.com/news/1494621

Rehman, I. A. (2014, October 9). Populism's second coming. *Dawn*. www.dawn.com/news/1136678

Rizvi, H.-A. (1993). *Pakistan and the geostrategic environment: A study of foreign policy*. Macmillan.

Rueda, D. (2020). Is populism a political strategy? A critique of an enduring approach. *Political Studies*, 69(2), 167–184. http://dx.doi.org/10.1177/0032321720962355

Shafqat, S. (1998). Democracy in Pakistan: Value change and challenges of institution building *The Pakistan Development Review*, 37(4), 281–198. http://dx.doi.org/10.30541/v37i4IIpp.281-298

Shah, A. (2019). Pakistan: Voting under military tutelage. *Journal of Democracy*, 30(1), 128–142. http://dx.doi.org/10.1353/jod.2019.0010

Shah, S. (2019, October 17). The middle-class person is dying. Pakistan's tax push is deflating its leader's political base. *The Wall Street Journal*. www.wsj.com/articles/the-middle-class-person-is-dying-pakistans-tax-push-is-deflating-its-leaders-political-base-11571313603

Shaikh, A. R. (2019, October 11). Remembering Benazir Bhutto's addressing Kashmir issue at the UNGA session. *Daily Times*. https://dailytimes.com.pk/481709/remembering-benazir-bhuttos-addressing-kashmir-issue-at-the-unga-session/

Shakil, K., & Yilmaz, I. (2021). Religion and populism in the Global South: Islamist civilisationism of Pakistan's Imran Khan. *Religions*, 12(9), 777. http://dx.doi.org/10.3390/rel12090777

Shams, S. (2019, July 14). Pakistani PM Imran Khan draws ire over taxes, rising inflation. *Deutsche Welle*. www.dw.com/en/pakistani-pm-imran-khan-draws-ire-over-taxes-rising-inflation/a-49585589

Siddiqui, T. (2019, July 27). Imran Khan's first year in office: U-turns and oppression. *Al Jazeera*. www.aljazeera.com/indepth/opinion/imran-khan-year-office-turns-oppression-190726091846779.html

Takeaways from Imran Khan's Speech at UN General Assembly. (2019, September 28). *Gulf News*. https://gulfnews.com/world/asia/takeaways-from-imran-khans-speech-at-un-general-assembly-1.1569641835080

Tanner, H. (1971, December 16). Zulfikar Ali Bhutto denouncing U.N. Security Council. *The New York Times*. www.nytimes.com/1971/12/16/archives/bhutto-denounces-council-and-walks-out-in-tears-weeping-bhutto.html

Tavernise, S. (2010, July 18). Pakistan's elite pay few taxes widening gap. *The New York Times*. www.nytimes.com/2010/07/19/world/asia/19taxes.html

Transfer of millions into Gulalai Ismael's accounts from India defected. (2019, July 17). *The News*. www.thenews.com.pk/print/499497-transfer-of-millions-into-gulalai-ismael-s-accounts-from-india-detected

Westcott, B. (2019, March 29). Pakistan's Khan dodges questions on mass Chinese detention of Muslims. *CNN*. https://edition.cnn.com/2019/03/28/asia/imran-khan-china-uyghur-intl/index.html

Zafar, I. (2020, June 15). Pakistan's fiscal budget leaves masses on their own. *Asia Times*. https://asiatimes.com/2020/06/pakistans-fiscal-budget-leaves-masses-on-their-own/

Zaidi, S. A. (2019, January 6). Special report: The triumph of populism 1971–1973. *Dawn*. www.dawn.com/news/1360571

Zaidi, S. M. Z. (2003). *The emergence of Ulema in the politics of India and Pakistan 1918–1949: A historical perspective*. Writers Club Press.

14
VARIANTS OF POPULISM IN BANGLADESH

Implications of charisma, clientelism, cronyism, and corruption

Habib Zafarullah

Introduction

Populist movements in the Global South began in the early 20th century at the height of anti-colonial campaigning. Nationalist leaders were embittered with alien rule and became wary of colonial tendencies that were being taken for granted in managing polities or governments—rulers' elitist inclinations, overbearing styles of governance and coercion, economic exploitation, cultural subjugation, and a wide state-people schism (Smith, 2013). The populists adopted anti-elitist and anti-establishment postures, derided colonial treatment of Indigenous sectors, and defended cultural traditions. These populist movements supported pro-independence campaigns as Indigenous politicians vigorously opposed the dominant power structures and sought to free the people from colonial rule and Western influences. Most anti-colonial leaders inspired their followers with their nationalistic commitment, charisma, and demagoguery, stirring their sentiments and beliefs (Willner & Willner, 1965). In general, they highlighted the significance of the 'will of the people' with whom they formed a special bond. Many were imbued with Marxist-Leninist principles, while some campaigned for representative democracy, people-centred growth, and prosperity. Primarily, the pro-independence populist movements aimed at eliminating elitist colonial control and mobilizing popular support for independence. Thereafter, their focus shifted to pro-people politics and nation-building, reducing inequality and exclusion, and supporting the basic requirements of the poorest and marginalized classes, especially those subsisting on agrarian production (De Cleen, 2017).

Generally, populism during the last decades of colonial rule was construed as 'political or social movements which challenge[d] the entrenched values, rules and institutions of democratic orthodoxy' (Mény & Surel, 2002, p. 3). Such political movements had the support of the majority of the urban working class and/or peasantry but were not the result of the autonomous organizational power of these two classes. Nonetheless, along with the non-working-class forces, they espoused an anti-status quo philosophy (di Tella, 1970).

In the post-colonial era, many nationalist leaderships departed from their quondam politics, disavowing their ideological leanings and values; rather, they essentially pursued their predecessors' authoritarian practices. Their pre-takeover 'rationale' of establishing citizen democracy and assuring equality of political rights and participation was forgotten. Their regimes mirrored those they had displaced and demonstrated a penchant for arrogating power by sidestepping the legislature, judiciary, and other constitutional authorities, disregarding the rule of law, and suppressing dissident voices and opposition to their authority (de la Torre, 2018). Initially, to garner the support of the people, these populist leaders demonstrated a commitment to establishing or consolidating democracy but eventually backtracked. Their populist agendas disappeared as pro-independence nationalist leaders lost their 'elite adversaries'—the colonial rulers—and substituted them with new political foes—communists, religious fundamentalists, people of other faiths, and liberals. They eventually became political elites themselves, inimical to the people's rights and needs (Mietzner, 2018).

Although populism in the Global South, as elsewhere, represents an antithesis to the ruling ideology (Laclau, 1997), it has rarely been effective on its own because of ideological shallowness, hence its need to blend with other ideologies (Mudde, 2004). This melding may have caused populism to lose its colour and get diluted, although as a concept, it continued to be equated with democracy (Tännsjö, 1992). Today, perhaps for good reasons, populism is viewed by many as an ideological aberration of democracy (Mény & Surel, 2002).

Whatever its form or ambiguity, populism helped generate an alliance of historically excluded social and political classes (di Tella, 1970). Essentially, these classes were mobilized politically by charismatic leaders of organized political entities using persuasive rhetorical oratory. After gaining political power through elections, the leaders maintained power, either fairly through institutional or procedural mechanisms, or fraudulently through electoral malfeasance by abrogating the rules of fair democratic contestation (Mény & Surel, 2002). This has been visible in many Asian, African, and Latin American countries, though in some cases, diluted forms of electoral ethics may have been present or pursued.

Today, populism has taken a different form in an environment of declining democratic practice and the missteps of capitalist economic arrangements. The people's will and the common good are undermined, and populism has emerged as a challenge to democratization (de la Torre, 2018). Ostensibly, leaders opposed to an incumbent 'elitist' and 'corrupt' regime seek to acquire political power and place it in the hands of the people. In reality, they appropriate more power and, as a political strategy, rely on clientelism, cronyism, and corruption to ensure their political survival.

Following this brief introduction, this chapter explains charisma, clientelism, cronyism, and corruption, which are now inextricably related to populism in the Global South. A detailed examination of these phenomena in Bangladesh, where populism has manifested itself in various forms and provided several implications for democracy, ensues. This is a historical-interpretive study informed by generalizations from relevant conceptual literature and an idiographic understanding of the specific Bangladesh case.

Populism and its relevance to charisma, clientelism, cronyism, and corruption

South Asian populism presents a peculiar assembly of diverse elements, some complementing and others contradicting one another. Thus, some populist regimes espouse secular principles while promoting the credo of a particular faith; some foster extreme nationalistic zealotry while succumbing to external pressures and global constraints; some set the stage for religious exclusivism while claiming to be unbiased towards other religions; some extol the virtues of democratic governance while pursuing non-egalitarian, exclusionary, and discriminatory practices; and some endorse socialistic approaches to poverty alleviation and economic management yet adopt capitalist market arrangements (Shakil & Yilmaz, 2021). Whatever their features or intended purposes, these populist leaders work in ways that do not reflect an unselfish concern for the state, society, and the people. Their brand of populism is ingrained by duplicitous methods of acquiring and retaining power through clientelism, cronyism, and corruption.

In general, populism claims to prioritize the people's supremacy over elites and the primacy of the 'public will' (Mudde, 2004, 2017). People with a low level of trust in political elites or the performance of political institutions are more likely to support populist leaders or parties (Fieschi & Heywood, 2004). Populist leaders pursue executive power with the direct support of a vast number of generally unorganized followers. Using their charisma and touting comprehensive reform initiatives, populist leaders solidify the bidirectional nature of their apparently direct relationship with the people, keeping intact the centrality of leadership. This relationship is based on leaders' social, cultural, and political traits—their style of interacting with followers and their attitudes representing deep social-psychological overtones (see, Forgas et al., 2021). In effect, populism that reflects the overall interests of the people defines the vectors of politics (Roberts, 2015).

Populism and charismatic leadership are symbiotically related. The personality and charisma of a populist leader are important, as populism affirms 'the ordinariness of its constituents and the extraordinariness of their leaders' (Taggart, 2000, p. 102). Populism believes in the strength of the people but relies on a charismatic leader to influence them. Populist parties count heavily on the charismatic connection between their leader and the unflinching support of their followers (Mény & Surel, 2002). People seek out leaders who are eager to listen to their concerns and capable of solving long-standing societal problems. Thus, charismatic leadership, internalized in democracy, is pivotal for populist parties and bonding with the masses. With their appeal, charismatic leaders can easily trigger a favourable emotive response from the people. In the legitimate use of authority, their charismatic qualities may be useful in steering the government and earning credence for its policies and actions. However, charisma is not always inbred in a populist leader, particularly in those fronting a hybrid regime displaying plebiscitary norms (Körösényi, 2018). So the equation between populism and charisma is not necessarily straightforward. Irrespective of how populist leaders are elected, perform, and present themselves, a charismatic relationship is established by the leader's image in the eyes of the people. Charisma is rooted in the perception of followers, not the leader's personality (Willner, 1984, pp. 14–15). It is not about what populists profess but what they actually do in regime maintenance.

At the core of populism, charismatic leadership often rests on a 'cult of personality' sentiment among the people, and populist leaders exploit this condition to their advantage. During nationalist movements in the colonial period, *the people* in their simplicity depended on leaders and placed their trust in them as their hope for liberation from colonialism. After independence, these charismatic leaders negated that trust, ensconced personal rule, and took complete control. Some charismatic nationalist leaders, such as Gandhi in pre-independence India, chose non-violent agitation against colonial rule and often had to depend on the rich business class for financial support (Low, 1991). Thus, over time, these charismatic leaders compromised, manipulated, and expanded their power and authority (see Shils, 1958). Even now, with the promise of providing economic and social improvements in return for the people's support, charismatic leaders often exercise leadership by overlooking defined rules and show an uncanny ability to convince the people of their unique qualities as a reason to be followed and obeyed (Tomayo, 2007).

Charismatic leaders take refuge in different forms of political clientelism, a cultural trend that reflects a complex viewpoint of interpersonal relationships, particularly between a charismatic leader and both dominant groups and vulnerable citizens (Piattoni, 2001). Personalized distribution networks of agents and intermediaries facilitate the exchange of goods and services (Hellmann, 2011). The organization of these networks and the methods of clientelism may take new forms with a change in populist regime (Holland & Palmer-Rubin, 2015). Such patterns have been evident in both India and Pakistan (Kochanek, 2010).

Clientelist practices are common in Asia. Political parties use such practices to garner citizen votes during elections in exchange for rewards, either in cash or kind. They may also be employed in dispensing patronage to party supporters. Due to the unequal weighting of interactions between patrons (those wielding power and authority) and clients (voting citizens), the bargaining chips are always with the powerful patrons. Clients on the receiving end depend on patrons for survival, and the 'true' loyalists are rewarded for their electoral support (Scott, 1972). Inversely, by fostering direct and politically unmediated interactions with followers not 'deeply embedded in existing party networks', populist leaders may deconstruct typical patron-client modes of political transaction. They may use effective political mobilization strategies that prevent clientelistic party building (Kenny, 2018, p. 3). Politicians in the subcontinent make huge investments to win elections with the potential for large returns later through kickbacks (Kochanek, 2010).

Clientelism, however, goes beyond electoral politics and thrives in the economic arena, taking the form of crony capitalism (Krueger, 2002). Capitalist arrangements may empower interest groups with strong links to the ruling party to influence politicians and the bureaucracy (Haber, 2002). Any conflicts of interest or backdoor deals have implications for governance and affect administrative efficiency, transparency, and accountability. The perverse effect of crony capitalism on economic growth, and its contribution to economic meltdowns, is due to corporate groups acquiring finance, expanding their size, and enlarging their political assets (Krueger, 2002). If bred and sustained, crony capitalism becomes ingrained in economic life, resulting in rent-seeking and corruption. In India, for instance, a close business-politics rapport boosts both partners' interests—the business community generously funds parties during elections in return for special advantages in their business pursuits, for example, tariff protection and monopolistic control of industries (Gowda & Sharalaya, 2016).

In populist regimes, cronyism is not confined to economic issues; it also encompasses social and political matters and manifests itself through patronage and nepotism, such as in recruiting candidates for public office, providing political and public sector appointments, managing bureaucratic careers, and issuing licenses and awarding contracts. In all these deviations of filling positions, personal connections, social networks, political allegiance, and other factors are crucial in undermining fairness by conferring unwarranted advantages on those not necessarily deserving. Credentials and competencies are compromised to serve political interests rather than safeguarding principles. Nepotism and favouritism are evident in South Asian civil services as political connections frequently influence recruitment and promotions, key assignments, and opportunities for overseas training (Kochanek, 2010; Blair, 2010).

In awarding contracts for goods and services, social cronyism or *chumocracy*—favouring friends or acquaintances using 'vague and broad-brush' measures—can cause a moral hazard and become a critical concern ('Boris Johnson's Profligacy', 2020). Thus, cronyism has adverse implications for public governance, especially ethics and integrity. Predominantly bereft of transparency and accountability, populist regimes make extraordinary use of cronyism to reward followers and protégés as a quid pro quo. Opportunistic cronies support politicians' agendas to advance their personal ambitions, while politicians, in turn, surround themselves with incompetent cronies whose interests align with their own (Kochanek, 2010).

In South Asia, neither political clientelism nor cronyism is uncommon at both the national and local levels. India presents a classic case of political mediators, elected officials, and a slew of politicians playing critical roles in advancing patron-client interactions in power relations within a structure of populism (Roy, 2017). The agents of the populist leadership at the central and state levels keep themselves busy distributing patronage, especially to the poor in the rural areas, for their support during elections (Anderson et al., 2015). In Pakistan, especially during Bhutto's populist rule, political power was localized by employing party activists in state institutions. Since then, patronage politics has grown, and populist leaders have taken advantage in pursuing their political ends (Akhtar, 2018).

Populist leaders gain political power in the Global South on anti-corruption platforms harping on rhetoric against social, political, and business malfeasance. Once in power, their regimes manifest the worst forms of corruption, both perceived and real. By design or default, populist regimes are prone to corruption invigorated and sustained by patronage networks, clientelist politics, cronyism, pork-barrelling, collusion, and conflicts of interest. There is a correlation between populist regimes and corruption scandals, giving unscrupulous people the scope for unbridled corruption to accumulate personal wealth (Chacko, 2018). Corruption has been rampant throughout South Asia to satisfy avarice, expedite government business, and accelerate economic development (Brass, 2010; Khatri et al., 2013).

The widespread abuse of authority in government facilitates corruption in the public sector, with a spillover effect in the non-state sector. Business-politician collusion drains national economies of billions of dollars to benefit the few (Perdomo & Burcher, 2017). Institutional weaknesses of the existing anti-corruption system are exploited, and political patronage is extended by co-opting favoured persons to key regulatory agencies to circumvent punitive measures rather than prevent fraudulent conduct. Populist leaders' concentrated power and bureaucratic self-indulgence contribute to inefficient performance, mismanagement, and white-collar crime. Inadequate state capacity, poor application of the rule of law, weak accountability mechanisms, and faulty integrity frameworks often enable malefactors to get away with impunity. In many countries of the Global South, corruption is 'seen as an affirmation of one's power, of one's ability to get away with such behavior' (Hindess, 2007, p. 808; see Smith, 2013). In general, the greater the public's perception of corruption, the weaker their trust in political institutions. The two are negatively correlated (Wang, 2016).

Corruption in populist regimes is not limited to the use of public office for undue or illegal personal gains; rather, it extends to financial crime—concealing assets, blackmailing, bribery, extortion, scams, delay or denial of justice, non-compliance with business standards, underhand dealings, and many more. In particular, the offshore investment of illegally obtained funds has been on the rise, and information regarding several politicians, including current and former heads of governments of countries in South Asia, or their cronies, has been leaked and reported in the *Panama Papers*, *Paradise Papers*, or *Pandora Papers* (Miller et al., 2021). These have social and economic ramifications.

On another plane, populist rulers expand the web of corruption to the electoral arena. Some turn to electoral fraud with the help of the bureaucratic apparatus and law enforcement agencies. Vote-buying, nomination-selling, voter intimidation and thwarting spontaneous participation, threats to opposition polling agents, ghost and surrogate voting, inflated turnout numbers, vote rigging, and fabrication of results are common during elections (Paul & Siddiqui, 2019). Such practices reduce confidence in the fairness of elections and undermine the integrity of the electoral machinery (Clausen & Nyiri, 2011). Political influence is scaled and distributed differently depending on the intensity of electoral competition—the fiercer the competition, the more widespread the dispersion (Scott, 2007). Engineered elections combined with clientelism and state-controlled media enable incumbent populist regimes to strengthen their grip on power (Smith, 2013).

The changing face of populism in Bangladesh

Bangladesh presents a unique case in *pendulating* populism, with populist leaders becoming authoritarian and losing support, but regaining popular appeal through either clean or stage-managed electoral contests. Since the pre-independence era, the country has experienced fluctuations between democratic populism and authoritarianism, with the character of populist leaders gradually changing and taking on the attributes of authoritarian rulers. Five regime types displaying variants of populism and non-populism have surfaced in Bangladesh since its independence.

From charismatic populism to personalized-authoritarian populism (1972–1975)

Before the liberation from Pakistani neo-colonial rule in 1971, Bengali nationalist leaders in Bangladesh (then East Pakistan) were highly critical of the governing elite comprising West Pakistani politicians, the military and civil bureaucracy, and a motley group of wealthy and highly influential businesspeople. Their marginalization of and dominance over East Pakistan in the social, political, economic, and cultural spheres were absolute. Bengali representation in politics, administration, and private sector investment was negligible. Instead of integrating and consolidating the country, the ruling elite prepared the stage for regionalism to take hold by default. The Awami League (AL), led by Sheikh Mujibur Rahman (Mujib) from the 1960s, pressed for East Pakistan's autonomy. Bengali antipathy and discontent found impassioned assertion in his party's six-point formula. In effect, this was a manifestation of emancipation from elite hegemony (LaPorte Jr, 1980).

Mujib's initial rise was not based on electoral success, but on his image as the vanguard of a popular movement to secure the Bengali people's political and economic rights. His rabble-rousing rhetoric against economic exploitation and cultural subjugation, along with pledges to establish a pro-people system, galvanized the masses to stand up against elite domination. He professed a belief 'in democracy; supremacy of the will of the people; government based on the consent of the governed; free-thinking, free expression, and other popular freedoms which help blossom human hearts and minds' (Khan, 1976, p. 111). Like other Third World populist leaders of his time, he developed a charismatic flair and was successful in political mobilization. After his party won the general elections by a landslide in 1970, he became resolute in his convictions and desire to serve the people as *Pakistan's* elected leader. But with the denial of that opportunity and imprisonment by the military dictatorship, his charisma and the cause he stood for became the rallying point for the East Pakistani people to take up arms and fight a nine-month-long guerrilla war against the regime. By that time, he had embodied the traits of a plebiscitary populist leader, perhaps as 'an icon or an oracle'. He was staunchly anti-elite, anti-establishment, faithful to the popular will, committed to promoting the people's welfare, protective of democratic ideals and social justice principles, and in possession of strong anti-corruption sentiments (Ziring, 1992; Maniruzzaman, 1980).

However, within a very short time as the leader of Bangladesh, Mujib began to rule with an iron fist, unleashing his paramilitary forces against any form of dissent and opposition to his regime, to sustain his authority. His operational style and policies were highly criticized in both popular and political circles. It became all too normal for his regime to flout the rule of law and deny justice. Apart from his nebulous commitment to populist socialism that would somehow alleviate the plight of the poor, Mujib lacked a clear ideological world view. His policy of nationalizing private sector industries, which were performing effectively before independence, miscarried due to managerial inefficiency and declining productivity. Ruling party lackeys became beneficiaries of patronage and cronyism, and they plundered the industrial enterprises and amassed wealth quickly (Kochanek, 1993). He alienated the core bureaucracy by placing his 'trusted' people in key positions (Zafarullah, 2003). The economy and law and order were in disarray, widespread starvation led to countless deaths, corruption became endemic, and many succumbed under a range of authoritarian measures (Maniruzzaman, 1980; Blair, 2010).

During the first general elections in independent Bangladesh, the opposition was terrorized, voters intimidated, and results manipulated to ensure an AL victory (see the January 1973 editions of the *Morning News*, *Bangladesh Observer*, and *Weekly Holiday*). The betrayal of public trust by the political leadership precipitated mounting opposition to the regime. The military and bureaucracy were despondent; this gradually distanced them from the regime.

Mujib's authoritarian inclinations came to the fore with his unilateral transformation of the political system into a one-party presidency that tore apart parliamentary democracy. All political parties were banned, fundamental rights curtailed, the judiciary became subservient to the executive, the state took total control of the media, and the military and bureaucratic personnel, and even academics were obligated to join the sole political party (Ziring, 1992). The changes came without the people's mandate, and Mujib consolidated his powers as the self-appointed, parliament-affirmed head of state. The Westminster system, which Mujib had battled so hard to establish during his political career, was abandoned. However, he was in power for less than four years before being assassinated by a section of the army colluding with some of his closest political aides (Maniruzzaman, 1980).

Mujib was a classic case of a charismatic populist turning totalitarian—giving up all that he stood for, simply to maintain himself in power. His policies and actions and the performance of his government reduced his legitimacy to govern. The country was branded a 'bottomless basket' for its economic failures (Sachs, 2005). In the eyes of his own people, including many of his party members, he was seen to have broken his democratic promises by stripping the people of their constitutional rights and deeply polarizing the country. He saw himself as a patriarch and made commitments he knew he could never keep (Ziring, 1992). Mujib, however, failed to routinize his charisma and continued to depend on his diehard followers for support and, in doing so, weakened his hold on formal party structures for reaching out to the people. Gradually, his charisma waned, and he lost the support of the masses while remaining largely reliant on party allegiance (Khan, 1976).

Transition from military leadership to quasi-populism (1975–1981)

The nation descended into political uncertainty and confusion in the wake of Mujib's demise, until a period of internal strife in the military brought General Ziaur Rahman to the fore. Zia was a Liberation War hero. His battalion was one of the first to revolt against the Pakistani military, and it was he who had announced the country's formal secession from Pakistan over the radio in March 1971 on behalf of interned Mujib. Zia led from the front in the many battles his forces fought, earning him a name and fame for valour. After the victory, he faded into the background, despite being active in the military and advancing to the highest position. Once saddled as the president, Zia's administration worked assiduously to re-establish order in society, economy, and government, albeit under martial law. Discipline was restored in the highly politicized military, and logistics, services, and facilities were upgraded to develop it into a modern force. His first cabinet was a collection of the finest people, all known for their excellent public service credentials (Zafarullah, 1996).

To improve the nation's economic productivity, Zia pursued a policy of denationalization and private sector development. He gradually reduced the sphere of public sector activity, encouraged foreign investment, restored stock trading, controlled inflation, turned to planning as a dynamic exercise, and streamlined the civil service (Kochanek, 1993; Zafarullah, 2003).

On the political front, Zia reinstituted multi-party democracy, lifted the ban on newspapers, removed secularism as a fundamental pillar of the state by making Islam the official religion, gradually civilianized his rule, and floated the Bangladesh Nationalist Party (BNP). He employed a variant of the liberal democratic framework in which multi-party politics could function (Ziring, 1992). Zia's vision of development and the programs he pursued—his appeal to the Muslim majority population, improvements in law and order, promotion of Bangladeshi nationalism, the elevation of the country's image, and his personal integrity—made him popular and won the people's confidence in his leadership (Franda, 1981). His popularity was evinced by the massive turnout and 'outpouring of grief' at his funeral, following his assassination by an aberrant section of the army in 1981 (Branigin, 1981).

Despite criticism of his motive to protect his position by whatever means, even if brutal, he stood out among Bangladeshi politicians as one free from avarice, who chose a simple, austere lifestyle, and possessed the ability to take tough decisions in the public interest (Ziring, 1992). Yet, at best, Zia can be labelled a military leader turned *pseudopopulist*, in that he lacked several populist attributes that Mujib possessed. He was not radically critical of the establishment he inherited, nor overly anti-elitist. His demagogy was not forceful, and he generally spoke cautiously to the point of being formal in his political speeches. With his military background and relatively short political career, he never mastered the art of fluent communication with the masses using their dialects. While Zia lacked Mujib's charisma, he mobilized ordinary folks by regularly touring rural areas and persuading the people to participate in development activities. Like other populist leaders of his time elsewhere, he undertook wide-ranging reforms. Each experience honed Zia's political acumen, and he impressed people with his desire to deepen democracy and enhance the country's stability (Ziring, 1992). However, even after civilianization, Zia's regime had military overtones;

it can, thus, best be described as *quasi-populist*. Despite the limitations of several of his policies and initiatives, like Mujib, Zia has remained a hero to his supporters after his assassination.

Militarized-authoritarian fiefdom (1982–1990)

Following Zia, another military general, Hussain Ershad, ruled the country for nearly a decade. During his rule, serious spontaneous political contestation was absent; instead, political manoeuvring by an opportunist leader to meet his parochial aspirations took centre stage. Like Zia, he had no political lineage, but unlike him, Ershad lacked the credibility to govern with the people's support. His most reliable and loyal constituency were the military and bureaucracy and, to some extent, religious-based organizations. He did, however, create opportunities for the private sector to thrive (Kochanek, 1993). To generate a power base for his rule, he launched his Jatiya Party along with renegades from the BNP and AL and undertook widespread reforms, the foremost being dismantling the colonial administrative structure, decentralizing authority, and devolving responsibility to the lower levels of the governmental hierarchy, right down to the grassroots (Bertocci, 1982). To give his regime a 'credible' political façade and gloss of 'legitimacy', he organized two *controlled* elections, with AL participation in the first, while the BNP boycotted both, being vehemently opposed to Ershad for his alleged complicity in Zia's assassination.

Despite his long rule and a series of reforms, Ershad could never attain popularity, due mainly to his quirky politics and overbearing handling of public affairs. Nonetheless, he was mercurial and flamboyant in presenting himself to the public—frequently changing his political position, bargaining with the opposition to secure their participation in elections, and initially agreeing to political concessions that he inevitably withdrew (Maniruzzaman, 1992). His Islamization strategy angered sceptics who doubted his sincere regard for the religion, while his pretence of being a poet—it was rumoured his verses were written by his aides—was regarded as a sham in cultural circles, considering his brash promiscuous and libertine nature that raised eyebrows in society. His probity was always questioned as he pursued personal riches, lavishly rewarded his adherents, and transferred his ill-obtained wealth to more secure offshore accounts (Kochanek, 1993; Ziring, 1992). His police force ruthlessly suppressed anti-government demonstrations and detained protesters. He was perpetually at odds with civil society organizations, and his attempts to impose his will on them failed. In the end, mounting public outrage, civil society alienation, and the bureaucracy's withdrawal of support culminated in his downfall (Maniruzzaman, 1992). The Ershad era in Bangladeshi political history was dominated by his personal will in every way.

Quasi-democratic populism (1991–2006)

Quasi-democratic populism (QDP) is a leader-oriented system in which citizens play a secondary role. Their participation does not go beyond the ballot box, as voters disappear after voting. Indeed, QDP undercuts the legitimacy of participation. Human agency in politics is latent or non-existent, open public discourse is limited, and public opinion formation strategies are neither scientific nor analytical. No one is permitted to voice an opinion, either in defence of the social-political order or the rule of law. QDP exhibits a notable lack of democratic entitlements, but not their abandonment. To a large extent, it resembles the early stages of authoritarianism (Pappas, 2019).

In Bangladesh, both Sheikh Hasina (Mujib's daughter) and Khaleda Zia (Zia's wife) rose to popularity during Ershad's rule. Hasina was cajoled into participating in Ershad's first election; Khaleda never compromised her stand against dictatorial rule. However, while the BNP and AL did not collaborate formally, they pursued a common cause to destabilize the Ershad dictatorship and restore democracy. In the 1991 parliamentary elections conducted by a neutral caretaker government, Khaleda's party won comfortably against Hasina's AL and formed the first government in the 'new' democratic era. Instead of paving the way for a broad consensus on key constitutional issues, as well as mutual respect and tolerance for each other's roles in government and opposition, the two sides became confrontational from the outset. Hasina slammed the election outcome as 'rigged' despite foreign observers attesting to its impartiality. By refusing to serve the purposes of a genuinely committed opposition, she created obstacles for the ruling party. Later, Khaleda, in opposition, emulated her adversary. Indeed, in the past two decades, both parties, whether in power or in opposition, have worked against the interests of democracy. Their unyielding confrontation resulted in parliamentary gridlocks, popular protests, and constitutional crises. Both Hasina and Khaleda and their parties have been responsible, to varying degrees, for creating the political impasse between 1991 and 2006.

As leaders of their respective parties, Khaleda and Hasina were able to garner widespread support within their ranks and the general population by drawing on their family backgrounds and invoking the memories of their political mentors—one's father, one's husband—who had ruled before them. Though they both censured past regimes and espoused anti-elite sentiments early in their political career, they both were part of the same 'political elite' sharing the same culture, educational background, and attitudes.

Both Khaleda (1991–1996, 2001–2006) and Hasina (1996–2001, 2009–) came to power through free and fair elections but made a mockery of democratic norms, exploiting religious and middle-class sentiment to further their political agendas. They successfully divided the nation into two acrimonious camps by resorting to political point-scoring and presiding over corrupt, inefficient, and unaccountable governments (Lewis, 2011). Despite their coteries of carefully chosen advisers sympathetic to their politics, neither could shed their highly centralized, visceral decision-making styles. Hasina, in particular, followed in her father's footsteps by adhering to 'intense familial and personalized authoritarianism' (Kochanek, 2000, p. 537). Their similar approaches to governance resulted in ineffective political management, limited concern for pressing policy issues, and a proclivity to meander from one political crisis to the next (p. 537). In effect, both Khaleda and Hasina turned out to be democratically-elected *sophomoric populists*, failing to make optimum use of their strong followings to consolidate democracy; rather, the period of 1991–2006 was transformed into competitive semi-authoritarianism. These two democratically-elected populists lacked the social concern and political trust that democracy required. Their enduring animus has hindered democratic consolidation.

Democratic backsliding, entrenched authoritarianism (2009–present)

After a two-year interregnum when a military-backed caretaker administration sought to clear the political, administrative, and economic quagmire that had ensued following months of political mayhem, fresh elections returned Hasina to power with a massive majority in parliament. Five years of BNP misrule had made it unpopular, and the electorate voted for a change, expecting Hasina to deliver on electoral pledges of establishing democratic governance, safeguarding fundamental rights and achieving economic stability.

Hasina took her popularity for granted and began materializing a grand plan of entrenching her rule à la Mujib. Apart from reversing several constitutional amendments made by Zia and Ershad, she abolished the non-partisan caretaker government system for conducting free and fair elections that she had fought so hard to establish, opting instead for a non-Westminster convention of holding elections without dissolving parliament. BNP, its allies, other opposition forces, and the attentive public were vehemently opposed to these changes, rubber-stamped by a lopsided parliament dominated by the ruling party. Clearly, Hasina eyed a prolonged stay in power without any strong opposition. A *virtual police state* has ridden roughshod over the nation for the past 12 years. Under Hasina's command, a highly centralized, politically indoctrinated bureaucracy has created a fearful environment fuelled by draconian laws such as the Information and Communications Technology Act, Digital Security Act, and Special Powers Act. These restrict the freedoms of expression and assembly, and are used to imprison critics and dissenters, suppress the media, and undermine academic freedom. Security force excesses, such as arbitrary arrests of opposition politicians, enforced disappearances, and extrajudicial killings and torture in custody, remain almost unaccounted for (HRW, 2021). Terror squads of the ruling party engage in anti-social activities, including violence against women, kidnapping for ransom, muggings at will, and drug peddling (Amnesty International, 2021).

Hasina's three-term rule has seen authoritarianism reach its zenith. Elections under party rule in 2014 and 2018 were astutely engineered to give AL activists carte blanche to seize polling booths, intimidate voters, stuff ballot boxes with pre-stamped papers, and coerce election officials into working for their party. More disconcerting was the electoral machinery's 'modifying' of the results under political influence. Crackdowns on dissent and the arrests of opposition candidates were pervasive ('Bangladesh's Election', 2014; 'Leaving Nothing to Chance', 2019). On all counts, the 2018 election was 'partially participatory, non-competitive, questionable and faulty' ('Polls Anomalies', 2019). Hasina's populism failed to translate the electoral process into spontaneous public engagement, as a substantial number of people opposed the two elections, which had already lost their credibility prior to taking place.

In her current term (2018–), Hasina has tightened her grip on power and ruled with autocratic alacrity. The bureaucracy, police and paramilitary forces, and state agencies are totally politicized and work towards regime maintenance. The frequent interference of the executive has weakened the judiciary to the point that victims are being denied justice. By utilizing the presidential clemency tool, Hasina has exonerated hardcore convicted criminals who were associated with her party. In the face of frequent executive intervention, popular trust in the judiciary has been weakened (Islam & Solaiman, 2003).

Apart from all the measures giving Hasina the leverage of state authority, the cult of her father is constantly and unabashedly apotheosized—observing year-long anniversary celebrations of his birth centenary, decreeing the hanging of her father's portrait in all public institutions, instructing the print and electronic media to glorify his name, capriciously assigning infrastructures and institutions his appellation, chastising those who fail to properly adulate him, and giving him the status of a deified mortal. Indeed, Hasina has used historical reconstruction to sculpt memories in specific ways that venerate her father for her political ends (Visser, 2019). Rewarding and celebrating the lives of her close relatives is just another of Hasina's political perversities—giving them exceptional security, releasing postage stamps to commemorate their birthdays, awarding them with supreme national honours, naming roads and structures after them—not to mention several honorary doctorates and other awards she herself has been acquiring from overseas over the years ('Sheikh Hasina Receives', 2020).

While autocracy has deepened during the current phase according to all governance indicators, Bangladesh has performed relatively well from an economic growth perspective and in a few social development areas (World Bank, 2021). This has been a positive achievement of the regime, given the political turmoil, antagonistic polarization in society, and democratic backsliding in recent times.

Unlike populism in Latin America (see di Tella, 1970; de la Torre, 2018), populism in Bangladesh failed as a medium for the people to express themselves politically. There has been no clear nationalistic ideology underpinning an interventionist state, except for a short time under Zia's quasi-populist period. As in the case of Latin America, however, there has been a mixed economy approach to boost industrialization since the 1990s. Populist leaders in Latin America successfully broadened the space for civic and political participation. Yet, during the term of quasi-democratic populism (1991–) in Bangladesh, the opposite has occurred—political space has shrunk, and genuine autonomous organizations with a definite class ideology have not emerged. As in Latin America (Tomayo, 2007), the executive has dominated all spheres of life, and the governing institutions have become fragile and lost their capacity to perform. The opposition parties have lost their ability to command public opinion under repressive controls.

While populism in Europe and Latin America has been a top-down anti-establishment construct of political elites, 'bottom-up populism' found expression in popular grassroots protests at often spontaneous eruptions (Aslanidis, 2017). In Bangladesh, such protests have largely been sporadic and failed to make any dent in the politics and policies pursued by hybrid quasi-populist regimes. While social movements for road safety and the removal of quotas in civil service recruitment had considerable support, they lacked a populist flavour because of their single objective character and the absence of structured leadership backing them (Jackman, 2020).

The protests of moderate Islamic groups, such as Hefazat-e-Islam, advancing an agenda of Islamic social transformation, caused tensions for the ruling elite. Given that these groups' support base lies mainly in the mosques and *madrasas* (Islamic schools), which constitute a large vote bank, the Hasina regime accepted many of their demands and virtually co-opted them into the AL fold. The presence of the militant groups, on the other hand, with their extremist modes of attaining goals through *fatwas* (religious edicts) and *shalishi* (*sharia*-based arbitration) do not augur well with the wider populace and are seen as tyrannizing society (Riaz, 2005). Formal Islamic political parties, such as Jamaat-e-Islami, are afflicted by a crisis of political mobilization and organizational inertia, rendering them incapable of securing electoral support (Islam, 2015). Thus, none of these disparate groupings has succeeded in establishing a popular base or fostering any form of bottom-up populism in the country.

Clientelism, cronyism, and corruption

Bangladeshi society is a complex web of mutual favours and obligations, and the patron-client nexus has been constant since pre-independence. However, the intensity of clientelism has increased due to the enduring interconnectedness between politicians, corporate interests, and cronies. This has crippled the economy and endangered governance. Wealthy and powerful groups dispense benefits to lackeys whose support has been essential for regime sustenance. Lobbying and persuasion are frequent among businesspeople, and they use their political and social connections to influence decision-making processes in favour of their corporate interests (Kochanek, 1993). The public sector has succumbed to the patron-client syndrome, with nepotism and cronyism influencing public sector recruitment and civil service management. Student activists affiliated with the ruling party are preferred over qualified candidates for employment in the civil service while serving officials loyal to the regime get accelerated promotions regardless of their performance (Zafarullah, 2003).

Populist politics has historically been a scourge on public integrity, with weak transparency and accountability mechanisms unable to check rent-seeking and corruption. Past populist leaders were complicit in allowing corruption to thrive among ruling party ranks despite their public condemnation of the vice. Familial corruption was evident during Mujib's rule, and although Zia was personally upright, he recognized social corruption as a fact of life and could not do much about it (Khan, 1976; Franda, 1981).

Corruption reached its apex during the so-called 'democratic era'. In several years from the mid-1990s, Transparency International placed the country in the bottom percentile in its Corruption Perception Index (Transparency International, 1996–2021). Despite constant rhetoric against corruption, the current leadership has been very casual in dealing with it, as countermeasures are rarely enforced appropriately or exploited to gain an advantage over political opponents. Any efforts to combat corruption have proved fruitless, with overbearing political influence deterring the work of anti-corruption and law enforcement agencies. The country remains one of the most corrupt in the world.

With creeping authoritarianism and the self-preservationist mindset of ruling politicians, political particularism combining clientelism, collusion, cronyism, and competing interests along with a laid-back attitude towards corruption became the populist credo. Neither Khaleda nor Hasina would shed this temperament. During their rule, banks and financial companies owned by groups politically connected to their parties mushroomed, providing easy loans and credit to unscrupulous people loyal to the regime (Kochanek, 2000). Licensed pyramid schemes run by politically connected businesspeople amassed enormous wealth while defrauding unsuspecting investors of millions. These scammers, along with bank loan defaulters, continue to be protected even after their activities are exposed and implicated ('Big Bank Scams', 2020).

Conclusion

Bangladesh has experienced several variants of political populism. Each displayed some common attributes and some that differed, mainly due to dissimilarities in their origins, developments, policy posturing, and operational styles. Mujib, the popular nationalist leader at independence, rose to power by rebelling against the existing order dominated by the military-civil oligarchy. He was staunchly anti-establishment, anti-elitist, and anti-malfeasance and was successful in mobilizing the people against political domination. Zia and Ershad rose to prominence within the military structure before gradually transitioning to a civilian system, but only the former could marshal mass support. Khaleda and Hasina used their popularity to wrest power from the ruling party through the ballot. In all five cases, however, populist politics succeeded via the anti-incumbency factor. The three democracy-oriented populist leaders—Mujib, Khaleda, and Hasina—gradually abandoned their campaign promises to defend democracy and displayed authoritarian leanings. Hardcore military rule, in Zia's case, became pseudo-democratic, while Ershad, as a military leader, retained his regime's military character behind a façade of electoral democracy. Hasina's current spuriously elected government (2009–present) has increasingly become autocratic and continues to rule with a heavy hand and a disregard for fundamental democratic institutions.

These Bangladeshi populist leaders have all displayed insensitivity to civil rights and liberties and resorted to manipulating the electoral process and obstructing spontaneous popular participation. Their overbearing intrusions have undermined the equilibria of political institutions—legislature, bureaucracy, judiciary, media—weakening the legitimacy and acceptability of their regimes in people's eyes. Two became victims of conspiracies and assassinations, followed by power vacuums, even if temporarily.

Populist movements of the 1960s were celebrated, but populism gradually transformed globally into a contra-democratic aberration. For 50 years since independence, Bangladeshi populist leaders, elected or otherwise, have pursued a strategy of wielding executive power and governing their way, often without popular support. Their foremost concern, unambiguously, was regime maintenance, and they shrewdly trod that path. Reliance on clientelism, cronyism, and patronage along with an indifferent attitude towards corruption served as catalysts for achieving this goal. Consequently, these regimes became disconnected from the people. In Bangladesh today, the axes of political struggle are determined by the predominant interpersonal antagonism of Hasina and Khaleda, to the detriment of major social, political, and economic issues. Over time, Machiavellianism encroached more and more into populist politics, while the people have shown reduced political participation and increased tolerance of arbitrary rule. Populism has all but conceded to autocratization.

References

Akhtar, A. S. (2018). *The politics of common sense: State, society and culture in Pakistan*. Cambridge University Press.
Amnesty International (2021). *Amnesty International Report 2020/21: The state of the world's human rights*. Amnesty International. www.amnesty.org/en/documents/pol10/3202/2021/en/
Anderson, S., Francois, P., & Kotwal, A. (2015). Clientelism in Indian villages. *American Economic Review*, 105(6), 1780–1816. https://doi.org/10.1257/aer.20130623
Aslanidis, P. (2017). Populism and social movements. In C. Rovira Kaltwasser, P. Taggart, P. Ochoa Espejo & P. Ostiguy (Eds.), *The Oxford handbook of populism* (pp. 304–325). Oxford University Press.
Bangladesh's election: Another beating. (2014, January 9). *The Economist*. https://www.economist.com/asia/2014/01/09/another-beating
Bertocci, P. J. (1982). Bangladesh in the early 1980s: Praetorian politics in an intermediate regime. *Asian Survey*, 22(10), 988–1008. https://doi.org/10.2307/2643756
Big bank scams, slow actions. (2020, March 4). *The Business Standard*. https://www.tbsnews.net/bangladesh/court/big-bank-scams-slow-actions-51496
Blair, H. (2010). Party overinstitutionalization, contestation, and democratic degradation in Bangladesh. In P. R. Brass (Ed.), *Routledge handbook of South Asian politics* (pp. 98–117). Routledge.
Boris Johnson's profligacy problem. (2020, November 14). *The Economist*. https://www.economist.com/britain/2020/11/14/boris-johnsons-profligacy-problem
Branigin, W. (1981, June 3). Vast crowds mourn at burial of Zia. *Washington Post*. https://www.washingtonpost.com/archive/politics/1981/06/03/vast-crowds-mourn-at-burial-of-zia/89b4bc88-ed0f-440c-a4f8-ef2e29970430/
Brass, P. R. (Ed.) (2010). *Routledge handbook of South Asian politics*. Routledge.

Chacko, P. (2018). The right turn in India: Authoritarianism, populism and neoliberalization. *Journal of Contemporary Asia*, 48(4), 541–565. https://doi.org/10.1080/00472336.2018.1446546

Clausen, B., A. K., & Nyiri, Z. (2011). Corruption and confidence in public institutions: Evidence from a global survey. *World Bank Economic Review*, 25, 212–249. www.jstor.org/stable/23029751

De Cleen, B. (2017). Populism and nationalism. In C. Rovira Kaltwasser, P. Taggart, P. Ochoa Espejo & P. Ostiguy (Eds.), *The Oxford handbook of populism* (pp. 342–362). Oxford University Press.

de la Torre, C. (2018). Global populism: Histories, trajectories, problems, and challenges. In C. de la Torre (Ed.), *Routledge handbook of global populism* (pp. 1–27). Routledge.

di Tella, T. (1970). Populism and reform in Latin America. In C. Veliz (Ed.), *Obstacles and change in Latin America* (pp. 47–74). Oxford University Press.

Fieschi, C., & Heywood, P. (2004). Trust, cynicism and populist anti-politics. *Journal of Political Ideologies*, 9(3), 289–309. https://doi.org/10.1080/1356931042000263537

Forgas, J. P., Crano, W. D., & Fiedler, K. (eds.). (2021). *The Psychology of populism: The tribal challenge to liberal democracy*. Routledge.

Franda, M. (1981). Ziaur Rahman and Bangladeshi nationalism. *Economic and Political Weekly*, 16(10–12), 357–380. www.jstor.org/stable/4369609

Gowda, M. V. R., & Sharalaya, N. (2016). Crony capitalism and India's political system. In N. Khatri & A. K. Ojha (Eds.), *Crony capitalism in India: Establishing robust counteractive institutional frameworks* (pp. 131–158). Palgrave Macmillan.

Haber, S. (2002). Introduction: The political economy of crony capitalism. In S. Haber (Ed.), *Crony capitalism an economic growth in Latin America: Theory and evidence* (pp. xi–xxi). Hoover Institution Press.

Hellmann, O. (2011). *Political parties and electoral strategy: The development of party*. Palgrave Macmillan.

Hindess, B. (2007). Corruption. In G. Ritzer (Ed.), *The Blackwell encyclopedia of sociology* (pp. 807–809). Blackwell Publishing.

Holland, A. C., & Palmer-Rubin, B. (2015). Beyond the machine: Clientelist brokers and interest organizations in Latin America. *Comparative Political Studies*, 48(9), 1186–1223. https://doi.org/10.1177/0010414015574883

HRW (2021). *World report 2021*. Human Rights Watch. https://doi.org/10.1177/0010414015574883

Islam, M. (2015). *Limits of Islamism*. Cambridge University Press.

Islam, M. R., & Solaiman, S. M. (2003). Public confidence crisis in the judiciary and judicial accountability in Bangladesh. *Journal of Judicial Administration*, 13(1), 29–64.

Jackman, D. (2020). Students, movements, and the threat to authoritarianism in Bangladesh. *Contemporary South Asia*, 29(2), 181–197. https://doi.org/10.1080/09584935.2020.1855113

Kenny, P. D. (2018). *Populism in Southeast Asia*. Cambridge University Press.

Khan, Z. R. (1976). Leadership, parties and politics in Bangladesh. *Western Political Quarterly*, 29(1), 102–125. https://doi.org/10.1177/106591297602900108

Khatri, N., Khilji, S. E., & Mujtaba, B. (2013). Anatomy of corruption in South Asia. In S. E. Khilji & C. Rowley (Eds.), *Globalization, change and learning in South Asia* (pp. 62–81). Chandos Asian Studies Series. Elsevier.

Kochanek, S. A. (1993). *Patron-client politics and business in Bangladesh*. Sage.

Kochanek, S. A. (2000). Governance, patronage politics, and democratic transition in Bangladesh. *Asian Survey*, 40(3), 530–550. www.jstor.org/stable/3021160

Kochanek, S. A. (2010). Corruption and the criminalization of politics in South Asia. In P. R. Brass (Ed.), *Routledge handbook of South Asian politics* (pp. 364–381). Routledge.

Körösényi, A. (2018). The theory and practice of plebiscitary leadership: Weber and the Orbán regime. *East European Politics and Societies and Cultures*, 33(2), 280–301. https://doi.org/10.1177/0888325418796929

Krueger, A. O. (2002). Why crony capitalism is bad for economic growth. In S. Haber (Ed.), *Crony capitalism and economic growth: Theory and evidence* (pp. 1–23). Hoover Institution Press.

Laclau, E. (1997). *Politics and ideology in Marxist theory*. Verso.

LaPorte Jr., R. (1980). Pakistan in 1971: The disintegration of a nation. *Asian Survey*, 12(2), 97–108. www.jstor.org/stable/2643071

Leaving nothing to chance: Biased institutions usher Bangladesh's ruling party to a third term. (2019, January 5). *The Economist*. https://www.economist.com/asia/2019/01/05/biased-institutions-usher-bangladeshs-ruling-party-to-a-third-term

Lewis, D. (2011). *Bangladesh: Politics, economy and civil society*. Cambridge University Press.

Low, D. A. (1991). The forgotten Bania: Merchant communities and the Indian National Congress. In D. A. Low (Ed.), *Eclipse of empire* (pp. 101–19). Cambridge University Press.

Maniruzzaman, T. (1980). *The Bangladesh revolution and its aftermath*. Bangladesh Books International.

Maniruzzaman, T. (1992). The fall of the military dictator: 1991 elections and the prospect of civilian rule in Bangladesh. *Pacific Affairs*, 65(2), 203–224. www.jstor.org/stable/2760169

Mény, Y., & Surel, Y. (2002). The constitutive ambiguity of populism. In Y. Mény & Y. Surel (Eds.), *Democracies and the populist challenge* (pp. 1–21). Palgrave.

Mietzner, M. (2018). Movement leaders, oligarchs, technocrats and autocratic mavericks: Populists in contemporary Asia. In C. de Torre (Ed.), *Routledge handbook of global populism* (pp. 370–384). Routledge.

Miller, G., Cenziper, D., & Whoriskey, P. (2021). *Pandora papers: A global investigation*. Washington Post.

Mudde, C. (2004). The populist Zeitgeist. *Government and Opposition*, 39(4), 542–563. https://doi.org/10.1111/j.1477-7053.2004.00135.x

Mudde, C. (2017). Populism: An ideational approach. In C. Rovira Kaltwasser, P. Taggart, P. Ochoa Espejo & P. Ostiguy (Eds.), *The Oxford handbook of populism* (pp. 27–47). Oxford University Press.

Pappas, T. S. (2019). Populists in power. *Journal of Democracy*, 30(2), 70–84. https://doi.org/10.1353/jod.2019.0026

Paul, R., & Siddiqui, Z. (2019, January 2). Western powers call for probe into Bangladesh election irregularities, violence. *Reuters Online*. https://www.reuters.com/article/uk-bangladesh-election-idUKKCN1OV1PC

Perdomo, C., & Burcher, C. U. (2017). Money, influence, corruption and capture: Can democracy be protected? In IDEA *The global state of democracy 2017: Exploring democracy's resilience* (pp. 126–156). International Institute for Democracy and Electoral Assistance. www.idea.int/gsod-2017/files/IDEA-GSOD-2017-CHAPTER-5-EN.pdf

Piattoni, S. (2001). Clientelism in historical and comparative perspective. In S. Piattoni (Ed.), *Clientelism, interests, and democratic representation: The European experience in historical and comparative perspective* (pp. 1–30). Cambridge University Press.

Polls anomalies in 47 of 50 seats. (2019, January 24). *The Daily Star*. https://www.thedailystar.net/bangladesh-national-election-2018/bangladesh-election-2018-irregularities-47-out-50-seats-tib-1687840

Riaz, A. (2005). Traditional institutions as tools of political Islam in Bangladesh. *Journal of Asian and African Studies*, 40(3), 171–196. https://doi.org/10.1177/0021909605055072

Roberts, K. (2015). Populism, political mobilizations, and crises of political representation. In C. de la Torre (Ed.), *The promise and perils of populism* (pp. 140–159). University Press of Kentucky.

Roy, I. (2017). From clientelism to citizenship? The politics of supplications. In I. Roy (Ed.), *Politics of the poor: Negotiating democracy in contemporary India* (pp. 187–237). Cambridge University Press.

Sachs, J. (2005). *The end of poverty: Economic possibilities for our time*. Penguin Press.

Scott, J. C. (1972). Patron-client politics and political change in Southeast Asia. *American Political Science Review*, 66, 91–113. https://doi.org/10.2307/1959280

Scott, J. C. (2007). Corruption, machine politics and political change. In A. J. Heidenheimer & M. Johnston (Eds.), *Political corruption: Concepts and contexts* (pp. 221–231). Transaction Publishers.

Shakil, K., & Yilmaz, I. (2021). Religion and populism in the Global South: Islamist civilisationism of Pakistan's Imran Khan. *Religions*, 12(9), 777. https://doi.org/10.3390/rel12090777

Sheikh Hasina receives 37 global awards. (2020, September 7). *The Bangladesh Post*. https://bangladeshpost.net/posts/sheikh-hasina-receives-37-global-awards-12212

Shils, E. (1958). The concentration and dispersion of charisma. *World Politics*, 11(1), 1–19. https://doi.org/10.2307/2009407

Smith, B. C. (2013). *Understanding third world politics: Theories of political change and development* (4th ed.). Palgrave Macmillan.
Taggart, P. (2000). *Populism*. Open University Press.
Tännsjö, T. (1992). *Populist democracy: A defence*. Routledge.
Tomayo, S. (2007). Caudillismo. In G. Ritzer (Ed.), *The Blackwell encyclopedia of sociology* (pp. 411–415). Blackwell.
Transparency International (1996–2021). *Corruption perception index*. Transparency International. www.transparency.org/en/cpi/2020/index/nzl
Visser, J. (2019). Bangladesh's 'Father of the Nation' and the transnational politics of memory: Connecting cross-scale iterations of Sheikh Mujibur Rahman. *International Journal of Politics, Culture, and Society, 32*, 162–179. https://doi.org/10.1007/s10767-018-9301-2
Wang, C.-H. (2016). Government performance, corruption, and political trust in East Asia. *Social Science Quarterly, 97*(2), 212–231. https://doi.org/10.1111/ssqu.12223
Willner, A. R. (1984). *The spellbinders: Charismatic political leadership*. Yale University Press.
Willner, A. R., & Willner, D. (1965). The Rise and role of charismatic leaders. *The Annals of the American Academy of Political and Social Science, 358*(1), 77–88. https://doi.org/10.1177/000271626535800109
World Bank (2021). *Overview*. The World Bank in Bangladesh. www.worldbank.org/en/country/bangladesh/overview#1
Zafarullah, H. (Ed.) (1996). *The Zia episode in Bangladesh politics*. South Asian Publishers.
Zafarullah, H. (2003). Public administration in Bangladesh: Political and bureaucratic dimensions. In K. K. Tummala (Ed.), *Comparative bureaucratic systems* (pp. 265–288). University Press of America.
Ziring, L. (1992). *Bangladesh: From Mujib to Ershad: An interpretive study*. Dhaka University Press.

15
GENDER, POPULISM, AND COLLECTIVE IDENTITY

A feminist analysis of the Maoist movement in Nepal[1]

Heidi Riley, Hanna Ketola, and Punam Yadav

Introduction

The global rise of right-wing populist movements has precipitated increasing scholarly interest in the political phenomenon. Far less attention has been paid to left-wing populist movements that contribute to the mobilization of marginalized groups for the purpose of armed struggle. Moreover, within existing scholarship, left-wing populism in South Asia remains notably under-explored. Left-wing populist movements that propagate armed violence tend to rely on ideologies constructed on radical agendas of social and progressive transformation to make sense of and justify their existence and means. They frequently incorporate a gender dimension. Building on critical feminist scholarship on populism, we explore this gender dimension not as an add-on to the ideologies of left-wing, violent populist movements, but as a key factor in defining a populist movement with left-wing or 'progressive' orientation. We argue that the gender dimension plays a crucial role in both constructing the identity of a populist movement and determining the support it can garner and retain over time.

Concurring with feminist scholarship on left-wing populism, we recognize how populist movements rely on a position of 'sameness' when appealing to 'the people', thus overriding differences and inequalities within the group (Kantola & Lombardo, 2019). Innovatively, we examine how women contribute to the gender agendas in such movements, as well as contest the potentially homogenizing rhetoric. To address these questions, we developed a bi-directional approach that examines the formulation of populist agendas as a two-way interaction between the leadership of a movement and its grassroots supporters. Taking this approach, we draw on the concept of 'collective identity' to understand the formation and fragmentation of a populist movement over time, centring on the transition from conflict to post-conflict (Brewer, 2001). A bi-directional approach thus allows us to examine how women both contribute to the development of the gender agenda and contest rhetorical homogenization at different stages of the conflict, impacting the movement's populist appeal over time (Giri, 2021; Yadav, 2021).

We address these questions through an empirical analysis focusing on the Nepali Maoist movement during the People's War (1996–2006) and the period of post-war transition.

The People's War was initiated by the Communist Party of Nepal (Maoist) (CPN(M)), who led the armed uprising against what they defined as the 'exclusionary' state (Adhikari, 2014; Agergaard et al., 2022, p. 96). The party and its military wing, the People's Liberation Army (PLA), secured widespread popular support, particularly from the economically marginalized, lower castes, ethnic minorities, and disadvantaged rural groups, with strong representation from women. Part of the CPN(M)'s success was its progressive appeal and promise of radical change, including the eradication of discrimination based on gender, caste, class, ethnicity, and religion (Riley, 2022; Shneiderman, 2017; Yadav, 2020; Zharkevich, 2009).

The chapter synthesizes complementary empirical research carried out by the three authors between 2011 and 2018, drawing on 100 in-depth interviews with ex-combatants, civil society members, and mainstream politicians. To analyze the discourses of Nepali Maoist leadership, the authors have also drawn on sources such as *The Worker*, an English-language publication disseminated by the CPN(M), and *Janadesh*, a popular Maoist Nepali-language publication.

Populism and collective identity

There is broad agreement that populism refers to a political endeavour built around the dichotomy of 'us—the people' and 'them—the elite' (Mudde, 2007; Palonen, 2018). However, there is divergence on how this polarity should be conceptualized. The 'ideational approach' considers it a 'thin ideology' that can be attached to more comprehensive ideologies across the political spectrum (Mudde, 2004). An alternative approach frames populism as a specific form of political strategy, paying close attention to how strategies differ and evolve over time (Weyland, 2017). However, most relevant to our analysis is the viewpoint that populism is a discursive style structured around this polarity (Laclau, 2005). Thus, rather than being a substantive ideology, populism is characterized as an empty core and populist rhetoric a chain of related 'empty signifiers' defining the collective 'us'. In the context of Nepal, the Maoist leadership used duplicitous signifiers that promoted their policies as 'progressive', 'humane', and representing a shift from the so-called 'backward' or 'semi-feudal' elite oppressors ('Political Line of CPN', 1993). This gave meaning to the Maoist populist agenda and constructed a vision of a *Naya* (New) Nepal, promising equality and dignity to its supporters.

Within the burgeoning literature on populism, the predominant focus in analyses is on political parties or their leaders. However, top-down approaches tend to overlook the important role that grassroots organizations play in institutionalizing populist movements and constructing populist agendas (Aslanidis, 2017; Panizza, 2017, pp. 414–415). Given that party-led populism may emerge as a 'corollary of its bottom-up incarnation', Aslanidis (2017) argues that a more complete understanding of populist movements can be developed by also engaging with the interactions between a populist leadership and its grassroots support base. For example, previously expressed grievances or demands at the grassroots level may be adopted and articulated through a populist leadership that 'infuses them with political importance, cultivating an appetite for action' (pp. 307–308).

Panizza (2017) argues that populism can be understood as a mode of political identification—that populist movements give meaning to 'the people' as a political actor, which is set in opposition to the antagonistic identity of 'the elite' or 'the other'. Despite the diversity of identities implicit in 'the people', the populist project aims at constructing a single, homogenous identity revolving around the nodal point of the anti-elite. Laclau has termed this the 'politics of equivalence' (de la Torre, 2017). It draws 'dispersed elements [agents, ideas, practices, demands] into a discourse by reinforcing what they have in common [their equivalence or sameness]' (Panizza, 2017, p. 409), and thus simplifies the political space between the two antagonistic camps (Laclau, 2005, p. 73). Taking account of constructions of sameness within populist discourse highlights how the reformulation of these constructions may contribute to breaking down traditional societal divisions between disparate identity groups, placing them within the sphere of the people. In doing so, this has the potential to elevate the demands or grievances of diverse identity groups within the broader antagonisms pitted as the anti—people or elite. As part of this agenda, gendered grievances may be included. Here, the frequent categorization of women's grievances in terms of 'sameness' is problematic in promoting a conceptualization of women as a homogeneous group (Kantola & Lombardo, 2019, p. 1110).

In Nepal, the core of Maoist populist appeal was the claim to support 'the people', oppressed by the elite on the basis of identity markers such as caste, ethnicity, and gender, as well as distance (geographic and socio-political) from those in positions of influence. Within their populist ambitions, the Maoist leadership was successful in grouping the grievances of multiple oppressed identity groups under a single 'class' banner in order to justify violent action perpetrated against the so-called elite. Groups classified as oppressed comprised marginalized castes, Indigenous peoples,[2] the rural population not aligned to the elite, and women. Operationalized together, 'the oppressed' became 'us', 'the people' that need to be emancipated, versus the 'oppressive state'.

The pronounced 'us' versus 'them' rhetoric was fundamental to the development of an inclusive collective identity amongst supporters and members of the PLA. In the literature on social movements, collective identity is understood as the critical link between 'social identity (at the individual and group level) and collective action' (Brewer, 2001, p. 119). Collective identity stems from the development of a common identity associated with a particular social group, in such a way that the identity of 'I myself' is merged into the group 'we' (Tajfel & Turner, 1982). In social movements, the group identity is constructed on collective action, which also incorporates group goals, ideology, norms, and values. Group members engage with this identity and seek to uphold it via an 'active process of shaping and forging an image of what the group stands for', what it wishes to achieve, and 'how it wishes to be viewed by others' (Brewer, 2001, p. 119).

Constructing collective identity is a crucial function of 'social movement entrepreneurship and populism constitutes an exemplary case of identity mobilization under the banner of "the people"' (Aslanidis, 2017, pp. 310–311). Key to this is the ability of leaders to identify with the people and their realities, or 'flaunt the low', as described by Ostiguy et al. (2017, p. 74). In the CPN(M), the leadership was particularly effective in its ability to appear attuned to the grievances of specific groups. This was key to gaining trust from diverse groups and constructing a collective identity that was inclusive of both the people and the leadership. In interviews with both ex-PLA men and women, author 1 was told how, during the war, many ex-PLA members felt their leadership 'could be trusted' to prioritize the people's interests. Others commented on the feeling of inclusion arising from being encouraged to speak out and provide criticism in group discussions. As expressed by an ex-PLA male member:

> If a commander made a mistake, we could raise that issue and ask for clarification. Everyone was allowed to point out the weaknesses of a commander. Even the commanders used to encourage us to figure out the weakness so that the person could improve themselves. It was a vice versa process, members could criticize commanders, and commanders too could point out the mistakes of members.[3]

Similarly, as written elsewhere (Riley, 2022), the level of commitment to Maoist ideology amongst cadre from diverse backgrounds was instrumental in constructing a sense of collective identity that crossed caste, ethnic, gendered, and hierarchical boundaries. In referring to the ideology as a bonding mechanism, another ex-PLA member noted:

> After being a part of the organization [PLA], there was no chance of dividing each other into the categories of various social groups such as Dalits or women. Women and Dalits both fulfilled their responsibilities and what made the organization strong was the criticism and review done at the end of each day.[4]

This sense of equality, therefore, was aided by a belief that members of the leadership were themselves participating in the same struggle and both furthered a sense 'equivalence' amongst recruits, thus facilitating the bi-directional relationship between the lower and upper echelons in the construction of the progressive identity.

Yet in post-conflict, the question remains as to what happens to this collective identity in the transition of a populist movement into a position of government. Panizza (2017) has argued that 'the people' takes on a different meaning when a populist leader, initially situated outside the government, enters mainstream politics, previously constructed as the realm of the elite. The leadership is no longer seen as 'flaunting the low', and thus becomes disconnected from the identity of 'the people', instead merging with what was once portrayed as 'the elite other' (Ostiguy et al., 2017, p. 74). This has implications for the multiple identities that were previously included in 'the people' and may lead to the re-orientation of inclusions and exclusions. It also has implications for the sense of collective identity experienced by participants in the movement during the conflict. This is particularly important in the case of Nepal, where the shift from a conflict to a post-conflict context led to a change in the positioning of Maoists from a revolutionary warring party fighting on behalf of the people to a mainstream political party with an ambition to stay in power.

Gender, violence, and populism: feminist lens

Analyses of the relationship between gender and populism within political science literature tend to either approach gender as a demographic factor or as a variable that can be measured. For example, gender has been invoked to study the 'gender gap' in electoral support for right-wing political parties (Immerzeel et al., 2015; Spierings et al., 2015) or as a variable in accounts based on regional comparisons and/or comparisons between left and right populism (Mudde & Rovira Kaltwasser, 2015). Whilst such deployment of gender has its merits, what goes missing is the gendered nature of populism *per se*, stripped of its 'host' ideology and the national culture in which it operates (Maiguashca, 2019). In contrast, an emerging field of feminist scholarship reveals how constructions of masculinity and femininity and framings of gendered hierarchies are at the core of how populism as an ideological construct operates (Kovala & Palonen, 2018; Wodak, 2015). Maiguashca (2019) argues:

> In a totalising politics of 'us' vs. 'them' there is no space or incentive to inquire into the internal conflicts or hierarchies that shape each camp or the way that gender might differentially impact on the lives of women and men in material ways as lived experience.
>
> p. 776

Whilst the existing feminist contributions differ in their conceptualizations of populism, there is a broad agreement that the opposition between 'us' and 'them' requires feminist scrutiny of how gendered power relations are implicated—entrenched, mobilized, or possibly navigated—in such a construction and in the politics it enables (Graff et al., 2019)

The strengthening of the populist right in Europe and the United States and the emergence of right populist parties touting explicitly anti-feminist agendas has generated urgent scholarly engagement (Graff et al., 2019; Keskinen, 2013). Crucially, there is also an emerging strand of feminist analysis that addresses right populism in the context of South Asia (Chacko, 2020; Sen, 2019; Singh & Féron, 2021). In contrast, the role of gender in left populism, and specifically the relation between left populism and feminism, has scarcely been researched. The few existing studies reveal a complex picture. In a comparative study of left populism in Spain (Podemos) and right populism in Finland (the Finns Party), Kantola and Lombardo (2019) argue that political ideology matters. They suggest that 'left-wing parties, though populist, are still better allies of feminist politics than right-wing parties, both in terms of empowerment and transformation' (p. 1124). Yet, their multi-dimensional analysis also shows that the 'ethos of hegemonic masculinity' endures in left populism, apparent in 'informal gendered institutions' (such as gender norms) and in the bellicose and confrontational style of politics that both of the populist parties under scrutiny articulate (ibid). Moving beyond the context of political parties, Emejulu (2011) reveals a problematic relationship between left populism and feminism also in grassroots organization. Examining left and right populism in the United States, the author shows how in the progressive populist discourse feminist claims are reconstructed from 'social justice' to 'special interest' claims, a move which labels feminism as an 'unrepresentative expression of elite partisan interests' (p. 145).

What appears clear from the feminist analysis is that left populism, when appealing to 'the people', is not exempt from the charge of erasing differences and inequalities that relate to potentially divisive issues such as gender and race to advance the ideology and maximize support (Kantola & Lombardo, 2019, p. 1110). To examine how this gendered character of left populism, specifically its tendency to homogenize, evolves and transitions from war to post-war, we build on feminist scholarship on peace and conflict.

Feminist peace and conflict scholarship offers crucial insights into conceptualizing both the contested question of women's agency within violent populist movements and the temporality of the post-war context. At the core of feminist scholarship on war is the acknowledgement that gendered discourses are invoked to legitimize war—to make war intelligible (Hutchings, 2008). In Nepal, mobilization for violence was underpinned by the production of specific femininities and masculinities—for instance representations of women as an oppressed group ready to stand up and fight against their oppressor or defining men as 'brave warriors' dedicated to fight for a new and more progressive nation (Lecomte-Tilouine, 2009; Yami, 2007, p. 63). Building on this, rich feminist scholarship explores how women who participate in non-state armed groups engage with such gendered discourses, whether in the context of ethnonationalism or class struggle (Parashar, 2014; Rajasingham-Senanayake, 2004). The question of instrumentalization emerges as central. Feminist analyses have exposed the ways in which agendas of gender equality, and indeed women's participation, are often strategically promoted by the leadership of such movements to broaden their recruitment pool and to garner popular appeal (Hedström, 2022; Viterna, 2013). We build specifically on feminist work that has examined how women interpret these militant agendas and conceive of their own contribution, including how the agenda of so-called 'sameness', constructed during the conflict period, provided a platform for women to contest the populist agenda in the post-conflict context (Berry, 2018; Gilmartin, 2018; Giri, 2021).

A prominent strand of feminist literature conceptualizes the 'postwar moment' (Cockburn & Žarkov, 2002) as one of fragile opportunity. In this interpretation, the myriad roles in which women engage in war, including as fighters and political organizers, may instantiate reconfigurations of gender norms and therefore create possibilities for transforming gendered relations of power, leading to various 'ambivalent gains' (Manchanda, 2004, p. 100). A crucial theme in the literature is the prevalent threat of a post-conflict backlash, a dynamic that involves a violent reinstating of regulatory gender norms (Afshar, 2003; Handrahan, 2004). What remains less explored are the complex legacies that women's participation in a militant movement generates, and how these legacies may be enacted upon when the armed struggle is over (Parashar, 2014). Here, we explore how women who are in various ways positioned within the Maoist movement navigate and contest exclusions and hierarchies that start to emerge in the post-war context. Such negotiations result both in withdrawing from the movement and in finding new ways to seize the legacy of the Maoist populist rhetoric of gender equality in the realm of parliamentary politics. We argue that taken together, these ways in which women have enacted upon the legacy of the Maoist movement in the post-war context significantly contribute to the deconstruction of the movement's populist appeal.

Gender and identity construction in Maoist populism

This section examines gender as central to the ways in which 'the people' was constructed and delineated in Maoist populist rhetoric during war. We argue that the way gender equality was framed as a key demand of the people within the rhetoric of the high-level leadership, as well as the way women were portrayed as a specific oppressed group amongst others, was significant in defining the movement as progressive and representing the aspirations of the *Naya* Nepal. What is highlighted as crucial in this section is that the portrayal of women in the populist agenda was built around sameness, both amongst women and in terms of the way women were celebrated as taking on masculine roles within the PLA. However, whilst problematic in terms of recognizing intersectionality and the diverse needs of women (Giri, 2021), in the extraordinary circumstances of conflict, this position of sameness actually facilitated the construction of a collective identity that transcended gendered boundaries and contributed to the success of the movement's populist appeal. Importantly, however, we highlight that the way women's emancipation was incorporated into the Maoist agenda was not purely driven by leadership ambition or instrumentalization but was the product of a bi-directional relationship between the leadership and grassroots women.

The Maoist position on women's emancipation was framed within the overarching focus on class struggle, which facilitated the use of the oppressed as the nodal point on which 'the people' was conceptualized (Pettigrew & Shneiderman, 2004). The rhetoric from the leadership constructed a narrative of women as an oppressed group, from which women's emancipation became part of the defining identity of the movement as progressive. This contrasted with the backward and semi-feudal framing of the state, which was portrayed as responsible for women's oppression. In 2003, the head of the women's department of the CPN(M) Central Committee, Comrade Parvati, defined women as 'doubly oppressed', by both the semi-feudal political system and the patriarchy, the latter of which was understood to be a product of the former (Parvati, 2003). Maoist rhetoric pinpointed the roots of women's oppression in customary patrilineal landownership and social norms of marriage and the family that marginalize women economically, socially, and politically (Parvati, 1999). Comrade Parvati explains how certain women have contributed to multiple nationalist struggles in the history of the Nepali state, but notes that 'it was only after CPN (Maoist) started the People's War that women from grassroots, mainly rural women, started getting mobilized' (Parvati, 1999). This statement portrays the CPN(M) as a progressive platform for women's emancipation via the vision of a *Naya* Nepal, in which all women would be freed from their oppressed status. 'Reports from the Battlefield' (1998) from the *Worker* magazine, states: 'The heroic exploits of hundreds of women who have joined the guerrilla squads and defence groups have been a source of inspiration and favourable anecdotes throughout the country'. Emphasizing how attuned the party was to the needs of women, the CPN(M) reported in 1998: 'The fact that women are the most inspired group emerging in the last 2 years of People's War itself indicates a definite victory for the Nepalese revolution' (cited in Karki & Sneddon, 2003, pp. 221–222). This position did not address the differences in women's needs or status as it intersects with caste or ethnicity, which has rightfully been a key critique of the ostensibly gender-positive agenda of the CPN(M) (Giri, 2021; Tamang, 2009; Yadav, 2016). Nevertheless, the 'sameness' posited in the 'women as an oppressed group' narrative was critical in defining the movement's progressive populist appeal. It portrayed the party as the voice of the downtrodden and was a link in 'the chain of equivalence' that pitted the people, as represented by the CPN(M), against the so-called exclusionary state.

Although it was the leadership through which the gender agenda and its homogenizing position were articulated, it is important to acknowledge the role of grassroots women in constructing and reifying the agenda. The All Nepal Women's Association (Revolutionary) (ANWA(R)), which was aligned to the party, and whose membership included grassroots women, was crucial in ensuring that the multiple harms and discriminations against women were recognized, exposed, and challenged by the party. In its early years, ANWA(R) campaigned in the villages against alcohol abuse, which was identified as a key driver of domestic violence in rural areas (Lohani-Chase, 2008, p. 84; Pettigrew & Shneiderman, 2004). As a result, an alcohol ban was implemented in the Maoist heartlands, and later became policy in other areas under Maoist control, as well as being imposed as policy amongst Maoist personnel (Manchanda, 2004; Yami, 2007). ANWA(R) also promoted policies banning polygamy, child marriage, and dowry. The association rejected the practice of 'son preference' and discouraged village women's participation in festivals such as *Teej*, in which women fast in honour of their husbands.

Beyond ANWA(R), other grassroots women's and student groups were also involved in defining Maoist approaches to challenging gender discrimination. In an interview with a former leader of one of the Women's Fronts, author 1 was told how grassroots women contributed to reformulating Maoist policy to combat *Chhaupadi* in the Far West region.[5] This practice banishes women and girls from the home during menstruation. They are then forced to sleep in a small hut outside, leaving them exposed to multiple harms (Amatya et al., 2018). She described how the Maoists first used to destroy the huts. However, local women then informed them how this negatively impacted the girls as they were made to sleep outside as a result. Instead, she explained, the Women's Front, together with local women, participated in a 15-day protest against the practice, marching through numerous villages, under the slogan of 'we have to open your minds and break down the hut'.

Women also contributed to shaping the agenda purely by joining the movement and legitimizing the way the ideology was perceived as addressing their needs. A former PLA woman explained: 'I joined the Maoist movement when I was a student. I had seen women suffering due to violence, poverty, dowry, polygamy and so on. I wanted to do something about it, so I joined the Maoist party'.[6] In many interviews carried out by all three authors, ex-PLA women stated similarly that gender-based violence and discriminatory practices had been important reasons for their joining the Maoist movement. Thus, whilst the leadership may have articulated the oppression of women, women at grassroots level also shaped the gender agenda and, in some cases, the way actions for women's emancipation were implemented.

Recruitment campaigns became more targeted towards women after the second year of the war, and it is estimated that by the end of the conflict, women formed between 33 and 40 percent of the PLA ranks (Yadav, 2016, p. 102). Key to understanding the success of the movement is recognizing the ability of the leadership to create a sense of collective identity amongst cadre that crossed gender, caste, ethnic, and hierarchical boundaries. Recruits were instructed to refer to one another as 'comrade' using bias-free language regardless of their organizational status (Riley, 2019, p. 553). In their interviews with author 1, former combatants noted that cooking and cleaning were rotational duties. An ex-PLA woman noted how 'work division was equal among both men and women. There was no discrimination'.[7] In narratives of training and 'battle', men and women ex-PLA spoke of how this was done 'with both men and women together'.[8] For men, this meant they experienced women carrying out activities normally only associated with men and masculinity. Ex-PLA men frequently recalled their initial surprise at the physical capabilities of women during the war (Riley, 2019, p. 556). For male members, participation in the PLA produced a sense of becoming a 'progressive man', which is exemplified in how they compared themselves with the state forces (Riley, 2022). In the interviews, the collective identity of 'us'—the enlightened liberators of the people—was frequently compared with the so-called 'feudal' and 'backward' police and army. The establishment's repressive treatment of women was frequently cited as evidence of their backwardness and contrasted with PLA men's own stories of respect for their female comrades or narratives of punishing villagers for the maltreatment of women (Riley, 2019). Thus, the role that gender played in defining the sense of collective identity as progressive was experienced by both men and women recruits. In turn, the group identity associated with what was perceived as a reformist agenda, in which recruits felt they had agency, was instrumental in maintaining cohesion and minimizing defections.

There have been numerous critiques of how the Maoists portrayed women in terms of a homogenous group (Tamang, 2009; Yadav, 2016). However, 'sameness' in the PLA justified the emancipation of women through the demonstration of equal capabilities. Maoist ideological rhetoric addressed cadres as 'the brave men and women of the People's Liberation Army', emphasizing that women were no less capable than men and celebrating those who became 'martyrs' for the movement. Although this is problematic in terms of women's realities, the 'sameness' position played an important role in creating a sense of collective identity that was constructed around empowerment of the 'oppressed' and that fed into the populist ambition. This was a collective identity that may have been facilitated by the leadership, but women of the PLA played a key part in its survival through their visibility in willingly taking on vital roles in the insurgency. Here again, it shows the contribution of women in the construction of a gender-positive agenda espoused by the leadership, which was instrumental in defining the Maoist identity as progressive in how it represented the people.

The Maoist movement in Nepal, in populist terms, is by no means exempt from feminist critiques of left-wing populism that expose the 'ethos of hegemonic masculinity' within them (Kantola & Lombardo, 2019, p. 1124). Despite claiming a progressive agenda, the Maoist leaders were predominantly men who led in a style associated with stereotypical masculine norms that celebrate warriorhood, power, and bravery (Riley, 2022). Moreover, it is well-documented that some women, both inside and outside of the movement, suffered harm or discrimination at the hands of the Maoists (Human Rights Watch, 2014). However, this does not overshadow the platform it provided for women to contribute to the progressive agenda and the movement towards change, despite this agenda being constructed around 'sameness'. Yet, as discussed in the subsequent section, the narrative of women as a 'single oppressed group', as a marker of a progressive agenda, may have been successful during the conflict when there was a clear goal of overthrowing the state, but becomes no longer tenable in the post-conflict context.

From peace agreement to gender gains and fragmentation

In this section, we examine how the movement's gender agenda is constructed differently in the post-conflict context as the CPN-M enters parliamentary politics and the movement's emphasis shifts from military to political goals. Our focus is explicitly on the bi-directional relationship between the leadership and the grassroots supporters through which the agenda is constructed, and how this relationship transforms in the post-conflict context. By focusing on the contributions of the women ex-PLA combatants engaged in the lower echelons of the movement, we show how the wartime collective identity starts to fragment as new hierarchies emerge along the lines of rank, including between women ex-PLA combatants. We argue that the way in which the women lower-level cadres started to contest the wartime homogenizing discourses and to withdraw their support from the movement in crucial ways contributes to the movement's loss of populist appeal.

After the signing of the peace agreement in 2006, the Maoists entered mainstream Nepali politics, which culminated in a landslide victory in the 2008 Constituent Assembly (CA) elections. Thus, Prachanda, Chairperson of the CPN(M), metamorphosed from clandestine populist revolutionary and became the prime minister of the world's youngest republic. The rallying call of 'us—the new progressive elite of the people' versus 'them—the old elite', was instrumental in the election success. Election success can also be attributed to a wartime rhetoric of inclusion, taking account of a legacy of political exclusion along gender and caste/ethnic lines. The significant shift towards greater inclusion of women and marginalized caste/ethnic groups in formal politics resonated with the Maoist leadership's wartime populist rhetoric of fighting for the people, as well as the agenda of women's liberation. As such, in entering mainstream politics, the party leadership could retain—at least on the surface—its populist discourse of inclusion, in which 'the people' continued to be embedded in the populist rhetoric (Rai & Shneiderman, 2019, p. 100).

The gains made regarding women's entry into formal politics and broader women's rights contrast with the prominent emphasis on backlash in feminist analysis of post-conflict contexts, particularly where women have contributed to militant movements (Handrahan, 2004). While the Maoist agenda brought more women into the political forum, inconsistencies in the agenda began to emerge—the CPN(M) failed to include any women in the peace negotiations. In response, women in the party, in particular ex-PLA, high-level commanders who had entered parliamentary politics after the peace agreement, sought to hold the party leadership accountable for their wartime promises. This pressure, combined with protests by women's rights organizations and a broad coalition of women in politics, led to legislation specifying a 33 percent minimum quota of representative women in the CA.

However, whilst crucial 'gains' (Manchanda, 2004, p. 100) were made with regard to women's increased participation in formal politics, what is striking is the emerging disconnect between the political leadership and the agendas of the lower echelons of the movement, of which we take the women lower-level cadres as an example. This disconnect led to the fragmentation of the collective identity that had upheld the party's populist appeal and contributed to many women in the lower echelons stepping away from the movement and disengaging from party activities. This tendency to 'withdraw' from the movement emerged strongly in interviews with women who participated in the PLA as low-level commanders and foot soldiers, conducted by author 2 in 2013 (Ketola, 2020). All the interview narratives were peppered with passionate critiques of party leadership, emphasizing the non-recognition of the contribution of lower-level cadres (see also: Robins & Bhandari, 2012). What was particularly striking was how these critiques were directed also at the 'women leaders', women who had fought in the PLA as high-level commanders and had since the peace agreement entered parliamentary politics, becoming members of the CA. Ambika, a lower-level commander during the war, expressed her thoughts about the 'women leaders' in this way:

> What else changed for women? We have women leaders in the parliament [gives a list of names of female politicians who had been high-level commanders in the PLA] and all, what did they do? . . . They used to shout saying 'women are not only made for household chores, they can fight and handle bombs, bullets as well', and 'women are not slaves' and many other things. At the end, everything remained same . . . What did they do? They became rich, got a luxury life, nobody bothered to care about us. Any republic or whatever has come for the rich, nothing around for the poor.[9]

These reflections demonstrate how the collective identity underwent a process of fragmentation in the post-conflict era. First, new identifications start to emerge along the lines of rank, distinctions being made between the 'lower level' and commanders or the 'lower level' and the 'leaders'. Second, whilst the wartime collective identity was organized around the notion of equality, in the post-conflict context, the leadership's commitment to this core principle became increasingly questioned. In intriguing ways, Ambika's reflections highlight how the wartime discourse that positioned 'women' as a homogenous group, based on their shared oppression, becomes contested when new hierarchies *between* women ex-PLA combatants start to emerge.

The shifts in the relationship between the leadership and the lower echelons of the movement we seek to capture are certainly entangled with broader changes in gendered power relations and norms that the post-conflict context generates (Friedman, 2018). In Nepal, norms around motherhood became central to how the position of women ex-combatants was constructed in both discourses of the Maoist leadership and in the international discourses around peacebuilding (Luna & Van Der Haar, 2019; Tamang, 2017). As many of the PLA fighters who had married during the war or soon after the peace agreement had children in the immediate aftermath of the war, the norms around childcare were debated and contested at different levels of the movement (Gayer, 2013). It would be tempting then to connect women's tendency to withdraw from the movement and party activities primarily with the restrengthening of gender norms in the post-conflict context, and specifically note how ex-PLA women were positioned as primarily responsible for childcare. However, there is value in taking a step back and considering how the women ex-combatants understood their relation to the party in the post-conflict context, and how they conceived of their own contribution and the withdrawal of it. This requires examining some of the concrete practices through which the women ex-PLA combatants were withdrawing their support.

The fragmentation we examine had begun to translate into concrete practices, through which many lower-level cadres were withdrawing their support from the party, including for election activities. A pivotal election was held in 2013 for a second CA after the first was dissolved in 2012, having failed to deliver a new constitution despite four extensions. The Maoists had held the majority of seats in the first CA and also held the premiership position for half of the term. However, in the second CA elections, the Maoist representation fell to third place (Gellner, 2014). An important factor that impacted the result was the high level of voter abstentions of former cadres and reduced efforts within this cohort to mobilize grassroots voters to rally around the former populist leadership. The telling impact of women cadres in the reduction of Maoist voter support emerged in author 2's interviews.

Renuka, who described herself as a 'seasoned cadre', explained that she had not voted and had refused to contribute to election activities in her home village, where she could have mobilized '100–150 people' to vote. In reflecting upon her decision, she noted how the party no longer respected the contribution of the seasoned cadre, pointing out the party's failure to offer economic support for her to travel to conduct election activities: 'We cannot sit like beggars'. Yet, what was striking about Renuka's narrative was how this refusal to contribute was combined with a continuing commitment to the 'fight for the country' and 'fight for the people':

> We are still hopeful towards the party; the only thing is that we are still watching and observing which politicians will do what. . . . Who will raise the issues that were of concern yesterday? Who is going to organize everyone together; we are going to follow that leader. We are not going to leave it. . . . We have already brought changes according to our capacity. Now we need to see what they will do.[10]

Extending from Panizza (2017), we argue that the kind of commitments and energies that the Maoist movement mobilized are not simply shaken off when the collective identity fragments and the movement starts to lose its populist appeal. Instead, they may take on new forms that do not necessarily resonate with the shifts in the discourses of the leadership. As Parashar (2014) and others have highlighted, what needs to be centred is how women active in militant movements interpret and contest agendas, including the discourse of gender equality, and how these interpretations may shift in post-war contexts. In critiquing the leaders and in withdrawing their support, both Ambika and Renuka draw on their capacities as ex-fighters and position themselves and those who had contributed to the struggle as part of the collective 'we'. It is in her capacity as a seasoned cadre and as someone who has 'brought changes' that Renuka evaluates 'who are the right leaders' deserving of her support. Similarly, Ambika articulates her critique of the leadership in a language that directly draws on the specific discourses of women's liberation propagated through the Maoist publications, simultaneously demonstrating fluency in this language and using it against the 'women leaders'. With such a positioning, she is able to question the sincerity of the leaders' commitment to the struggle and to the women lower-level cadres whom they had encouraged to fight.

It is by centring the bi-directional relationship through which the populist discourse is constructed and deconstructed that we are able to highlight how the femininities produced in the wartime discourses are negotiated and contested by women in the lower echelons of the movement, and to point to the fractures in the collective identity as the leadership pursues parliamentary politics. In a context in which these fractures emerge along the lines of rank, also between women ex-combatants, the homogenized wartime discourses that portray women as a group with shared interests and experiences of oppression become increasingly untenable. Examining these contestations that target the leadership's adherence to its own principle of equality, along with the micro-level practices through which the lower-level cadres withdraw their support, is crucial to understanding how the movement starts to lose its populist appeal.

Conclusion

This chapter has illustrated the important role of gender agendas in defining left-wing populist movements in their progressive orientation by examining the case of the Maoist movement in Nepal. We framed the Maoist campaign as a populist movement that produced and relied on the dichotomous construct of the 'oppressed people' versus 'the elite' and propagated an armed struggle as a means of social transformation. Our aim was to capture the central role that gender ideology played in defining the trajectory of the movement; explore how the movement's populist agenda was constructed, retained, and fragmented; and to examine the trajectory across conflict to post-conflict. As our main theoretical move, we centred the bi-directional relationship between the leadership of populist movements and their grassroots supporters by operationalizing the concept of collective identity. This allowed us to offer the following key insights.

First, the populist agenda of the Maoist movement produced a homogenizing discourse of 'sameness' in two specific ways: primarily, in terms of how 'women' were integrated into the broader category of the 'oppressed' *as* a homogenous group, and second, how women were acknowledged through fulfilling masculine functionalities within the PLA and demonstrating the same capacities as men. Unpacking this gendered, homogenizing discourse is central to understanding the trajectory of the movement across conflict to post-conflict. The analysis has shown that under the extraordinary circumstances of armed struggle, this discourse had certain uptake and resonance amongst the grassroots supporters and enabled the construction of a cohesive collective identity, especially within the PLA. Moreover, the movement's populist appeal and its ability to retain support during the conflict was intricately linked to its gender agenda and, more specifically, enabled by the way this agenda overwrote multiple forms of difference—between Nepali women generally, and between members of the PLA.

Second, the discussion demonstrated the importance of examining the construction of populist movements' gender agendas over time. This was done by revealing the way in which the collective, progressive identity of the Maoist movement fragments in the post-conflict context. Centring on the experiences of the ex-PLA cadres, we were able to illustrate how new identifications emerge along the lines of rank, as well as the concrete practices through which the women withdrew their support for the movement. These emergent identifications directly contested the homogenizing discourses that position 'women' as an oppressed group, with new hierarchies being articulated between the 'women leaders' entering the realm of formal politics and the lower-level cadres.

Our argument contributes to feminist and critical approaches to populism by offering a more nuanced understanding of how gender agendas of left-wing populist movements are constructed and deconstructed through the participation of grassroots supporters over time. First, feminist approaches to populism have argued that left-wing populism—both at the party and grassroots levels—tend to silence feminist agendas and women's lived experiences in order to bolster and retain the unity of the people. Whilst such analyses have merit, they fail to inform on how and why women actively participate in the construction of such homogenizing agendas and, as circumstances shift, contribute to their deconstruction. Second, whilst thematic strands of the broader populist literature argue for centring the interaction between leadership and grassroots support to examine the evolution of populist movements, these accounts rarely focus on constructions of femininities and masculinities as central to the movement's trajectory.

Notes

1 This chapter is an edited version of our published paper, 'Riley, H., Ketola, H., & Yadav, P. (2022). Gender, Populism and Collective Identity: A Feminist Analysis of the Maoist Movement in Nepal. *Journal Of Human Security*, 18(2), 35–46'. The original article was published under the Creative Commons Attribution License (http://creativecommons.org/licenses/by/4.0), which allows for partial or total reproduction, where the original source is acknowledged.
2 Nepal is a multi-ethnic, multi-lingual country with 125 castes/ethnic groups who speak 123 languages. Caste is one of the principal systems of social stratification, with those in the lower castes typically facing exclusions and marginalization (Yadav, 2016).
3 Interview with author 1, Surkhet, November 2015
4 Interview with author 1, Kailali, November 2015
5 Interview with author 1, Kathmandu, 25 November 2015
6 Interview with author 3, Kathmandu, May 2012
7 Interview with author 1, Kailai, November 2015
8 Interview with author 1, Sindhuli, January 2016
9 Interview with author 2, Nawalparasi, 23 May 2013
10 Interview with author 2, Banke, 29 November 2013

References

Adhikari, A. (2014). *The bullet and the ballot box: The story of Nepal's Maoist revolution*. Verso.

Afshar, H. (2003). Women and wars: Some trajectories towards a feminist peace. *Development in Practice*, *13*(2–3), 178–188. https://doi.org/10.1080/09614520302949

Agergaard, J., Subedi, B. P., & Brøgger, D. (2022). Political geographies of urban demarcation: Learning from Nepal's state-restructuring process. *Political Geography*, *96*. https://doi.org/10.1016/j.polgeo.2022.102605

Amatya, P., Ghimire, S., Callahan, K. E., Baral, B. K., & Poudel, K. C. (2018). Practice and lived experience of menstrual exiles (Chhaupadi) among adolescent girls in far-western Nepal. *PloS One*, *13*(12), 1–17. https://journals.plos.org/plosone/article?id=10.1371/journal.pone.0208260

Aslanidis, P. (2017). Populism and social movements. In C. Rovira Kaltwasser, P. Taggart, P. Ochoa Espejo & P. Ostiguy (Eds.), *Oxford handbook of populism* (pp. 305–325). Oxford University Press.

Berry, M. E. (2018). *War, women, and power: From violence to mobilization in Rwanda and Bosnia-Herzegovina*. Cambridge University Press.

Brewer, M. B. (2001). The many faces of social identity: Implications for political psychology. *Political Psychology*, *22*(1), 115–125.

Chacko, P. (2020). Gender and authoritarian populism: Empowerment, protection, and the politics of resentful aspiration in India. *Critical Asian Studies*, *52*(2), 204–225. https://doi.org/10.1080/14672715.2020.1711789

Cockburn, C., & Žarkov, D. (2002). *The postwar moment: Militaries, masculinities and international peacekeeping*. Lawrence & Wishart.

de la Torre, C. (2017). Populism in Latin America. In C. Rovira Kaltwasser, P. Taggart, P. Ochoa Espejo & P. Ostiguy (Eds.), *The Oxford handbook of populism* (pp. 195–213). Oxford University Press.

Emejulu, A. (2011). Can 'the people' be feminists? Analysing the fate of feminist justice claims in populist grassroots movements in the United States. *Interface: Special Issue on Feminism, Women's Movements and Women in Movements*, *3*(2), 123–151. www.interfacejournal.net/wordpress/wp-content/uploads/2011/12/Interface-3-2-Emejulu.pdf

Friedman, R. (2018). Remnants of a checkered past: Female LTTE and social reintegration in post-war Sri Lanka. *International Studies Quarterly*, *62*(3), 632–642. https://doi.org/10.1093/isq/sqy019

Gayer, L. (2013). 'Love—marriage—sex' in the People's Liberation Army: The libidinal economy of a greedy institution. In M. Lecomte-Tilouine (Ed.), *Revolution in Nepal: An anthropological and historical approach to the people's war* (pp. 333–366). Oxford University Press. https://doi.org/10.1093/acprof:oso/9780198089384.001.0001

Gellner, D. (2014). The 2013 elections in Nepal. *Asian Affairs*, *45*(2), 243–261. https://doi.org/10.1080/03068374.2014.909627

Gilmartin, N. (2018). *Female combatants after armed struggle: Lost in transition?* Routledge. https://doi.org/10.4324/9781315227696

Giri, K. (2021). Do all women combatants experience war and peace uniformly? Intersectionality and women combatants. *Global Studies Quarterly*, *1*(2), ksab004. https://doi.org/10.1093/isagsq/ksab004

Graff, A., Kapur, R., & Walters, S. D. (2019). Introduction: Gender and the rise of the global right. *Signs: Journal of Women in Culture and Society*, *44*(3), 541–560. www.journals.uchicago.edu/doi/full/10.1086/701152

Handrahan, L. (2004). Conflict, gender, ethnicity and post-conflict reconstruction. *Security Dialogue*, *35*(4), 429–445.

Hedström, J. (2022). Militarized social reproduction: Women's labour and parastate armed conflict. *Critical Military Studies*, *8*(1), 58–76. https://doi.org/10.1080/23337486.2020.1715056

Human Rights Watch (2014, September 23). *Silenced and forgotten: Survivors of Nepal's conflict-era sexual violence*. www.hrw.org/sites/default/files/reports/nepal0914_ForUpload_0.pdf

Hutchings, K. (2008). Making sense of masculinity and war. *Men and Masculinities*, *10*(4), 389–404. https://doi.org/10.1177/1097184X07306740

Immerzeel, T., Coffé, H., & Van der Lippe, T. (2015). Explaining the gender gap in radical right voting: A cross-national investigation in 12 Western European countries. *Comparative European Politics*, *13*(2), 263–286.

Kantola, J., & Lombardo, E. (2019). Populism and feminist politics: The cases of Finland and Spain. *European Journal of Political Research*, 58(4), 1108–1128. https://ejpr.onlinelibrary.wiley.com/doi/full/10.1111/1475-6765.12333
Karki, A., & Sneddon, D. (2003). *The people's war in Nepal: Left perspectives*. Adroit Publishers.
Keskinen, S. (2013). Antifeminism and white identity politics. *Nordic Journal of Migration Research*, 3(4), 225–232. http://doi.org/10.2478/njmr-2013-0015
Ketola, H. (2020). Withdrawing from politics? Gender, agency and women ex-fighters in Nepal. *Security Dialogue*, 51(6), 519–536. https://doi.org/10.1177/0967010620906322
Kovala, U., & Palonen, E. (2018). Populism on the loose: Seminal preflections on the condition of differentiality. In U. Kovala, E. Palonen, M. Ruotsalainen & T. Saresma (Eds.), *Populism on the loose* (pp. 13–26). University of Jyväskylä. http://urn.fi/URN:ISBN:978-951-39-7401-5
Laclau, E. (2005). *On populist reason*. Verso.
Lecomte-Tilouine, M. (2009). Fighting with ideas: Maoist and popular conceptions of the Nepalese people's war. In C. Jaffrelot & L. Gayer (Eds.), *Armed militias of South Asia: Fundamentalists, Maoists, and separatists* (pp. 65–90). Hurst & Company.
Lohani-Chase, R. S. (2008). *Women and gender in the Maoist people's war in Nepal: Militarism and dislocation* [Doctoral dissertation]. Rutgers University (RUcore). https://doi.org/10.7282/T3QV3MWG
Luna, K. C., & Van Der Haar, G. (2019). Living Maoist gender ideology: Experiences of women ex-combatants in Nepal. *International Feminist Journal of Politics*, 21(3), 434–453. https://doi.org/10.1080/14616742.2018.1521296
Maiguashca, B. (2019). Resisting the 'populist hype': A feminist critique of a globalising concept. *Review of International Studies*, 45(5), 768–785. https://doi.org/10.1017/S0260210519000299
Manchanda, R. (2004). Maoist insurgency in Nepal: Radicalizing gendered narratives. *Cultural Dynamics*, 16(2–3), 237–258.
Mudde, C. (2004). The populist zeitgeist. *Government and Opposition*, 39(4), 541–563. https://doi.org/10.1111/j.1477-7053.2004.00135.x
Mudde, C. (2007). *Populist radical right parties in Europe*. Cambridge University Press.
Mudde, C., & Rovira Kaltwasser, C. (2015). Vox populi or vox masculini? Populism and gender in Northern Europe and South America. *Patterns of Prejudice*, 49(1–2), 16–36.
Ostiguy, P. (2017). Populism: A socio-cultural approach. In C. Rovira Kaltwasser, P. Taggart, P. Ochoa Espejo & P. Ostiguy (Eds.), *The Oxford handbook of populism* (pp. 73–97). Oxford University Press.
Palonen, E. (2018). Performing the nation: The Janus-faced populist foundations of illiberalism in Hungary. *Journal of Contemporary European Studies*, 26(3), 308–321. https://doi.org/10.1080/14782804.2018.1498776
Panizza, F. (2017). Populism and identification. In C. Rovira Kaltwasser, P. Taggart, P. Ochoa Espejo & P. Ostiguy (Eds.), *The Oxford handbook of populism* (pp. 406–425). Oxford University Press. https://doi.org/10.1093/oxfordhb/9780198803560.001.0001
Parashar, S. (2014). *Women and militant wars: The politics of injury*. Routledge. https://doi.org/10.4324/9780203628669
Parvati, C. (1999, October). Women's participation in the People's War in Nepal. *The Worker*, 5. www.bannedthought.net/Nepal/Worker/Worker-05/WomenInPW-Parvati-W05.htm
Parvati, C. (2003, January). The question of women's leadership in People's War in Nepal. *The Worker*, 8. www.bannedthought.net/Nepal/Worker/Worker-08/WomensLeadershipInPW-Parvati-W08.htm
Pettigrew, J., & Shneiderman, S. (2004). Women and the Maobadi: Ideology and agency in Nepal's Maoist movement. *Himal Southasian*, 17(1), 19–29.
Political line of CPN (Unity Centre): Significance of the three instruments of revolution. (1993, February). *The Worker*, #1. https://www.bannedthought.net/Nepal/Worker/Worker-01/PoliticalLine-CPN-UC-W01.htm
Rai, J., & Shneiderman, S. (2019). Identity, society, and state: Citizenship and inclusion in Nepal over time. In D. Thapa (Ed.), *The politics of change: Reflections on contemporary Nepal* (pp. 83–108). Himal Books.
Rajasingham-Senanayake, D. (2004). Between reality and representation: Women's agency in war and post-conflict Sri Lanka. *Cultural Dynamics*, 16(2–3), 141–168.

Reports from the battlefield. (1998, May). *The Worker*, #4. https://www.bannedthought.net/Nepal/Worker/Worker-04/ReportsFromBattlefield-W04.htm

Riley, H. (2019). Male collective identity in the People's Liberation Army of Nepal. *International Feminist Journal of Politics*, 21(4), 544–565. https://doi.org/10.1080/14616742.2019.1577153

Riley, H. (2022). *Rethinking masculinities: Ideology, identity and change in the People's War in Nepal and its aftermath*. Rowman & Littlefield. https://go.exlibris.link/BhxsvDxG

Robins, S., & Bhandari, R. (2012). *From victims to actors: Mobilising victims to drive transitional justice process*. Berghof Foundation.

Sen, A. (2019). 'Teach your girls to stab, not sing': Right-wing activism, public knife distribution, and the politics of gendered self-defense in Mumbai, India. *Signs: Journal of Women in Culture and Society*, 44(3), 743–770.

Shneiderman, S. (2017). The formation of political consciousness in rural Nepal. In A. Shah & J. Pettigrew (Eds.), *Windows into a revolution: Ethnographies of Maoism in India and Nepal* (pp. 60–88). Routledge. https://doi.org/10.4324/9781315145723

Singh, S., & Féron, É. (2021). Towards an intersectional approach to populism: Comparative perspectives from Finland and India. *Contemporary Politics*, 27(5), 528–549. https://doi.org/10.1080/13569775.2021.1917164

Spierings, N., Zaslove, A., Mügge, L. M., & De Lange, S. L. (2015). Gender and populist radical-right politics: An introduction. *Patterns of Prejudice*, 49(1–2), 3–15. https://doi.org/10.1080/0031322X.2015.1023642

Tajfel, H.& Turner, J. C. (1982). Social psychology of intergroup relations. *Annual Review of Psychology*, 33(1), 1–39.

Tamang, S. (2009). The politics of conflict and difference or the difference of conflict in politics: The women's movement in Nepal. *Feminist Review*, 91(1), 61–80. https://doi.org/10.1057/fr.2008.50

Tamang, S. (2017). Motherhood containers: Cantonments and the media framing of female ex-combatants in Nepal's transition. In M. Hutt & P. Onta (Eds.), *Political change and public culture in post-1990 Nepal* (pp. 223–252). Cambridge University Press. https://dx.doi.org/10.1017/9781316771389.011

Viterna, J. (2013). *Women in war: The micro-processes of mobilization in El Salvador*. Oxford University Press.

Weyland, K. (2017). Populism: A political-strategic approach. In C. Rovira Kaltwasser, P. A. Taggart, P. Ochoa Espejo & P. Ostiguy (Eds.), *The Oxford handbook of populism* (pp. 48–72). Oxford University Press.

Wodak, R. (2015). *The politics of fear: What right-wing populist discourses mean*. Sage.

Yadav, P. (2016). *Social transformation in post-conflict Nepal: A gender perspective*. Routledge.

Yadav, P. (2020). When the personal is international: Implementation of the National Action Plan on Resolutions 1325 and 1820 in Nepal. *Gender, Technology and Development*, 24(2), 194–214. https://doi.org/10.1080/09718524.2020.1766187

Yadav, P. (2021). Can women benefit from war? Women's agency in conflict and post-conflict societies. *Journal of Peace Research*, 58(3), 449–461. https://doi.org/10.1177/0022343320905619

Yami, H. (2007). *People's war and women's liberation in Nepal*. Janadhwani Publication.

Zharkevich, I. (2009). A new way of being young in Nepal: The idea of Maoist youth and dreams of a new man. *Studies in Nepali History and Society*, 14(1), 67–105.

16
CONTEMPORARY SRI LANKA
Nationalism meets 'soft populism'

D. B. Subedi and Siri Hettige

Introduction

A persisting debate in populism studies concerns a critical question: in what ways are nationalism and populism similar or dissimilar? Do they portray and represent a similar political phenomenon? Why do these movements co-evolve or intersect in some nation-states but not in others? In this chapter, we engage with these questions using the case of contemporary Sri Lanka.

One line of argument suggests nationalism and populism have a close affinity, and many prominent populist movements, both left- and right-wing, have embraced nationalist ideologies and movements (see Ionescu & Gellner, 1969; Canovan, 1981, Stewart, 1969, p. 183). Nationalism in this sense provides a host ideology for populism to evolve. Populism benefits from nationalism's ethnic homogenization project and the horizontal cleavages it creates among *ethnos* based on their ethnicity, race, religion, and language. Populists claim to represent the 'will of the people' and the 'pure people', who are arguably considered *insiders* having historical connections with the land, traditions, and culture (Mudde, 2004; Katsambekis, 2022). This entails exclusionary politics, using nationalism as a political platform to construct and reinforce social polarizations between the pure people and the 'others'. In the Asian context, the so-called 'outsiders' or social 'others' are actually ethnic, religious, and cultural minorities within the boundaries of a nation-state (see Subedi & Scott, 2021; Varshney, 2021). The phenomenon, however, manifests differently in right-wing populism in Western Europe where the 'others' are immigrant, cultural, and religious minorities (Kende & Krekó, 2020).

A counter-argument suggests that although populism and nationalism claim to represent the people and express the idea of popular sovereignty, they represent two distinct political phenomena (see De Cleen, 2017). At the core of this argument lies the concept of *the people* and how populist parties and leaders define and mobilize them.

For populists, *demos* (the people) are the key actors in a horizontal social polarization— a precondition for populist politics to thrive. This involves a Manichean view of moralistic politics that divides a society into the morally-correct 'pure' people (insiders) and the 'others' (Müller, 2016). In contrast, *ethnos* (ethnicity) provides the conceptual core of nationalism and revolves around the question of how a nation-state and national identity are defined, formed, and routinized. Often embedded in state institutions, such as laws, school textbooks, symbols, museums and maps, nationalism can become a state ideology, taking routinized forms (Gellner, 2008). Thus, it has been argued that conflating populism with nationalism blurs the meanings of *ethnos* and *demos* and provides little conceptual clarity by which to distinguish a populist from a nationalist mobilization (de Cleen, 2017). *Ethnos* and *demos* easily elide in the real world (Mann, 2005).

Concomitant is the role elites play in populism and nationalism. Populists frame political elites as 'enemies' of the people; hence, anti-elitism is at the core of populism (Brubaker, 2020; Levitsky & Loxton, 2013; Mudde, 2004). The political antagonism rooted in anti-elitism facilitates vertical social conflicts between the people and political elites, who are often portrayed as immoral and corrupt and therefore accountable for the misery of the masses. Alternately, nationalism is often led by elites and consequently involves a top-down process of popular political mobilization of ethnos (Gellner, 2008).

The idea of anti-elitism, however, can be contested in the Asian context where the elites are themselves populist politicians, although there are some exceptions in the West, such as Trump in the United States. In Asia, many past and present populist-charismatic leaders—Jawaharlal Nehru and Indira Gandhi in India, Thaksin Shinawatra in Thailand, and Imran Khan in Pakistan—are elites who mobilized popular support to dislodge elite political opponents (see Kenny, 2018; see Chapters 12, 13, and 17 in this volume). Several pro-independence elite nationalist leaders in Asia were populist (Mietzner, 2019).

There is also a middle-ground argument recognizing the differences and similarities between nationalism and populism. Ashutosh Varshney (2021), for example, argues that despite some differences, both populism and nationalism are rooted in the idea of popular sovereignty. They 'look alike when populism gravitates toward the right'; right-wing populism identifies those 'with an ethnic or racial minority' (Varshney, 2021, p. 131) as an easy target and potential scapegoat. Populist exploitation and mobilization of ethnicity-based identities is a characteristic shared with nationalism and results in the phenomenon of 'ethnopopulism' (see Cheeseman & Larmer, 2015). Nationalism expresses 'exclusionary ethnopopulism' in embracing majoritarianism, attacking internal minorities, and seeking secessionist independence (Varshney, 2021).

In this chapter, we take the middle-ground approach to analyze the relationship between populism and nationalism in Sri Lanka. In particular, we analyze the populist politics of the former president and prime minister, Mahinda Rajapaksa, and his younger brother, the former president, Gotabaya Rajapaksa, who were in power for more than a decade until June 2022 (excluding 2015–2019). Both were nationalists, politically-driven by their Sinhala Buddhist identity. The populist element in their nationalist politics has largely gone unnoticed, although the recent analyses of Jayasinghe (2020) and Subedi (2022) have focused on the nationalist ideology and populist political style of the brothers.

We preface our analysis of the case of the Rajapaksa brothers, acknowledging that it may only qualify as a case of 'soft populism', which we define as a form of populist politics which travels with a host ideology. The thin ideology and populist political style are overshadowed by the dominant host ideology. In other words, even though populist elements are very much present in the politics, they can seem invisible due to the dominance of the host ideology.

In the case of Sri Lanka, the Rajapaksas' soft populist politics has been overshowed by their Sinhala Buddhist nationalist ideology (see Subedi, 2022). Thus, unlike hard populism, soft populism can include an ideational dimension driven by a host ideology and a political-strategic dimension dependent on the political style of the leaders. As we will elaborate later, soft populism also presents several elements of a hard case of populism: it thrives on social and vertical polarization, benefits from the rhetoric and narratives of an existential crisis faced by the pure people, and enables a populist-nationalist leader to centralize power in ways that undermine democratic checks and balances. Moreover, populist-nationalism as a form of soft populism requires the plebiscitary element of democracy as a precondition.

We show that in a hybrid democracy, when or if reinforced by a host ideology, soft populism becomes a fragile and unstable category primarily because of the unstable nature of people's emotions, devotions, and support for the leader. The fragility and instability mean that soft populism can either morph into hardcore populism that establishes the leader in the power for a relatively long period or slide back when the people withdraw their support. The latter results in the decline of a populist leader, as has been the case for the Rajapaksa brothers. The fragility of populist leaders has become a universal phenomenon, such as the case of Donald Trump in the United States, Rodrigo Duterte in the Philippines (see Chapter 19 in this volume), and Imran Khan in Pakistan (see Chapter 13 in this volume).

We argue that populism and nationalism in Sri Lanka come closer and blend together when nationalist political elites look for an alternative political strategy and narrative to consolidate their support base and construct a bounded political community of 'insiders' based on ethnic, religious, and cultural identity. The so-called 'outsiders'—Tamils and Muslims—constitute ethnic and religious minorities who have lived in Sri Lanka for centuries. To capture the nuances of political leadership that combines nationalist ideologies with populist political orientation, we use the term *populist nationalism*, a subcategory of soft populism. In Sri Lanka, this form of exclusionary soft populist politics shares certain elements with right-wing populism, which thrives on social polarization, undermines cultural and religious pluralism, and serves one specific goal for nationalist elites: regime survival.

In the next section, we analyze the contested notions of a 'pure people' in light of ethno-linguistic nationalism in post-independence Sri Lanka. This will be followed by an analysis of the political shift and the rise and fall of Mahinda Rajapaksa as a populist-nationalist leader. In the third section, we examine the politics of the Rajapaksas and the way it benefitted from the emergent 'new social polarization', ostensibly based on ethnic and religious identities and the narratives of existential crisis. The fourth section addresses the strengths and fragility of the populist-nationalist leadership style of the Rajapaksas. In the fifth section, we discuss post-war reconstruction as an example in which a nationalist ideology blended with populist development projects. The final section concludes our argument.

Nationalism, identity, and the contested notions of 'pure people' in Sri Lanka

Sri Lanka is a multi-ethnic country with a population of 21 million. The Sinhala population constitutes roughly 75%, the vast majority of whom (about 69%) follow Theravada Buddhism, while the rest follow different Christian denominations. The majority of the roughly 15% Tamils are Hindus, with a small section of Tamil Christians. Muslims, including the descendants of Arab traders and Tamil Muslims, make up roughly 9% of the population. The language divide is significant: Tamil and Muslim minorities speak Tamil, while the Sinhalese speak Sinhala. Both are official national languages.

Ethnic identities and languages have fuelled social conflict and nationalist movements since the pre-independence period. This social polarization based on ethnicity and language predates the Buddhist (Anagarika Dharmapala) and Hindu (Arumuga Navalar) revivalist movements of the late 19th century (Russell, 1982).

Post-colonial Sri Lanka has witnessed multiple claims for recognition of their national identity and political inclusion by the Tamil minority in the North and East and the Sinhalese majority in the South. Central to these claims is the quest for ethnic-based nationalisms and the contentions around the origins of races and religions. The origins of the Sinhalese are elaborated in the *Mahavamsa*, which associates the race with the introduction of Buddhism to Sri Lanka, roughly between 250 and 210 BC (de Silva, 2017). The co-origin and co-evolution of the religion and race forms the foundation of Sinhala Buddhist culture and civilization, and had been under attack by colonial invaders—namely, the Portuguese, Dutch, and British—from the early 16th century onwards (de Silva, 1981; Ivan, 2009). The disintegration of Sinhala kingdoms in the colonial period fuelled Sinhala Buddhist religious and cultural revivalist movements in the 19th and 20th centuries, initially led by Anagarika Dharmapala, a founder and staunch advocate of Sinhala nationalism (Ivan, 2009). The colonial rulers introduced and protected minorities, Christianity, and the business elites—notably the Muslims, who had gradually taken business opportunities away from Sinhala traders and merchants. Accordingly, the Sinhala Buddhist nationalist movement led by Anagarika Dharmapala had identified Tamils and Muslims as the principal enemies of the Sinhalese race (Dewaraja, 1994; Ivan, 2009), and religious/cultural protectionism and economic competition became the fundamental elements of the Sinhala Buddhist nationalist movement in the 19th and 20th centuries. The Sinhala interpretation of the history of their people, in accord with the *Mahavamsa*, holds the Sinhalese to be an ancient chosen race and Theravada Buddhism to be the purest form of the religion. This historical narrative has provided the Sinhalese with the rationale to regard Sinhala Buddhists as the 'sons of the soil' (i.e., 'pure people') and continues to form the central ideology of Sinhala Buddhist nationalism in contemporary Sri Lanka.

The ethno-religious underpinnings of the anti-colonial nationalist movement led to the fragmentation of native political elites who emerged during the colonial period, particularly the British period (Roberts, 1982), despite the fact that certain elements of Westernization such as modern Western education, anglicization, and a Western lifestyle, became integral to the elite identity. The dominance of schools established by Christian religious denominations, though used by Sinhala elite families to educate their children, and the increasing ethno-religious consciousness of many Indigenous elites encouraged them to contribute from their accumulated wealth toward the establishment of privileged schools with a distinct ethno-religious orientation in Colombo and many regional towns. Thus, the privatization and elitization of the school system still continues to play a major role in the formation of ethno-religious identities, particularly among the Sinhalese Buddhists (Little & Hettige, 2013). It is significant that these elite schools in Sinhala-dominated areas, including Colombo, are largely named after popularly-known Buddhist historical figures.

This notion of nationalism is, however, contested by non-Sinhalese minorities. Most notable are the Sri Lankan Tamils, the descendants of racially 'Dravidian' migrants from south India, who have lived in the North and East of the country since the second century BC (Pfaffenberger, 1994). By the 13th century, a separate Tamil kingdom consisting of the Jaffna peninsula and peripheries in the North had been established. By the middle of the 14th century, the influence of this Hindu kingdom had reached as far south as Puttalam (de

Silva, 2017, p. 27). In the colonial period, Tamil nationalism in the North evolved for two reasons: first, the ethnic and religious consciousness of the Tamils competed with the burgeoning dominant Sinhala Buddhist nationalism in the South, and second, a social reaction formed in response to the unprecedented Christianization of Tamil society and culture by Christian missionaries, supported and funded by the colonial rulers. This fuelled a Hindu revivalism in the North, which has sharpened Tamil ethnic and cultural consciousness since the colonial era. In the post-colonial period, the focus of Tamil nationalism widened from religion to politics as the Tamil leaders began to demand equality and greater political inclusion in Sri Lankan post-independence state formation.

The Sri Lankan Muslims, the third largest ethno-religious group, have lived in the country since as early as the 8th century (Dewaraja, 1994) and claim their collective identity through Islamic religious association, although even in terms of religious faith and practice, they are by no means a homogeneous group. They follow Islam but speak Tamil and, consequently, their ethnic identity is often confused with that of the Tamils. Even though Sri Lankan Muslims have always sought to articulate a separate collective ethnic identity—one that is different from that of the Tamils—the emergence and articulation of Muslim nationalism has suffered from the group's internal religious and political fragmentation (Subedi, 2022). Until a separate Muslim party, the Sri Lanka Muslim Congress (SLMC), was formed in 1981, the Muslim communities mostly relied on the Sinhala Buddhist leadership for their political representation (International Crisis Group [ICG], 2007).

Currently, there are as many as ten Muslim political parties competing to represent the Muslim communities. The rise of Muslim political parties and leadership challenged the traditional leadership held by Islamic authorities and religious associations which had been influential in allocating resources for community development and wellbeing. In the meantime, both types of leadership seemed to either ignore or be unaware of dramatic religious fragmentation among Muslim groups based on their religious-philosophical orientations and associated practices. As a result, the Muslim community in contemporary Sri Lanka is significantly fragmented ideologically between conservative Islamists and modern moderate Muslims. An example of this divide is the emergence of Saudi-based movements such as *the Thawheed Jamaat* and the conflict between radical 'Wahabism' (Thawheed) and moderate 'Sufism' (Faslan & Vanniasinkam, 2015). The Thawheed ideology was allegedly involved in the Easter Sunday bombings in 2019, which dramatically transformed the public's perception of the entire Muslim community as violent. In the absence of a central political authority representing the Muslim communities and with traditional religious authorities such as All Ceylon Jamiyathul Ulama losing its political and social influence (Faslan & Vanniasinkam, 2015), religious factions such as the *Thawheed Jamath*, the *National Thawheed Jamath*, and the *Thablighi Jamaat* have competed to exercise power in the social and political arenas. This has factionalized Muslim identity and hindered the rise of a unified Muslim nationalism.

The history of ethno-religious identity formation and the competing claims for social and national identities by majority and minority groups make it difficult to define the pure people in Sri Lanka. Alternately, this social division provided a major political toolkit for populist-nationalists like the Rajapaksas as they mobilized religion in addition to ethnicity as the major markers of a new social divide (Subedi, 2022), which in turn produced a perceptible shift in Sinhala nationalist discourse. Before delving into how the new social polarization created a conducive environment for populist-nationalist leaders, exemplified by Mahinda Rajapaksa and his brother Gotabaya Rajapaksa, we first discuss the political shift that facilitated their rise to prominence.

The populist-nationalist shift and the rise of Mahinda Rajapaksa

Although Sinhala Buddhist nationalism has always shaped contentious identity politics in Sri Lanka, it first acquired a Sinhala chauvinistic character in the late 1980s and early 1990s. To a large extent, this shift was driven by the growing ethno-religious consciousness within the Sinhalese communities due to the threat posed by Tamil militant separatism led by the Liberation Tigers of Tamil Eelam (LTTE). Moreover, a section of Sinhala Buddhists was also frustrated with the failed 'peaceful solution to the war' experiment, as well as the civil war-induced economic hardships and inequalities. This coincided with the presence of a fragile and unconsolidated democratic system exploited by a few English-educated, elite Sinhala families (see Tambiah, 1986). Nepotistic politics and elite rivalry hampered democratic consolidation and created a conducive environment for the emergence of a populist political leadership. This phenomenon, in which the plebiscitarian element of a democratic system served as a precondition for populism, was not unlike precedents elsewhere in Asia, as well as in Europe (see Mueller, 2019; Subedi & Scott, 2021).

The LTTE-led war was an extreme manifestation of militant Tamil nationalism underpinned by separatism. Tamil separatism and militant nationalism are, however, different from the up-country Tamil quest for nationalism based on culture, civilizational history, and language. The failure to clearly differentiate between the two forms of Tamil nationalism—nonviolent and militant—was integral to the violent responses to the civil war of the Sinhala Buddhist nationalist government, which fundamentally shifted the landscape of ethnic relations by framing the entire Tamil population in the North and East as an enemy of the state (de Silva, 2000).

As the civil war deeply divided the Tamil and Sinhala communities, the rise of Sinhala Buddhist nationalism in the South further facilitated anti-Tamil and anti-peace process sentiment and created a nationalist political platform supported by the ideology of Sinhala Buddhism. While the LTTE's indiscriminate attacks on civilians, political leaders, and infrastructure turned Sinhala Buddhist nationalists against the peace process (Shastri, 2009), some monks affiliated with the *Jathika Hela Urumaya* (JHU), a Sinhala nationalist/heritage party, staunchly advocated for a 'just war' they deemed necessary to eliminate the LTTE (Subedi, 2022).

There was a remarkable link between the growing demand for a just war and the military capitalism that had flourished since the late 1980s, which further contributed to establish Mahinda Rajapaksa as an arguably 'strong man'. Apart from relying on nationalist ideology, Mahinda's populist politics also benefitted from the military labour market (Venugopal, 2011).

Notwithstanding the extent of the war-driven economic, physical, and human destruction, Sri Lanka experienced continued economic growth during the war, facilitated by neoliberal market reforms and structural adjustment programmes. During the first 15 years of the war (1983–1998), the country experienced an average annual economic growth of 4.6 % (Venugopal, 2011). As Venugopal (2011) further argues, despite the long-term decline in small-holder farming, rising rural-urban disparities, and the diminishing role of civilian state employment as a viable route for upward social mobility, military employment increased drastically, making the Sinhala-dominated military the largest single employer in the country. Thus, on the one hand, the military labour market prevented economic decline during the war. On the other hand, it also averted possible resistance by unemployed middle-class Sinhalese youth in the rural areas. Because the lower middle-class Sinhalese youth provided the recruitment base for both the military and the Sinhala Buddhist nationalist leaders, in the 1990s, military capitalism based on the military labour market was crucial for Mahinda Rajapaksa to consolidate and centralize state power by controlling the military as well as loyal Sinhala Buddhist constituencies.

In this context of the civil war, military capitalism, ethnic division, and the resurgence of Sinhala Buddhist nationalism created a conducive social and political environment for Mahinda Rajapaksa to emerge as a strong nationalist leader whose political style clearly embraced aspects of populism.

In November 2005, the Sri Lanka Freedom Party built an alliance with Sinhala nationalist parties—namely, the *Janatha Vimukthi Peramuna* (JVP) and JHU—and fielded Mahinda as its presidential candidate. Although the LTTE boycotted the polls in the North and East, Rajapaksa won the election with the strong support of his allies and Sinhala Buddhist voters from the South. In the face of the LTTE's growing insurgency and violent behaviour, President Rajapaksa abrogated the ceasefire agreement in 2006 and declared all-out war in January 2008. The defeat of the LTTE in May 2009 glorified the 'war victors' and established new narratives of victorious Sinhala Buddhist nationalism. While a significant section of Sinhala Buddhists who have lived in harmony with other ethno-religious groups were uncomfortable with the idea of victorious Sinhala nationalism, the Sinhala political elites trumpeted this idea to consolidate the voter base and mobilize the majority constituency, claiming to represent the 'will' of the 'sons of the soil'.

At the heart of this populist shift is the *Mahavamsa* narrative of Sinhala Buddhist origins and heritage and their portrayal as Sri Lanka's 'pure people'. The historical and civilizational narrative of national identity has been a central strategic instrument supporting the populist political mobilization of the Rajapaksa brothers (Subedi, 2022). We explain this populist-nationalist shift by focusing on three key aspects of their politics: re-articulation of new social polarization and existential crisis and populist-nationalist leadership, along with populist development projects.

New social polarization and the notion of crisis in contemporary Sri Lanka

As Sri Lanka entered the stage of post-independence state formation in the 1950s, social polarizations were deepened by contentious politics around language, religion, and education.

At independence, there was a powerful *swabhasha* (own vernacular) movement, which advocated for Sri Lanka to have its own official language. Although the original aim of the movement was to recognize both Sinhala and Tamil as official languages, the Sri Lanka Freedom Party (SLFP), dominated by Sinhala elites, fervently advocated a Sinhala-only language policy in its 1956 election campaign. Ultimately, the SLFP government passed the Sinhala Only Language Act in 1956, replacing English with Sinhala as the official language. The Language Act is one of the early examples of a populist policy that the SLFP leader and then Prime Minister S. W. R. D. Bandaranaike employed to form a bounded political community of the masses—the Sinhala Buddhists—at the expense of marginalizing minorities.

There was a disproportionate Tamil representation in government services at that time, as the British favoured the Tamil minorities to assert social control. Moreover, Tamils had greater fluency in English acquired through missionary education in the North (Pieris, 2019), and therefore were in an advantageous position to become public servants under the colonial system. In this situation, the Language Act was a powerful tool for the SLFP government to unite its core support base—the rural and middle-class, Sinhala-speaking population. Even though the 13th Amendment to the Constitution in 1987 belatedly recognized Tamil as an official language, its implementation was weak.

The Standardization Policy of 1971 had replaced the previous fully merit-based system with a new system in which about half of university admissions were merit-based, with the remainder based on district quotas (Anuzsiya, 1996). Although intended to increase educational opportunities not only for Sinhalese youth, but for all those from backward districts, the reduction in placements by merit had a disproportionately negative impact on Tamil students from Jaffna, a non-backward district. Political opposition toward the discriminatory Language Act mounted in Tamil-speaking communities. Eventually, it led to the radicalization of Tamil youth, who were later recruited by revolutionary militant groups, most notably the LTTE, which waged a civil war between 1983 and 2009 (Richardson, 2005, p. 279). It is important to note that the language issue extended far beyond access to higher education. In the increasingly state-dominated economy of the 1960s and 1970s, access to white-collar employment in state institutions became contentious as educated but underprivileged youths from all communities competed for limited employment opportunities.

Consequently, the language policy had significant implications for the education system and created further social divisions. By the early 1960s, Sri Lanka had already abandoned the Free Education Policy introduced in 1945. This policy enabled Sri Lanka to achieve high literacy rates and economic development in the 1970s (Isenman, 1980). The shift from free education to the *Swabhasha* education system also had discernible cultural and societal impacts. Free education had contributed to a bilingual society in the North and South. However, segregation of the education system based on language denied children from both ethnic groups exposure to one another's language and cultural traditions. Thus, social alienation of the two ethnic groups was maintained in the face of the threat to religious, ethnic, and cultural pluralism. Despite the country's adoption of liberal democracy, ongoing cultural and ethnic homogenization continued to threaten democratic practices. Frustration with the liberal political system and neoliberal economy translating into socio-economic inequalities grew among all ethnic groups, who began to look for alternative strong leadership to navigate the country away from messy politics and pervasive civil war. The political liberalism of the 1950s was replaced by ethno-nationalism from the 1960s onward until the centre-left politics of President Chandrika Kumaratunga arose in the 1990s. Common to these three political eras was the adaptation of neoliberal economic policies that resulted in declining exports, economic downturn, and rising socio-economic inequalities and social disintegration due to the LTTE war (Venugopal, 2011). Thus, the adverse economic, structural, and cultural conditions favourable to the rise of a populist leader were readily present in Sri Lanka in the late 1990s.

In this context, Mahinda Rajapaksa emerged from outside the Colombo elite as a popular leader claiming to represent Sinhala Buddhists from urban, rural, and regional Sri Lanka. Emboldened by his election victory in 2005, Mahinda upped the internal struggle to a full-scale war in 2008, eliminating the LTTE in 2009 and establishing himself as a national hero. Staunch Sinhala nationalist supporters compared Mahinda, the national hero and strong yet benevolent leader, with the legendary Sinhalese King Dutugamunu—the greatest king of the Anuradhapura Kingdom—who ruled from 161 BC to 137 BC. Mahinda exploited and mobilized this popular sentiment to defame and dislodge political opponents based on their 'failures' to defend the Sinhala Buddhist race and religion.

There was an emerging perception among many Sinhalese communities that the Tamils, as the enemy of the state, had been defeated, but there was another ethno-religious group—the Muslims—readily available to be cast as the new enemy. This perception shifted the social polarities, as well as the landscape of Sri Lankan populist-nationalist politics.

The shift toward a new social polarization in the post-war period

Post-civil war, Sri Lanka shifted away from ethnolinguistic nationalism to more pragmatic, populist nationalism. This 'new social polarization' highlighted religious and cultural differences. During the civil war, religion was rarely a subject of social division (or cohesion). The LTTE carefully avoided bringing religion into the war due to the religious heterogeneity of the Tamil-speaking community. Comprising Hindus, Christians, and Muslims, mobilizing on the basis of religion would have fragmented the LTTE support base. However, religion and culture became the new fault lines for social conflict after the war, with Sri Lankan Muslims identified as a 'new social enemy' of Sinhala Buddhism (Holt, 2016) and targeted by radical Buddhist organizations such as the Bodu Bala Sena (BBS).

The ties between populist-nationalist parties, such as the Sri Lanka Podujana Peramuna (SLPP), and radical religious organizations, such as the BBS, are ambiguous. However, like the SLPP, the BBS emphasizes Sinhala Buddhist 'religious and cultural protectionism' (Subedi, 2022). The BBS acts as the 'moral police', committed to safeguarding the Sinhala people's race and religion from outsiders. So, Sri Lankan Muslims have been indiscriminately labelled by a section of BBS leaders and members as an 'extremist group' and thus a principal enemy of Sinhala Buddhists.[1]

The notion of cultural protectionism, adopted first by the JHU and subsequently by the BBS, has influenced specific policy outcomes. For instance, in September 2020, the Rajapaksa government announced that it would ban the slaughter of cows, a policy that the BBS had actively lobbied for. Likewise, some radical BBS monks argued that the widespread construction of new mosques, allegedly funded by Islamic countries and charities from the Middle East, exemplified a 'cultural invasion' and the globalization of Islamic religion and culture (Silva, 2016). In February 2013, a former BBS leader, Kirama Wimalajothi, called for a cultural war, and demanded a national ban on *hijabs* and *burqas*. Following the Easter Sunday attacks in April 2019, President Sirisena approved a ban on all types of *burqas* and face coverings. The ban was provoked by Islamic fundamentalism, but the government seemed to accept the portrayal by radical Buddhist groups of Muslim culture as a threat to national security and integrity. In other words, Sirisena implicitly supported the BBS cultural war against Muslims.

This new social polarization was manipulated to rationalize the need for a 'strong' populist-nationalist leader to move the country forward. Amidst enduring social divides, the majority of Sri Lankans supported the Rajapaksa brothers' claims to charismatic, strong leadership and altered electoral politics. Gotabaya's 2019 presidential election victory was the first in Sri Lankan history won with an outright majority of Sinhalese votes. Previously, with the political division along class lines, a Sinhalese presidential candidate could not have won an election without some support from minority communities. However, as the Easter Sunday attack galvanized Sinhala solidarity, it benefitted Gotabaya who contested the election on a national security ticket. This was similar to Modi's populist approach in India in 2019, where his campaign shift from development to national security was the key to his victory (Subedi & Scott, 2021).

Leadership and political personalism

Populist nationalism is a *leader-centric* political discourse, central to which is the relationship between leader and followers that has both *relational* and *acclamatory* qualities (Pappas, 2016). In other words, a populist-nationalist leader's claim to extraordinary leadership qualities must ultimately be validated by the followers (Subedi & Scott, 2021). These are the qualities originally formulated by Max Weber (2019 [1922]) in his classical account of charismatic leadership (see Chapters 3 and 7 in this volume). Most populist-nationalist leaders demonstrate *some* form of charisma, but not all are necessarily charismatic (Pappas, 2016). They tend to have the characteristics of popular 'strongmen', claim extraordinary powers to lead, and dominate political and cultural discourses.

The relationship between populist-nationalist leaders and their followers is often determined by what Pappas (2016) calls *personalism* and *radicalism*. While personalism refers to the abilities of leaders to dominate political organizations and movements and to establish unmediated relationships with their followers, radicalism refers to how they articulate radical worldviews and visions for social and economic transformation to attract the masses (Pappas, 2016).

Populist-nationalist leaders often benefit from the plebiscitary element of democracy (Scott, 2018) and thus usually emerge by (mis)using or manipulating democratic systems. Once in power, they subvert these systems, for example by centralizing power in their own hands (Subedi & Scott, 2021). They often confect the idea that the nation is in crisis and claim to be able to address the crisis via simplistic solutions, which can involve extraordinary and unrealistic promises of socioeconomic transformation. The notion of crisis also provides political cover to monopolize state power beyond the party and political system (Pappas, 2016).

Mahinda Rajapaksa was president from 2005 to 2015. During his tenure, state power was personalized, largely centralized in and patronized by his family. Political personalism and the idea of national crisis were instrumental to Mahinda claiming charismatic leadership and promoting an agenda for radical socioeconomic transformation and cultural protectionism for Sinhala Buddhism.

His victory over the LTTE significantly increased his popularity as a nationalist leader, and he was re-elected in 2010. In his second term, Mahinda initiated a constitutional change to consolidate his position. Through the 18th Amendment to the Constitution in 2010, he reintroduced a presidential system that enabled him to control the administrative, legislative, and judicial arms of government ('Eighteenth Time Unlucky', 2010). Furthermore, by promoting cultural protectionism and Sinhala nationalism, Mahinda sought to institutionalize political personalism and cultivate a populist style of politics. Initially, he had embraced the nationalist cultural notion of the *Sinhalanization* of national identity after coming to power in 2005. The implication was that the Sinhalese were the pure people or insiders. By distinguishing insiders from outsiders (Tamils and Muslims), Mahinda's populist-nationalist politics constructed a bounded political community of Sinhala Buddhists. In merging nationalist and populist styles, he claimed to represent the pure people and sought to establish a direct and institutionally unmediated relationship with his followers. He perfected a system of patron-client politics, distributing almost all types of public resource through his political and personal networks that ranged from politically loyal business, administrative, professional, cultural, and intellectual elites to local and regional networks of politicians, activists, and supporters, often micro-managing state institutions for this purpose. He politicized institutions, appointing his loyalists to lead such institutions and facilitate the process. This drew in many ambitious academics, public officers, and professionals in the hope that they would be handpicked to head one of the public institutions, including universities.

Populist political ambitions were integral to Mahinda's nationalist notion of *Jathika Chinthanaya* (roughly translated as 'nationalist thought'). *Jathika Chinthanaya* represented the political psychology of Sinhalese majoritarianism and became partially institutionalized in governance. *Mahinda Chinthanaya* ('The Vision of Mahinda's Thought') was promoted as the 'Vision for the Nation's Future' and a guiding philosophy for development planning.[2] While *Jathika Chinthanaya* fostered cultural protectionism in the emerging populist-nationalist political discourse, *Mahinda Chinthanaya* sought to institutionalize political personalism.

Despite the dominance of the Rajapaksa family, Mahinda was defeated in the 2015 presidential election. Maithripala Sirisena, formerly a minister in Mahinda's government, won by a narrow margin and formed a coalition government with the prime minister, Ranil Wickremasinghe. Discord between the coalition partners over power-sharing, however, resulted in a new alliance between Sirisena and Mahinda and the disintegration of the coalition government. In November 2019, Mahinda's younger brother, Gotabaya Rajapaksa, was elected president, and the 'war victors' returned to power.

Gotabaya's victory re-established Sri Lanka's divisive, leader-centric populism. Mahinda was immediately appointed Prime Minister, and several other Rajapaksa brothers were given key positions in government or parliament. In October 2020, the legislature passed the 20th Amendment to the Constitution, proposed by the Rajapaksa government, negating the separation of powers between president and government provisioned in the 19th Amendment. This made the president the most powerful person in Sri Lanka, with the capacity to remove the prime minister, members of the cabinet, and other ministers or deputy ministers. The president may dissolve parliament after a term of one year and has sole power to appoint the chief justice, supreme court judges, and other key positions such as attorney general, auditor general, election commissioner, and human rights commissioner. Thus, the amendment undermined all democratic checks and balances and institutionalized a leader-centric populist-nationalist political order. Indeed, the centralization of power was originally articulated by the 1978 Constitution: the 19th Amendment reduced the power of the executive president, but the 20th Amendment redirected where it was centralized. By centralizing power in the hands of the president, Gotabaya Rajapaksa extended his elder brother's political personalism.

Nonetheless, there was a dramatic shift in the people's support away from the Rajapaksas in early 2022. Sri Lanka's economic crisis—mounting debt and soaring inflation—had deepened in early 2021. The country experienced unprecedented daily power cuts and shortages of basic items such as food, fuel, and medicines. The crisis followed the president's promise of technology-driven socioeconomic transformations and triggered nationwide anti-government protests in April 2022. Worsened by nepotistic politics, unsustainable investments in post-war reconstruction, and monopolization of economic resources, the new economic crisis gave the people no choice but to withdraw their support from the Rajapaksas. The government initially responded by mobilizing its key ally, the military, and using force against what was tantamount to its former support base, urging the president to step down. Mahinda resigned as prime minister in May 2022, while Gotabaya struggled to maintain political order by sharing power with other political elites. In the face of a growing revolution, Gotabaya resigned as president and fled the country in July 2022.

As this case study shows, the notion of crisis is a double-edged sword in populist politics. While articulation of a national crisis can help bring a populist leader to power, failure to address a crisis inevitably leads to a worsening situation and to withdrawal of the people's support for the leader. Thus, it can be argued that the meaning, significance, and depth of a crisis and the populist leader's response determine the degree of fragility of the populist leadership and the future of soft populism.

Nationalist politics and populist project investments

The defeat of the LTTE undoubtedly saw Mahinda's fame soar, at least among the Sinhalese communities, who regarded him as the saviour of the nation. He was awarded the highest Buddhist religious honour, the *Vishwa Keerti Sri Sinhaladhishwara*, by the Karaka Sangha Sabhas of the Malwatta and the Asgiriya chapters of the Siyam Maha Nikaya, which not only attested to his fame but added to the personification of his nationalist politics. Mahinda proceeded to make populist but unrealistic promises for socioeconomic transformation in the post-war period, intending to expand and consolidate his Sinhala support base.

For example, between 2010 and 2015, several large and costly infrastructure projects were undertaken, including the A9 highway linking Kandy and the Buddhist capital city, Anuradhapura, with Jaffna, the North-South linking transport project, and the Jaffna-Colombo railway service, which was abandoned upon the escalation of the war in 1990 but reopened in 2014. Although the highway was expected to facilitate post-war reconciliation between the Tamil-dominated North and Sinhala-dominated South, in the absence of political moderation and openness, Mahinda's populist developmental path to reconciliation failed to achieve reunion.

The Ministry of Economic Development commenced a series of exorbitant costly projects under its 2010 *Divineguma* (reawakening) scheme. These included electricity, education, health, roadworks, water, sports, religious activities, social welfare, fisheries, and school rehabilitation projects, mainly funded by foreign loans. However, in the absence of elected provincial councils in the Northern and Eastern Provinces, these reconstruction and development projects were not decentralized, nor did they receive public support from Tamils (Subedi & Bulathsinghala, 2018). Instead, Rajapaksa used them to distribute patronage to his populist support base and state resources to his political loyalists through diverse means, including construction contracts.

Indeed, numerous post-war construction projects had less economic and more populist political significance, alongside alleged corruption. The Mattala Rajapaksa International Airport, the second international airport in the country, was built in Mahinda's political constituency, the Hambantota District of the Southern Province. Built at a cost of approximately USD 200 million, since its opening in March 2013, it has proven to be a 'ghost airport'. Likewise, the Magam Ruhunupura Mahinda Rajapaksa Port, the first phase of the new harbour also built in Hambantota at a cost of around USD 400 million and opened in late 2010 (first phase), has produced minimal business given the scale of investment (Sarvanantham, 2016).

In spite of the massive infusion of public capital into the Eastern, Northern, and Southern Provinces after 2009, only 7.3% of the total employment in Sri Lanka was created from this expenditure. Only 5.8% of the total jobs created accrued to the Northern Province

(24,303 jobs), while the national unemployment rate of 4% in 2013 was the lowest since independence (Sarvanantham, 2014, 2016). Mahinda's populist reconstruction and rural development projects between 2010 and 2015 are textbook examples of how populist leaders monopolize state resources by making unrealistic promises of revolutionary socio-economic transformations. These infrastructure investments did not generate significant sustainable employment, while their benefits largely remained confined to a close circle of people within the patron-client network built around the ruling party and its leaders. This is reminiscent of the classical discussion of megaprojects and the risks they pose to politics, developed by Flyvbjerg et al. (2003), although in the Sri Lankan case, risks were downplayed and populist ambitions were central in making investment decisions.

Instead of transforming the economy of the war-torn country, populist investments between 2010 and 2015 sowed the seeds of steady economic inflation, which ultimately led to uncontrollable inflation and unprecedented foreign debt. The inflation rate increased significantly by 3.3% between 2009 and 2013 (Sarvanantham, 2014), reaching 10% in December 2021. In January 2022, Sri Lanka had USD 4.5 billion in sovereign debt, the highest in the country's history, and the foreign currency reserve hit its lowest recorded level. It must be acknowledged that the inflation and sovereign debt did not happen overnight, and successive governments are responsible for the economic mismanagement, which has brought the country near to collapse. The decline in tourism and exports, two major national economic sectors, due to the effects of the COVID-19 pandemic must be factored into this crisis.

However, as noted above, ambitious populist post-war reconstruction and development projects funded by soft loans, government bonds, and commercial borrowing pushed the country into an unprecedented debt crisis and unprecedented inflation rate in 2022. The crisis had worsened with the onset of the COVID-19 pandemic in early 2020, when regular sources of much-needed foreign currency such as tourism, worker remittances, and export earnings began to dry up, making it increasingly difficult not only to service the accumulated foreign debt, but also to pay for essential imports such as fuel, food, and medicines.

Although the current economic crisis is partly a consequence of long-standing economic mismanagement and unfavourable neoliberal economic policies since the 1980s, Mahinda and Gotabaya became victims of their own economic policies that failed to yield benefits for the masses. The devotion of their followers became fluid and extremely unstable as a result of the new economic crisis. The case of the Rajapaksa brothers shows that soft populism inherently carries the seeds of its own destruction.

Conclusion

Focusing on the political ideology and style of governance of former President and then Prime Minister Mahinda Rajapaksa and his younger brother, the subsequent President, Gotabaya Rajapaksa, the chapter shows that nationalism provides a host ideology for right-wing populist politics. However, the host ideology often appears so dominant that it masks populist elements. We highlighted the subtle interaction between nationalism and populism in the form of populist nationalism, a political phenomenon in which populism is hosted by nationalism, as well as the tendency for nationalist politics to incorporate a populist political style to survive in power. We demonstrated that through the dominance of a nationalist ideology, populism manifests what we labelled 'soft populism'. Soft populism travels with a dominant host ideology, but also shares the core elements of hard populism. Notable among these elements is the binary dialectic of 'us' versus 'them' rooted in the discourse of social polarization, the amplified notion of crisis facing the pure people, and the personification of politics by populist leaders, arbitrarily undermining core principles of democracy such as democratic checks and balances and ethnic, cultural, and religious pluralism. Populist nationalism can therefore manifest as a typical example of soft populism.

As the case of Sri Lanka demonstrated, populist nationalism shares several elements manifested by right-wing populism in Western Europe and the United States. Its antiminority and anti-pluralist character dominated by a populist leader that emerged within the context of minimal liberal democracy indicate it approximates the recent right-wing populism in the aforementioned contexts. However, there are certainly exceptions. Several conclusions can be drawn from Sri Lanka.

First, populist nationalism embraces both ideology and political style, therefore becoming a complex phenomenon to define conceptually. It shares the theoretical and conceptual boundaries of the ideational approach (Mudde, 2004) and stylistic approach (Weyland, 2001) of populism. In the case of Sri Lanka, Mahinda Rajapaksa's nationalist politics provided him an ideological basis—specifically a nationalist ideology—for his politics, while his populist political style was expressed in post-war reconstruction projects and populist appeal to the Sinhalese majority. Thus, as a populist-nationalist leader, Mahinda combined both ideology and style, enabling him to survive in power from 2005 until the abysmal end in 2022. Nevertheless, there were significant structural conditions that underpinned the sense of vulnerability felt by the majority Sinhala Buddhist community, in particular its disadvantaged members who constituted the majority within the majority ethno-religious constituency. This sense of vulnerability was a product of post-1977 neoliberal economic and social policies adopted by the right-wing United National Party (UNP) regime that came to power in that year. The significant contraction of the state sector and the rapid expansion of the private sector that followed adversely affected the life opportunities of many Sinhalese Buddhists, who were disproportionately disadvantaged. The entry of private capital into the previously state-dominated education, health, and transport sectors created a more unequal and competitive environment where ethno-religious factors had no significant impact. Despite the UNP regime's defeat in 1994 by the left-of-centre coalition led by Chandrika Bandaranaike Kumaratunga, intensification of the ethnic war precluded her regime from introducing policy to significantly change economic and social conditions during the two terms of her presidency. Mahinda Rajapaksa, as the prime minister during this period, trained his eye on the presidency in 2005.

The loss of opportunities for economic and social advancement, the serious threat posed by the continuing war—not just in the North East but also in other parts of the country, in particular the border villages inhabited by Sinhalese Buddhist settlers—and the mobilization of Sinhala Buddhist nationalist forces against the intensifying Tamil separatist struggle led by the LTTE helped Mahinda emerge as a strong competitor to win the presidential election with the overwhelming support of the majority ethnic community. Yet, the economic and social policies he adopted following his election did not deviate significantly from pre-existing neoliberal ones, except that his policies became distinctly more pragmatic and populist than those of previous regimes. His style of governance also clearly attested to this, made evident from the fact that, following the end of the war, his ethno-nationalist propagandists gradually shifted their focus from the Tamil community to the Muslim community as the new enemy of the Sinhalese Buddhists.

Second, in a multi-ethnic country like Sri Lanka, the dialectics of insider and outsider are highly complex. Unlike right-wing populism in the West, in which the outsiders are religious and cultural minorities and immigrants, excluding long-standing residential groups such as U.S. Hispanics, in Sri Lanka, the minorities are actually 'insiders', politically labelled 'outsiders'. Both Tamil and Muslim minorities have lived in Sri Lanka for centuries, but their national and cultural identities have been denied by the Sinhala political elites in the process of post-independence state formation. The fluidity and controversy of the pure people forced populist-nationalist leaders to articulate new social polarizations as demanded by the changing social and political contexts. This has happened in Sri Lanka with a new social polarization constructed by replacing the enemy of the majority. In the political arena, this new polarization enabled populist nationalist leaders to construct a politically and culturally bounded national identity to serve as a resource for both populist and nationalist politics.

Third, soft populism is a subtype—a fragile and unstable category which has the propensity to either evolve into hardcore and relatively durable populism or slide back to a hybrid democratic form. This is primarily due to the power of the people and their unstable, fragile, and potentially changeable moral and emotional support, as well as their devotion to the leader. Central to this fragility is the notion of crisis. Crisis can support populist leaders in mobilizing a bounded political community and consolidating power, but the nature of crisis can shift depending on the social and economic circumstances. The inability to handle such crises constrains the leader's ability to routinize populist politics and ultimately dislodges the leader from power.

Finally, as is the case with right-wing populism in Western Europe, anti-elitism is a core element of populist nationalism in Sri Lanka. However, a key difference is that historically, Sri Lanka's national politics has been dominated by a few elite Sinhala families. The centrality of elitism and nepotism in the national polity implies populist nationalism is a political discourse led by elites against other elites. In this sense, like nationalism, populist nationalism in Sri Lanka is an elitist discourse which *appears* to differ from populism when a populist leader emerges from the masses or is the underdog. This phenomenon is not much different from elite-driven populist politics in India, Pakistan, Bangladesh, and Myanmar (for the respective national cases, see Chapters 12, 13, 14, and 18 in this volume). Nonetheless, in the case of Sri Lanka, populist nationalism has shown its capacity to serve one fundamental political goal: regime survival for elite politicians like the Rajapaksa brothers.

Notes

1 Interviews with a Christian Sinhala woman and Muslim man in Colombo, September 2019.
2 Interview with a male Sinhalese academic in Colombo, October 2019.

References

Anuzsiya, S. (1996). Standardisation in the university admissions and ethnic crisis in Sri Lanka. *Proceedings of the Indian History Congress, 57*, 799–807.
Brubaker, R. (2020). Populism and nationalism. *Nations and Nationalism, 26*(1), 44–66. https://doi.org/10.1111/nana.12522
Canovan, M. (1981). *Populism*. Harcourt Brace Jovanovich.
Cheeseman, N., & Larmer, M. (2015). Ethnopopulism in Africa: Opposition mobilization in diverse and unequal societies. *Democratization, 22*(1), 22–50. https://doi.org/10.1080/13510347.2013.809065

Cheran, R. (Ed.) (2009). *Pathways of dissent: Tamil nationalism in Sri Lanka*. Sage.
De Cleen, B. (2017). Populism and nationalism. In C. Rovira Kaltwasser, P. Taggart, P. Ochoa Espejo & P. Ostiguy (Eds.), *The Oxford handbook of populism* (pp. 342–362). Oxford University Press.
de Silva, K. M. (1981). *A history of Sri Lanka*. University of California Press.
de Silva, K. M. (2000). *Reaping the whirlwind: Ethnic conflict, ethnic politics in Sri Lanka*. Penguin Books.
de Silva, K. M. (2017). *The island story: A short history of Sri Lanka*. International Centre for Ethnic Studies.
Dewaraja, L. (1994). *The Muslims of Sri Lanka: One thousand years of ethnic harmony, 900–1915*. Lanka Islamic Foundation.
Eighteenth time unlucky. (2010, September 9). *The Economist*. www.economist.com/leaders/2010/09/09/eighteenth-time-unlucky
Faslan, M., & Vanniasinkam, N. (2015). *Fracturing community: Intra-group relations among the Muslims of Sri Lanka*. International Centre for Ethnic Studies.
Flyvbjerg, B., Bruzelius, N., & Rothengatter, W. (2003). *Megaprojects and risk: An anatomy of ambition*. Cambridge University Press.
Gellner, E. (2008). *Nations and nationalism*. Cornell University Press.
Holt, J. C. (Ed.) (2016). *Buddhist extremists and Muslim minorities: Religious conflicts in contemporary Sri Lanka*. Oxford University Press.
ICG (2007). *Sri Lanka's Muslims: Caught in the crossfire*. Asia Report No. 134. International Crisis Group (ICG). www.crisisgroup.org/asia/south-asia/sri-lanka/sri-lanka-s-muslims-caught-crossfire
Ionescu, G., & Gellner, E. (Eds.) (1969). *Populism: Its meaning and national characteristics*. Macmillan.
Isenman, P. (1980). Basic needs: The case of Sri Lanka. *World Development*, 8(3), 237–258. https://doi.org/10.1016/0305-750X(80)90012-1
Ivan, V. (2009). *Revolt in the temple: The Buddhist revival up to Gangodawila Soma Thera*. Ravaya Publication.
Jayasinghe, Pasan (2020). Hegemonic populism: Buddhist nationalist populism in contemporary Sri Lanka. In S. J. Lee, C-e. Wu & K. K. Bandyopadhyay (Eds.), *Populism in Asian Democracies* (pp. 176–196). Brill.
Katsambekis, G. (2022). Constructing 'the people' of populism: A critique of the ideational approach from a discursive perspective. *Journal of Political Ideologies*, 27(1), 53–74. https://doi.org/10.1080/13569317.2020.1844372
Kende, A., & Krekó, P. (2020). Xenophobia, prejudice, and right-wing populism in East-Central Europe. *Current Opinion in Behavioral Sciences*, 34, 29–33. https://doi.org/10.1016/j.cobeha.2019.11.011
Kenny, P. D. (2018). *Populism in Southeast Asia*. Cambridge University Press.
Levitsky S., & Loxton J. (2013). Populism and competitive authoritarianism in the Andes. *Democratization*, 20(1), 107–136. https://doi.org/10.1080/13510347.2013.738864
Little, A. W., & Hettige, S. T. (2013). *Globalisation, employment and education in Sri Lanka: Opportunity and division*. Routledge.
Mann, M. (2005). *The dark side of democracy: Explaining ethnic cleansing*. Cambridge University Press.
Mietzner, M. (2019). Movement leaders, oligarchs, technocrats and autocratic mavericks: Populists in contemporary Asia. In C. de la Torre (Ed.), *Routledge handbook of global populism* (pp. 499–518). Routledge.
Mudde, C. (2004). The populist Zeitgeist. *Government and Opposition*, 39(4), 541–563. https://doi.org/10.1111/j.1477-7053.2004.00135.x.
Mueller, A. (2019). The meaning of 'populism'. *Philosophy & Social Criticism*, 45(9–10), 1025–1057. https://doi.org/10.1177/0191453719872277
Müller, J.-W. (2016). *What is populism?* University of Pennsylvania Press.
Pappas, T. S. (2016). Are populist leaders 'charismatic'? The evidence from Europe. *Constellations*, 23(3), 378–390. https://doi.org/10.1111/1467-8675.12233
Pfaffenberger, B. (1994). Introduction: The Sri Lankan Tamils. In C. Manogaran & B. Pfaffenberger (Eds.), *The Sri Lanka tamils: Ethnicity and identity* (pp 1–27). Routledge.

Pieris, G. (2019). The contribution of education to Tamil separatism and to the ethnic conflict in Sri Lanka. *Aleph, UCLA Undergraduate Research Journal for the Humanities and Social Sciences, 16*(0), 144–157. https://doi.org/10.5070/L6161045562

Richardson, J. M. (2005). *Paradise poisoned: Learning about conflict, terrorism, and development from Sri Lanka's civil wars.* International Centre for Ethic Studies.

Roberts, M. (1982). *Case conflict and elite formation: The rise of Karava elite in Sri Lanka, 1500–1931.* Cambridge University Press.

Russell, Jane (1982). *Communal politics under the Donoughmore Constitution 1931–1947.* Tissa Prakasakayo.

Sarvanantham, M. (2014). Comparison of post-war development in Nepal and Sri Lanka [Paper presentation]. *13th annual symposium of the centre for poverty analysis on post war development in Africa and Asia.* Centre for Poverty Analysis (CEPA).

Sarvanantham, M. (2016). Elusive economic peace dividend in Sri Lanka: All that glitters is not gold. *Geo Journal, 81*(4), 571–596. https://ssrn.com/abstract=2619811

Scott, A. (2018). (Plebiscitary) leader democracy: The return of an illusion? *Thesis Eleven, 148*(1), 3–20. https://doi.org/10.1177/0725513618800120

Shastri, A. (2009). Ending ethnic civil war: The peace process in Sri Lanka. *Commonwealth & Comparative Politics, 47*(1), 76–99. https://doi.org/10.1080/14662040802659025

Silva, K. T. (2016). Gossip, rumour and propaganda in anti-Muslim campaigns of Bodu Bala Sena. In J. C. Holt (Ed.), *Buddhist extremism and muslim minorities: Religious conflicts in contemporary Sri Lanka* (pp. 119–139). Oxford University Press.

Stewart, A. (1969). The social roots. In G. Ionescu & E. Gellner (Eds.), *Populism – its meanings and national characteristics* (pp. 180–196). Weidenfeld and Nicolson.

Subedi, D. B. (2022). The emergence of populist nationalism and 'illiberal' peacebuilding in Sri Lanka. *Asian Studies Review, 46*(2), 272–292. https://doi.org/10.1080/10357823.2021.1983519

Subedi, D. B., & Bulathsinghala, F. (2018). Sri Lanka's developmental path to reconciliation: Narratives and counter-narratives from the margins. In B. Jenkins, D. B. Subedi & K. Jenkins (Eds.), *Reconciliation in conflict-affected communities: Practices and insights from the Asia Pacific* (pp. 91–110). Springer.

Subedi, D. B., & Scott, A. (2021). Populism, authoritarianism, and charismatic-plebiscitary leadership in contemporary Asia: A comparative perspective from India and Myanmar. *Contemporary Politics, 27*(5), 487–507. https://doi.org/10.1080/13569775.2021.1917162

Tambiah, S. J. (1986). *Sri Lanka—Ethnic fratricide and the dismantling of democracy.* University of Chicago Press.

Varshney, A. (2021). Populism and nationalism: An overview of similarities and differences. *Studies in Comparative International Development, 56*(2), 131–147. https://doi.org/10.1007/s12116-021-09332-x

Venugopal, R. (2011). The politics of market reform at a time of civil war: Military fiscalism in Sri Lanka. *Economic and Political Weekly, 46*(49), 67–75. www.jstor.org/stable/41319460

Weber, M. (2019). *Economy and society: A new translation* (K. Tribe, Editor-Translator). Harvard University Press (Original work published 1922).

Weyland, K. (2001). Clarifying a contested concept: Populism in the study of Latin American politics. *Comparative Politics, 34*(1), 1–22. https://doi.org/10.2307/422412

17
ISLAMIC NATIONALISM, POPULISM, AND DEMOCRATIZATION IN THE MALDIVES

Mosmi Bhim

Introduction

The Maldives resumed its transition to democracy after the electoral autocratic president, Abdulla Yameen, lost the September 2018 presidential election. However, populism has skewed the democratization process of this atoll nation of 1192 islands. The overlapping of nationalism and populism is not a new phenomenon in Asia (see Chapters 2, 16, and 18 in this volume). In the Maldives, the simultaneous rise of Islamic fundamentalism and Islamic extremism over the past two decades, as well as the manipulation of these ideologies for political mileage, has seen populist politics subvert democracy by preventing pluralism, obstructing justice, and curtailing human rights (Bhim, 2020). In this ethnically homogeneous nation of over 400,000,[1] Islam is the only permitted religion, and citizenship is restricted to descendants of Maldivians (or Muslims married to local women). Influential political leaders have used religious populism at different times by invoking Islamic ideologies and practices to differentiate between the true followers of Islam, alluding to them as 'pure people'. 'Pure people' are mobilized against moderate and/or liberal followers of Islam as well as non-religious Maldivians who are portrayed as 'enemies of Islam'. This strategy, embracing a populist style, has benefitted nationalist leaders aiming to attract the political support of the masses, justify their rule, and shield them from prosecution for corruption.

Nationalism, rooted in Islamic ideology and identity, rather than populism, is the dominant political ideology of the mainstream political parties and the state in the Maldives. However, as this chapter shows, from time to time, Maldivian nationalist leaders have drawn on populism to garner popular support from below and retain power. To elaborate on this point, this chapter discusses the political styles and strategies of the Maldives' post-independence leaders, namely the former presidents Ibrahim Nasir, Maumoon Abdul Gayoom, Mohamed Nasheed, Abdulla Yameen, and the current president, Ibrahim Mohamed Solih. It analyzes why Islamic nationalism took root in the Maldives and how leaders, in particular authoritarian ones, manipulated faith and religious ideology, adding a populist dimension to their politics.

Dehanas and Shterin (2018, p. 180) defined populism as 'a political style that sets "sacred" people against two enemies: "elites" and "others"'. The stylistic approach stresses the performative aspect of populism, which manifests as an actor-mediated, strategic, and often dramatized form of political action and strategy (see Chapter 3 in this volume). This approach is relevant in studying the political styles of the Maldivian presidents, for some of whom religion, and in this case Islam, is as much an instrument of political mobilization as it is an ideology of their nationalist politics. This means that while Islamic nationalism took precedence, it also hosted certain elements of religious populism—a subtype of populism driven by religious faith, identity, symbolism, morality, and norms (see Chapter 9 in this volume). In other words, Islamic nationalism hosted populism, leading to an exclusionary political discourse and social othering in the post-independence Maldives.

In Western states, *others* could be immigrants, cultural minority groups, or Muslims. But in non-Western nations, *others* could be Western intruders or secularists who threaten the domestic culture (Dehanas & Shterin, 2018, p. 178). Thus, Islamic nationalism resonates with populism, as non-Muslims can be shunned as enemies or others. But Islam as a source of nationalism is rooted in political Islam and pan-Islamism, making it incompatible with the territorial nation-state (Zubaida, 2004). This makes Islamic nationalism different from civic forms of nationalism because it seeks fidelity to the Islamic faith globally by transcending nation-state borders.

In the Maldives, an imaginary threat posed by Christianity and other religions to that nation's Muslim identity has been employed by political leaders over the past decades to undermine support for democracy and human rights. These leaders include beneficiaries of the former dictator Maumoon Abdul Gayoom. They used religious populism to incite protests and violence against Gayoom's successor, Mohamed Nasheed, the Maldives' first democratic president, who was elected in 2008 but forced to resign in 2012. Nasheed's successor, Yameen, and his Progressive Party of Maldives (PPM) deployed Islamic fundamentalism to portray Nasheed's Maldivian Democratic Party (MDP—the Maldives' first political party) as anti-Islam to undermine the legitimacy of that party (Bhim, 2020). Yameen lost the 2018 elections, but the ostensibly democratic MDP government of President Ibrahim Mohamed Solih continues to exercise restraint in response to Islamic nationalism. The freedom of choice inherent in civil and political rights is a cornerstone of democracy. However, nationalist populism leads to exclusionary practices that discriminate based on nationality and religion, as well as gender and sexual preference (UNGA, 2018). This chapter will discuss how Islamic nationalism, exploited by populist politicians, has exacerbated such exclusionary acts in the Maldives. The Maldives remained an authoritarian society post-independence, where the leaders felt justified in determining the will of the people.[2] As such, the post-independence leaders' political styles are analyzed vis-à-vis approaches to populism. In addition to secondary literature, this chapter utilizes primary data from news media and interviews conducted in 2017 and 2018 with prominent Maldivians.

Populism propels the Maldives to independence

There is a stark contrast in the style of populism adopted by the Maldives' first post-independence president, Ibrahim Nasir, and that of his successor, Maumoon Abdul Gayoom. In the campaign for independence, Nasir invoked the central feature of populism—*the people*—who are betrayed, wronged, or left vulnerable to indomitable forces (Gagnon et al., 2018, p. viii). In contrast to Nasir, Gayoom sought popularity with the people by mobilizing religious populism, a subtype of populism driven by religious ideologies and faith, which is examined in the next section. Nasir, as the prime minister (1957–1968), a man of monarchical descent, encouraged hostile sentiments against British colonial rule, thus pressuring Britain to grant the Maldives independence in 1965. The Maldives had been a British protectorate since 1887, but monarchical rule continued because Britain practiced indirect rule through the sultanate. As the first post-independence president from 1968–1978, Nasir classifies as a dictator (Bhim, 2020) because the *Majlis* (parliament) chose him as the sole candidate for the referendum to determine the president, thus depriving voters of the right to choose from alternative contenders. Even after independence, political parties were prohibited and civil society was non-existent, meaning that the Maldives was not a plural democratic society. Nevertheless, Nasir amassed populist support from the nationalist movement that arose in the last decade of British rule. In other words, nationalism facilitated populism during Nasir's time.

Nasir's populist style of politics is shown in two key events that galvanized national unity—the leasing of Gan Island in the Addu Atoll, and the secessionist movement to make Addu Atoll a separate state. The British faced hostility from Maldivian ministers when a 100-year lease of Gan Island to Britain's Royal Air Force (RAF) was signed without parliamentary consent by Prime Minister Ibrahim Faamudheri Kileygefaanu in 1956 (Rasheed, 2014, p. 18). Opposition by Nasir and fellow ministers led to rejection of the agreement in 1957, followed by Faamudheri Kileygefaanu's resignation, at which time Nasir became Prime Minister. The second incident was when residents of Addu Atoll, whose lives had been improved by the RAF presence on Gan, launched a secessionist movement that lasted from 1959 to 1963 (Maloney, 2013, pp. 203–205). Nasir, leading the military, crushed the uprising but was outraged by Britain's protection of the movement's leader, Abdulla Afeef, whom they secretly shipped to exile in the Seychelles (Ashraf, 2012, p. 33). Britain's political interference generated a nationalistic fervour, thus giving Nasir the popular support he needed to spearhead the Maldives' independence movement. Nasir mobilized the people and invoked nationalism to promote the attainment of state sovereignty.

The scant literature for this period shows that Nasir's patriotism aroused nationalist sentiments and reciprocal trust by the people. He prevented secession, fought for independence, and introduced many developments, including the construction of the first international airport, the Maldives' tourism industry, and English language education. Although Nasir was of monarchical descent, he removed the monarchical head of state and reigned as President after the nation became a republic in 1968. This enabled him to rule as a dictator and protect himself from being forcibly ousted, as had happened to President Ameen in 1953. Populist politics was thus deployed by a member of the elite against other elites. Despite the majority *Majlis* vote in his favour, Nasir declined to stand for the presidency in 1978 and instead nominated Gayoom, who won that election. Subsequently, Nasir permanently relocated to Singapore.

Gayoom—the pious dictator who ruled with an iron fist in a velvet glove

Unlike Nasir, Gayoom was in no position to evoke anti-colonial nationalist populism. Commencing his presidency in Nasir's shadow, Gayoom ruled as a personalist dictator for 30 years until 2008. Gayoom was respected as a renowned scholar of Islam, which he studied at the Al Azhar University in Egypt and taught at a Nigerian university and in the Maldives. He creatively employed Islamic symbols, tropes, and ideas to generate a feeling of belonging among Maldivians (Dehanas & Shterin, 2018, p. 182). National landmarks, such as the Islamic Centre in the capital Malé, displayed his Arabic calligraphy (Ellis, 1998, pp. 171–172). His strategic orchestration of religious populism led to Gayoom being revered by the public. Albeit of noble lineage, he needed this reverence because, unlike previous Maldivian heads of government, he was not from the monarchical family. Being a doyen of Islam bestowed him with legitimacy and stature.

Gayoom manipulated Islam to gain political support and discredit his predecessor, Nasir. The Maldives was regarded as a moderate Islamic nation prior to, and for a decade after, independence. Nasir's rule was considered brutal due to his repression of political freedoms. However, Nasir had allowed greater individual liberties for commoners and women (Timeline, 2015). The Western tourism and alcohol consumption permitted during Nasir's rule were criticized by Gayoom as anti-Islam. The Maldivian cultural tradition of brightly coloured clothes and a liberal practice of Islam were prevalent under Nasir. In contrast, under Gayoom, garments for women became increasingly conservative and more men grew beards (Roul, 2013). Gayoom's approach to religious populism induced people to overtly display loyalty to Islam, despite there being no other religion present in the Maldives. Thus, he differentiated between true followers of Islam, and the 'enemy'—namely, those who failed to uphold his strictly interpreted conservative religious tenets.

Gayoom entrenched Islam in Maldivian society through initiatives such as the Islamic institute Mauhadu-al Dhiraasaathul Islamiyya, created in 1980, and the Islamic Centre of Maldives, established in 1984 with the assistance of other Islamic nations (Hassan, 2011, p. 28). Youths were sent to study Islam in Asian and Middle Eastern nations. Textbooks conveying a stricter version of Islam were introduced into schools (Ningthoujam, 2015). Gayoom created the 1994 Protection of Religious Unity Act, which restricted the practice of other religions and established the Supreme Council for Islamic Affairs in 1996 (Ningthoujam, 2015). Islam was proclaimed the official religion in the 1997 Maldives Constitution. In practice, the Sunni branch of Islam became the national religion. Gayoom banned nightclubs and presided over religious events, including the delivery of sermons. His official biography claims he revived the spirit of Islam in the Maldives but also discouraged religious extremism (Ellis, 1998, p. 117). Political dissidents were dubbed 'enemies' of Islam and repressed, as were Islamist extremists. To the outside world, Gayoom promoted a purportedly moderate and tolerant Islam to safeguard tourism. Yet he also introduced policies to nurture his image as the supreme authority of Islam in the Maldives (Hassan, 2011, p. 28–30). This led to the ascendency of political Islam, which seeks solidarity with other parts of the global *Ummah* by the re-Islamization of Muslims corrupted by Western values (Altuntaş, 2010, p. 424). Gayoom's policies promoted religious intolerance in the Maldives by instilling Islamic fundamentalist values. Gayoom utilized religious populism to justify his rule and maintain support for himself as a 'holy' ruler. It fostered intolerance as he compelled Maldivians to be vigilant against, and resist, outsiders (Dehanas & Shterin, 2018, p. 182) with a pragmatic exception made for tourists. Despite his political repression, Gayoom launched a populist charm offensive. A former elections commissioner described Gayoom as 'a benevolent dictator, doing enough for the people in terms of economy and welfare. Only political, civil liberties were restricted' (Former elections commissioner, personal communication, November 6, 2017).

Gayoom used several populist strategies to entrench himself as ruler. In Gayoom's official biography, he was portrayed as a consultative leader who transformed the Maldives into a democracy (Ellis, 1998, p. 122). He opened the *Majlis* to the public and, from 1979, gave immunity to legislators for expressing opinions that did not transgress Islam (Luithui & Phadnis, 1985, p. 43). He developed an open leadership style by holding public meetings, mass prayers, and press conferences around the country (Luithui & Phadnis, 1985, pp. 43–47). Such actions to win the admiration of the public are among the hallmarks of populist leaders who derive legitimacy through large rallies and election victories (Dehanas & Shterin, 2018, p. 182).

A senior Maldivian human rights professional described Gayoom as being 'very high in narcissistic self-importance', with a determination to hold onto power that prevented him from taking up opportunities for peaceful democratization sooner:

> Gayoom and his supporters somehow believed the infallibility of the regime and lacked accountability. Gayoom was a very grandiose person, a person who has such self-admiration. . . . He built his regime around his personality as a sort of cult trying to make people believe that everything Gayoom has done, said or thought about, is always right, there are no questions asked. Whether he was cruel or not cruel, good or bad, he's always right.
> *Senior human rights professional, personal communication, November 6, 2017*[3]

Although Gayoom claimed to have democratized Maldives, there were no political freedoms and dissent could lead to arbitrary disappearance, torture, and death. Former MDP parliamentarian Hamid A. Ghafoor described Gayoom's rule as an 'iron fist in a velvet glove', because he appeared sophisticated, but in reality, opponents were being tortured:

> There were about 120 unaccounted people, mostly disappeared while detained in prison. The President controlled all appointments to government. If anybody talked about anything the government did not like, they may not get promoted.
> *H. A. Ghafoor, personal communication, December 8, 2017*

To ensure control over and support from the people, a wide range of decisions required Gayoom's personal approval. This strategy approximates the populist tendency to centralize state power and authority and undermine democratic checks and balances once they are in power. Dr. Azra Naseem, a Maldivian researching Islamic radicalization, described this as having to 'beg' Gayoom for certain things:

> Most families in Malé would have written Gayoom a letter, as it was the norm to request his help for things such as education assistance, money for medicine or overseas treatment, and to get land or divide land.
> *Dr. A. Naseem, personal communication, February 2, 2018*

Human rights advocate, Ahmed Tholal,[4] confirmed that the presidential office's approval was required for a wide range of matters:

> permits for house construction; commuting sentences or releasing arrested relatives so they wouldn't end up in prison where there was rampant torture. If it was a political arrest, they had to ask for the President's forgiveness.
> *A. Tholal, personal communication, November 8, 2017*

Dependency on Gayoom's approval made people less willing to oppose his rule. It demonstrated the president's domination of society by authoritarian personal rule (Geddes, 1999).

Gayoom kept in personal touch with the people, but also engaged in brutal repression through arbitrary detentions, torture, and unjust convictions. He controlled the executive, judiciary, atoll councils, and the legislature through appointments and, until 2003, he was Commander-in-Chief, as well as Minister of Finance and Defence (Ashraf, 2012, p. 24). Yet piety and Gayoom's all-pervasive personal power were insufficient to prevent protests by Maldivians desiring democracy. In addition, the collapse of the Soviet Union, the catastrophic 2004 tsunami, and the global financial crisis increased the need for aid from democratic countries. Gayoom was thus compelled to introduce democratic reforms through changes to legislation and institutions. The arrest of a Maldivian, Ibrahim Fauzee, at an Al-Qaeda hideout in Pakistan by U.S. forces in 2004 drew international attention to a new problem—the tiny atoll nation's involvement in global terrorism (Hassan, 2011, p. 51). Moreover, Islamists portrayed the devastation from the 2004 tsunami as God's wrath for not practicing their version of the 'right Islam', which was fundamentalist and puritanical (The long road, 2014). The social disruption from the tsunami and underlying social conditions combined with new democratic freedoms of expression and association provided the necessary context for radicalism to spread (Hassan, 2011, p. v). Actions against democratization by radicals included the bombing of Sultan Park in Malé in September 2007, which wounded 12 tourists. Suspects included Maldivian youth with a connection to radical Islamist terror groups in Pakistan (Didi, 2012, p. 207). Notwithstanding such instability, the Maldives' first democratic multiparty election was held in 2008, which Gayoom lost (Bhim, 2020, pp. 166–171).

Undoubtedly, the utilization of religious populism sanctified Gayoom's rule as a personalist dictator. In conjunction with direct control and brutal repression, Gayoom portrayed himself as charming and generous. His use of Islamic nationalism was akin to the populist style, as Maldivians not following his rules of Islam qualified as outsiders or enemies. Political Islam in the Maldives served to legitimize Gayoom's self-aggrandizement. Re-Islamization during this era created the foundation for instability that derailed the Maldives' efforts to democratize its laws, institutions, and society.

Political Islam and democratization

Re-Islamization was detrimental to the Maldives, as freedoms of thought, conscience, and religion were thus excluded from the democratization agenda. The 'democratic' 2008 Maldives Constitution prohibits non-Muslims from becoming citizens and requires members of the executive and legislature to be Muslim. Thus, being of Maldivian descent no longer sufficed for citizenship. Moreover, laws and freedom of expression could not contravene the tenets of Islam. This meant the nation had not genuinely become a plural society despite the first multiparty elections in 2008, when the MDP's Nasheed was elected President. Nasheed, a democracy activist, had been jailed and tortured many times by the Gayoom regime (Didi, 2012, p. 149). Yet Nasheed's rule was encumbered by having to pander to and placate Islamic fundamentalists that democracy was not a threat to Islam.

The 2008 Maldives Constitution enshrines Islam as the state religion. This explains Nasheed's launch of a constrained human rights reform agenda that excluded religious freedom. He also felt compelled to drop his female running mate for the 2008 elections when her potential appointment was criticized as un-Islamic by MDP advisors. Furthermore, after becoming president, Nasheed created the Ministry of Islamic Affairs and let the Adhaalath Party (AP)—a Muslim nationalist party—control it to secure conservative Muslim support (Larsen, 2009). Nasheed's deference implied that the AP was the authority on Islam. Evidently, Nasheed attempted to appease Islamic fundamentalists and implemented a compromised form of democracy in the Maldives, where freedom of religion was excluded to accommodate the hate speech of Islamic fundamentalists. Increasing intolerance towards other religions left non-Muslim Maldivians fearful to practice freedom of religion (Didi, 2012, p. 207). Such restrictions on freedom of religion and failure to safeguard non-Muslim Maldivians meant that a diverse plural society was not being allowed to develop in the Maldives.

Nasheed's rule encountered a challenge in the rise of Islamic fundamentalism that grew unchecked during the transition to democracy. Further challenges arose from accumulating debts that necessitated financial intervention by the International Monetary Fund in 2009, and a decline in tourism revenue due to the global financial crisis. Nasheed implemented public sector reform that required slashing civil service jobs and instigating new taxes to mitigate the financial crisis. This threatened the power and privilege of the beneficiaries of three decades of Gayoom's authoritarian rule (Zahir, 2016). Gayoom had largely kept radical Islam and Saudi Arabia's influence at bay. But during the last years of his rule, Gayoom made no concerted effort to control the growth of Islamic terror groups. Instead, he and his supporters accused the opposition of trying to introduce foreign religions to the Maldives (Larsen, 2009).

As a liberal, Nasheed refused to restrict social movements. This allowed the growth of the new 'glocalized' political Islam, referring to the many Islamists who think globally but act locally (Karagiannis, 2018, pp. 1–4). They identify with their communities and regard Western governments, secularists, and other Islamic denominations as enemies (Karagiannis, 2018, p. 11). Democratic freedoms allowed puritanical Islam, aligned to Wahhabi organizations such as the Jamiyathul-Salaf (JS) and the Islamic Foundation of Maldives (IFM) established in 2009, to spread across the Maldives. It also contributed to more widespread head-covering among women and to female circumcision (Hassan, 2011, pp. 59–61). Maldivians joined Al-Qaeda and fought as terrorists in Pakistan between 2009 and 2013 (Hassan, 2011). The internet, accessed by 43% of Maldivians, was the chief facilitator for Maldivians joining terror groups (Naseem, 2015). In 2009, President Nasheed bemoaned the fact that hundreds of Maldivians had joined terrorist groups in Pakistan and Afghanistan (Sharma, 2019).

Gayoom capitalized on this by portraying Nasheed as anti-Islamic to move the public against him. To wrest executive power back from Nasheed, Gayoom formed partnerships with conservative Islamic organizations and opposition parties (Arora, 2014). Gayoom's loyalists in politics and business manipulated Islamic extremism to ignite anti-Nasheed protests. This was a crucial element in the armed forces' mutiny in February 2012 by factions loyal to Gayoom, which forced Nasheed's resignation. During the 'Defend Islam' protests in December 2011, opposition parties and religious groups had accused Nasheed's government of defiling Islam and promoting Western ideals (Roul, 2013). The Wahhabi and Salafist organizations, the JF and IFM, promoted Islamism to political parties that protested against Nasheed in 2011 (Roul, 2013).

The AP terminated its coalition with Nasheed's government in September 2011 and organized massive rallies against the MDP (Musthaq, 2014, p. 168; Hassan, 2011, pp. 32–34). The AP played a key role in Nasheed's removal from power by joining with radicals in labelling Nasheed 'an enemy of Islam' and creating the rhetoric of 'Nasheed's devious plot to destroy Islam' (The long road, 2014). Qasim Ibrahim, the leader of another coalition partner, the Jhumhooree Party, called for *jihad* against the MDP while the Dhivehi Qaumee Party accused Nasheed's government of undermining Islam (Musthaq, 2014, p. 169).[5] At the height of the armed forces' mutiny in February 2012, when President Nasheed was forced to resign, pre-Islamic Hindu and Buddhist relics at the National Museum were destroyed by radicals.

Thus, the Islamic nationalism that had cemented Gayoom's one-man dictatorship was utilized to bring down the Maldives' democratically elected government. The political parties' manipulation of Islamic fundamentalism provoked protests and ultimately mutiny against Nasheed. His truncated rule was a casualty of 'glocalized' political Islam, whereby three kinds of agents—activists, politicians, and militants (Karagiannis, 2018, p. 16)—modified global Islamic extremist incantations to accord with Maldivian local practices, thereby inciting violent demonstrations with fatal consequences for democracy. It reflects the pan-Islamic logic of Islamic nationalism, which is globalized opposition to the West, but with particular or localized practice (Zubaida, 2004, p. 409; Altuntaş, 2010, p. 432). Maldivians became enmeshed in identity politics by being made to feel that they had to choose between democracy and Islam. Nasheed's resignation showcases the interface of Islamic nationalism and populism in the Maldives, where the fundamentalists portrayed themselves as the 'sacred' people, and moderate Muslims as the 'enemy'. Islamic nationalism differs from populism insofar as it is not the people against the elites, but a case of fundamentalist Muslims against the 'enemy' of moderate Muslims and non-Muslims. In this sense, Islamic nationalism became an instrument of populist politicians in the Maldives for acquiring political support through their display of fundamentalism and undermining support for their moderate political opponents.

Yameen's blood-and-faith nationalism

The 'Islam under threat' rhetoric was used to justify Nasheed's abrupt removal from power and paved the way for a reversion to authoritarianism in the Maldives. Gayoom's half-brother, Yameen, was elected president in November 2013 in polls obstructed by the police and delayed by Supreme Court judgements (Bhim, 2019). Yameen's Islamic extremist rhetoric during the election campaign and his tenure as president portrayed Nasheed as bent on destroying Islam in the Maldives (Johansson, 2018). Yameen's populist strategies portrayed his coalition government as the protector of 'the sacred religion of Islam' and Nasheed as 'an enemy of the nation's Islamic unity' (Arora, 2014). Such inflammatory rhetoric has become a feature of populism in Asian nations. It is blood-and-faith nationalism based on race and/or religion whereby foreigners are blamed for a nation's economic problems and adulterating their culture (Gunasekara, 2017).

Yameen's autocratic government, which served from November 2013 to September 2018, is a classic case of how two characteristics of populism—anti-pluralism and illiberalism—gradually broke down democracy (Diamond, 2017, pp. 5–7). Following his election, Yameen established stronger relations with authoritarian states, Saudi Arabia and China, and distanced the Maldives from democracies such as long-time ally India. Arabic was introduced to Maldivian schools, and an agreement was signed with Saudi Arabian scholars to improve the study of the Quran (Arora, 2014). Assistance from Saudi Arabia in 2015–2016 included U.S.$50 million to construct apartments for the security forces, a

U.S.$80 million loan for development ventures, budget support of U.S.$20 million, and an agreement to maintain the Maldives as a 100% Muslim nation ('Saudi Arabia Pledges', 2016). The Maldives reciprocated by joining a Saudi-led Islamic alliance in December 2015 to combat terrorism. Yameen thus exhibited a pronounced tendency for forging closer ties with illiberal states.

During Gayoom's tenure, there was not only re-Islamization but also a promotion of moderate Islam. In contrast, under Yameen, Islamic fundamentalism was encouraged to spread, including its teaching in schools. According to Tholal:

> There's more focus on fundamental religious ideals in the curriculum. If you look at a school textbook now, it has been laced with religious undertones . . . there's a lot of segregation between girls and boys in schools and extra-curricular activities like theatre, drama, singing, are discouraged.
> *A. Tholal, personal communication, November 8, 2017*

Under Yameen, radical Maldivian imams, funded by Saudi Arabia, spread Wahhabist doctrines unhindered in the Maldives, whereas Sufism was discouraged (Johansson, 2018). Additionally, civil society organizations (CSOs) were treated as forces created by the Western un-Islamic countries, according to parliamentarian, Ali Hussain:

> Their voices are not being heard. I've seen in government they are considered as evil. They are being portrayed as *Laadheeni*—as against the religion. For that reason, we have very few actively working CSOs.
> *A. Hussain, personal communication, November 16, 2017*

As Islam is the state religion, critics of government faced challenges as Maldivians were increasingly accustomed to lives regulated by Islam, whereas the promotion of freedom was associated with Western values. Dr. Azra Naseem believes that such regulation limited freedom of thought and expression in the Maldives:

> You have to conform, you have to be a Muslim, you have to follow rules. Anybody who does not follow the prescribed rules and regulations is considered an outlaw, a misfit or an apostate.
> *Dr. A. Naseem, personal communication, February 2, 2018*

Political leaders claiming to protect Islam openly used hate speech, threats of violence, and murder during Yameen's rule. Unpunished crimes that created fear among supporters of democracy and human rights included the murder of the prominent blogger and social media commentator Yameen Rasheed in 2017; extremists stabbing the former editor of *Haveeru* newspaper Ismail Khilath Rasheed in 2012; extremists murdering the journalist Ahmed Rilwan Abdulla; and the assassination of moderate lawmaker Dr. Afrasheem Ali in 2012 (Bhim, 2020, pp. 195–196). The nonconformists and the opposition were derided as anti-Islamic, while Yameen's party benefitted politically by depicting themselves as the protectors of Islam. These crimes against liberals show that although the Maldives claims to be a 100% Muslim nation, a minority of Maldivians are either non-Muslim, non-religious, or atheist, but have not been allowed to practice their beliefs under successive governments.

Increased aid from Saudi Arabia contributed to re-Islamization and the diminution of women's rights. Dr Azra Naseem observed that women's oppression increased under Yameen:

> Twenty years ago, we were a more equal society. . . . There's a regression; freedoms that we used to have are being taken away. . . . A particular brand of conservative Islam, Wahhabism and Salafi, from Saudi Arabia, Pakistan and Afghanistan, had a major impact on women. . . . A lot of women chose to wear black *niqabs* influenced by the radicals. On some islands, you will find women wearing head to toe black clothes, going into the sea in them.
> Dr. A. Naseem, personal communication, February 2, 2018

Yameen's government, in benefitting from re-Islamization, did not publicly acknowledge that the nation's security was under threat from radicals, including Maldivian returnees from Syria. In 2015, an Islamic State (IS) trio threatened in a video message to kill Yameen and demanded the release of jailed politician, Sheik Imran Abdulla. In 2017, several IS sympathizers were arrested in connection with local and international terror conspiracies (Sharma, 2019). However, instead of acting against Islamic terror groups, Yameen forged closer ties with authoritarian countries in the Middle East.

Yameen's brutal repression was presented as a defence of Islam, although essentially it was to eliminate all opposition. In the lead-up to the 2018 elections, the armed forces and judiciary acted against opposition parliamentarians through detentions, convictions, and a parliamentary lock out (Bhim, 2020, p. 208). Parliamentarian Ali Hussain and former MDP parliamentarian Ghafoor revealed (2017, pers. comm) that Nasheed was portrayed by the incumbent government as very *Laadheeni*, or anti-Islam. PPM supporters threatened to behead Nasheed and other opposition figures if they returned to the Maldives (Bhim, 2020, p. 208). Yameen's repression led to him losing the September 2018 presidential election to the MDP's Solih.

Yameen was an electoral autocratic ruler who used blood-and-faith nationalism to manipulate Maldivian sentiments towards Islam. Similar to Gayoom, Yameen used religion selectively to rally Maldivians to be vigilant and resist elites and outsiders (Dehanas & Shterin, 2018, p. 182). Through the rhetoric of 'us versus them', Yameen amplified the fear of outsiders with the political propaganda that Islam was endangered in the Maldives. He drew on Islamic nationalism, as well as sympathized with Islamic extremists, to the detriment of human rights and freedom of expression. Despite these tactics, Yameen lost the 2018 elections due to the harsh repression during his rule and widespread high-level corruption. Thus, religious populism was insufficient for him to retain power, as he did not nurture the patron—client relations that had enabled Gayoom's lengthy rule (Bhim, 2020).

Challenges to democracy

The election of Ibrahim Solih[6] as president in 2018 returned the government to transitional democracy, although it has been adversely impacted by Islamic nationalism. Solih won the election on his pledges to fight corruption, end dictatorship, and return to justice (Bhim, 2020, p. 210). However, the politicized Islam ingrained in the Maldivian psyche necessitated that Solih go to great lengths to show commitment to Islam and prevent a coup against his fledgling government. Solih's rule depicts the populist characteristic of 'real or perceived reaction to a deep crisis' (Gagnon et al., 2018, p. viii). While Yameen exemplified a populist actor subjectively constructing a crisis of their nation's religious and cultural identity under threat, Solih's mitigating policies were a reaction to contain the crisis created by Yameen's xenophobic schema (see Gagnon et al., 2018, p. ix).

The symbols and tropes of religion that were entrenched under post-independence authoritarianism have been retained by emerging democratic leaders. At independence, the presidential oath required a pledge to respect and be faithful to Islam (Luithui & Phadnis, 1985, p. 38). This remains the case in contemporary Maldives as President Solih, in his inaugural address on November 17, 2018, pledged not only to 'uphold the doctrines of Islam' but also to maintain 'governance that upholds the exemplary principles of Islam' (Solih, 2018). Solih assured the public that his government would practice democratic governance that would not alienate any race, sex, sect, or class. He omitted explicit references to religious freedom, thus making his commitment to democracy incomplete.

Solih's government denied entry to the controversial Islamic preacher Zakir Nair, known for hate speech and inciting youth to terrorism (Sudhakar, 2019), but the following incident shows that secularists are far from safe under Solih's government. Islamic extremists threatened a former parliamentarian, Ibrahim Ismail, who had questioned the Islamic punishment of adultery by stoning, after a Maldivian woman was sentenced to this form of death in January 2019 (Ganguly, 2019). Instead of providing him with protection, police questioned Ibrahim over his related social media posts. The Solih government thus reacted in the same manner as Yameen's government, which took no action to protect Ibrahim's sister, Shahinda Ismail, the executive director of the Maldivian Democracy Network (MDN) from threats by extremists in 2018. Solih's government caved in to protests by religious scholars against the 2016 MDN report that challenged Islamic principles and dissolved the MDN in November 2019 (Balachandran, 2019). Meanwhile, political and religious leaders persisted with their campaign of exploiting Islam to provoke violence against Solih and Nasheed, who was now the speaker of parliament (Bhim, 2020, p. 212). By bowing to majority Muslim demands at the expense of the non-religious Maldivian minority, the Solih government showed it was leaning expediently towards populism to ensure its survival. Solih's populist reaction excluded the interests of dissenting voices and minorities, thus demonstrating how populism can effectively undermine democracy (Dehanas & Shterin, 2018, p. 183).

The Solih government has reacted to identity politics by showing loyalty to Islam, rather than democracy. However, while vowing to defend Islam, the government did take decisive actions to penalize Islamic extremist and jihadist crimes. This was evident when Mohamed Ameen was charged in December 2019 for allegedly conducting ten recruitments for Jihadist terror groups (Hadi, 2019). The MDP government has taken strict measures against Islamic extremism by placing 17 terrorist groups on a watch list, including Islamic State (IS), Al-Qaeda, Jabhat Al-Nusra, and Lashkar-e-Taiba (Aiham, 2019). Individuals associated with these organizations face up to 15 years imprisonment if convicted under the Terrorism Prevention Act. Through these measures, Solih is striving to persuade Maldivians that moderate Islam is the right Islam for the Maldives, whereas extremist Islam is classified as a criminal activity.

Nonetheless, Islam continues to provide a vehicle for opposition parties to try to incite violence and hatred against Solih and Nasheed by portraying them as anti-Islamic, as well as to fend off the prosecution of Yameen and his allies for their past crimes. The opposition Progressive Congress Coalition has been touting the 'Islam in danger' slogan to portray

MDP leaders as having a sinister plan to diminish Islam (Balachandran, 2019). Following his election victory, Solih renewed the formerly warm bilateral ties with India while forging strong relations with Muslim nations including Saudi Arabia, the United Arab Emirates, and Bangladesh. These nations aided the Maldives as it grappled with the COVID-19 pandemic that saw 9,000 cases by September 2020 and 77,000 cases by July 2021, with a recovery rate of over 95% ('Home Minister Tests Positive', 2021). Renewing ties with India was a strategic economic move for the Maldives as the reopening of the borders to tourism in July 2020 during COVID-19 brought the highest number of tourists from India. Conversely, strengthened ties with India provide fodder to fundamentalist politicians such as the PPM party, under whose rule relations with India became estranged.

Contending with extremists, notably the returning Maldivian *jihadists* from Syria, remains a major hurdle for Solih (Bhim, 2020, p. 214). The Maldives had the highest per capita representation of foreign fighters who went to Syria, and officials estimated the nation had 1,400 extremists in 2019 (Gough, 2021). The Maldives' political and security challenges were drawn into stark relief when suspected Islamic extremists seriously injured the former democratic president Nasheed in a bomb blast on May 6, 2021.

Nevertheless, Solih's humility and the priority he accords to social harmony, inclusivity, and stability have earned the trust of the MDP's ultra-religious coalition partner, the AP ('AP Hits Back', 2021). Thus, while Solih still falls short of granting the religious freedom crucial for democracy, his efforts to promote consensus and moderation show he is not seeking populist admiration. Rather, he is cracking down on extremists and engaging with reason to convince Maldivians that they are already Muslim and do not need to become Islamic extremists to prove their faith.

Conclusion

This chapter examined the varying recourses to a populist style of politics in the Maldives over six decades under different leaders and changing political circumstances, which have had a divisive impact on the nation. A common factor is that the populist style was vital, particularly for authoritarian leaders, to enhance their legitimacy and popular support, thus enabling them to stay in power. However, an analysis of the interplay between nationalist politics and Islamic ideology and practice shows that the populist political style of the leaders was tactical and reactive. Islamic nationalism was the main political platform on which their populist politics played out.

The post-independence dictator, Nasir, gained support through anti-colonial nationalism, which also included elements of populism, such as mobilization of the people against the political elites and others—namely, the colonial rulers and Westerners. This helped Nasir to retain public loyalty due to the trust he accrued as the country's national hero who had led the independence campaign. Hence, Islam under Nasir was regarded as the primary source of a homogeneous national identity rather than a populist trope.

Unlike Nasir, Gayoom was the first leader to utilize religion for populist purposes. It helped him to gain legitimacy in that, unlike previous rulers, he was not from a monarchical family. Through symbols and tropes of Islam, such as sermons and calligraphy on prominent mosques, Gayoom gained respect as a revered Islamic scholar. The re-Islamization under Gayoom saw other religions outlawed and liberal practices labelled as un-Islamic and criminalized, which fostered religious intolerance among Maldivians. This created a condition in which the Islamic faith and Islamic ideologies were readily available to exploit for advancing nationalism as well as populist politics. Both Nasir and Gayoom centralized power by controlling the executive, judiciary, atoll councils, and legislature.

The nation's first democratic president, Nasheed, was forced to resign prematurely following violent demonstrations instigated by extremist politicians claiming he was a threat to Islam. The rise of Islamic extremism and fundamentalism posed a challenge for Nasheed. His successor, Yameen, was a half-brother of Gayoom. He was not an Islamic scholar but portrayed himself as a protector of Islam to justify his rule. Nevertheless, he was defeated in the 2018 election as he failed to nurture patron-client relations during his volatile reign.

The chapter reveals that the interface of religious populism and Islamic nationalism has caused divisions in the Maldives. Among the conservative followers of Islam, this interface has created suspicion and hatred towards moderate Muslim citizens, measured against the more stringent new standards of Islam. Gayoom and Yameen utilized religious populism in conjunction with authoritarianism to maintain their rule. Their rhetoric as protectors of Islam may have deflected attention away from their repression, which could be justified by its safeguarding of Islam. The nexus between Islamic nationalism and populism in the Maldives is that both were utilized to win support and retain political power for the authoritarian old guard and their beneficiaries, who comprised former clients of Gayoom and supporters of Yameen.

The current president, Solih, is differentiating moderate Islam from that of violent extremism. Despite having only one religion, the Maldives is grappling with identity politics and extremists who are creating violence and instability. The populist politics of the authoritarian leaders was tactical and reactive rather than strategic and used to overcome anti-elitist political opposition. It remains to be seen whether the false populist rhetoric of the 'people' (fundamentalist Muslims) versus the 'outsiders' (non-fundamentalists) can triumph, or whether Solih's politics of moderation is able to overcome the scaremongering tactics of extremist politicians.

Notes

1 With the inclusion of non-Maldivian residents, the World Bank (2019) estimated the population at 531,000 prior to the onset of COVID-19. See https://data.worldbank.org/indicator/SP.POP.TOTL?locations=MV.
2 See Subedi and Scott's discussion of Othmar Spann's justification for authoritarian leaders' legitimacy (Subedi & Scott, 2021).
3 Anonymity of respondents is maintained at the request of the interview participants.
4 Interviewed in the Maldives. Tholal was Vice-Chair of the Human Rights Commission of Maldives (HRCM) from 2010–2015. In 2017, he was the senior project coordinator of the human rights project with Transparency Maldives.
5 See Bhim, 2020, pp. 171–177, for discussion of events leading up to the 2012 coup.
6 Solih, a founding member of the MDP, shares a close friendship with former President Nasheed. Solih had been a parliamentarian during Gayoom's rule.

References

Aiham, A. (2019, September 19). Maldives places 17 organisations on 'terror watchlist'. *The Edition*. https://edition.mv/news/12476
Altuntaş, N. (2010). Religious nationalism in a new era: A perspective from political Islam. *African and Asian Studies*, 9(4), 418–435. https://doi.org/10.1163/156921010X534805
AP hits back at Nasheed over statement. (2021, July 18). *Avas*. https://avas.mv/en/103787

Arora, V. (2014, February 17). Maldives: A return to religious conservatism. *The Diplomat*. https://thediplomat.com/2014/02/maldives-a-return-to-religious-conservatism/

Ashraf, I. (2012). *Civil-military challenges for a consolidating democracy: The Maldives* (Master's thesis, Naval Postgraduate School (NPS)). http://hdl.handle.net/10945/27786

Balachandran, P. K. (2019, November 5). Islam becomes a political issue in the Maldives again. *MENAFN*. https://menafn.com/1099229143/Islam-becomes-a-political-issue-in-the-Maldives-again

Bhim, M. (2019). Does electoral authoritarianism persist? A comparison of recent elections in Fiji, Seychelles and Maldives. In J. I. Lahai, K. von Strokirch, H. Brasted & H. Ware (Eds.), *Governance and political adaptation in fragile states* (pp. 243–270). Palgrave Macmillan.

Bhim, M. (2020). *Authoritarian regimes in small island states: The anomalous cases of electoral autocracies in Fiji, the Maldives and Seychelles* (Unpublished Doctoral thesis, University of New England).

Dehanas, D. N., & Shterin, M. (2018). Religion and the rise of populism. *Religion, State & Society*, 46(3), 177–185. https://doi.org/10.1080/09637494.2018.1502911

Diamond, L. (2017, November 3–4). When does populism become a threat to democracy? [Paper presentation]. *FSI Conference on Global Populisms*. Stanford University. https://fsi-live.s3.us-west-1.amazonaws.com/s3fs-public/when_does_populism_become_a_threat_to_democracy.pdf

Didi, A. (2012). *The Maldives in transition: Human rights and voices of dissent* (Unpublished Doctoral thesis, Curtin University). https://espace.curtin.edu.au/bitstream/handle/20.500.11937/604/191527_Didi2013.pdf?sequence=2&isAllowed=y

Ellis, R. (1998). *A man for all islands—A biography of Maumoon Abdul Gayoom, President of the Maldives*. Times Editions.

Gagnon, J., Beausoleil, E., Son K., Arguelles, C., Chalaye, P., & Johnston, C. N. (2018). What is Populism? Who is the Populist? *Democratic Theory*, 5(2), v–xxvi. https://doi.org/10.3167/dt.2018.050201

Ganguly, M. (2019, January 28). Expressing religious views is risky in the Maldives. *Human Rights Watch*. www.hrw.org/news/2019/01/28/expressing-religious-views-risky-maldives

Geddes, B. (1999). What do we know about democratization after 20 years? *Annual Review of Political Science*, 2(1), 115–44. https://doi.org/10.1146/annurev.polisci.2.1.115

Gough, A. (2021, March 22). The Maldives—An unlikely ISIS haven. *Global Risk Insights*. https://globalriskinsights.com/2021/03/the-maldives-an-unlikely-isis-haven/

Gunasekara, T. (2017, May 21). Blood-and-faith populism & Sri Lanka's future. *Colombo Telegraph*. www.colombotelegraph.com/index.php/blood-and-faith-populism-sri-lankas-future/

Hadi, A. A. (2019, December 3). Local recruiter for Islamic state to be charged for terrorism. *Sun Siyam Media*. https://en.sun.mv/56941

Hassan, A. (2011). *Islamism and radicalism in the Maldives* (Unpublished Master's thesis, Naval Postgraduate School).

Home minister tests positive for COVID-19. (2021, July 30). *Avis*. https://avas.mv/en/104298

Johansson, A. (2018, February 10). Maldives crisis: A bitter religious divide comes to the fore. *The Conversation*. https://theconversation.com/maldives-crisis-a-bitter-religious-divide-comes-to-the-fore-91455

Karagiannis, E. (2018). *The new political Islam: Human rights, democracy and justice*. University of Pennsylvania Press.

Larsen, O. (2009, February 18). Maldives: Reform excludes freedom of religion or belief. *Forum 18 News Service*. www.refworld.org/pdfid/499bbf7c0.pdf

Luithui, E. L., & Phadnis, U. (1985). *Maldives—Winds of change in an Atoll state*. South Asian Publishers.

Maloney, C. (2013). *People of the Maldive Islands*. Orient Blackswan.

Musthaq, F. (2014). Shifting tides in South Asia: Tumult in the Maldives. *Journal of Democracy*, 25(2), 164–170. www.journalofdemocracy.org/articles/shifting-tides-in-south-asia-tumult-in-the-maldives/

Naseem, A. (2015, May 13). Leaving 'paradise' for Jihad: Maldivian fighters in Syria and the internet. *VOXPol*. www.voxpol.eu/leaving-paradise-for-jihad-maldivian-fighters-in-syria-and-the-internet/

Ningthoujam, A. S. (2015, March 2). *Maldives is no longer a 'paradise'*. International Institute for Counter-Terrorism (ICT). www.ict.org.il/UserFiles/Ningthoujam-Apr15.pdf

Rasheed, A. A. (2014). Historical institutionalism in the Maldives: A case of governance failure. *The Maldives National Journal of Research*, 2(1), 7–28.

Roul, A. (2013, March). The threat from rising extremism in the Maldives. *CTC Sentinel*, 6(3). https://ctc.usma.edu/the-threat-from-rising-extremism-in-the-maldives/

Saudi Arabia pledges US$50m for military housing project. (2016, March 14). *Maldives Independent*. https://maldivesindependent.com/politics/saudi-arabia-pledges-us50m-for-military-housing-project-122779

Sharma, A. (2019, October 16). *Radical Islam in the Maldives: Hotbed for al-Qa'ida and Islamic State*. Vivekananda International Foundation. www.vifindia.org/article/2019/october/16/radical-islam-in-the-maldives-hotbed-for-al-qaida-and-islamic-state

Solih, I. M. (2018, November 17). *Unofficial translation of the inaugural address by his excellency Ibrahim Mohamed Solih, President of the republic of Maldives*. The President's Republic of Maldives. https://presidency.gov.mv/Press/Article/20274

Subedi, D. B., & Scott, A. (2021). Populism, authoritarianism, and charismatic-plebiscitary leadership in contemporary Asia: A comparative perspective from India and Myanmar. *Contemporary Politics*, 27(5), 487–507. https://doi.org/10.1080/13569775.2021.1917162

Sudhakar, K. (Ed.) (2019, December 14). Maldives Govt Denies entry to controversial Preacher Zakir Nair. *India.com*. www.india.com/news/world/maldives-govt-denies-entry-to-controversial-islamic-preacher-zakir-nair-says-if-you-want-to-preach-hate-we-cant-allow-that-3877444/

The Long Road (2014, May 30). The long road from Islam to Islamism: A short history. *Dhivehi Sitee*. www.dhivehisitee.com/religion/islamism-maldives/4/

Timeline (2015, July 26). Timeline—Story of independence. *Maldives Independent*. https://maldivesindependent.com/politics/timeline-story-of-independence-115638

UNGA (2018, August 6). *Report of the Special Rapporteur on contemporary forms of racism, racial discrimination, xenophobia and related intolerance*. A/73/305. United Nations General Assembly (UNGA). Seventy-third session.

Zahir, A. (2016). Does Islam have a problem with democracy? The case of the Maldives. *The Conversation*. https://theconversation.com/does-islam-have-a-problem-with-democracy-the-case-of-the-maldives-58040

Zubaida, S. (2004). Islam and nationalism: Continuities and contradictions. *Nations and Nationalism*, 10(4), 407–420. https://doi.org/10.1111/j.1354-5078.2004.00174.x

18
DEMOCRACY ICON OR DEMAGOGUE? AUNG SAN SUU KYI AND AUTHORITARIAN POPULISM IN MYANMAR (BURMA)

Johanna Garnett

Introduction

Populist politics emerged in the multi-ethnic nation state of Myanmar (formerly Burma)[1] in Southeast Asia. Myanmar was, until recently, a nascent democracy following decades of military dictatorship, but democratic hopes were dashed with the military takeover of February 1, 2021. The military had ruled Myanmar in various guises following a 1962 coup prompted by unrest in the wake of colonial rule and World War II (see Callahan, 2003; Fink, 2001; Holliday, 2011; Steinberg, 2013; Myint-U, 2011). After political reforms instigated in 2011, a democratically elected civilian government was installed in early 2016 as a result of the landslide victory of the National League for Democracy (NLD) in the November 2015 general election. Populist political elements, such as appeals to the masses and promises of revolutionary socioeconomic transformation, played a considerable role in this electoral success due to the leadership of the charismatic democracy icon, Aung San Suu Kyi.[2] Since 1988, the vast majority of the populace had been encouraged by her promises of equal rights for all nationalities and religions and for a future free from fear. The elections were an outright rejection of the authoritarian regime (Clements, 2008; Ellis-Petersen, 2018; Fisher, 2017; Thawnghmung, 2016). However, following establishment of the NLD government in 2016, real power was never transferred.

The military retained considerable influence at the national level in Myanmar due to the military-drafted 2008 Constitution that ensured 25% of parliamentary seats were reserved for the military and that guaranteed it operate unfettered by civilian oversight (Selth, 2018, 2019; Than, 2016). To cement that role, the military was granted the power to veto constitutional amendments (Barany, 2018, p. 6). This dominance resulted in shared ministerial portfolios and, as a result, the NLD-led government struggled to institute political and economic reforms. Further, under the Constitution, Aung San Suu Kyi's marriage to a foreigner precluded her from the role of president (Crouch, 2019), so she therefore took on the mantle of State Counsellor, together with the Ministry of Foreign Affairs. She was supported in this role by her close aide Win Myint as the president, as well as key NLD advisers. However, the Ministries of Defence, Home Affairs, and Border Affairs remained under direct control of the military commander-in-chief, Senior General Min Aung Hlaing, effectively giving him control over the police, intelligence services, and border guards.

In the last few years preceding the 2021 coup, Myanmar, under Aung San Suu Kyi and Senior General Min Aung Hlaing, had shifted to the right, falling back upon exclusionary populism and authoritarianism. This chapter seeks to highlight the distinctive features of populist politics in Myanmar by focusing on three core areas: the Rohingya crisis in Rakhine State, the media, and the judiciary. This chapter argues that Aung San Suu Kyi's authoritarian turn, influenced by her charismatic leadership and the desire for centralization of power at the expense of ethnic exclusion, was not surprising given the hierarchical and reactionary nature of politics in Myanmar, together with an upsurge in Buddhist nationalism (Subedi & Garnett, 2020; Walton & Hayward, 2014). She utilized a populist approach for the purpose of political mobilization—setting up a monist, ethno-nationalist, non-inclusive, and majoritarian political system in an effort to maintain power. However, whilst the strategy attracted followers from the Bamar Buddhist constituency, it did not bode well for ethnic minorities, human rights activists, and proponents of secular and liberal politics due to ongoing human rights abuses.

This chapter was first considered in 2020 as a commentary on the politics surrounding Myanmar's tentative transition to democracy. This analysis was overtaken by the military coup of 1 February 2021, signalling the return to military rule under the leadership of Senior General Min Aung Hlaing. The outcome of the military takeover was devastating for the vast majority of the Myanmar population, who not only had to endure the ravages of the COVID-19 pandemic, but also brutal attacks on their human rights, including displacement, impoverishment, imprisonment, torture, abuse, and death (Human Rights Watch, 2022; UNHRC, 2022).[3] This surprising turn towards renewed authoritarianism and re-establishment of the junta supports this chapter's argument for the importance of decentralization and the failure of emerging populist politics to promote democracy.

This chapter is grounded in an analysis of the literature surrounding politics in Myanmar together with related media commentary. It also draws on personal observations and discussions with civil society actors as part of the author's involvement in the democracy and human rights movement in Myanmar,[4] including her experiences living and working in the country at intervals between October 2013 and November 2019. The discussion begins by situating the analysis within the literature pertaining to populism—in particular, populism as a political strategy.

Populism as political strategy

The most widely cited definition of populism is 'a "thin" ideology that considers society to be ultimately separated into two homogeneous and antagonistic groups, "the pure people" versus "the corrupt elite", and which argues that politics should be an expression of the general will of the people' (Mudde, 2004, p. 543). However, as Mudde and Rovira Kaltwasser (2017) note more recently, populism is an essentially contested concept with a range of approaches in addition to the ideational. These include popular agency, the Laclauian, socioeconomic, politically strategic, and a folkloric style of politics (pp. 2–4). This chapter agrees with Kenny's 'organizational' approach to conceptualizing populism (2017, 2019, and Chapter 3 in this volume), which is closely related to the 'political-strategic' approach (Weyland, 2017). Populism is therein defined as 'the charismatic mobilization of a mass movement in pursuit of political power' (Kenny, 2019, p. 1). The focus of this analysis is not on what populists say, but on what they actually do; i.e., the methods and instruments utilized in pursuing and sustaining political power (Müller, 2016; Weyland, 2017, p. 50). More specifically—'how a political actor maintains the government and ensures the support and obedience of citizens' (Weyland, 2017, p. 55).

Populist parties, by this understanding, are those headed by charismatic leaders who seek to gain and retain power by mobilizing mass constituencies that are typically free of other political constraints (Kenny, 2019). Although populists can and do have parties, they are highly personalist in that the interests of the party are virtually equivalent to the interests of the party leader, who, in turn, is not constrained by organizational rules and has (near) total authority over personnel and strategic decisions within the organization (Kenny, 2020, pp. 262–263; Kenny, 2019, p. 12). Populist support is thereby mobilized and maintained primarily through direct communication between the leader and the people, in the form of traditional and social media, public rallies, and other forms of mass communication (Kenny, 2017, 2019). Populism, so defined, is simply a strategy to mobilize support.

One of the key aspects of populism discussed in the literature is whether it is exclusive, inclusive, or both (Mudde & Rovira Kaltwasser, 2013, p. 147). Exclusionary populism stresses a focus on an ethnically homogenous nation or people (Müller, 2016, pp. 80–81). It considers 'the people' as a monolithic group without internal differences—except for some very specific categories that are subject to an exclusion strategy (Jagers & Walgrave, 2007, p. 3). It has been noted that European populism is predominantly exclusive (Mudde & Rovira Kaltwasser, 2013, p. 148), whilst as a rule, Southeast Asian populism has, until quite recently, mostly resembled the inclusionary populism of Latin America (Mudde & Rovira Kaltwasser, 2013). However, Pepinksy provides a caveat in relation to Myanmar and the Rohingya Muslims, noting the exclusionary nature of politics in the country (2019, p. 2). There are various dimensions of exclusion and inclusion:

- the material dimension refers to the distribution of state resources, both monetary and non-monetary, to specific groups in society;
- political exclusion means that specific groups are prevented from participating (fully) in the democratic system and they are consciously not represented in the arena of public contestation; whilst,
- the symbolic dimension refers to when populists define 'the people', in their rhetoric and symbols without referring to (the characteristics and values of) certain groups, resulting in the latter being symbolically excluded (Mudde & Rovira Kaltwasser, 2013, pp. 158–164). It is here that populists define the main crisis facing the nation as a cultural one with emphasis on race, ethnicity, religion and/or identity.

Finally, it is argued that populism, both left and right, corrodes democratic institutions, undermining checks and balances and paving the way to some form of authoritarianism (Aslanidis, 2016, p. 94; Kenny, 2019). Populists attack and delegitimize any possible opposition to their rule and there are often serious negative implications of populist party government for the rule of law, electoral quality, and other liberal democratic institutions (Kenny, 2020, p. 273). Kenny (2020) found that 'populist rule is associated with a decline in press freedom and freedom of expression' (p. 270), and this is closely related to discrimination within the judiciary/law. To understand how and why this dynamic is playing out in

Myanmar, the discussion proceeds with an overview of the country's political history and political economy.

Myanmar: The Golden Land

Myanmar is home to around 53 million people comprising 135 officially recognized ethnic groups, resulting in a multicultural society with extensive cultural, linguistic, and religious diversity, with about two-thirds of the population assumed to be Bamar Buddhists (Cheesman, 2017; Wade, 2019). Around 70% of the population lives off the land or relies on traditional agriculture in some way, although this was shifting prior to the coup as the country embraced an industrialized modernization programme. Myanmar has a monarchical history, with a traditionally stratified social structure (Steinberg, 2013; Taylor, 2009), and Theravada Buddhism, practiced by 89% of the population, is integral to the society and culture (Schober, 2011), hence the moniker 'The Golden Land', referring to the thousands of glittering Buddhist pagodas and stupas that dot the landscape. The country was colonized by the British[5] and gained independence on January 4, 1948, following the efforts of the nationalist leader, General Aung San (father of Aung San Suu Kyi), who was assassinated on July 19, 1947, before his plans for a united and independent nation under a new constitution came to fruition. The ensuing years were ones of strife and ethnic conflicts (Callahan, 2003; Fink, 2001) that led to the military coup on March 2, 1962 when the junta seized power, abolished the elected government of U Nu, who had been voted in two years earlier, and established a socialist one-party rule under the *Burma Socialist Programme Party* (BSPP) (Walton, 2017, p. 30). The BSPP sought to implement the 'Burmese Road to Socialism', an idiosyncratic blend of Marxist, Buddhist, and nationalist ideologies, and the country turned inward, limiting political organization and cracking down on dissent (Fink, 2001; Smith, 1999, p. 24; Walton, 2017, p. 30).[6] The outside world responded by imposing political and economic sanctions, virtually closing off the country (Steinberg, 2013, p. 101). However, China, which had ratified the coup, continued as a powerful supporter. Aung San achieved martyrdom and is acknowledged annually as a national hero on July 19, Burmese Martyr's Day.

Myanmar is one of the world's least developed countries, despite being rich in natural resources (UNDP, 2019).[7] An ostensibly free-market system was established in 1988, but in the subsequent decades, the state was extremely interventionist (Steinberg, 2013, p. 20; Taylor, 2009), and the defining feature of the political economy of Myanmar has been the highly instrumental nature of capitalist control of state power by oligarchs and/cronies—a ruling hierarchy of self-appointed leaders and groups taking power at will (Jones, 2014, p. 149; Turnell, 2014, 2011, p. 84). Throughout its contemporary history, the state in Myanmar has consistently failed to deliver political goods to 'the people', culminating in a broad range of social, economic, and environmental injustices, impoverishment of the vast majority of the population, and serious human rights abuses (Fink, 2001; Petrie & South, 2014, p. 88). These include rape, torture, assassination, bayoneting, land confiscation, burning of villages, displacement of whole villages, use of child soldiers, and arbitrary detention (see for example Fink, 2001, p. 78).

As well as ongoing ethnic conflicts, impoverishment and oppression have contributed to a number of people's uprisings, comprising the Bamar, certain ethnic groups, and members of the *sangha*, the monastic society. The most notable political insurgency was the student protests of August 8, 1988—the *8-8-88 Nationwide Popular Pro-Democracy Protests*.

This historically momentous event began in March 1988 with a brawl in a bar, leading to student protests that gained momentum and quickly escalated to violence (Smith, 1999, p. 16). By mid-August, millions of citizens had taken to the streets. The junta responded with force, leaving an estimated 1,000 people dead and over 2,000 injured, with thousands more imprisoned (Clements, 2008, pp. 17–19). At this stage, the government's leadership was in turmoil and the economy in shambles. The junta, determined to ensure its continued pre-eminence and control, enacted a second coup on September 18, 1988 (Smith, 1999, p. 424). The military dictators established the *State Law and Order Restoration Council* (SLORC) followed by the *State Peace and Development Council* (SPDC) in 1997, and the *Union Solidarity and Development Party* (USDP) in 2010 (Fink, 2001, p. 62; Hlaing, 2012, p. 198; Smith, 1999, p. 424). The SPDC reigned until 2011, when political reforms were instigated by then president and moderate, Thein Sein, leading to the 2015 democratic elections. It was from this socioeconomic milieu and state-led violence that the democracy leader Aung San Suu Kyi and the NLD emerged (Clements, 2008; Smith, 1999, p. 16).

The lady—Aung San Suu Kyi—8.8.1988 onwards

Aung San Suu Kyi was born in Rangoon (now Yangon), Burma, in 1945 and continued to live there after her father's assassination until 1960, when her mother was appointed Ambassador to India, the first Burmese woman to hold such a position. Her family is from the majority Bamar ethnic group and her moral legacy is rooted in Theravada Buddhism—she is a devout Buddhist (Houtman, 1999; Mon Mon Myat, 2019). Well-educated and well-travelled, she settled in the UK to study and raise a family after marrying Michael Aris, a British national (Harriden, 2012, p. 207). In 1988, she returned to Rangoon to care for her dying mother, and was confronted with the decline of the economy, the hardships of the people, and the corrupt authoritarian rule of the junta (Silverstein, 1990, pp. 1010–1011). She was catapulted to the leadership of a popular movement against the tyrannical regime in mid-August 1988, when she was approached by democracy activists due to her status as the daughter of Aung San. Her August 26 address to a rally near Shwedagon Pagoda attracted around 500,000 supporters (Bengtsson, 2010; Clements, 2008; Houtman, 1999; Silverstein, 1996, p. 212; Smith, 1999, p. 9).

In seeking to return to the democratic ideals of her father, Aung San Suu Kyi quickly came to dominate the political scene (Houtman, 1999, p. 16; Silverstein, 1996, p. 212). She co-founded the NLD in September 1988 with a core group of retired army officers: U Aung Shwe, U Win Tin, U Tin U, and U Kyi Maung, among others. She was supported in the early years by older men such as these, viewing them as her 'truest of friends and companions' (Aung San, 1997, pp. 71–73; 201). Her popularity grew, due not only to her heritage as the daughter of the father of independence and 'inherited charisma' (Harriden, 2012, p. 207; Silverstein, 1990, p. 1007) but also because of her *awza*—her charisma, wisdom, and perceived high morality (Houtman, 1999, pp. 157–176).[8] As Harriden (2012) notes, 'people with *awza* can exercise considerable political influence, even if they do not hold any formal political office' (p. 7). In response to her increasing influence, and sensing that she had the potential to unite the disparate elements of an emerging political opposition, the junta began a campaign of intimidation (Aung San & Aris, 2010; Silverstein, 1990, pp. 1013–1014). In July 1989, she was placed under house arrest, and other party leaders were incarcerated. Aung San Suu Kyi was to be held incommunicado, with an offer of freedom only if she agreed to leave Myanmar (Clements, 2008, p. 145). She refused to do so until the country returned to civilian government and political prisoners were freed, and subsequently endured repeated periods of house arrest, 15 years in total, which did not end until 2010 (Bengtsson, 2010). Whilst incarcerated, she maintained close contact with the people and held weekend rallies, mounting a table behind the front gate of her home to speak to crowds of supporters through a loudspeaker. During her periods of release, she met with journalists and authors, all keen to document and disseminate her experiences and insights (see Clements, 2008). Her popularity grew primarily due to her promotion of the Buddhist ideals of non-violence, compassion, and loving kindness, all of which provided her with a moral authority, one that stood in stark contrast to the morally corrupt power of the military (Harriden, 2012, p. 45).

The NLD won the first election it contested on May 27, 1990, with more than 80% of the vote, indicating unequivocal support from the people (Aung San, 1997, pp. 123–164; Thawnghmung, 2016, p. 135), but the results were ignored by the military government.[9] The party subsequently boycotted the 2010 general election, the first poll since 1990. However, it contested the 2012 by-elections, winning 43 out of 45 seats ahead of its landslide victory in the national election of 2015 (Than, 2016). This political success was all due to the popularity and charisma of Aung San Suu Kyi, whose sacrifices won the hearts and minds of human rights and democracy activists around the world, subsequently earning her the Nobel Peace Prize, together with a raft of other awards and honours. However, upon becoming Myanmar's de facto leader in 2016, she was rounded on by the same international leaders and activists who once supported her ('Aung San Suu Kyi,' 2021), and this is for one startling reason—the Rohingya crisis.

2017 and the Rohingya crisis

The Rohingya are a minority Muslim group of around 1.3 million individuals, primarily from northern Rakhine State (formerly Arakan) in the west of the country (Ware & Laoutides, 2018, pp. 25–30). They have not been recognized as one of the country's 135 official ethnic groups, nor as part of the national races of Myanmar, the *taing-yin-tha*, despite the fact that the majority have lived in Myanmar for generations (Cheesman, 2017). They consequently have no citizenship rights and have been portrayed as an existential threat to the survival of Buddhists, as the majority religious group in Myanmar (Schonthal & Walton, 2016; Wade, 2019). The term *Rohingya* is banned in the country, and they are officially referred to as *Bengalis*.

The Rohingya crisis, comprising communal violence in southern Rakhine State, began in June 2012, triggered by an allegation that a Rakhine Buddhist woman had been raped and killed by three Rohingya Muslim men. Attempting to bring the situation under control, the government declared a state of emergency including an extended curfew, but conditions soon deteriorated, with increasing conflict between the Rohingya and security forces, as well as with Rakhine Buddhists. Between 2012 and 2016, the Burmese authorities treated the crisis as a law-and-order problem, acting with force and brutality and displacing many Rohingyas internally, whilst others fled to neighbouring countries. The situation escalated dramatically in August 2017, when a new Muslim militant group, the Arakan Rohingya Salvation Army (ARSA), allegedly linked to Muslim radical groups in the Middle East, attacked three border guard police posts in Maungdaw and Rathedaung in the northern Rakhine state. The government responded swiftly, labelling the attack an 'act of terrorism', a narrative that enabled the government to justify indiscriminate attacks on Rohingyas, along with an even more brutal area clearance operation (Wade, 2019; Ware & Laoutides, 2018, pp. 36–58). By January 2018, some 700,000 Rohingya had fled over the border into Bangladesh in the wake of a sustained campaign of extrajudicial killings, torture, systematic rape, and the burning down of villages, crops, and livestock by the federal security agencies. This massive persecution of the Rohingyas was labelled 'a text book example of ethnic cleansing' by the United Nations Independent International Fact-Finding Mission on Myanmar (UNHRC, 2019).

While Aung San Suu Kyi was not responsible for the military crackdown, in her role as State Counsellor, she did not publicly condemn the anti-Rohingya pogrom in Rakhine State. Rather, during this time, she propagated assertions that the military's actions were an appropriate response to a militant Rohingya uprising, and was quoted as describing the generals, later accused of genocide, as 'quite sweet' (Ellis-Petersen, 2018). In late 2019, she took it upon herself to defend her government against the accusation of genocide of the Rohingya in a case filed at the International Court of Justice (ICJ) in The Hague by Gambia on behalf of the Organisation of Islamic Cooperation. Whilst many Rohingya looked on hoping for justice, inside Myanmar it appears that Aung San Suu Kyi received massive support from Burmese Buddhist communities (Aung, 2019). Further, the government was silent on the repatriation of the Rohingya, despite the instigation of a joint working group, the involvement of China, and claims that repatriation was welcomed by Myanmar. As Subedi and Scott (2021) note in their analysis of Aung San Suu Kyi's populism, her efforts to form a bounded political community excluded the Rohingyas, as well as other ethnic and religious minorities. The unresolved Rohingya crisis is one of the most recent iterations of the interface between organized violence and state-building in Myanmar (Subedi & Garnett, 2020, p. 12). An extension of the state reaction was the wide-ranging crackdown on criticism and dissent, particularly in the media's coverage of this conflict.

The media

Myanmar experienced ruthless censorship under the various regimes (Selth, 2019), and media freedom prior to the coup was only initiated in 2012 as part of the political and social reforms, in the form of the *Media Law No. 12/2014*.[10] This law offered a framework for the media that included: the freedom from censorship and the right to express, publish, or distribute freely, as part of rights and privileges granted to every citizen in compliance with regulations incorporated into the national constitution; the need to ensure that news media could stand firmly as the fourth estate of the nation; and the guarantee that news media workers were fully granted such entitlements and freedom (Pyidaungsu Hluttaw, 2014). The law did, however, emphasize that 'ways of writing which may inflame conflicts regarding nationality, religion and race shall be avoided' (Provision 9(h)). Further, 'if any news media worker is considered to violate these restrictions, he/she will be taken proper actions by applicable existing laws' (Provision 26)—and that was what occurred.

Prior to the coup, journalists were increasingly vulnerable to arrest and prosecution, together with the closure of media outlets (Athan, 2020; Barany, 2018, p. 13). The media were prevented from travelling to conflict-affected areas, and journalists who tried to investigate ended up in prison (Human Rights Watch, 2019). There were several widely publicized cases, including the arrests of three journalists charged with Article 17(1) of the Unlawful Association Act, the arrest of Reuters reporters under the Official Secrets Act, and the indictment of Rakhine political leader, Dr. Aye Maung, under article 17(1) of the

Unlawful Association Act and Sections 121 and 505 of the Penal Code on charges related to high treason and incitement. Maung received a prison sentence of 20 years (Mangshang, 2018). Prosecutions were also filed under Section 66(d) of the Telecommunications Act, primarily related to contraventions of internet restrictions in the conflict-affected Rakhine and Chin States, together with the exertion of controls over social media (Human Rights Watch, 2019). As a result, there was a sharp increase in defamation cases filed against people who criticized the government online (BBC Online, 2019; Freedom House, 2019). Both the military and the NLD repeatedly used legal provisions to silence their critics, expanding their crackdown on freedom of expression and the right to protest (FEM, 2018; Human Rights Watch, 2019).

Further, prior to the coup, those wishing to hold an assembly or protest were required to adhere to the Peaceful Assembly and Peaceful Procession Law (2011). Amendments in 2014 promised greater freedom of expression, and the government did consent to protests, albeit with onerous conditions. Demonstrators were arrested for failing to comply with these conditions, as well as for violating various vague and broadly-phrased restrictions imposed on speech under the statute, primarily the rule that they 'must not say things . . . that could affect the country or the Union, race, or religion, human dignity and moral principles' (Rule 12(e)). Further, they 'must not spread rumours or incorrect information' (Rule 12(f)). Such vague and subjective terms were misused by officials looking for a way to silence government critics and deal with anti-government sentiments.

The NLD's 2015 election manifesto promised to protect news media as the eyes and ears of the people (Aung, 2020). However, despite the rhetoric, a deterioration in the levels of press freedom and freedom of expression was evident, with many arguing it had reached a critical level (FEM, 2018; Aung, 2020; Mangshang, 2018). Myanmar was ranked as 'not free' by Freedom House in 2020, with the score declining, reversing a three-year trend in improvement. Underlying the situation was the ongoing state-media monopoly, with the state controlling the main broadcasters and publications as well as telecommunications. Myo Nyunt, an NLD spokesperson, stated that Myanmar's laws restricting the freedom of expression were necessary to maintain law and order as the country transitioned to democracy. Acts that violated the statutes were, therefore, deemed undemocratic (Mangshang, 2018) and demanded prosecution.

The judiciary

The three top parallel courts in Myanmar are the Constitutional Tribunal, the Courts Martial, and the Union Supreme Court. The Supreme Court is the most powerful and active, with oversight of all 14 High Courts (one in each region or state), which in turn oversee the District Courts and Self-Administered Zones or Division, Township Courts, and other specialized courts below it (Crouch, 2016, p. 251). The Supreme Court (as it exists at the time of writing) was constituted in 1988, in the wake of a previous military takeover, and its focus historically became that of watchdog over the lower courts (Cheesman, 2015). Despite the political reforms, there was evidence of persistent interference with judicial independence—a form of 'procedural authoritarianism' had emerged, enabling overt executive control over the courts (Crouch, 2016, p. 248). The judicial framework had moved towards centralization and executive-military control, in which the military retained substantial power to intimidate officials and influence outcomes. As Dunant (2019) notes, the cooperation of core elements of the civilian government—willing or otherwise—was required to put its enemies in prison. The Supreme Court played the role of supervising prisons, including upholding the rights of those incarcerated, but it did not appear to actively exercise this authority; given the scale of political prisoners and concerns of multiple human rights organizations, this aspect was neglected (Crouch, 2016, p. 251).

Overall, as Cheesman (2015) has noted, the law in Myanmar has not been used to protect the people as one would expect under the rule of law but instead to restrict them under 'law and order'. Such law and order depends on 'particularistic commands and directives in response to exigencies', the pivotal role of 'authoritative institutions act(ing) upon specific injunctions to intervene directly with people's lives', and the 'exogenous imposition of discipline'. Law and order has as its primary concern the elimination of restlessness; its ultimate objective is quietude (Cheesman, 2015, p. 241). Politicians and office bearers motivated to act on a law and order agenda are not climbing the same ladder as their counterparts, who hold to the values of the rule of law. They are on a different ladder altogether (Cheesman, 2015, p. 243). Courts may be used to intimidate and silence political opponents, activists, dissenters, and victims of land laws and abuses.

Those marked as 'public enemies' in Myanmar, regardless of who is in government, pass through an 'administrative continuum' that, however protracted, reliably takes them from the police station through the courtroom to the prison cell. It is noted by Selth (2019, ch. 93) that Aung San Suu Kyi relied on similar mechanisms and methods of the previous military regime to tackle the challenges of government, noting that 'the vast intelligence apparatus that underpinned military rule was still in place' (p. 458). Aung San Suu Kyi indicated a 'presupposed competence in a judiciary she had previously disparaged', expressing support and noting that 'the courts, however flawed, must be given space to breathe if the rule of law is to flourish in Myanmar' (Dunant, 2019). Yet, it was a judicial system still beholden to the law and order mindset that characterized five decades of military rule (Lakhdir, 2019), and was not what one would expect in a society free from fear, which had been her stated aim for three decades (Aung San & Aris, 2010).

Discussion—democracy icon or demagogue?

Aung San Suu Kyi was not readily identified as a populist leader (see Kenny, 2019; Pepinsky, 2020, p. 4; Subedi & Scott, 2021, and Chapter 7 in this volume). However, all three dimensions suggested by Mudde and Rovira Kaltwasser (2017) as necessary and sufficient for identifying populism—the exaltation of a 'noble people', the condemnation of 'corrupt elites', and the appeal to the value of popular sovereignty—have been evident in Myanmar. Forced into a power-sharing role, Aung San Suu Kyi, as State Counsellor and effectively the leader of the country, dominated the landscape of civilian politics (Barany, 2018, p. 7) and utilized populist tools as a strategy for political mobilization in an effort to consolidate power. She was assisted in this project by her charismatic authority, which, as Kenny (2019) notes, 'is characterized by the concentration of arbitrary control in the person of a popularly acclaimed leader' (pp. 9–10). Charismatic leadership here describes a relationship or a type of formal or informal organization, not a set of character traits. However, she has undoubtedly been the most charismatic politician in the country, and the people were mobilized through a direct affinity to her as the daughter of the charismatic populist General Aung San (David & Holliday, 2015; Kenny, 2019, p. 17).

Populists, as charismatic leaders, frequently undermine liberal institutional constraints on their authority (Hawkins & Rovira Kaltwasser, 2017; Mudde, 2004), and this has been highlighted in the case of Myanmar by the discussions of the Rohingya crisis, crackdowns on freedom of expression in various forms, and a shift to law and order rather than rule of law. Aung San Suu Kyi established a monist, non-inclusive, and majoritarian political system, and central to her populist strategies is ethnic nationalism; in other words, her populist strategy benefitted from nationalist politics. Burmese nationalism is conflated with Buddhist religious identity; to be authentically a citizen of Myanmar is to be Buddhist and ethnically Burman (Walton & Hayward, 2014, p. 6). The identity of the Buddhist majority effectively overlaps with national identity; the roots of constructing a Burmese Buddhist national culture run deep, as does the protection of the *sasana*, the Buddhist religion (Walton & Hayward, 2014, p. 22). The resulting narrative was that non-Buddhist, non-Burmans were a threat to the state, or at least the stability of the state, and this materialized in the case of U *Wirathu* and the *MaBaTha* nationalist movements (Schonthal & Walton, 2016; Subedi & Garnett, 2020; Walton & Hayward, 2014, p. 19). Many Buddhists in Myanmar perceive Muslims as a threat.

Aung San Suu Kyi fed into nationalistic sentiments and found a new ally in the far-right, nationalist Hungarian prime minister and populist leader, Viktor Orbán. The two leaders found common ground on the subject of co-existence with continuously growing Muslim populations (Ellis-Petersen, 2019). Like Orban, she established direct relations with voters, 'the noble people', and her policy-based appeals[11] and support for her defence at the ICJ in the Hague indicate that her followers had developed an affinity for a collective project. She was well aware that being seen as a defender of Rohingya interests could cost her the elections held in November 2020, which the NLD won in a landslide victory, and speaking out in defence of the Rohingya would have been political suicide (Barany, 2018, p. 14). Through exclusionary populism, she was protecting the *sasana* or teaching of the Buddha (albeit by supporting violent and exclusionary mechanisms) (Walton & Hayward, 2014, p. 46) and exaltation of the noble people, namely the Bamar Buddhist community—but she was also protecting herself.

On taking over the government in early 2016, Aung San Suu Kyi began to consolidate power. A small circle of insiders effectively ran the country, sidestepping formal institutions (Fisher, 2017). The junta's power is characterized by *ana* (authority)—it is both centralized and institutionalized—and she sought to take and consolidate some of that structural power. The author's in situ research supports the widespread perception that she was in full control; nothing of importance relating to the economy or development, even at the very local level, was approved unless by Ntaypidaw (the seat of government). During an interview in November 2019, a former 1988er remarked to the author: 'She has set herself up as a Queen. We fear repression now more than we did when we came back (from exile) in 2012, after Thein Sein's reforms'.[12] Unrequested advice and constructive criticism were clearly unwelcome. Furthermore, legislators complained that Aung San Suu Kyi personally made all important decisions; their own roles seemed trivial by comparison, and the idea of voting against the government was unheard of (Barany, 2018, p. 8). Meanwhile, the cronies—the so-called elite that were supposedly a danger to the people—appeared to enjoy her protection (Barany, 2018, p. 11).

It was in these spaces that Aung San Suu Kyi cast off the mantle of human rights and her role of democracy icon and embraced a form of demagoguery. She increasingly sought support by appealing to the desires and prejudices of ordinary people, exploiting emotions and ignorance, but also the vulnerabilities of a large majority of the populace to external shocks, including natural disasters and inter-ethnic conflicts, often resulting in theft and eviction from land, physical assault, and threats. These vulnerabilities stem from poverty and the inadequate capacity to mobilize resources to deal with hazards and externalities. For someone who 'advocated a democracy with a human face, one that embodied dialogue over domination, kindness over cruelty and compassion over killing' (Clements, 2008, p. 12), her turnaround was disappointing.

In conclusion, all forms of populism involve a battle between the elite and the people, and the battle in Aung San Suu Kyi's Myanmar was monumental, having played out in a highly complex political scene (Selth, 2021). Her turn to the right and to populism, whilst regrettable, was not surprising. Deep-rooted issues have plagued this multi-ethnic nation state, and public opinion veers towards the kind of intolerance that was profoundly difficult for her to manage (David & Holliday, 2015). The people expressed the desire for a strongman-style leader and raw majority rule. Aung San Suu Kyi was strategic in supporting the Buddhist majority, which generally supported her stance towards the Rohingya, and her refraining from intervention in the crisis was politically expedient (Thawnghmung, 2016, p. 139). However, populism is dangerous, as highlighted by democracy guided by religious strictures and nationalism, the campaign against the Rohingya, and social controls against journalists and minorities (Fisher, 2017). As a result of this populist turn, prior to the coup, the country appeared to be converging on a democratic-authoritarian hybrid—an illiberal democracy, a version of majority rule that excludes minorities, curtails freedoms, and governs arbitrarily (Fisher, 2017)—not the democracy promised in the heady days of the democracy movement and the nascent NLD political party.

The hierarchical nature of Myanmar society, with its dynastic legacy, cannot support both a Queen and a King. The motivation for Min Aung Hlaing taking control in 2021 has been debated. Some contended it was purely for personal reasons (Regan, 2021); others, like Selth (2021), argued that it was embedded in the military's strategic concerns, its long-term plans, and the role it perceives for itself. Either way, had Aung San Suu Kyi been open to power-sharing, she would not have proved such a central target for the military and might still be in power. Her utilization of popular prejudices and engagement in populist politics contributed to her personal downfall, and the return of the regime put paid to the yearning of the people of Myanmar for a 'future free from fear'.

Notes

1 The country's name was changed from Burma to Myanmar by the military leaders in June 1989. The term Myanmar reportedly means a 'fast and strong people', claiming to represent the multiracial country. However, the term has been criticized by ethnic groups, as Myanmar was simply the historic ethnic Burman name, representing the Bamar ruling majority (Smith, 1999, p. 21). Myanmar remains the official name, but is still contested by human rights organizations and ethnic groups.
2 Myanmar people refer to her as Daw Aung San Suu Kyi. Daw means 'aunt' and is an honorific for any older and revered woman, akin to 'madam'. She is sometimes addressed in country as Daw Suu or Amay Suu—Mother.
3 The execution by hanging of four democracy activists attracted worldwide condemnation, with fears that many more faced a similar fate.
4 This includes working with Alan Clements, journalist, writer, human rights activist, and author of the book *The Voice of Hope*, 2008. He lived in Burma for many years in the 1970s and 80s, including nearly five years as a monk. He was co-founder and director of the *Burma Project USA/Canada*, as well as a political satirist, performing his theatrical monologues to audiences around

the world. I studied and worked with him, online and in Australia, for a period of six years between 2009 and 2015.
5 Following the First Anglo-Burmese War of 1824, although they did not gain full control of the region until 1886. Their legacy is evident in the grand colonial buildings and infrastructure, particularly in the major city of Yangon (formerly Rangoon).
6 The fearful events following the coup exist in living memory. In late 2017, a retired professor spoke about a military crackdown on students in July 1962. He took me to a gutter on the Yangon University campus where he had huddled with some friends in fear for his life, telling me: 'We were so scared—I thought I would die' (pers. comm., November 29, 2017).
7 It is ranked 145th out of 187 countries in the 2019 UN's Global Human Development Indicators concerning health, education, and income (UNDP, 2019). It is also one of the most corrupt countries in the world (Transparency International, 2020), and deemed to be one of the least peaceful globally (Institute for Economics and Peace, 2019, p. 9).
8 The concept of *awza* denotes influence—that which is associated with self-purification through moral practice. *Awza* contrasts with *ana*, the idea of order, command, or authority, in Myanmar Buddhist politics. *Ana* is most commonly associated with the top-down disciplining power of the military, but it is argued that the two are not complete opposites because they are ideally combined in a model of righteous and ethical rule. However, the story of political authority throughout Burmese history is one of primarily *ana-based*, centralizing power and *awza-based* moral opposition (Walton, 2014, p. 4).
9 In 2010, the military government formally annulled the results of the 1990 election.
10 This law, like the Broadcasting Law and Privacy Law, was later amended by the military.
11 These include NLD policies targeting the Rohingya and denying them citizenship; Aung San Suu Kyi, as State Counsellor, refusing to condemn the state's violence towards the Rohingya and to refer to the ethnic group by its name; centralization of political and economic power and material wealth, focusing on the majority Bamar Buddhists, and Bamar middle classes, and as a result, sidelining predominant ethnic groups; and the inclusion of only two Muslims among the NLD's 1,143 candidates for the 2020 election.
12 (pers. comm., 23 November 2019)

References

Aslanidis, P. (2016). Is populism an ideology? A refutation and a new perspective. *Political Studies*, 64(1), 88–104. https://doi.org/10.1111/1467-9248.12224
Athan Myanmar (2020). Analysis on freedom of expression situation in four years under the current regime. *Athan Myanmar.* www.athanmyanmar.org/analysis-on-freedom-of-expression-situation-in-four-years-under-the-current-regime/
Aung, S. H. (2019, November 22). Mixed reaction to State Counsellor's ICJ decision. *The Myanmar Times.* www.mmtimes.com/news/mixed-reaction-state-counsellors-icj-decision.html
Aung, S. H. (2020, January 1). Freedom of speech remains elusive under NLD regime. *The Myanmar Times.* www.mmtimes.com/news/freedom-speech-remains-elusive-under-nld-regime.html
Aung San, S. K. (1997). *Letters from Burma*. Penguin.
Aung San, S. K., & Aris, M. (2010). *Freedom from fear: And other writings*. Penguin.
Aung San Suu Kyi: Myanmar democracy icon who fell from grace. (2021, December 6). *BBC news.* www.bbc.com/news/world-asia-pacific-11685977
Barany, Z. (2018). Burma: Suu Kyi's missteps. *Journal of Democracy*, 29(1), 5–19. https://doi.org/10.1353/jod.2018.0000
Bengtsson, J. (2010). *Aung San Suu Kyi: Struggle for freedom*. Harper Collins.
Callahan, M. P. (2003). *Making enemies: War and state building in Burma*. Cornell University Press.
Cheesman, N. (2015). *Opposing the rule of law: How Myanmar's courts make law and order*. Cambridge University Press.
Cheesman, N. (2017). How in Myanmar 'national races' came to surpass citizenship and exclude Rohingya. *Journal of Contemporary Asia*, 47(3), 461–483. https://doi.org/10.1080/00472336.2017.1297476
Clements, A. (2008). *Aung San Suu Kyi, the voice of hope: Conversations with Alan Clements*. Rider.

Crouch, M. A. (2016). The judiciary in Myanmar. In A. Simpson, N. Farrelly & I. Holliday (Eds.), *Routledge handbook of contemporary Myanmar* (pp. 248–256). Routledge.

Crouch, M. A. (2019). *The constitution of Myanmar: A contextual analysis*. Hart Publishing.

David, R., & Holliday, I. (2015, July 23). From icon to politician: Aung San Suu Kyi's choice. *The Interpreter*. www.lowyinstitute.org/the-interpreter/icon-politician-aung-san-suu-kyis-choice

Dunant, B. (2019, May 31). How the rule of law was lost. *Frontier Myanmar*. https://frontiermyanmar.net/en/how-the-rule-of-law-was-lost

Ellis-Petersen, H. (2018, November 23). From peace icon to pariah: Aung San Suu Kyi's fall from grace. *The Guardian*. www.theguardian.com/world/2018/nov/23/aung-san-suu-kyi-fall-from-grace-myanmar

Ellis-Petersen, H. (2019, June 6). Aung San Suu Kyi finds common ground with Orbán over Islam. *The Guardian*. www.theguardian.com/world/2019/jun/06/aung-san-suu-kyi-finds-common-ground-with-viktor-orban-over-islamFink, C. (2001). *Living silence: Burma under military rule*. Zed Books.

Fisher, M. (2017, October 19). Myanmar, once a hope for democracy, is now a study in how it fails. *The New York Times*. www.nytimes.com/2017/10/19/world/asia/myanmar-democracy-rohingya.html

Free Expression Myanmar (FEM). (2018). *Myanmar's media freedom at risk, The results of a nationwide survey of journalists' opinions*. http://freeexpressionmyanmar.org/wp-content/uploads/2018/05/myanmars-media-freedom-at-risk.pdf

Freedom House (2019). *Freedom in the world 2019 Myanmar*. https://freedomhouse.org/country/myanmar/freedom-world/2019

Harriden, J. (2012). *The authority of influence: Women and power in Burmese history*. NIAS Press.

Hawkins, K. A., & Rovira Kaltwasser, C. (2017). The ideational approach to populism. *Latin American Research Review*, 52(4), 513–528. https://doi.org/10.25222/larr.85

Hlaing, K. Y. (2012). Understanding recent political changes in Myanmar. *Contemporary Southeast Asia*, 34(2), 197–216. www.jstor.org/stable/41756341

Holliday, I. (2011). *Burma redux*. Columbia University Press.

Houtman, G. (1999). *Mental culture in Burmese crisis politics: Aung San Suu Kyi and the national league for democracy* (Institute for the Study of Languages and Cultures of Asia and Africa (ILCAA), Monograph Series 33). Tokyo University of Foreign Studies.

Human Rights Watch (2019). *Dashed hopes: The criminalization of peaceful expression in Myanmar*. https://reliefweb.int/sites/reliefweb.int/files/resources/myanmar0119_web2.pdf

Human Rights Watch (2022). *World report 2022—Myanmar*. www.hrw.org/world-report/2022/country-chapters/myanmar-burma

Institute for Economics and Peace (2019). *Global peace index, measuring peace in a complex world*. http://visionofhumanity.org/app/uploads/2019/06/GPI-2019-web003.pdf

Jagers, J., & Walgrave, S. (2007). Populism as political communication style: An empirical study of political parties' discourse in Belgium. *European Journal of Political Research*, 46(3), 319–345. http://dx.doi.org/10.1111/j.1475-6765.2006.00690.x

Jones, L. (2014). The political economy of Myanmar's transition. *Journal of Contemporary Asia*, 44(1), 144–170.

Kenny, P. D. (2017). *Populism and patronage. Why populists win elections in India, Asia, and beyond*. Oxford University Press.

Kenny, P. D. (2019). *Populism in Southeast Asia*. Cambridge University Press.

Kenny, P. D. (2020). 'The enemy of the people': Populists and press freedom. *Political Research Quarterly*, 73(2) 261–275. https://doi.org/10.1177/1065912918824038

Lakhdir, L. (2019, September 23). Critics of Myanmar government facing prison time: Civilian officials' intolerance of criticism rivalling military's. *Human Rights Watch*. www.hrw.org/news/2019/09/23/critics-myanmar-government-facing-prison-time

Mangshang, Y. B. (2018, May 30). Myanmar's freedom of expression as a broken promise of the NLD. *Tea Circle*. https://teacircleoxford.com/2018-year-in-review/myanmars-freedom-of-expression-as-broken-promise-of-nld/

Mudde, C. (2004). The populist zeitgeist. *Government and Opposition*, 39(4), 542–563. https://doi.org/10.1111/j.1477-7053.2004.00135.x

Mudde, C., & Rovira Kaltwasser, C. (2013). Exclusionary vs. inclusionary populism: Comparing contemporary Europe and Latin America. *Government & Opposition*, 48, 147–174. https://doi.org/10.1017/gov.2012.11

Mudde, C., & Rovira Kaltwasser, C. (2017). *Populism: A very short introduction*. Oxford University Press.

Müller, J.-W. (2016). *What is populism?* Penguin.

Myat, M. M. (2019). Is politics Aung San Suu Kyi's vocation? *Palgrave Communications*, 5(1), 1–8. https://doi.org/10.1057/s41599-019-0258-1

Myint-U, T. (2011). *Where China meets India: Burma and the new crossroads of Asia*. Faber and Faber.

Pepinsky, T. (2020). Migrants, minorities, and populism in Asia. *Pacific Affairs*, 18, 593–610. https://doi.org/10.5509/2020933593

Petrie, C., & South, A. (2014). Development of civil society. In M. Gravers & F. Ytzen (Eds.), *Burma/Myanmar: Where now?* (pp. 87–94). NIAS Press.

Pyidaungsu Hluttaw (2014). *News media law—Pyidaungsu Hluttaw law no. 12/2014*. Online Burma/Myanmar Library. www.burmalibrary.org/en/news-media-law-pyidaungsu-hluttaw-law-no-122014-english

Regan, H. (2021, February 8). Why the generals really took back power in Myanmar. *CNN*. https://edition.cnn.com/2021/02/06/asia/myanmar-coup-what-led-to-it-intl-hnk/index.html

Schober, J. (2011). *Modern Buddhist conjunctures in Myanmar*. University of Hawai'i Press.

Schonthal, B., & Walton, M. J. (2016). The (New) Buddhist nationalisms? Symmetries and specificities in Sri Lanka and Myanmar. *Contemporary Buddhism*, 17(1), 81–115. https://doi.org/10.1080/14639947.2016.1162419

Selth, A. (2018). All going according to plan? The armed forces and government in Myanmar. *Contemporary Southeast Asia*, 40(1), 1–26. https://muse.jhu.edu/article/692007.

Selth, A. (2019). *Interpreting Myanmar: A decade of analysis*. ANU Press. http://doi.org/10.22459/IM.2020

Selth, A. (2021). *Myanmar's Military Mindset: An exploratory survey*. Griffith Asia Institute, Griffith University.

Silverstein, J. (1990). Aung San Suu Kyi: Is she Burma's woman of destiny? *Asian Survey*, 30(10), 1007–1019. https://doi.org/10.2307/2644786

Silverstein, J. (1996). The idea of freedom in Burma and the political thought of Daw Aung San Suu Kyi. *Pacific Affairs*, 69(2), 211–228. https://doi.org/10.2307/2760725

Smith, M. (1999). *Burma: Insurgency and the politics of ethnicity*. Zed Books.

Steinberg, D. (2013). *Burma/Myanmar: What everyone needs to know* (2nd ed.). Oxford University Press.

Subedi, D. B., & Garnett, J. (2020). De-mystifying Buddhist religious extremism in Myanmar: Confrontation and contestation around religion, development and state-building. *Conflict, Security & Development*, 20(2), 223–246. https://doi.org/10.1080/14678802.2020.1739859

Subedi, D. B., & Scott, A. (2021). Populism, authoritarianism, and charismatic-plebiscitary leadership in contemporary Asia: A comparative perspective from India and Myanmar. *Contemporary Politics*, 27(5), 487–507. https://doi.org/10.1080/13569775.2021.1917162

Taylor, R. H. (2009). *The State in Myanmar*. NUS Press.

Than, T. (2016). Myanmar's general election 2015: Change was the name of the game. In M. Cook & D. Singh (Eds.), *Southeast Asian Affairs 2016* (pp. 241–264). ISEAS—Yusof Ishak Institute.

Thawnghmung, A. (2016). The Myanmar elections 2015: Why the National League for Democracy won a landslide victory. *Critical Asian Studies*, 48(1), 132–142. https://doi.org/10.1080/14672715.2015.1134929

Transparency International (2020). *Myanmar*. www.transparency.org/country/MMR.

Turnell, S. (2011). Myanmar's fifty year authoritarian trap. *Journal of International Affairs*, 65(1), 79–92.

Turnell, S. (2014). Burma's economy and the struggle for reform. In M. Gravers & F. Ytzen (Eds.), *Burma/Myanmar where now?* NIAS Press.

United Nations Development Programme (UNDP) (2019). *Human development reports: Myanmar*. http://hdr.undp.org/en/countries/profiles/MMR

United Nations Human Rights Council (UNHRC) (2019, September 16). *Detailed findings of the independent international fact-finding mission on Myanmar (online)*. www.ohchr.org/sites/default/files/Documents/HRBodies/HRCouncil/FFM-Myanmar/20190916/A_HRC_42_CRP.5.pdf

United Nations Human Rights Council (UNHRC) (2022, June 13). Losing a generation: How the military junta is attacking Myanmar's children and stealing their future. *Conference Room Paper of the Special Rapporteur on the Situation of Human Rights in Myanmar*. A/HRC/50/CRP.1. www.ohchr.org/en/documents/thematic-reports/ahrc50crp1-conference-room-paper-special-rapporteur-losing-generation

Wade, F. (2019). *Myanmar's enemy within: Buddhist violence and the making of a Muslim 'other'*. Zed Books.

Walton, M. J. (2014). Burmese Buddhist politics. In Oxford Handbooks Editorial Board (Eds.), *Oxford handbook topics in religion* (online ed.). Oxford University Press. https://doi.org/10.1093/oxfordhb/9780199935420.013.21

Walton, M. J. (2017). *Buddhism, politics and political thought in Myanmar*. Cambridge University Press.

Walton, M. J., & Hayward, S. (2014). *Contesting Buddhist narratives: Democratization, nationalism and communal violence in Myanmar*. East-West Centre.

Ware, A., & Laoutides, C. (2018). *Myanmar's 'Rohingya' conflict*. Hurst & Company.

Weyland, K. (2017). Populism: A political-strategic approach. In C. Rovira Kaltwasser, P. Taggart, P. Ochoa Espejo & P. Ostiguy (Eds.), *The Oxford handbook of populism*. (pp. 48–72). Oxford University Press.

19
THE DUTERTE PHENOMENON AS AUTHORITARIAN POPULISM IN THE PHILIPPINES

Bonn Juego

Introduction

Former President Rodrigo Duterte of the Philippines was Southeast Asia's most prominent representative of the so-called 'strongmen era' in recent world politics. After winning the country's presidential election in May 2016, he drew loud attention from the international media, which often covered him for his foul mouth and his government's even fouler 'war on drugs' that resulted in thousands of extrajudicial killings of mostly small-time drug dealers. Despite mainstream media's portrayal of him as an odious character, Duterte remained a nationally popular president, including among Filipinos living and working abroad, during his constitutionally limited single six-year term.

Survey results show that Duterte had maintained excellent satisfaction ratings: starting at a record high 70%–86% range during the height of his administration's controversial anti-drug crusade in 2016–2017; peaking at 91% in 2020 despite a mediocre performance in the management of the COVID-19 pandemic; and concluding at 78% when he finished his term in 2022 (see Chapter 11 in this volume). In the absence of an appropriately designed scientific survey to empirically determine the major factors behind his popularity among the majority of Filipinos, who continued to trust and be satisfied by Duterte's leadership, it can be plausibly argued that his administration actively mobilized support for undemocratic ideas and practices through a combination of legitimation by the active, passive, manufactured, and coerced consent of citizens. Whereas his loyalists, known as the Diehard Duterte Supporters (DDS), promoted active consent, sections of the less engaged electorate lent passive consent to his politics. While the government apparatus can manipulate public information and communication channels to manufacture consent, a state-orchestrated climate of fear can secure coerced consent to the regime.

Duterte's rise to power in one of the earliest democracies in post-colonial Asia, which underwent transitions through both colonialism and authoritarianism, is a significant event in the trajectory of Filipino and Asian politics. Philippine historiography offers heroic stories of its people in their struggle for independence from the sequence of Spanish, American, and Japanese colonization between the 16th century and the mid-1940s. To a large extent, since becoming an independent nation-state, the institutional design of its political system has been patterned after U.S.-style democracy, including the principles of liberalism in the constitution and the presidential form of government. During the past 50 years, Western media and foreign academics generally divided post-colonial Philippine political history into two periods: the dictatorship of Ferdinand Marcos after martial law was declared in 1972, and its overthrow and the restoration of democracy through the peaceful People Power uprising in 1986. Duterte's eventful presidency is bound to be a further defining moment in the historical narrative of the evolution of Philippine politics.

It can be inferred that Duterte's popular election and government favourably impacted the historic victory of his successor, Ferdinand Marcos Jr., the son and namesake of the former dictator, in the May 9, 2022 elections. Nevertheless, answers to whether the Duterte regime marked merely an aberration in the process of democratization, a dangerous disruption towards autocratization, or an alternative political development will be determined by the governance activities and political outcomes during the Marcos Jr. administration in the coming years.

Pundits and researchers have largely associated the case of the Philippines in the time of Duterte with the emergence of illiberalism in the West, punctuated by the crises of liberal and social democracy in the United States and parts of Europe (Bremmer, 2018; Regilme, 2021). However, Duterte-style populism had its own conjunctural particularities. Studies in political science and sociology have described and attempted to explain specific facets of the Duterte regime's illiberal populist characteristics, notably 'penal populism' (Curato, 2016), 'fascist original' (Bello, 2017), 'populist revolt against elite democracy' (Heydarian, 2018), 'new populist politics' (Putzel, 2018), and 'violent populism' (Thompson, 2022). This chapter builds on this existing literature and contributes to a contemporary reading of Philippine politics by analyzing the Duterte phenomenon as *authoritarian populism*, which has had multiple dimensions (Juego, 2018a).

Conceptually, populism is understood here as a phenomenon whose causal explanation is in doubt. The following account is thus more descriptive than explanatory. The concept of authoritarian populism is also analyzed as an emergent socio-political process rather than as a governance style, coherent ideology, state form, or public policy. The analytical focus is on the history and tendencies of the current conjuncture (cf. Hall, 1979, 1985; Jessop et al., 1984). In particular, the chapter centres on the idea that Duterte-led authoritarian populism was a self-contradictory phenomenon in which anti-democratic ideology and autocratic politics gained popular legitimacy.

Twelve dimensions of Duterte-style populism

A study on populism, especially the specificity of the Duterte phenomenon, needs to be clear about the timeframe of analysis to understand its evolving form and manifestation. Evaluating a populist leader like Duterte necessitates tracking his rhetoric and actions during specific periods of election (the campaign) and tenure in office (policies), thereby examining their consequences (both intended and unintended).

With the benefit of hindsight, at least a dozen dimensions of Duterte's phenomenal candidacy and presidency are pertinent for populism studies. These multifaceted dimensions constitute an analytical framework that reveals significant features of the Duterte phenomenon and its attendant regime of authoritarian populism in terms of (1) reasons for election and popularity; (2) leader's personality; (3) position in the populist spectrum; (4) language and gendered discourse; (5) ideology; (6) mode of participation and means of communication;

(7) class dynamics and support base; (8) governance approach; (9) strategy for hegemony; (10) political philosophy; (11) foreign policy and international relations; and (12) political economy and economic policy.

1. Peculiar electoral victory and popularity

Duterte's initial political capital consisted of 39% of the 42 million total votes cast in the May 2016 presidential elections. To top this, surveys registered a 91% trust rating after his first 100 days in office. His hardline supporters used these election and survey results as a strong argument for a majoritarian principle to settle any political and moral issues of the day. The claim was that Duterte's opinions and decisions embodied the sentiments of the majority.

Three factors stand out among many considerations that can explain the impressive electoral victory and consistent domestic popularity of Duterte. The first is the agential factor, which suggests that Duterte's campaign team executed a more effective and efficient campaign strategy than its rivals. The messaging connected well with the resentments and hopes of the electorate at the time, touching on both the most basic day-to-day concerns (like heavy traffic in Metro Manila and horrifying street crimes) and the fundamental social problems (including class inequalities, feudalism, and U.S. colonialism). The catch-all anti-corruption and law and order platforms also generated a big-tent coalition of voters.

The second aspect concerns the institutional mechanism of the first-past-the-post plurality voting rule, the personality-oriented party system, and the presidential set-up in the Philippines. The political fate of Duterte would probably have been different had there been run-off voting, platform-based party discipline, and a parliamentary form of government. He may well have lost in a two-round voting rule. He may have remained an obscure persona in a mature political party system. His crass opinions conveniently expressed through the media would also have been subjected to scrutiny and censure in a parliamentary setting. A genuinely democratic institution of justice may well have nipped his political career in the bud, especially since he had achieved notoriety in the early 1990s for his violence-ridden leadership in the provincial City of Davao.

While these agential and institutional explanations are counterfactual scenarios, the third and most important factor is the structural reason why Duterte's brand of populism has gained hegemonic status. His landslide election represents a protest vote against the perceived hypocrisies, shortcomings, or failures of the so-called 'EDSA Republics' (i.e., the successive administrations from the 1986 People Power revolution that toppled the dictatorship of Marcos in favour of the democratic and developmental ideals of liberal democracy). Duterte's rhetoric successfully exploited not only the general perception, but also the reality of the failings of the 30-year liberal-democratic order (Juego, 2018a).

2. Personality cult and charisma

The history of populism in the Philippines suggests that this phenomenon is organized around charismatic leaders rather than political party ideologies. Prior to Duterte, the populist figureheads regarded as 'strongmen' were Manuel L. Quezon, President of the U.S.-managed Commonwealth of the Philippines from 1935 to 1944, and Marcos, initially elected for the 1965–1972 presidential tenure, who stayed in the position until 1986 (McCoy, 2017). In the late 1990s, the 'celebrity superstar' Joseph Estrada represented the Filipino face of populism in

Southeast Asia (Hedman, 2001; Thompson, 2010). Both the protracted dictatorship of Marcos and the short-lived presidency of Estrada were terminated through extra-constitutional means at a time of increasing dissatisfaction with their governments. In contrast, Duterte sustained his popularity and was able to command a faithful following despite constant negative publicity from both international and local media. This is indicative of his charisma, which is a key mobilizing source of power in Filipino political culture.

Arguably, however, there are social institutions and economic conditions that make a leader's charismatic persona a compelling force in Asian societies like the Philippines (Bello, 2020). Charisma is often viewed as a personal gift, but in political sociology, it should be understood in relational terms, as the interaction between the leader and followers (Subedi & Scott, 2021). Charismatic authority becomes problematic in a democracy if it leads to a cult of the leader's personality in which voters turn into fans, citizens into fanatics, and citizenship into fanaticism.

Only the zealous followers of Duterte would be able to fully account for the specifics of their attraction to him (Arguelles, 2019). But he can be described as a heterodox politician who combined a traditional political background with an unorthodox political style. He was a traditional politician, a veteran local political boss who thrived on patronage politics and had the capacity for violence using guns and goons. Even though he presented himself as an outsider to the country's mainstream power bloc, he came from an elite political clan based in two of the three main island groups, namely, Visayas and Mindanao (Bagares, 2016; Parreño, 2019). Thus, it can be assumed that he had been party to the wheeling and dealing of money politics and clientelism at the national level (Juego, 2017).

For someone holding the highest political office, Duterte had an unorthodox demeanour, such as uncouth public behaviour and speeches. But it was his bold criticism and repudiation of established actors in the Philippine power structure—the United States, the oligarchy, and the Catholic Church—that most clearly distinguished him from other elected Filipino political figures.

3. A mix of left- and right-wing populisms

As a candidate and newly elected president, Duterte projected a mixture of both left- and right-wing populism. But shortly after completing his first year in office, he swung to right-wing populism due to the predisposition towards authoritarianism in his rhetoric, governance style, and support base.

Duterte was rhetorically 'socialist' and 'leftist,' strongly criticizing the historically established power institutions of U.S. imperialism, the landed oligarchy, and the hierarchy of the Catholic Church. In a video clip released just a few days before the election, then presidential front-runner Duterte was shown to have had a friendly conversation via Skype with Jose Maria Sison, the founder of the Communist Party of the Philippines (CPP) in exile in the Netherlands, where he committed to facilitating a peaceful resolution to the decades-long armed insurgency. Duterte said to Sison in a mix of Tagalog and English:

> The elites, supposedly the prim and proper, in our nation haven't done anything. They say there's economic growth, but we don't feel it in the grassroots. We only see the oligarchs and the poor. There's no middle class. Everybody is suffering, so I said to myself, this has to end. We have to bring in the middle class, we have to make it stronger.
>
> *'Duterte, Joma Sison', 2016*

He concluded with a reassurance to Sison that:

> I will follow the pattern of socialism in my government. I said this in public, in every meeting, that I am socialist, and though I am not a member of the communist party . . . I belong to the left. This will be the first time in the history of our country that there is a leftist President. There is nothing wrong with being left.
>
> *'Duterte, Joma Sison', 2016*

In the early days of his administration, Duterte opened peace negotiations with communist rebels and Islamist separatist groups. He went even further, arguing that these were ideological organizations with legitimate grievances rather than criminal bands. A peace agreement was reached between the Philippine government and the Moro Islamic Liberation Front that led to the legislation of the Bangsamoro Autonomous Region in Muslim Mindanao in July 2018. But Duterte had already broken ties with left-leaning groups, citing continued attacks by the CPP's armed wing, the New People's Army (NPA), against government police and armed forces in the countryside. By late 2017, Duterte had issued official proclamations declaring the 'termination of peace negotiations' with the CPP-NPA, which was soon to be classified as a 'terrorist organization'. In December 2018, he signed an executive order creating the National Task Force to End Local Communist Armed Conflict (NTF-ELCAC), which supposedly institutionalized a 'whole-of-nation approach,' rather than a 'purely military option,' as the government policy for securing peace (Office of the President, 2021). This was followed by the signing of the controversial Anti-Terrorism Act of 2020. The act's constitutional lawfulness with respect to basic rights and freedoms was challenged in the Supreme Court, which made a final ruling that almost all its provisions were constitutional. The NTF-ELCAC, acting on the pretext of the anti-terror law, was strongly criticized for orchestrating a series of red-tagging drives against Duterte's civil society critics from the universities, media, and entertainment industry.

While on some occasions Duterte spoke for the cause of social justice to resolve the roots of historical conflicts, his speeches were often replete with anti-democratic themes, especially the disregard for human rights and the repeated threats to impose Marcos-era martial law. By his actions, it is evident that he had resorted to state violence—coercive military and police actions—to address problems of insurgency, criminality, illegal drug addiction, as well as the COVID-19 pandemic, instead of thoroughgoing social and economic reforms (Juego, 2018a; Hapal, 2021; Thompson, 2022).

4. *The macho populism of Duterte-speak*

The communication style known as 'Duterte-speak' started to emerge during the election campaigns, and as Duterte's years in office went by, it became normalized in everyday media and discourse. It was messianic, domineering, and unconstrained by norms of political correctness. With 'change is coming' as his slogan, his messaging was full of motherhood statements. Sounding as if possessed by a messiah complex in his assertion that his reason for running was 'to save the republic,' he offered simple solutions to complex social problems, specifically the promise to end criminality and illegal drugs in three to six months. The message also spoke of the all-embracing objectives of law and order and anti-corruption that can easily be supported by every citizen. Importantly, the main thrust of the campaign to package Duterte's masculinity and authenticity proved compelling to voters (McCargo,

2016). After his election, his supporters promoted a familial analogy in which Duterte was hailed as the father of the nation (*Tatay Digong*). The call for national unity created binaries between friends and enemies of the state, between good citizens and bad criminals, and between ordinary people and the elites.

Duterte often made the headlines through his outrageous comments. He had the habit of digressing from his written speeches with expletive-laced ad libs. The attention of the international media was drawn to his controversial utterances (e.g., the rape jokes, the remark about shooting female rebels in the vagina, the warning that he would physically assault critics, the order to kill anyone who resisted police arrest, and the threat to slaughter millions of drug addicts). As Mayor of the City of Davao for more than 20 years, Duterte had mastered socio-political communication skills in provincial and local contexts, where street language lends voice to macho culture and as such celebrates social deviance emanating from masculine peer pressures (Abinales, 2015; Rocamora, 2017). However, as a manager of societal affairs and a leader of government, Duterte's 'macho populism' was not only paternalistic towards the governed and punitive towards lawbreakers but it also embodied patriarchal conservatism and gendered moralizing, especially towards women and sexual minorities who opposed him (Parmanand, 2020; Encinas-Franco, 2022).

Duterte-speak spread from local to national politics. His tongue was *Bisaya*; thus, he connected well with Visayan-speaking Filipinos, both domestically and overseas, who, in turn, were among his strongest defenders in the face of criticisms of his obscene remarks and anecdotes. His vulgar speeches appeared to be a non-issue for the general population, arguably because these were the public expression of dominant discourses and popular sentiments in Filipino culture, and as such are deeply ingrained in the psyche of the majority of the people: machismo, sexism, violence, the desire for social order, and the need to discipline the citizenry (Juego, 2018a). Duterte defended his use of colourful language and frequent swearing by labelling it 'slang'.

5. Critique of liberal democracy

In terms of its ideological dimension, a consistent theme in Duterte's authoritarian populism was the critique of both the theory and practice of liberal democracy. He and his supporters particularly criticized the ideals of human rights by emphasizing their unsuitability for the Filipino, Asian, and developing country contexts. Whether this criticism was a deliberate autocratic offensive or plain ignorance concerning the principles of liberalism, it was a 'scorched-earth rhetoric' that attacked the very foundations of human rights: universality, inalienability, indivisibility, and interdependence (Juego, 2018b). Yet what most forcefully impacted social discourse was Duterte's disparagement of the ideas, institutions, and personalities associated with the liberal-democratic order. In the case of the Philippines, this attack was targeted specifically at the failure of the hypocritical liberal elites who ruled the country's government, politics, economy, and society to address the issue of corruption prior to his ascent to the highest echelons of power.

Duterte's authoritarian-populist discourse expanded into a strongly partisan and ideological echo chamber against the social forces for liberal democracy. Its drawing power could not be reduced to mere consequences of political propaganda intended to deceive the population, to false consciousness, or interpreted as the result of emotional populism. Rather, his social embedding of authoritarian populism was a manifest response to real problems affecting people's lives. The legitimate feelings of fear, insecurity, resentment, anxiety, and hope were derived from real material conditions and lived experiences of the Filipino majority.

A notable example of this was the interrelations between feelings, beliefs, perceptions, and social reality in the Duterte administration's flagship war on drugs, which was internationally controversial but domestically popular. A fieldwork survey carried out by Pulse Asia (2017) suggests that the bloody campaign was initially supported by around 88% of Filipinos, even though 73% believed that it involved extrajudicial killings. Bearing in mind variations in estimates across different sources, the anti-drug campaign resulted in the death of somewhere between 5,000 and 30,000 people between 2016 and 2021. Multiple psychological factors explain the popularity of the drug war: fear and hatred among actual and potential victims, frustration and anger at the failure of previous administrations, a yearning for personal safety and public security against crime, and a high level of trust in and positive perception of Duterte's political will (Juego, 2018a).

Neither the term authoritarianism nor populism was uttered by Duterte during his candidacy. In fact, there were instances when he named socialism and German-type social democracy as his ideology. Even though Duterte did not label his thinking authoritarian-populist, his election to power by projecting himself as a strongman leader may be construed as a popular vote for authoritarianism. It is indicative that Duterte's authoritarian populism coincided with his fast-tracking the political rehabilitation of the family of late dictator Ferdinand Marcos, the so-called 'Marcos Restoration' that spanned the period from their ousting in 1986 to their return to Malacañang Palace in 2022.

6. *The populist moment and social media*

The Duterte phenomenon ushered in the populist moment in contemporary Philippine politics. There emerged some remarkable patterns in the articulation of political communication between citizens using the interactive technologies of social media. Cyberspace serves as a battleground for electioneering and shaping public opinions, especially in the Philippines, where social media use increased rapidly from 56% of the population in 2017 to around 72% (78.5 million users) in 2020. The Duterte camp overcame rivals in the online war in the run-up to the 2016 presidential election thanks to its effective social media campaign backed by a budget of U.S.$200,000, which was used to initially hire cyber influencers, troopers, and trolls that subsequently led to the mobilization of passionate internet warriors across many different locations (Gavilan, 2016; Williams, 2017; Bradshaw & Howard, 2017). These paid professional PR strategists and celebrity pundits, together with the netizens they influenced, carried on their operation after the election to amplify support for the Duterte government (Ong & Cabanes, 2018).

Digital age interest groups have utilized social media in different ways as a communicative means to achieve specific political ends. In the case of the Duterte phenomenon, social media served as a convenient platform to facilitate the appeal of an authoritarian-populist personality and disseminate bits of information with a far-reaching impact on minds and emotions. Moreover, while the populist moment is characterized by a considerable increase in citizen participation in public debates online, it is also replete with harmful activities such as fake news, disinformation, trolling, and character assassination that are endemic in social media.

From the 2016 electioneering to the Duterte presidency, Philippine political cyberspace was preoccupied with the 'DDS (Diehard Duterte Supporters) versus Dilawan (Yellows)' conflict. Hurling insults at one another, pro-Duterte supporters called the opposition 'Yellowtards,' with reference to their symbolic yellow political colour, while the opposition called the DDS 'Dutertards.' The fierce rivalry between the two camps evinced what social psychologists call 'groupthink'—each camp engaged in exclusivist friend/enemy distinction and discursive exchanges processed through confirmation biases, cognitive dissonance, and the logical fallacies of straw man and ad hominem arguments.

The process of political consciousness formation during the populist moment may be described using Albert Hirschman's conceptual 'exit, voice, and loyalty' framework (Hirschman, 1972). Before Duterte's election, the liberal political agenda for apathetic citizens who chose to *exit* from participating in the democratic decision-making process was to encourage them to *voice* their views as an exercise of active citizenship. However, during his presidential term, his supporters further strengthened their *loyalty* to their patron as a basis for active participation in political and governmental affairs.

7. From cross-class alliance to centre-right

Over time, the Duterte support base shifted from a cross-class alliance to the centre-right bloc. During Duterte's candidacy and first year in office, the composition of his populist movement cut across class, gender, generations, and the political spectrum (Juego, 2018a). This catch-all politics and big-tent coalition had a divide-and-rule effect on different sectors of the population. For example, criticisms against his misogynistic and homophobic remarks were responded to by his supporters from women's groups and the LGBTQIA+ community. In comparison to the earlier populist, former president Estrada's pro-poor posturing, Duterte projected himself as a leader for all classes despite his anti-elite rhetoric, while the administration's drug war and economic policies were criticized as anti-poor.

After winning the election, Duterte forged a broad coalition of different political factions, while keeping his own clique of long-time friends from the City of Davao and former law school classmates. But a couple of initial controversies—namely, the series of deaths in the course of the anti-drug campaign and his support for the interring of Ferdinand Marcos at the Heroes' Cemetery—caused divisions among Duterte supporters, as not everyone condoned extrajudicial killings or believed that Marcos should be honoured as a hero.

Although every newly inaugurated president had tried to make some degree of accommodation of leftist groups, Duterte was the most daring in nominating individuals proposed by the far left to work for his cabinet as departmental secretaries. However, a little over a year after the establishment of the purported tactical alliance between them, Duterte severed ties with the left. First, the activist nominees were not confirmed by the Commission on Appointments, whose members were political allies of Duterte from both the Senate and House of Representatives. Second, Duterte formally ended the peace talks with the Communist Party of the Philippines—New People's Army—National Democratic Front (CPP—NPA—NDF) and ordered that their leaders be re-arrested. Thereafter, in several speeches, he taunted communism for its irrelevance, ordered soldiers to kill communist rebels, and reminded the police to ignore human rights.

It became increasingly clear that Duterte had sided with the more aggressive faction within his supporters, whose ideological leaning was to the right. Among the notable members of the right-wing power elite backing, exploiting, and riding Duterte's popularity were the family of ex-dictator Marcos and allies of former President Gloria Macapagal Arroyo. The Duterte regime created a conducive climate for the Marcos family to promote authoritarian nostalgia for their 21-year political dominance and their loud disdain for their Yellow opponents via social media. Arroyo, who served as Speaker of the House of Representatives from 2018 to 2019, admitted that Duterte's election provided an atmosphere of goodwill that supported a favourable court decision releasing her from her four-year incarceration for election fraud and plunder charges. As the policies and priorities of his government made it clear, Duterte always valued the interests and viewpoint of the coercive apparatuses of the police and military.

8. Securitization: police-centric and militaristic governance approach

Duterte had a police-centric and militaristic approach to governance. The 'law of the instrument'—'if all you have is a hammer, everything looks like a nail'—captures well Duterte's over-reliance on the police and military as his favoured means of resolving major governmental problems. Securitization was the state's response to intractable social and long-term pathologies. Societal challenges—from criminality and substance abuse to rebellion and the pandemic health crisis—were treated as security issues requiring forceful methods of policing and further militarization (Juego, 2018a; Hapal, 2021; Thompson, 2022; Teehankee, 2022).

The Philippine National Police (PNP) became the central planning and implementing agent of the Duterte administration's centrepiece programme, the war on drugs. Duterte would often warn drug peddlers: 'Those who destroy my country . . . And those who destroy the young people of our country, I will kill you' (Duterte, 2021). The government's official statistics provided by the Philippine Drug Enforcement Agency for the period July 1, 2016, to September 30, 2021, reported 216,138 anti-illegal drug operations conducted; 311,686 persons arrested; and 6,201 deaths during anti-drug operations. The report of the United Nations High Commissioner for Human Rights noted that since July 2016, 'killings related to the anti-illegal drugs campaign appear to have a widespread and systematic character' and 'the most conservative figure . . . suggests that . . . 8,663 people have been killed—with other estimates of up to triple that number' (OHCHR, 2020, p. 5). These reports and other relevant information form the basis for cases filed against Duterte at the International Criminal Court (ICC), whose designated prosecution believed 'that the Crime Against Humanity of Murder was committed from at least 1 July 2016 to 16 March 2019' and 'that state actors, primarily members of the Philippine security forces, killed thousands of suspected drug users and other civilians during official law enforcement operations,' where the 'total number of civilians killed . . . appears to be between 12,000 and 30,000' (Office of the Prosecutor, ICC, 2021, p. 3). Duterte's government deposited a written notification to the ICC announcing the Philippines' withdrawal as a State Party to the Rome Statute on March 17, 2018. This took effect the following year. The ICC still claims jurisdiction to investigate and prosecute crimes against humanity in the Philippines prior to its withdrawal.

Duterte touted the anti-illegal drugs campaign as a solution to a whole range of individual, family, community, generational, societal, and economic problems. While the government's Dangerous Drugs Board estimated that there were about 1.8 million drug users in the country, in his speeches Duterte would refer to three to four million addicts. Research suggests that most of these drug users came from vulnerable sectors. Hence, by assigning the police as the main problem-solver of both the supply and demand for illegal drugs rather than implementing vital socio-economic reforms, the war on drugs criminalized the poor, the unemployed, the sick, and other victims of social pathology (Juego, 2018a, pp. 143–144).

The Duterte administration also militarized its orientation towards historical conflicts, insurgencies, and radicalization. This can be observed not only in the government's eventual termination of the peace negotiations with the CPP—NPA—NDF, but also in its relentless military response to radical Islamists during the five-month siege of Marawi and its aftermath. Duterte's military carried out air strikes against the ISIS-linked Maute group in the Islamic City of Marawi in May 2017 and imposed an extended martial law over the whole island of Mindanao for two and a half years. Even though there was recognition from Duterte himself and top officials of the Armed Forces of the Philippines of the complexity of conflicts in the Muslim Mindanao region, their counter-insurgency strategy placed military authority over relevant social considerations. Such a manner of conflict management, derived from a tactical warfare perspective, is contradictory to the need for more comprehensive and cohesive programmes that draw lessons from past peace processes with Moro and Islamic rebel groups (Juego, 2018a, pp. 144–145).

9. Hegemony by coercion, lawfare, and mass mobilization

In order to secure political and social hegemony, the Duterte regime depended not only on typical authoritarian methods of repression but also on creative lawfare and proactive mass mobilization. Duterte's populist discourse came with mortal threats and actual violence against individuals he deemed to be a danger to the stability of the state and society. Perhaps owing to his profession as a lawyer, he also utilized legalism and the legal system as disciplinary tools against dissenters. Pro-Duterte cyber troopers—and the many social media users they had influenced—drowned out criticisms of government policies (Billing, 2020).

Duterte's angry tirades against old oligarchs, dissenting officials, opposition politicians, human rights activists, and the critical news media usually came with government-orchestrated and legalized action against them. Initially, the Department of Justice and the Department of Finance prepared tax evasion cases against the business tycoon Lucio Tan (Marcos's former crony) and the Mighty Corporation (a large cigarette manufacturer). Eventually, however, both were resolved through amicable settlement. Tax and cyber libel cases were also filed against the journalist Maria Ressa, CEO of the social news site Rappler, who was awarded the 2021 Nobel Peace Prize for her efforts to safeguard freedom of expression. Former opposition Senator Leila de Lima, who as Chair of the Commission on Human Rights (2008–2010) had investigated Duterte's Davao record of abuses, has been detained since February 2017, accused of involvement in illicit drug trading during her stint as Secretary of the Department of Justice (2010–2016). The Office of the Solicitor General initiated *quo warranto* action in the Supreme Court against Maria Lourdes Sereno. This resulted in the nullification of her appointment as Chief Justice. Congressional proceedings, supported by pro-administration legislators in the House of Representatives, made it possible for Duterte to maintain his long-running threat to reject the ABS-CBN (the country's largest media network) application to renew its franchise. In addition to the familiar repressive practice of filing trumped-up charges such as illegal possession of firearms and explosives against opponents, anti-terror measures made human rights defenders, community journalists, and social critics vulnerable to harassment and arrest on the mere suspicion that they were terrorists.

Selective justice, lawfare, and legalism were not new to Duterte's Philippines. They have been ever-present features of an enduring culture of impunity, often utilized by incumbent governments to stifle dissent and undermine political opposition. What appears unprecedented was the tactic of mass mobilization through active online presence and social media engagement to arouse and organize popular support for the Duterte regime (see also Chapter 8 in this volume). Political dissenters, critics, and the opposition were subjected not only to verbal assault and legal prosecution but to cyberbullying and defamatory labelling as 'destabilizers' and 'enemies of change'. Thus, it can be said that in the battle for social and political hegemony, Duterte's authoritarian-populist strategy was not just a revolution from above, but also a project of bottom-up mass mobilization.

10. *Biopolitics of exception*

In the terms of political philosophy, the Duterte regime's government through securitization underpinned a certain biopolitics of exception. Duterte's authoritarian populism exemplified Foucauldian 'governmentality' in the sense that disciplinarian power over life-and-death policies were popularly legitimized through his election on a campaign platform to rule with an iron fist, as confirmed by his consistently high trust survey ratings. At the heart of the populist biopolitics of the incumbent government was the normalization of the exceptional disciplinary methods used to subjugate and control the population. This state of exception, exercised as violent measures in response to national crises, was not only police-centred and militarist, but also juridical. It involved various coercive yet legal measures such as the criminalization of drug users, the prolonged imposition for two and a half years of the putatively temporary martial law across the whole island of Mindanao, the labelling of communist insurgents as terrorists, and the policing strategy enforcing one of the world's longest COVID-19 lockdowns (Juego, 2018a; Hapal, 2021; Agojo, 2021; Thompson, 2022). Duterte was forthright about this rationality of governance for the purpose of protecting both the sovereign state and society: 'It is never, never wrong for a President and the police and the military to protect its citizens. It is self-preservation' (Office of the Press Secretary, 2016).

The Duterte government assumed its sovereign mandate by deciding on the exception and by using the narrative of crisis as legal and political justification for heavy-handed intervention in civil rights and civic life (cf. Juego, 2018c; Rafael, 2022). Duterte would incite the discontented and opposition groups to defy, rebel, or launch a coup d'état (Musico, 2018). The suspicion here is that any ensuing social chaos and disorder provided a pretext and opportunity for a militarily calibrated intervention to establish a regime of exception and restore order. Duterte, together with his inner circle of lawyers and military men, must have calculated the risks of any possible confrontation with prospective enemies of the state and concluded that the opportunities outweighed the threats.

The passage of the Anti-Terrorism Act of 2020 exemplified the biopolitical aspect of the governmentality of authoritarian populism under Duterte. The act alarmed proponents of democracy and human rights, as it signified the regime's autocratic political project on securitization and threatened the democratization process. Its legality was challenged in the Supreme Court on the grounds that it violated the Bill of Rights and undermined checks and balances, judicial oversight, and the indispensable role of the judiciary. Duterte, military officials, and other supporters defended this security legislation by promoting the 'nothing to fear, nothing to hide' argument. Yet, there was a fundamental tension between the government's security-based interests, embodied in the Anti-Terror Act that conceivably permitted abuse and circumvented due process and privacy (e.g., warrantless arrest on mere suspicion, arbitrary detention without trial, and surveillance) on the one hand and the limitations on the state prerogatives and exceptional powers required to democratize the relations between state and civil society on the other.

11. Peaceful coexistence between authoritarian-populists

The international relations aspect of the Duterte phenomenon produced a few interesting narratives: first, the palpable foreign policy shift from idealistic nationalism to pragmatic realism; and second, the emergent trend in relationships among illiberal state leaders, which may be referred to as 'authoritarian peace' and/or 'populist peace,' that is, peaceful coexistence among authoritarian-populists.

Typical of the populist in a formerly colonized country, Duterte campaigned on a nationalist ticket, accompanied by grandiloquent statements such as the assertion that the Philippines is no longer a vassal of the U.S. imperialist system and the absurdity of jet skiing to plant the national flag on the disputed territories in the South China Sea. His speeches about geopolitics were, in general, articulated within the frames of nationalism and anti-colonialism, whether topically a neo-colonial analysis critiquing core-periphery dependency, hedging between great power rivals U.S. and China, a strategy of non-alignment for a Third World nation, or a version of 'Look East' to Asian neighbours as priority partners.

As head of state, faced with hard geopolitical and social-structural realities, Duterte soon changed his tune and stance. In terms of relations with China, he opted to focus on economic diplomacy through trade and investment rather than national security. Both in discourse and action, he was reluctant to robustly defend the ruling awarded to the Philippines by the Permanent Court of Arbitration (PCA) in The Hague on July 12, 2016, which adjudicated that China's claims to historical rights, particularly encompassing the maritime areas within the 'nine-dash line' of its sovereign jurisdiction, were contrary to the 1982 United Nations Convention on the Law of the Sea (Permanent Court of Arbitration, 2016). He hardly protested against China's reported dredging, reclamation, artificial island-building, and militarization in the South China Sea. Criticism of the Duterte administration's alleged absence of an independent foreign policy was couched in a sarcastic message: 'Welcome to the Philippines, Province of China,' printed on tarpaulin banners installed in parts of Metro Manila on the second anniversary of the PCA judgement.

While Duterte might have had the option of keeping the United States at bay and forging closer friendships with China and Russia, Filipino soldiers cooperated closely with U.S. intelligence operatives during the Marawi siege. If anything, the government under Duterte maintained Philippine-U.S. military pacts: the 2014 Enhanced Defense Cooperation Agreement, the 1999 Visiting Forces Agreement, and the 1952 Mutual Defense Treaty. All these stemmed from the Americanized orientation and socialization of the Philippines and its people. Social institutions had long been associated with the United States, including the diplomatic corps, military, police, mass media, and academia (Juego, 2018a). Nevertheless, a 2017 Pew Research Center study was instructive about how Duterte's populism altered the impact of domestic political dynamics on foreign affairs (Poushter & Bishop, 2017). The study showed that Filipinos still favoured the United States over China, but that the gap was narrowing because popular support for Duterte correlated with increased positive perception towards China.

Unsurprisingly, Duterte maintained very friendly relationships with leaders generally regarded as autocratic—Chinese President Xi Jinping and Russian President Vladimir Putin—and avoided clashes with presidents and premiers of authoritarian, semi-authoritarian, or less democratic regimes in the Southeast Asian region (Juego, 2015). Among the discourses that Duterte shared with his strongmen counterparts were a critique of Western double standards in the doctrine of humanitarian interventionism, governance narratives of patriotism and sovereignty, and rhetoric on the principle of non-interference in domestic affairs (Juego, 2018a).

Furthermore, Duterte displayed contrasting attitudes towards two former U.S. presidents. Global media covered how Duterte disparaged liberal Barack Obama but was amiable with populist Donald Trump. Modern-day populists like Duterte, Trump, and those from European far-right parties converged on a number of issues: anti-elite and/or anti-establishment discourse, criticism of liberalism, foreign policy rhetoric of non-interventionism, alarmist talk on crisis and change, platforms on law and order, and political incorrectness in speeches. However, the appeal to ethnonationalism—a staple of Trump's and Europe's right-wing populists—was only deployed by Duterte during his election campaign (Juego, 2018a).

12. Authoritarian neoliberalism and economic populism

The political economy of the Duterte phenomenon demonstrated three compelling characteristics: (1) the continuity of neoliberal policies; (2) the logic of the social regime of authoritarian neoliberalism; and (3) the tension between economic populism and competitive capitalism. To a large extent, the popularity of Duterte's illiberal politics was a social response to the crisis of neoliberalism, which is the long-standing policy framework of the Philippines, based on a capitalist market-oriented ideology. Yet the Duterte government's economic priorities, policy choices, and selection of technocrats indicated the country's business as usual, neoliberal development paradigm (Juego, 2020).

First, since the mid-1990s, the Philippines had ardently instituted neoliberal policies of privatization, deregulation, fiscal discipline, and liberalization, supposedly to replace the Marcosian dictatorship and crony capitalism with institutions that would support liberal democracy and capitalist competition in the age of globalization. Duterte's populist discourse was framed as a critique of all these ingrained socioeconomic structures: oligarchy, political liberalism, and economic neoliberalism. His successful campaign illustrated that such an anti-elite project resonated powerfully with deepening insecurities and widening inequalities affecting everyday economic existence. In power, however, the Duterte regime continued with neoliberalism and likewise created its own coterie of favoured oligarchs (Almendral, 2019; Ramos, 2021).

In its first year, the Duterte administration adopted two major economic policies: the Philippine Development Plan (PDP) 2017–2022 and the Tax Reform for Acceleration and Inclusion (TRAIN). The PDP did not fundamentally depart from the vision of previous administrations for an open market economy and was intended to implement Duterte's 10-point socioeconomic agenda and initiate the multi-stakeholder AmBisyon 2040 for the reduction of poverty from 21% in 2015 to 13% by 2022. Rather than being seen as a bold initiative for income transfers and asset redistribution, TRAIN, as the initial instalment of the Comprehensive Tax Reform Program, was opposed on the grounds of its potential impact on inflation and its myopic view of consumption.

Second, 'Dutertenomics' was launched in April 2017 as the overarching project heralding a 'golden age of infrastructure' through the so-called 'Build, Build, Build' (BBB) programme. The proposed expenditure amounted to around U.S.$36 billion initially, with the aim of attaining upper-middle income country status by 2022. Funding for these big-ticket infrastructure projects came from taxes, official development assistance, and commercial loans. The government allotted a minimum of 5% of GDP annually. In the last two months of the Duterte administration, the chief implementer of BBB from the Department of Public Works and Highways reported that 'only 12 out of 119 infrastructure flagship projects (IFP) were completed,' totalling U.S.$1.2 billion, or 1.4% of the U.S.$89.5 billion total cost of investments (Cordero, 2022). But Dutertenomics was not to be viewed simply as an infrastructural plan; it was political through and through.

The *logic* of Dutertenomics was that of authoritarian neoliberalism—i.e., a capitalist accumulation regime in which a neoliberal economy operates within an authoritarian political framework. The state's role is to enforce neoliberal policies by guaranteeing law and order for the sake of business stability. This configuration is akin to German *Ordoliberalismus*, underscoring that a strong state does not by necessity control market activity, but intervenes in societal affairs to secure economic freedom and competition (Juego, 2018c). The process of capitalist development in the contemporary Philippines was undertaken at the point of interplay between the coexisting realities of an insurgent populist moment, the durable oligarchic structure, and the predominance of neoliberal policies. Institutionally, authoritarian neoliberalism under Duterte's populist regime manifested itself as a combination of anti-oligarchy assertions with the conscious appointment of both retired military generals and neoliberal technocrats in the bureaucracy.

Economic conditions and market signals were favourable at the outset of Dutertenomics. This was combined with the considerable political and social capital of a popularly elected president. However, between Duterte's inauguration in 2016 and the coronavirus-induced recession year of 2020, there was a significant decline in economic performance: the growth rate fell from 7.1% to -9.6%; foreign and local debt went from 42.2% to 58% of the GDP; balance of trade from U.S.$ -15.92 billion to U.S.$ -21.84 billion; and inflation from 1.3% to 2.6% (Manuel, 2021; Marasigan, 2021). Battered by the pandemic, the economy remained consumer driven and import dependent, rather than attaining the more desirable outcome of a strengthened manufacturing and productive structure.

Third, during the 2016 election, Duterte claimed to belong to the centre-left and made several economic populist promises such as the end of labour contractualization, universal health cover, free tuition for state universities, a hike in pensions, and increased salaries for government personnel, especially the police and military. The left-wing elements in his campaign discourse on the national economy included ideas about the necessity of protectionism for agriculture and manufacturing industries, criticism of the deleterious effects of the World Trade Organization (WTO) rules on the livelihood of local farmers, and condemnation of large-scale mining extractivism.

Even though Duterte officially enacted the socialistic Universal Health Care Act and the Universal Access to Quality Tertiary Education Act, as well as the Salary Standardization Law, he vetoed the pro-worker Security of Tenure Bill. As President, he prioritized and signed the Rice Tariffication Law of 2019, removing quantitative restrictions on the importation of rice and liberalizing the rice value chain. In the final year of his term, he appealed to the Association of Southeast Asian Nations (ASEAN) to keep the WTO relevant and uphold the free-market trading system through the Regional Comprehensive Economic

Partnership in the Asia Pacific and lifted the ban on operating mines and open-pit mining. Peddled as a pandemic response, the Duterte administration brought down taxes for corporations and businesses through the Corporate Recovery and Tax Incentives for Enterprises Act of 2021, while the TRAIN Law of 2018 increased excise taxes that mostly affected the purchasing power of the poor and middle class. In March 2022, economic managers finally succeeded in their push for the legislation of amendments to the Public Service Act, which aimed to rationalize, liberalize, and redefine public utilities and critical infrastructure to permit 100% foreign ownership.

Duterte's nationalist and leftist economic populism contended with the compulsions of contemporaneous global capitalist competitiveness and the influence of his appointed neo-liberalist technocrats. His politics may have been populist, but he had 'very conservative economic policies' (Department of Finance, 2020). Indeed, in response to questions related to Duterte's unfulfilled campaign promise to increase pensions of members of the social security system, which would entail using taxpayers' money to support private funds, the affirmation of the administration's economic team was telling: 'Candidate Duterte is different from President Duterte' ('Candidate Duterte Different', 2017).

Conclusion

The Duterte phenomenon initiated an ongoing social process of authoritarian populism in the Philippines, in which popular consent to illiberal politics and anti-democratic policies increased. Duterte retained abiding national popularity despite the intensification of local and international opposition to his autocratic style of governance. Though perceptions concerning his presidential legacy will remain sharply contentious, his tenure, for better or worse, was certainly a momentous point in Filipino politics.

Duterte inspired and led an authoritarian-populist movement, which was elected democratically but wielded state power through manifold undemocratic practices. The Philippine experience of the Duterte phenomenon tilted the social configuration of forces towards autocratization, thereby threatening freedoms hard won in the period of deepening democratization that commenced in the mid-1980s. The supposedly liberal-democratic EDSA Republics, which governed during the 30 years between the Marcos dictatorship and the Duterte populist regime, also, though to a lesser degree, left harmful legacies: corruption, impunity, elitism, human rights violations, selective justice, executive dominance, and ineptitude.

While the dictator Marcos inflicted long-lasting damage to Philippine society and the economy, the crucial political-economic faults and flaws of the succeeding EDSA Republics spawned the resurgence of nostalgia for Marcosian authoritarianism and the sustained appeal of Duterte's anti-liberalism (Juego, 2018a). Indeed, the election of Marcos Jr. by a historic majority of 58.77% votes in the May 2022 election can be said to have signified a familiar cycle of dynastic politics redux or historical amnesia about the country's authoritarian past. However, this does not signal an outright drift into autocracy. The presidential performance of Marcos Jr. and the social response to it will be a gauge of the impact of Duterte's authoritarian-populist regime on the evolution of Filipino political relations and institutions.

The Philippines during Duterte's presidential tenure represents a particular case with distinct dynamics in the study of varieties of populism in the Asia Pacific and the world. This chapter has outlined an analytical framework built upon the 12 observed dimensions of populism evinced by the Duterte phenomenon that can inform subsequent analyses and research on populism in comparative national contexts. The chapter has described how each dimension was manifested in and by the regime in descriptive, conceptual, and discursive terms. In doing so, the regressive attributes and contradictions of the political, social, economic, cultural, linguistic, ideological, gendered, and policy aspects of authoritarian populism have also been uncovered. This is a step towards a much-needed rethinking of progressive strategies for democracy.

References

Abinales, P. (2015, December 6). Digong's mouth. *Rappler*. www.rappler.com/voices/thought-leaders/115071-duterte-mouth-censorship/

Agojo, K. (2021). Policing a pandemic: Understanding the state and political instrumentalization of the coercive apparatus in Duterte's Philippines. *Journal of Developing Societies, 37*(3), 363–386. https://doi.org/10.1177/0169796X21996832

Almendral, A. (2019, December 4). Crony capital: How Duterte embraced the oligarchs. *Nikkei Asia*. https://asia.nikkei.com/Spotlight/The-Big-Story/Crony-capital-How-Duterte-embraced-the-oligarchs

Arguelles, C. V. (2019). 'We are Rodrigo Duterte': Dimensions of the Philippine populist publics' vote. *Asian Politics and Policy, 11*(3), 417–437. https://doi.org/10.1111/aspp.12472

Bagares, G. S. (2016, May 29). 'Kanto boy'? Duterte is so 'de buena familia ('sa totoo lang'). *Lifestyle.INQ*. https://lifestyle.inquirer.net/229627/kanto-boy-duterte-is-so-de-buena-familia-sa-totoo-lang/?fbclid=IwAR1D61Uf_sI70No5-zLh8_RZiwjJQdtrK7snTDG2TOTkvd5Fpr_By2_Ycdg

Bello, W. (2017, January 19). *Rodrigo Duterte: A fascist original*. Transnational Institute. https://www.tni.org/en/article/rodrigo-duterte-a-fascist-original

Bello, W. (2020). A dangerous liaison? Harnessing Weber to illuminate the relationship of democracy and charisma in the Philippines and India. *International Sociology, 35*(6), 691–709. https://doi.org/10.1177/0268580920942721

Billing, L. (2020, July 21). Duterte's troll armies drown out Covid-19 dissent in the Philippines. *Coda Story*. www.codastory.com/disinformation/philippines-troll-armies/

Bradshaw, S., & Howard, P. N. (2017). *Troops, trolls and troublemakers: A global inventory of organized social media manipulation*. Oxford University (Computational Propaganda Project Working Paper No. 2017.12). https://ora.ox.ac.uk/objects/uuid:cef7e8d9-27bf-4ea5-9fd6-855209b3e1f6

Bremmer, I. (2018, May 3). The 'strongmen era' is here. Here's what it means for you. *Time*. https://time.com/5264170/the-strongmen-era-is-here-heres-what-it-means-for-you/

Candidate Duterte different from President Duterte, says Diokno. (2017, January 3). *ABS-CBN News*. https://news.abs-cbn.com/business/01/03/17/candidate-duterte-different-from-president-duterte-says-diokno

Cordero, T. (2022, April 27). DPWH: 12 out of 119 build, build, build projects completed. *GMA News*. www.gmanetwork.com/news/money/economy/829909/dpwh-12-out-of-119-build-build-build-projects-completed/story/

Curato, N. (2016). Politics of anxiety, politics of hope: Penal populism and Duterte's rise to power. *Journal of Current Southeast Asian Affairs, 35*(3), 91–109. https://doi.org/10.1177/186810341603500305

Department of Finance (2020, April 12). PHL 'financially able' to meet COVID challenges—Dominguez. *Government of the Philippines*. www.dof.gov.ph/phl-financially-able-to-meet-covid-challenges-dominguez/

Duterte, R. (2021, July 26). *Sixth state of the nation address*. Presidential Communications Operations Office. https://www.officialgazette.gov.ph/2021/07/26/rodrigo-roa-duterte-sixth-state-of-the-nation-address-july-26-2021/

Duterte, Joma Sison chat online. (2016, May 4). *ABS-CBN News*. https://news.abs-cbn.com/halalan2016/nation/05/03/16/watch-duterte-joma-sison-chat-online

Encinas-Franco, J. (2022). The presidential kiss: Duterte's gendered populism, hypermasculinity, and Filipino migrants. *NORMA: International Journal of Masculinity Studies, 17*(2), 107–123. https://doi.org/10.1080/18902138.2022.2026107

Gavilan, J. (2016, June 4). Duterte's P10M social media campaign: Organic, volunteer-driven. *Rappler*. www.rappler.com/newsbreak/podcasts-videos/rodrigo-duterte-social-media-campaign-nic-gabunada

Hall, S. (1979, January). The great moving right show. *Marxism Today*, pp. 14–20.

Hall, S. (1985). Authoritarian populism: A reply to Jessop et al. *New Left Review*, 151, 115–124.

Hapal, K. (2021). The Philippines' COVID-19 response: Securitising the pandemic and disciplining the pasaway. *Journal of Current Southeast Asian Affairs*, 40(2), 224–244. https://doi.org/10.1177/1868103421994261

Hedman, E. (2001). The spectre of populism in Philippine politics and society: Artista, masa, eraption! *South East Asia Research*, 9(1), 5–44. https://doi.org/10.5367/000000001101297306

Heydarian, R. J. (2018). *The rise of Duterte: A populist revolt against elite democracy*. Palgrave.

Hirschman, A. O. (1972). *Exit, voice, and loyalty*. Harvard University Press.

Jessop, B., Bonnett, K., Bromley, S., & Ling, T. (1984). Authoritarian populism, two nations, and Thatcherism. *New Left Review*, 147, 32–60.

Juego, B. (2015). *The political economy of the ASEAN regionalisation process*. Heinrich Böll Stiftung. https://th.boell.org/en/2015/10/29/political-economy-asean-regionalisation-process.

Juego, B. (2017, February 22). *Demystifying Duterte's populism in the Philippines*. University of Nottingham Asia Research Institute. https://theasiadialogue.com/2017/02/22/demystifying-dutertes-populism-in-the-philippines/

Juego, B. (2018a). The Philippines 2017: Duterte-led authoritarian populism and its liberal-democratic roots. *Asia Maior*, 28, 129–164.

Juego, B. (2018b). *Human rights against populism: A progressive response to the politics of Duterte and Mahathir*. Heinrich Böll Stiftung. www.boell.de/en/2018/12/28/human-rights-against-populism-progressive-response-politics-duterte-and-mahathir

Juego, B. (2018c). Authoritarian neoliberalism: Its ideological antecedents and policy manifestations from Carl Schmitt's political economy of governance. *Administrative Culture*, 19(1), 105–136. https://doi.org/10.32994/ac.v19i1.209

Juego, B. (2020, June 13). Addressing the pandemic in the Philippines necessitates a new economic paradigm. *Developing Economics*. https://developingeconomics.org/2020/06/13/addressing-the-pandemic-in-the-philippines-necessitates-a-new-economic-paradigm/

Manuel, P. (2021, July 25). SONA 2021: The economy under President Rodrigo Duterte. *CNN Philippines*. www.cnnphilippines.com/business/2021/7/24/SONA-2021-economy-under-President-Rodrigo-Duterte.html

Marasigan, A. (2021, July 18). Why Dutertenomics weakened the economy. *BusinessWorld*. www.bworldonline.com/why-dutertenomics-weakened-the-economy/

McCargo, D. (2016). Duterte's mediated populism. *Contemporary Southeast Asia*, 38(2), 185–190. https://doi.org/10.1355/cs38-2a

McCoy, A. (2017). Global populism: A lineage of Filipino strongmen from Quezon to Marcos and Duterte. *Kasarinlan: Philippine Journal of Third World Studies*, 32(1–2), 7–54.

Musico, J. (2018, September 12). Duterte's oust dare to military an 'expression of confidence'. *Philippine News Agency*. www.pna.gov.ph/articles/1047753

Office of the President (2021). *The president's final report to the people 2016–2021: Sustaining our nation's gains amidst unprecedented challenges*. Presidential Management Staff, Republic of the Philippines. https://mirror.officialgazette.gov.ph/downloads/2021/11nov/1PRP20162020_072621.pdf

Office of the Press Secretary (2016, October 7). *President Duterte on drug war: 'We are fighting for self-preservation'*. https://pcoo.gov.ph/president-duterte-on-drug-war-we-are-fighting-for-self-preservation-07-oct-2016/

Office of the Prosecutor, ICC. (2021, May 24). *Situation in the Republic of the Philippines: Public redacted version of 'Request for authorisation of an investigation pursuant to article 15(3)'*, ICC-01/21-7-SECRET-Exp. www.icc-cpi.int/court-record/icc-01/21-7-anx4

OHCHR. (2020, June 29). *Situation of human rights in the Philippines: Report of the United Nations High Commissioner for Human Rights*. 44th Session of the UN Human Rights Council. A/HRC/44/22. https://digitallibrary.un.org/record/3879531?ln=en

Ong, J. C., & Cabanes, J. V. C. (2018). *Architects of networked disinformation: Behind the scenes of troll accounts and fake news production in the Philippines* (Communication Department Faculty Publication Series No. 74). UMassAmherst. https://scholarworks.umass.edu/communication_faculty_pubs/74/

Parmanand, S. (2020). Duterte as the macho messiah: Chauvinist populism and the feminisation of human rights in the Philippines. *Review of Women's Studies, 29*(2), 1–30.

Parreño, E. G. (2019). *Beyond will and power: A biography of President Rodrigo Roa Duterte*. Optima Typographics.

Permanent Court of Arbitration. (2016). *The South China Sea Arbitration (Philippines v China) (Award) PCA Case No. 2013-19*. https://www.pcacases.com/pcadocs/PH-CN%20-%2020160712%20-%20Award.pdf

Poushter, J., & Bishop, C. (2017, September 21). *People in the Philippines still favor U.S. over China, but gap is narrowing* (Global Attitudes and Trends). Pew Research Center. www.pewresearch.org/global/2017/09/21/people-in-the-philippines-still-favor-u-s-over-china-but-gap-is-narrowing/

Pulse Asia. (2017, October 16). *September 2017 nationwide survey on the campaign against illegal drugs*. www.pulseasia.ph/september-2017-nationwide-survey-on-the-campaign-against-illegal-drugs/

Putzel, J. (2018, May 25). *The Philippines as an extreme case in the worldwide rise of populist politics*. LSE Southeast Asia Forum (SEAF). https://blogs.lse.ac.uk/seac/2018/05/25/the-philippines-as-an-extreme-case-in-the-worldwide-rise-of-populist-politics/

Rafael, V. L. (2022). *The sovereign trickster: Death and laughter in the age of Duterte*. Duke University Press.

Ramos, C. (2021). The return of strongman rule in the Philippines: Neoliberal roots and developmental implications. *Geoforum, 124*, 310–319. https://doi.org/10.1016/j.geoforum.2021.04.001

Regilme, S. (2021). Contested spaces of illiberal and authoritarian politics: Human rights and democracy in crisis. *Political Geography, 89*. https://doi.org/10.1016/j.polgeo.2021.102427

Rocamora, J. (2017). Philippine President Rodrigo Duterte: The good, the bad and the ugly. *SocDem Asia Quarterly, 6*(3), 4–13.

Subedi, D. B., & Scott, A. (2021). Populism, authoritarianism, and charismatic-plebiscitary leadership in contemporary Asia: A comparative perspective from India and Myanmar. *Contemporary Politics, 27*(5), 487–507. https://doi.org/10.1080/13569775.2021.1917162

Teehankee, J. (2022). *Duterte's pandemic populism: Strongman leadership, weak state capacity, and the politics of deployment in the Philippines* (UNU-WIDER Working Paper 2022/63). United Nations University World Institute for Development Economics Research. www.wider.unu.edu/sites/default/files/Publications/Working-paper/PDF/wp2022-63-Duterte-pandemic-populism-strongman-leadership-weak-state-capacity-politics-deployment-Philippines.pdf

Thompson, M. R. (2010). Populism and the revival of reform: Competing political narratives in the Philippines. *Contemporary Southeast Asia, 32*(1), 1–28.

Thompson, M. R. (2022). Duterte's violent populism: Mass murder, political legitimacy and the 'death of development' in the Philippines. *Journal of Contemporary Asia, 52*(3), 403–428. https://doi.org/10.1080/00472336.2021.1910859

Williams, S. (2017, January 4). Rodrigo Duterte's army of online trolls. *The New Republic*. https://newrepublic.com/article/138952/rodrigo-dutertes-army-online-trolls.

20
GENDER, MEDIA, AND POPULISM
The vilification of first lady Ani Yudhoyono in the Indonesian online news media

Jane Ahlstrand

Introduction

In contexts of socio-political change and rising populist sentiment, prominent political figures can emerge as heroes or villains. These figures function symbolically as a discursive site of ideological division, representing either the in-group or out-group. Under conditions of populist-driven change, the villain commonly represents the loathsome elite, who oppresses and exploits the common people. By virtue of their difference from the male political norm, political women become highly visible figures, particularly in populist movements (Ahlstrand, 2022). In turn, their public images are susceptible to manipulation across a range of discursive platforms. The study of the discursive representation of an iconic political woman, therefore, becomes a salient way of identifying and examining the ideological boundaries and relations of power in a society undergoing transition.

In the digital age, online news media organizations play an increasingly influential role in spurring populist movements. Converging with social media, online news media reporting contributes to the formation of ideological groupings and political polarization, as well as the symbolic personalization of individual political figures (Lim, 2017; Widholm, 2016). Focusing on a prominent female political figure, this chapter examines how the discursive representation of the former first lady of Indonesia, Ani Yudhoyono, in the online media became a way of constructing an ideological divide and fuelling a populist agenda within the Indonesian population. It highlights the intersecting roles of gender, social media, and online news discourse within a populist movement taking place in democratic Indonesia as it is about to experience a change in national leadership.

Specifically, this chapter focuses on the portrayal of Ani Yudhoyono in the discourse of the mainstream Indonesian news site, Kompas.com, from August 2013 to September 2014, encompassing the lead-up to the hotly-contested 2014 presidential election and her final 12 months in the role after serving for a decade as first lady. This period was characterized by a groundswell of anti-elite, populist sentiment, reflected in the campaign styles of the two presidential candidates, Joko Widodo (Jokowi) and Prabowo Subianto. In this context, Ani Yudhoyono became a target of public ire, embodying the undesirable characteristics of the perceivably stagnant, elitist political regime of her husband, President Susilo Bambang

Yudhoyono (SBY). Her ill-fated attempts at closing the elite-public divide by engaging with the public on the social media site Instagram resulted in a series of clashes, which were covered extensively by news outlets, including Kompas.com. This study thereby aims to capture the discursive reproduction of an elite-non-elite divide between Ani Yudhoyono and the public that occurred on social media, refracted through the language of mainstream online news media. In so doing, it will demonstrate how news discourse gave momentum to the populist movement and justified a change in leadership through the vilification of one female political figure.

Using the theoretical framework of critical discourse analysis (CDA) and, in particular, van Leeuwen's (2008) model of social actor analysis, this chapter draws attention to the role of media language in transforming a female political figure into a key target of ideological contestation that contributed to a populist-driven realignment of power taking place in Indonesia. It demonstrates how the Kompas.com discourse strategically constructed a divide between Ani Yudhoyono as a member of the incumbent elite and Instagram users as the Indonesian public, or the non-elite. It also illustrates how the discourse disempowered Ani Yudhoyono while empowering the public and delegitimizing her participation in the online community, the political realm and, more broadly, undermined her husband's leadership. The strategies of division and exclusion employed by Kompas.com are built upon sets of social actor representations derived from van Leeuwen's framework of analysis, as well as van Leeuwen's framework of legitimation (2009). The functions of the strategies are illustrated through samples of text derived from Kompas.com news reports. Going beyond linguistic analysis, this chapter also evaluates the causes and consequences of these representations within the surrounding socio-political context, incorporating an imminent regime change and the predominant populist agenda.

Populism and the 2014 presidential election

Populist tactics became the overwhelming feature of the 2014 Indonesian presidential race. While conceptions of populism may vary, an appeal to a distinction between 'the people' and an undesirable 'other' rests at its core (Hatherell & Welsh, 2020). Indeed, rather than a distinct ideology, populism is best described as a political style, which relies on discourse peppered with symbolic acts that construct a dichotomy between the 'pure people' and the 'corrupt elite', which in turn serve political interests (Moffitt, 2016; Mudde, 2007). The construction of this dichotomy requires the representation of an enemy other, or multiple others, unworthy of acceptance or even engagement, while emphasizing the threat they pose to the people (Hatherell & Welsh, 2020; Wodak, 2015, p. 4).

The act of othering legitimizes the power of populist leaders and the in-groups they represent. It also seemingly empowers the people by defining what they are not and, particularly, whom they oppose (Hatherell & Welsh, 2020). From a CDA perspective, van Dijk (1998, p. 267) explains that this form of polarizing ideological discourse is guided by the concept of the ideological square, which emphasizes the 'good things' of the in-group and the 'bad things' of the out-group, while de-emphasizing the 'bad things' of the in-group, and the 'good things' of the out-group. Those included are empowered through the process of exclusion. This chapter describes the various discursive strategies engaged in Kompas.com discourse to malign Ani Yudhoyono within a populist agenda, framed by van Dijk's concept of the ideological square.

In the presidential race, the former governor of Jakarta, Joko Widodo (Jokowi), fashioned himself as a symbolic figure of hope for political renewal, working on behalf of the people. He tapped into the widespread public disillusionment with the SBY presidency and turned it into political capital (McRae, 2013). His campaign emphasized his simple demeanour to downplay any traces of elitism and increase his appeal to the ordinary people. His rival, the former military general and son-in-law of Suharto, Prabowo Subianto, also employed a populist approach. In this case, he appealed to the rural and lower classes through a pro-poor message, by claiming 'that the rich and powerful were looting Indonesia's natural resources' (Mietzner, 2015, p. 2). He promised tougher leadership and a return to the indirect elections of the New Order as a way to provide security in uncertain times (Mietzner, 2015). Similar to the populism of the pink-tide governments of Latin America (Madrid, 2019; Salgado & Sandrin, 2021), Prabowo promised to stand for the everyday people who were impoverished and ignored by the excessively democratic elite. Eventually, Jokowi won the election, claiming a win of 53.15% against Prabowo's 46.5% (Mietzner, 2015, p. 39).

First lady Ani Yudhoyono

While serving as first lady from 2004 to 2014, public perception of Ani Yudhoyono was invariably tied to that of her husband, Susilo Bambang Yudhoyono (SBY), who gained immense support in his initial term in office and was seen as a bringer of hope and change to Indonesia's nascent democracy. He served the permissible maximum of two five-year tenures as president, but by the end of his second term, the public had become increasingly frustrated with his cumbersome, elitist approach to politics, and began to demand change (Mietzner, 2015). This emerging desire for change turned into a populist movement, exploited heavily by Jokowi and Prabowo in their presidential campaigns mentioned above. As the populist movement gained momentum, Ani Yudhoyono became a target because of her perceived inadequacies as first lady and poor relationship with the public, which helped fuel acrimony towards the incumbent government and justify a change in leadership. Nevertheless, Ani remained loyal to her husband and supported him throughout his presidency and continuing leadership of the Democratic Party (*Partai Demokrat*).

Ani Yudhoyono's venture onto the social media platform Instagram began in April 2013, before public sentiment had turned sour. She used the account to upload and share her amateur photographic work, document her day-to-day activities, and provide an intimate look into her family life. Uniquely, she appeared to moderate the account herself and interact directly with the public in the comments section. In a domain dominated by young people, Ani Yudhoyono faced the challenge of adapting to and gaining acceptance in a new and largely foreign community of practice. As a female political figure on social media, Ani was scrutinized intensely as she navigated the intrinsically masculine political and online realms (Gudipaty, 2017; Marshall, 2020). While online communications with the public may have worked in her favour in the midst of rising populism, from mid-2013 onwards, her attempts at online engagement began to flounder. Unprecedented conflict relating to her social media account ensued, providing an abundant source of fodder for the Indonesian media.

As first lady, Ani Yudhoyono's image was not only anchored to her husband's profile, but also to traditional, state-sanctioned gendered expectations. In Indonesia, the title of *first lady* translates literally to 'mother of the nation' (*ibu negara*) and thereby embodies traditional ideals of womanhood founded in motherhood or *ibuisme* (lit. 'motherism'). This concept can be traced back to the authoritarian New Order regime (1966–1998) (Bennett, 2005; Blackburn, 2004; Robinson, 2009) in which Indonesia was conceived as a *family state*. Men and women were directed to gender-specific roles which, in turn, helped reproduce the structures of state power. Women were depoliticized and bound to the domestic realm, imagined as dutiful wives and nurturing mothers. Elite men were able to engage more actively in the public realm, serving as leaders of the family, as well as the nation.

The traditional narrow view of womanhood attached to the role of first lady is not unique to Indonesia. In the United States, for example, the first lady is expected to display the qualities of domestic femininity and uphold traditional values of middle to upper-class womanhood (Mayo & Meringolo, 1994). The idealized representation of the domesticated woman in the political realm is reinforced by the undesirable image of an outspoken, politically active woman. Mass media discourses perpetuate this simplified dichotomy, which makes female political actors more easily identifiable as heroes or villains. These discourses encourage vilification and scapegoating, thus perpetuating a superficial political narrative (Vasby Anderson, 2004, p. 28). The analysis of Ani Yudhoyono's portrayal in Kompas.com discourse therefore contributes to understanding the role of online news media in constructing this political narrative within a populist agenda.

The news media in the digital era in democratic Indonesia

The online news site Kompas.com is produced by the influential Indonesian media conglomerate Kompas Gramedia, which owns a range of businesses, including Indonesia's longest-running national print newspaper, *Kompas*. As a highly reputable Indonesian-language national news source, the daily print newspaper has maintained its leading position for half a century. Through its cautious, middle-of-the-road reporting, Kompas was able to continue operating during the repressive New Order regime (1966–1998). While under a different editorial board and running to a different news production schedule, Kompas.com undeniably benefits from the well-established image of the Kompas brand.

In the digital age, the shift to an online format and the ability to share across multiple platforms and devices have inevitably changed the relationship between news production and consumption. While elite groups like news media organizations traditionally had greater access to influential discourse and communication (van Dijk, 1995, pp. 12–13), as news media and social media converge, the reader as a consumer also plays a major role in determining content. Journalists monitor and adjust their coverage according to audience engagement in a bid to remain competitive. They aim for immediacy, audience reactivity, and the likelihood of the story being spread through shares across online platforms. Readers tend to skim, engage in reactive commenting and sharing, and move swiftly between online media platforms, predominantly on a mobile device (Costera Meijer & Groot Kormelink, 2015; Lim, 2013).

In contrast to the slower production schedule and more focused reading of print, the click-driven model of online news has impacted the quality of production and depth of reader engagement. Lim (2017) argues that, like elsewhere around the world, this new form of production and consumption in the digital era generates *algorithmic enclaves* in Indonesia. An algorithm responds to reader preferences as they engage with the media, adapting content to suit their pattern of engagement. In turn, the range of media stories made available to the user narrows, otherwise known as a *filter bubble* (Lim, 2017). Lim links this practice of media consumption to van Dijk (1998, p. 267) concept of the ideological square.

Users fall into self-perpetuating 'us against them' ideological groupings through repeated exposure to a certain ideological perspective. Ahlstrand's (2021) study of the representation of Megawati Soekarnoputri demonstrated the occurrence of polarization in the discourse of Kompas.com, pointing to the relevance of both a prominent woman in politics and the online news media as sources of ideological contestation in Indonesia.

The analysis of Ani Yudhoyono in Kompas.com discourse

Having described the Indonesian political context, the significance of the role of first lady, and the characteristics of the online news media, the following section outlines findings from the analysis of 50 news texts published by Kompas.com featuring Ani Yudhoyono as the main social actor from August 2013 to September 2014. Van Leeuwen's social actor analysis (2008) provides a framework for the analysis of her representation and other social actors as individuals and members of groups as they interact in the text. This approach also draws on the work of Halliday (1985) on transitivity, or the grammatical representation of agency. The type of social action, along with the allocation or concealment of agency, will demonstrate a social actor or social group's level of involvement in certain social actions.

Overall, as the findings show, Kompas.com strategically foregrounds or backgrounds information, including the actions, agencies, and identities of social actors. This strategic construal of information facilitates the dissemination of power relations and the construction of ideological boundaries according to an underlying ideological vision. In this regard, van Dijk's model of the ideological square (van Dijk, 1998) discussed earlier supports the identification of ideological boundaries between the different groups represented in the discourse. Complementary to the core focus on social actor analysis, the examination of the texts also incorporates van Leeuwen's concept of legitimation (van Leeuwen, 2007) to determine how Kompas.com portrayed the legitimacy of Ani Yudhoyono's participation in both the political and online realms.

The analysis uncovered two major discourse strategies which are labelled: *constructing an elite-public divide* and *delegitimation through authorization and trivialization*. Both strategies are formed by 'building blocks' of social actor representations derived from van Leeuwen's framework of social actor analysis. These representations are clustered according to a shared socio-political function relevant to the surrounding socio-political context to form a strategy. The second strategy also draws upon van Leeuwen's legitimation techniques (2007), which will be discussed in further detail herein. The components and socio-political functions of both strategies are explained through illustrative examples derived from the news texts translated into English for the sake of readability, with some of the original Indonesian features highlighted when pertinent. Linkages are made between the social actor representations, as well as the immediate and broader historical trends, to understand their causes and consequences for Ani Yudhoyono, notably the role of the mainstream online media and the surrounding political agenda.

Strategy 1: constructing an elite-public divide

In Kompas.com coverage of the conflict over Ani Yudhoyono's Instagram account, the strategy of constructing an elite-public divide portrayed her as the source of the conflict and members of the public as witty adversaries and occasional victims of her harsh outbursts.

The coverage of events in which this strategy emerged chiefly involved Ani defending photographs of her family she had uploaded to Instagram from public criticism. Initially portraying the conflict in a less provocative manner, the discourse gradually began to demonize her while absolving the public of any wrongdoing. The increasingly direct discourse both reflected and fuelled a sense of growing public disdain for Ani Yudhoyono and, more broadly, her husband's presidency.

Excerpt (1) herein documents the initial 'debate' that occurred between Ani and the public over the authenticity of a photograph she had taken of her granddaughter, Aira, and uploaded to Instagram. The photo itself was clearly the work of an amateur, but some Instagram users went so far as to claim it looked photoshopped. She responded vigorously to these comments, defending the authenticity of her photographic work, which only prompted further contest. As the first in a series of spats that took place on her Instagram account, Kompas.com conveyed the disparity in the conduct of Ani Yudhoyono and the public subtly. As further clashes ensued, however, Kompas.com shifted the responsibility for the conflict more blatantly to Ani Yudhoyono, while showcasing the innocence of the public. In contrast to her reactive and later aggressive attitude, Kompas.com positioned the public in a comparatively empowered role, focusing on responses that demonstrated self-control and mastery of the rules of the game on social media. Excerpt 1 captures this apparent difference between the two groups.

Excerpt 1

Other accounts, @evi_ira and @dvsagita also made comments that expressed doubt over the authenticity of the photo of Aira. However, not long after that, the first lady quickly responded and gave a clarification.

Kompas.com identified two members of the public responsible for criticizing the photograph by referring to their Instagram account names, complete with the '@' sign, effectively anonymizing them. Contrastingly, Ani Yudhoyono was clearly identified by her title as first lady, which indicated her online actions were completed in her official capacity. The two Instagram users were associated with the seemingly innocuous verbal process of 'making comments'. Moreover, these comments did not directly claim that the photograph was inauthentic, but instead 'expressed doubt'. Contrastingly, Kompas.com activated Ani Yudhoyono in a more explicit verbal process of 'quickly responding', which positioned her in a reactive role.

As the conflict escalated, Kompas.com apportioned greater blame to Ani and highlighted her failings on social media more directly. This drove a wedge between her and the public. Kompas.com continued to maintain the integrity of the members of the public, victimized by her aggression. With each new incident documented, Kompas.com reports included intertextual references to earlier related reports, thus compiling a body of evidence as proof of Ani's offensive persona, which also justified the more direct approach to reporting. Four months after the initial debate over the authenticity of the photograph of her granddaughter and a serIes of other online altercations, controversy erupted when an Instagram user questioned Ani Yudhoyono's ongoing Instagram activity during severe flooding in Jakarta. Excerpt 2 demonstrates the unfavourable portrayal of her, corroborated by intertextual references to interrelated coverage on Kompas.com.

Excerpt 2

While previously Ani 'got angry' at her followers because of comments on a photo of her granddaughter, Aira, a photo of her youngest son, Ibas, and a photo of the Yudhoyono family wearing batik to the beach, this time Mrs Ani behaved the same way towards one of her followers who wrote a comment on a photo of her grandchild, Airlangga Satriadhi Yudhoyono.

In an increasingly bold reporting style, Kompas.com held Ani Yudhoyono directly to account, positioning her as the agent responsible for the explicit verbal act of 'getting angry' with her followers. Ani's emotional verbal reaction violated the ideal of first lady as the nurturing 'mother of the nation' as well as the expected code of conduct for social media engagement. Just as in excerpt (1), Kompas.com downplayed the responsibility of the public for the conflict, portraying a followernlyveved in an innocuous act of 'writing a comment' as a victim of Ani's anger. Including the growing list of Ani's prior offences also helped readers update their knowledge of her pattern of negative behaviour while legitimizing a more critical reporting style. In a paragraph beneath this excerpt, Kompas.com embedded links to the reports on Ani's prior offences.

Kompas.com also demonstrated the divide between Ani Yudhoyono and the public through the use of direct and indirect quotations extracted selectively from her Instagram account. These quotations provided direct evidence of her aggressive behaviour and her followers' comparatively polite and witty comments. By using quotations, Kompas.com also avoided a perception of bias, by attributing the contentious content to a third party. In the report entitled, 'The Moment Ani Yudhoyono Called a Comment "Stupid" on Her Instagram', Kompas.com reiterated her use of *bodoh* (stupid) in the headline to highlight her provocative act. Indeed, the word carries entrenched socio-political connotations dating back to the New Order. The elite was viewed as *insyaf* or *terpelajar* (enlightened, educated), while the people were perceived as *masih bodoh* (still stupid), and thereby 'worthy' of domination (Anderson, 1990, p. 56). Ani's use of this term in the democratic era thus implied the perpetuation of this elite-non-elite divide.

In excerpt 3, Kompas.com used a direct quotation to capture an Instagram user's highly cynical remark in response to Ani's use of the word *bodoh* against him.

Excerpt 3

Erie then responded, 'Yes, madam, I may in fact belong to the category of Indonesians who are still stupid. I hope that you (*ibu*) are willing to provide me with enlightenment so that I can then become clever like you (*ibu*).'

Kompas.com presented Instagram user Erie's comment in a direct quotation, which enables its socio-political salience to shine through while showcasing his audacious act of addressing the first lady directly. Erie's active self-categorization as an Indonesian from the *masih bodoh* social group reinforces the gap between the public and the first lady. His sarcastic request to be 'provided with enlightenment' alludes to the enduring divide between the educated, powerful elite and uneducated, disempowered non-elite. While Kompas.com regularly identified members of the public on Instagram by their username, in this case, the follower was only identified by his given name, Erie. Erie thus appears more human and potentially evokes greater empathy from readers, who may also see themselves at the receiving end of elite oppression. Overall, by demonstrating that Ani Yudhoyono failed to remain calm and respectful on social media in contrast to the polite and clever Erie, Kompas.com challenges the historical concept of the enlightened elite and ignorant public.

While Kompas.com frequently portrayed members of the public in a witty and relatively empowered role, it also constructed them as victims of Yudhoyono's actions, often simultaneously. This seemingly contradictory representation evoked an extraordinary blend of respect and sympathy for the public. That ultimately perpetuated the dichotomous narrative of the evil elite and innocent public. In a follow-up report to the original from which excerpt 3 was derived, excerpt 4 herein highlights the personal impact of the conflict on Erie.

Excerpt 4

After First Lady Ani Yudhoyono called him stupid on Instagram, Erie Prasetyo, the owner of the account @erie_nya, has often suffered bullying. Cynical comments from supporters of the first lady take turns in attacking him.

Kompas.com allocated full culpability to Ani Yudhoyono, positioning her as the perpetrator, responsible for the verbal process of 'calling him stupid'. Erie, as the direct target of her verbal act, was positioned as the victim. As in excerpt (1), Kompas.com refers to Ani Yudhoyono by her proper name and title, again associating her online misconduct with her official role. Kompas.com then referred to him by his full name, Erie Prasetyo, demystifying his identity and enhancing his relatability. Kompas.com then compounded his 'victim' status by activating him in the mental process of 'suffering bullying', undertaken in a coordinated attack upon him by 'supporters of the first lady'. Erie was constructed as both savvy and a victim deserving of sympathy, while both Ani and her supporters were represented as the enemy.

Strategy 2: delegitimation through authority and trivialization

Concurrent with the representation of the series of online altercations constructing an ideological divide between the elite and the non-elite, Kompas.com adopted a strategy of delegitimation, undermining Ani Yudhoyono's participation in both the political and online realms while reinforcing her status as a member of the self-serving enemy elite. Kompas.com drew on authority figures, often exaggerating their statuses with grandiose titles, to voice the right to critique Ani's performance on social media. Kompas.com also emphasized Ani Yudhoyono's incongruity with the formal norms of politics by referring to her appearance and self-centred, even absurd behaviour.

Excerpt 5 invoked the voice of a political communications expert from Mercu Buana University, Heri Budianto. The provocative headline declared 'Ani Yudhoyono not Ready to Join Cyberspace', but navigated constraints of objectivity by relying throughout on the voice of an authoritative expert to undermine Yudhoyono's eligibility to participate in the online realm. In the excerpt below, Heri Budianto defined the behavioural expectations governing Ani's online engagement.

Excerpt 5

When entering the cyber community, continued Heri, Ani should be able to accept the consequences, including criticism. If Ani responds to the criticism, Heri sees that as being extremely detrimental.

As an academic at a tertiary institution, Heri embodies the authoritative role of the professor who sets the rules and places Ani in the subordinate role of the student, despite the defence demanded by her status. In an ambiguously presented quote devoid of quotation marks, Kompas.com activates Budianto in an act of advice-giving, albeit unsolicited, which naturally positions him in a powerful role, while positioning Ani in a subordinate role as the target of the advice. The double modals 'should be' (*harus*) and 'able to' (*bisa*) implore her to behave herself online and act to further disempower her while urging her to accept the consequences of her actions and 'take criticism'. While the conflict involved both the public and Ani Yudhoyono, she is singled out as the cause, while the public are included indirectly by reference to 'criticism', which minimizes their responsibility.

Excerpt 6 also demonstrates how the use of an authoritative voice enabled Kompas.com to navigate constraints of objectivity in publishing a negative opinion of Ani's conduct as first lady on social media. Quoting Musni Umar, a sociologist at the prestigious University of Indonesia, Kompas.com again claims the right to publish a harsh criticism of the first lady.

Excerpt 6

Sociologist from the University of Indonesia (UI) Musni Umar has criticized the attitude of First Lady Ani Yudhoyono who frequently makes reactive comments on her Instagram account. According to Musni, the attitude of the wife of President Susilo Bambang Yudhoyono (SBY) is ridiculous.

While audaciously describing Ani Yudhoyono's attitude as 'ridiculous', this news report was published without controversy. A close analysis reveals that Kompas.com assumes the authority to publish this criticism not only by indirectly quoting the expert but further through its careful choice of terms. Rather than quoting the expert directly, her 'attitude' is positioned as 'ridiculous'. Moreover, naming her 'First Lady Ani Yudhoyono' and 'the wife of President Susilo Bambang Yudhoyono' when referring to her 'reactive comments' reminds readers of her inappropriate online behaviour as both the 'mother of the nation' and wife of the president.

Trivialization also served to undermine Ani Yudhoyono's legitimate participation in the political realm and highlight the disparity between her and the people. In global political contexts, through a range of tactics, trivialization draws attention to women's incongruity with politics and thus challenges their legitimacy as political participants (Adcock, 2010; Ibroscheva & Raicheva-Stover, 2009; van Acker, 2003; van Dembroucke, 2014). In Kompas.com reports, trivialization involved the transformation of Ani into an object of scrutiny, drawing attention to her body and behaviour—a common form of trivialization occurring in media representations of political women (Ibroscheva & Raicheva-Stover, 2014, p. 47). While scrutinizing her body and behaviour, the discourse also disempowered Ani Yudhoyono by limiting her agency and influence.

Excerpt 7 is from a report covering the seemingly inconsequential story of Ani's attendance at a technology fair; however, rather than covering the event itself, the report scrutinized Ani in minute detail, describing her movement around the stalls, her attire and, most importantly, her use of a small hand-held fan in the tropical Indonesian heat. While focusing on Ani, it also emphasized the role of her aide in operating the fan on her behalf, which establishes her privilege and self-indulgent use of state resources.

Excerpt 7

It certainly wasn't an easy job. The aide had to maintain a constant distance. Too far, the breeze wouldn't be felt on Ani's body. Too close and the rotating blades would come into contact with the first lady's back.

In this scenario, Kompas.com objectifies Ani Yudhoyono and conceals her agency, which constrains her at the mercy of the reader and reporter's gaze. In 'the breeze wouldn't be felt on Ani's body', the agentless passive verb 'felt' eliminates Ani's control of the situation. In 'Ani's body', Kompas.com engages somatization, or the representation of a social actor by reference to a part of the body (van Leeuwen, 2008, p. 47), which contributes to her objectification. Somatization reappears in the next sentence, referring to 'the first lady's back', which carries the same alienating effect as 'Ani's body'. By both discursively objectifying her and removing her agency, Kompas.com demobilizes Ani Yudhoyono and limits the scope of her participation. Through this process, it becomes much easier to portray her as an object of ridicule and delegitimize her contribution to the political realm as first lady and representative of the SBY presidency.

The focus on Ani Yudhoyono's inconsequential and self-oriented behaviour also contributed to her trivialization, and in turn, her delegitimation. As part of this practice, Kompas.com tended to activate Yudhoyono in self-serving acts, at odds with her expected demeanour as first lady, and absurd in the eyes of the everyday people. In particular, the discourse activated her behavioural processes, which are social actions that relate to a person's deportment or conduct and are usually grammatically intransitive, meaning they do not have an impact on a direct object (van Leeuwen, 2008). Kompas.com also activated her in mental processes, in relation to the expression of thoughts and feelings (van Leeuwen, 2008). While activation in both processes can humanize a social actor, in the strategy of delegitimation, it emphasized Ani's incompatibility with, and limited impact on, the political realm, by juxtaposing her inconsequential actions against a formal political backdrop. Excerpt 8 was gleaned from the lead sentence of a report covering a large public Democrat Party rally held as part of the 2014 legislative election campaign.

Excerpt 8

First Lady Ani Yudhoyono appeared cheerful and danced around enjoying the rhythm of the music in the Democrat Party campaign in Pukon Field, Magelang Jawa Tengah.

Kompas.com began the report by identifying Ani Yudhoyono according to her official title and then immediately describing her as 'cheerful'. It then portrays Yudhoyono in the behavioural process of 'dancing around', and the mental process of 'enjoying' the music. Later in the report, Kompas.com describes her clothing choices on stage, which again serves to objectify her. When placed in the context of a campaign event, her portrayal bore no relation to the Democratic Party goal of winning seats at the upcoming legislative election. Instead, her 'undignified' behaviour detracted from the image of the party she represented, as well as her image as first lady. Overall, Ani was transformed into a target of ridicule, which undermined not only her persona but also her husband's leadership.

Conclusion

The illustrative excerpts explored provide evidence of the relationship between the online media, gender, and populism, achieved through the innovative use of social actor analysis within a CDA framework. The portrayal of Ani Yudhoyono as a reactive, cruel, and frivolous character placed her at odds with gendered expectations of a nurturing and self-sacrificing 'mother of the nation' in relation to the people. When covering her online activity, Kompas.com also positioned her in violation of expected codes of conduct governing social media communication. While personally responsible for her online actions, Kompas.com went to great lengths to gradually construct Ani Yudhoyono as the source of the conflict and a tiresome, unlikable member of the elite. In the process, it drew a distinct wedge between her and the public.

Kompas.com created this polarized representation by selectively reporting on Ani's actions and allocating responsibility strategically. The allocation of blame to Ani was reinforced by the contrasting positive representation of the public, who appeared rational and witty, exemplary participants in the online realm and, at times, undeserving victims of her aggression. As if building a convincing legal case against Ani, intertextual references, supported by embedded hotlinks, presented readers with a growing body of evidence of her online misdemeanours. From a commercial perspective, this technologically-facilitated form of intertextuality encouraged further engagement with other similar news reports, increasing the hit rate and advertising revenue. It potentially contributed to the formation of self-perpetuating algorithmic enclaves, as discussed by Lim (2017), and a one-sided view of Ani. Also facilitated by technology, featuring the voice of the public through direct quotations from Ani's Instagram account elevated the value of non-elite opinion. Including the voice of the non-elite empowered the public to actively challenge elite authority in the digital realm, an area dominated by young, urban-based, and educated Indonesians.

Kompas.com also created an illusion of objectivity to criticize and ridicule Ani Yudhoyono's engagement in both the political and online realms. The cautious use of language is a historical characteristic of Kompas' reporting and surfaces in the online format. The strategic construal of responsibility for controversial actions enabled Kompas.com to navigate constraints governing objectivity in the news media while constructing a divide between Ani, as a member of the elite, and the Instagram users as members of the non-elite. While not allocating blame directly, Kompas.com still managed to do so through contrasting representations of the two parties involved in the conflict. Moreover, when focusing on Ani Yudhoyono's triviality, the strategic concealment of her human agency alongside her objectification enabled Kompas.com to disempower her and transform her into a target of derogation while upholding an impression of objectivity.

The use of the authoritative expert as a source of delegitimation is a well-known discourse strategy (van Leeuwen, 2007) and served to shield Kompas.com from any suspicion of bias when publishing scathing critiques of the first lady. A remnant of New Order oversight, the Indonesian news media relies heavily on this tactic (Steele, 2011) to maintain a sense of objectivity and to enhance the credibility of a story. While the constant privileging of authoritative voices can undermine democratic participation in political discourse, in this case, the inclusion of the voice of everyday people as participants innlyine and offline realm in other reports helped to recalibrate hierarchical relations of power.

Gender norms played an undeniable role in demonizing and belittling Ani and, in turn, facilitating the elite-public divide. Referring to Ani as 'first lady' or 'wife of President Yudhoyono' in association with her negative social actions suggested a violation of the expected gendered obligations of submissive, nurturing wifehood and motherhood attached to the role of first lady. Relying on the voice of authority to delegitimize her took on a patronizing tone, whereby university-based male 'experts' doled out unsolicited advice to Ani on how she should conduct herself on social media. Trivialization delivered a further blow, using typically gendered tactics, focusing on appearance, and scrutinizing her intensely to undermine her participation in the political realm.

In a broader sense, while not necessarily fair, Ani Yudhoyono's portrayal as an aggressor in violation of her traditional role and acceptable online conduct, as well as an object of ridicule, served to undermine her husband's flailing presidency and justify a need for a new form of leadership with an anti-elite populist agenda. The coverage of Ani pointed to a potential shift in the balance of power between the political elite and non-elite and to a desire to empower the public to stand up to perceived elite tyranny. Moreover, the events demonstrated the importance of the digital realm as an annex to the public realm and a site of political contestation among Indonesia's urban middle class. In her own efforts to bridge the gap and engage with Indonesia's tech-savvy youth, Ani inadvertently became the target of anti-elite sentiment and, ultimately, the embodiment of the perceived problems of the SBY presidency.

Epilogue

In September 2014, after fulfilling the maximum two terms in office and the victory of Jokowi, Ani and SBY left the presidential palace. In the lead-up to their departure, news reports took a gentler stance towards Ani, portraying her in a more vulnerable, submissive role as she prepared to leave. This change in coverage likely reflected a change in attitude towards Ani, as political change had already been achieved through the presidential election and she no longer posed a threat. When Joko Widodo was sworn in as the new president, Indonesians were introduced to first lady, Iriana Widodo. In line with the new down-to-earth political persona of the Jokowi presidency, the first lady projected a decidedly more reticent public image and avoided social media, possibly having learned from Ani Yudhoyono's experience. Both Ani and her husband SBY quickly faded from media headlines as the new political era began.

The 2019 presidential election campaign became a rematch between Jokowi and Prabowo, both of whom employed reformulated populist tactics. The image of the incumbent president, Jokowi, as a democratic reformer had been overshadowed by a more technocratic and development-focused approach to leadership. He nevertheless maintained an ongoing grassroots orientation, claiming that economic development and the defence of national sovereignty were tantamount to the welfare of the Indonesian people. Prabowo maintained his pro-poor, anti-elite message of the 2014 presidential campaign, but this time coupled it with authoritarian Islamic rhetoric. In the end, Jokowi defeated Prabowo, promising to defend Indonesia's development and uphold pluralistic values.

As the presidential campaign gained momentum, in February 2019, Ani Yudhoyono suddenly reappeared in the media spotlight when she was diagnosed with leukaemia. She underwent intensive treatment in a private hospital in Singapore, but only lived for four more months. The news media coverage during this period differed starkly from her portrayal in her final year as first lady discussed in this chapter. As a cancer patient, she became acutely vulnerable and was treated with the highest respect as a much-loved former first lady. The revisionist, eulogizing portrayal of Ani Yudhoyono is worthy of further analysis, especially considering the context of the ever more authoritarian political climate five years into the Jokowi presidency.

Note

Some of the data in this chapter was drawn on in a recently published article by the author: Ahlstrand, J. L. (2023). Challenging the elite-public divide; Representing former Indonesian first lady, Ani Yudhoyono in online news discourse,. *Wacana, Journal of the Humanities of Indonesia, 24* (1) DOI: 10.17510/wacana.v24i1.1165

References

Adcock, C. (2010). The politician, the wife, the citizen, and her newspaper. *Feminist Media Studies, 8*(2), 135–159. https://doi.org/10.1080/14680771003672254

Ahlstrand, J. L. (2021). Strategies of ideological polarisation in the online news media: A social actor analysis of Megawati Soekarnoputri. *Discourse & and Society, 32*(1), 64–80. https://doi.org/10.1177%2F0957926520961634

Ahlstrand, J. L. (2022). *Women, media, and power in Indonesia*. Routledge.

Anderson, B. (1990). *Language and power: Exploring political cultures in Indonesia*. Cornell University Press.

Bennett, L. R. (2005). *Women, Islam and modernity*. Routledge.

Blackburn, S. (2004). *Women and the state in modern Indonesia*. Cambridge University Press.

Costera Meijer, I., & Groot Kormelink, T. (2015). Checking, sharing, clicking and linking. *Digital Journalism, 3*(5), 644–679. https://doi.org/10.1080/21670811.2014.937149

Gudipaty, N. (2017). Gendered public spaces: Online trolling of women journalists in India. *Comunicazione Politica, 2*, 299–310. http://dx.doi.org/10.3270/87226

Halliday, M. (1985). *An introduction to functional grammar*. Edward Arnold.

Hatherell, M., & Welsh, A. (2020). Populism and the risks of conceptual overreach: A case study from Indonesia. *Representation, 56*(1), 53–69. https://doi.org/10.1080/00344893.2019.1663904

Ibroscheva, E., & Raicheva-Stover, M. (2009). Engendering transition: Portrayals of female politicians in the Bulgarian press. *Howard Journal of Communications, 20*(2), 111–128. https://doi.org/10.1080/10646170902869429

Ibroscheva, E., & Raicheva-Stover, M. (2014). The girls of parliament: A historical analysis of the press coverage of female politicians in Bulgaria. In M. Raicheva-Stover & E. Ibroscheva (Eds.), *Women in politics and media: Perspectives from nations in transition* (pp. 47–64). Bloomsbury Academic.

Lim, M. (2013). Many clicks but little sticks: Social media activism in Indonesia. *Journal of Contemporary Asia, 43*(4), 636–657. https://doi.org/10.1080/00472336.2013.769386

Lim, M. (2017). Freedom to hate: Social media, algorithmic enclaves, and the rise of tribal nationalism in Indonesia. *Critical Asian Studies, 49*(3), 411–427. https://doi.org/10.1080/14672715.2017.1341188

Madrid, R. L. (2019). The emergence of ethno-populism in Latin America. In C. de la Torre (Ed.), *Routledge handbook of global populism* (pp. 163–175). Routledge.

Marshall, J. (2020). Trolling and the orders and disorders of communication in '(dis)information society'. In P. Budka & B. Bräuchler (Eds.), *Theorising media and conflict* (pp. 137–157). Berghahn Books.

Mayo, E., & Meringolo, D. (1994). *First ladies: Political role and public image*. National Museum of American History.

McRae, D. (2013). Indonesian politics in 2013: The emergence of new leadership? *Bulletin of Indonesian Economic Studies*, 49(3), 289–304. https://doi.org/10.1080/00074918.2013.850629

Mietzner, M. (2015, January 1). Reinventing Asian populism: Jokowi's rise, democracy, and political contestation in Indonesia (Policy Studies 72). *East-West Center*. www.eastwestcenter.org/publications/reinventing-asian-populism-jokowis-rise-democracy-and-political-contestation-in

Moffitt, B. (2016). *The global rise of populism: Performance political style, and representation*. Stanford University Press.

Mudde, C. (2007). *Populist radical right parties in Europe*. Cambridge University Press.

Robinson, K. (2009). *Gender, Islam and democracy in Indonesia*. Routledge.

Salgado, C., & Sandrin, P. (2021). A 'pink tide' then a 'turn to the right': Populisms and extremism in Latin America in the twenty-first century. In B. De Souza Guilherme, C. Ghymers, S. Griffith-Jones & A. Ribeiro Hoffmann (Eds.), *Financial crisis management and democracy* (pp. 265–280). Springer.

Steele, J. (2011). Indonesian journalism post-Suharto: Changing ideals and professional practices. In K. Sen & D. Hill (Eds.), *Politics and the media in twenty-first century Indonesia: Decade of democracy* (pp. 85–103) Routledge.

van Acker, E. (2003). Media representations of women politicians in Australia and New Zealand: High expectations, hostility or stardom. *Policy, Organisation & Society*, 22(1), 116–136. https://doi.org/10.1016/S1449-4035(03)70016-2

Van Dembroucke, C. (2014). Exploring media representations of Argentina's president Cristina Fernandez de Kirchner. *Feminist Media Studies*, 14(6), 1056–1070. https://doi.org/10.1080/14680777.2014.882858

van Dijk, T. A. (1995). Power and the news media. In D. Paletz (Ed.), *Political communication and action* (pp. 9–36). Hampton Press.

van Dijk, T. A. (1998). *Ideology: A multidisciplinary approach*. Sage.

van Leeuwen, T. (2007). Legitimation in discourse and communication. *Discourse and Communication*, 1(1), 91–112. https://doi.org/10.1177%2F1750481307071986

van Leeuwen, T. (2008). *Discourse and practice: New tools for critical discourse analysis*. Oxford University Press.

Vasby Anderson, K. (2004). The first lady: A site of American womanhood. In M. Meijer Wertheimer (Ed.), *Inventing + voice: The rhetoric of American first ladies of the twentieth century* (pp. 17–30). Rowman & Littlefield.

Widholm, A. (2016). Tracing online news in motion. *Digital Journalism*, 4(1), 24–40. https://doi.org/10.1080/21670811.2015.1096611

Wodak, R. (2015). *The politics of fear: What right-wing populist discourses mean*. Sage.

21
WEAPONIZING POPULISM
How Thailand's civil society went from anti-populism to anti-democracy campaigns

Janjira Sombatpoonsiri

Introduction

Despite the association of populism with *demos* (the people), contemporary analysts tend to view it as a threat to liberal democracy. Based on policy studies and the rhetoric and manners of contemporary populist figures such as Donald Trump, Nigel Farage, Rodrigo Duterte, Recep Tayyip Erdoğan, and Viktor Orbán, populism is negatively attributed to democratic backsliding. Jan-Werner Müller (2016), for instance, argues that populist leaders may fan the rhetoric that characterizes the 'people' as an authentic and homogenous entity, neglected by their elites and exploited by outsiders. By claiming to represent 'the people', populist leaders can reinforce the social divide, pitting their popular base against critics accused of disrespecting the people's voice. Populist anti-pluralism potentially sows the seed of autocracy by utilizing electoral mandates to undermine institutions that provide checks and balances, and by clamping down on civil society organizations as well as the media, which populists claim intrudes between them and their constituents. This populist onslaught on democracy has already been evident in Poland (Strzelecki, 2016), Hungary (Dunai, 2017), and Turkey (Cagaptay & Aktas, 2017). In addition, populists with xenophobic inclinations tend to capitalize on a generated sense of crisis and collective anxiety to justify their persecution of minority scapegoats (Moffitt, 2015).

Anxiety that populists are threatening democracy has thus far led many analysts and activists to call for defiance of demagogues in power. Particularly in the United States, civil society networks protested nationwide against President Trump directly following his electoral victory. Most notably, millions of ordinary Americans joined the Women's March in 2017 and 2018 in Washington DC as well as other cities and towns across the United States (Hartocollis & Alcindor, 2017; Lopez, 2018). Other protests focused on varying issues, ranging from Trump's Muslim ban (Taylor, 2017) to his cuts of the science research budget (Milman, 2017) and his repealing of the Patient Protection and Affordable Care Act (Wiegel, 2017). Based on the Crowd Counting Consortium, there were over 4,000 protest events between January 2017 and October 2017, the majority of which targeted Trump's policies (Caruso, 2017). Although on a smaller scale, similar protests have also occurred in a number of European countries that have witnessed a populist surge such as Poland, Austria, Germany, the United Kingdom, and Hungary (Aziz & Rehman, 2017; Chase, 2018; Kelly, 2017; Peto, 2018). In this milieu, analysts project populism's detrimental effects on democracy (Finchelstein, 2019; Kyle & Mounk, 2018; Levitsky & Ziblatt, 2018; Mounk, 2018; Müller, 2016; Norris, 2017, pp. 13–16), at times encouraging a popular overthrow of *authoritarian populists* (Beauchamp, 2017; Chenoweth, 2017).

In this chapter, I argue that while resisting right-wing and authoritarian populism is necessary, it can harm, rather than save, democracy if the power struggle surrounding populist politics is overlooked. To date, civic activism against populism has generally been driven by the assumption that authoritarian populists may directly cause democratic erosion. Toppling them should simply restore democracy. Expressed differently, anti-populism should essentially be democratic. However, political upheavals in Thailand over the past two decades demonstrate a different trajectory. Populism has been used as a political weapon (hereafter, 'weaponized') by the establishment elites, who are inherently sceptical of representative democracy. Disguised as critics of populism, these elites aligned their agenda with segments of civil society, whose disruptive protests set the stage for two episodes of military coups. In the end, anti-populist civil society became a handmaiden for the elites' crusade against popular sovereignty. The Thai case invites us to rethink our assumptions on populist threats and inquire deeper into the existing *gatekeepers* that populist supporters resent and seek to change.

What is populism? Does it threaten democracy?

Studies on populism offer diverse definitions with democratic and autocratic connotations. Key scholars suggest that populism is a vehicle for expressing the grievances of those identified as *the people* against the loosely defined *elites*. The people are generally portrayed as authentic and the elites as unresponsive and self-serving (Canovan, 1984; Inoescu & Gellner, 1969; Kazin, 1995). According to Laclau (2005), populism emerges through the elites' failure to fulfil particular demands. It constitutes a 'thin ideology' that can be incorporated into both left and right spectrums of political thought (Stanley, 2008). On the left, populism is an antidote to liberal democracy, which has increasingly imposed the economic framework and cultural values on the people without popular consent. Established political systems, moreover, respond to demands by transnational but unelected institutions, rather than constituents who call for redistribution and participation in decision-making (Mouffe, 2005, 2018). Based on these conceptions, populism bridges the gulf between elites and constituents by recalling the *demos* or *people* to the discussions on democracy (Mudde, 2007).

However, on the right, scholars argue that populism potentially threatens democracy in two ways. First, culturally, populist politics runs counter to democratic pluralism, as it is based on the demarcated boundary between *us*, the people, and *them*, the elites, and the rhetoric that the latter is the adversary of the former. Right-wing populists inject the cultural element into this equation by additionally identifying the foreign 'other' as a threat to the people. Second, procedurally, populists contribute to the ongoing democratic backsliding trend (Levitsky & Ziblatt, 2018; Mounk, 2018). Although democratically elected, populists can exploit the electoral mandate to undermine checks and balances, strangling the expression of oppositional opinion. Populists justify these moves by claiming to represent the voice of the people and discrediting their critics as meddling between them and the people. By weakening the institutional and civic forces that oppose populists, the latter can concentrate executive power, stay in power longer, and possibly refuse to leave office following free and fair elections (Kyle & Mounk, 2018).

However, the challenge to democracy of populism reveals only half of the story, as the populist surge is conditioned by broader socio-political contexts that shape popular dissatisfaction with the establishment. Generally, economic grievances and cultural backlash are attributed to the growth of support for contemporary populist movements in the United States and Europe. Neoliberal policies introduced in the late 1970s, deregulation of business, privatization of state-owned enterprises, and cutbacks in social welfare expenditure (aka austerity) led to the state playing a reduced role in providing social safety nets. Neoliberal globalization that followed the Cold War worsened the socioeconomic circumstances of many, as industries cut costs by transferring manufacturing to developing countries with less rigid labour laws and lower wages than in the West, or through the import of cheaper labour (Brown, 2015; Harvey, 2007). Two decades after venturing into neoliberal economics, the workforce of the most affluent country on earth has earned 134 times more than that of the most impoverished (Milanovic, 2016). In addition, a widening of the income gap between the richest and the rest in developed countries has increased inequality. The hardest hit have been not only the poor, as the middle classes have also experienced downward mobility ('The American Middle Class', 2015). A shift away from the Democrats by middle class voters with declining status and working-class voters in deindustrialized areas who had previously supported Barack Obama contributed to the victory of the Republican Trump in 2016. Similarly-affected groups made the difference in the United Kingdom referendum decision to exit from the European Union in the same year (Dorling et al., 2016).

These economic grievances have been accompanied by identity politics that shaped the perception of *us* against *them*. The majority of supporters of European populist parties are typically patriotic males without college degrees and a world-view esteeming group loyalty, traditional family values, and traditional gender roles. Post-industrial societies saw rapid social changes that have threatened these values (Inglehart & Norris, 2016, pp. 29–30). Moreover, open borders and cultural globalization saw the emergence of a cosmopolitan society with values that threaten the preservation of a single national identity. The increasing trend of the young adult population toward overseas travel and toward living and working in urban areas offers an exposure that generally produces greater tolerance of cultural and gender diversity and the embracing of migrancy. Reflection on these new values is a hallmark of the progressive lifestyle associated with this group and tends to regard traditional values as deplorable (Müller, 2017). Such globalist discourse concerning cultural diversity and political correctness creates a backlash by pushing those questioning these discourses toward the right. Accordingly, the cultural grievances of conservative populists not only focus on foreign threats, but also on those liberal advocates perceived to undermine their values and police their behaviours (Haidt, 2016).

These factors compounded in the rise of populists exemplify layers explaining democratic erosion. Exacerbating economic inequality has undermined the popularity of the notion that a liberal economy tied to democracy can improve livelihoods. Meanwhile, prioritizing liberal, cosmopolitan values has alienated many local patriots whose sense of community belongingness is labelled as *nativism*. The increased distance between alienated population sectors and democratic institutions can be considered an early sign of democratic recession. Populist leaders promise to remedy this by listening and responding to the so-called silent majority. As such, civic efforts to address the populist challenge to the rule of law and freedom of expression may risk overlooking conditions that nurture popular mistrust in democracy (Canovan, 1999). At worst, these efforts may play into the hands of anti-populist elites who are simultaneously anti-democratic. The Thai case illustrates how these dynamics can unfold in a series of democratic breakdowns.

Thailand: weaponizing populism

The term *populism* gained traction in Thailand as the country underwent the longest period of democratic experiments and witnessed the effects of changing power relationships between the old and new political forces. Traditional elites comprising the palace, bureaucrats, the army, and allied businesses had long dominated Thai politics. Excluding brief intervals after the 1932 revolution that toppled the absolute monarchy and 1973 mass demonstrations, the Thai political system was characterized by variations of non-democratic governance, from military rule to civilian autocracy. Traditional elites, particularly, relied on military coups to counter intra-elite conflict and external threats such as communism in the 1970s (Isarabhakdi, 1989). Thus far, there have been thirteen successful military coups and seven coup attempts in Thailand between 1932 and 2016, with twenty constitutions and charters (Chambers, 2015). The 1992 popular uprising broke this vicious cycle briefly by pushing the army back to its barracks and paving the way for the 1997 people's constitution, which was conducive to strengthening the electoral system (Pongsudhira, 2008). Despite some major democratic changes, traditional elites have effectively occupied reserve domains, or bastions of non-democratic political power that allowed them to constrain an elected government's control over the passage, implementation, and enforcement of its own policies (McCargo, 2005).

This veto power remained unchallenged until the emergence of the tycoon-turned-politician Thaksin Shinawatra, categorized as a populist based on his and the elites' political usage of the term. Thaksin's Thai Rak Thai Party (TRT) won a landslide victory in the 2001 and 2005 elections. By holding the supermajority in both lower and upper houses and absorbing smaller parties, the TRT effectively secured its ruling position. Despite overwhelming electoral support, at least initially in his administration, Thaksin showed little sign of becoming a populist. During his 2001 campaign trail, he hardly mentioned the term *the people*. Nor did he express resentment of the establishment (Phongpaichit & Baker, 2008, p. 64). Moreover, Thaksin's allies were broad-based in the 2001 election and included the Bangkok middle class, civil society, and corporate businesses, who praised Thaksin for navigating Thailand through the aftermath of the 1997 economic crisis (McCargo & Pathmanand, 2005, p. 5). However, this pattern changed due to allegations of populism made against Thaksin and his responses to them.

Allegations of populism

Thaksin's policies such as the provision of universal healthcare, agrarian debt relief, and soft loans for communities appealed to the rural population, who had little access to state welfare. These were seen as a source of social mobility and social dignity. Certainly, the image of an empowered rural populace contrasted with the traditional elites depicting them as underdeveloped and thus deserving charitable aid and development projects from the state and especially the palace. This treatment by elites is in line with the portrayal of rural communities as naïve and incapable of electing moral leaders. Contrary to these perceptions, the livelihood and values of rural Thais have been radically transformed by Thailand's economic modernization and urbanization. Thais from rural villages have increasingly migrated to urban areas or other countries in search of better lives, adopting new identities as urbanized or cosmopolitan villagers (Keyes, 2012; Thabchumpon & McCargo, 2011). TRT's policies reflected an understanding of these changing dynamics and accordingly attracted unprecedented support (Phongpaichit & Baker, 2008).

Armed with this static image of the rural constituency, traditional elites and some critics blamed Thaksin's welfare policies for, among other things, brainwashing rural villagers in order to increase his personal popularity and his likelihood of electoral triumph. Immediately after TRT developed an electoral platform, a prominent Thai academic coined the term *poppiewlit* as the Thai adaptation of the English term *populism*. Later, he used the Thai term *pracha-niyom* (literally translating as *people-popular*). A variation, equivalent to *pluto-populist*, was adopted to explain Thaksin's appeal not only to the poor but to small and medium-sized entrepreneurs, brought into an alliance through their nationalism (Phongpaichit & Baker, 2002). At some point, as Hewison (2017, p. 343) notes, populism was linked to the ills and evils that the TRT policies came to represent. These policies were criticized for:

> creating a 'welfare state' *or* being insufficiently welfarist; fostering dependence, reducing self-reliance and self-sufficiency whereby poor citizens were clients queuing up to receive handouts from TRT; being too expensive and emptying state coffers; encouraging consumerism and indebtedness, especially in rural areas where villagers were brainwashed; . . . making Thaksin too popular, leading to a monopolisation of power and a parliamentary dictatorship termed 'Thaksinocracy;' weakening the bureaucracy, technocrats and independent organizations; establishing a populist capitalism to further the interests of big business while also weakening the market mechanism; providing a front for 'policy corruption' enriching Thaksin's cronies.
>
> *Hewison, 2017, p. 343*

University professor turned conservative politician, Anek Laothamatas, warned against the peril of *majoritarian dictatorship*, thus associating populist, but elected, leaders like Thaksin and his rural support with authoritarian underpinnings of populism. In his book *Thaksina-prachaniyom* [*Thaksin-style populism*] published in 2006, Anek argued that

> the rural electorate supported Thaksin because his populist policies were in their self-interest . . . rural voters were not free agents but bound by patron-client ties. . . . In this social setting, a pure democracy was bound to lead to . . . [the] tyranny of the majority and irresponsible populism.
>
> *Laothamatas, 2006, p. 177*

Anek's solution was to counteract representatives of the lower classes who formed the majority with the middle and upper classes (Laothamatas, 2006, pp. 178–179). The latter was identified as 'a small number of upper class people who are leaders or governors of the country at the highest level . . . who command the trust of the majority'—in the Thai context, this clearly implies the monarchy. He also included aristocrats defined as 'the leaders with wisdom and experience in politics and administration, including senior bureaucrats, top intellectuals, and senior journalists' (Laothamatas, 2006, pp. 179, 181).

Anek's thoughts echo Thailand's royal nationalist ideology that dismisses popular sovereignty. As an ideology that provides political legitimacy for such an ancient institution as the Thai monarchy, the royal nationalist ideology places the King at the top of a hierarchical social order as the soul of the nation. Perceived as natural and fixed, this hierarchy also provides a justification for socioeconomic inequality. According to this ideology, charismatic, powerful, and wealthy figures are associated with merit accumulated in their past lives, in line with an interpretation of Buddhist teachings (Ferrara, 2015, p. 5). This ideological order has little room for the notion of popular sovereignty defined as the people; as citizens with equal rights whose consent is the basis for governance (Ferrara, 2015, p. 5). As we shall see, the royalist rhetoric featured powerfully in anti-Thaksin campaigns, eventually overshadowing concerns regarding Thaksin's illiberal tendencies evident in his war on drugs, hawkish approach to ethnic conflict in the south, and crackdown on oppositional NGOs (Chaiwat, 2006). Royalist antagonism toward Thaksin would stoke his turn to populist politics.

Populist responses

In boosting his political legitimacy in the face of growing opposition, Thaksin embraced the populist rhetoric and mass mobilization typical of populist leaders. By late 2004, Thaksin came under increasing attack over a wide range of issues, including alleged corruption. In response, he embarked on a series of nationwide tours, transported by motorcade into villages to receive reports on local problems (Phongpaichit & Baker, 2008, p. 66). On several occasions, he personalized the relationship with his support base by, for instance, promising students in a TRT stronghold that he would spend his own money to buy them laptops. Prior to the 2005 election, TRT had highlighted its connection with the people through a novel slogan: 'The heart of the TRT is the people'. In addition, Thaksin showed his affinity to the people via live broadcasts of his cabinet meetings and favourable scenes from his national campaign tours, for example, with images of him emerging from a village bath-house in a *pakoma* (common male lower cloth), transported on a village tractor, and riding a motorcycle down a dusty village street (Phongpaichit & Baker, 2008, p. 67). By the end of his administration in 2005, he claimed to work for the people, while side-lining critics' allegations of his human rights violations, executive overreach, and corruption. In a public speech, he stressed: 'We want politics with meaning, don't we? We want politics that have something for the people, don't we? And this politics which is destructive, can we get rid of it yet?' (cited in Phongpaichit & Baker, 2008, p. 70).

Only after his ousting by the 2006 military coup did Thaksin become seriously involved in mobilizing mass supporters who viewed themselves as underdogs rebelling against the establishment. In the coup's aftermath, Thaksin went into exile, while the Constitutional Court dissolved the TRT and banned its politicians from running again. Remaining TRT politicians founded the United Front for Democracy Against Dictatorship (UDD), whose members were also known as 'Red Shirts'. The movement mobilized public support to oppose the military junta and pressure it to hold elections. The Red Shirts criticized the social hierarchy that traditional elites were defending by defining themselves as *prai* (peasants), who had revolted against the injustice of *ammart* (aristocrats). During the Red Shirt street protests, Thaksin would phone in from abroad in support of the movement. In these speeches, he deliberately expressed populist sentiment against the elites:

> Providing opportunities for the poor is like invigorating your body. To be strong, you need to invigorate the dying cells. That was what I tried to do. But one day, the military coup took away everything, and people chose to rise against it. When people were hungry, democracy was only for the elite. But now, people have filled their stomachs. And they want more. But the elite don't want change that will affect their already happy lives . . . I am a political victim here, because the elite saw that I'm the one who pushed for democracy. I represent the working class people from rural area[s].
>
> cited in Hewison, 2017, p. 436

Beyond Thaksin, the Red Shirts challenged the royalist social hierarchy by insisting they be granted equal rights to the *ammart* because they are the *people*. Their mobilization represented bottom-up populism, an approach common among leftist grassroots movements (Meade, 2019). When the new Thaksin-backed party won the December 2007 elections, the former prime minister's opponents mobilized once again. In 2008, the Constitutional Court disbanded the Thaksin-affiliated party, allowing the Democrat Party, a long-time ally of the royalist establishment, to lead the governing coalition. For the enraged Red Shirts, this was a plan concocted by elites to dismiss *the will of the people*. Taking to the streets in 2009 and again in 2010, the Red Shirts started explicitly expressing their contempt for traditional elites, especially those within the army and the palace. Leading activists compared the Red Shirts with *dirt* and the elites with the *sky*, cynically asking the latter 'to recognize the Red Shirts' worthless existence' (Phuaphansawat, 2018, p. 371). The Red Shirt 2010 protests turned disruptive, suggestive of a peasant uprising. Elites moved swiftly to quell them, with military forces killing nearly 100 protesters. The entire populist movement was virtually wiped out after the 2014 coup, for which protests by an anti-populism-cum-anti-democracy civil society provided a pretext (Charoenmuang, 2016).

From anti-populism to anti-democracy

Emerging as an anti-Thaksin network, the People's Alliance for Democracy (PAD) set out mainly to oppose populist politics, but its successor, the People's Democratic Reform Committee (PDRC) morphed into an anti-democratic movement. The PAD generally comprised three components banded together in the form of anti-populist, anti-majoritarian, and royalist rhetoric. The first group consisted of NGOs critical of Thaksin's economic policies, including the state-enterprise labour union, AIDS Network, Southern Federation of Small Scale Fishers, Northern Farmer Alliance, Ecology Movement, Alternative Agricultural Network of Isan, Thai Volunteer Service, Consumers' Association, and Slum Dwellers group (Pye & Schaffar, 2008, p. 41). Some of these groups were former Thaksin allies whose pro-poor policies were perceived to empower rural communities. However, the alliance was broken for two reasons. First, parallel with pro-poor policies, Thaksin pursued a neoliberal economic approach that was geared toward the privatization of state-owned enterprises, corporate encroachment on natural resources, and free trade with foreign capital (Kasian, 2006, p. 37). Many NGOs grew critical of these policies, deemed to undermine economic sustainability.

Together with oppositional journalists, they faced a string of police crackdowns (Chaiwat, 2006). Second, many NGOs opposing Thaksin's economic and social policies were driven by a communitarian ideology based on a rural-urban dichotomy and the romanticization of rural community self-reliance (Hewison, 2017, p. 431). Thaksin's welfare policies were simply perceived as cash transfers. Meanwhile, his neoliberal platform disrupted the NGOs' idealized image of a submissive and self-sufficient rural populace. As Pitidol (2016) asserts, this NGO ideology was in line with royalist thinking that eternally places the rural poor under traditional elites' tutelage. Hence, the upward mobility of this population sector is not welcome.

The second component was the urban middle class, who despised Thaksin's virulent *money* politicking, with corruption and cronyism being seen as his greatest sins. Although corruption in Thailand permeates most institutions, accusations in public discourse focus mainly on elected politicians accused of exploiting public funds and positions for their vested interests and of buying votes from the naïve rural masses. As Winichakul (2008, pp. 26–27) notes, the discourse equating elections with corruption emerged at the historical juncture when electoral politics gained traction in the 1980s, thereby threatening the political legitimacy of unelected bodies such as the army and the palace. The notion is based on the comparison of corrupt (thus dirty) elected politicians with moral leaders. As such, the solution is to cleanse politics. This conception fits well with urban prejudices against the rural electorate generally perceived as too uneducated to choose their own leaders (Saxer, 2014, p. 16). Nonetheless, as the country's majority, the rural populace always gets the representatives they voted for. But since these politicians are allegedly corrupt, the middle class believes that they contaminate the *clean* (transparent) politics they prefer (Walker, 2008; Winichakul, 2008, p. 25).

Lastly, the ultra-royalist chapter of the PAD effectively used the royal nationalist discourse to unite the forces against Thaksin and eventually set the scene for the 2006 military putsch. As foremost PAD leaders, the media tycoon Sondhi Limthongkul and retired General Chamlong Srimuang built their media and protest campaigns on the rhetoric of Thaksin as the enemy of 'the nation, the Buddhist establishment, and the King' (Kasian, 2006, p. 36). By politicizing national identity, these figures successfully drew support from sections of the NGOs, urban middle class, and royalist elites, including civil servants and business groups excluded from Thaksin's patronage network. Due to Chamlong's leadership in the Dharma Army section of the *Santi Asoke*, a radical Buddhist sect, members of the Dharma Army joined the ranks of the PAD (Pawakapan, 2013, pp. 58–59). Despite the PAD's diverse advocacies, with some highlighting Thaksin's illiberal practices, royalist criticism of Thaksin eventually prevailed. The Thaksin-led government was analogous to an *electocracy, moneytocracy*, and 'elected capitalist absolutism' (Kasian, 2004) that contrasted with an inherently Thai political system with the righteous King as the head of the state (Winichakul, 2008, p. 27). From late 2005 through to 2006, the PAD called for the restoration of the Royal Prerogative and the King's appointment of a new prime minister and cabinet in Thaksin's place. The palace took note (Kasian, 2006, p. 36). As the PAD protests intensified, Thaksin announced a snap election in April 2006, seeking to restore his mandate. He again won at the polls, but the Constitutional Court annulled the election results. Meanwhile, in a military gathering, a leading member of the King's Privy Council delivered a speech reminding the army of its allegiance to the monarch. In September 2006, amid rising political tensions, the army staged a coup that many civil society members applauded as a 'good coup' (Connors & Hewison, 2008).

Although its political agenda overlapped with that of the PAD, the PDRC represented a more radical stance, not only against populism but against electoral democracy as a whole. The 2006 coup did not completely uproot the TRT and Thaksin. As described earlier, the party reincarnated in the nexus of a grassroots movement and political party that won the 2007 elections. And despite the 2010 crackdown on the Red Shirts, the party currently known as Pheu Thai struck another victory in 2011. By this time, the PAD had faded out, followed by the rise of the PDRC to oppose the Pheu Thai-led government in 2013. The key trigger event was the then government's attempt to pass an amnesty bill seen by critics as a ploy to vindicate self-exiled Thaksin, and another example of murky electoral politics. Spearheaded by Suthep Thaugsuban, a leading politician in the Democrat Party, the movement launched nationwide campaigns entitled *Reform Before Election* that demanded an indefinite end to electoral democracy until the country could rid itself of corrupt politicians (Sinpeng, 2019). In other words, the PDRC's main target was the political system that empowered figures such as Thaksin; the election slogan became a shorthand for the *Thaksin regime*.

The movement attracted support from three segments of society, with some crossover with members of the PAD. The first group comprised student activists and NGOs such as the Student People Network Thailand Reform, the Green Group, and the People Networks from 77 provinces. The second group comprised civil servants and the armed forces. While the latter played no explicit role in the PAD, former generals founded the Pitak Siam, later known as the People's Army to Uproot the Thaksin Regime, which became the PDRC's pivotal ally (Sinpeng, 2019; Sae Chua, 2014). Lastly, former politicians and their constituents constituted a pillar of support for the movement. Suthep, along with eight other MPs of the Democrat Party, quit the party and formally led the PDRC. Suthep, in particular, from being regarded as a rather unpopular politician became a beloved *uncle* or *kamnan*, championing the cause of many disgruntled Thais upset with the Thaksin regime (Sinpeng, 2019). Many participants in the PDRC were from the upper southern provinces, a stronghold of the Democrat Party.

While claiming to represent the *muan maha prachachon* (great mass of people), the PDRC's activism focused on annihilating electoral democracy associated with populism, aiming to cleanse politics and resurrect political morality. First, the movement's campaign messages attacked elected representatives as fundamentally corrupt and thus immoral, in contrast with the good nature of protesters (Kongkirati, 2017). Many justified their antidemocratic activism as a crusade against evil. According to a militant Buddhist monk who spearheaded an extremist chapter of the movement:

> The politicians' behaviours are utterly disgusting. . . . When evil politicians are damaging our country, taking advantage of society and the people, undermining the rule of law, we have to collectively draw on the moral force to wipe them out. . . . I insist that we are doing the right thing.
>
> *cited in Kongkirati, 2017, p. 17*

The PDRC's self-assessment of being morally superior to and more intelligent than the Red Shirts led its members to question the merits of universal suffrage. The PDRC adopted elite prejudices against the rural poor deemed incapable of electing leaders. During their protest speeches, PDRC activists often hurled derogatory expressions that dehumanized Red Shirts; for instance, as the *khon chan tam* (low cast/unwashed), *kwai* (stupid), and *hen gae ngeun* (greedy). According to a PDRC celebrity, the PDRC members were more reasonable than the rural poor, Pheu Thai's support base, because they were more educated and socially more respectable. Although Pheu Thai represented the parliamentary majority, the celebrity, along with other *high society* members of the PDRC, contended that the rural population sector was not qualified to cast votes in the first place (Marshall, 2013). Accordingly, the principle of *one man one vote* could not be applied in Thailand because the quality of lower and upper classes citizens was considered different (Kongkirati, 2016).

Consistent with these thoughts, the PDRC deliberately designed protest actions to hamper an election viewed as a symptom of political corruption. PDRC activists frequently intimidated passers-by and journalists and engaged in head-on clashes with the police and political opponents (Sombatpoonsiri, 2017a). When the government announced snap elections in February 2014, the PDRC mobilized its supporters nationwide to block registration venues and polling stations and attacked voters on site. Approximately 400,000 people were prevented from advance voting, and the election turnout was historically low, mainly due to the obstructions by PDRC protesters. Typically, the Constitutional Court subsequently declared the election result null (Kongkirati, 2016, p. 479). The PDRC ultimately paralyzed Bangkok for nearly seven months. As tensions rose at protest sites, armed clashes between the PDRC and Red Shirt activists escalated. These incidents accounted for the general perception that Thailand was on the brink of civil war, and eventually provided the pretext for the army's seizure of power in May 2014. This was the second episode of a democratic breakdown that Thailand had experienced in less than a decade (Sombatpoonsiri, 2017b, p. 139).

Conclusion

Right-wing and authoritarian populism should be resisted, but without taking into account broader socioeconomic structures that shape the power struggle surrounding populist politics, that resistance can be detrimental to democracy. The Thai case demonstrated that the populist surge corresponded with the upward socioeconomic mobility of rural population sectors, whom traditional elites had designated the *uneducated poor*. Thailand's political liberalization during the 1990s created an opportunity for major parties such as Thai Rak Thai to capture new sectors of support among the electorate. These were the so-called *cosmopolitans*, or urban villagers who demanded that the political elites recognize popular sovereignty. Nonetheless, the advent of the Thaksin administration was characterized not only by grassroots support, but also by broad-based endorsement from the corporate sector and progressive NGOs. As Thaksin came under attack from traditional elites and segments of civil society, he increasingly relied on populist rhetoric by claiming to represent the people. The 2006 coup and its aftermath pushed Thaksin to fully embrace the populist nexus of anti-elite sentiment and mass mobilization. The Red Shirts emerged from this milieu, evolved from an anti-coup network to a grassroots populist movement that effectively challenged the traditional elites.

In this chapter, I have shown that anti-populist discourses in Thailand are rooted in the elite struggle against democracy. The elites patronized rural communities representing the majority of the population as too unready, unintelligent, and impoverished to decide their political fate. This has been the mode of thinking that has underpinned Thailand's long history of authoritarianism until the rise of Thaksin who, one could argue, repainted the image of a vast rural majority to represent an oppressed people pursuing better livelihoods and social upward mobility. This change goes against the grain of the existing political order, thus provoking a reactionary attitude from the elites and conservative traditionalists. The PAD campaigns and PDRC advocacy exemplified how an anti-populist movement could metamorphose into an anti-democracy network. Ultimately, these campaigns justified the military coups of 2006 and 2014. The most recent coup had a disastrous impact on democracy as the junta ruled for five years, imposing draconian laws to strangle all opposition. This led to one of the most anti-democratic constitutions in Thailand's history, and concentrated wealth, as well as power, in a handful of royalist elites. As the 2016 constitution was crafted to the electoral advantage of the pro-junta party, the 2019 elections did little to heal the legacy of the 2014 coup. While the new opposition party, Move Forward, and Pheu Thai Party, respectively won the largest and second largest share of parliamentary seats in the 2023 election, the constitution's authoritarian roots prevented them from forming a ruling coalition. The establishment elites have once again stalled Thailand's democratic progress.

Global anxiety equates rising populism with authoritarianism. The Thai case questions this nexus. Populism is a vehicle, a conversation, a veiled ideology that facilitates the expression of popular demands in the face of elitist obduracy. Whereas a surge of mass populism can threaten a democracy; an elite-captured democracy that fails to represent the interests of the majority can also account for such a surge. In the contemporary socio-political context, an elite-captured democracy drives an increasingly unequal society and growing anger toward cultural minorities deemed allies of the liberal elites. In this sense, populist aspirations demand an overhaul of a failing democracy. Without directly addressing the grievances, the removal of a Trump or Erdoğan figure will not prevent the next wave of populist demagogues. Worse, as the Thai case has illuminated, movements against populist leaders can easily mutate into movements against the fundamental element of democracy, the *demos*.

References

The American middle class is losing ground. (2015, December 9). *Pew Research Center*. www.pewsocialtrends.org/2015/12/09/the-american-middle-class-is-losing-ground/

Aziz, S., & Rehman, A. (2017, December 20). Donald Trump should expect a carnival of resistance on the streets of London. *New Statesman*. www.newstatesman.com/world/2017/12/donald-trump-should-expect-carnival-resistance-streets-london

Beauchamp, Z. (2017, Janurary 20). White riot: How racism and immigration gave us Trump, Brexit, and a whole new kinds of politics. *Vox*. www.vox.com/2016/9/19/12933072/far-right-white-riot-trump-brexit

Brown, W. (2015). *Undoing the demos: Neoliberalism's stealth revolution*. Zone Books.

Cagaptay, S., & Aktas, O. R. (2017, July 7). How Erdoganism is killing Turkish democracy. The end of political opposition. *Foreign Affairs*. www.foreignaffairs.com/articles/turkey/2017-07-07/how-erdoganism-killing-turkish-democracy?cid=int-lea &pgtype=hpg

Canovan, M. (1984). 'People', politicians and populism. *Government and Opposition*, 19(3), 312–327. https://doi.org/10.1111/j.1477-7053.1984.tb01048.x

Canovan, M. (1999). Trust the people! Populism and the two faces of democracy. *Political Studies*, 47(1), 2–16. https://doi.org/10.1111/1467-9248.00184

Caruso, C. (2017, November 15). Count love project reveals protest patterns. *The Brink*. www.bu.edu/articles/2017/counting-american-protests/

Chaiwat, S. (2006). Fostering authoritarian democracy: The effect of violent solutions in southern Thailand. In V. R. Hadiz (Ed.), *Empire and neoliberalism in Asia* (pp. 169–187). Routledge.

Chambers, P. (2015). Civil military relations in Thailand since the 2014 coup. The tragedy of security sector 'deform'. *Peace Research Institute Frankfurt (RRIF), Report* 138. www.hsfk.de/en/publications/publication-search/publication/civil-military-relations-in-thailand-since-the-2014-coup/

Charoenmuang, T. (2016). The Red Shirts and their democratic struggle in northern Thailand, April 2010 to May 2015. In *Trends in Southeast Asia*. ISEAS.

Chase, J. (2018, May 27). AfD outnumbered 4–1 in Berlin demo. *Deutsche Welle*. www.dw.com/en/in-berlin-20000-detractors-shout-down-5000-afd-protesters/a-43948489

Chenoweth, E. (2017, February 1). It may only take 3.5% of the population to topple a dictator with civil resistance. *The Guardian*. www.theguardian.com/commentisfree/2017/feb/01/worried-american-democracy-study-activist-techniques

Connors, K. M., & Hewison, K. (2008). Introduction: Thailand and the 'good coup'. *Journal of Contemporary Asia*, *38*(1), 1–10. https://doi.org/10.1080/00472330701651929

Dorling, D., Stuart, B., & Stubbs, J. (2016, December 22). Brexit, inequality and the demographic divide. In *LSE Blog*. London School of Economics and Political Science. http://blogs.lse.ac.uk/politicsandpolicy/brexit-inequality-and-the-demographic-divide/

Dunai, M. (2017, April 26). Hungarian opposition struggles to build on anti-Orban sentiment. *Reuters*. www.reuters.com/article/us-hungary-soros-politics-opposition-ana-idUSKBN17S1FB

Ferrara, F. (2015). *The political development of modern Thailand*. Cambridge University Press.

Finchelstein, F. (2019). *From fascism to populism in history*. University of California Press.

Haidt, J. (2016, July 10). When and why nationalism beats globalism. *The American Interest*, *12*(1). www.the-american-interest.com/2016/07/10/when-and-why-nationalism-beats-globalism/

Hartocollis A., & Alcindor Y. (2017, January 21). Women's march highlights as huge crowds protest Trump: 'We're not going away.' *New York Times*. https://www.nytimes.com/2017/01/21/us/womens-march.html

Harvey, D. (2007). Neoliberalism as creative destruction. *The ANNALS of the American Academy of Political and Social Science*, *610*(1), 22–44. https://doi.org/10.1177/0002716206296780

Hewison, K. (2017). Reluctant populists: Learning populism in Thailand. *International Political Science Review*, *38*(4), 426–440. https://doi.org/10.1177/0192512117692801

Inglehart, R. F., & Norris, P. (2016). *Trump, Brexit, and the rise of populism: Economic have-nots and cultural backlash* (HKS Faculty Research Working Paper Series RWP16–026). Harvard Kennedy School. www.hks.harvard.edu/publications/trump-brexit-and-rise-populism-economic-have-nots-and-cultural-backlash

Inoescu, G., & Gellner, E. (Eds.) (1969). *Populism: Its meaning and national characteristics*. Macmillan.

Isarabhakdi, V. (1989). *The man in khaki—debaser or developer? The Thai military in politics, with particular reference to the 1976–1986 period* [PhD Dissertation]. Tufts University.

Kasian, T. (2004). *But kap thaksin: Rabop amnatniyom khwa mai thai-amerikan* [*Bush and Thaksin: Thai and US neoconservative authoritarianism*]. Kopfai.

Kasian, T. (2006). Toppling Thaksin. *New Left Review*, *39*, 5–37.

Kazin, M. (1995). *The populist persuasion: An American history*. Basic Books.

Kelly, L. (2017, May 7). Several thousand Poles protest against right-wing ruling party. *Reuters*. www.reuters.com/article/us-poland-politics-protests/several-thousand-poles-protest-against-right-wing-ruling-party-idUSKBN1820JN

Keyes, C. (2012). 'Cosmopolitan' villagers and populist democracy in Thailand. *South East Asia Research*, *20*(3), 343–360. https://doi.org/10.5367/sear.2012.0109

Kongkirati, P. (2016). Thailand's failed 2014 election: The anti-election movement, violence and democratic breakdown. *Journal of Contemporary Asia*, *46*(3), 467–485. https://doi.org/10.1080/00472336.2016.1166259

Kongkirati, P. (2017). *Virtuous warfare, moral violence and uncivil disobedience: The politics of 'good' people in Thailand's crisis (2013–2014)*. Unpublished research paper.

Kyle, J., & Mounk, Y. (2018, December 26). *The populist harm to democracy: An empirical assessment*. Tony Blair Institute for Global Change. https://institute.global/policy/populist-harm-democracy-empirical-assessment

Laclau, E. (2005). *On populist reason*. Verso.

Laothamatas, A. (2006). *Thaksina-prachani yom* [*Thaksin-style populism*]. Matichon Books.

Levitsky, S., & Ziblatt, D. (2018). *How democracies die: What history reveals about our future*. Penguin.

Lopez, G. (2018, January 23). A year after the first Women's March, millions are still actively protesting Trump. *Vox New*. www.vox.com/policy-and-politics/2018/1/23/16922884/womens-march-attendance

Marshall, A. R. C. (2013, December 14). High society hits the streets as prominent Thais join the protests. *Reuters*. www.reuters.com/article/thailand-protests-idUKL3N0JS1TC20131213

McCargo, D. (2005). Network monarchy and legitimacy crises in Thailand. *The Pacific Review*, 18(4), 499–519. https://doi.org/10.1080/09512740500338937

McCargo, D., & Pathmanand, U. (2005). *The thaksinization of Thailand*. NAIS Press.

Meade, R. (2019). Populist narratives from below: Occupy Wall Street and the Tea Party. *Populisms dans les Amériques*, 14. https://doi.org/10.4000/ideas.5833/

Milanovic, B. (2016). *Global inequality: A new approach for the age of globalization*. Harvard University Press.

Milman, O. (2017, April 22). March for science puts Earth Day focus on global opposition to Trump. *The Guardian*. www.theguardian.com/environment/2017/apr/22/march-for-science-earth-day-climate-change-trump

Moffitt, B. (2015). How to perform crisis: A model for understanding the key role of crisis in contemporary populism. *Government and Opposition*, 50(2), 189–271. https://doi.org/10.1017/gov.2014.13

Mouffe, C. (2005). *The democratic paradox*. Verso.

Mouffe, C. (2018). *For a left populism*. Verso.

Mounk, Y. (2018). *The people vs. democracy: Why our freedom is in danger and how to save it*. Harvard University Press.

Mudde, C. (2007). *Populist radical right parties in Europe*. Cambridge University Press.

Müller, J.-W. (2016). *What is populism?* University of Pennsylvania Press.

Müller, J.-W. (2017). A majority of 'deplorables'. *Social Europe Journal*, 11, 20–21. https://social-europe.eu/a-majority-of-deplorables

Norris, P. (2017). *Is western democracy backsliding? Diagnosing the risks* (HKS Faculty Research Working Paper Series RWP17–012). Harvard Kennedy School. https://doi.org/10.2139/ssrn.2933655

Pawakapan, P. R. (2013). *State and uncivil society in Thailand at the temple of preah vihear*. ISEAS—Yusof Ishak Institute.

Peto, S. (2018, April 22). Tens of thousands of Hungarians protest against PM Orban's rule. *Reuters*. www.reuters.com/article/us-hungary-protest/tens-of-thousands-of-hungarians-protest-against-pm-orbans-rule-idUSKBN1HS0KN

Phongpaichit, P., & Baker, C. (2002). *The only good populist is a rich populist: Thaksin Shinawatra and Thailand's democracy* (Working Paper Series No. 36). City University of Hong Kong, Southeast Asia Research Centre.

Phongpaichit, P., & Baker, C. (2008). Thaksin's populism. *Journal of Contemporary Asia*, 38(1), 62–83. https://doi.org/10.1080/00472330701651960

Phuaphansawat, K. (2018). Anti-royalism in Thailand since 2006: Ideological shifts and resistance. *Journal of Contemporary Asia*, 48(3), 363–394. https://doi.org/10.1080/00472336.2018.1427021

Pitidol, T. (2016). Redefining democratic discourse in Thailand's civil society. *Journal of Contemporary Asia*, 46(3), 520–537. https://doi.org/10.1080/00472336.2016.1164229

Pongsudhirak, T. (2008). Thailand since the coup. *Journal of Democracy*, 19(4), 140–153. http://dx.doi.org/10.1353/jod.0.0030

Pye, O., & Schaffar, W. (2008). The 2006 anti-Thaksin movement in Thailand: An analysis. *Journal of Contemporary Asia*, 38(1), 38–61. https://doi.org/10.1080/00472330701651945

Sae Chua, B. (2014, September 23). Revisiting 'people's politics.' *Society for Cultural Anthropology*. https://culanth.org/fieldsights/revisiting-peoples-politics

Saxer, M. (2014). *Fighting corruption in transformation societies*. Friedrich Ebert Stiftung. https://library.fes.de/pdf-files/bueros/thailand/10744.pdf

Sinpeng, A. (2019). From the yellow shirts to the whistle rebels: Comparative analysis of the People's Alliance for Democracy (PAD) and the People's Democratic Reform Committee (PDRC). In P. Chachavalpongpun (Ed.), *Routledge handbook of contemporary Thailand* (pp. 145–155). Routledge.

Sombatpoonsiri, J. (2017a). The 2014 military coup in Thailand: Implications on political conflicts and resolution. *Asian Journal Peacebuilding*, 5(1), 131–154. https://doi.org/10.18588/201705.00a022

Sombatpoonsiri, J. (2017b). The policing of anti-government protests: Thailand's 2013–2014 demonstrations and a crisis of police legitimacy. *Journal of Asian Security and International Affairs*, *4(1)*, 95–122. https://doi.org/10.1177/2347797016689224

Stanley, B. (2008). The thin ideology of populism. *Journal of Political Ideologies*, *13(1)*, 95–110. https://doi.org/10.1080/13569310701822289

Strzelecki, M. (2016, December 14). Polish leader marks crackdown with plans to curb opposition. *Bloomberg*. www.bloomberg.com/news/articles/2016-12-13/polish-leader-marks-communist-crackdown-by-plan-to-curb-dissent

Taylor, A. (2017, January 30). A weekend of protest against Trump's immigration ban. *The Atlantic*. www.theatlantic.com/photo/2017/01/a-weekend-of-protest-against-trumps-immigration-ban/514953/

Thabchumpon, N., & McCargo, D. (2011). Urbanized villagers in the 2010 Thai Redshirt protests: Not just poor farmers? *Asian Survey*, *51(6)*, 993–1018. https://doi.org/10.1525/AS.2011.51.6.993

Walker, A. (2008). The rural constitution and the everyday politics of elections in northern thailand. *Journal of Contemporary Asia*, *38(1)*, 84–105. https://doi.org/10.1080/00472330701651978

Wiegel, D. (2017, January 15). Democrats rally across the country to save and expand Obamacare. *The Washington Post*. www.washingtonpost.com/news/powerpost/wp/2017/01/15/democrats-rally-across-the-country-to-save-and-expand-obamacare/?utm_term=.537283dfdc8d

Winichakul, T. (2008). Toppling democracy. *Journal of Contemporary Asia*, *38(1)*, 11–37. https://doi.org/10.1080/00472330701651937

22
SOUTH KOREA
Still the 'politics of the vortex'?[1] A historical analysis of party solidarities and populism

Kan Kimura

Introduction

In South Korea, much of the conversation about populism came after the 2016/2017 presidential impeachment, as it ignited a fierce debate about whether or not the event should be considered populist and, if so, to what extent South Korea was likely to fall prey to the evils associated with populism.

Harris, 2022, p. 40

In 2017, media company Intelligence Squared presented an online debate with the sensational title, 'Western Democracy Is Threatening Suicide' (2017). The same year, South Korean President Park Geun-hye was impeached after massive demonstrations across the country, with media commentators and scholars suggesting that an international wave of populism was impacting the country.

Is South Korea really moving towards populism and, if so, does this reflect an international trend? To examine the concept of populism in the context of a particular country, we first need to define the term. However, even among academics, the range of applicability of the term remains contested. For example, Mueller describes it as follows:

The term 'populism' is agreed among journalists, theoreticians and participants in *contemporary* political discourse to stand for a kind of platform or politician who engages in confrontational anti-establishment politics aimed at displacing the governing elites in representative liberal constitutional democracies and everything that politically enabled them. In this generic sense, populism is a particular phenomenon, a *stance* exercised towards liberal democracy and not merely an *anomaly*—like a transitory anti-system protest vote intended to shake traditional parties up—owed to special circumstances. Instead, it is a sort of permanent possibility in liberal representative democratic politics, like 'democracy's shadow'.

Mueller, 2019, p. 1026 (emphasis in original)

The concept of populism has been used in diverse ways to explain a variety of political situations. Populism is a political phenomenon that is invariably associated with political leaders. There are several examples in the post-independence political history of South Korea of leaders who effectively used a populist strategy, the best-known being Syngman Rhee and Roh Moo-Hyun. Weyland redefined this wide-ranging concept by ascertaining where different usages of the word overlapped and concluded the following:

> Populism is best defined as a political strategy. Political strategies are characterized by the power capability that types of rulers use to sustain themselves politically. Under populism the ruler is an individual, a personalistic leader, not a group or organization. Populism rests on the power capability of numbers, not special weight. Populism emerges when personalistic leaders base their rule on massive yet mostly uninstitutionalized support from large numbers of people.
>
> *Weyland, 2001, p. 18*

Weyland thus defines populism as a leadership strategy in which the political leader attempts to mobilize people directly, often bypassing intermediate organizations. He further identifies the following points related to populism that we will explore: (1) how political leaders set up relations with the people, (2) the roles that political leaders assign to intermediate organizations, and (3) how political leaders' strategies actually work. This chapter will explain the historical relationship between politics and populism in South Korea, focusing mainly on these three elements from the country's independence in 1948 to the end of the Moon Jae-in administration in 2022.

Populism under the *father of the nation*

How South Korea gained independence in 1948 is fundamental to understanding the context of populism in the country's political history. As was the case in other countries formerly under colonial rule, the basic framework of politics in South Korea was established in the process of decolonization (Kimura, 2021).[2] The implication here is that decolonization was tantamount to a revolution that significantly shifted the balance between society and politics (Geertz, 1973, pp. 234–238).

While the set of historical, demographic, social, and political factors governing the independence of each formerly colonized country was unique, how these factors impacted on post-colonial politics and related institutions can be grouped into three comparative categories. For example, in countries that experienced armed struggles in the process of gaining independence (such as Vietnam), strong political parties—some even with their own military institutions—were essential for the transition. This meant that political leaders in those countries could use these parties as instruments even after independence (category A).

A similar situation can be found in nations that experienced peaceful mass movements in the process of decolonization, such as India. In such cases, a large national organization had to be established for mobilization purposes. Political leaders could use this as the parent organization of the ruling party after the nation had acquired independence (category B).

Alternately, in countries where independence was *granted* by the colonial power after peaceful negotiation, such as the Philippines, a powerful organization that could mobilize the masses was unnecessary. The process of decolonization was smooth rather than revolutionary, and the social systems established under colonial rule were largely preserved. This meant that after independence, political leaders in these nations could rely on the colonial and/or traditional system as a means of control. Typically, political leaders were colonial elites who effectively exercised control via the patron-client system fostered under the colonial regime through intermediate organizations (category C).

Decolonization also affected political leaders. In countries in categories A and B, political leaders were heroes of the independence movements, thus enjoying national adulation as the *fathers of the nation*. In countries belonging to category C, however, political leaders had to rely directly on the old patron-client system to establish and maintain control, in the absence of heroic roles in independence movement.

South Korea does not fall under any of the three aforementioned categories, and compared to the decolonization process in other nations, the South Korean process was unique (Kimura, 2021). Although South Koreans also had a national movement against the ruling colonial power, local nationalists were severely dealt with. As a result, no strong national organization was ever established in South Korea before the country gained independence.

For South Korea's political leaders, it was almost impossible to find a national organization sufficiently powerful in scope to be the parent of the upcoming ruling party. The country's unique decolonization process also damaged the old patron-client system fostered under Japanese rule because colonial elites on the Korean Peninsula had collaborated with the colonial power in the total war system. This collaboration heavily damaged the legitimacy of the colonial elites and made it inconceivable for them to use the existing patron-client system as an *intermediate organization* for their leadership after the nation gained independence.

In short, the political development of post-independence South Korea was burdened from the start by two systemic constraints. First, there were no influential intermediate organizations on which political leaders could depend, and second, the colonial elites lacked the legitimacy enjoyed by the leaders of other independence movements.

It was against this backdrop that Syngman Rhee became the first president of South Korea. He was elected because he had an important advantage over other political leaders at the time in terms of legitimacy as the leader of a new nation (Lew, 2017; Kimura, 2003). Rhee was one of the oldest leaders of the independence movement against the Japanese occupation. More importantly, he spent most of Korea's years under colonial rule in exile in the United States and thus had no record of collaboration with the Japanese. To his advantage, the United States had occupied the southern half of the Korean Peninsula after the defeat of Japan in World War II. This created a widespread popular expectation of continuing good relations with the United States.

Rhee could have gained overwhelming legitimacy as *father of the nation* after South Korea's independence, but despite his popularity, he could find no dependable political organization to support him in the manner that the Congress Party had backed Nehru in India (Tharoor, 2003). The old colonial elites in South Korea continuously realigned themselves and failed to establish such an organization.

Consequently, Rhee adopted a populist strategy, appealing to the people directly and not relying on political parties, which he went to the extent of publicly criticizing (Kim,

2019). As part of his administration's official ideology called *Ilminism*, or the *One People Principle*, he insisted that:

> Korea is a nation and has to be unified to survive in the international society. We call this 'Ilminism'. We have to terminate partisanism and develop this ideology. For that, we also have to disseminate it to all the people, to make them fully understand it. Just by doing this, our thirty-million-strong nation can obtain happiness.
>
> Rhee, 1947, p. 7

Trial and error in establishing a *governmental party*

It was not easy for Rhee to maintain his popularity in the long term using only the conception that he was 'father' of the nation. As the leader of a divided nation on a major Cold War front, he struggled to preserve the promised political and economic stability. The Korean War, which broke out in 1950, destroyed the nation, creating widespread frustration and a sense of despair. Rhee repeatedly used physical violence to suppress the people's dissatisfaction and maintain political stability.

Rhee thus abandoned his original populist strategy (Kim, 2019, pp. 12–14). In 1951, he established his own political party, the Liberal Party, despite criticizing political parties in the late 1940s as part of his official ideology of Ilminism. However, he could not find any reliable social base or intermediate organization for the party, which had to depend directly on its own power to mobilize government organizations. In the late 1950s, Rhee formed a *governmental party system* in which the ruling party and government organizations were integrated. Government officials were directly mobilized to campaign for the ruling party, while in the counting of votes in elections, cheating was rampant.

The above experience of South Korea, characterized by a shift from the populism of the father of the nation to an authoritarian regime supported by the governing party, was not unique among newly independent nations after World War II. Many 'national fathers' in such countries enjoyed considerable popularity at the beginning of their regimes based on the people's post-independence hopes but could not maintain their popularity for long due to the dire post-colonial economic and political conditions in their countries. As a result, the population soon became disillusioned with the leader's performance.

The fathers of these nations, however, were generally unwilling to relinquish leadership. They strongly believed that having led their associated independence movements, they were the legitimate and rightful leaders of their countries and attempted to entrench their power using government organizations. We find typical examples in Indonesia and Ghana. In Indonesia, seeing disorder after the general election in 1955, Sukarno introduced a system of 'guided democracy' from above (Tan, 1967). Ghana's national father, Nkrumah, also repressed the anti-government movements and established a one-party system (Omari, 1971).

Ironically, these organizations were inherited from the colonial era and had previously been used to suppress independence movements. The fathers of these nations became dependent on the same system once used to suppress the anti-colonial movements they had led in order to quell post-independence anti-government movements and preserve their power.

The government organizations that the South Korean government inherited from the Japanese empire, via the U.S. occupation from 1945 to 1948, were originally used to sustain Japan's total war and were efficient and robust for mobilization purposes (Choi, 1998).

For several years, Rhee's administration seemed to have successfully entrenched his political leadership in South Korea with support from strong government organizations. However, the overt mobilization of government organizations to suppress the opposition triggered a harsh backlash against his administration. During the April Revolution in 1960, Rhee was forced to resign as president in the face of a massive anti-government demonstration against allegations of cheating in the presidential election, which he was officially declared to have won, to secure a third consecutive term. As South Korea belonged to the Western bloc during the Cold War, and its people considered their country democratic, Rhee's rough dependence on government organizations to prop up his rule impacted his legitimacy as a democratic leader and finally caused the demise of his administration.

After Rhee's fall, the unstable political situation continued because the new political leaders in the country could likewise not find any stable political support base. Again, the political elites kept realigning, and this chaotic situation paved the way for the military coup of Park Chung-Hee in 1961 (Pyeonjipbu, 1997, pp. 145–155).

The establishment of reliable political bases that befit a democratic system was also a daunting task for the Park administration. From the start, Park lacked legitimacy as the leader of a democratic nation, as he had seized power by means of a coup. His career history also proved to be a handicap (Kim & Vogel, 2013). Prior to independence, Park was a military officer of the Manchurian Empire, which was under the control of the Japanese, and thus, he had no legitimacy in terms of the independence movement. He had also been a member of the Workers Party of South Korea, a sister party of the North Korean ruling party, in the late 1940s. This allegiance was repeatedly raised by his political rivals, who insisted that Park was unsuitable to lead an *anti-communist country* on a major Cold War front.

Park's lack of legitimacy precluded the use of a populist strategy to maintain power, as Rhee had done. He thus established his own intermediate organization, which developed into the Democratic Republican Party (DRP), to support his administration. To broaden his support base, he recruited several former opposition leaders and touted the success of his economic development measures (Pyeonjipbu, 1997, pp. 155–161).

Despite the significant economic development initiated under Park's administration, he failed to obtain adequate public support to sustain the long-term regime he wanted. In the National Diet election of 1971, the DRP failed to obtain the required two-thirds majority vote to amend the Constitution and give Park an additional term as president. In 1972, he staged a *coup from above*, known as the Yushin coup d'état, that ushered in another authoritarian era for South Korea (Kleiner, 2001).

Park was assassinated in 1979 and Chun Doo-Hwan seized power by means of another military coup the following year, after a short period of democracy referred to as the *Spring in Seoul*. Facing severe criticism at home and internationally for his coup and the subsequent tragic Gwangju massacre, in which hundreds of people against the coup and martial law installed by the military government were killed, Chun announced his plan to 'restore justice in the government and remove the fraud and corruption of Park's tenure'. As a result, the democratic system was partially restored, along with democratic competition between the ruling and opposition parties (Kimura, 2013, pp. 107–108).

The major arena of political competition under the Chun administration was the National Diet election. Chun introduced direct elections to the Diet but continued the government-controlled indirect electoral system for the presidency. To win the National Diet election, however, Chun required some form of support (Kimura, 2013). In this regard, he committed the same mistake as Park and organized a new ruling party, the Democratic

Justice Party (DJP), recruiting old opposition leaders to impart some degree of legitimacy. Still hampered by the tragic Gwangju massacre, the DJP failed to obtain adequate popular support. In 1985, the National Diet election outcome reflected the DJP's continuing failure against the dramatic impact of the newly formed opposition party, the New Korean Democratic Party (NKDP), led by prominent opposition leaders such as Kim Young-Sam and Kim Dae-Jung. Although the NKDP did not gain a majority, its unforeseen breakthrough in becoming the major opposition party after the election served as a clear signal of the start of a renewed democratic movement, placing South Korea once a again on a path towards democratization in 1987.

Democratization and regionalism

As we have seen, one of the major characteristics of South Korean political history is the absence of strong intermediate organizations for political mobilization. Theoretically, in such a situation, political leaders have only two options. The first is to adopt a populist strategy, as Syngman Rhee had done early in his political career, appealing directly to the public by issuing personal messages and relying on the leader's personal legitimacy, in Rhee's case as father of the nation.

In South Korea, this strategy worked for Rhee due to his long career as a leader of the independence movement. The leaders who followed, Park and Chun, were forced to deploy alternative strategies. However as political leaders who seized power via a military coup, using their personal past records to obtain the peoples' support in democratic elections was futile.

Hence, the only option for both Park and Chun was to establish a new political organization. This is the second option for political leaders lacking strong intermediate organizations for political mobilization. This was undertaken through two approaches. The first was to invite former opposition leaders to join their parties, which was generally unsuccessful, as these leaders soon lost their personal popularity after being seen to betray the opposition and democracy. The other and more important method was to use government organizations. However, Park and Chun's mobilization of such organizations for their own ends further damaged their legitimacy as leaders of a democratic nation. It was for this reason that a group of political leaders decided to subvert the democratic system with a coup, as Park had done in 1972.

Henderson (1968) aptly referred to the political and social situation in South Korea as *the politics of the vortex*. The term captures the overreliance on patronage and family and its consequences, namely the corresponding weakness of intermediate organizations and institutions. This term has thus been borrowed for the title of this chapter. The lack of an intermediate organization as a stable support base was also a dilemma for opposition leaders. As had been the case prior to the April Revolution of 1960 and the Spring in Seoul of 1980, opposition leaders repeatedly changed allegiance and failed to formulate a solid political base against the authoritarian regime. This was another reason why South Korea experienced political instability for decades.

There was a manifest change after democratization in 1987. The major political leaders of the period, Roh Tae-Woo, Kim Young-Sam, Kim Dae-Jung, and Kim Jong-Phil, represented different provinces and mobilized people on the basis of their regional identities to consolidate support (Kwon, 2004). There had been a long history of regional rivalry in South Korea, which intensified under authoritarian regimes. Park and Chun were both from Kyeongsampuk-do Province, and under their rule, they appointed officials from their province to major national government posts. Similarly, a disproportionate share of the fruits of state-led economic development was also distributed to their province, which became a source of frustration for the remainder of the population.

Roh Tae-Woo, who, like Chun, was from Kyeongsampuk-do Province and an important ally of his in the military coups, inherited the network established under authoritarian administration. The two major political heroes of the democratization movement, Kim Young-Sam and Kim Dae-Jung, from Kyeongsangnam-do and Cholla-do respectively, founded their own political parties, together with supporters with strong local identities and a prominent record of advocacy for democratization. The husband of Park's niece, Kim Jong-Phil, who had served as Prime Minister under the Park administration, was originally a successor of the political faction led by Park Chung-Hee, but also mobilized his home province, Chungcheong-do, to establish his own party.

In the late 1980s and 1990s, the aforementioned political leaders, collectively known as *One Roh and Three Kims*, monopolized the political arena in South Korea, establishing a stronghold in their respective home provinces on the basis of *regionalism*. Although their parties experienced realignments during election periods due to political opportunism, their party bases in the provinces remained largely intact, facilitating party realignments without fear of losing local support.

The Asian financial crisis and populism

By the time of the 1997 Asian financial crisis, South Korea seemed to finally manifest reliable and stable intermediate organizations rooted in local identities. However, the situation changed once again at the beginning of the 2000s for several reasons.

The first was the retirement of major political actors. The political parties organized after democratization were originally founded to support key actors from their regions who embodied local identity, as in the case of Kim Dae-Jung from Cholla-do Province. However, one by one during the 1990s, they were forced to retire from the political arena. Roh Tae-Woo, Kim Young-Sam, and Kim Dae-Jung were successively elected president in the 1987, 1992, and 1997 elections, respectively, after which they retired from politics due to the constitutional prohibition against re-election. The last major political actor in this league, Kim Jung-Phil, whose support base was insufficient for election as president, lost his seat in the 2004 National Diet election and decided to call it a day. In losing their founders, the political parties gradually lost their solidarity.

The second and more important reason for the change in the political outlook at the beginning of the 2000s was the after-effects of the Asian financial crisis. As Haggard (1990) noted, South Korea was by then one of the most successful state-led economies in East Asia, and the people's trust in their political representatives was linked to this success. However, the 1997 crisis revealed that their state-led economy was becoming dated in the face of globalization. During the crisis, the Kim Young-Sam administration repeatedly mismanaged the economy and was finally forced to surrender to the dictates of the International Monetary Fund (IMF) at the end of 1997, in exchange for standby credits (Onishi, 2004). The government accepted the conditions of the IMF, and the population had to endure economic austerity for several years, in accordance with the measures prescribed by this financial body. The Kim Young-Sam administration's day of surrender to the IMF is widely referred to as *the second day of national humiliation*, the first being the day when Korea was conquered by Japan in 1910. South Korea's national identity was severely damaged by this experience.

It was natural for the Korean people to lose confidence in the political elites, blamed at the time for the crisis. However, the decline in the people's trust in the political elites after the Asian financial crisis was not unique to South Korea; it could also be observed in other countries in East Asia. This situation led to the emergence of new political leaders, such as Chen Sui-bien in Taiwan, Shinawatra in Thailand, Estrada in the Philippines, and Koizumi in Japan, who exhibited several similarities in their political strategies and messaging. They emerged during a time of economic difficulties, became popular using rhetoric criticizing the old elites, advocated social reform, and attempted to deliver messages directly via social media, bypassing the old-fashioned party systems. In short, they displayed the typical political characteristics of populist leaders on their paths to leadership in their respective countries (Kimura, 2007).

While conditions in South Korea at the time were similar to those in many other East Asian countries after the Asian financial crisis, the nation's experience was the most negative in the region. At the start of the millennium, levels of trust in the government were the lowest in the region at 10% (Kimura, 2007, pp. 287–288). Trust in South Korean national politics had thus collapsed, and political elites were severely criticized. Support for political parties declined, as did their symbolic provincial character. Consequently, the political arena in South Korea was returning to the politics of the vortex.

In the early 2000s, it was up to South Korean political leaders to restore the legitimacy of politics. However, in light of the circumstances that prevailed after democratization, restoration could not be achieved through mobilization of government organizations, as was done by Rhee, Park, and Chun and their authoritarian administrations. This was prohibited by the Constitution and the nation would never have accepted a repeat of this strategy.

South Korean political leaders again resorted to a populist strategy. Two factors underpinned the use of this strategy. The first was that the old elites were extremely unpopular, as mentioned earlier. It is well known that criticizing old elites is one of the most effective populist strategies. Such messaging reinforces the distance of current leaders from the old elites and instructs the audience that they are on their side. The approach is particularly effective after a severe economic crisis, in which it is likely that the legitimacy of the old elites will have been destroyed. That was what occurred in South Korea in the wake of the 1997 Asian financial crisis and the time was therefore ideal for current and emerging leaders to adopt a populist strategy.

Another factor that can persuade political leaders to use a populist strategy is an adequate level of internet infrastructure. After the financial crisis, the South Korean government found that online diffusion was a key tool that could be deployed for economic recovery and made huge investments in internet infrastructure (Lee et al., 2003). In 2002, broadband coverage in the country had reached 21.3%, and South Korea ranked number one globally in this category. Like many other politicians around the world, those in South Korea also found the internet to be a very effective tool for conveying their messages directly to the public, bypassing party organizations and the mainstream media.

The new populist leaders appealed directly to the public using social media and delivering strong messages of criticism for the old elites. Roh Moo-Hyun did this during the 2002 presidential election. He was a lawyer who had played an important role in the country's democratization movement, although not at the level of prominence of Kim Young-Sam or

Kim Dae-Jung. At the beginning of the election year, he was considered a minor candidate of the ruling party, and it was generally expected the party would choose a candidate from among the seasoned politicians such as Lee In-je, the governor of Kyeongsangnam-do Province, who had run for president in 1997. However, Roh's discourse calling for reform, along with powerful criticism of the old elites, including those in the same party, caused an explosion in the political arena. This was boosted by his candour and liberal image based on his involvement in democratization. The people, still vexed and burdened by post-financial crisis economic constraints, welcomed this new star in the political arena. A social media group known as *Nosamo* ('gathering of people who love Roh Moo-Hyun') was formed and eagerly volunteered to support Roh's campaign (Sheafer, 2008).

Nationalist sentiment in South Korea also favoured Roh Moo-Hyun's campaign. In June 2002, a U.S. army vehicle struck and killed two 14-year-old South Korean schoolgirls, an incident that triggered strong anti-U.S. sentiment. Large demonstrations occurred on the streets, and Roh insisted that the incident reflected South Korea's *unequal relations* with the United States, calling for reform of the U.S.-South Korean alliance.

Against this backdrop, Roh was elected president and maintained his populist style of leadership even after his victory. Roh and his allies in the ruling party continued their criticism of mainstream politicians under the previous Kim Dae-Jung administration, including those in their party, and finally split the party in November 2003. The remaining members of the party aligned with the opposition to impeach Roh, and his presidency was terminated in March 2004. Two months later, amid strong popular opposition, the Constitutional Court overruled the impeachment. In April 2004, immediately after the decision, Roh's new Uri Party gained a landslide victory in the National Diet election, and Roh appeared to have stabilized his political base (Lee, 2005).

The overturning of Roh's impeachment marked a renewal political instability in the country. The popularity of his administration depended heavily on his personal popularity, which soon began to ebb. For one, as the constitution prohibited his re-election, he became a political lame duck as he neared the end of his term. Although people welcomed Roh's messaging about social reform, they soon learned that he did not have effective prescriptions for such reform. As the Asian financial crisis had shown, the South Korean economic slump was closely linked to the globalization of the world economy since the 1990s, and there was no quick national solution. Roh's ambition to reposition South Korea in relation to the growing rivalry between the United States and China, along with its bilateral relations with the two superpowers, caused concern among the public about the country's alliance with the United States, and he eventually abandoned this ambition.

Thus, Roh's administration eventually lost its centripetal force as his popularity declined. His populist strategy had worked effectively in breaking up the hegemony of the old elites and ushering in his presidency, but his personal popularity and dynamism could not sustain a stable base of support for his leadership.

As a result, Roh's ruling party took a hammering from the conservative opposition Grand National Party (GNP) in the 2007 presidential election. This did not mean, however, that the GNP had successfully restored its party political base, and the party remained dependent on the popularity of individual members. The party had suffered in its failure to impeach Roh, but it was Park Geun-hye who saved the day. Park, the elder daughter of former President Park Chung-Hee, had a high national popularity rating and the intention to reactivate national economic development as it had been in the 1960s under her father's leadership (Hahm & Heo, 2013). Park was elected party leader before the National Diet elections of 2004, and she staved off a major party defeat.

However, it was not Park who ultimately led the GNP to the mantle of national leadership. Lee Myong-bag, noted as the legendary manager of Hyundai Construction during the country's high-growth era, entered the political arena in the 1990s. In 2002, he was elected mayor of Seoul and further advanced his reputation through his urban reconstruction projects. Whereas Park's economic development was linked to the legacy of her father, Lee's economic development was based purely on his own management record (Lee, 2011). Park and Lee competed for the 2007 GNP nomination, which went to Lee.

While Roh's 2002 election victory was secured by his populist messaging calling for reform as an extension of democratization, Lee's 2007 victory lay in his populist projects for rebuilding infrastructure—an extension of the doctrine of *development from above* of the 1960s—foremost of which was the Grand Korean Waterway from Busan to Seoul, which he contended would revive South Korea's economy. Although his political opponents criticized the project as unrealistic and too costly, Lee easily won the presidential election in the same year. What is fundamental here is that there were two major historical lines of success in South Korea after independence (Kimura, 2003). One was the legacy of democratization, which progressive parties used to sustain their administrations. It was natural for the conservatives to depend on an alternative historical course—economic development.

Yet, like Roh, Lee could not fulfil his populist promises to the nation. Although he displayed his superior management skills during the 2007–2008 global financial crisis, he was unable to recover the former level of economic growth. Lee's support gradually declined from 2010, and he too ended up a political lame duck in his last years in office.

Throughout the period from the advent of Rhee's presidency to the end of Lee's tenure, the support bases of parties were relatively weak and representation in South Korean politics was heavily dependent on the personal popularity of political leaders. As mentioned earlier, however, this phenomenon was also observed in many other countries in East Asia after the Asian financial crisis, including Japan, and led to political instability and the rise of populism in those countries.

Ideological division and party identities

The situation in South Korea changed after 2012, when Park Geun-hye was elected President, due to the fact that her support base was far more stable than those of the country's previous presidents. A similar phenomenon was evident in Japan with the re-election of Shinzo Abe as Prime Minister the same year.

Graph 22.1 depicts the support rates of leaders in one year after their inauguration. The trends in the support rates of both Park and Abe indicate greater stability than those of previous leaders in the two countries.

What political, social, and/or economic changes had occurred in South Korea and Japan during that period that led to the support rates of their leaders stabilizing? One answer to this question is the existence of ideological divisions in these countries at the time. In South Korea, the ideological division between the progressives and conservatives began to widen in 2004, when Roh eliminated the old political system and established his own ruling party. Roh expelled conservative elements from his new party to make it more reformist and criticized the opposition, calling them remnants of the country's past authoritarian administrations. This strategy of the ruling party worked, producing a tidal wave that swept away

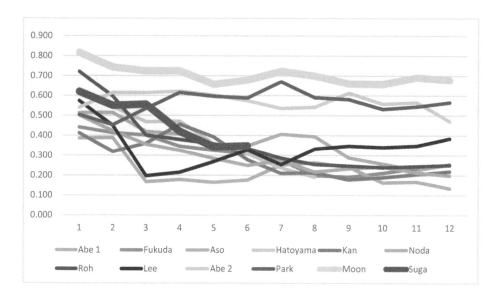

Graph 22.1 Approval Rates of Political Leaders
Source: Jiji News, retrieved from www.jiji.com/, and Korea Gallup, retrieved from www.gallup.co.kr/

the other side of the political arena—that is, the ruling party underscored its ideological identity as progressive, while the opposition depicted its ideology as conservative.

The ideological division between the main political parties also created ideological divisions among the population. Faced with severe competition between the two party blocs, people gradually became wedded to one of the two ideological positions. Middle-of-the-roaders repeatedly attempted—unsuccessfully—to realize a third force. In South Korea, which has a presidential electoral system, 80% of the seats in the National Diet are elected from single-member districts, where smaller parties are traditionally at a disadvantage in relation to the major parties. To realize their political aspirations, the electorate was forced to vote for either the progressives or the conservatives. As the ideological division grew, the political arena became torn between two extremes, which generally precluded voters from shifting their party support.

However, the important point here in the context of populism in South Korea is that the situation described above worked in favour of the major political parties. It enabled them to establish more stable support bases and thus do away with their high dependence on the personal popularity of their leaders, as in the early 2000s. In South Korea, the people call this solid support base for presidents a *rock support layer*.

Although Park was impeached for corruption and expelled from office in 2017, the rock support layer was not weakened. According to a survey by Realmeter,[3] South Korean society today is built on three blocs: the progressives (about 30% of the population), the conservatives (25%), and others. This ratio has proved more consistent than the approval rates of previous presidents, and the parties are supported by stable bases. As a result, the approval rating of the 12th South Korean president, Moon Jae-in, who completed his term in May 2022, was the most stable since the period following democratization in 1987 (Korea Gallup, 2022).

Thus, no South Korean president since 2012 has been forced to adopt a populist strategy. Unlike Roh, who spoke directly to the people, Park and Moon closed the doors of the Blue House (presidential residence until the end of Moon's tenure) and refused to hold regular press conferences. Neither appears to have had any dream of development or reform, unlike Lee and Roh, because in an ideologically divided South Korean society, they could count on the stable support of those on the same side of the ideological divide. In such situations, political leaders should not place undue emphasis on winning over voters with different ideologies, but rather ensure that they do not lose their own 'rock support layer', as Park Geun-hye did in 2016.

Conclusion: an end to the politics of the vortex?

Clearly, the political history of post-independence South Korea has been one of trial and error in re-establishing the political arena. The most important finding of this chapter is that the country's political context was never a simple reflection of that of other countries.

The democratic governments that followed the independence of South Korea in 1948 lacked well-organized intermediate organizations and political parties to sustain leadership due to the country's unique process of decolonization—the Japanese colonial rulers were forced to withdraw from the Korean Peninsula immediately after surrendering to the United States at the end of World War II. The father of the nation, Syngman Rhee, naturally depended on a populist strategy. He relied on his personal legitimacy from his involvement in the independence movement and rejected intermediate organizations, regarding them as obstacles to unifying the people as a nation.

However, Rhee's popularity, which stemmed from his prominent role as a nationalist in exile, did not last long. He was forced to change his strategy and ended up using government organizations to mobilize support for his administration. The leaders who followed, such as Park Chung-Hee and Chun Doo-Hwan, also relied on government organizations as both gained power by means of a military coup, precluding any democratic legitimacy from the beginning of their administrations.

Their attempts to compensate for their lack of legitimacy by using government organizations inevitably further damaged their reputations as leaders of a democratic nation. As a result, South Koreans repeatedly experienced political instability under authoritarian administrations. Henderson called this phenomenon the politics of the vortex.

The situation did not change dramatically, even after democratization. In the late 1980s and 1990s, major political leaders successfully mobilized local identities and were able to solidify their respective political bases, but only temporarily. The solidarity of the parties dissipated after the retirement of the leading lights in each region. In addition, the 1997 Asian financial crisis undermined people's confidence in government and politics, weakening the solidarity of South Korean political parties.

The country welcomed populist leaders in the 2000s. Roh and Lee were from different political parties, the progressives and conservatives respectively, though both achieved major political success. As a lawyer with a history in the democratization movement, Roh called for social reform as a continuation of democratization, whereas with his record as a legendary manager in the 1970s and 1980s, Lee inspired the people with his planned investment in ambitious projects, contending that these could put the nation back on track in regard to economic development.

Notably, such populist competencies clarified the ideological positions of these leaders' respective parties. Roh's call for radical reform did not change society significantly but made the party radical. Lee's investment in projects reflected the party's focus on economic growth. In the competition between progressives and conservatives, South Korean society became sharply divided between the two polarized ideologies, and the potential to strike a compromise decreased.

Of course, this ideological division in society is a well-known phenomenon worldwide and is especially pronounced in the United States. In South Korea, it has assumed different meanings because the political parties, which had been weak and unstable for decades, now seem to have finally achieved internal solidarity given their clear party identities. Have the trials and errors in establishing stable intermediate organizations in South Korean politics finally come to an end, and are we also seeing the end of populism in the country? Or is politics going back to the status quo ante in which political leaders could not find solid support bases? Are political leaders in South Korea trying to mobilize populist strategies again?

What needs to be emphasized is that the country's current political leaders can no longer rely on the legacies of independence movements, democratization, and economic development as Syngman Rhee, Roh Moo-Hyun, and Lee Myung-Bak were able to do. The age of enthusiasm has long passed, and a deep distrust of politics is spreading in South Korea once more. This means that if and when party solidarities are lost, political leaders such as President Yoon Suk-Yeol, who worked as a prosecutor and had no involvement with democratization and business activities, will find it challenging to recover them using populist strategies. Indeed, any future political leaders will face considerable challenges building support.

Notes

1 The 'politics of the vortex' refers to the title of Henderson, 1968 book, which is discussed briefly herein.
2 On the social system and decolonization, see also Kimura, 2021.
3 Realmeter is one of the major survey companies in South Korea. Retrieved from www.realmeter.net/.

References

Choi, J.-J. (1998). Hangugui chogi gukgasuribui seonggyeokgwa gujo, 1945–1948. [The characteristics and structures in the state formation of South Korea, 1945–1948]. *Goryeodaehakgyo sahoegwahangnonjip*, p. 14.
Geertz. C. (1973). *The interpretation of cultures: Selected essays*. Basic Books.
Haggard, S. (1990). *Pathways from the periphery: The politics of growth in the newly industrializing countries*. Cornell University Press.
Hahm, S. D., & Heo, U. (2013). The first female president in South Korea: Park Geun-hye's leadership and South Korean democracy. *Journal of Asian and African Studies*, 53(1), 649–655. https://doi.org/10.1177/0021909617722376
Harris, S. K. (2022). Populist attitudes in South Korea: Implications and definitions. *Transcience*, 13(1), 40–63. ttps://www2.hu-berlin.de/transcience/Vol13_No1_40_64.pdf
Henderson, G. (1968). *Korea, the politics of the vortex*. Harvard University Press.
Kim, B.-K., & Vogel, E. F. (2013). *The Park Chung Hee era: The transformation of South Korea*. Harvard University Press.
Kim, H.-G. (2019). Kankoku no Tochi Ideorogii 'ichiminshugi' no Tojyo to Henyokatei. [Ilminism as a political ideology in South Korea]. *Ajia Kenkyu*, 65(2), 1–18.

Kimura, K. (2003). *Kankoku ni okeru Kenisyughiteki Taisei no Seiritsu* [Authoritarianization in South Korea]. Minervashobo.

Kimura, K. (2007). Nationalistic populism in democratic countries of East Asia. *Journal of Korean Politics, 16*(2), 277–299.

Kimura, K. (2013). Shihaiseito ni miru Pakuchonhiseiken kara Chondofanseiken heno Renzoku to Danzetsu [Continuity of the military governments? From the Park Chung-hee government to the Chun Doo-hwan government]. *Journal of International Cooperation Studies, 20*(2–3), 105–127.

Kimura, K. (2021). Decolonization and governmental parties in post-World War II era: The newly independent states and democratizaion in perspective. *Asian Journal of Arts, Humanities and Social Studies, 4*(2), 92–105.

Kleiner, J. (2001). *Korea: A century of change*. World Scientific.

Korea Gallup. (2022). *Deilli opinieon [Daily Opinion]*, 506. www.gallup.co.kr/.

Kwon, K. (2004). Regionalism in South Korea: Its origins and role in her democratization. *Politics & Society, 32*(4), 545–574. https://doi.org/10.1177/0032329204269982.

Lee, H., O'Keefe, R. M., & Yun, K. (2003). The growth of broadband and electronic commerce in South Korea: Contributing factors. *The Information Society, 19*(1), 81–93. https://doi.org/10.1080/01972240309470

Lee, M.-B. (2011). *The uncharted path: The autobiography of Lee Myung-Bak*. Sourcebooks.

Lee, Y.-J. (2005). Law, politics, and impeachment: The impeachment of Roh Moo-hyun from a comparative constitutional perspective. *The American Journal of Comparative Law, 53*(2), 403–432. https://doi.org/10.1093/ajcl/53.2.403.

Lew, Y.-I. (2017). *The making of the first Korean president: Syngman Rhee's quest for independence*. University of Hawaii Press.

Mueller, A. (2019). The meaning of 'populism'. *Philosophy and Social Criticism, 45*(9–10), 1025–1057. https://doi.org/10.1177/0191453719872277

Omari, T. P. (1971). *Kwame Nkrumah: The anatomy of an African dictatorship*. Africana.

Onishi, Y. (2004). Korea: Trade polity to draw political support. In J. Okamoto (Ed.), *Trade liberalization and APEC* (pp. 156–176). Routledge.

Pyeonjipbu. (1997). 516gunsajeongbyeongwa je3gonghwagung [516 Coup d'état and the Third Republic], Hangukjeongchioegyosahakoe. *Hangukjeongchioegyosanonchong, 15*, 143–202.

Rhee, S. (1947). *Ilminjuui Gaeseol* [The outline of Ilminism]. Ilminjuui Bogeupoe.

Sheafer, S. A. (2008). *Roh Moo Hyun*. Chelsea House.

Tan, T. K. (Ed.) (1967). *Guided democracy: Sukarno's guided Indonesia*. Jacaranda Press.

Tharoor, S. (2003). *Nehru: The invention of India*. Arcade Publishing.

Western democracy is threatening suicide. (2017, October 3). *Intelligence²debates* (Formerly known as Intelligence Squared U.S. is now known as Open to Debate). www.intelligencesquaredus.org/debate/western-democracy-threatening-suicide-/#/

Weyland, K. (2001). Clarifying a contested concept: Populism in the study of Latin American politics. *Comparative Politics, 34*(1), 1–22. https://doi.org/10.2307/422412.

23
PATRIOTIC SONGS AND POPULISM IN CHINESE POLITICS

Xiang Gao

Introduction

Since the ascent of Xi Jinping to the Presidency in 2012, the Chinese Communist Party (CCP) has sought to further entrench its authority and legitimacy by subtly embracing populist politics along with a performance-based and ideologically-validated commitment to government legitimacy. Certainly, the institutional power of the party, the impression of economic competence, and the patron-client commissioning of political action remain. Still, the CCP under Xi has increasingly incorporated populist tropes and rhetoric into its government programme. On the rhetorical level, the CCP appeals to various anti-Western campaigns and the notion of the 'Chinese Dream' that ties the successes of individuals to China's grand national rejuvenation strategy. At a policy level, the implementation of a widely popular anti-corruption campaign, constitutional changes, and a more assertive foreign policy has aimed to position Xi as a symbol of hope in the realization of the political aspirations of fellow citizens.

This chapter starts with a discussion of populism and its application in the context of contemporary Chinese politics, focusing on the conceptualization of *the people*, *the elite*, and *the general will* through the medium of patriotic *Red songs*—an essential component of China's state propaganda. Through an analysis of changes made to the content of the lyrics, the associated imagery, and the staging of performances of the patriotic song repertoire over the past four decades, it is asserted that contemporary populism in China has adopted both moral and ethnic appeals and supportive images. Case studies illustrate the trends of depersonalization and depoliticization in the repertoire, especially from the second to fourth generations of Chinese leaders. The parameters of artistic performance have also changed to facilitate mass participation. These trends signal the evolving style of leadership, approach to discourse and propaganda, and conceptualization of populism. Contemporary populist politics in China, as fostered by the CCP, values and incorporates the role of elites in contrast to Western populist anti-establishment discourse. Additionally, the establishment of an ethnically-defined Chinese nation and people has significantly impacted the ethnic minority policy, as well as foreign policy involving the Chinese diaspora and citizens of Chinese descent in other countries.

Populism in contemporary Chinese politics

Populism is a complicated and slippery concept. Yet, political scientists are seemingly undeterred by its elusiveness when they define it. Populism can be traced back to the philosophical ideas of the Enlightenment, especially the radical forms of popular sovereignty and direct democracy (Verbeek & Zaslove, 2019, p. 3). From the French Revolution to post-WWII political trends of decentralization and referenda to the recent Occupy Movement, populism has been embraced by political parties and some civil societies across different times and spaces. At the most basic level, populism as a form of politics puts *the people* at the centre (Featherstone & Karaliotas, 2019, p. 31). The conceptualization of populism varies. First, populism can be understood as a political strategy, which either consistently focuses on select issues such as immigration, race, trade protectionism, and political leadership or moves towards the spectrum of political opportunism, where politicians make radical promises to deliver policies that fulfil what the people want (Verbeek & Zaslove, 2019, p. 5). Second, populism is alternatively defined by the broader public's distrust of elites and established conventions, such as laws, political institutions, and government officials (Vickers, 2017, p. 59). Third, populism can be presented in various forms to differentiate 'us' from 'them'. Early agrarian populism in the United States, which viewed small-holder farmers and mid-American townspeople as the *authentic* people, was a rural response to late 19th-century industrialization. Furthermore, populism can also be found in both right- and left-wing politics: the former takes a nativist perspective, arguing that the corrupt ruling class does not represent the *native* people's interest, and the latter considers the people underprivileged compared with the economic, political, and cultural elites (Verbeek & Zaslove, 2019, p. 7). Contemporary socioeconomic populism (left-wing) in Latin America advocates for greater state involvement in the economy and criticizes the adverse effects of neoliberalism on local communities; while xenophobic populism (right-wing) focuses on issues such as immigration, crime, and employment, as well as featuring nativism and authoritarianism (Mudde & Rovira Kaltwasser, 2013, pp. 495–497).

Although populism is often associated with political distrust, economic disparity, and cultural alienation in the West, in the East Asian context, populism has manifested in different forms. Populism in East Asian countries was conceived in the political discourses of historical wartime trauma and built upon national identities that are more ethnically constructed and biologically homogeneous. Japan created a post-war national identity based on the pacifist notion and atomic victimhood, brushing away the historical narrative of imperialist aggression (Vickers, 2017, p. 60). China and South Korea both hold grievances against Western and Japanese imperialism, which has been reflected in both countries' nationalistic sentiments and populist discourses. Moreover, populism in China also adopts the rhetoric that China is a united multinational state, and that the Chinese nation is comprised of 56 ethnic groups, emphasizing the shared 'Chineseness' of the enumerated groups despite the overwhelming demographic dominance of the Han ethnic group. This populist discourse promoted by Chinese government in turn reinforces its assimilation policy.

Recognizing its complexity, this chapter investigates populism in contemporary Chinese politics through a thin-centred ideological approach (Mudde, 2004), which views populist politics as having three core components: the people, the elite, and the general will. This approach is built upon the premise that all populist politics presents a conflict between the *pure* people and the *corrupt* elite. Focusing on the people-elite dichotomy and the notion of a shared 'general will' enables us to closely examine political leadership, the CCP, political discourses, and civil society in contemporary China.

The people

Populist politics constructs *the people* as a political actor whose demands cannot be accommodated within the existing institutional order (Laclau, 2005, p. 122). The interpretation of the people differs across political contexts, histories, and social realities. As a collective body, the people or the sovereign people are the 'ultimate source of political authority' especially in democracies (Canovan, 2005, p. 68). The legitimacy of political power is built upon the consent of the sovereign people, who can transfer this legitimacy and power from one regime to another if they are not well represented (Canovan, 2005, p. 84). The notion of a sovereign people in populist politics is usually associated with mass mobilizations or even upheavals such as the Arab Spring, the pro-democracy uprisings which spread across the Arab world in the early 2010s. The people can also convey the meaning of *the common people* as those of a specific socioeconomic status or as a group sharing a common cultural tradition, values, and history (Mudde & Rovira Kaltwasser, 2013, p. 502). Contrary to elitism, the idea of the common people embodies the notion of popular culture in opposition to the dominant culture of the elites—a culture from which *the people* are excluded due to their lower socioeconomic status, shared culture, or history. This identification with popular culture, and the corresponding rejection of elite cultural sentiments, is an important aspect of populist leadership (Panizza, 2005, pp. 26–27). For example, the frequent media coverage of former U.S. President, Donald Trump, devouring Big Macs added a subtle cultural touch, suggesting that President Trump is one of *the people*, the previously marginalized group in the elitist cultural context. Similarly, in Chinese media, President Xi Jinping has often been seen casually dressed and mingling with workers in factories or farmers in the fields. Finally, the concept of the people can be understood as a whole national community (Featherstone & Kaliotas, 2019, p. 39). This interpretation can ostensibly include the entire population of a particular state, but sometimes refers to a narrower group—the natives—selectively defined. The idea of people as a nation is often reinforced by national mythology such as that describing all Chinese people as descendants of the Yan and Yellow Emperors. Yet, because different ethnic groups exist in the same country, the proper boundaries of the people and the definition of the nation become a salient issue, especially when it concerns questions as to who belongs to the people (Näsström, 2011, p. 19). In populist politics, the view of 'the people as a nation' is linked to patriotism and nationalism.

The elites

Research into populism generally addresses *the elites* comparatively in relation to *the people* and their collectively held *general will*. Hypothetically, the underlying distinctions between the elites and the people are normative and material (Mudde & Rovira Kaltwasser, 2013, p. 503). In short, the two groupings or classes are totally antithetical, aside from the common humanity shared by members of both. Under the populist lens, the elites are irretrievably 'bad' and the people unassailably 'good'. The elites have power, holding leading positions in the political, economic, and cultural spheres. Populist discourses maintain that corrupt elites from many sectors advance one another's interests, instead of the interests of the people and the country. Though populist leaders can also be elites, such as Thaksin in Thailand and Imran Khan in Pakistan, it is often presumed that most elites possess considerable economic power, while populist leaders, claiming to represent the people, are often seen as deprived of both resources and political success (Mudde & Rovira Kaltwasser, 2013). The second distinction between the elites and the people is ethnic. The elites are often considered either agents of a foreign power or aliens promoting the interests of immigrants rather than the native population. For example, the historic 'White Australia' and 'White New Zealand' policies not only rejected the non-white labourers attracted by goldmining in Australia and New Zealand but also shaped a more 'native' national identity operating against the 'distant colonial ruler' in London (Schwarz, 2011, pp. 145–148).

The general will

The distinction between the people and the elite is reflected in the *general will*, which is the capacity of the people to form a community and pursue their collective interests with legislative support (Mudde & Rovira Kaltwasser, 2013, p. 505). The idea of the general will is framed as a representation of popular demands that are often not met by the establishment. The concept is also used for political construction of a popular identity that differentiates the people from *the enemy* (Laclau, 2005, p. 86). The enemy takes various forms depending on the scenarios: government ministry, business corporations, city council, university authority, media, and so on. Adopting the notion of the general will, populism agrees with the Rousseauian critique of representative democracy and usually supports an unmediated relationship between populist leaders and the people. Moreover, a populist leader should be 'enlightened enough to see what the general will is' and represent the 'will of a collective people' (Canovan, 2005, p. 115). In other words, populist leaders purport to solve the real problems of the people directly, rather than through representatives. For example, the North Korean media has projected the image of the late Kim Jong-Il, the 'dear leader', as showing a real interest in and care for the North Korean people's daily lives, by publishing photographs of Kim inspecting various consumer products, such as pencils, nylon stockings, groceries, and a roasted pig. Indeed, in a 2011 photo, the late leader demonstrated his concern by publicly testing the quality of bras in a garment factory in Pyongyang using a manual examination technique. By emphasizing the general will, populist politics arguably contributes to democratization as it gives voice to marginalized groups. However, populist politics can also lead to, or sustain, authoritarianism through an exclusionary notion of general will and a purported unity of a collective people under populist leadership.

Examining populism in contemporary China through patriotic songs

Chinese patriotic *Red Songs* have evolved across the historical succession of eras, from the anti-imperialist May Fourth Movement (1919) to the second Chinese-Japanese War (1937–45), the Cultural Revolution (1966–76), and the Reforming and Opening Up (1978 onward). Patriotic songs in China share a common theme: love and praise for the country, the people, and the political regime. These songs cover various topics and subjects: war history and heroes, the People's Liberation Army (PLA), the CCP, political leaders, the nation's unification, specific government policies, ethnic minorities, as well as the common people (Wang, 2012, pp. 133–136). The songs are written for different musical genres, usually folk or popular music, but sometimes in an operatic style for formal concert presentation. Despite the diverse subjects and performance styles, the patriotic songs referred to here are selected on the basis that they present a political viewpoint related to the populist context in China.

Patriotic songs are used to examine populism in China for three main reasons. Firstly, the use of music is particularly important to authoritarian states, 'making people forget, believe or be quiet' (Lee, 1995, p. 100). Patriotic songs in China are significant components of the popular culture, demonstrating an admixture of popular artistic taste and government political propaganda. Second, patriotic songs are more widely known and learned among ordinary Chinese citizens than popular literature, which is also censored by the State. Factory workers, peasants in the field, and soldiers patrolling the border can generally hum the same patriotic tunes. Lastly, unlike the artificial insertion of political propaganda into mainstream media discourses, patriotic songs often describe inspiring images of the magnificent Chinese rural scenery and the proud, hardworking Chinese people. In contrast to the boringly repetitive propaganda messages embedded in daily news broadcasts, these songs are much closer to the hearts and minds of individual Chinese, be they old or young, at home or abroad. Given their accessibility, popularity, and political nature, patriotic songs are an ideal cultural genre through which to study populism in contemporary China.

This analysis of selected Chinese patriotic songs reflecting populism in contemporary Chinese politics identifies three key ideological elements. First, the concepts of a *sovereign people* as the source of regime legitimacy and the *common people*, too often rejected by elitist culture, are examined in terms of changes in the lyrics of traditional songs and the related historical periods of the People's Republic of China. The changes in the lyrics also demonstrate the evolving concept of the general will of the people. Second, many patriotic songs promote down-to-earth popular perceptions of top Chinese political leadership, suggesting that they can be portrayed as both elites and populists in representing the will of the people. This duality eliminates the elite-versus-people polarization that often characterizes Western populist politics. Finally, scrutinizing the popular identification of the people as the nation facilitates our understanding of contemporary Chinese nation building. Chinese populist politics promotes the perception of an 'imagined Chinese community' that emphasizes the shared allegiance to the Chinese state regardless of an individual's ethnic background.

Chinese people: 'our workers have the power'[1]

Populism claims that the source of power and regime legitimacy lies in the pure people. China's 'Reforming and Opening Up' initiative, introduced in 1978, has reduced state ownership, built a market-oriented economy, and promoted international trade. The initiative has also profoundly impacted wealth distribution, employment opportunities, and individual lifestyles through large-scale industrialization, urbanization, and a burgeoning middle class. This has produced countrywide growth in populist concerns—namely, the widening income gap, rising unemployment, and misconduct under various guises perpetrated by elite groups. Populism in China manifests as a grassroots movement, disseminating netizen and online media watchdog reactions to nepotism and corruption among government officials that intensifies in cases of leniency and non-punishment (Liu, 2017, p. 48).

The belief that true power is derived from the people and should be used appropriately for the people is fundamental to the modified patriotic song lyrics of the post-Mao era. The revised lyrics reveal a trend towards depersonalization, most notably under the political leadership of Deng Xiaoping, Jiang Zemin, and Hu Jintao. The tendency has been to move away from venerating individual charismatic leaders with references to name, personality traits, and association to political policies. Instead, the collective leadership and, more often, the collective Chinese people are praised. For example, the 1963 song 'We are Marching Along the Wide Road' was revised in the 1990s to replace the direct references in the lyrics to the leadership role of Chairman Mao with references to the CCP. Thus, the line 'Chairman Mao is leading the revolutionary troops' has transitioned to 'the Communist Party is leading the revolutionary troops'.[2] Similarly, the 'Song of Praise' no longer glorifies 'the great Communist Party and Chairman Mao' as did in the 1964 setting, but since 1984 celebrates 'brothers of all ethnic groups'.[3] 'China, China, the Bright Red Sun Never Sets', composed in 1977, exhorted the people to adopt 'Mao Zedong's thought' as the 'weapon to destroy all invaders'; in the revision, the weapon of destruction has become the 'heroic people in full battle array'.[4]

Generally, revisions have depoliticized the lyrics without impairing the patriotic nature of the song. Through imagery depicting the daily lives of the masses, the power of the people and their heroic nature are exalted. The 1975 version of the Mongolian song 'The Beautiful Grassland is My Home' highlighted the CCP's influence across inner Mongolia, closing evocatively with 'the light of the Party shines on the grassland'. The close of the depoliticized 1978 version—'pleasant singing fills the world'—extols the harmonious simplicity of the lives of the regional population.[5] 'Happy Holiday' was written in 1954 to celebrate International Children's Day. The original lyrics invited Chairman Mao to celebrate the joyful day in the company of Chinese children. In the version of the 1990s, the same invitation was extended to the 'dear uncles and aunts'.[6]

The style of performing patriotic songs was also adapted to suit the tastes of the masses. Prior to the 1980s, patriotic songs were generally performed by prominent soloists or choirs in a conventional concert stage setting, to serve a dual purpose as entertainment and patriotic education. Since the 1980s, popular music has gained greater popularity in China through the introduction of commercial films and television from Hong Kong, Taiwan, and Japan. As the popular music audience began to widen, the performance styles of patriotic songs changed. For example, the Tang Dynasty Band, founded in 1988, is a Beijing rock group. Beyond its rock repertoire, the band has become renowned for repackaging patriotic songs such as *L'Internationale*, the anthem of the international socialist movement and the CCP, into the genre of heavy metal rock. Moreover, the formal concert stage settings where professional soloists sang arrangements of patriotic songs in the classical *bel canto* style, backed by a chorus, have given way to naturalistic settings such as a park, where the patriotic repertoire is delivered in modern popular styles that encourage audience participation. The improvisatory *flash mob* phenomenon, in which a group, often motivated via social media, gathers in a public place for the purpose of entertainment or artistic expression, has become one of the prominent methods of promoting patriotic songs. Prior to the outbreak of COVID-19, a meticulous arrangement of 'My Motherland and I', the most popular patriotic song for flash mob staging, was performed by thousands of Chinese citizens assembled in airports, railway stations, universities, streets, and shopping malls. The lyrics describe the strong bond between citizenry and their motherland. Free of any reference to political leadership or the CCP, the lyrics present a series of evocative rustic images of the Chinese countryside, popular across successive generations and certain to arouse feelings of nostalgia and, thereby, patriotic sentiment.[7] Overall, the adaptations of the lyrics and innovations in the styles of performance of patriotic songs have substantially accommodated the cultural and artistic preferences of younger generations of the Chinese populace. The revised lyrics of the 1990s and 2000s have contributed to diminishing the roles of political elites and the dominance of elitist cultural content and performance styles. What is noteworthy is that levels of political and social transformation have been realized, and yet the fundamental tradition and repertoire of patriotic songs have been preserved.

Chinese elite: 'serving people wholeheartedly while leading them to a bright future'

Populist politics elsewhere generally has an anti-establishment and anti-elitist stance. From this perspective, populists encounter an inevitable paradox in acquiring and maintaining power, as wielding power potentially lands them in the realm of the corrupt elite, perpetually in opposition to the people (Mudde & Rovira Kaltwasser, 2013, p. 503). However, populism in China does not exhibit a truly anti-elitist nature, especially when it is closely moderated by the CCP-led government. On the contrary, the elites—and thereby the CCP ('vanguard of the working class' according to the CCP's doctrine) and top political leaders—portray themselves as destined to lead the people. This is evident in the song, 'Without the Communist Party There Would Be No New China', written during WWII and sung by successive generations at official events. The song praises the CCP leadership for its role in building a new China, for winning the anti-Japanese war, and for liberating the Chinese people and leading them to a brighter future.[8] Another song created in the 1960s, 'Sing a Folk Song to the Party' goes even further in acclaiming the CCP leadership's role in leading the Chinese revolution. The song compares the Party with a mother, stating, 'My mother only gave birth to my body, but the light of the Party shines on my heart'.[9] In 1997, the song 'Entering Into the New Era' was created to celebrate Hong Kong's return to China. Without explicitly naming the political leaders (then Deng Xiaoping and Jiang Zemin), the song describes the smooth transition from the second to third generations of Chinese political leadership, acclaiming the manner in which Chinese leaders had advanced tradition in steering the people into a new era.[10] Thus, the patriotic songs have evolved, but the mission of the CCP leadership remains unchanged.

Since Xi Jinping's rise to power in 2012, there has been increasing personalization and centralization of power, reassertion of CCP dominance in Chinese politics and the economy, and promotion of nationalist sentiment (Jaros & Pan, 2017, p. 111). This is reflected in song lyrics which have positive references to President Xi, in contrast with the trend of depersonalization from the second to fourth generations of CCP leaders (Deng Xiaoping, Jiang Zemin and Hu Jintao). New patriotic songs have been released to celebrate Xi Jinping's leadership, pointing to the unmediated relationship between the paramount leader and the people. 'Being a Good Soldier for President Xi', released in 2017, encourages novice Chinese soldiers to aspire to future battlefields and pursue victory.[11] 'President Xi's Message' was originally a school song that encouraged youth to 'discover and pursue what inspires them'. The song was later made into a music video with accompanying sign language for nationwide presentation and performance at the United Nations.[12]

Xi Jinping instituted an anti-corruption campaign in 2014 that embraced populist themes in expressing the will to punish corrupt bureaucrats and senior political representatives and to strictly enforce CCP disciplinary measures. It has become the cornerstone of Xi's continuing popularity among the public and elicits admiration countrywide, especially on social media. The campaign has led to a change of heart among political elites, who portray themselves as ordinary citizens of the Chinese people in the egalitarian sense, dutiful and diligent in their service. This attitude that takes pride in serving echoes the CCP constitution's stated goal, 'to serve the people wholeheartedly'. New patriotic songs emerged to reinforce this populist political trend. Several patriotic songs written in the 2010s, all sharing the same title—'Serving the People'—gained popularity. All embody transformation, advocating that government officials as representatives of the elite, are *servants* of the people and work for the benefit of the people. One of the songs uses an extended metaphor to describe the transition.

> The people are the mountain and the earth. The people are the life's roots and backbone. We cannot forget that the people have raised us. We must always remember that we serve the people because we are the Communist Party.[13]

Populist politics in China is pro-establishment and is controlled and regulated by the government. Chinese elites, most of whom are CCP members, comprise the establishment possessing political, economic, or cultural power. The leader-servant complex is reflected in the populist relationship between the CCP leadership function and the people. The elites have been described in patriotic songs as leaders—and even saviours—of the nation and the people. This self-identified aggrandizement of the elites became a generally accepted feature of Chinese governance, reinforced through the political institutions and culture. As Confucius advised, 'those who excel in study should pursue political careers'—historically, the demand for positions in government has far exceeded their availability. Nevertheless, as embodied in the revised lyrics of patriotic songs, a good leader represents the general will and undertakes to serve the people. This revisionary approach was introduced by Mao Zedong and has been followed by successive generations of Chinese political leadership.[14]

Chinese nation: 'wearing a Western outfit, I still have a Chinese heart'

Populist politics builds a political community that continues to maintain the 'us versus them' dichotomy. The term *Chinese people* refers not only to all who are native to the Chinese territory, irrespective of ethnicity, but also those foreign-born and expatriate Chinese people, who fulfil one of the national foundational myths—for example, descendancy from the Yan and Yellow Emperors. These broadly defined Chinese people, wherever they may be located, are conceived as together forming what Canovan (1984, p. 351) describes as 'a community with a common life'. After the student-led 1989 Tiananmen Square mass pro-democracy demonstrations were suppressed, the Chinese government introduced a patriotic education campaign to secure CCP leadership and offset Western influences in China (Zhao, 1998, pp. 291–293). A Han-based ethnocentric construction of the Chinese nation has been reflected in many patriotic songs since the 1990s. The 1991 release, 'Love My Chinese Nation' is a song celebrating Chinese national unity. The song declares that the 56 ethnic groups in China belong to the same nation-family and share the affection of the Chinese nation equally.[15] The song gained such popularity in China that it was uploaded as an artefact of Chinese culture to the satellite Chang'E-1, which was launched in 2007. The 1994 ballad 'A Big China' mentions the symbolic images of Yangtze River, Yellow River, Mount Qomolangma, and the Great Wall and reflects that 'we are all brothers and sisters who have endured hardships, and we form a big China that is a big family for all.[16] These patriotic songs use the metaphor of brothers and sisters in the same family to demonstrate national unity and to weaken the distinct identities of ethnic minorities in China. By emphasizing the shared Chineseness among different ethnic groups, the populist politics of the CCP promotes the notion of an inclusive Chinese nation, which operates hand-in-hand with the government's assimilation policy towards ethnic minorities in China.

The populist construction of a Chinese nation changes when it is directed at Chinese persons abroad. In this case, the Han-ethnocentric notion of the Chinese nation discussed earlier is replaced by a more reified notion of Chinese nation and the shared Sino ancestry, which includes all people of Chinese descent. Some patriotic songs, written outside mainland China, have also gained much popularity since the 1980s for their contribution to national unification. Such songs often share similar themes: a sense of nostalgia and unwavering love for the 'motherland' despite the individual's foreign citizenship. 'My Chinese Heart' was written and first performed by Hong Kong artists in the early 1980s. The song confesses that despite having been far from their motherland for a long period, and dressing in Western outfits daily, they can still maintain a Chinese heart due to their ancestors having branded their hearts with a Chinese mark. The sustained metaphor declares that their individual heartbeats 'echo the sound of the Chinese nation', and that being born overseas does not change one's Chinese heart.[17] This ethnologically defined Chinese identity also resonates in other Chinese patriotic songs that originated in Taiwan and further abroad. Written and composed in Taiwan in the late 1970s, 'The Descendants of Loong (the Dragon)' draws upon the national mythology. The narrative recounts that a community of people in the East are the descendants of Loong. All members of the community are endowed with the same physical features—dark hair, dark eyes, and yellow skin—which forever identifies them as 'The Descendants of Loong'.[18] A Chinese American artist and singer, Wang Leehom, revised the lyrics and incorporated elements of jazz and rap into his performance in 2000 (Gao, 2015, p. 482). Wang's adaptation is based on his own experience as an immigrant in the United States: 'On a silent night many years ago, my family arrived in New York. Wild fire cannot burn out the longing for home day and night. I grew up in the foreign land, and became a descendant of Loong'. The personal nature of Wang's experience and his sincerity of expression has led to its popularity throughout the Chinese diaspora and among domestic Chinese citizens.

The populist perception of the Chinese nation is meticulously constructed and presents two aspects. First, the *imagined* Chinese community includes different ethnic identities that are united under citizenship and state-led political interactions. Their common Chineseness permeates the 56 ethnic groups that comprise the definitive Chinese people. In official rhetoric, the nation and people are the foundation of China, the unified, multi-ethnic state. This leaves little room for the expression of ethnic minority group interests. Second, the ethnic construction of the Chinese nation goes beyond the national boundary and transcends an individual's citizenship. The Chinese nation therefore is broadly defined as including all people with Chinese ancestry, which confers a potential 'patriotic duty' on all these people, regardless of being citizens of China or not. The risk of building this imagined Chinese community is that it can lead to the extremes of ethno-cultural nationalism and xenophobic populism based on a racialist conception of nationhood. Moreover, the broadly identified 'Chinese people' includes the diaspora. This has recently become a sore point in Western countries, where an increasing number of residents and citizens of Chinese origin have been scrutinized over their loyalty and commitment to their current country of residency or citizenship.

Conclusion

This chapter examined populism in contemporary China through the lens of popular patriotic songs. In reviewing the lyrics and styles of performance, it highlighted a focus on populist concepts in the specific Chinese context of *the people*, *the elites*, and *the nation*. Many patriotic songs created before 1978 were revised in the 1990s to emphasize the power and legitimacy of the people. The revised or adapted lyrics demonstrate a trend in depersonalization and depoliticization, hence diminishing the personal references to the most senior political leaders, their policies, and their achievements. However, in some respects, this trend has been reversed under Xi Jinping, and many recent patriotic songs have been intended to personalize Xi's policies. Performances now follow popular contemporary commercial styles including jazz, hip hop, and rock, thus reflecting the changing tastes of the people and encompassing more youths. Many patriotic songs are suitable for square dancing, a form of group exercise in China taking place in parks and other public open spaces. Similarly, patriotic songs are performed by flash mobs that encourage massive assemblies of active citizens of all ages across the country.

Patriotic songs across different time periods reveal the leader-servant roleplay of Chinese elites and the CCP. In contrast to the anti-establishment populist sentiments in other countries, Chinese populist politics values the elites' dual role as leaders and servants of the people. This was supported by the growing institutionalization of Chinese politics, which sought to eliminate the egregious abuse of power based on charisma, personal influence, and patron-client relationships. Chinese political institutionalization since 1978, particularly in terms of transitioning to power sharing and collective leadership, ironically may be deemed a populist exercise as it underscores the inherent *serving* aspect of the leadership. Rather than focusing on the populist leader *per se*, Chinese populism seeks to identify the entire CCP within this fundamental populist relationship. This gives Chinese populism an institutional character that is lacking in many other states. Nevertheless, as President Xi has consolidated his political power, the personalization trend has returned and is reflected in many new patriotic songs celebrating Xi's leadership. This has occurred despite the fact that the notion of an unmediated relationship between the leader and the citizenry has had a particularly troubled past in China, as evidenced by Mao Zedong's launch of the Cultural Revolution. Additionally, in assuming the role of a paramount leader, rather than one of seniority in a collective leadership, Xi shoulders more personal responsibility in terms of the policy outcomes. This trend in personalizing policy has also contributed to increasingly tighter control over media, information, and political discourses in China. From this perspective, populism in China reflects the authoritarian political system from which it arises and blends into nationalist discourse.

Populist politics constructs the *Chinese nation* and the *Chinese people* as all who share a common *Chineseness*, irrespective of ethnic group or foreign citizenship. The patriotic songs emphasize and consolidate the official political discourse of a unified multi-ethnic state and ethnic minorities being 'inseparable components' of the Chinese state. Individual ethnic identities and unique experiences, such as being Hui, Uyghur, or Tibetan, are portrayed in these patriotic songs as less important compared to being a member of the Chinese nation and Chinese people. The construction of a homogeneous national identity reflects the government's policy of assimilating ethnic minorities and can also be found in other East Asian states, such as Japan. Moreover, the ethnically-defined *Chinese peoples* has been extended to include all people of Chinese descent. In accordance with this broad definition, anyone who shares the ethnic features—dark hair, dark eyes, and yellow skin—classifies as Chinese. As China strengthens its political and economic influence, the inherent vagueness of the definition has raised concern in some states over the trustworthiness of the Chinese diaspora and persons of Chinese origin residing in other countries. Globally scattered Chinese communities and organizations, as well as foreign citizens of Chinese descent, have experienced increasing scrutiny and even faced discrimination due to the expanded definition of citizenship and allegiance to China. In the extreme, there is a fear that ethnic Chinese living in other countries may be faced with a 'patriotic' duty if summoned by the Chinese government to form a united front in their country of residency. In the current global environment, where universal values are at risk and normative values are contested, an unbridled Chinese populist politics fuelled by contentious domestic politics and assertive foreign policy may further challenge a rules-based world order.

Notes

1. 'Our Workers Have the Power': music and lyrics by Ma Ke (1947). It describes the Chinese factory labourers working hard to support the CCP and its army in the Chinese Civil War (1945–49). The song is sung in praise of the Chinese working class. [All lyrics referred to in this chapter have been translated into English by the author.]
2. 'We Are Marching Along the Wide Road': music and lyrics by Li Jiefu (1963). The original first verse was 'We are marching along the wide road full of high spirit, Chairman Mao is leading the revolutionary troops, hacking our way through difficulties and moving towards the future'.
3. 'The Song of Praise', in the Mongolian style: music and lyrics by Hu Songhua (1964). The original lyrics start, 'From the [Mongolian] grassland to Tiananmen Square, we raise the golden glass and sing a song of praise. We thank great Communist Party, and wish Chairman Mao a long life'. In 1984, the lyric was changed to 'From the [Mongolian] grassland to Tiananmen Square, we raise the golden glass and sing a song of praise. Brothers of all ethnic groups happily get together, to celebrate our liberation'.
4. 'China, China, the Bright Red Sun Never Sets': music by Zhu Xinan, lyrics by Ren Hongjiu and He Dongjiu (1977) to celebrate the end of the Cultural Revolution. A part of the original lyric was 'Mao Zedong Thought arms us to be ready at all times to perish all the invaders'. The new version was changed to 'heroic people are in full battle array, ready at all times to perish all the invaders'.
5. 'The Beautiful Grassland is My Home' was written by Huo Hua in 1975 and the lyrics were substantially revised in 1978. Political imagery associated with the Cultural Revolution, such as the 'electricity power lines', was replaced by references to the pure natural beauty of Inner Mongolia, such as birds, butterflies, waterscapes, and the sunset. The original last line, 'the light of the Party shines on the grassland', was revised to 'The pleasant singing fills the world'.
6. 'Happy Holiday' was composed by Li Qun with lyrics by Guan Hua (1954). The original lyric ended with 'respectful Chairman Mao, come to spend the happy holiday with us'. It was changed in the 1990s to 'dear uncles and aunts, come and spend the happy holiday with us'.
7. 'My Motherland and I': music by Qin Yongcheng, lyrics by Zhang li (1985). The first verse states, 'My motherland and I can never be apart. I sing a song of praise wherever I travel. I sing for every mountain, every river, a curl of smoke rising from houses, a small village and a track on the country road. My dear motherland, I always cling to your heart, listening to your motherly pulse'.
8. 'Without the Communist Party There Would Be No New China': music and lyrics by Cao Huoxing (1943). The lyrics were based on an editorial in the CCP's *Liberation Daily*, which was a response to the slogan 'without the Nationalist Party, there is no China' proposed by Chiang Kai-Shek in his book 'China's Destiny'. A part of the lyric is 'Communist Party aims to save China. The Party pointed out to the people a path to liberation and led China into the bright future'.
9. 'Sing a Folk Song to the Party': music by Zhu Jianer, lyrics by Jiao Ping (1963). A verse in the original stated, 'Sing a folk song to the Party; the Party is like my mother. My mother only gave birth to my body. The light of the Party shines on my heart'.

10 'Entering Into the New Era' was written by Jiang Kairui and composed by Yin Qing in 1997. A part of the lyric is that 'our guide carries forward the tradition and forges ahead into the future. He leads our entering the new era'.
11 'Become a Good Soldier for President Xi' was created by some newly recruited trainees in the military police force in 2017. It quickly gained popularity in the armed forces.
12 'President Xi's Message' was created in 2013. A verse states, 'When you are young, you must find and pursue great inspiration. You must endure the storm before you gain skills and competence'. See '"President Xi's Message" will be sung at UN headquarters. The key choir team looks forward to performing at the Spring Festival Gala for Year of Goat', 31 January 2015, *China Daily*, www.chinadaily.com.cn/.
13 The song's music is by Chen Li and the lyrics by Yi Jiancheng.
14 In memoriam of Zhang Side, a soldier who died in an accident in 1944, Mao Zedong gave a speech entitled 'Serve for People' which emphasized the CCP's goal of 'serving the people wholeheartedly'.
15 'Love My Chinese Nation': music by Xu Peidong, lyrics by Qiao Yu, was created as a theme song for the 4th Traditional Games of Ethnic Minorities in 1991. A verse states, '56 starts and 56 flowers. Brothers and sisters from 56 ethnic groups are a family. 56 languages are transformed into one sentence: Love my Chinese nation, love my Chinese nation, and love my Chinese nation'.
16 'A Big China': music and lyrics by Gao Feng (1994). The song won several national awards and was performed at the Spring Festival Gala in 1998. The lyrics state, 'We all have a family, called "China". We have a lot of brothers and sisters, as well as great scenery. We have two dragons guarding our house, and they are Yangtze River and Yellow River . . . Our big China is like a big family. I want to be with her forever and ever'.
17 'My Chinese Heart': music by Wang Fuling, lyrics by Huang Zhan, was composed in Hong Kong to mark the start of the Chinese-British bilateral negotiations in 1980 regarding Hong Kong's return to China in 1997. An extract from the lyrics states, 'In my dreams, the sceneries are so divine. I've been far from my homeland for so many years, but nothing can ever change my Chinese heart. Though I wear Western outfits, I still have a Chinese heart. My ancestors branded my heart with a Chinese mark . . . The blood that flows through my veins roars "China"'.
18 'The Descendants of the Dragon' was written and composed by Taiwanese artist, Hou Dejian, in 1978. A part of the lyric is that 'There is a Loong (dragon) in the ancient East; His name is "China". There are a group of people from the ancient East; They are all descendants of the Loong. I grew up in the Loong's land and became a descendant of the Loong. Dark eyes, dark hair, and yellow skin, I am a descendant of the Loong forever and ever'.

References

Canovan, M. (1984). 'People', Politicians and Populism. *Government and Opposition*, 19(3), 312–327. https://doi.org/10.1111/j.1477-7053.1984.tb01048.x
Canovan, M. (2005). *The people*. Polity.
Featherstone, D., & Karaliotas, L. (2019). Populism. *Soundings*, 72, 31–47. https://doi.org/10.3898/SOUN.72.02.2019
Gao, Z. (2015). When nationalism goes to the market: The case of Chinese patriotic songs. *Journal of Macromarketing*, 35(4), 473–488. https://doi.org/10.1177/0276146715573079
Jaros, K., & Pan, J. (2017). China's newsmakers: Official media coverage and political shifts in the Xi Jinping era. *The China Quarterly*, 233, 111–136.
Laclau, E. (2005). *On populist reason*. Verso.
Lee, G. (1995). The 'East is red' goes pop: Commodification, hybridity and nationalism in Chinese popular song and its televisual performance. *Popular Music*, 14(1), 95–120. www.jstor.org/stable/853344
Liu, X. (2017). On the internet populism mobilisation and its governance in contemporary China. *Socialism Studies*, 234(4), 46–56.
Mudde, C. (2004). The populist zeitgeist. *Government and Opposition*, 39(4), 541–563. https://doi.org/10.1111/j.1477-7053.2004.00135.x
Mudde, C., & Rovira Kaltwasser, C. (2013). Populism. In M. Freeden & M. Stears (Eds.) *The Oxford handbook of political ideologies* (pp. 493–512). Oxford University Press.

Näsström, S. (2011). The challenge of the all-affected principle. *Political Studies*, *59*, 116–134. https://doi.org/10.1111/j.1467-9248.2010.00845.x

Panizza, F. (2005). *Populism and the mirror of democracy*. Verso.

Schwarz, B. (2011). *Memories of empire volume 1: The white man's world*. Oxford University Press.

Verbeek, B., & Zaslove, A. (2019). Contested issues surrounding populism in public and academic debates. *The International Spectator*, *54*(2), 1–16. https://doi.org/10.1080/03932729.2019.1606513

Vickers, E. (2017). All quiet on the eastern front? Populism, nationalism, and democracy in East Asia. *Georgetown Journal of International Affairs*, *18*(2), 59–68. https://doi.org/10.1353/gia.2017.0021

Wang, Q. (2012). Red songs and the main melody: Cultural nationalism and political propaganda in Chinese popular music. *Perfect Beat*, *13*(2), 127–145.

Zhao, S. (1998). A state-led nationalism: The patriotic education campaign in post-Tiananmen China. *Communist and Post-communist Studies*, *31*(3), 287–302.

24
TAIWANESE POPULISM IN THE SHADOW OF CHINA[1]

Guy C. Charlton and Yayut Yi-shiuan Chen

The ambiguous international status of Taiwan, the long period of authoritarian rule under the Kuomintang government, and the subsequent peaceful transition to a vibrant liberal polity have profoundly shaped forms of democratic mobilization and discourse in Taiwan. Nevertheless, this democratic trajectory overlays deep political and cultural fissures among political parties, non-governmental movements, Indigenous groups, and civil society. These include fundamental issues about the nature of Taiwanese identity and nationalism, corruption, the scope of constitutionally guaranteed rights and human rights more generally, the rule of law, and the place of Indigenous groups within the Taiwanese polity and state. Coupled with growing social and economic inequality and a slowing economy, the cleavages have posed significant challenges to liberal democratic institutions, a situation most recently demonstrated by the 2014 'Sunflower Movement', in which activists and student protestors occupied the Legislative Yuan in opposition to a proposed free trade agreement with China.

An important aspect of Taiwanese political competition and discourse has been the use of *mincui* or 'populist' discourses, tropes, and political performance by various political actors. These appeals and discourses have come from both the left and right of the political spectrum. Among other things, they have reflected a dissatisfaction with the inequalities and costs of Taiwan's economic development, corruption, and threats to the rule of law; a disenchantment with representative institutions; and a gamut of particular political issues of the day. Populist appeals have been utilized by major political parties—Kuomintang (KMT) and Democratic Progressive Party (DPP)—minor political parties—New Power Party (NPP) and Social Democratic Party (SDP)—various political movements, such as the Taiwan March [*daoguo qianjin*]), and politicians such as the recently recalled Kaohsiung mayor and defeated KMT presidential candidate, Han Kuo-yu. This chapter analyzes the populist impulse in Taiwanese politics and reviews the development of populist politics and discourse over the past two decades. It argues that populism in Taiwan has been infused with contested notions of Taiwanese identity and nationalism, which various actors have insisted are part of a larger Chinese identity coincident with the People's Republic of China (PRC), versus a more geographically limited national identity which is composed of independent and separate Taiwanese cultural and political elements. This ideational fragmentation of the Taiwanese 'people', which cannot be papered over by sentimental appeals to history to ground an 'imagined' national collectivity or bucolic primordial identity, has moderated populist appeals across the political spectrum. At the same time, there has not been the anti-elite impulse that has characterized populist political expressions in other states. There are the class and socio-economically-based realities of political, economic, and cultural inequalities, yet resentment against elite privilege, as well as strong leadership and unmediated politics, which have channelled that resentment in other states, has not found traction in the electorate. To this extent, Taiwanese populism, as a frame for political mobilization and governance, is significantly different to, and far less prominent than, the left and right populism evident in Europe, the United States, and Latin America.

Populism as political framing or an ideology

As is evident from the discussion in other chapters in this volume, populism has a range of meanings and connotations—the content and scope of 'populist' political action, strategies, and discourse cross ideological divides, states, and cultures without losing their ostensible usefulness to political analysts. From the perspective of this chapter, populism can be understood as a mental structure(s) or schemata (i.e., frame) which captures the 'emergent, contested, and socially constructed quality of cognitive frames as they are molded in interaction' (Oliver & Johnston, 2005, p. 5). This ideological structure is characterized by a limited number of core concepts: the people, the elite, and the general will, plus related adjacent and peripheral concepts. The proliferation of populism is partly due to its simplification of complexity and its conceptual elasticity (Freeden, 1996, p. 77). Populism as a framing device enables individuals to 'locate, perceive, identify and label occurrences' and experiences within their present and past environments, thereby providing meaning and structuring social action—'by rendering events or occurrences meaningful, frames function to organize experience and guide action' (Snow et al., 1986, p. 464).

Despite these homonymous characteristics, populism at all times involves a unitary anti-pluralist 'moral' claim for populist representation in the polity coupled with some version of identity politics (Müller, 2016, pp. 2–4), as well as appeals that resonate with the 'heartland' (Mudde & Rovira Kaltwasser, 2013, p. 150). These notions underlie the three core concepts of populist politics and discourse: The idea of 'the people' and the rhetorical appeals to the people, the idea of the 'elite' as contraposed to the people, and the idea of the 'general will'. At the bottom of populist rhetoric lies an integrative, or in the case of right-wing xenophobic populism, exclusionary (Mudde & Rovira Kaltwasser, 2013, p. 147), appeal to 'the people'. The ambiguity of this term, which can include such notions as 'the nation', the whole political community, the 'common man' or the 'underdog', in part allows for the wide use of populist discourse (Canovan, 1984, p. 315). Irrespective of how the concept of 'the people' is understood, populist communication involves 'a conspicuous exhibition of closeness to (ordinary) citizens', and this self-presentation 'can take different guises—using casual or colloquial language or adopting an informal dress code' (Jagers & Walgrave, 2007, pp. 322–323).

Canovan (1984, p. 322) has noted that the malleable nature of 'the people' makes it 'an ideal concept in terms of which neglected grievances can be expressed'. Populist grievances are directed at technocratic, political, financial, and cultural elites perceived to control state and representative institutions, the economy, the media, and social values. These elites, while able to exercise hard economic and coercive power, can also 'shape the conditions within which power can be exercised—to manipulate and indoctrinate or to condition power' (Cudworth & McGovern, 2007, p. 77). Whether these elites constitute a single, cohesive social group/class or a set of interlinking and overlapping dominant groups (Mills, 1956, pp. 157–161), populist thought typically perceives them as malevolent and self-interested, contraposing the purported liberal and cosmopolitan elite interests as antagonistic towards those of the virtuous 'people'.

While populism is 'predicated on the assumption that elite rule can and should be eliminated', the interest which replaces narrow elite interest is that of the presumed 'general will' (Cudworth & McGovern, 2007, p. 70). In short, for a populist, democracy should embody and effectuate the general will. The task is to find the will of the people and follow it. How this 'general will' is to be ascertained is beyond the scope of this paper. However, unlike other forms of authoritarianism, it posits a need to be legitimized in the electoral process, which is conceived as an articulation of that popular sovereignty. This is contrary to liberal notions of elections, which are seen as providing a 'check' on rulers, thus protecting liberty and/or providing a set of preferences for rulers to implement. Populist leadership from this perspective 'is theoretically defined as the representative of the people by the people' in that it is not dependent upon representative institutions or constitutional conventions (Finchelstein, 2017, p. 229). The populist leader, both the crucible and voice for the articulation of this popular sovereignty, acts as a personification of the popular will. In this sense, populism rejects pluralist politics because pluralism embraces the normative vision of a diverse society, where different interests and conflicts are mediated by cross-cutting loyalties and multiple identities.

Populism in the Asian context: Taiwan

Populist theory and case studies in the Asia Pacific do not have a long pedigree compared with those in Europe and Latin America. This is not due to the lack of populist appeals and strategies adopted by individuals and political parties in the region. Populist frames and ideologies arise in numerous socio-political contexts. For example, deposed Prime Minister Thaksin Shinawatra and his Thai Rak Thai (Thais Love Thais) party unabashedly used populist policies and discourse as part of his (and his family's) political platform. In the Philippines, President Rodrigo Duterte was highly successful with his populist 'common person' authenticity and his capacity to visualize the poverty and misery of the common person (Arguelles, 2019, p. 417). Even stodgy Japan has been impacted. In July 2019, the populist Reiwa Shinsengumi, an anti-establishment party running on an anti-capitalist platform calling for the creation of 'a society that does not judge people by their productivity' while blaming the existing system for ignoring the poor and the vulnerable, won 4.6% of the total votes and two seats in the upper house (Minami, 2019). Rather, it seems that some of the underlying socioeconomic conditions, collective and individual mentalities, national identities, and cultural factors have militated against the more broadly based populism experienced in other regions.

Taiwan has likewise been influenced by populist appeals, language, tropes, and strategies since the lifting of martial law in 1989 and the subsequent transition to a democratic polity. Indeed, Shyu (2008, p. 131) argues that Taiwan's electoral politics has 'long been embedded with populist elements'. These populist appeals have veered across the political spectrum. Huang (2014), for example, argues that KMT President Lee Teng-hui used populist appeals to justify his democratic reforms in the 1990s, while DPP President Chen

Shui-bian shrewdly used populist appeals to polarize conflicts between native-born Taiwanese and Mainlanders and to promote Taiwanese independence. Indeed, Chen's policy program, which he used to manipulate public opinion and rationalize his cross-strait trade and economic agenda, was characterized as both populist and nationalist. Schaffer, who canvassed popular media and academic commentary from 1980 to 2008, noted that *mincui* discourse in Taiwan has reflected various elements of 'destructive populism', 'populist Jiang Jing-guo (Chiang Ching-kuo, the son of Chiang-Kai-shek)', 'radical populism', 'populist authoritarian', and 'populist fascism' across the decades (Schaffer, 2010, p. 145). He argues that these various types of populism have been associated with particular leadership styles and socio-political and/or party configurations. Nevertheless, while Schaffer has found an extensive record of populist discourse across the decades, he argues that most populist discourse is simply rhetoric without a significant accompanying populist political program (Schaffer, 2010, pp. 145–147).

Populism and Taiwanese identity

Populism in Taiwan has not been all rhetoric and political stratagem—rather, it has surfaced in unique ways in relation to Taiwan's particular historical experience. Populist imagery and policies have been intermixed with notions of Taiwanese national identity and emerging nationalism, consequently manifested in Taiwanese political activity. National identity is 'the perception of the difference between "we" (in-group) and "they" (out-group)', and a nation or national identity is the consequence of people's subjective construction of this bifurcated reality (Yu & Kwan, 2013, p. 261). It involves not only a sense of place but also a sense of history or shared culture and is generally accompanied by a national narrative or mythology (Poole, 1997, p. 436). From a populist perspective, a national identity or consciousness is a romanticized part of a nation's repository of 'common' virtue and acts as a historic touchstone or consensus for the 'common' person in that society. It is often an integral element in populist appeals, but a notional populist 'identity' is essentially backward-looking and static, privileging primordial associations and allegiances in the face of newer identities or narratives.

Taiwanese identity, which has been undergoing a shift since democratization, does not fit well within this notion. It lacks the historical consensus or primordial antecedents that can be harnessed by populist movements. Conceptually, the ongoing development of Taiwanese identity involves a complex combination of Confucianism, post-colonialism, Indigenous non-Chinese values and political expressions, and Western liberal democracy, as well as emerging multiculturalism. The dynamic emergent nature of Taiwanese national identity, coupled with its conceptual ambiguity and political cleavages, enable Taiwanese citizens and government to pursue contradictory concepts such as: 'modernity and Confucianism, pro-independence and pro-unification, and status quo pitted against an accessible future' (Shih, 2007, p. 120). This conceptual ambiguity is accompanied by a political cleavage relating to the various political positions taken by the KMT and DPP over Taiwanese independence. Politically, the issue devolves into whether the PRC represents the 'true' China and Taiwanese independence is compatible with this unitary notion of Chinese identity and nationalism, or whether there is a separate Taiwanese identity altogether (Stockton, 2007, p. 51). While some commentators have argued that nationalist identity politics is no longer a salient issue of contestation because Taiwanese national identity has stabilized under the DPP, the latest presidential election suggests that the issue remains contested, although it is important not to reduce notions of Taiwanese identity to simply 'Taiwanese vs. Chinese' or 'pro-independence vs. pro-unification'. These dualist notions of Taiwanese identity do not sufficiently encompass the views of the electorate.

This awareness of separate national identity or consciousness, officially discouraged by the ruling KMT rule for decades prior to the 1990s, has been increasingly embraced by the Taiwanese population. Since the 1990s, there has been a significant increase in the percentage of individuals who consider themselves 'Taiwanese' only. This moniker appeared in official discourse with President Lee's discussion of a new Taiwanese identity during the 1998 legislative elections, which sought to induce people to 'localize' their sense of cultural and national identity. In 2008, when President Ma of the KMT took office, a National Chengchi University (NCCU) survey indicated that 48.4% of respondents in Taiwan identified as predominantly Taiwanese, 43.1% identified as both Chinese and Taiwanese, and 4% identified as predominantly Chinese (Ho, 2018). An NCCU study undertaken after the 2014 municipal election, in which the KMT suffered significant losses, found that approximately 60% of individuals identified themselves as 'Taiwanese' only, while those who held dual identity (Chinese and Taiwanese) had decreased to 32%, and those identifying themselves as Chinese only dropped to 3.5% (Election Study Center of NCCU). From the perspective of this new national identity, mainland China is perceived as 'backward, authoritarian and irrational', and the desire of the PRC to re-incorporate the island is simply another effort to colonize Taiwan (Zhong, 2000, p. 60). More recently, an admixture mingling national identity concerns and populism was evidenced in the 'Sunflower Movement' (太陽花) which arose in the face of unpopular governmental activity and policies relating to trade with the PRC. In 2020 (Graph 24.1), individuals who identify themselves as solely 'Taiwanese' reached a historic high, with nearly 70% of respondents identifying themselves as Taiwanese.[2]

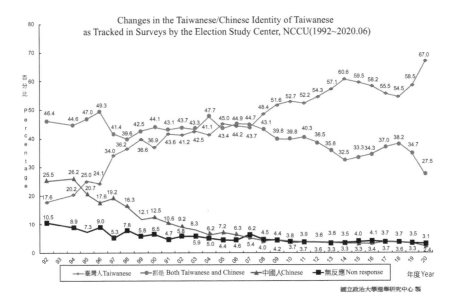

Graph 24.1 Changes in the Taiwanese/Chinese Identity of Taiwanese
Source: Election Study Center, National Chengchi University (2022)

This rising national consciousness has informed legislative activity. For example, in September 2020, several amendments to the Additional Articles of the Constitution (憲法增修條文) were proposed in the Legislative Yuan (legislature). These proposals included changing the definition of the nation's territory, eliminating the Taiwan Provincial Government as an entity (thus dispensing with the institutional representation that Taiwan is part of wider China, notably the mainland), prioritizing the use of the term 'Taiwan' for national groups at international events, (as opposed to 'Chinese Taipei' and 'Taiwan, Province of China') and removing various restrictions on defining the national emblem, flag, and anthem (Yang & Chung, 2020).

Populism and Taiwanese nationalism

While populist appeals can involve an explicit nationalist element, and indeed are often inseparable from nationalist appeals, due to the historical context in Taiwan, populist nationalist appeals have had little political traction. Nationalism as a politically efficacious appeal or as a conception of an 'imagined community' is simply too contested. In addition, to the extent that there is Taiwan nationalism, the concept is bound up in the ongoing notion of democratic transition and the development of liberal state institutions. Nationalist sentiment is then defined in part by its adherence to the symbolic and institutional aspects of liberal democracy and democratic transition. Shyu (2008) has argued the election-driven democratic transition in Taiwan has been facilitated by three political changes. First, traditional authoritarian political and cultural values were replaced gradually by liberal values relating to autonomy, personal choice, and self-fulfilment. Second, there has been an increasing entrenchment of 'the psychological aspects of party politics, partisanship, and psychological attachments to political parties' in the population, a process that facilitated and deepened party competition and competitive elections. Finally, a competitive party system that includes effective and legitimate legislative opposition has developed. These party and electoral systems have already occasioned three peaceful transfers of power (Shyu, 2008, p. 135). As such, while issues of Taiwanese national identity and nationalism are often essentialized into a conflict between opposing Chinese and Taiwanese identities, the notion of Taiwanese nationalism, directed outward in opposition to the strident nationalism of the PRC, includes an element of liberal pluralism and ascription to representative democracy. In the Taiwanese setting, populism can neither co-opt nor trump nationalism with its alternative non-populist unitary notion of community interest as a political movement, nor can it overcome the ascription to liberal institutions. These institutions are an essential aspect of Taiwanese identity and nationalism.

That the ruling KMT regime initiated and actively participated in democratic reforms while in power, and its continued electoral successes despite its adherence to a pan-ethnic Chinese Republic of China (ROC) nationalism, demonstrates the ambiguities of Taiwanese identity and nationalism, which made populist appeals to nationalism politically ineffective (Lin, 1999, p. 1). After democratic reforms were undertaken by KMT President Chiang Ching-kuo in 1986 and 1987, the KMT candidate in the first democratic presidential election, incumbent President Lee Teng-hui, who had succeeded Chiang after his death in 1988, won in 1996 by a landslide margin. After eight years of DPP rule under Chen Shui-bian commencing in 2000, the KMT was returned to the presidential office under Ma Ying-jeou. Ma's electoral success was based on a party platform that called for either reunification with the PRC or some form of a 'Two Systems One State' arrangement under pan-ethnic

Chinese nationalism. The 2016–2020 electoral cycles saw nationalist appeals coming from both the DPP and the KMT. On one hand, followers of DPP President Tsai Ing-wen supported the formal creation of an independent Taiwanese state. For their part, the KMT and the 2019 supporters of presidential candidate Han Kuo-yu offered increased support for the ROC, with the ROC flag as an alternative form of Chinese nationalism to that proffered by the PRC. During the run-up to the 2020 elections, both of these alternative nationalist formulations used the 'sense of national doom' (亡國感) to attack the other camp (Hsieh, 2020). The KMT accused the DPP of attempting to erase the ROC from Taiwan, thus eliminating the ROC as the legitimate repository of Chinese nationalism and national identity. This reaching towards China or Chinese nationalism as inherent in the ROC has been strongly contested by other Taiwanese and Indigenous groups. Conversely, the DPP argued that the KMT's ties with the CCP and pro-unification narratives would end Taiwan's democratic way of life in the event of a Han victory (Hsieh, 2020).

The consequence of this contestation of rival 'nationalisms' is that populist nationalist appeals, which have a consensual or majoritarian basis, are difficult to use. From one perspective, Taiwanese nationalism is 'ROC' nationalism, a comprehensive notion of an imagined community encompassing the entire Chinese community in mainland China and Taiwan, ideally with the recognition of a ROC government. From another perspective, nationalism is the notion of unitary Chinese nationalism sought by the PRC, which does not conceive of a separate ROC or Taiwanese nationalism—a notion evident in the PRC's interpretation of the 'One China' idea or the 1992 'One China Consensus' A third perspective, as advocated by the DPP, encompasses the notion of an autonomous and singular Taiwanese nationalism and Taiwanese community.

Anti-elitism in the Taiwanese context

Along with the hybrid nature of emerging Taiwanese identity and nationalism, Taiwanese populism has, in comparison to populism manifest elsewhere, exhibited less anti-elitism. Vickers has asserted that Taiwanese populism does not exhibit the same primal suspicion of political, economic, and cultural elites as evidenced in other societies (Vickers, 2017, p. 59). The KMT party has been perceived as 'full of elites' (in contrast to the common person), a situation reversed in the 2018 election and attempted unsuccessfully in the KMT's 2019 Ho campaign. However, it is evident that the Taiwanese electorate and politicians remain pluralist in their consideration of social interests, rejecting the populist elite/common person polarity in favour of a more nuanced range of societal interests and interactions.

Initially, extensive protests throughout the period of democratic transition and constitutional reform in the late 1980s and early 1990s, which typically provide fertile grounds for populist appeals and rhetoric, did not exhibit the anti-elite animus, anti-liberal bias, and populist idealization and nostalgia of the people that characterize populist movements in Europe and the Americas. While particular protest movements utilized populist rhetoric, they were generally centred on social concerns regarding instrumental moral, policy, and constitutional objectives. For example, the 1990 Wild Lily student movement (野百合學運) set forth four programmatic demands through the use of populist rhetoric: 1) dissolve the National Assembly (國民大會) and re-establish a new National Assembly infrastructure; 2) nullify the Temporary Provisions Against the Communist Rebellion (動員戡亂時期臨時條款) and re-establish constitutional order; 3) hold a National Affairs Conference (國是會議); and 4) establish a political reform timetable (Wild Lily Student Movement, n.d.). As democratic institutions became firmly rooted, populist rhetoric and social protest incorporated more typical populist elements and programs. Populist elements were evident in the response to a series of corruption scandals that involved DPP President Chen and his family in 2006. As investigations revealed abuses of power such as bribery and Chen's alleged misuse of the Discretionary State Affairs Fund in the second wave of financial reform, public discontent with the government and the direction in which the country was heading boiled over. This saw the emergence of the 'Red Shirt Movement' led by Shih Ming-teh, the first anti-state 'populist' movement since Taiwan's democratization. A wave of protests with numerous instances of civil disobedience saw nearly a million Taiwanese citizens take to the streets to voice their disapproval of Chen's regime and demand his resignation (Restall, 2006, p. 43). However, even these protests did not exhibit the full-throated anti-elitism evident in other countries, as they were not regarded as partisan but rather as reflecting a wider desire to restore moral order to the political system.

Similarly, the rhetoric and agenda of the 2014 'Sunflower Movement' (太陽花), the largest political protest in the history of democratic Taiwan, did not reveal an entrenched anti-elitist bias or the concomitant populist celebration of the 'common person'. The movement erupted in response to KMT President Ma's proposed Cross-Strait Service Trade Agreement (CSSTA) with the PRC, which was part of a longer policy process that sought closer economic integration and rapprochement with the PRC. Driven by student activists, the initial protests arose due to the Ma Administration's insistence that the CSSTA be passed by the Legislative Yuan without a clause-by-clause review. The protests started with an occupation of the Legislative Yuan that lasted 23 days, eventually drawing hundreds of thousands of people onto the streets in peaceful solidarity. Two months later, the CSSTA was withdrawn. The Sunflower Movement came into being as an anti-free trade coalition, formed by activists concerned about the potential economic impact of the CSSTA and the political effects of closer economic relations with the PRC, as well as Ma's non-transparent 'black box' governance. The movement soon attracted numerous ancillary groups who perceived it as a mechanism to achieve other political and social objectives, including Indigenous, gender, and land rights; democratic reform, transparency, and independence; and anti-nuclear activities. The protests were driven by extensive populist rhetoric and programming, as exemplified by the convening of a citizens' constitutional conference (*gongmin xianzheng huiyi*) (Ho, 2019, p. 112). For many participating groups, the protests and wider movement were seen as an exercise in popular sovereignty against the KMT 'elites' conspiring to undermine Taiwanese sovereignty and national identity. They were directed against the appropriateness of the CSSTA and the motivations of the KMT government. The events leading to the protest, such as the Ma administration's attempt to fast-track the agreement without legislative approval, suggested to many that Taiwanese sovereignty was in crisis and could only be rescued by the people themselves, not the 'delegitimized' government of Ma—a belief manifested in the popular slogan 'Our Country, Ours to Save' throughout the movement (Hsu, 2019, pp. 248–249; Ho, 2019, pp. 100–103).

The 2019–20 presidential campaign

That identity issues and anti-elitist political appeals have little political traction was evident in the January 2020 presidential election, won by DPP incumbent Tsai Ing-wen (蔡英文), who received 57.1% of the vote, trouncing the KMT candidate Han Kuo-yu (韓國瑜) who won only 38.6% (Hale, 2020).

In early 2019, Tsai's re-election prospects looked grim. During the 2018 local elections, the ruling DPP had been soundly defeated. Opposition KMT mayoral candidates had triumphed in Taiwan's three largest cities—New Taipei City, Taichung, and Kaohsiung. While there was significant evidence that the PRC was actively influencing the election and favouring the KMT, there were also local obstacles faced by the DPP, including wage stagnancy and severe air pollution in the southern region of the island. Included on the ballots was a set of referendum questions on topics such as same-sex marriage (rejected by the electorate), removal of gendered content from school textbooks, and a question asking whether the country should be referred to as 'Taiwan' rather than 'Chinese Taipei' at international sporting events. These problems and the controversial nature of the referendum questions created voting blocs that cut across traditional bases of DPP support (Horton, 2018). Tsai resigned as DPP chairperson following the 2018 election, and her approval rating remained low in early 2019.

Han was elected Mayor of Kaohsiung in November 2018—the first KMT politician since 1998 to hold that office. Prior to his election, he had been General Manager of Taipei Agricultural Products Marketing Corporation (TAPMC), jointly owned by Taipei City and the Council of Agriculture, and served in the Legislative Yuan from 1992 to 2002. Despite his prior service in the more elitist KMT, Han was generally known for his 'non-elite' style as he rose to prominence. During his 2018 mayoral campaign, he drew attention as a non-traditionalist KMT politician, emphasizing that he was not from a prominent political family. His mayoral campaign for Kaohsiung was best known for a few simple slogans: 'Making Kaohsiung Great Again' (which unsurprisingly won him the title of the 'Taiwanese Trump') and 'Export goods out. Welcome people in. Let Kaohsiung prosper!' (Wang, 2020). This campaign appealed to a large cross-section of the city's voters. Given his pro-PRC political standing, he was keen to further strengthen cross-strait economic ties, arguing that engagement with the PRC would foster economic prosperity and should not be regarded as a political preference. He argued that the KMT—DPP disagreement surrounding relations with the PRC was elite-driven and unreflective of the interests of ordinary citizens.

Han's victory in Kaohsiung City reflected the rise of the populist-driven 'Grass-roots Blue' faction within the KMT. 'Grass-roots Blue' describes KMT politicians not from the KMT 'Elite Blue', who come from well-connected political families and generally dominate the party platform and government policy. Han's 'Grass-roots Blue' background made him a viable alternative candidate as the party's presidential nomination in the likelihood that he would resonate with pan-blue voters within the KMT, who had expressed dissatisfaction with corrupt practices associated with the party during the Ma administration. He was also seen to appeal to independents as well as disenchanted DPP voters.

Nathan Batto has described Han's presidential campaign strategy as presenting politics as a 'moral choice between himself, the representative of the *shumin* [ordinary people], and a corrupt elite who control the DPP and sap the country of its vitality' (Nachman, 2020). At a rally in early December 2020, Han denounced 'a small cabal' at the helm of the DPP. 'They feast and feast', he railed. 'The factions divide the spoils among themselves' (Batto, 2020). In running with this theme, Han explicitly incorporated populist performance into his campaign. He harkened back nostalgically to Taiwan's boom days when mere construction workers earned lucrative wages and a large sector of the public was playing the stock markets. Consistent with the patriotic aspect of populist politics, he publicized his great love for the ROC flag, even opining that 'flag platforms' should be installed on 'all the nation's mountains with peaks 3,000m or higher so flag-raising ceremonies could be held on them' (Hsu, 2019). His campaign slogan, 'safety for Taiwan, money for the people', and his campaign platform—to defend the ROC, to love Chinese culture, to uphold freedom and democracy, and to never forget the struggling people—echoed populist platforms from other counties. This Manichean world view, which calls for dramatic change, evokes nationalism and outlines an 'us vs them' duality is a populist feature that is often used by populist campaigns where the focus is not on particular issues (Hawkins, 2009).

At the same time, Han's campaign relied heavily on his 'common-man' image and populist discourses. Voters cited Han's 'humility, use of plain language and displays of affection' as likeable traits. In the words of a supporter, 'He has also exhibited genuine care for the socially disadvantaged and people at the grassroots level, unlike those political elites who only pay lip service' (HAN FANS, 2019). In his first campaign address, in which he interrupted former President Ma's speech to introduce himself, Han implored 'the country to support his campaign platform' and promised the people that, if elected, his government would 'truly serve the people' (DeAeth, 2019). Like many other populist politicians around the globe, he used racist tropes and rhetoric against immigrants, such as domestic workers from the Philippines (employing a racial slur), and he regularly courted controversy with his gendered and misogynistic comments. This was reminiscent of a speech to a women's association in 2018 on attracting foreign investment, during which Han stated: 'If you create 1,000 job opportunities, I'll give you a kiss. If you create 10,000, I'll sleep with you for one night' (Horton, 2019).

Han also sought to appeal to the electorate's sense of nationalism and the importance of ROC sovereignty. This perception of sovereignty under attack, which should be defended at all costs, is a popular topic in populist campaigning (Jenne, 2016). Unsurprisingly, as the KMT nominee, he advocated forging closer ties with the PRC. In an emotional speech after his formal nomination, he noted, 'This won't be a polite gentleman's race. The election is about the life and death of the Republic of China (ROC) and Taiwan's next generation', referring to the island by its official name (Shi, 2019). Han contended that better ties with China would reduce the risk of conflict and improve the economy, thus ensuring the long-term prosperity of the ROC. He maintained that the China policy pursued by Tsai and the DPP (including Tsai's refusal to ascribe to the 1992 One China Consensus) threatened the very existence of the ROC. He contrasted his common appeal and his belief in ROC sovereignty to the policies of the Tsai Administration and the Green (DPP) elites which, he argued, threatened to draw Taiwan into an unwinnable conflict with the PRC. 'Economic prosperity and stable cross-strait relations rather than the colours of the island's political parties', he argued, should be the determinant of ROC-PRC cross-strait policies (Shi, 2019).

Nevertheless, despite his early popularity, Han's populist-centred campaign did not work for him during the presidential election. As the year progressed, his pro-PRC stance supported by President Xi Jinping's January 1, 2020, speech, which called for Taiwan's unification with China under a 'One Country, Two Systems' framework similar to that ostensibly granted to Hong Kong, was undercut by Xi's insistence that force remained an option in reunification. In that speech, Xi noted to applause, 'We make no promise to abandon the use of force, and retain the option of taking all necessary measures' (Buckley & Horton, 2019). Moreover, the attractiveness of 'One Country, Two Systems' was seriously damaged by Beijing's moves to suppress dissent in Hong Kong, which led subsequently to the introduction of the new National Security Law in Hong Kong in June 2020 criminalizing secession and subversion. These actions, as well as the PRC's effort to damage the Taiwanese economy and moves to internationally isolate Tsai's Taiwan over the previous years, made clear that Beijing's version of the 'One China' vision was different from that presented by the KMT to Taiwanese voters. In the face of protests and the implied consequences for Taiwan, Tsai strongly asserted her support for liberal democratic politics in Hong Kong as well as Taiwanese democratic institutions and autonomy, allowing her to regain political support. In response, Han struggled to articulate a coherent cross-strait policy and position on Taiwanese/ROC autonomy, and he was soundly defeated in the January 2020 election. President Tsai was re-elected with 57.1% of the popular vote and the DPP won 61 of the 113 seats in the national legislature.

Populism in Taiwan

As Batto suggests, the international and domestic contexts resurrected the election issues of sovereignty and identity, as conventionally understood. However, this is not to say that populist appeals were irrelevant or that they had no political traction (Batto, 2020). It was evident from Han's rise that a populist program could appeal to a broad section of voters. Nor was Han's failure a repudiation of populism, as he was clearly incapable of sustaining his populist strategy, partly due to the shadow of China. Under the spotlight of his presidential campaign, it became evident that Han was far from an ideal candidate. The DPP was able to portray him as detached and ineffectual, and, contrary to his common-man image, media reports revealed real estate transactions from which he had allegedly benefited through his political connections. The result was that levels of trust in Han among the public, a core element in a populist programme or political campaign as a populist leader, declined dramatically throughout 2019.[3] Conversely, Tsai successfully clothed herself and the DPP with the accoutrements of Taiwanese autonomy and to a lesser extent Taiwanese/ROC identity. The threat from the PRC throughout that year enabled her to prove her competence as a leader of the Taiwanese/ROC state. She was further able to claim credit for various bread and butter accomplishments such as higher wages, lower taxes, and greater investment in social welfare programs (Batto, 2020).

Despite the populist rhetoric and use of populist motifs by Han, the failure of the KMT to harness populist energies suggests that conceptually, Taiwanese nationalism and identity remain bound up in liberal democratic institutions and pluralist politics. These political perspectives make it difficult to sustain the anti-elitism found in many populist discourses. For example, less than a week before the election, Tsai's campaign released a video presenting the election as a choice between a vibrant Taiwanese democracy and a dictatorship, represented by a photo of Chinese President Xi Jinping. The narrator intoned:

> No matter the differences between us, we all love the quiet life here.... We still love this country with its democracy and its freedom. Now it's our turn to speak. The whole world is watching how Taiwan makes its voice heard.
>
> *Fifield, 2020*

This perspective, simultaneously plural and unified, is the basis of a plural liberal democracy.

Naturally, the continued and growing threat of the PRC and seemingly intractable nature of the conflict, coupled with the emergent nature of Taiwan's democratic transition, could provide an opportunity for the rise of a more inclusive form of populism and the recrudescence of authoritarian government. More prosaically, a society can lose faith in democratic institutions and plural politics when corruption and minoritarian self-interest are manifest, such as during the President Chen scandals. While democratic processes and discourse remain robust, the institutional base of Taiwanese democracy remains contested and emergent. The rule of law, the apolitical nature of the civil service and judiciary, constitutional norms, and the legitimacy of political opposition and constitutional rules continue to be the object of political and social discord. In this environment, where the population is confounded by foreign threats, discord, and anxiety, a simple populist program (particularly as a discursive style and political strategy) could be utilized by power-seeking leaders who have little interest in maintaining the current democratic transition. Once in power, the government could then eliminate threats to their power (i.e., special interests and political and social opposition) as part of a set of alternative domestic and foreign policies designed to assuage the anxieties of the electorate. Yet, given the attention that the population has paid to creeping authoritarianism in Hong Kong, the continued presence of political opposition both in Taiwanese society and in the legislature—developing multiculturalism and reconciliation with Indigenous peoples—there is good reason to be optimistic as to the robustness of Taiwanese liberal institutions and politics.

Conclusion

At its core, populism conceives of the world in stark contesting dualities: us vs them, people vs the elite, nationalism vs globalism, common virtue vs malignant special interest. While populist language and programs have been an important aspect of democratic competition and protest movements since the 1980s, the dualities and rigid categorizations of populist politics and populist leaders do not easily fit the historical context and present-day challenges of Taiwan. The populist notions of the people, the common will, and the state—whether defined inclusively or exclusively—remain too contested in Taiwan to have broad appeal across the political spectrum. Moreover, the democratic transition since the 1980s has entrenched a respect for democratic institutions and political pluralism. This allegiance to liberal constitutionalism is an important aspect of Taiwanese identity and nationalism militating against populist politics.

Notes

1 The authors would like to thank Tobie Openshaw and Cat Thomas for their insights and helpful comments.
2 https://esc.nccu.edu.tw.
3 According to surveys conducted by Tai Li-an (Batto, 2020), one of Taiwan's most respected pollsters, and published by the news site Formosa, the percentage of respondents who said they distrusted Mr. Han rose from more than 27% in February to about 57% in November 2019. His support among independent voters withered from more than 41% in February to less than 15% in December. Even among supporters of the Kuomintang camp, his base, support dropped from nearly 89% to a little over 66% over the same period.

References

Arguelles, C. V. (2019). 'We are Rodrigo Duterte': Dimensions of the Philippine populist publics' vote. *Asian Politics and Policy*, 11(3), 417–437. https://doi.org/10.1111/aspp.12472

Batto, N. (2020, January 12). When populism can't beat identity politics. *The New York Times*. www.nytimes.com/2020/01/12/opinion/taiwan-election-tsai-han-populism.html

Buckley, C., & Horton, C. (2019, January 1). Xi Jinping warns Taiwan that unification is the goal and force is an option. *The New York Times*. www.nytimes.com/2019/01/01/world/asia/xi-jin-ping-taiwan-china.html

Canovan, M. (1984). 'People', politicians and populism. *Government and Opposition*, 19(3), 312–327. https://doi.org/10.1111/j.1477-7053.1984.tb01048.x

Cudworth, E., & McGovern, J. (2007). The state and the power elite. In E. Cudworth, T. Hall & J. McGovern. (Eds.), *The modern state: Theories and ideologies*. Edinburgh University Press.

DeAeth, D. (2019, September 9). Han Kuo-yu offers core campaign message at mass rally in New Taipei. *Taiwan News*. www.taiwannews.com.tw/en/news/3773147

Election Study Center, National Chengchi University (2022). *Taiwanese core political attitude trend (1992–2014/06)*. https://esc.nccu.edu.tw/PageDoc/Detail?fid=7436&id=6532

Fifield, A. (2020, January 7). As Taiwan goes to the polls, Tsai says the choice is democracy or dictatorship. *The Washington Post*. www.washingtonpost.com/world/as-taiwan-goes-to-the-polls-tsai-says-the-choice-is-between-democracy-or-dictatorship/2020/01/07/2119a620-310a-11ea-971b-43bec3ff9860_story.html

Finchelstein, F. (2017). *From fascism to populism in history*. University of California Press.

Freeden, M. (1996). *Ideologies and political theory: A conceptual approach*. Clarendon.

Hale, E. (2020, January 11). Tsai Ing-wen wins landslide in Taiwan presidential election. *Aljazeera*. www.aljazeera.com/news/2020/1/11/tsai-ing-wen-wins-landslide-in-taiwan-presidential-election

HAN FANS: Why Han Kuo-yu Appeals to People Who do Not Have Time for the Political 'Elite'. (2019, July 29). *Taipei Times*. www.taipeitimes.com/News/taiwan/archives/2019/07/29/2003719541

Hawkins, K. (2009). Is Chávez populist?: Measuring populist discourse in comparative perspective. *Comparative Political Studies*, 42(8), 1040–1067. https://doi.org/10.1177/0010414009331721

Ho, M.-S. (2018, August 2). *The activist legacy of Taiwan's Sunflower Movement*. Carnegie Endowment for International Peace. https://carnegieendowment.org/2018/08/02/activist-legacy-of-taiwan-s-sunflower-movement-pub-76966

Ho, M.-S. (2019). *Challenging Beijing's mandate of heaven: Taiwan's Sunflower Movement and Hong Kong's umbrella movement*. Temple University Press.

Horton, C. (2018 November 25). Taiwan's president quits as party chief after stinging losses in local races. *The New York Times*. www.nytimes.com/2018/11/24/world/asia/taiwan-election-results.html

Horton, C. (2019, April 16). The Taiwanese populist advancing China's interests. *The Atlantic*. www.theatlantic.com/international/archive/2019/04/taiwanese-populist-han-kuo-yu-china/587146/

Hsieh, M. (2020, January 22). Despite Tsai's victory, nationalism and populism are still strong in Taiwan. *Taiwan Insight*. https://taiwaninsight.org/2020/01/22/despite-tsais-victory-nationalism-and-populism-are-still-strong-in-taiwan/

Hsu, L., Chu, P., & Hetherington, W. (2019, November 24). Han likes idea of national flags on top of peaks. *Taipei Times*. www.taipeitimes.com/News/taiwan/archives/2019/10/24/2003724550

Huang, Y. T. (2014). A study of the transition of Taiwan's populism: the formation of populist electoralism. *Hongguang Journal of Humanities and Social Sciences*, 17, 52–73.

Jagers, J., & Walgrave, S. (2007). Populism as political communication style: An empirical study of political parties' discourse in Belgium. *European Journal of Political Research*, 46(3), 319–345. https://doi.org/10.1111/j.1475-6765.2006.00690.x

Jenne, E. (2016). *How populist governments rewrite sovereignty and why*. Central European University. www.ceu.edu/sites/default/files/attachment/event/15587/erinjennepolberg-consec-2016.pdf

Lin, J. W. (1999). Democratization under one-party dominance: Explaining Taiwan's paradoxical transition. *Issue & Studies*, 35(6), 1–28.

Mills, C. W. (1956). *The power elite*. Oxford University Press.

Minami, D. (2019, July 31). Is populism finally coming to Japan? The success of the leftist Reiwa Shinsengumi marks a turning point in Japanese politics. *The Diplomat*. https://thediplomat.com/2019/07/is-populism-finally-coming-to-japan/

Mudde, C., & Rovira Kaltwasser, C. (2013). Exclusionary vs. Inclusionary populism: Comparing contemporary Europe and Latin America. *Government & Opposition*, 48(2), 147–174. https://doi.org/10.1017/gov.2012.11

Müller, J.-W. (2016). *What is populism*? University of Pennsylvania Press.

Nachman, L. (2020, January 13). Taiwan's voters show how to beat populism. *Foreign Policy.* https://foreignpolicy.com/2020/01/13/china-tsai-han-trump-boris-taiwans-voters-show-how-to-beat-populism/

Oliver, P., & Johnston, H. (2005). What a good idea! Ideologies and frames in social movement research. In H. Johnson & J. A. Noakes (Eds.), *In frames of protest. Social movements and the framing perspective* (pp. 185–204). Rowman and Littlefield.

Poole, R. (1997). National identity, multiculturalism, and Aboriginal rights: An Australian perspective. *Canadian Journal of Philosophy, 26*(1), 407–438. https://doi.org/10.1080/00455091.1997.10716823

Restall, H. (2006). Taiwan's red shirt rebel. *Far Eastern Economic Review, 169*(10), 43–55.

Schaffer, C. (2010). Populism in East Asia's new democracies: An analysis of the Taiwanese discourse. In M. Parvizi (Ed.), *State, society and international relations in Asia* (pp. 133–147). Amsterdam University Press.

Shi, J. (2019, July 29). KMT presidential candidate Han Kuo-yu says 2020 election will be life-or-death battle for Taiwan. *South China Morning Post.* www.scmp.com/news/china/politics/article/3020407/kmt-presidential-candidate-han-kuo-yu-says-2020-election-will.

Shih, C.-Y. (2007). *Democracy (made in Taiwan). The 'success' state as a political theory.* Lexington Books.

Shyu, H. (2008). Populism in Taiwan: The rise of a populist-democratic culture in a democratising society. *Asian Journal of Political Science, 16*(2), 130–150. https://doi.org/10.1080/02185370802204073

Snow, D. A., Rochford, E. B., Worden, S. K., & Benford, R. D. (1986). Frame alignment processes, micromobilization and movement participation. *American Sociological Review, 51*(4), 446–481. https://doi.org/10.2307/2095581

Stockton, H. (2007). Taiwan: Political and national security of becoming 'Taiwanese'. In S. Horowitz, U. Heo & A. C. Tan (Eds.), *Identity and change in East Asian conflicts: The cases of China, Taiwan, and the Koreas.* Palgrave Macmillan.

Vickers, E. (2017). All quiet on the eastern front? Populism, nationalism and democracy in East Asia. *Georgetown Journal of International Affairs, 18*(2), 59–68. https://doi.org/10.1353/gia.2017.0021

Wang, Z. (2020, January 10). Populism comes to Taiwan in election focused on future relationship with China. *The Conversation.* https://theconversation.com/populism-comes-to-taiwan-in-election-focused-on-future-relationship-with-china-129198

Wild Lily Student Movement. (n.d.). *Oftaiwan.* https://oftaiwan.org/social-movements/wild-lily-student-movement/

Yang, C., & Chung, J. (2020, Februrary 25). Poll finds 62.6% identify as Taiwanese. *Taipei Times.* www.taipeitimes.com/News/front/archives/2020/09/25/2003744036

Yu, F., & Kwan, D. (2013). Social construction of national reality: Tibet and Taiwan. *Journal of Chinese Political Science, 18*(3), 259–279. https://doi.org/10.1007/s11366-013-9249-z

Zhong, Y. (2000). Taiwan's presidential election and Sino-U.S. relations. *Journal of Chinese Political Science, 6*(1), 55–69. https://doi.org/10.1007/BF02876899

25
POPULISM IN JAPAN
Actors or institutions?

Toru Yoshida

Japan has long been seen as an exception to the populist waves around the world that began in the 1990s. Chairman of the Asia-Pacific Initiative and award-winning journalist, Dr Yoichi Funabashi, observed that in contrast to other developed democracies, Japan has been spared the rash of 'sweeping and virulent populism' and has enjoyed unprecedented political stability, particularly since the Abe Shinzo government took office in 2012 (Funabashi, 2017). Similarly, Japanese political scholar and Brookings Fellow Dr Mireya opined that Japan has escaped 'the disruption of populism and the temptation of economic nationalism' that has plagued advanced democracies elsewhere (Solís, 2019, p. 2). Clearly, Japan has not been exposed to the boom of culturally authoritarian and economically interventionist populist figures that has reverberated in the West. A range of explanations have been proffered to account for the absence of populism in Japanese national politics: budgetary expansion policies despite a huge budget deficit, minimal political participation partly due to the ageing society, lack of cultural and ethnic cleavage, less impactful economic and cultural globalization, and less economic inequality despite a relatively low level of GDP growth compared with that of other industrialized countries. These hypotheses only raise the overwhelming question that studies on populism have long tried to explain—why, when, and how does populism occur, and in what particular context does it gain and sustain power?

In this chapter, I try to clarify rather than answer the questions by providing a contextual background that facilitates an understanding of Japanese politics. At the start, it is demonstrable that populism has not been absent in Japan and is firmly grounded in the political arena. Those insights are prerequisites to support a discussion on the institutional (i.e., the electoral systems) and sociological (e.g., increasing non-affiliated voters in metropolitan areas) factors that facilitate the rise of populism, and not the *ideational* aspect that is so prominent in the academic literature.

Is Japan an exception?

Focusing on the changing parameters of political conflict and economic and social inequality, as evidenced in an empirical analysis of post-electoral statistics for France, the United Kingdom, and the United States since World War II, Thomas Piketty (2018) recently introduced the phrase 'Brahmin left vs merchant right' to explain how modern *hyper-capitalism* has widened disparities within countries. In this longitudinal study of voting behaviour, he shows that social democrat and labour left-wing parties in Western Europe, which through the 1950s and 1960s were supported by a lower-income, less-educated working-class voter base, have become the preserve of high-education elites (Brahmin left) and the better-educated middle class, while the right-wing, conservative parties have become dominated by high-income business-oriented elites (merchant right) (Piketty, 2018, p. 2). The resultant 'multiple-elite stabilization' since the 1990s has given rise to a form of populism linked to a growing sense of alienation from established political parties and thus a lack of democratic representation among less-educated and low-income voters who have consequently turned to right-wing populist parties (Piketty, 2018, p. 4). Piketty's findings coincide with other recent research describing the mechanisms of electoral support for populist parties and leaders in Western countries (for example, Norris & Inglehart, 2019; Mudde, 2007).

Notably, Piketty finds that this changing pattern of voting behaviour has not been observed in Japan. One study on Japanese political development *à la* Piketty claims that the long-term dominance of the conservative Liberal Democratic Party (LDP) from 1955 to 1993 led consecutive governments to adopt catch-all strategies, and despite rising inequality and social unrest following the end of the economic boom (i.e. since the early 1990s), no single political actor has succeeded in forming a dominant political cleavage (Gethin, 2018, Ch. 7).

Yet, we must not overlook a typical populist phenomenon that Japan has witnessed in recent decades. Firstly, as we shall see below, Prime Minister Junichiro Koizumi, who held office from 2001 to 2006, was widely appraised as a typical populist politician, like his Italian counterpart, Silvio Berlusconi, and the former French President, Nicolas Sarkozy (Otake, 2003). Secondly, we have to pay attention to regional and local populist figures in Japan, generally bypassed by the international media, who represent an original Japanese archetypal populism. Indeed, Yuriko Koike, Tokyo governor since 2016, and Toru Hashimoto, who served as Osaka governor and then city mayor between 2008 and 2015, have been widely cited (and criticized) as populist politicians. What makes Japan unique is that its populism is a mostly forgotten type, namely a reformist and neoliberal version, which arose in the shadow of the political hegemony of the LDP. In other words, the pronouncements that Japan is immune to populism are only relevant in regard to culturally authoritarian and economically protectionist types of populism. Populism, however, has several forms and styles, as the case of Japan illustrates. Thirdly, Japan is currently experiencing a new type of populism, namely left-wing populism, which conforms to recent developments in some Latin American and Southern European countries. Although it will not be discussed in this chapter, a brand new party, *Reiwa-Shinsengumi*,[1] making extensive use of social networks in their campaign, gained two seats in the 2019 Senate (House of Councillors) election against all media expectations (Klein, 2020).

While Japan has not manifested the types of populism common in other countries, it certainly has its own type of populism. The next section will explore in detail why these reformist and neoliberal forms of populism have arisen in Japan.

Incumbent populist: the Koizumi phenomenon

Junichiro Koizumi was designated by the National Diet and appointed by the emperor as the 87th Japanese prime minister on 26 April 2001. It was the third time he had contested the LDP presidential election, having been unsuccessful in 1995 and 1998. Ex-Prime Minister Ryutaro Hashimoto, leader of the party's largest faction, had been tipped as the winner, but Koizumi, by appealing to party members rather than Members of Parliament (MPs), was able to triumph in spite of his perceived inferior position.

Until this time, Koizumi was regarded as a lone wolf within the LDP. The eldest son in a family of politicians, he began serving as an MP in 1972 when he belonged to *Seiwa-kai*, one of the bigger factions of the party, and one which, at the time of Koizumi's election, projected a strong reformist and anti-communist agenda. His key commitment on assuming office was the privatization of the postal service, which was contrary to the party's position, since the LDP from the time of its creation was committed to rural interests. Merging savings and insurance services, the Japan Post had historically been an important resource for electoral mobilization, as well as for regional development. However, Koizumi embarked on a vast agenda of *structural reform* in privatizing the Japan Post as well as the Highway Road Corporation. Several other important reforms, inter alia deregulation of the labour market, introduction of special economic zones, and placing a ceiling on government bonds, were promised for his first term. Reforms during his premiership covered over six policy domains—namely, budget reforms, bank debt disposal, medical and pension reforms, privatization, regional budgetary constraint, and deregulation (Hook, 2010).

Uchiyama (2010) asserts that Koizumi introduced a new political style in Japan, as his frank and personal political discourse, illustrated by statements such as 'forces of resistance' and 'smashing the LDP' referring to his personal view of the party through which he had come to power, was based on *pathos* rather than *logos*, while his policies were driven by *ideas* and not *interests*, as had been the case with his predecessors (p. 22). The expression 'one-phrase politics' was attributed to his style of political communication (p. 9). And it was almost unprecedented in the long history of LDP governments that controversial governmental policies had been attributed to a single political leader.

It is therefore not surprising that the term *populism* became widely circulated for the first time in Japan during his premiership. The centre-left national newspaper Mainichi Shimbun had used this term only 35 times between 1990 and 2000. Usage became more frequent after that, rising to 103 times by 2010.[2] Before Koizumi, the term was applied to foreign political leaders, who fitted the bill, or to specific policies regarded as popular but unfeasible in budgetary terms. Lindgren claims that 'certainly high-quality research on Japanese populism exists, however the literature is limited' (Lindgren, 2005, p. 589), and that research only starts with Koizumi's tenure.[3]

Some commentators have asserted that Koizumi embodies a Japanese model of populism. Otake defines Koizumi as a political outsider, and claims that he brought a moral dimension to politics and favoured direct communication with the electorate, which he expressed in his own unique 'theatrical style' (Otake, 2003). According to Otake, the powerful former prime minister, Kakuei Tanaka (1972–1974), with his vast infrastructure investment plan and introduction of a generous welfare system, might also have been described as a populist politician, but his style was an 'interest-led populism', which differs considerably from the modern neoliberal type of populism represented by Koizumi.[4]

As is often the case for a populist, Koizumi was much criticized by quality newspapers and by intellectuals, but he was nevertheless a *popular* politician. His average approval rating during his tenure was 50.7% (based on Jiji-Press opinion polls), the second highest rating after the Hosokawa government (1993–1994)[5]. As Hosokawa was in power for only eight months, and as Koizumi's tenure (2001–2006) was the third-longest in post-war

Japan, the latter's record is exceptional. In another opinion poll, conducted by Asahi-Shimbun in 2009, Koizumi was placed sixth among the most highly regarded politicians of the post-war period. But the five above him on the list had all benefited from the unprecedented economic growth or the economic bubble of earlier decades. A detailed electoral and opinion poll survey shows that people who felt a sense of 'blockage' or 'entrapment' and favoured economic redistribution were the Koizumi government's biggest supporters (Sugawara, 2009; Hamada, 2013). This might seem paradoxical, since Koizumi's period in power coincided with the economic downturn which began in the 1990s (referred to as Japan's lost decade), but he represented a political aspiration for more fair and free competition, breaking down the old vested interests to allow people access to economic and social resources that had been denied them, ensuring a positive reaction to his reforms.

Koizumi's populism as an outcome of institutional reforms during the 1990s

Do these details demonstrate that Koizumi was a popular populist solely because of his political style and policies? Certainly not, because one also needs to pay attention to the institutional reforms of the 1990s, which created the conditions that made it possible for Koizumi to be a successful populist.

The Japanese lower-house electoral system was changed in 1994 after several financial scandals had shaken public opinion and resulted in the LDP losing its majority in the Diet in 1993. The government-opposition reformists agreed to modify the electoral system from multi-seat districts (*Chûsenkyoku*, based on single non-transferable votes) allowing three to five candidates to gain a seat to a single-member district-based system.[6] The new electoral system profoundly muted not only the inter-party competition structure, resulting in a reduction of the number of political parties, but also the intra-party competition structure by reducing the historically powerful influence of LDP factions. The latter was made possible because the party leader could now control the party organization, as he had the authority to nominate the candidates for each district (Reed, 2007). The political reforms also introduced public financing of political parties, which added further to the power of party leaders, giving them the authority to distribute money to their preferred candidates (Kobayashi, 2012).

Other important reforms had been undertaken by the Hashimoto government (1996–1998), which endorsed a wide-ranging administrative reform plan. The number of ministries was reduced from 22 to 12, and the functions of the prime minister and the chief cabinet secretary were institutionally reinforced. Those reforms included an increase in the number of public servants working for the prime minister and the chief cabinet secretariat, the establishment of the independent advisory council, and the introduction of the formal agenda initiative by the Prime Minister (Iio, 2007). One of the consequences of these reforms was the increased power of the core executive (Shinoda, 2005), who could now largely bypass the party committee that had previously dominated the policy agenda and delegate responsibility to the prime minister's advisory council, which comprised civilian reformists.

These political reforms created the conditions that enabled Koizumi to seize his political opportunity and propose his policies. For the first time in LDP history, he was able to ignore the party's factions to form his government. Most of the ministerial portfolios were given to his allies, with the exceptions of a few appointments to small coalition partners. Traditionally, the prime minister had to consider the power balance of five to eight factions inside the party in order to secure his position, as the faction leaders' cooperation was the key to securing and retaining the party presidency. However, Koizumi was able to ignore this custom, as factional influence had been curbed by the electoral reforms.

In 2005, Koizumi dissolved the assembly when the majority of the Senate rejected his daring Postal Privatization Bill. In the ensuing controversial snap election, which was criticized as anti-constitutional, Koizumi likened himself to Galileo Galilei, implying that the privatization of Japan Post was as necessary as a belief in Copernican heliocentricity. He disendorsed the 37 LDP MPs who opposed the bill and designated new candidates (described as *assassins* by the media) in their districts. Labelled the 'Koizumi theatre' by the media, this strategy resulted in a landslide victory for the LDP, the second most convincing election win in the party's history. Koizumi's reforms were thus the fruit of the political and administrative reforms implemented in the 1990s.

It has become common to describe Koizumi as a populist, and since his period in office, the term has become much more widely used in Japan. It is also true that, as an outsider in a powerful governmental party environment where faction leaders had exercised strong influence, Koizumi is fit to be denoted as such. But it has to be stressed that his populism could only flourish because of the structural changes made within Japanese politics during the 1990s. First, the interest-led, pork-barrel politics had been dismissed, no longer necessary as the rural areas of Japan had developed thanks to the long-term one-party dominance. Ironically, however, the rising influence of the rural sector had weakened the LDP's hegemony. Then, in the mid-1990s, the electoral reforms irrevocably reduced the power of the mighty factions within the party. The administrative reforms made it possible for the prime minister to introduce policies even if they were unpopular within the party. Koizumi's populism was assessed as rebellious and antagonistic to the majority of LDP MPs but received massive support from the electorate. The call by Koizumi for 'smashing the LDP' could only be reform-driven, opposing the old values and long-established policy styles of the party. In sum, Koizumi's populism did not emerge and become successful simply because it was populism but as the result of prior mid-term institutional changes to the Japanese political system.

Local populism in Osaka and Tokyo

The same schema can be applied to the tide of Japanese populism, the regional populism of metropolitan governors and big-city mayors (Yoshida, 2020).

Following Matsutani's (2017) argument, we can identify three criteria to apply to populist politicians in Japan: ideology, style, and strategy. The first refers to the ideological approach of populism that posits the idea of 'the good people and evil elites', the second refers to the political discourse that praises 'the people' in general, and the third refers to the political communication strategy targeting the working class. Matsutani considered ten Japanese politicians commonly regarded as populist and identified five who met all the criteria. Four of the five are local politicians, with Koizumi as the fifth: Yasuo Tanaka, Governor of Nagano (2000–2006); Toru Hashimoto, Governor of Osaka (2008–2011) and then Mayor of Osaka City (2011–2015); Takashi Kawamura, Mayor of Nagoya (since 2009); and Yuriko Koike, elected and re-elected Governor of Tokyo with landslide victories in 2016 and 2020. As this list shows, one of the traits of Japanese populism is that it is predominantly a regional phenomenon.

Regional politicians have not been totally excluded from populism studies. For example, in her classic work on populism, Margaret Canovan identifies 'populist dictatorship' as one of seven types of populism, citing as an archetype Huey Long, Governor of Louisiana (1928–1932) (Canovan, 1981). Thus, populism can be generated in the sub-national political arena, which is particularly the case in Japan. To examine this form of Japanese populism, we will focus on two recent popular figures, Toru Hashimoto and Yuriko Koike, both denounced as populists by their adversaries.

Toru Hashimoto was born in 1969 and first came to the attention of the public as a lawyer on popular TV programmes. He was elected Governor of Osaka prefecture, the second largest local government area in Japan, as an independent candidate in 2008. He has a sharp tongue and is noted for his vicious criticisms (often through local TV programmes or Twitter) of intermediate organizations such as local councils, labour unions, and public schools. After establishing his personal party, *Osaka-Ishin-no-Kaî* (The Osaka Restoration Association) in 2010, he fiercely denounced the prefectural bureaucracy and the local bureaucratic system as structured by the central government (see Pekkanen & Reed, 2018 for a detailed discussion). He then teamed up with several MPs from established parties to form *Nihon-Ishin-no-Kaî* (Japan Restoration Party) a few months before the 2012 general election. The party manifesto called for reforms that included regionalization, the direct election of the prime minister, a downsizing of government, the introduction of an internet voting system, a pay-as-you-go pension system, a flat tax, the easing of immigration, and increased market competition in the public sector. Hashimoto stated prior to the election: 'It is my firm conviction that we need to go further with the Koizumi and Takenaka [Minister of Economy under Koizumi] way of structural reform' (cited in Nakakita, 2020, p. 289). After the heavy defeat of the Democratic Party of Japan (DPJ), which had governed between 2009 and 2012, these neoliberal policies proved very popular with voters, and *Ishin-no-Kaî* became the third biggest party in the Diet. However, following alignments and realignments with small factions of right-wing and neoliberal parties, it lost momentum and ended up in sixth position in the parliament after the 2017 general election.

Hashimoto resigned from the party presidency and the governorship of Osaka in late 2011 in order to serve as Osaka city mayor. Ichiro Matsui, his colleague from *Osaka-Ishin-no-Kaî*, succeeded him as governor. Hashimoto announced his retirement from politics in 2015, when his long-time programme to establish a new administrative entity ('*Osaka-tô*', similar to *Tokyo-tô*) was rejected by a local referendum.

Still, *Osaka-Ishin-no-Kaî* remains active and dominant in the region, holding the majority in both the Osaka city and prefecture assemblies. A number of members have also been elected as mayors in suburban cities of the region, further evidence of the party's wide and robust electoral support. Voters identified as core supporters of *Ishin* show a strong defiance of public administration and a preference for neoliberal policies. In the 2011 Osaka city mayoral election, nearly 90% of full-time workers and 85% of managers supported Hashimoto (Zenkyo, 2018). Support from other groups was a little lower, with 75% of the unemployed, part-time workers, and sociocultural professionals backing him. This electoral base is confirmed when analyzing voter educational and income levels, which show that 70% of university graduates supported Hashimoto compared to 60% of college graduates and 53% of middle school graduates. Based on income, well over 70% of all voters earning above the average Osaka household annual income of 3.2 million yen supported Hashimoto (Matsutani, 2012).

Tokyo has also evidenced neoliberal populism in its local politics. In 2016, Yuriko Koike—TV news anchor turned MP, who later became one of Koizumi's designated *assassin*

MPs—stood as an independent and was convincingly elected the first female governor of Tokyo. Koike had an established reputation as a politician prepared to change her party affiliation. She was first elected as a candidate of *Nihon Shintô* (Japan New Party) led by the then prime minister, Morihiro Hosokawa, but switched her affiliation to the LDP in 2002. Like Hashimoto with *Ishin-no-Kaî*, she established a national political party, *Kibo-no-tô* (Party of Hope), based on her own metropolitan party, *Tomin-first-no-Kaî* (Tokyoites First Party), in 2017. This new party welcomed 14 MPs, notably those from *Minshintô* (Democratic Party), the successor of the DPJ, in order to fight the 2017 general election. But her political entrepreneurship failed when a small, leftist faction of *Minshintô* refused to join. Yet another new party, *Rikken-minshutō* (Constitutional Democratic Party) was formed and actually won additional seats.

As governor, Koike has enjoyed strong support from Tokyoites. Her COVID-19 leadership was highly praised, and she won the 2020 election comfortably. The policies of Koike and her *Tomin-First* party remain rather vague but include a major renovation of Tokyo; an emphasis on assemblies, transparency, the promotion of work efficiency, and wise spending; and the establishment of a world financial market to promote foreign investment.

Although studies of her electoral base distribution are limited, it is known that more than half of all independent voters preferred Koike during the 2016 election. In regard to her policies, the renovation of urban transportation and infrastructure attracted the greatest support among independent voters (64%), while her administrative and budgetary reforms also held great appeal (52%). On the other hand, only 27% of Tokyoites expected Koike to tackle the problem of poverty in the city (Tokyo Shimbun, 2016).[7]

Hashimoto and Koike's strategies differ to some extent. Hashimoto was hostile to traditional parties and intermediate groups, while Koike is more cooperative with other political groups, including the LDP and labour unions, which gained her the backing of *Rengô*, the Japanese Trade Union Confederation during her campaign. Yet the similarities are striking. Both formed their own local political parties that emphasized political and administrative reforms and then tried to elevate those parties onto the national level. They both established cooperative relationships with local assembly members of *Komeîtô*, the 'political arm' of *Soka-Gakkai*, the Japanese Buddhist movement and a junior partner in government since 2012.

The political activities, associations, and achievements of Hashimoto and Koike illustrate that Japanese populists are more likely to manifest in local or regional politics under a neoliberal, reformist banner. The question that follows in the next section is why and how those features are generated by the country's institutional structure.

The dual-representation system as a source of executive's populism

The regional executives (governors and mayors) and assembly members (councillors) are elected separately in Japan. This unique political system is called the dual-representation system (*Nigen-Daihyo-seî*), and the executives and the councillors are elected as political representatives sharing power in related competencies. This system was established by the Supreme Commander for the Allied Powers during the occupation, with the aim of developing grassroots democracy in Japan (Steiner, 1965). The decentralized government comprises four levels of local assembly (prefecture, city, town, and village) as deliberative organs. Local governments have an elected head—a governor for prefectures or a mayor for municipalities—as executive. Constitutionally, the Japanese post-war system of government is a hybrid of the pre-World War II local assembly system and an American-style executive branch. However, the Japanese system is not comparable to that of the United States, where individual state legislatures differ in their system of representation.

The assembly has the authority to issue resolutions, establish or amend bylaws, make budgetary decisions, approve statements of accounts, endorse expenditures, and deal with local matters. Members have the right to submit a motion of no confidence in the executive with the support of at least three-quarters of the assembly. The executive branch is the only authority that can submit the budget but shares power with the assembly on proposing bylaws. The executive may object to an assembly resolution and insist on reconsideration, amendment, or abolition. Following a successful vote of no confidence, the executive can resign but alternatively has an option to dissolve the assembly. Both the executive and local assembly have democratic authority and legitimacy, as each is directly elected by voters. Interpretations of the power relationship between the two branches differ. Some commentators point to the predominance of the executive (Yoda, 1995), while others contend that greater power resides in the assembly, in particular, the no-confidence motion challenge (Natori, 2004). Irrespective, the dual-representation system inherently supports the power of each branch to check and curb excesses in the other (Kitamura et al., 2017, p. 36).

This strong dual system is unique to Japan. There are similarities between the Japanese local assemblies and the U.S. presidential and French semi-presidential systems, though only the Japanese assembly is empowered to pass a vote of no confidence in the executive, and the Japanese executive can dissolve the assembly. This relationship between the executive and councillors maintains the balance of the two branches.

When considering populism, it is important to note that that the executive and the assembly are elected separately through two distinct electoral systems. In the case of the executives, each municipality constitutes one electoral district, the size of which determines the strategies of candidates; for example, the governors of Tokyo and Osaka are chosen by over ten million and seven million voters, respectively. In both cities, the commercial wholesale sector employs the most workers—18% of the Tokyo electorate and 17% of the Osaka electorate in 2012—while service industries represent about 80% of total employment. In Tokyo, over 70% of males are employed, and nearly half have university degrees. Roughly 40% of the city's inhabitants are between 25 and 55 years of age, and the majority of voters are independent; a 2014 survey showed that about 58% of Tokyo voters were non-affiliated (*mutô-ha*) (Seijiyama, 2015). This characteristic extends beyond Tokyo and is an important consideration in devising a winning strategy. Only three independent governors were elected in 1995, but this number had risen to 20 by 2015 (i.e., in about 40% of the country's prefectures).

Under these conditions, candidates for governorship require not only the recognized essential levels of achievement that include educational qualifications, proven service, and social and financial status, as well as the obvious personal qualities such as popularity, eloquence, communicability, and media visibility, but additionally a campaign strategy that includes a programme that appeals to independent voters. Any attempt to define and evaluate the political style and programmes adopted by populist candidates for governorship requires an understanding of the electoral system and the composition of the electorate (i.e., the voters). In general, large constituencies with a high proportion of independents generate a wider range of voter preferences and expectations that favour candidates who adopt a populist approach and strategy.

The local assembly electoral system is different. Local councillors are elected under a single non-transferable vote (SNTV) system where multiple candidates contest between one and ten seats, proportionate to the district population.[8] For prefectural assemblies, the electoral district is the county (*gûn*) or a city. In 2013, there were 1,139 constituencies (polling districts) making up the 47 prefectural assemblies. Single-seat constituencies exist only in big cities and towns; in 2011, there were 431 such seats, constituting approximately 40% of the total number of constituencies. In the remaining 614 districts (2,046 seats), the councillors are elected by SNTV. Under these political conditions, much different from those of the executive elections, candidates seeking an assembly seat need only receive 20–30% of the vote to be elected. Therefore, their rational strategy is to represent specific organized or occupational interests. In assessing data on LDP's councillors, Toai (2017) found strong evidence that councillors representing particular interest groups are positioned to control the assembly committees directly associated with those interests. In practice, therefore, it is to be expected the members of the committees that implement policies, for example, on agro-fisheries, construction, and commerce, will receive election support and the promise of votes from organizations directly related to or representing those sectors, industries, or services. As local elections are more candidate-centred than national elections, personal networks become more relevant. In addition, prefectural assembly elections generally tend to still be contested on the traditional conservative-progressive party-based cleavage, which is no longer the case with executive elections. Normally, LDP councillors rely on professional organizations such as chambers of commerce, while those on the left often depend on trade union support (Nishizawa, 2012; Shinada, 2013).

Weiner (2008) notes there was a durable absence of competition in elections during the 1990s, even at the prefectural level, observing that about half of the nation's districts lacked viable challengers to the incumbents, and that a quarter of all districts were uncontested. For constituencies in prefectural assembly elections with more than five seats, even parties struggling to gain seats in the national assembly, such as the Socialist Party and Communist Party, were able to win approximately 70% of the seats they contested (Sunahara, 2017). At the national level, the party system has been inclined toward a two-party contest since the electoral reforms of 1994, but competition at local level has stagnated as the electoral system has remained unchanged since World War II.

Once the institutional and electoral structures are explained in relation to their historical evolution and capacity to restructure, it becomes clear that it is a logical strategy for local executives to adopt a neoliberal populist-reformist position. Candidates for executive office must appeal to geographically dispersed constituencies, as well as the vast numbers of resolutely-independent urban voters, averse to a needless commitment to support the policies of an established political party. In order to mobilize independent-voter support, it becomes logical to project a self-determinism that aligns with community improvement and welfare, while exposing the negative social community impact of politicking that prioritizes private interests and polarizes society.

Political vacuum from the 1990s leading to populism

Another factor that led to an increase in local populists in Japan, as well as the populism represented by Prime Minister Koizumi, is the hegemony lost by the long-running governmental party, the LDP, and other established parties in regional politics.

At the national level, the de-alignment of Japanese voters has been observed since 1993, when the LDP lost power for the first time since its formation in 1955. As a result, Japan witnessed a growth in the number of so-called 'independent governors' (*Mûtoha Chiji*), unaffiliated with any established party (Tanaka & Martin, 2003). One consequence was an increase in conflicts between governors and assemblies.

Tsuji (2015) finds that after 1993, these conflicts were mainly caused by 'reformist governors' (*Kaîkakuhā Chiji*) trying to enforce their programme regardless of the assembly's composition. Many of these governors' policies centred on public utilities, administrative reforms, and information disclosure. Using Tokyo as an example, Soga and Machidori (2007) specified the policy areas where the conflicts between the two bodies have arisen. Prior to the 1990s, reflecting the old conservative-progressive cleavage, social security issues were a major source of conflict. However, disputes in the 1990s mainly concerned issues such as deregulation, environment, and information disclosure. These were all issues which had been politicized by independent governors.

These two studies demonstrate that a new antagonistic relationship has been established between the two representative branches. The assembly opts for increased spending as the conservatives pursue their routine *pork-barrel* political agenda and the progressives favour increasing welfare provision; both enhance the council candidates' election prospects. Despite the concomitant economic downturn, general expenditure across the prefectures was stable for the 1995–2000 period. However, prefectural tax revenue gradually declined as local economies shrank, most notably after the 2008 recession (Somusho, 2017). Under these conditions, independent governors called for 'small government orientation' (Soga & Machidori, 2007, p. 309), which has become the basic political orientation of populist executives.

These new conflicts arose due to the de-alignment of urban electorates, which had previously manifested volatility in voting behaviour and low party affiliation—preconditions for the creation of a large reservoir of independent voters to whom a populist leader could appeal. The LDP still received support in rural areas but experienced a rapid loss of hegemony in metropolitan areas. For example, in the 2012 Lower House elections, the LDP secured 35% of the rural vote, but only 25% in more densely populated areas (Sugawara, 2013). In the same election, *Nihon-Ishin-no-Kaî* gained around 15% of the vote in the countryside, and slightly more, about 20%, in urban areas. The main opposition party at the time, the DPJ, received fewer votes at the prefectural level than at the national level. These variations, with no one party dominant in either rural or metropolitan areas, created room for the emergence of populist politicians.

This gradual decline of the LDP's hegemony and the absence of a credible opposition in the city electorates created a political vacuum in which new entrepreneurial aspirant politicians were able to employ neoliberal and reform-oriented populist strategies, promoting administrative reforms and cost-cutting measures. These reforms matched those introduced by Koizumi at the start of his tenure as prime minister. He had vowed during his 2001 LDP presidency campaign to smash the LDP, depart from the traditional interest-led politics, and implement the vast structural reforms he had envisioned, and in doing so, he attracted fresh support in urban areas where LDP support had been dwindling. Although the LDP was defeated by the DPJ in 2009, they adopted Koizumi's reform agenda (Taniguchi, 2020).

Conclusion: the reform programme

The recent literature on populism studies tends to stress its culturally authoritarian and economically protectionist characteristics, which reflect the preferences of the declining middle class (Gidron & Hall, 2017; Gest, 2016). Seen from this perspective, some observers assert that Japan is immune to this type of populism. An alternative conception is a political movement led by an outsider that distinguishes the *good people* from the *evil elites*, ostensibly to realize the people's will (Mudde & Rovira Kaltwasser, 2017).

This chapter has demonstrated that populism does exist in Japan but in a neoliberal, regionally-rooted form. In doing so, it has shown also that the style and programmes of Japanese populists emerge from certain institutional settings, conditions to which actors have adapted. Former Prime Minister Koizumi, a typical example of Japanese populism in the 2000s, moved the LDP away from the outmoded factional, interest-led politics, a leadership strategy that could only emerge after the political and administrative restructuring of the 1990s. His angry, one-phrase, party-smashing style of discourse facilitated his reforms and, in turn, resulted in increased urban support for the LDP where it had been losing ground for about a decade.

In regional politics, notably in metropolitan areas, the dual-representation system, in which local executives and assembly members share power and authority but are elected under two different systems, generates an incentive among governors to adopt the same neoliberal form of populism that characterized Koizumi's tenure. Thus, while the elected councillors generally represent sectoral interests, the rationale for executives is to appeal directly to independent urban voters and drive reforms that benefit the wider society. This supports the classification of Japanese local populism as a political strategy, rather than an ideology.

If our conclusion is valid, we could not have understood *populism* in a Japanese political setting through an ideational or ideological lens. Rather, the validity, extent of application, and development of the term can be conceived of as a matrix that reflects an evolving multi-level political system and its parties, coalitions, politicians, and electorate, within the changing parameters of socioeconomic conditions. That signifies the need to take into account different types of populism, as well as the institutional and sociological contextual factors that generate the differences, in order to grasp properly this contentious term, and in the case of this study, its appropriateness and relevance for Japan.

Notes

1 *Reiwa* is the name of the era that commenced starting on 1 May 2019, and *Shinsengumi* is a private military force organized by the Ancien Regime Bakufu in the 1860s. It is commonly regarded in Japan as a symbol of a romantic rebellion.
2 Limited to the Tokyo morning edition.
3 This trend is now increasing, as more than 100 books dealing with populism, including translations, have been published in Japan since 2010.
4 In another publication. Otake compares Koizumi with Ronald Reagan, who was, in his view, a neoliberal populist (Otake, 2006).
5 Note that the average survival rate of the cabinet in post-war Japan is about two years. There have been 35 prime ministers since 1948.
6 Three hundred seats were apportioned to the single-member districts and 200 to the proportional system.

7 A survey revealed that among the Tokyoites who voted for Koike in 2016, many did not have a populist attitude (Hieda et al., 2021).
8 The number of councillors is laid down in bylaws and varies according to the size of the municipality. Representation ranges from 12 for a village with fewer than 2000 inhabitants to 127 in metropolitan Tokyo. The average number of seats is around 55 in a prefectural assembly and 75 in the assembly of a city with a population that exceeds 1.3 million.

References

Canovan, M. (1981). *Populism*. Harcourt Brace Jovanovich.
Funabashi, Y. (2017, February 8). Japan, where populism fails. *The New York Times*. www.nytimes.com/2017/02/08/opinion/japan-where-populism-fails.html.
Gest, J. (2016). *The new minority. White working class politics in an age of immigration and inequality*. Oxford University Press.
Gethin, A. (2018). *Cleavage structures and distributive politics: Party competition, voter alignment and economic inequality in comparative perspective* (Masters thesis, Paris School of Economics). http://piketty.pse.ens.fr/files/Gethin2018.pdf
Gidron, N., & Hall, P. A. (2017). The politics of social status: Economic and cultural roots of the populist right. *The British Journal of Sociology*, 68(1), 57–84. https://doi.org/10.1111/1468-4446.12319
Hamada, K. (2013). Shin-jiyushugiteki kaikaku ni taisuru ishikikozo no sedaikan kakusa [The Intergenrational perception gap on the Neo-liberal reforms]. *Gendaishakaigaku Kenkyu*, 1(17), 1–17.
Hieda, T., Zenkyo M., & Nishikawa, M. (2021). Do populists support populism? An examination through an online survey following the 2017 Tokyo Metropolitan Assembly election. *Party Politics*, 27(2), 317–328. https://doi.org/10.1177/1354068819848112
Hook, G. D. (Ed.). (2010). *Decoding boundaries in contemporary Japan*. Routledge.
Iio, J. (2007). *Seikyoku kara Seisaku he* [From politics to policy]. NTT Shuppan.
Kitamura, W., Aoki, E., & Hirano, J. (2017). *Chiho Jichiron*. Yuhikaku.
Klein, A. (2020). Is there left populism in Japan? The case of Reiwa Shinsengumi. *The Asia-Pacific Journal*, 18(10), 1–18. https://apjjf.org/2020/10/Klein.html
Kobayashi, Y. (2012). *Seiken kotai* [Leadership change]. Chuokoron shinsa.
Lindgren, P. Y. (2005). Developing Japanese populism research through readings of European populist radical right studies: Populism as an ideological concept, classifications of politicians and explanations for political success. *Japanese Journal of Political Science*, 14(4), 574–592. https://doi.org/10.1017/S1468109915000328
Matsutani, M. (2012). Populism no shiji kozo. *Rekishi Hyoron*, 751, 36–47.
Matsutani, M. (2017, September 23). Nihon ni okeru populist shijiso to sono henka ni tsuite [On the populist attitudes in Japan and its transformation]. *Paper Presented at the Annual Conference of the Japanese Political Science Association*. Japanese Political Science Association.
Mudde, C. (2007). *Populist radical right parties in Europe*. Cambridge University Press.
Mudde, C., & Rovira Kaltwasser, C. (2017). *Populism: A very short introduction*. Oxford University Press.
Nakakita, K. (2020). Ti-iki kara no populism [Populism from the region]. In J. Mizushima (Ed.), *Populism to iu Chosen*. Iwanami Shoten.
Natori, R. (2004). Fuken Level no Rieki Haibun Kozo [The interest distribution on the prefectural level]. *Kansai Daigaku Hogaku Kenkyujo*, 27, 31–75.
Nishizawa, Y. (2012). Todofuken gikai giin no senkyo senryaku to tokuhyoritsu [The electoral strategies and vote share of the prefectural parliament members]. *Leviathan*, 15, 33–63.
Norris, P., & Inglehart, R. (2019). *Cultural backlash: Trump, Brexit, and authoritarian populism*. Cambridge University Press.
Otake, H. (2003). *Nihongata Populism*. Chuokoronshinsha.
Otake, H. (2006). Neoliberal populism in Japanese politics: A study of prime minister Koizumi in comparison with President Reagan. In K. Mizuno & P. Phongpaichit (Eds.), *Populism in Asia*. Kyoto University Press.
Pekkanen, R. J., & Reed, S. R. (2018). The opposition: From third party back to third force. In R. J. Pekkanen (Ed.), *Japan decides 2017*. Palgrave.

Piketty, T. (2018). *Brahmin left vs merchant right: Rising inequality and the changing structure of political conflict* (World Working Paper Series 2018/7). World Inequality Database, WID. http://129.199.194.17/files/Piketty2018.pdf

Reed, S. (2007). Duverger's law is working in Japan. *Japanese Journal of Electoral Studies*, 22, 96–106.

Seijiyama. (2015, February). *Dai 15 kaî Seijiyama chosa* [15th Survey of Chosayama]. Seijiyama. https://seijiyama.jp/research/investigation/inv_15_1.html

Shinada, H. (2013). Todofuken gikai giin no shiji kiban [The electoral base of prefectural parliament members]. *Leviathan*, 15, 10–13.

Shinoda, T. (2005). Japan's cabinet secretariat and its emergence as core executive. *Asian Survey*, 45(5), 800–821. https://doi.org/10.1525/as.2005.45.5.800

Soga, K., & Machidori, S. (2007). *Nihon no chiho seiji: Nigen daihyiisei seifu no seisaku sentaku* [Local politics in Japan: Policy choices in presidential systems]. Nagoya Daigaku Shuppankai. Sornusho [Ministry of Internal Affairs and Communications].

Solís, M. (2019). *Japan's consolidated democracy in an era of populist turbulence*. Policy Brief, Brookings Institute. www.brookings.edu/wp-content/uploads/2019/02/FP_20190227_japan_democracy_solis.pdf

Somusho. (2017). *Chiho Zaisei no Jokyo* [The State of the regional budget]. Ministry of Internal Affairs and Communications.

Steiner, K. (1965). *Local government in Japan*. Stanford University Press.

Sugawara, T. (2009). *Yoron no Kyokkai* [The distortion of the public opinion]. Kodansha.

Sugawara, T. (2013, June). Sangiin senkyo seido saidai no mondai [The biggest problem of the upper house electoral system]. *Huffington Post Japan*. www.huffingtonpost.jp/takussugawara/post_5076_b_3520362.html

Sunahara, Y. (2017). *Bunretsu to Togo no Nihon Seiji* [Integrity and division in Japanese politics]. Chikura Shobo.

Tanaka, A., & Martin, S.(2003). The new independent voter and evolving Japanese party system. *Asian Perspective*, 27(3), 21–51. www.jstor.org/stable/42704420

Taniguchi, M. (2020). *Gendai Nihon no Daihyo-sei Minshushugi* [Representative democracy in contemporary Japan]. Tokyo University Press.

Toai, D. (2017). Jiminto Chiho Giin to Iinkai Shozoku. *Rokkodai Ronshu*, 64(1), 19–51.

Tokyo Shimbun (2016, August 1). *Jiminto mo Koike-shjii he* [The LDP supprts Ms. Koike]. https://static.tokyo-np.co.jp/tokyo-np/archives/senkyo/tochiji2016/list/CK2016080102100032.html

Tsuji, A. (2015). *Sengo Nihon Chiho Seiji Ron* [On the regional politics in postwar Japan]. Bokutakusha.

Uchiyama, Y. (2010). *Koizumi and Japanese politics: Reform strategies and leadership style*. Routledge.

Yoda, H. (1995). Chiho seijika to seito [Regional politicians and political parties]. *Nenpo Gyoseigaku Kenkyu*, 30, 1–13.

Yoshida, T. (2020). Populism 'made in Japan': A new species? *Asian Journal of Comparative Politics*, 5(3), 288–299. https://doi.org/10.1177/2057891119844608

Zenkyo, S. (2018). *Ishin Shiji no Bunseki* [Analysis of ishin supporters]. Yuhikaku.

26
FROM POPULISM TO AUTHORITARIANISM? THE CONTEMPORARY FRAME OF POLITICS IN AUSTRALIA

Tim Battin

Almost all commentary on *populism* will include a statement about the indefinability of the term, which Marco Revelli has proclaimed 'almost unusable' (Revelli, 2019, p. 4). Indeed, as many writers have noted, some aspects of what is construed to be *populist* contradict others, while those who admit to the elusive nature of establishing a definitive characterization contend that the task is nonetheless an important one. Part of the problem, at least in the political science profession, is that until relatively recently, it was considered de rigueur to adopt a negative view of populism (D'Eramo, 2013, pp. 5–7 and p. 19; Dunleavy, 2018, p. 327). However, it was not always regarded as shameful to label oneself a populist. The late 19th and early 20th century North American period is one example of self-identified populism, and it sits easily with what is suggested in the etymology of the Greek *demos* and Latin *populus* for the synonymous term: *the people* (Revelli, 2019, p. 3). The negative ascription given to populist movements need not have led to inattention towards the phenomenon of populism itself, but it did, and more importantly, it may have delayed the formulation of an analytical frame centred on significant questions: how is the term used? How has it changed? Who uses it? For what purpose? (D'Eramo, 2017, p. 134).

That we are dealing with a paradox or outright contradiction is obvious enough. The term is essentially contested because the manner in which populism is defined will determine the subject matter to be analyzed, revealing or concealing aspects of power. It follows that the argument advanced by some (e.g., Müller, 2017) that most expressions of populism come from political actors strategically and opportunistically adopting populist techniques to acquire and use state power—Margaret Canovan's (1981) *politicians' populism*—is deserving of support. For this reason, if for no other, it is useful to think of populism as a discursive activity or method rather than an ideology. It arises out of specific political economic conditions. We shall extend the case for seeing contemporary populism 'as a response to a structural malaise' brought about by social upheaval and political disorder (Robison & Hadiz, 2020; see also Lynch, 2019). One factor to be explored in this essay is how right populism depends upon the abrogation of representation by nominally left political actors.

A sound definition will be broad enough to be applied to various situations which are prima facie similar and narrow enough to carry meaning so that analytical distinctions can be made between populist and non-populist phenomena. Marco D'Eramo observes that in the contemporary era covering WWII to the present, populists tend not to self-identify (2017, p. 131),[1] and so it may be more useful to ask what the label says about the labeller rather than the labelled (2013, p. 8).[2] This contrasts with the earlier American populism already mentioned; populists then happily called themselves populist since conservatives at that time were openly elitist (in the Schumpeterian sense) and not yet engaged with the politicians' populism that would later be employed by conservative and reactionary elites.

If a particular use of *the people* is a convenient designation of populist expression, as numerous scholars (Canovan, 1981; Mudde, 2004; Laclau, 2005; Müller, 2017; Revelli, 2019) rightly contend, it is a revealing and empirically demonstrated paradox that the 'systematic use of the term [populism] develops in exact proportion to the disuse of the term *the people*: the more peripheral the people in political discourse, the more central populism becomes' (D'Eramo, 2013, p. 15). An explanation for this paradox is offered in what follows.

It is commonplace to observe the malleable and contradictory attributions given to *the people*. While this observation is certainly accurate, there are objective conditions that assist in understanding the contradictions. When a central feature of populism—the people—is invoked, it is immediately counterpoised against something else, as in Cas Mudde's valuable juxtaposition of 'the pure people' against 'the corrupt elite' (2004, p. 543). But it is more than this; in populist use, *the people* subsumes other categories, such as objective sociological and/or economic categories. It is this lack of analysis of what constitutes the people that sits beside a dearth of commentary on power. The identification of objective conditions that obtain in societies where groups are labelled populist can also assist in understanding some puzzles. Left vs. right, genuine vs. false, upwards vs. downwards are some of the conundrums that can be addressed by insisting—as much as is possible—on analyzing the objective underlying conditions in societies now open to populist method and discourse. Geoff Dow (2020, p. 334) best sums up the contradictions when he depicts populism as 'drawing on both legitimate and illegitimate, genuine and contrived grievances'. A stance adopted along these lines is more likely to clarify the similarities and differences between the various forms of populism.

The common ground is that although all populists (rightly) see that elites are to be criticized, sometimes severely so, the critique they offer is, at best, invariably too selective and, some would say, simplistic, while claiming to be an adequate, if not complete, analysis. In cruder cases, the partiality can extend to anti-pluralism. International observers of Australian politics sometimes seek an analysis of the Pauline Hanson One Nation (PHON, formerly One Nation Party) phenomenon with the expectation it can explain a large part of Australian populism. However, the case is made here that PHON, to the extent it is examined, plays an attendant role in terms of agency. It was once successful in tapping the grievances of those who saw themselves as declining in status, a prerequisite of populism, but its right-populist agenda has largely been incorporated by the Coalition of the Liberal and National Parties. More recently, multi-billionaire Clive Palmer has competed for right-populist support, particularly in Queensland via the United Australia Party, largely on the basis of anti-taxation, pro-developmentalist, and anti-environmental policies. The much smaller Katter Australia Party has adopted some economic interventionist elements of ONP/PHON and is the only populist party that now openly advocates for economic interventionism. More important than PHON's role are the preconditions of Australia's right populism.

In what follows, the argument is made that an improperly recognized precondition of right populism, and much of what is being observed, results from the involvement of the Australian Labor Party (ALP) in a state-led neoliberal project, from the Hawke and Keating governments to the present (Maddox, 1989; Battin, 1993, 1997; Humphrys, 2019). In elaborating on this line of argument, the central organizing concept of depoliticization is used. In the final section, rather than arguing that Australia is subject to authoritarian rule, which limitation of space does not permit, some criteria are outlined as part of a basis for any such assessment in the future.

An outline of the Australian frame of politics

In the Australian context, right, downwards, or politicians' populism is the means through which neoliberalism has been consolidated. The important contribution of Rae Wear (2008) documents the Howard Coalition government's continual populist technique of politicians' populism employed between 1996 and 2007. What Ernesto Laclau (2005) calls the discursive construction of elites was on full display. Howard's targets were to be found in sections of the public sector and national and international organizations pursuing human rights and cultural or environmental protection. Other targets included Indigenous representatives, public broadcasters, universities, the arts sector, trade unions, and other institutions of social justice advocacy (Johnson, 2018). These entities were depicted as sources of economic and social malaise and juxtaposed against Howard's 'battlers', a deliberately vague notion deployed to eschew objective classification. Exploitation of racial tension and outright racism was particularly instrumental, while culture wars and identity politics were placed at the centre of public discussion. Notwithstanding the adept handling of such discursive construction, the question remains as to why it was so successful.

The technique was so effective and, despite much less proficient execution after Howard, it continues to meet with success, because of the deleterious impact of neoliberal restructuring between 1983 and 1996 by the ALP, the political party that later stood in opposition to Howard (Battin, 1997; Quiggin, 2001; Woodward, 2005). Equally important, such a programme has not subsequently been renounced by the ALP (see below). So, in this context, in contrast to a countermovement enunciating a class framework, right populism emerges as the clearly discernible response to the neoliberal project. The analysis by Lynch (2019) of populist technique in displacing *class* discourse with terms cognitively associated with *status* points to one obvious indication of a political vacuum. Precisely because the ALP has vacated the role of highlighting the structural conditions of inequality, since it had a hand in creating them, right-populist actors make appeals to the people by fixating on the status of experts, bureaucrats, intellectuals, and most politicians. Ironically, perhaps, in a polity in which the major parties avoid analysis on the basis of class, and in which society is depicted as a collection of status and identity groups, PHON supporters are by far the most likely to see themselves as working class (see citation of Australian Election Study (AES) data (Marr, 2017)).

The attempt by right political actors to erase class idioms is not new, but what mitigated the success of such technique in the past, as in the hands of former Liberal Party Prime Minister Malcolm Fraser, was a more-or-less robust left politics. Essential to the contemporary eradication of class discourse, to the extent that mild policy proposals addressing inequality are now met with the derisory 'politics of envy' or the preposterous 'class warfare', is the inability or unwillingness of numerous left elites, parties, or groups purporting to subscribe to progressive and reformist ideas to offer a coherent alternative to neoliberalism. In the meantime, ideas that are more radical remain even more on the margins, never mobilized to challenge the norms and values underpinning neoliberalism.[3]

The deeper process sustaining these phenomena is the depoliticization of state affairs. Political economy, industrial relations, and the general questions of who gets what, when, and how, are matters over which there is necessary division, and when such questions are not asked or the sources of conflict and contestation are not identified and openly debated, effective representation is denied and democracy is hollowed out (Mair, 2013). An indicator of how bereft of left ideas some writers have been was the apparent (at least partial) acceptance of Clive Hamilton's one-time attempts to argue that affluence was so widespread in the contemporary developed world that the left needed to abandon notions of deprivation, and that those believing themselves deprived had mainly themselves to blame (Hamilton, 2006). Although in many ways peculiar, the stance shares a more general disposition, which has been antagonistic to political economy and approaches based on the structural nature of injustice. Over time, neoliberal ideas have become so hegemonic that any public challenge to most proposals to redistribute wealth or income upwards is quickly cut down by invoking the notion of choice. That is to say, matters of *structural* inequality, such as the fact women retire, on average, with 43% less superannuation than men, are not considered structural in nature, but a result of women's choices. Housing unaffordability is similarly treated as open to individual remedy. Further examples of such depoliticized ways of seeing the world can be cited.

The literature on depoliticization is substantial, growing, and important (see Burnham, 2001, 2014; Hay, 2007, 2014; Wood, 2015). For our purposes, there is little need to cross-examine it, since we use the term in an uncontroversial manner. By *depoliticization*, we mean the attempt or act of erasing or obscuring the political character of a decision or activity when, for normatively stated reasons, it is desirable that its political character is retained and made explicit. Depoliticization involves obscuring the real relations of power and the interests that are advanced or regressed by a policy decision or state activity. This view is not inconsistent with the definition of depoliticization of Peter Burnham (2001, p. 128) 'as a process whereby state managers may seek to place at one remove the politically contested character of governing and in so doing paradoxically enhance political control'.[4] Indeed, the point about paradox is amplified. Depoliticization is one of the most political processes possible. Accepting this proposition, then, means that *politics* is necessarily pulled in two antithetical directions: politics as a publicly explicit argument about how society ought to be organized (the kind of politics the agents of depoliticization seek to remove) and politics as a hyper-partisan, often concealed exercise of power—indeed an abuse of power—by or on behalf of the powerful. Such a definition of depoliticization can deal with the apparent contradiction in its co-existence alongside trends (usually associated with the term politicization in a different context) in the civil realm, such as the diminution of the rule of law or compromising the independence and/or security of the public service or executive interference in the legitimate aims of statutory authorities. In general, erstwhile mediating institutions are weaponized against political opponents. This apparent contradiction is considered briefly before resuming the main argument.

There *appears* to be a contradiction in first maintaining that the present period is marked by depoliticization, and second characterizing the same period as overly politicized or hyper-partisan. Rather than contradictory, the claim is paradoxical—a paradox explained by the use of two quite different meanings of politics. In terms of the present argument, to speak critically of depoliticization is to decry the degree to which the ALP, a notionally left party, is unwilling and/or unable to articulate or represent the interests of those who have little or no control over their working conditions, along with some other aspects of their lives. The ALP continues to dismiss *political* possibilities that would countermand the neoliberal programme—an economically monist stance that would be destructive to democracy even if a functional form of neoliberalism were possible (Battin, 2017). Meanwhile on the right, as the neoliberal programme runs up against its logical and electoral limits, incoherent policy positions accumulate (Denniss, 2018). There are simply not enough votes to be gained by fulfilling a consistent neoliberal programme, and faced with widespread disaffection with policies, institutions, and decision-making (Dow, 2020, p. 341; Hay, 2007), the Coalition's modus operandi is to settle on a mixture of contradictory policy across the social and economic spheres and on hyper-partisan practices in the civil sphere (politicization in the negative sense). Defunding and weakening public broadcasters, perverting the Administrative Appeals Tribunal, organizing a secret trial against a former intelligence officer, Witness K and his lawyer, who exposed the criminal conduct of the Howard Coalition government in 2004 against Timor-Leste, attempting to discredit the president of the Human Rights Commission in 2015, defunding the office of the Auditor-General, interfering with charities who step into the activity of politics, instituting royal commissions to undermine past and present political opponents, corruptly administering monetary grants for purely partisan reasons, and abolishing the Family Court of Australia are some examples of a hyper-partisanship pursued, obviously, to reduce accountability, but also designed to marshal support from individuals and social groups that might not otherwise favour the Coalition.

One such group contains voters who give, or once gave, PHON their first preference. That group has shrunk (from 8.4% in the House of Representatives in 1998 to 3.1% in 2019, and from 9% to 5.4% over the same period in the Senate), and so it is useful to think of the Hanson phenomenon in two iterations. The first, from 1996 to 2004, was a classic populist movement which posed policy positions from across the spectrum and made its appeal accordingly (Moore, 1997). The second, from 2016 to the present, is marked by a more straightforwardly right-wing platform, and one from which the movement increasingly seeks to control the flow of voting preferences away from candidates associated with progressive identity politics. In lower-house divisions (state or federal), this approach can be pivotal where PHON candidates gain a third-place position on the primary ballot. In close elections at the national level, that is, in the House of Representatives, a strong performance by PHON in just one of six states, namely Queensland, where its potential is greatest, can determine the outcome by controlling its preference flow. In upper-house elections, PHON is still capable of picking up a seat here or there. At the present time, however, PHON's right populism has been incorporated by the Coalition.[5]

Disenchantment, populism, and depoliticized neoliberalism

State elites are now confronted with a reduced capacity to create forms of legitimacy and consent, and so find it increasingly difficult to manage day-to-day troubles, let alone crises (Chacko & Jayasuriya, 2018). Weaponization and politicization (hyper-partisanship), then, coexist with a deeper-seated, four-decade depoliticization in which the primacy of politics—that is, the necessary argument about how a society is organized, and deliberation on the policy options it possesses—has been denied.

The disaffection of various publics with formal systems of politics and political representation, as demonstrated in falling voter turnout, volatile electoral results, declining party affiliation and membership, and condemnatory responses in surveys, is now widespread (Hay, 2007; Hay & Stoker, 2009; Mair, 2013; Stoker, 2017; Stoker & Hay, 2017). On the question of trust in government over a 20-year period, or on the nearest equivalent question in Australia (Cameron & McAllister, 2019a, pp. 15–16; Cameron & McAllister, 2019b), data place Australia somewhere between what Gerry Stoker calls the 'steep decliners'—Ireland, Portugal, and Spain—and the 'modest decliners', the Netherlands, Sweden, Finland, and Luxembourg (Stoker, 2017, pp. 41–46).

The process in which disaffection with a society's socio-economic direction and disenchantment with left elites' seeming unwillingness to provide alternatives is followed by social groups turning to right political parties (Frank, 2004, 2016; Moore, 2019) is not without historical precedent. Sheri Berman (2006) argues that the near-collapse of liberal capitalism in the inter-war years in Italy and Germany, along with the dearth of democratic statecraft, or any likelihood of the latter transpiring, contrasted with the case of Sweden. In the case of the former, accordingly, the situation provided at least some of the fuel for fascism to foment a support base; whether coherently articulated or not, people want governments to intervene in a crisis so that societal needs are met and will opt for a party of whatever political stripe that proposes plausible solutions.

In the contemporary era, in Australia and elsewhere, a debilitating irony is that right elites seem more aware of the implications of neoliberal policy failure, and are consequently more willing to contradict the neoliberal programme, all the while masquerading a commitment to free markets (Denniss, 2018), than are left elites (Galbraith, 2008).[6] Notionally left political actors continue to be ideologically committed to the neoliberal framework (Battin, 2017), while denying such a characterization,[7] or are too intellectually and politically timid to develop and argue for an alternative.

While analytically distinct, there are connections which can be made between depoliticization, populism, and what some scholars have called anti-politics (Humphrys et al., 2021). Scope does not permit an examination of where anti-politics makes its points of departure from depoliticization and/or populism, but suffice to say the broader phenomenon of anti-politics is inextricably bound to the political disenchantment that marks the contemporary era (Lilla, 2017, pp. 19–55). What is more to the point of the present argument is that the right tends to flourish in an environment in which politicians are distrusted if for no other reason that private interests will be privileged, and/or that allocation will be less than transparent. The natural appeal of most left political actors, in contrast, relies on at least a public perception of a functional political system. For right actors this is not crucial, since their appeal is more individualistically targeted; in a neoliberal setting combined with populism, electoral appeal can be pitched disjointedly and implemented capriciously. Regardless of whether we refer to the top-down technique (Canovan's politicians' populism) or the general trend (market populism), we encounter 'the notion that markets are a more democratic form of organization than governments, and that they disempower elites' (Hart, 2019, p. 315). For those on the right practising politicians' or market populism, such as the Howard, Abbott, Turnbull, and Morrison governments, the public's trust in government per se is not as important as it is for non-populist right governments or governments of the left. Indeed, many governments on the right, from those of Thatcher and Reagan in the 1980s to the Australian Coalition governments between 1996 and 2007, and 2013 and 2022, have relied heavily and consciously on distrust in government. In an environment in which the public thinks that all politicians are the same, it is near impossible for a left political party to make a breakthrough. Insofar as this pertains, the political framework is biased towards politicians' populism.

In the relevant literature, a prominent competing argument to explain the rise of populism at any given time centres on the gap that sometimes emerges between *redemptive* democracy on the one hand and *pragmatic* or *transactional* democracy on the other (Canovan, 1999). When the tension between democracy's redemptive promise to rescue the polity and, in contrast, the day-to-day, transactional, sometimes sordid, deal-making that accompanies democratic politics, is intolerably evident, the emergence of populism is said to be more likely. Such a theoretical stance has some merit, but left at that does not explain enough about what causes the gap to open in the first place. Here again, power ought to be considered. When Martin Parkinson, former Secretary of the Department of Climate Change, offered his view of why Australia had not resolved climate change policy over more than a ten-year period, his summation was that the 'political class was incapable of grappling with [such policy]' (Australian Broadcasting Corporation, 2020). Alternatively, Parkinson could have observed that political actors attempting to counteract the power of fossil-fuel industries and their allies had failed to devise a *political strategy* to pursue climate change policy. Parkinson's comments betray a technocratic, depoliticized stance and a disregard for the interests that will organize against a reforming government. Here was an archetype elite criticizing the elite, using language devoid of power. His criticism of the Greens' position as purist exemplifies exactly the gap between what Canovan terms the redemptive and transactional faces of democracy (Canovan, 1981). Similarly, the propensity of some to cast the removal of prime ministers between 2010 and 2018 as a psychologically fickle reaction to polling, rather than at least partly as the result of the plutocratic power wielded by fossil-fuel interests, derives from the mainstream media and the Murdoch media in particular.

This brings the discussion back to neoliberalism and the question of its inherent features. As suggested above, in a formal democracy dominated by a two-party system, a comprehensive implementation of a stand-alone and internally consistent neoliberal programme carries considerable political risk of insufficient electoral support. A programme that reverses the gains of social democracy by entrenching wage stagnation, job insecurity, and supposed deregulation by neutering institutional support for very different outcomes, imposing arbitrary (and non-democratic) constraints on government spending and public debt, prolonging and expanding privatization and reducing the capacity for public provision, and attempting to hold back the growth of progressive taxation (cf. Dow, 2020, p. 335)—without incorporating any offsetting strategy—would be a high-risk, foolhardy plan. (Australian state governments with large majorities that have pursued neoliberal policies have been bundled out of office.) Right populism, and more specifically politicians' populism, then, is a distortionary and indispensable tool for political actors carrying out a neoliberal programme. This is not to suggest that right populism, when it comes to its compatibility with neoliberalism, is at every point a square peg in a round hole. As suggested above, market-populist ideas sometimes draw as easily from (neo)liberal, individualist concepts of freedom as they do from the notion of the ordinary person pitted against privileged elites. However, the fit is far from neat. Whereas the neoliberal programme drives economic inequality (Stilwell, 2019, pp. 115–136), right populists necessarily divert attention towards (real or imagined) changing relativities in status, displace discussion of objective measurement of social inequality with what is owed to those who consider themselves (morally) worthy,[8] and generally inundate public discussion with the grievances of those who, against considerable evidence, see themselves as the more marginalized.

From right populism to authoritarianism?

Whether by design or mere effect, such a dynamic alters perceptions of (potential) political bases. The alteration of perception has been particularly acute on the ALP side of the electoral equation. One view is that the alliance of blue- and white-collar groups, feminized occupations, and groups emphasizing post-materialist concerns, an alliance supporting the ALP from the 1960s until the 1990s, has dissolved. This disintegration is claimed to be at the centre not only of the ALP's present electoral difficulties but its capacity for renewal as well. If the ALP moves left, some suggest, it will lose votes from its traditional base to the Coalition or other right parties; if it moves right, it will sacrifice yet more of its base to the Greens (although it knows primary votes lost to the Greens in federal elections will be returned via preference flow). Rather than offering a counterargument, which space does not permit, the discussion is concerned with the general effect of these claims and perceptions.

As suggested above, a consistently implemented neoliberal programme is not likely to meet with electoral success in a two-party system. Populist appeal has been used to garner more votes for right parties than they would otherwise draw. In this environment, the anti-pluralism that is often expressed by right populists, or in Müller's analysis (2017, p. 20), the sine qua non of populism, becomes more prominent. To claim that one group, and that one group alone, represents the people is the anti-pluralist step taken by populists. There are important differences between this understanding of populism and authoritarianism, to be sure. For one thing, some elements of authoritarianism precede the rise of populism, and the links are worth exploring. One link—and at the same time distinction—is whether it is *the way we do politics* that is detested, or *democracy itself*, or whether a sufficient proportion of the public makes this distinction. (Surveys suggest the public did once make a distinction between politics which was disliked, and democracy which was valued, but a trend of a declining proportion in support for the latter is emerging.) Another important link exists between an angry, anti-pluralist mood amongst sections of the public in the first place and furtive changes of an anti-pluralist kind. Institutional changes acted upon by elites to hinder political opponents or constrain the legislature's check on the executive are qualitatively different from the anti-pluralist public expression often associated with populist society, and they point towards authoritarian trends.

With a background of 15 years of comparative and historical research into the factors that stifle democracies in poorer parts of the world, Steven Levitsky and Daniel Ziblatt (2018) have urged those in longstanding democracies to jettison complacent beliefs that authoritarianism could never happen there. The path to authoritarian rule need not involve guns and coups, and these days, it resembles less of that in the global South in any case (2018, p. 5). Levitsky and Ziblatt distil four criteria (2018, pp. 23–24, *passim*) to ascertain whether or to what extent a party, ruling elite, or regime displays authoritarian behaviour:

1. rejection of (or weak commitment to) democratic rules of the game;
2. denial of the legitimacy of political opponents;
3. toleration or encouragement of violence; and
4. readiness to curtail civil liberties of opponents, including media.

In Australia, a most dramatic realization of criteria 1 and 2 was enacted in the 1975 dismissal of a constitutionally elected government, an event assumed by many to be too remote to apply to current times. The wrongdoing of those behind the dismissal, however, has never been acknowledged by the perpetrators, nor by other elites who were, and are still, in a position to influence public debate (Maddox & Battin, 2019). This is despite new evidence having been unearthed by Jenny Hocking (2017, 2020) about the systematic nature of constitutional and political destruction. A more recent display of the degree to which the Coalition is willing to deny the legitimacy of its political opponents is found in the remark of Joe Hockey, newly-installed treasurer when the Coalition returned to power in 2013, that 'the tenants trashed the joint and now we're trying to fix it'. The implication was that the rightful owners of the Australian government would have to restore its furnishings (Maddox, 2016). Other examples of denying legitimacy, some to which we have already referred, such as the use of royal commissions to pursue opponents, would follow in due course. Curtailing the civil liberties of individuals and media organizations has also occurred in recent times, with the raid on the home of a journalist being yet another disturbing development.

Of course, of some importance in how these strategies play out is whether the key actors are in government or opposition. As the examples cited here will have made clear, the seemingly never-ending arrogation of power to the executive branch has obvious implications for the ease with which authoritarian actions can be pursued. However, the fate of the Abbott opposition, which failed to make a transition to efficacious government, suggests the process of presenting oneself as an outsider once in government has its complications.

Perhaps the only difficult criterion to establish is the toleration or encouragement of violence, either in the past or present, at home or abroad; however, the reticence of the ALP—and the outright refusal of the Coalition—to condemn all historical violence on Indigenous peoples or to denounce and desist from the contemporary violence governments themselves have perpetrated upon asylum seekers means the criterion cannot be set aside. When right populism takes an extreme form, and where acts of violence are normalized as based on mainstream thinking, the threat of authoritarianism cannot be denied.

One can agree with the proposition of Levitsky and Ziblatt that 'the erosion of . . . democratic norms began in the 1980s . . .' (2018, p. 9), but missing from their reckoning is any naming of the underlying cause. Indeed, rather than locating the problem with a depoliticization of questions dealing with the production and distribution process, they lament an excessive polarization afflicting the United States (pp. 145–75). To be fair, much of their description and critique of this polarization—including stacking the Supreme Court or blocking the appointment of nominees, filibustering in Congress, impeaching Bill Clinton, and making baseless and extremist statements about political opponents—can be compared to what has been referred to in the Australian context as hyper-partisanship (politicization of an acrimonious, tribalist form). However, the authors do not sheet home the responsibility for polarization or partisan intolerance to anyone other than those practicing such intolerance. Populism is discussed briefly (p. 22, p. 46) and several excellent points are made throughout, but the remedy recommended by Levitsky and Ziblatt is tantamount to elites doing a better job of gatekeeping.

In the foregoing argument, the concept of depoliticization was employed to direct a number of propositions. Rather than sneering at populists, we have agreed with Müller that there is a need to understand them. However, we go further than Müller in his depiction of populism as the permanent shadow of democracy: populism has emerged in its current form because democracy is in peril. Any sneering should be saved for politicians' populists—those who cynically play to people's grievances while entrenching inequality and reinforcing the same social relations that have led to the malaise. The main proposition is that populism is a symptom of denied representation and repressed class antagonism, and that such denial and repression have come about through the means of a depoliticized neoliberalism. For four decades, the primacy of politics itself has been denied. The central reason for the emergence of right populism is that a relevant left economic programme has not been successfully articulated, let alone gathered to itself a strategy of mobilization.

Acknowledgement

The author thanks Andrew Brown and the referees of this volume for some very helpful comments on an early draft.

Notes

1 Although there are some contemporary exceptions. See Zúquete (2019).
2 When the term *populism* is used by the journalists and editors of the *Australian Financial Review* or News Corp newspapers, it is meant to denote the misguided thoughts of people who wish to return to a form of democratic interventionism, rather than to continue along the neoliberal path (in which interventions and subsidies are not made publicly explicit). When used by Coalition politicians, the term is employed for even greater duplicity. So, Prime Minister Scott Morrison, in denigrating his own profession while pretending to be outside it when referring to 'the Canberra bubble', participating in cruelty towards asylum seekers, extending a policy based on xenophobic and racist views of a significant section of the populace, overseeing an automated debt recovery programme ('robo-debt'), causing indescribable distress to welfare recipients, and relying on support from ignorant members of the voting public, did not blush when he earlier disparaged the calls for a royal commission into the commercial banks in August and September 2016 as a 'populist whinge' and 'crass populism'.
3 Interestingly, right populists selectively persist with some terms, such as *middle-class welfare*, *class warfare*, and *Aussie battlers*, which are re-politicized to pervert a proper understanding of class and inequality.
4 The period of depoliticization in Australia dates back to the 1980s and is at least coterminous with neoliberalism. Paul Barratt (2021) outlines changes to the Australian public service, including those of the Hawke-Keating period, and considers the 'nonsensical objective', stated in the mid-1980s, of establishing mega-departments to reduce political conflict between departments and within the cabinet.
5 One indicator of shifting support from PHON to the Coalition points to gender. In 1998, One Nation's male support resulted in no less than a 30-percentage point gender gap. By 2016, this had reduced to 12 points (Marr, citing AES data, 2017). Figures for PHON's gender gap in 2019, if it existed, cannot be discerned from the aggregated figure for 'Other', but the measure of the coalition male/female support is available. The 10-point gender gap of male support for the Liberal Party is the highest on record, having reversed from small gaps of female support in the 1990s.
6 So, for example, the coalition continues to preference fossil-fuel industries to the point of subsidizing the massive consortium behind the Adani coalmine, and has proposed at various times to nationalize coal-fired power stations.
7 See, for example, former Treasurer Wayne Swan's views (2017), and similar ideas in Dyrenfurth and Zelinsky (2020), cited in McLoughlin (2021).
8 Following the 2019 federal election, profuse media commentary preceded any reliable electoral data when claiming that the ALP's franking credits policy, falsely referred to during the campaign by some media as a 'retiree tax', was responsible for the result and constituted a disincentive and/or was unfair. The ALP's policy proposed to end a rort costing the public some $8 billion per annum, through which individuals who pay no income tax receive a tax rebate.

References

Australian Broadcasting Corporation (2020, May 18). Climate wars: How brutal politics derailed climate policy in Australia [TV series episode]. In *Four Corners*. ABC Television.

Barratt, P. (2021). My, how things have changed. *Meanjin Quarterly*. https://meanjin.com.au/essays/my-how-things-have-changed/

Battin, T. (1993). A break from the past: The Labor Party and the political economy of Keynesian social democracy. *Australian Journal of Political Science*, 28(2), 221–241. https://doi.org/10.1080/00323269308402238

Battin, T. (1997). *Abandoning Keynes: Australia's capital mistake*. Macmillan.

Battin, T. (2017). Labouring under neoliberalism: The Australian Labor government's ideological constraint. 2007–2013. *Economic and Labour Relations Review*, 28(1), 146–163. https://doi.org/10.1177/1035304616687951

Berman, S. (2006). *The primacy of politics: Social democracy and the making of Europe's twentieth century*. Cambridge University Press.

Burnham, P. (2001). New Labour and the politics of depoliticisation. *British Journal of Politics and International Relations*, 3(2), 127–49. https://doi.org/10.1111/1467-856X.00054

Burnham, P. (2014). Depoliticisation: Economic crisis and political management. *Policy and Politics*, 42(2), 189–206. https://doi.org/10.1332/030557312X655954

Cameron, S., & McAllister, I. (2019a). *The 2019 Federal election: Results from the Australian election study*. Australian National University. https://australianelectionstudy.org/.

Cameron, S., & McAllister, I. (2019b). *Trends in Australian political opinion: Results from the Australian election study 1987–2019*. Australian National University. https://australianelectionstudy.org/.

Canovan, M. (1981). *Populism*. Harcourt Brace Jovanovich.

Canovan, M. (1999). Trust the people: Populism and the two faces of democracy. *Political Studies*, 47(1), 2–16. https://doi.org/10.1111/1467-9248.00184

Chacko, P., & Jayasuriya, K. (2018). Asia's conservative moment: Understanding the rise of the right. *Journal of Contemporary Asia*, 48(4), 529–540. https://doi.org/10.1080/00472336.2018.1448108

D'Eramo, M. (2013). Populism and the new oligarchy. *New Left Review*, 82, 5–28.

D'Eramo, M. (2017). They, the people. *New Left Review*, 103, 129–138.

Denniss, R. (2018, June). Dead right: How neoliberalism ate itself and what comes next. In *Quarterly Essay*, QE 70. Black Inc. www.quarterlyessay.com.au/essay/2018/06/dead-right.

Dow, G. (2020). The retreat from statist political economy in Australia: Neoliberalism, populism, and social democracy. *Journal of Australian Political Economy*, 86, 333–354. https://doi.org/10.3316/informit.664638103406446

Dunleavy, P. (2018). 'Build a wall'. 'Tax a shed'. 'Fix a debt limit'. The constructive and destructive use of populist anti-statism and 'naïve' statism. *Policy Studies*, 39(3), 310–333. https://doi.org/10.1080/01442872.2018.1475639

Dyrenfurth, N., & Zelinsky, M. (2020). *The write stuff: Voices of unity on labor's future*. Connor Court Publishing.

Frank, T. (2004). *What's the matter with America?* Secker & Warburg.

Frank, T. (2016). *Listen, liberal or what ever happened to the party of the people?* Metropolitan Books.

Galbraith, J. K. (2008). *The predator state: How conservatives abandoned the free market and why liberals should too*. Free Press.

Hamilton, C. (2006, March). What's left? The death of social democracy. *Quarterly essay*, QE21. Black Inc. www.quarterlyessay.com.au/essay/2006/03/whats-left

Hart, G. (2019). From authoritarian to left populism? Reframing debates. *The South Atlantic Quarterly*, 118(2), 307–323. https://doi.org/10.1215/00382876-7381158

Hay, C. (2007). *Why we hate politics*. Polity.

Hay, C. (2014). Depoliticisation as process, governance as practice: What did the first wave get wrong and do we need a second wave to put it right? *Policy and Politics*, 42(2), 293–311. https://doi.org/10.1332/030557314X13959960668217

Hay, C., & Stoker, G. (2009). Revitalising politics: Have we lost the plot? *Representation*, 45, 225–236. https://doi.org/10.1080/00344890903129681

Hocking, J. (2017). *The dismissal dossier: Everything you were never meant to know about November 1975*. Melbourne University Press.

Hocking, J. (2020). *The palace letters: The Queen, the Governor-General, and the plot to dismiss Gough Whitlam*. Scribe Publications.

Humphrys, E. (2019). *How Labour built neoliberalism: Australia's accord, the labour movement and the neoliberal Project*. Haymarket Books.

Humphrys, E., Copland, S., & Mansillo, L. (2021). Anti-politics in Australia: Hypotheses, evidence and trends. *Journal of Australian Political Economy*, 86, 122–156. https://doi.org/10.3316/informit.664712635291479

Johnson, C. (2018). The Australian right in the 'Asian Century': Inequality and implications for social democracy. *Journal of Contemporary Asia*, 48(4), 622–648. https://doi.org/10.1080/00472336.2018.1441894

Laclau, E. (2005). *On populist reason*. Verso.

Levitsky, S., & Ziblatt, D. (2018). *How democracies die*. Crown Publishing Group.

Lilla, M. (2017). *The once and future liberal: After identity politics*. Harper Collins Publishers.

Lynch, T. (2019). Pauline Hanson's one nation: Right populism in a neoliberal world. In B. Grant, T. Moore & T. Lynch (Eds.), *The rise of right populism: Pauline Hanson's one nation and Australian politics* (pp. 43–61). Springer.

Maddox, G. (1989). *The Hawke government and labor tradition*. Penguin.

Maddox, G. (2016). *Stepping up to the plate: America, and Australian democracy*. Melbourne University Press.

Maddox, G., & Battin, T. (2019). Interpreting the dismissal: Paul Kelly's influence, *Australian Quarterly*, 90(3), 22–30. https://doi.org/10.3316/agispt.20190710013921

Mair, P. (2013). *Ruling the void: The hollowing out of Western democracy*. Verso.

Marr, D. (2017, March 27). Looking back, and angry: What drives Pauline Hanson's voters. *The Guardian*. www.theguardian.com/australia-news/2017/mar/27/looking-back-and-angry-what-drives-pauline-hansons-voters

McLoughlin, L. (2021, February 5). The Australian Labor Party needs to ditch neoliberalism instead of doubling down. *Jacobin*. https://jacobinmag.com/2021/02/australian-labor-party-alp-right-faction-neoliberalism

Moore, T. (1997). Economic rationalism and economic nationalism. In B. Grant (Ed.), *Pauline Hanson: One Nation and Australian politics* (pp. 50–62). University of New England Press.

Moore, T. (2019). Once as tragedy and again as farce: Hansonism, backlashers, and economic nationalism after 20 years. In B. Grant, T. Moore & T. Lynch (Eds.), *The rise of right populism: Pauline Hanson's One Nation and Australian politics* (pp. 43–61). Springer. https://doi.org/10.1007/978-981-13-2670-7_10

Mudde, C. (2004). The populist Zeitgeist. *Government and Opposition*, 39(4), 541–563. https://doi.org/10.1111/j.1477-7053.2004.00135.x

Müller, J.-W. (2017). *What is populism?* Penguin.

Quiggin, J. (2001). Social democracy and market reform in Australia and New Zealand. In A. Glyn (Ed.), *Social democracy in neoliberal times: The left and economic policy since 1980* (pp. 80–109). Oxford University Press.

Revelli, M. (2019). *The new populism: Democracy stares into the abyss*. Verso.

Robison, R., & Hadiz, V. (2020). Populism in Southeast Asia: A vehicle for reform or a tool for despots. In T. Carroll, S. Hameiri & L. Jones (Eds.), *The political economy of Southeast Asia: Politics and uneven development under hyperglobalisation* (pp. 155–175). Palgrave.

Stilwell, F. (2019). *The political economy of inequality*. Polity.

Stoker, G. (2017). *Why politics matters*. Palgrave.

Stoker, G., & Hay, C. (2017). Understanding and challenging populist negativity towards politics: The perspectives of British citizens. *Political Studies*, 65(1), 4–23. https://doi.org/10.1177/0032321715607511

Swan, W. (2017, May 14). The Hawke-Keating agenda was laborism, not neoliberalism, and is still a guiding light. *The Guardian*. www.theguardian.com/commentisfree/2017/may/14/the-hawke-keating-agenda-was-laborism-not-neoliberalism-and-is-still-a-guiding-light

Wear, R. (2008). Permanent populism: The Howard government 1996–2007. *Australian Journal of Political Science*, 43(4), 617–634. https://doi.org/10.1080/10361140802429247

Wood, M. (2015). Puzzling and powering in paradigm policy shifts: Politicization, depoliticization and social learning. *Critical Policy Studies*, 9(1), 2–21. https://doi.org/10.1080/19460171.2014.926825

Woodward, D. (2005). *Australia unsettled: The legacy of neo-liberalism*. Pearson Longman.

Zúquete, J. P. (2019). From left to right and beyond: The defense of populism. In C. de la Torre (Ed.), *Routledge handbook of global populism* (pp. 416–34). Routledge.

27
MAN ALONE
Winston Peters and the populist tendency in New Zealand politics

Luke D. Oldfield and Josh van Veen

Introduction

A frequent pitch made to young New Zealanders as they traverse the high school curriculum is one of a nation whose history is daring, bold, and progressive. New Zealand was, after all, among the first countries to provide old-age pensions to those of 'good moral character' and the very first to provide all women with the right to vote. Historian Neill Atkinson eloquently detailed this brave leap in a young nation's politics in his 2003 book, *Adventures in Democracy: A History of the Vote in New Zealand*. Thus, a sort of banal nationalism of *firsts* has permeated throughout the lore of New Zealand society, so much so that the image of suffragist Kate Shepherd is now emblazoned on the nation's currency, a blue $10 note. Balanced against this narrative is another facet of New Zealand's past that is at best contradictory but often inimical: fraught relations between the *Māori* (the nation's Indigenous population) and *Pākehā* (the nation's population of European descent) and a populist tendency in the nation's politics, which plays off each side of this bicultural identity against the other.

The politics of New Zealand's pre-eminent populist, long-standing member of parliament (MP), and minor party leader, Winston Peters, is an amalgamation of this history and the nation's broader political culture. Peters is of both Māori and Pākehā descent. Despite many critics, he enjoys a political longevity unrivaled by other party leaders. Peters served as Deputy Prime Minister on two occasions (1996–1998 and 2017–2020), Foreign Minister (2005–2008 and 2017–2020) and, most recently, acting Prime Minister while Jacinda Ardern took maternity leave. As well as having been an MP for 36 of the past 43 years, he has led his own party for 29 years.

A temptation for those taking a cursory look at politics in New Zealand might be to transpose the electoral strategy of Peters onto existing theoretical literature, particularly that which has been used to define populist right-wing parties in Europe. Indeed, Peters and his New Zealand First (NZ First) party have been described by political commentators as populist and noted for their exclusionary, anti-immigrant rhetoric. To follow this literature, populism has up to four inherent, minimalist traits: an 'us vs. them' dualism, advocacy of direct democracy, anti-pluralism, and a penchant for straight-forward or 'common sense' solutions (Akkerman et al., 2014; Mudde, 2007; Mudde & Rovira Kaltwasser, 2012). Superficially, there may appear to be some utility in applying an ideological framework. Peters himself has provided countless examples of how political mavericks might weaponize seemingly popular opinion in a way that would conjure up images of firebrand politicians in democracies elsewhere.

However, significant limitations also arise in utilizing an ideological framework in a New Zealand context. Focusing on Peters and his contemptuous style of campaigning ignores the structural differences between Peters and his NZ First party compared to exclusionary populists and their respective parties in other countries. It also risks obscuring how Peters initially rose to prominence, the backdrop of which can be found in the nation's messy colonial history, including the Treaty of Waitangi signed in 1840 (an agreement under which some Māori tribes ceded powers to the British in return for protection, property rights, and citizenship[1]); its periods of often distressing economic upheaval, in particular the 1930s, 1970s and 1980s; and its electoral system, which fundamentally changed in 1996. Such minimalist interpretations also do not allow for evaluation of the extent to which this exclusionary-type populism has interacted with democracy in New Zealand.

It is argued, through careful examination of this nuance, that a distinct New Zealand style of populism has emerged, albeit one which might come with an expiration date. The way that this brand of populism has manifested itself in the corridors of power has been different even from that of New Zealand's much larger geographical neighbour, Australia.[2] This chapter starts by setting out the historical genesis of this New Zealand style of populism before codifying the populism of Peters and the NZ First. Following the October 2020 general election and the departure of NZ First from parliament, it is unclear what is next for Peters, his party, and this New Zealand brand of populism.

A brief history of populism in New Zealand

In *New Zealand Literature: A Survey* (1959, p. 130), E. H. McCormick described a 'solitary, rootless nonconformist' stock character that turns up persistently in New Zealand fiction. The so-called *Man Alone* was most vividly portrayed in John Mulgan's (1939) eponymous novel. Benson (1998) identified this archetype with existentialist philosophy. At its heart is a belief that the world is inherently meaningless and that individuals must find their own way in life. That concept resonated in Pākehā early settler society, where the adult population was largely male and single. Phillips (1987) demonstrated how many of the traits we identify in the stereotypical 'Kiwi bloke' came from the itinerant workforce of rural labourers who drifted around colonial New Zealand.[3]

Such men were a core constituency of the radical Liberal Government elected in 1890. They would find a strong champion in the publican-turned-premier, Richard John Seddon (1893–1906, who idealized the New Zealand male as 'strenuous, independent and humane' (in Burdon, 1955, p. 313). Despite his reputation for crude opportunism, Seddon articulated a coherent and succinct political philosophy: the objective of government was to make life easier for the poor and dispossessed while preserving a spirit of independence. Seddon, like many of his contemporaries, imagined New Zealand as a 'rural arcadia' of self-sufficient landholders (Vowles, 1987, p. 219). During the 20th century, politicians on both the left and right would stake claim to Seddon's legacy. Thus, the Man Alone theme can also be discerned in the country's political history, and traces of it are evident in contemporary New Zealand politics.

Here the link between liberalism and populism is important. At its core, 19th-century popular liberalism was a belief in self-realization through progress. Key to progress was development and economic growth. However, the goal was not simply material wealth. It was, in the words of Seddon, 'the life, the health, the intelligence and the morals of a nation' (in Brooking, 2014, p. 390). Wealth redistribution was subject to a belief in the virtuosity of hard work and personal responsibility. The egalitarian rhetoric belied an individualism that was always willing to take from the hand of the state when circumstances required, but much less willing to give back in good times. During the 1890s, for example, the cause célèbre was land reform. Following a series of dubious acquisitions, land wars, and confiscations of land from the Māori, much of the country was owned by a small, wealthy Pākehā elite and so the stage was set for a populist uprising among less wealthy Pākehā against these wealthier enemies of progress, the *squattocracy*. Once land had been nationalized and subdivided, however, the debate soon turned to property rights, and a new constituency of small farmers demanded freehold against the Liberal reformers' expectations. Thus, the first great populist moment in New Zealand politics foundered on contradiction.

Michael Joseph Savage, the country's first Labour prime minister, was another politician who embodied the fears and aspirations of Pākehā settler society. While Savage may have identified as a socialist, his later career suggests he was not an ideologue. During the 1920s, Labour was divided on property rights. In keeping with socialist principles, most Labour activists wanted the state to own land, leasing it to farmers in perpetuity rather than granting freehold titles. Yet Savage grasped that this position was untenable in a country of rugged individuals and set out to broaden Labour's appeal with rural voters (Gustafson, 1986). In 1927, he led other pragmatic Labour members in rewriting the party's land policy to accept 'full recognition of owners' interest in all land including tenure, the right of sale, transfer and bequest' (Franks & McAloon, 2016, p. 91). Savage's ascension to leadership in 1933 completed this shift from socialism to a popular liberal stance.

A key figure in Labour's 1935 victory, aside from Savage, was the former soldier turned author John Alfred Alexander Lee. A powerful orator, the charismatic Lee was unmistakably a populist of the left. He would later fall out with Savage and Labour; Lee's expulsion in 1940 and subsequent career provide yet another illustration of the Man Alone theme. With many of his ideas rejected by the Labour hierarchy, Lee fulminated on the sidelines, criticizing the lack of internal democracy but unwilling to make concessions. In protest, he formed the Democratic Labour Party (DLP) with considerable support from Labour's rank and file. Despite Lee's popularity, the DLP failed to win any seats in the 1943 general election, and he turned his attention to writing.

Lee's rabble-rousing speeches certainly made an impression on Robert David Muldoon. Writing in his 1974 autobiography, *The Rise and Fall of a Young Turk*, Muldoon professed a great admiration for the socialist politician whom he 'rarely disagreed with'.[4] According to Muldoon, the two diverged in one respect only: he had come to believe that it was possible to achieve social justice without the 'levelling down' of socialism (Muldoon, 1974, p. 26). Inspired by Seddon and Lee, Muldoon fashioned an identity that appeared to cross the traditional party divide but in fact was consistent with the country's dominant ideology of popular liberalism. Upon returning from war service in 1947, Muldoon joined the centre-right National Party and went on to have a long career. He served as Prime Minister from 1975 to 1984.

Muldoon spoke in plain language and appealed directly to the 'ordinary New Zealander' (Muldoon, 1974, p. 145). Populist themes based on fear and othering such as crime and immigration also featured prominently in the National Party's 1975 election campaign. But so too did notions of freedom and choice. With the help of American cartoonist Hanna-Barbera, the National opposition produced a highly effective television advertisement that made allusions to a communist takeover of New Zealand. National won by a landslide, and Muldoon went on to govern until 1984. Although his opponents portrayed him as a right-wing reactionary, Muldoon passionately supported the welfare state and was an outspoken critic of neoclassical economic theories. Muldoon's support for Māori gangs, use of *te reo Māori* (Indigenous language) in speeches, and his personal friendship with land rights activist Whina Cooper suggest that he was at least sympathetic to biculturalism (Gustafson, 2006, pp. 206–207).

Muldoon, like Seddon and Savage, represented a populist tendency that was essentially liberal in character but with a strong sense of social justice. Moving into the contemporary era, a clear lineage exists between Peters and the former prime ministers—Seddon (1893–1906), Savage (1935–1940), and Muldoon (1975–1984). While Savage and Muldoon came from opposing sides of the political divide, both men identified with Seddon. Both used populist rhetoric that appealed to the archetypal New Zealand male described here. Although a socialist in his youth, Savage respected New Zealanders' individualism and refashioned the Labour Party accordingly. By contrast, Muldoon reconciled support for the welfare state and social justice, with a conservative outlook as the leader of the centre-right National Party.

Populist, statesman, and 'kingmaker'?

Born in 1945, Winston Peters belongs to a generation that grew up in the shadow of war and depression yet had good reason to be optimistic about the future. Throughout the 1950s and 1960s, New Zealanders enjoyed some of the highest living standards in the world. Historian Keith Sinclair (1969, p. 285) declared the country 'nearly classless'.[5] Peters joined the National Party as a student in 1967 because it aligned with his 'philosophy of independence' (Booth, 1990, p. 48), and Muldoon was to become a significant influence on him over the next decade. Although the two men were never close, they shared a mutual admiration (Hames, 1995). Further, many have remarked on their similarities, and one recent commentator labelled Peters 'the last Muldoonist' (Thomas, 2017). Understandably, these comparisons tend to focus on a particular campaign style. However, as we have seen, the Man Alone theme provides an important cultural dimension to populism in New Zealand.

By the time Peters began his political career, the 'golden age of capitalism' was over. New Zealand, like other developed countries, experienced stagnant growth and high rates of inflation throughout the 1970s. These problems were exacerbated by falling export prices and the loss of trade with the United Kingdom after it joined the European Economic Community in 1973. During the 1980s, a period of economic transformation took place under the Fourth Labour Government (1984–1990). In particular, the dismantling of trade protections freed up the economy but put many New Zealanders out of work. The social dislocation caused by economic reform also triggered a political backlash that culminated in the rise of anti-establishment sentiment and support for new minor parties. Those parties would eventually be represented in parliament.

It was in this climate that Peters reached maturity as a politician. For a time, many believed it was his destiny to become New Zealand's first Māori prime minister. However, fierce independence and contempt for authority undermined his ambition to lead the National Party (Hames, 1995, pp. 75–78). While Peters' highly emotive public statements were almost certainly intended to elicit media attention, his outrage at government ministers 'looking after their mates', and his disdain for those profiting from the sale of public assets may have been acutely felt as someone who grew up believing in the welfare state (Hames, 1995, p. 55). In one of his more introspective moments, Peters spoke of 'the almost irreplaceable quality called hope' that infused his childhood and which younger generations have been denied (in Moir, 2020). Loss and betrayal are, therefore, recurrent themes in Peters' speeches over the past 30 years.

Moves to reinstate the rights of Indigenous peoples have been a fertile breeding ground for resentment in settler societies (Moffitt, 2017; Pearson, 2001), and New Zealand has been no different. By leading a view on Indigenous affairs that has oscillated between support for and opposition to Indigenous self-determination, Peters has at different times attempted to court conservative voters who are of European and/or Māori ancestry. By doing so, Peters has often rubbed against a more conciliatory tone taken by the government toward the Māori. For example, while still a cabinet minister in the National government, Peters commissioned the *Ka Awatea* report of 1991, aimed at addressing low educational achievement, high representation in crime and imprisonment, and high state dependency among Māori (Mahuika, 2011). Much of the report, ignored by that National Government, included proposed remedies that Peters would himself reject a decade later (Mahuika, 2011).

In the 1996 election campaign, Peters promised a simple solution to Māori constituents: a vote for his three-year-old NZ First party would sweep the ruling National Party from power. Pitting Māori constituents against what he had framed as the ruling Pākehā elite, which he claimed had become complicit in the neoliberal reform agenda since taking office, aided NZ First in winning each of the five Māori electorate seats. Six weeks and a series of intense negotiations later, NZ First formed a coalition government with the National Party. By the 1999 election, however, all five Māori electoral seats returned to Labour, who formed the government. In 2002, Peters pivoted back toward Pākehā voters, delivering a speech to the party faithful titled *Treaty Lunacy and Treaty People*, in which he compared the reparation process for past colonial injustices, known colloquially as 'treaty settlements',[6] to 'a noxious weed, a malignant cancer, this industry thrives on certain conditions that promote its growth' (Peters, 2002). By 2005, it had become NZ First policy to abolish the functions of the Waitangi Tribunal, a quasi-legal body designed to guide the nation's bicultural relationship between Māori and Pākehā with reference to the Treaty of Waitangi (Berry, 2002).[7]

Peters also weaponized immigration policy, in much the same way as populist politicians in other liberal democracies. During the late 1990s and early 2000s, Peters' anti-immigration rhetoric often emphasized demographic change in New Zealand society as a result of Asian immigration (Moffitt, 2017). In 2002, he claimed the country would soon be 'unrecognizable' and stoked fears that multiculturalism would lead to racial tension. Since then, NZ First has reframed the debate in economic terms by highlighting the impact of immigration on wages, unemployment, and housing affordability (in ways similar to Muldoon some four decades earlier). These concerns received support from some mainstream commentators and experts (see Garner, 2017; Larson, 2017). Paradoxically, despite record high immigration prior to the closing of borders due to the COVID19 pandemic in

2020, the issue appears to have declined in perceived importance among voters. Although immigration has lacked salience in recent years, it nevertheless remains a powerful theme for NZ First.

The 2017 election campaign suggested that Peters and his party continued an indecorous politics, a performative style which Ostiguy (2009) characterized in other liberal societies as an appeal to the low. In one particular campaign rally, notable in local media outlets for the presence of dog whistle politics, Peters revisited the 'us vs. them' dualism, stating to a raucous crowd of party faithful: 'We have a government that works only for the elite few— not for you!' (Murphy, 2017). Only weeks earlier, in a distinctly anti-pluralist pitch, Peters had questioned comments made by the race relations commissioner, claiming that his plain speaking on immigration matters was not racist and that her concerns regarding inflammatory rhetoric were without cause.[8] As the election neared, the party promoted a referendum on whether Māori electorate seats should be abolished, dusting off its long-standing appeal for contentious matters of policy to be decided through direct democracy. The party also utilized the campaign slogan 'it's just common sense', thus reaffirming the ease with which Peters and NZ First can be codified through the minimalist, populist frame.

Such examples, some decades old and others more recent, demonstrate that the durability of Peters as a political figure was not necessarily found in the consistency of those he targeted for support, but rather in the consistency of his style and messaging. It is a theatrical and often irreverent politics, which operates alongside a rebuke to the fast-paced transformation of New Zealand, both socially and economically. It is again a populist contradiction: Peters is himself part of the political elite and for many years a political insider, yet he has reached out to different groups of largely disparate outsiders. As part of the political elite, Peters made himself a spokesman for those he once described as 'relegated, denigrated and forgotten' (in McLachlan, 2013, p. 22) by the establishment. Throughout his time in the National Party, and following his subsequent exit to form NZ First, Peters has been the outsiders' insider. In that respect, Peters has fashioned himself as the quintessential Man Alone.

The illusion of independence is crucial here; it was a recurrent theme throughout his career, whether in relation to the National Party, the establishment more generally, and even, at times, the Māori. Peters' dismissal from the Bolger National Government in 1991, followed by his 'walk out' from the Shipley National-NZ First coalition government in 1998, and public disagreements with the Ardern Labour-NZ First coalition government between 2017 and 2020 suggest a clear pattern of behaviour. While this behaviour is often seen as calculated and expedient, with one business leader describing him as 'the ultimate opportunist on the political front' (McCready, 2017), such reductionism tells us nothing about Peters' underlying motives or outlook, let alone why this particular approach has been successful. A more critical insight may be gained from the application of psychosocial concepts such as those developed by the so-called Melbourne School (t'Hart & Uhr, 2008, p. 11).

Little (1986), for example, hypothesized that there are three distinct types of political leadership: strong, group, and inspirational. Each represents a solution to what Little called the 'self/other dilemma' or the question of how individuals should relate to one another. The type of leader a person gravitates to will reflect their own psychosocial orientation. In this regard, the leader becomes an exemplar of how to behave. One may choose to elevate the self above others (strong) or see others as an extension of the self (group). But some will attempt to have it both ways and look for a leader who appears to exist both outside social life and inside it, thus transcending the self/other dilemma.

This third type of leader is typically 'considered a narcissist and his charisma is a threat to politics because it takes away from the legitimacy of institutions and traditions' (Little, 1986, p. 140). The inspiring leader and their followers 'resist ties that bind and rules that restrict' (Little, 1986, p. 139). Despite superior communication skills, however, the inspiring leader may become 'stuck on cliched slogans and abstract formulas', making a 'once fresh approach an old, familiar trick' (Little, 1986, p. 153). Little's description is apt for Peters who, more than any other New Zealand politician, succeeded in having it both ways. While he once provided a stimulus to debate in the 1990s and inspired a large following, his later years have seen this appeal diminish and his style become old-fashioned. Yet the psychosocial basis for Peters' leadership has remained consistently strong.

A contemporary man alone? Codifying a New Zealand populism

New Zealand's dance with populism over the 20th century is remarkable for being tepid in application, despite its occasional grasp of incendiary language. The most useful theoretical positioning might be found in Arditi (2004), who identifies a form of populism that departs from the etiquette of political salons without apologizing for its brashness:

> The archetypal image of its followers is that of excited football fans unconcerned with the ritualized table manners of public life. Whether as a reaction against 'politics as usual' or as a response to the failures of elitist democracy, populism would designate a form of intervention that has the potential to both disturb and renew the political process without necessarily stepping outside the institutional settings of democracy. Its politics unfolds in the rougher edges of the liberal-democratic establishment.
> *Arditi, 2004, p. 142*

It is this reactive constituency which Peters has reached for since the introduction of a mixed member proportional (MMP) electoral system. The nation's MMP electoral system was introduced in 1996 and affords proportional representation (a party's nationwide vote as a percentage of 120 seats in the legislature) to any party reaching a minimum 5% of the overall party vote or winning at least one electorate seat.[9] To reach this threshold, NZ First relies on protest voters, an amorphous group, perhaps feeling a sense of economic or social alienation. According to data from the New Zealand Attitudes and Values Survey, a longitudinal study which asks participants who they voted for in the preceding election, we can estimate the number of NZ First true believers to be somewhere around 2% of the voting population. This means that at election time, Peters is reliant on his party either winning an electorate seat or marshalling support from a further 3% or more of voters nationwide. Critical, then, for the longevity of NZ First and its influence is the need to carefully nurture their 'outsider' characterization, even as a part of government (see also Miller & Curtin, 2011).

For a populist leader of a minor party, Peters has maintained a remarkable proximity to executive power. On all but two occasions, the 2008 and 2020 elections, a sufficiently large segment of the electorate found some coherence in his approach to politics, allowing NZ First to pass the 5% representation threshold.[10] Had election results been based on the preceding First Past the Post Westminster electoral system, which was last used in 1993, NZ First would not have been represented in parliament since 2005. The heightened status of Peters and his party is therefore inextricably linked to MMP, and the position of NZ First as 'kingmaker', a power derived from being able to decide which of the two major parties, National or Labour, would form the next government.

A notable feature of exclusionary populists has been the assembling of ramshackle party structures that revolve around the incendiary politics of their own personal profile (Schedler, 1996; Taggart, 2002). This is evident elsewhere in the world and in particular Australia in the case of Pauline Hanson's One Nation. While NZ First has had a high turnover of officials, candidates, and advisors, the party's structure has remained comparatively robust. Evidence of internal competition is on display at the party's annual convention, where members openly debate and vote on policy remits. It is an important difference from populist parties that emerge around the popularity of their leader, understanding the need to balance internal competition with collaborative decision making (see Abedi & Lundberg, 2009).

NZ First's internal process for selecting office-holders and policies is reminiscent of the American tradition of political conventions whereby delegates are selected to represent localities at a national forum. During these conventions, it is not uncommon for delegates to challenge the leadership on salient issues. In 2019, for example, delegates voted with members of the youth wing to liberalize the party's position on drug quality testing at music festivals, which was opposed by some MPs. A board of directors, elected from the convention floor, plays another crucial role in holding the leadership accountable to members. In the aftermath of the 2017 election, the board was closely involved in coalition negotiations and is likely to have influenced the decision to form a government with the centre-left Labour Party rather than the centre-right National Party. A sub-committee of the board is also responsible for approving candidate selection and determining candidates' list rankings.

While the annual party convention and elected board are a significant check on the leader, Peters nevertheless maintains a near iron grip on the party. The survival of Peters as party leader makes NZ First a peculiarity among modern political parties, though perhaps less so among populist parties. However, the party leadership has not been without contestation. During its first term in government (1996–98), a schism emerged between Peters and other NZ First MPs, resulting in a failed attempt to unseat Peters by the then deputy leader Tau Henare. While Peters' leadership has not been seriously challenged since, the offices of party president and deputy leader have on occasion been fiercely contested. One interpretation of the leader-party relationship is the popular image of Peters as a lone rebel, standing up to the establishment in a David and Goliath-like struggle for justice. The image originated in the early 1990s when Peters, then a cabinet minister, broke ranks with the National Party.

The closest threat to the support base of NZ First arose in 2004, when former Reserve Bank Governor Don Brash took over leadership of the National Party and delivered what was later referred to as the 'Orewa speech'. Brash's speech borrowed many of the key tenets of NZ First's platform, including its claim that the treaty settlement process is limitless and affords unfair advantages to Māori. Nevertheless, NZ First survived the 2005 election, albeit with a much-reduced representation, seeing off the attempt from Brash to mainstream the party's policy agenda. The absence of mainstreaming is important in a comparative sense with Australia and the United Kingdom, where larger parties have co-opted policies from smaller populist rivals, leading to their eventual decline (Abedi & Lundberg, 2009; Snow & Moffitt, 2012).

While other politicians have challenged Peters' dominance in the sphere of Māori-Pākehā relations, no major rival has emerged in the immigration debate. Attempts by the Labour Party to adopt a more nationalistic outlook prior to the 2017 election did not galvanize support and sat uncomfortably with the liberal, cosmopolitan image of leader Jacinda Ardern. According to the New Zealand Election Study (NZES), only 5% of respondents named immigration as 'the single most important issue' in 2017 (Vowles et al., 2017). Of these, a majority (57%) considered NZ First to be the party 'best at dealing with that issue'. Thus, Peters has at least continued to enjoy strong support among voters who oppose mass immigration, and there is evidence that the issue is dormant rather than dead. When asked what should happen to the number of immigrants allowed into New Zealand, some 19% of 2017 NZES respondents said the number should be 'reduced by a lot'. Furthermore, 18% agreed with the proposition that New Zealand culture is 'generally harmed by immigrants'. These figures suggest that Peters has not mobilized the anti-immigration vote to the extent that right-wing populists have in Britain, the United States, and continental Europe.

Despite an occasional flourish of racial rhetoric, Peters' hostility to ethno-demographic change has been tempered by a respect for liberal democracy and biculturalism. His Man Alone style of politics may represent a distinct New Zealand populism. But whether it survives Peters is an open question. At nearly 80, he has passed the apotheosis of his career. Ill health in the run-up to the 2020 election prompted speculation as to when the NZ First leader might leave politics, a question Peters himself was quick to rebuff. The alternative is that Peters' inevitable departure will give way to a more extreme form of populism based on ethnic-majority grievance and illiberal attitudes.

When NZ First was voted out of parliament in 2020, a prevailing media narrative was that firearm owners had abandoned the party in large numbers over its support for a gun register in the aftermath of the Christchurch terrorist attack (Vance, 2020). In its place, the ACT New Zealand party (originally Association of Consumers and Taxpayers but now known simply as ACT), who had previously captured less than 1% of the vote in 2017,[11] surged to 7.6% following its opposition to gun control laws and its criticism of the Labour-NZ First Government's response to COVID-19. ACT leader David Seymour also garnered attention for his provocative style of leadership and his party's brand of free-market populism. At first glance, the rise of ACT mirrored the decline of NZ First. However, the NZES again provides critical insight. Of those who reported voting for NZ First in 2017, 35.8% went to Labour in 2020, while only 12.1% went to ACT and 7.2% to National. Just under a quarter (22.8%) remained loyal. It is perhaps also significant that 11.6% did not vote at all (Vowles et al., 2020). Previous research has found NZ First supporters to be more authoritarian than average (Vowles, 2020).[12] Given their preference for conformity and security, it would not be surprising if these voters found Ardern's rhetoric of national unity appealing, especially during a pandemic, while the rise in support for ACT is better explained by the decline in support for the National Party.

The codification of New Zealand populism, at least that which has carried NZ First to success in seven election campaigns between 1996 and 2020, is probably more easily quantifiable by noting the omissions. It is neither forceful nor a threat to representative democracy, at least not yet; it does not display disorganization and amateurish political behaviour (by its leader); and, thus far, it has been resistant to mainstreaming by the two major political parties. That is not to say Peters and NZ First are on the fringe; rather, they have been critical players both in government and opposition.

Conclusion

The populism of Winston Peters and NZ First can be described as an idiosyncratic representation of themes recurrent throughout the nation's history and its more recent political culture. The antecedents of these can be traced back to the country's colonial beginnings and subsequent attempts by the Pākehā ethnic majority to reconcile a desire for individual freedom with the need for security while rejecting calls to provide redress to the Māori for the ongoing impacts of colonization. Much of this early 20th-century political outlook was based on a conception of quintessential New Zealanders—rugged individuals struggling against the world but determined to live by their own means. War and depression undermined these goals and led to the New Zealand electorate voting for welfarism and government intervention, thus illuminating what had been a contradiction inherent in the Man Alone theme.

Political scientist Jack Nagel (1993) took a retrospective look at Richard Seddon's ability as prime minister to defeat competing policy outcomes, sometimes through attracting the support of different majority coalitions, by introducing new issues, or by redefining old ones (i.e., shifting his support to women's suffrage and balancing settler land rights). Written at the time NZ First was formed, Nagel's characterization of New Zealand's first populist leader was in many ways a prognosis of what Winston Peters would become, not as prime minister but as lead agitator within parliament, following the lineage of Seddon, Savage, and Muldoon. For almost three decades preceding the 2020 election, Peters and his NZ First party were in parliament for all but three years, attracting diverse coalitions of voters and negotiating deals with the government of the day.

Peters' brand as the outsiders' insider—ill-mannered and non-conforming to established political etiquette—is perhaps quaint when set against the more incendiary variants of populism observed in other countries, including Australia. A New Zealand populism might then be characterized as a moderate form because the representative structures of government have not been disrupted, and the movement's leader moved only partway toward the locus of power. This should not, however, diminish the sometimes hidden social costs of language, tone, and advocacy delivered by Peters when out on the campaign trail, much of which is likely to validate prejudices toward ethnic minorities, especially those who are non-Māori.

With NZ First managing only 2.6% of the party vote and failing to win an electorate seat in the 2020 election, they were, for the second time in their history, a registered party outside of parliament. In a speech to party faithfuls in June 2021, Peters declared that NZ First would be back at the next election, and confirmed his intention to continue as leader (Husband, 2021). However, throughout 2021, the newly invigorated ACT party polled higher than its result on election night, attracting further support by demanding a referendum on proposed hate speech legislation. It is a position that might assist the party in shutting Peters and NZ First out of parliament in 2023, replacing a populism rooted in economic protectionism with a populist free-market agenda.

Populism in New Zealand politics is then at a juncture. If NZ First regains parliamentary representation, Peters and his eventual successor might continue to steer the party in a way that publicly skirts the edges of democracy but stops short of seeking to dismantle core democratic institutions. Alternatively, the party might disappear altogether and leave behind a vacuum for new political mavericks to muscle in on disaffected voters, to the point where, as Arditi (2004) opined, the spectre of populism might begin to threaten democracy itself. The most recent election also saw the emergence of two other unsuccessful parties, both utilizing a populist platform. The New Conservatives, a right-wing, Christian-oriented party, exhibited many of the minimalist traits synonymous with populism in Europe but fell well short of the 5% threshold with only 1.5% of the vote. Meanwhile, a composite of smaller parties promulgating conspiracy theories, anti-vaccine messaging, and a sceptical view of government institutions ran under the Advance New Zealand banner but managed only 1% of the vote.

While it seems unlikely that a more incendiary populism will disrupt New Zealand political institutions in the immediate future, it should not be dismissed entirely. Concern about society's ethnic structure, typically expressed in views on immigration, is the strongest predictor for populist voting in other anglophone jurisdictions (see Kaufmann, 2018). Given that the Pākehā majority continues to decline in numbers relative to ethnic minorities, and the broadly Asian population is growing at a much faster rate than the Māori and Pasifika group (Spoonley, 2020), an ethnonationalist populism could mobilize collective grievances in the future. Such possibilities lead to an uncomfortable hypothesis—Peters, who for decades stoked reactionary sentiments among disillusioned voters, might until now have functioned as a firewall, keeping at bay a variant of populism that will inevitably be more harmful to democracy.

Notes

1. Māori and English language versions of the Treaty of Waitangi have crucial differences that, among other things, cast significant doubt over the extent to which Māori knowingly ceded power to the British in 1840 (for a more complete history of the treaty see Orange, 2015).
2. While there are similarities in how populism is operationalized in each country (Moffit, 2017 argues the existence of an Antipodean populism), there are also important differences linked to the history of politics in New Zealand.
3. See also Fairburn (1989).
4. Muldoon's affinity for Lee can probably be explained by the strong influence of his maternal grandmother, Jerusha Browne, who had been active in both the Liberal and Labour Parties.
5. Despite the implementation of a welfare state by the Savage government, the ongoing impacts of colonization, including a failure to redress the loss of land, meant that Māori often fared worse than their Pākehā counterparts throughout the 20th century.
6. With reference to breaches of the Treaty of Waitangi.
7. The policy has been conspicuously absent from the NZ First policy manifesto in recent years, suggesting it is no longer considered to be of strategic importance.
8. In 2017, *The Spinoff*, a left-leaning online news platform, published a satirical column outlining a variety of demonstrably racist comments made by Peters, including a joke with the punchline 'two Wongs don't make a right' in reference to foreign ownership of land in New Zealand (see Donnell, 2017).
9. Eligible New Zealanders get two votes: a party vote for the political party of their choosing, and an electorate vote for the local representative of their choosing. The total number of seats a party receives depends on their percentage share of the party vote. That share of seats is filled first by those in the party who were successful in winning an electorate seat, with the balance drawn from a party list. If a smaller political party fails to reach the 5% threshold, it can still win its share of seats below 5% by winning an electorate, a process known colloquially as 'coat tailing'.
10. NZ First also failed to reach the 5% threshold in the 1999 election, but Peters was successful in winning the Tauranga electorate, meaning the party returned to parliament with a total of five seats under MMP's coat tailing provision.
11. ACT is an acronym of Association of Consumers and Taxpayers, founded in 1993, which became a political party for the 1996 election. ACT maintained a presence in parliament between 2011 and 2020 by winning their sole electorate seat of Epsom, despite falling well short of the 5% party vote threshold.
12. For a critique of the relationship between authoritarianism and voting NZ First, see Donovan (2020).

References

Abedi, A., & Lundberg, T. C. (2009). Doomed to failure? UKIP and the organisational challenges facing right-wing populist anti-political establishment parties. *Parliamentary Affairs*, 62(1), 72–87. https://doi.org/10.1093/pa/gsn036

Akkerman, A., Mudde, C., & Zaslove, A. (2014). How populist are the people? Measuring populist attitudes in voters. *Comparative Political Studies*, 47(9), 1324–1353. https://doi.org/10.1177/0010414013512600

Arditi, B. (2004). Populism as a spectre of democracy: A response to Canovan. *Political Studies*, 52(1), 135–143. https://doi.org/10.1111/j.1467-9248.2004.00468.x

Atkinson, N. (2003). *Adventures in democracy: A history of the vote in New Zealand*. Otago University Press.

Benson, D. (1998). Marilyn Duckworth: Existentialism was in the air. *Journal of New Zealand Literature (JNZL)*, 16, 149–155. www.jstor.org/stable/20112300

Berry, R. (2002, July 1). NZ First to ignore Maori seats. *Evening Post*, p. 3.

Booth, P. (1990, June 14). Winston Peters: The man you want as Prime Minister. *North & South*, 40–55.

Brooking, T. (2014). *Richard Seddon: King of God's own: The life and times of New Zealand's longest-serving prime minister*. Penguin.

Burdon, R. M. (1955). *King Dick: A biography of Richard John Seddon*. Whitcombe and Tombs Ltd.

Donnell, H. (2017, July 11). Two Wongs don't make a right. *The Spinoff*. https://thespinoff.co.nz/politics/11-07-2017/revealed-winston-peters-has-never-had-a-racist-approach-to-anything

Donovan, T. (2020). Misclassifying parties as radical right/right wing populist: A comparative analysis of New Zealand First. *Political Science*, 72(1), 58–76. https://doi.org/10.1080/00323187.2020.1855992

Fairburn, M. (1989). *The ideal society and its enemies: The foundations of modern New Zealand society, 1850–1900*. Auckland University Press.

Franks, P., & McAloon, J. (2016). *Labour: The New Zealand labour party, 1916–2016*. Victoria University Press.

Garner, D. (2017, December 23). Duncan Garner: Dear NZ, how do we want to look in 20 years? *Stuff*. https://www.stuff.co.nz/national/politics/opinion/97625919/duncan-garner-dear-nz-how-do-we-want-to-look-in-20-years

Gustafson, B. (1986). *From the cradle to the grave: A biography of Michael Joseph Savage*. Reed Methuen.

Gustafson, B. (2006). Populist roots of political leadership in New Zealand. In R. Miller & M. Mintrom (Eds.), *Political leadership in New Zealand* (pp. 51–69). Auckland University Press.

Hames, M. (1995). *Winston first: The unauthorised account of Winston Peters' career*. Random House.

Husband, D. (2021, June 27). Will Winston rise again? *E-Tangata*. https://e-tangata.co.nz/korero/will-winston-rise-again/

Kaufmann, E. (2018). *Whiteshift: Populism, immigration and the future of white majorities*. Penguin.

Larson, V. (2017). The economics of immigration in NZ. *Noted*. www.noted.co.nz/currently/currently-social-issues/the-economics-of-immigration-in-nz

Little, G. (1986). *Political ensembles: A psychosocial approach to political leadership*. Oxford University Press.

Mahuika, N. (2011). 'Closing the gaps': From postcolonialism to Kaupapa Māori and beyond. *New Zealand Journal of History*, 45(1), 15–32. https://researchcommons.waikato.ac.nz/handle/10289/6579

McCormick, E. H. (1959). *New Zealand literature: A survey*. Oxford University Press.

McCready, T. (2017, September 12). Mood of the boardroom: Kingmaker or queenmaker? *The New Zealand Herald*, D9. www.timmccready.nz/2017/09/12/kingmaker-or-queenmaker/

McLachlan, B. T. (2013). *In search of a New Zealand populism: Heresthetics, character and populist leadership* (Master's thesis, Victoria University of Wellington). https://researcharchive.vuw.ac.nz/xmlui/handle/10063/2653?show=full

Miller, R., & Curtin, J. (2011). Counting the costs of coalition: The case of New Zealand's small parties. *Political Science*, 63(1), 106–125. https://doi.org/10.1177/0032318711407294

Moffitt, B. (2017). Populism in Australia and New Zealand. In Rovira Kaltwasser, C., P. Taggert, P. Ochoa Espejo & P. Ostigay (Eds.), *The Oxford handbook of populism* (pp. 121–139). Oxford University Press.

Moir, J. (2020, February 5). Winston Peters talks growing up in rare sit-down interview [Interview Transcript]. *RNZ*. www.rnz.co.nz/news/political/408874/winston-peters-talks-growing-up-in-the-north-in-rare-sit-down-interview

Mudde, C. (2007). *Populist radical right parties in Europe*. Cambridge University Press.

Mudde, C., & Rovira Kaltwasser, C. (2012). Populism and (liberal) democracy: A framework for analysis. In C. Mudde & C. Rovira Kaltwasser (Eds.), *Populism in Europe and the Americas: Threat or corrective for democracy?* (pp. 1–26). Cambridge University Press.

Muldoon, R. D. (1974). *The rise and fall of a young Turk*. AH & AW Reed.

Mulgan, J. (1939). *Man Alone*. Penguin.

Murphy, T. (2017, September 27). Winston Peter's little black book. *Stuff*. www.stuff.co.nz/national/politics/97281948/winstons-little-black-book

Nagel, J. H. (1993). Populism, heresthetics and political stability: Richard Seddon and the art of majority rule. *British Journal of Political Science*, 23(2), 139–174. https://doi.org/10.1017/S0007123400009716

Orange, C. (2015). *The treaty of Waitangi*. Bridget Williams Books.

Ostiguy, P. (2009). *The high and the low in politics: A two-dimensional political space for comparative analysis and electoral studies* (Working Paper No. 360). Kellogg Institute. https://kellogg.nd.edu/documents/1670

Pearson, D. (2001). *The politics of ethnicity in settler societies: States of unease*. Palgrave Macmillan.

Peters, W. (2002, May 29). Treaty lunacy and treaty people [Speech Transcript]. Delivered by the Rt Hon Winston Peters at New Zealand first, Clevedon electorate public meeting, Auckland. *Scoop*. www.scoop.co.nz/stories/PA0205/S00640/treaty-lunacy-and-treaty-people.htm

Phillips, J. (1987). *A man's country? The image of the Pakeha male, a history*. Penguin.

Schedler, A. (1996). Anti-political-establishment parties. *Party Politics*, 2(3), 291–312. https://doi.org/10.1177/1354068896002003

Sinclair, K. (1969). *A history of New Zealand* (2nd ed.). Penguin.

Snow, D., & Moffitt, B. (2012). Straddling the divide: Mainstream populism and conservatism in Howard's Australia and Harper's Canada. *Commonwealth & Comparative Politics*, 50(3), 271–292.

Spoonley, P. (2020). *The new New Zealand: Facing demographic disruption*. Massey University Press.

t'Hart, P., & Uhr, J. (2008). *Public leadership: Perspectives and practices*. ANU Press.

Taggart, P. (2002). Populism and the pathology of representative politics. In Y. Mény & Y. Surel (Eds.), *Democracies and the populist challenge* (pp. 62–80). Palgrave Macmillan.

Thomas, P. (2017). The last Muldoonist has his final stand in Government. *Noted*. www.noted.co.nz/currently/currently-politics/the-last-muldoonist-has-his-final-stand-in-government

Vance, A. (2020, October 28). Election 2020: The strategic error that cost Winston Peters—and boosted a determined, wily David Seymour. *Stuff*. www.stuff.co.nz/national/politics/300140171/election-2020-the-strategic-error-that-cost-winston-peters--and-boosted-a-determined-wily-david-seymour

Vowles, J. (1987). Liberal democracy: Pakeha political ideology. *New Zealand Journal of History*, 21(2), 215–227.

Vowles, J. (2020). Populism, authoritarianism, vote choice and democracy. In J. Vowles & J. Curtin (Eds.), *A populist exception? The 2017 New Zealand general election* (pp. 107–135). ANU Press.

Vowles, J., Barker, F., Krewel, M., Hayward, J., Curtin, J., Greaves, L., & Oldfield, L. (2020). *New Zealand Election Study 2020* [Data set]. New Zealand Election Study. www.nzes.net/home-2/the-2020-election/

Vowles, J., McMillan, K., Barker, F., Curtin, J., Hayward, J., Greaves, L., & Crothers, C. (2017). *New Zealand Election Study 2017* [Data set]. New Zealand Election Study. www.nzes.net/home-2/the-2017-election/

28
ARE FIJI'S TWO MILITARY STRONGMEN POPULISTS?

Thomas A. J. White

This chapter inquires into the 'conceptual overstretch' of a comparative populism (Sartori, 1970; Moffit, 2016, p. 13) and its relevance for political description in Oceania, specifically in the nation-state of Fiji. To date, the politics of the island nations of Oceania have not so much as made a scratch in global populism studies. For example, with the exception of Aotearoa New Zealand, *The Oxford Handbook of Populism* (2017) makes no mention of Melanesian, Micronesian, or Polynesian states, and the polities of this region go missing again in *The Routledge Handbook of Global Populism* (2019). Moreover, while populism studies have paid scant attention to the politics of Oceanic states, in Fiji at least, this indifference has been mutual. Through fifty years of independence from British colonialism, Fiji's racially-charged politics of coups and serial constitutions have included behaviours that appear populist. Yet this term is rarely used to define or critique such a politics. The most common use of this term in Fiji's national newspapers is found in Reuters reports in the World News sections, describing populist leaders, regimes, and movements *elsewhere* in the world.[1]

What insights then does a populist analysis provide to understanding Fijian political behaviour? Or alternatively, what blind spots does it create? Does its local non-use for denoting populist-type activities invalidate any such theoretical intervention? At the least, it cautions that a focus on populism in Fiji may overwrite more probing, alternative explanatory accounts. Variously pitched as a thin ideology, strategy, discourse, performance, and even the grounds of 'the political' itself, the polysemy of populism led Peter Wiles (1969) to state fifty years ago: 'To each his own definition of populism, according to the academic axe he grinds' (p. 166). Far from scuttling comparative populism, however, this observation returns us to the core objective of social inquiry: to understand human behaviour, rather than defend conceptual forts. The task at hand, therefore, is to assess how the various theoretical approaches in the populist studies tool kit might advance or hinder our understanding of Fiji's politics.

This chapter evaluates the analytic merits and costs of applying a populist reading to Fiji's two most significant contemporary politicians: the Indigenous military strongmen, former coup-makers, and repeat-elected prime ministers Sitiveni Rabuka and Voreqe Bainimarama. While these two leaders are not necessarily the most *populist* of all Fiji's political figures—the

2000 coup-leader George Speight could probably best advance such a claim—they remain ideal cases for thinking through the contemporary relevance of a comparative populism in Fiji. First, the two leaders have been politically pre-eminent in Fiji across the last thirty-five years. Speight, by contrast, is twenty years into a life sentence for treason and never took control of the state. Second, both leaders have clearly employed populist-like speech and behaviour in their politics, and yet they are rarely described as populists. These two leaders' more ambivalent relations to populist description offer greater nuance for specifically evaluating the analytic value of populism for interpreting Fiji's politics than a hard case would.

The following analysis is split into four parts: (i) an overview of the two leaders' political careers, summarizing Fiji's last thirty-five years of political division; (ii) the utility of a populist description for these two leaders; (iii) an analysis of what a populist description misses in these leaders' politics; and (iv) an alternative account for interpreting the populist characteristics of Fijian political behaviour.

The political careers of Rabuka and Bainimarama

Lieutenant-Colonel Sitiveni Rabuka burst onto Fiji's political scene in the country's first military coup on May 14, 1987. Storming parliament with masked soldiers, Rabuka ousted the month-old Coalition government, comprising the newly-formed, multiracial Labour Party and the National Federation Party, the traditional party of the Indo-Fijians (Lal, 1988, pp. 1–2). Ruggedly handsome, a lay Methodist preacher, military officer, and former national rugby player, Rabuka was the archetype for Indigenous iTaukei (Fijian) masculinity (Teaiwa, 2005). Rabuka claimed to be of *bati* (warrior) rank and presented himself as defending the honour of Fiji's chiefs (Scarr, 1988, p. 56). Indigenous support rallied behind his military takeover with slogans such as *Noqu kalou, noqu vanua* (My God, my land) and *Rerevaka na kalou ka duka na Tui* (Fear God and honour the chief) while Rabuka claimed Fiji for Jehovah, the chiefs, and the Indigenous iTaukei, over and against *heathen* Hindu and Muslim Indo-Fijians and the *intellectuals* in Fiji's capital, Suva (Norton, 1990, p. 139).

Rabuka claimed that the Indo-Fijian community—primarily the descendants of indentured sugar plantation labourers (1879–1920)—had forgotten their place in Fiji's colonially constructed racial hierarchy. After release from indenture, Indo-Fijians had persevered as the backbone of Fiji's sugar industry but also came to underpin Fiji's local economy of shopkeepers and white-collar professions in the colony's growing townships. Colonial rule was careless of Indo-Fijian well-being. This left many Indo-Fijians destitute yet also comparatively free to incorporate, establish credit and labour unions and schools, and contest elections for the few Indian seats on the Legislative Council. By contrast, British policies of Indigenous protectionism sought to insulate the iTaukei from the human attrition of plantation capitalism by restricting commoners to their villages under the combined care of the Methodist Church and the chiefs, with the latter representing Indigenous interests to the colonial state through the Great Council of Chiefs (GCC). Indigenous Fijians widely perceived this *privileged* status of Indigenous culture and interests as continuing after independence in 1970, whereafter the Indigenous-led Alliance Party and the high chief, Prime Minister Ratu Kamisese Mara, held office for seventeen years. Mara's shock loss at the hands of iTaukei commoners and Indo-Fijians in the April 1987 elections upended a century of institutionalized inter- and intra-ethnic political hierarchies. It also led Rabuka and his ethno-nationalist supporters to declaim Indo-Fijians as making a grab for political as well as economic hegemony.

In the aftermath of the coup, Rabuka invited Mara back to lead an interim government, but then, from the safety of his barracks, publicly admonished Mara's rule whenever he perceived a backtracking on the coup's goal of securing Indigenous paramountcy. When Mara agreed to a power-sharing arrangement between his Alliance Party and the deposed Labour Coalition, Rabuka executed a second coup in late September 1987. Rabuka established his own Council of Ministers, abrogated the London-drafted 1970 constitution, and declared Fiji a Republic—severing Fiji's ties to the British monarchy. Having now turned against Mara and the chiefly elite, Rabuka allied himself with the nationalist wing of the Methodist Church, as well as anti-Mara nationalist politicians, such as Sakeasi Butadroka of the marginal Fiji Nationalist Party. Amidst a flurry of draconian military decrees, in early October, Rabuka instituted the Sunday Ban, which prohibited all non-worship activities on Sundays for Christians and non-Christians alike.

Rabuka's Council of Ministers lasted only two months before he again turned to Mara to save the economy and lead Fiji through a redrafting of the constitution. The new 1990 Constitution reserved top government positions and allocated a fixed majority of parliamentary seats for the Indigenous iTaukei, and exempted Indigenous affirmative action policies from anti-discrimination law. Still in his barracks, Rabuka continued to intervene opportunistically on political issues, adding to his folk-hero status as the man who saved Fiji from a government of *vulagi* (foreigners). For example, Rabuka chose to join the pickets of the 1990 nurses' strike against Mara's interim government, contrasting sharply with his military harassment of the trade unions during his coups (Keeling, 1991). In the lead-up to fresh elections in 1992, Rabuka officially left military life for politics and, despite his status as a commoner, won control of the newly-formed *Soqosoqo ni Vakavulewa ni Taukei* (SVT) party, the new party of Fiji's chiefs, outmanoeuvring Mara's wife, Ro Lala Mara (a high chief in her own right), for the leadership. Still highly popular amongst the Indigenous masses and benefiting from the changes to the 1990 Constitution, Rabuka won repeat elections in 1992 and 1994, cementing his transition from rebel coup-maker to national prime minister.

Rabuka's ethno-nationalism tempered during his time in office, and by 1997, he had shifted towards ideals of statesmanship, pushing through parliament reforms to the 1990 Constitution that promoted multiracialism and reframed Indigenous paramountcy from an ideology of political dominance to one of cultural defence (Lal, 2000). The multiracial compromises of Fiji's 1997 Constitution scandalized many iTaukei while, conversely, many Indo-Fijians attacked the new laws for falling short of full political equality. During his premiership, Rabuka's programmes for Indigenous economic uplift suffered unprecedented graft and nepotism, haemorrhaging huge sums from unsecured, defaulting loans (Robertson, 1998, pp. 139–143). Rabuka's 1999 election coalition with the Indo-Fijian National Federation Party, which stood with Rabuka in solidarity for the 1997 Constitution, suffered a humiliating defeat to a resurgent Labour party, which gave Fiji its first Indo-Fijian prime minister, Mahendra Chaudhry. Rabuka resigned his parliamentary seat and left party politics. He did not return until 2016, to stand as the principal political opponent to the ruling Fiji First government led by our second leader for analysis, Voreqe Bainimarama.

Commodore Voreqe Bainimarama, or Frank, as he is referred to in Fiji, is likewise iTaukei, a commoner and a military man, and became Fiji's military commander in 1999. Bainimarama was soon thrust into the political spotlight when he assumed control of government in response to the parliament hostage crisis in 2000. On May 19, businessman George Speight led a rebel company of elite soldiers into parliament and held captive Prime Minister Mahendra Chaudhry, along with the ministers of his one-year-old Labour coalition government. The siege lasted eight weeks and sparked an epidemic of violence and looting, especially in and around Suva (Robertson & Sutherland, 2001; Trnka, 2008). Speight's coup was distinctive for its chaos and its mobilization of Indigenous villagers, who set up camp in the parliamentary complex itself, establishing a civilian shield preventing the military from attempting a rescue (Field et al., 2005). Roaming bands of young iTaukei men would sortie out from the complex and pillage Indo-Fijian shops and farmsteads. The 2000 coup was also remarkable for its intra-ethnic conflict. As law and order collapsed across the country, rival *mataqali* (fraternal clan-groups) settled scores, and contending noble chiefly lineages rebelled against the hegemony of then-President Ratu Mara's Lauan establishment based in Eastern Fiji.

Whereas Rabuka's supporters claim he saved 'Fiji for the Fijians', Bainimarama's intervention in the 2000 coup was broadly fêted as saving Fiji from inter-ethnic and intra-ethnic anarchy. Bainimarama negotiated the release of Speight's hostages, then later arrested Speight and his supporters for weapons violations of their amnesty agreement. Speight was convicted of treason and imprisoned for life. Bainimarama subsequently returned to the barracks and installed an iTaukei banker, Laisenia Qarase, as Interim Prime Minister to steward Fiji back to fresh elections and explore revisions to the 1997 Constitution, including new affirmative action policies for the iTaukei. Chaudhry's Labour government was never reinstated. Bainimarama, however, was drawn back into national politics in November 2000, when he narrowly escaped assassination in an army mutiny by soldiers supporting Speight. Some mutineers had been released from prison as part of Qarase's evolving policy of Christian forgiveness for those involved in the coup, as advised by ethno-nationalist chiefs and Methodist churchmen. Much to Bainimarama's disgust, instead of stepping down before the 2001 elections, Qarase used the resources of the state to help secure victory for his newly-formed Indigenous unity party, *Soqosoqo Dua ni Lewenivanua* (SDL). While Qarase persevered with customary practices of apology and reconciliation for Fijians involved in the 2000 coup, Bainimarama publicly demanded a zero-tolerance approach, driving a growing wedge between Qarase's SDL government and Bainimarama's military.

Bainimarama's leadership style developed in the context of leading his near-exclusively Indigenous military into increasing conflict with Qarase's Indigenous-privileging SDL government. Purges and tests of personal and institutional loyalty were combined with a latitude towards high-ranking officers, upon whose support he felt assured. Bainimarama's political values also took new form in his antagonism to the Qarase government. Whereas Qarase deferred to the chiefs and commissioned a new building for the Great Council of Chiefs, Bainimarama came to view the majority of chiefs as corrupt, uneducated, and racist, infamously remarking that they should 'go drink homebrew under a mango tree' (Lal, 2009, p. 32). While Qarase drew on customary values and Christian institutions for public events and policy-making, Bainimarama came to emphasize modernization, economic development, and later, secularism. When the SDL was re-elected in May 2006 and Qarase sought to remove Bainimarama as military head (Lal, 2009, p. 30), Bainimarama initiated his 'clean-up campaign', seizing control of the Fijian state via a coup in December 2006. In an interview with Maori Television several years later, Bainimarama justified his takeover by stating:

> In Fiji, you don't come up with your own vote. Your vote is dictated by the chiefs, it is dictated by the Great Council of Chiefs, it is dictated by the [chiefly] provincial councils, and it is dictated by the [Methodist] Church. So it's not your vote. So don't tell me that's democracy.
>
> *Robie, 2009*

Bainimarama's initial logic for his coup was anti-corruption and natural justice, whereby the professional soldier would hold corrupt and incompetent chiefs and politicians to account, but its mission parameters quickly expanded. A prompt return to elections would merely re-elect the still popular but deposed SDL government. As such, Bainimarama began a top-down programme to reconfigure Fijian democracy and free Fiji from its toxic 'politics of race'. A new project of sweeping liberal social and political reform offered the rationale for postponing elections and for dismantling the political base of the deposed Qarase government. Bainimarama abolished the 'colonial' GCC, harassed the Methodist Church leadership, and purged the civil service of anti-coup dissidents. Key vacated positions, such as the regional development positions of divisional commissioner, were then awarded to loyal military officers (Ratuva, 2013, p. 172). Following his regime's abrogation of the 1997 Constitution in 2009, Bainimarama introduced a series of military decrees that clamped down on free speech, free assembly, and free association, giving the regime increased control of the media to push through its anti-racism agenda. Fiji's judges were replaced, Qarase was imprisoned for minor corruption offences, and political opponents fled the country.

By 2013, Bainimarama's military regime had drafted a new constitution that centralized executive power and rejected the consociational multiracial compromises of the 1997 Constitution, favouring an integrationist approach, returning Fiji to a winner-takes-all Westminster system, and removing systems of separate Indigenous representation. Many post-coup military decrees were simply absorbed into the new constitutional order, such as heavy regulation of the press and restrictions on organized labour. Government media outlets trumpeted Bainimarama's new ethnically-blind constitution with the catchphrase 'We are all Fijians' and heralded the dawn of Fiji's first 'genuine democracy'. These reforms, however, were often received by Indigenous Fijians as an all-out assault on their cultural integrity. For example, all new political parties were required to register under an English name, and English became the mandatory language of parliament. Any protests against these reforms, moreover, were quickly rebranded by Bainimarama's regime as perpetuating the racist, chiefly politics of divide and rule. With the trauma of the 2000 Speight coup still etched deep in the national psyche, Bainimarama's zero-tolerance, anti-racism strategy resonated with many Fijians across the ethnic divide and his Fiji First party won the 2014 elections emphatically. In addition to the overwhelming support from Indo-Fijians, Bainimarama received a substantial percentage of the urban, middle-class iTaukei vote, attracted to his vision of a 'modern and progressive' Fiji. Bainimarama was re-elected in 2018 by a much tighter margin following Rabuka's political return to lead Fiji's main Indigenous opposition party, SODELPA, the successor party to Qarase's SDL. Rabuka is likely to be Bainimarama's primary opponent again in the 2022 general elections. This time, however, Rabuka will lead the newly-formed People's Alliance Party, a name that harks back to a halcyon pre-coup era of Mara's Alliance Party and signals a more consensus-oriented, multiracial approach, conceived in opposition to the authoritarian one-nationism of Bainimarama and his Fiji First government.

The utility of populist description in Fiji

The details in these biographical accounts repeatedly gesture at political behaviours that we *could* call *populist*. But what does a *populist lens* actually add to interpreting the politics of these two leaders? The most significant advantage is enabling an analysis that transcends their enmity and policy differences, instead highlighting their *shared* populist discourse instantiating 'the people versus a malign other' (see, for example, Hawkins, 2009), as well as their matching populist political styles (Moffit, 2016, pp. 27–37). That is, despite being on opposite ends of Fiji's dominant political spectrum of race, we may see how during their coups and in their post-coup governments, the early Rabuka and the contemporary Bainimarama adopted the same populist-type speech and behaviour to seize and hold onto power.

In terms of their common populist discourse, both leaders operationalized a partisan rhetoric that conceptualized the Fijian people in opposition to either *racial others* (Indo-Fijians) or *racist others* (ethno-nationalist chiefs and churchmen). This political speech propagated a sense of crisis which enabled these leaders to reject election results and usurp governing authority in the name of cleansing Fiji of this other's distorting influence. The conceptual flexibility of populism to include both a racially exclusive and racially inclusive politics (Mudde & Rovira Kaltwasser, 2017) helps maintain focus on these two leaders' common illiberalism and their 'us versus them' polemics that heightened the political stakes (Moffitt, 2015) in order to excuse their coups and win subsequent elections.

In Rabuka's ethno-nationalist discourse during the 1987 coups, Indo-Fijians dominated the economy, and with a faster population growth, would dominate democratic politics too.[2] The notion of Indo-Fijian economic dominance is flawed (Kumar & Prasad, 2004), yet the high visibility of Indo-Fijian small businesses gives the impression of bustling Indo-Fijian affluence, particularly when juxtaposed against the quiet, comfortable, albeit cash-poor subsistence life in Indigenous villages. An Indigenous politics of grievance drew deeply on stereotypes of wealth-worshipping Indo-Fijians, who served as scapegoats for an increasing Indigenous social dislocation as the strict hierarchical structures of a chief-led village life disintegrated in the face of advancing capitalist modernity (Ernst, 1994). Rabuka's politics of crisis played to the perceived calamity of an Indian political takeover, in which Fiji would cease to be a Christian country, chiefly *mana* (power or effectiveness) would be diminished by *vulagi* (foreigner) rule, and Indigenous-held land would be converted to freehold, then plundered by Indo-Fijians and foreign capital. The Sunday Ban reveals how this politics interlocked ideals of racial paramountcy and a nostalgia for a past uncomplicated by a globalized modernity. The ban clearly discriminated against Indo-Fijians and recognized in law the authority of one ethnicity's religious doctrines over the nation as a whole. It also, however, pushed against iTaukei bourgeois lifestyles that increasingly used Sundays for leisure as well as worship (Rutz & Balkan, 1992, pp. 62–85) by recalling the strict Sabbatarianism of colonial village life introduced by early Wesleyan missionaries and imposing this onto Fiji's urban centres too (Heinz, 1993, p. 428). In addition to Rabuka's attack on Indo-Fijians, therefore, he also targeted the urban middle-classes, especially those connected to the newly-formed Labour Party. This included the violent harassment of leftist academics based at the University of the South Pacific in Suva (Howard, 1991, pp. 244–252; Robertson & Tamanisau, 1988, pp. 68–71).

By contrast, Bainimarama's anti-elitism attacked Fiji's Indigenous cultural elite, with Qarase's network of chiefs and Methodist *talatala* (ministers) vilified as the toxifying other. This Indigenous elite was portrayed as manipulating their customary high rank and religious authority to hijack the democratic process, playing the 'politics of race' to secure privileged access to iTaukei development funds. Crucial to Bainimarama's narrative is the crisis of a repeat of the 2000 coup, which recalls both the worst aspects of Indigenous ethno-nationalism and Bainimarama at his most heroic. Thus, corruption, ethnic division, and violence before his 2006 coup are contrasted by him with justice, unity, and good governance after it. Bainimarama's military enthusiastically pursued any rumour of malfeasance in Qarase's government, which in turn justified the replacement of key senior public officials with coup loyalists (Larmour, 2005, pp. 11–12). This concentration on the vices of the old order facilitated nepotism in the new one. When encountering Indigenous resistance to his integrationist policies, such as his abolition of the GCC, Bainimarama's regime dismisses this as 'racism' and resituates these Indigenous claims of cultural vandalism as an ethno-nationalist dog-whistle for resurrecting the politics of race.

By identifying these two discourses as populist, we see not only their similar techniques of exclusion and misrepresentation but also the dynamic reciprocity of the two discourses: how they intensified one another. Despite being on opposite sides of Fiji's politics of race, both leaders' rhetoric hinged on a zero-sum relation between racial equality and the political integrity of Indigenous cultural institutions. Whenever political opponents defended the one, they were blasted for doing down the other. This entrenched and confirmed an irreconcilable opposition that justified the trashing of constitutional democracy and affirmed a preference for non-dialogue and rule by force. Indeed, it is notable that a feature of Rabuka's return to national politics in 2016, without military backing, is that his political speech placed much greater emphasis on dialogue and pluralism.

The label of populism also usefully draws attention to the two leaders' common political style. Despite their ideological differences, Rabuka and Bainimarama set themselves up as *non*-politicians. Their claim to be no-nonsense soldiers not only sought to excuse an impatience with consensus-seeking and public deliberation and to assert a self-narrative of men of action, but may also be seen to position them as more authentically 'of the people', and not of the political elite. In this regard, their self-presentation as reluctant national leaders who would rather be back in the barracks matches the populist figure of the 'patriotic soldier', discussed most often with reference to the 'generals' of Latin America (Casullo, 2019, p. 58). Simultaneously, however, both leaders acquired a saviour status from their radical overhaul of the constitutional status quo. Rural Indigenous Fijians christened Rabuka their Moses, who saved them from becoming vassals in a 'little India', whereas the now pro-government newspaper, the *Fiji Sun*, happily reported local descriptions of Bainimarama as a 'messiah' who saved Fijians from the colonial politics of race (White, 2013, p. 97).

Due to this profound personal capital, Fijian citizens frequently petitioned these leaders directly, circumventing the normal state institutions of redress. This direct relation, unmediated by tribal loyalties or honorific protocols (qua chiefs), or institutionalized systems of representative government (qua politicians), added to their populist appeal and style. One absurd but real example of this is when Prime Minister Bainimarama's office telephoned my department at the Fiji National University to enquire about a student who had complained to the prime minister about their zero mark due to plagiarism. Framing this behaviour as populist emphasizes the matching personality politics of these two leaders: their similar aesthetics of martial masculinity, and their politics of crisis and exclusion, as well as their disregard for legal institutional norms and structures in their military takeovers. It also points to how this approach, as is the case with other populist regimes, degrades accountability, transparency, and the separation of powers, leading towards nepotism, patron-clientelism, and authoritarianism. The common marker of populism across the two regimes helps see past their rhetoric of opposition, or, as Robert Robertson laments on the frustrating familiarity of Bainimarama's new order, despite its revolutionary reforms: '*plus ça change, plus c'est la même chose*'[3] (Robertson, 2017, p. 211).

How a populist description in Fiji misses

The examples of Bainimarama and Rabuka are instructive because both leaders *appear* as attractive candidates for populist description. They both look the part of the contemporary populist strongmen we see elsewhere in the world. Both leaders used a discourse of 'us' and 'them', which they map out as 'the people' against an economic or customary 'elite'. Both are political outsiders who cultivated a saviour status. They both shared a low regard for the rule of law, operated an aesthetic of charismatic transgression, and propagated a public sense of crisis to justify their grab for power. Yet there are good reasons for caution regarding populist description too, not least because populism is typically viewed as a feature of democracies (or at least a politics that dresses in the language of popular sovereignty), and Fiji, thus far, has only been *contingently* democratic.

While Fiji's liberals strongly reject the old refrain of traditionalist chiefs that 'democracy is a foreign flower' (Larmour, 2005), political scientists might well affirm it. Despite holding thirteen competitive elections since independence from Britain in 1970, Fiji has never had a successful, democratic *transfer* of power, never mind the twice turnover criterion for 'democracy' required by Samuel Huntington (1991, p. 266). Incumbent governments get re-elected in 'free and fair' elections, but when opposition parties win, they never complete a full term before their ejection at the barrel of a gun. Historically, this has been limited to new governments with substantive representation by Indo-Fijians. However, with Bainimarama continuing his post-coup reign with electoral successes in 2014 and 2018, his new 'democracy' under the 2013 Constitution has yet to veer from this 'remorseless power of incumbency' (Fraenkel, 2015).

In his introduction to his collected volume *Populism and the Mirror of Democracy*, Panizza argues that 'the notion of the sovereign people as an actor in an antagonistic relation with the established order, as the core element of populism, has a long tradition in the writings of the topic' (Panizza, 2005, p. 4). Either as the exceptional, integral moments of political regeneration or as the illiberal self-portrait hiding in the attic, populism is strongly tied to a fundamental logic of democracy—power must flow from the agency and sovereignty of the people. This makes the translation of populism into Fiji's 'democratic' politics somewhat problematic, as coups and constitutions, not elections, have been the principal engines of political change, and when Fiji's two coup-makers overturned elections and overthrew governments, such acts were not conceived primarily as 'of the people'. Alternative sovereigns of Jehovah and the divine right of chiefs, and natural justice and anti-corruption figured more centrally in these coup-makers' claims to power. The authority to rule in Fiji, then, is gained not so much by harnessing the general will but by first invalidating it. Indeed, for both leaders, their charisma arguably lies less in the embodiment of the popular will, and more as the expression of their personal *mana* in defying it.

Bainimarama and Rabuka seized control of the state by military force—not through a strategic mobilization of the popular will—and only secured their popular mandates after first remaking Fiji's constitutional order from the top-down. Global norms of modern constitutionalism required these leaders to subsequently cast their interventions within a legal grammar of popular sovereignty, with Indigenous paramountcy (Rabuka) or racial equality (Bainimarama) given special emphasis. This is not to say that these later acclamations of a sovereign people were insincere or merely self-interested, but that they were not the primary means by which these political upheavals were initially achieved. Indeed, in what we might call Fiji's *coupstitutions* of 1990 and 2013, a competing sovereignty of a 'right of might' is tacitly acknowledged. Unlike in Fiji's 1970 and 1997 constitutions, these two texts issued the military with the role to ensure both national security and the 'well-being of Fiji and all Fijians' (Constitution of Fiji, 1990, 94.3; Constitution of Fiji, 2013, 131.2). Given Fiji's history of military takeovers, such a vaguely-worded competency to ensure Fijians' 'well-being' remains a backdoor for military interference. With Rabuka's 2022 election bid increasingly perceived as a major threat to the Bainimarama military establishment, we should expect to see growing efforts by the government to paint Rabuka as not merely sorely lacking as a replacement prime minister, but as an existential threat to Fiji's basic political order.

We find further warning of the shortcomings of populist description in Fiji on the few occasions when Fijians do use 'populism' to remark on local politics. Here, the term denotes behaviours quite distinct from the standard juxtaposition of a sovereign people antagonistic to the established political order. In parliament, Fiji's opposition Members of Parliament (MPs) cry 'populism' at government promises of free laptops for schoolchildren, abrupt announcements of new public holidays, reckless infrastructure expenditure, and VAT reductions.[4] Bainimarama's Fiji First ministers counter-accuse opposition MPs of 'populism' for latching onto trivial trending issues, such as plastic bag levies or cheaper mobile phone data,[5] and not focusing on long term policy concerns. In a rare article that actually addresses this topic, albeit briefly, Scott Macwilliam critiques this usage as erroneous, and as merely denoting what is considered *popular*, not what is genuinely populist (Macwilliam, 2015, p. 6). Fijian use of 'populism', therefore, is not one that sees the spectre of illiberalism lurking in the majoritarian biases of democratic decision-making. Instead, it reveals the fear that a democracy too representative of the masses will jeopardize 'good governance'.

Through British colonialism to the neoliberal advocacy of development actors such as the World Bank, Fiji has long been subjected to *discourses of governance*. These may (or may not) aim to advance the people's best interests, but they rarely prioritize their voice. In Bainimarama's 'clean-up campaign', there is a similar focus on governing efficacy, based on a perception of a superior military technocratic know-how. Fiji's military is well-funded and cherishes its international reputation for professionalism. Fiji contributes more United Nations peacekeepers per capita than any other country in the world,[6] and its soldiers are prized recruits in the global security industry (May, 2014). Fiji's military class, both officers and privates, have developed skill sets and gained work experience well beyond that of village life. Officers sent to military academies in Britain, Australia, New Zealand, India, and, after Bainimarama's coup, China and Malaysia, return better educated and worldlier than most of Fiji's chiefs (Firth & Fraenkel, 2009, pp. 118–120). Such life experience can lead to a marked condescension towards both customary and democratic leadership. This is evident in Bainimarama's 'homebrew' remarks, and statements by him and his officers at the time of the 2006 coup. When Bainimarama's soldiers took to Suva's streets during the 2006 elections, Colonel Piti Driti promoted their superior military efficacy, saying: 'Politicians are politicians, but we are professionals', while Bainimarama later justified his overthrow of the government by stating 'only the military can bring about real social change' (Baledrokadroka, 2016, p. 179). After Bainimarama seized power, his contrast between his regime doing 'governance' and 'developing' Fiji versus his opponents 'playing politics' figured frequently in rebuttals to criticism of his rule (see, for example, Rasoqosoqo, 2011). While such speech acts might be read as populist for their monological style, adopting an ad hominem hostility to dialogue, they also demonstrate a prioritization of governing efficacy over representational legitimacy.

To emphasize a populist description for these two leaders because they most closely match the charisma, authoritarianism, and divisiveness of other populist leaders in the world overlooks their founding anti-democratic strategies reliant on military force and their appeals to alternative sovereigns to merely that of 'the people'. Note, the argument here is not that Rabuka and Bainimarama are not 'populists per se', but that stamping these leaders with this label risks concealing as much as it reveals. It may successfully perceive typically populist characteristics in the behaviours of Rabuka and Bainimarama, but it arguably loses considerable explanatory power when making assumptions regarding the underlying ideological and strategic causes of such behaviours.

An alternative account for populist behaviour in Fiji

Given the populist character of these two leaders—deep partisanship, anti-elitism, clientelism, extra-institutional rule, authoritarianism, accountability deficits, and a heavy emphasis on charisma and personality—combined with only a limited appeal to a sovereign popular will or a politics premised on the mobilization of the masses, what non-populist accounts are there for Rabuka and Bainimarama's populist-like behaviour? Or in other words, what alternative descriptive or explanatory accounts would a populist lens potentially occlude?

First, we might consider the locally prominent models of Oceanic leadership, which Marshall Sahlins presents as two contrasting sociological types: the feudal Polynesian Chief and the entrepreneurial Melanesian Big Man (Sahlins, 1963). This binary model resonates with the contrast between charismatic and customary authority in Fiji's recent history, manifest in the waxing careers of commoner coup-makers versus the waning authority of Fiji's high chiefs. With the steady erosion in the governing authority of Fiji's eastern chiefs, marked first by the electoral defeat of Ratu Mara in 1987, then by Rabuka's ascendency as party leader of the chiefly SVT party, and finally Bainimarama's coup and his abolition of the GCC, one might say the ascribed status of Fiji's Polynesian chiefs has given way to the attained status of Fiji's Melanesian big men. Fiji's cultural and physical geography sits at the colonially-imagined divide between Oceania's Polynesian East (e.g., Hawaii, Tahiti, Tonga, Samoa, Raratonga, and Aotearoa New Zealand) and its Melanesian West (e.g., Vanuatu, the Solomon Islands, and Papua New Guinea). The angry, brash style of politics by Rabuka and Bainimarama has drawn scholars of Fiji's politics towards this binary comparison (for example, Garrett, 1990). When reading Sahlins' caricature of Melanesian big men, we can see why.

> The Melanesian big-man seems bourgeois, so reminiscent of the free enterprising rugged individual of our own heritage . . . the indicative quality of big-man authority is everywhere the same: it is personal power. Big-men do not come to office, nor succeed to, nor are they installed in existing positions of political groups. The attainment of the big man status is rather a series of acts that elevate a person above the common herd.
>
> *Sahlins, 1963, p. 289*

Does populist-type behaviour in Fiji simply reflect the reassertion of a more Melanesian form of leadership? Conceptually, this position is tricky to maintain. Sahlins never intended this binary to serve as a hard category distinction, admitting it as 'obviously imprecise' (Sahlins, 1963, p. 286). Moreover, critique of the big man/chief binary, which draws on Sahlins' own later work 'The Stranger-King or Dumézil Among the Fijians' (1981), points out that Fijian chieftainship itself operates a 'kingly/populist' duality (Marcus, 1989, p. 198).

> The opposed forces in play *celeritas* and *gravitas* . . . perfectly fit in the Fijian case [of chiefly authority]. *Celeritas* refers to the youthful, active, disorderly, magical and creative violence of conquering princes; *gravitas* to the venerable, staid, judicious, priestly, peaceful and productive dispositions of an established people.
>
> Sahlins, 1981, p. 121

In Sahlins' account, chiefs are outsiders from across the sea, 'sharks who travel on land' (1981, p. 112). These aliens take political power but consolidate their rule by becoming bound to 'the people of the land,' often through betrothal to the previous chief's daughter. The 'disorderly' politics of 'creative violence' of Fiji's two coup-makers, their status as political outsiders, and their usurping of the old constitutional order only to then ground their leadership in law anew resonates with this cultural logic. Rabuka and Bainimarama are not publicly discussed as chiefs in Fiji, but as Baledrokadroka has argued, the military is now in effect its own '[chiefly] super-confederacy' (Baledrokadroka, 2016, p. 179). Sahlins's observation that within Fiji's chiefly system, 'rather than a normal succession, usurpation itself is the principle of legitimacy' (Sahlins, 1981, p. 113), offers an apt prediction for Fiji's later cycle of coups and constitutions. Such an explanatory account based on cultural logic is important for centring actor perspectives and their frames of meaning (Enfield, 2000), but it also remains hazy how exactly such logic drives specific behaviour, particularly when multiple cultural logics appear to be in play. For example, Rabuka's and Bainimarama's populist common touch is a reflection on their non-chiefliness—their lack of strangeness. Are Rabuka and Bainimarama then 'big men' capitalizing on a politics of 'stranger chiefs' or something else entirely? It is not obviously clear how one might resolve this lack of clarity, or how such a theorizing of Fijian politics might actually inform policy.

Another account for the apparently populist character of Fiji's military strongmen, and one that suffers less from the imprecise causality of explanatory accounts based on cultural logics, concerns the specifics of Fiji's human geography. Namely, the more intimate political ecologies of very small nation-states (such as those of Pacific Island countries) can establish norms of populist-type behaviour—a strong connection between individual leaders and constituents, a limited private sphere, a limited role for ideology and programmatic policy debate, strong political polarization, the ubiquity of patronage, the capacity of individual leaders to dominate all aspects of public life—by dint of their smallness alone (Corbett & Veenendaal, 2018, pp. 8–11). Such an observation is crucial for a comparative populism, for while very small nation-states—which Corbett and Veenendaal (2018) enumerate as countries with populations of less than a million—make up nearly 20% of the world's nation-states, the framing assumptions of populism studies, and political science more generally, rest pretty much exclusively on the experiences of much larger countries.

These populist characteristics, which emerge because of the micro-scale of a nation-state, repeatedly show similar outcomes deriving from different causes. For example, the inevitably proximate social relations between political actors and the public in very small states mean that there is already less institutional distance between politicians and the people for populist leaders to disdain and symbolically collapse. Populist leaders override the separation of powers and may concentrate power by combining a multitude of cabinet portfolios. In very small states, however, a similar circumvention of institutional checks may be less an egregious power-grab and more a quotidian habit of responsive and cost-effective government. Though this is not to say ministry-hoarding is never criticized. Public dissent directed against Fiji First's 'minister for everything', Attorney-General Aiyaz Sayed-Khaiyum, shows such portfolio-hoarding has its limits. Populist authoritarianism occurs when actors claim to embody the homogenized, sovereign will of the people, establishing a charismatic authority to roll over institutional norms. In very small states, such authoritarianism also appears to be a feature of the out-sized role of the state compared to other civil society institutions, where, for example, state-compliant newspapers, like the *Fiji Sun*, tailor their reports to guarantee continued government advertising for income. Moreover, where personalization of politics is a core feature of populism, it is also a pattern of behaviour in small Oceanic states in general, in 'face-to-face societies' where 'everybody knows everybody' (Corbett, 2015, p. 5). Instead of this necessarily making politics less partisan, familiarity may breed contempt, particularly where political divisions cut through family ties (Corbett, 2015, p. 8).

Conclusion

In this chapter, the relevance of populist description for Fiji's two military strongmen has been evaluated in terms of both what such a description reveals and what it obscures. Given the wide polysemy with which populism circulates in contemporary global politics, and yet its relative absence or divergent use in Fiji, the focus has fallen on what populism studies offer for understanding Fijian politics, more than what Fijian politics has to offer populism studies. As such, descriptive accuracy has been prioritized over conceptual precision. The benefit of this approach, on the one hand, has been to skirt the contested semantics that besets a comparative populism. On the other hand, it has enabled analyses to dig into Fiji's politics and navigate around the ideological differences of its two pre-eminent military strongmen—Rabuka and Bainimarama—to reveal their commonalities in discourse and style. And in contrast, by showing what populism misses, this approach has also drawn attention to Fiji's *ongoing* democratic deficit despite its much-touted 'return' to democracy in 2014 (Ratuva & Lawson, 2016)—where popular sovereignty merely confirms political authority rather than establishes it. It is an anti-democratic trend that is revealed in Fijians' own idiosyncratic use of the term 'populism', which is bound up in Fiji's colonial and neo-colonial discourses of governance pursuant of a capitalist productive efficiency. Where Fiji's particular cultural logics, such as Sahlins's 'stranger chief', may partially help explain the more confirmatory role that populist appeals to 'the people' fulfil in Fiji, the recent scholarship of Corbett and Veenendaal offers a more comprehensive account of Rabuka's and Bainimarama's apparently populist behaviour—namely, that it may be productively explored as a function of scale. The small size of Fiji's polity encourages behaviours that resemble populist practices—including personality politics, authoritarianism, extra-institutional governance, and nepotism, but also broad political participation at elections—that need not be rooted in ideologies of popular sovereignty or strategies of mass mobilization.

Corbett and Veenendaal's comparative work on small states has emphasized their democratic resilience, yet their scholarship bears relevance for exploring the quality of populist politics in larger states too. Indeed, this potential crossover is an opportunity Corbett and Veenendaal consider themselves (2018). Their comparative analysis draws on the personalized politics of small democratic states to anticipate the future democratic integrity of large states experiencing a wave of populist politics. The comparison may also, however, identify something that appears integral to the core logic of populism more generally: its nostalgia for a more proximate politics. Populisms tend to be anti-globalization and anti-bureaucratic, grounding their appeal in the promise of a more demanding and more intimate form of political representation. These political preferences for norms of authority are more consistent with smaller polities than with larger ones. Populist leaders are often 'family' figures, such as Don Pepe Jose Figueres[7] or Uncle Bernie.[8] Emotional closeness is prioritized over distant rational argument. Populist behaviour takes high politics and pulls to the low familiarities of common life, whether this is Big Macs on Air Force One[9] or swearing in press statements. Comparative populism has so far largely ignored the experiences of small states, especially in Oceania. These case studies, however, may not only present as instructive outliers or illuminating contrasts; they may embody the very proximate politics that big-state populists idealize in their speech and behaviour.

Epilogue

Fiji's subsequent national politics have fulfilled and overtaken the anticipations of this chapter. In a repeat electoral face-off between Fiji's two strongmen in December 2022, the final count tied Sitiveni Rabuka's People's Alliance Party (twenty-one seats)—allied with his old 1999 elections partner, the National Federation Party (five seats)—with Bainimarama's Fiji First Party (twenty-six seats). With the three remaining seats won by SODELPA, this fixed the successor party to the Indigenous government usurped in Bainimarama's 2006 military takeover to now deliver the *coup de grace* to his sixteen-year rule. Remarkably, however, the ill-will Rabuka generated by abandoning SODELPA to start his own party had split the SODELPA hierarchy over whether to support their old leader or rally behind Bainimarama. An initial vote of SODELPA's thirty-member board narrowly chose Rabuka sixteen to fourteen, yet this vote was declared null and void by Mohammed Saneem, the Supervisor of Elections and nephew to Fiji First's General Secretary Aiyaz Sayed-Khaiyum. That SODELPA's party leader Viliame Gavoka was also Sayed-Khaiyum's father-in-law layered the party's internal politics with further intrigue. At the same time, Police Commissioner, Sitiveni Qiliho—a former military officer and close ally to Bainimarama—circulated reports of inter-ethnic violence triggered by the prospective return of Rabuka as prime minister. Decrying these reports as false flags, the deputy police commissioner Abdul Khan resigned in protest, offering a crucial counter narrative at this pivotal moment for Fijian democracy. The military commander, Major-General Jone Kalouniwai, also refused requests by Fiji First loyalists to militarily intervene. On December 23rd, the now-reduced SODELPA board voted a second time, and narrowly chose Rabuka again, with votes split thirteen to twelve. On Christmas Eve, parliament elected Rabuka's new cabinet, with Bainimarama resigning from parliament in the new year, having little enthusiasm for life on Fiji's opposition benches. Though with charges of corruption and sedition being assembled by Rabuka's ruling coalition—a rare source of common ground in a government including Indigenous nationalists and Indo-Fijian liberals—Bainimarama is unlikely to get a quiet retirement from public life.

Notes

1. A search for the terms *populism* and *populist* over the last five years in Fiji's oldest and most respected national newspaper, *The Fiji Times*, returned ninety-seven hits. Of these, 79 were in Reuters or other international news agency reports. The remaining mentions turned on local debates, but here, the meaning varied significantly from how the term is understood in comparative contexts. This is further discussed later in this chapter.
2. Population ratios between the Indigenous iTaukei and the Indo-Fijian have influenced, and been influenced by, Fiji's political upheavals. At the time of the 1987 coup, Indo-Fijians outnumbered the iTaukei, with their population share at 49% compared to 46% for the iTaukei (Fiji Bureau of Statistics, 1986). Primarily due to Indo-Fijian emigration following the 1987 and 2000 coups, though also due to shifting birth rates, this population ratio changed to 37% Indo-Fijian and 57% iTaukei by the time of Bainimarama's 2006 coup (Fiji Bureau of Statistics, 2008).
3. The more things change, the more they stay the same.
4. See National Parliament of Fiji, *Parliamentary Debates*, July 11, 2017 (Prem Singh, Opposition MP); April 12, 2018 (Biman Prasad, Opposition MP); June 18, 2019 (Jese Saukuru, Opposition MP).
5. For example, National Parliament of Fiji, *Parliamentary Debates*, August 8, 2019 (Aiyaz Sayed-Khaiyum, Government MP)
6. Figures taken from United Nations (2018) 'Summary of Troop Contributing Countries by Ranking', 31 December 2018, https://peacekeeping.un.org/sites/default/files/2_country_ranking_8.pdf. At the end of 2018, Fiji's deployment stood at 458, though this is a drop from 655 in 2016. In 2005, deployment numbers were at 767. On the 2018 figures, Fiji is very closely tied with Rwanda for the top spot, and one's choice of population statistics could call it either way.
7. José María Hipólito Figueres Ferrer, thrice president of Costa Rica.
8. Bernard Sanders: U.S. Senator who sought the Democratic Party nomination in the 2016 presidential election.
9. Donald Trump's projected preference for eating McDonald's fast foods.

References

Baledrokadroka, J. (2016). The Fiji military and the 2014 elections. In S. Ratuva & S, Lawson (Eds.), *The people have spoken* (pp. 177–189). National University Press.

Constitution of Fiji (1990). *Constitution of the sovereign democratic Republic of Fiji (promulgation) decree 1990*. http://www.paclii.org/fj/promu/promu_dec/cotsdrofd1990712/

Constitution of Fiji (2013). *Constitution of the Republic of Fiji*. https://www.laws.gov.fj/ResourceFile/Get/?fileName=2013%20Constitution%20of%20Fiji%20(English).pdf

Casullo, M. E. (2019). How to become a leader: Identifying global repertoires of populist leadership. In F. Stengal, D. MacDonald & D. Nabers (Eds.), *Populism and world politics* (pp. 55–72). Palgrave Macmillan.

Corbett, J. (2015). 'Everybody knows everybody': Practicising politics in the Pacific Islands. *Democratization*, 22(1), 51–72. https://doi.org/10.1080/13510347.2013.811233

Corbett, J., & Veenendaal, W. (2018). *Democracy in small states: Persisting against all odds*. Oxford University Press.

Enfield, N. (2000). The theory of cultural logic: How individuals combine social intelligence with semiotics to create and maintain cultural meaning. *Cultural Dynamics*, 12(1), 35–64. https://doi.org/10.1177/092137400001200102

Ernst, M. (1994). *Winds of change: Rapidly growing religious groups in the Pacific Islands*. Pacific Conferences of Churches.

Field, M., Baba, T., & Nabobo-Baba, U. (2005). *Speight of violence*. Reed Books.

Fiji Bureau of Statistics (1986). *1986 census*. Government of Fiji.

Fiji Bureau of Statistics (2008). *2007 census*. Government of Fiji.

Firth, S., & Fraenkel, J. (2009). The Fiji military and ethno-nationalism: Analyzing the paradox. In J. Fraenkel, S. Firth & B. Lal (Eds.), *The 2006 military takeover in Fiji* (pp. 117–138). ANU Press.

Fraenkel, J. (2015). The remorseless power of incumbency in Fiji's September 2014 election. *The Round Table*, 104(2), 151–164. https://doi.org/10.1080/00358533.2015.1017255

Garrett, J. (1990). Uncertain sequel: The social and religious scene in Fiji since the coups. *The Contemporary Pacific*, 2(1), 87–111. http://ezproxy.une.edu.au/login?url=www.jstor.org/stable/23701519

Hawkins, K. (2009). Is Chávez populist? Measuring populist discourse in comparative perspective. *Comparative Political Studies*, 42(8), 1040–1067. https://doi.org/10.1177/0010414009331721

Heinz, D. (1993). The Sabbath in Fiji as guerrilla theatre. *The Journal of the American Academy of Religion*, 61(3), 415–442. https://doi.org/10.1093/jaarel/LXI.3.415

Howard, M. (1991). *Fiji: Race and politics in an island state*. University of British Columbia Press.

Huntington, S. (1991). *The third wave: Democratization in the late twentieth century*. University of Oklahoma Press.

Keeling, D. (1991). Rabuka's turn. *Australian Left Review*, 131, 26–27.

Kumar, S., & Prasad, B. (2004). Politics of race and poverty in Fiji: A case of Indo-Fijian community. *International Journal of Social Economics*, 31(5), 469–486. https://doi.org/10.1108/03068290410529335

Lal, B. (1988). *Power and prejudice*. Institute of International Affairs.

Lal, B. V. (2000). Review: Rabuka of Fiji Coups, constitutions and confusion. *The Journal of Pacific History*, 35(3), 319–326. www.jstor.org/stable/25169505

Lal, B. V. (2009). 'Anxiety, uncertainty and fear in our land': Fijis road to military coup, 2006. In J. Fraenkel, S. Firth & B. V. Lal (Eds.), *The 2006 military takeover in Fiji* (pp. 21–41). ANU Press.

Larmour, P. (2005). *Foreign flowers: Institutional transfer and good governance in pacific islands*. Hawaii University Press.

Macwilliam, S. (2015). *Bonapartism in the South Pacific: The Bainimarama government in Fiji, state, society and governance in Melanesia discussion paper 2015/10*. Australian National University.

Marcus, G. (1989). Chieftainship. In A. Howard & R. Borofsky (Eds.), *Developments in Polynesian ethnology* (pp. 187–223). University of Hawaii Press.

May, S. (2014). *A fighting people? Fijian service in the British army and the production of race and nation* (PhD thesis, University of Chicago).

Moffitt, B. (2015). How to perform crisis: A model for understanding the key role of crisis in contemporary populism. *Government and Opposition*, 50(2), 189–217. https://doi.org/10.1017/gov.2014.13.

Moffitt, B. (2016). *The global rise of populism*. Stanford University Press.

Mudde, C., & Rovira Kaltwasser, C. (2017). *Populism: A very short introduction*. Oxford University Press.

National Parliament of Fiji, *Parliamentary debates*, July 11, 2017 (Prem Singh, Opposition MP); April 12, 2018 (Biman Prasad, Opposition MP); June 18, 2019 (Jese Saukuru, Opposition MP); and August 8, 2019 (Aiyaz Sayed-Khaiyum, Government MP).

Norton, R. (1990). *Race and politics in Fiji* (2nd ed.). University of Queensland Press.

Panizza, F. (2005). Introduction: Populism and the mirror of democracy. In F. Panizza (Ed.), *Populism and the mirror of democracy* (pp. 1–31). Verso.

Rasoqosoqo, L. (2011, June 14). Bainimarama: No room for dirty politics. *Fiji Sun*. http://fijisun.com.fj/2011/06/14/bainimarama-no-room-for-dirty-politics/

Ratuva, S. (2013). *The politics of preferential development*. ANU Press.

Ratuva, S., & Lawson, S. (Eds.) (2016). *The people have spoken*. ANU Press.

Robertson, R. (1998). *Multiculturalism & reconciliation in an indulgent republic*. Fiji Institute of Applied Studies.

Robertson, R. (2017). *The generals goose: Fijis tale of contemporary misadventure*. ANU Press.

Robertson, R., & Sutherland, W. (2001). *Government by the gun: The unfinished business of Fiji's 2000 coup*. Pluto Press.

Robertson, R. T., & Tamanisau, A. (1988). *Fiji: Shattered coups*. Pluto Press.

Robie, D. (2009, September 17). Bainimarama won't be bullied. *Pacific Islands Report*. Center for Pacific Island Studies.

Rutz, H. J., & Balkan, E. M. (1992). Never on Sunday: Time-discipline and Fijian nationalism. In H. J. Rutz (Ed.), *The politics of time* (pp. 62–85, American Ethnological Society Monograph Series 4). American Anthropological Association.

Sahlins, M. (1963). Poor man, rich man, big-man, chief: Political types in Melanesia and Polynesia. *Comparative Studies in Society and History*, 5(3), 285–303. www.jstor.org/stable/177650

Sahlins, M. (1981). The Stranger-king or Dumézil among the Fijian. *Journal of Pacific History*, 16(3), 107–132. www.jstor.org/stable/25168469

Sartori, G. (1970). Concept misformation in comparative politics. *American Political Science Review*, 64, 1033–1053. www.jstor.org/stable/1958356

Scarr, D. (1988). *Politics of Illusion: The military coups of Fiji*. New South Wales University Press.

Teaiwa, T. (2005). Articulated cultures: Militarism and masculinity in Fiji during the mid 1990s. *Fijian Studies*, 3(2), 201–222.

Trnka, S. (2008). *State of suffering: Political violence and community survival in Fiji*. Cornell University Press.

United Nations (2018, December 31). *Summary of troop contributing countries by ranking*. https://peacekeeping.un.org/sites/default/files/2_country_ranking_8.pdf

White, T. A. J. (2017). How novel is the secularism of Fiji's 2013 constitution. *Journal of South Pacific Law* (Special Edition), *2017*, 73–100. https://doi.org/10.3316/agispt.20180927002522

Wiles, P. (1969). A syndrome, not a doctrine. Some elementary theses on populism. In G. Ionescu & E. Gellner (Eds.), *Populism: Its meanings and national characteristics* (pp. 166–179). Weidenfeld and Nicolson.

INDEX

Note: Pages with "n" refer to endnotes.

Aalberg, T. 108–109
Acosta, P. 152–153
Adhaalath Party (AP) 245, 246
ad hoc decisions 68
Adventures in Democracy: A History of the Vote in New Zealand 383
Afeef, A. 242
Ahlstrand, J. L. 292
Ahmed, F. A. 169
algorithmic enclaves 291
All Ceylon Jamiyathul Ulama 227
All India Congress Committee (AICC) 165
All Nepal Women's Association (Revolutionary) (ANWA(R)) 213, 214
al-Qaeda 144, 245, 246
ambiguity, source of 51
ammart (aristocrats) 307, 308
ana (authority) 264
Anderson, B. 24
anti-authoritarian 91
anti-colonialism 69
anti-elitism 4, 179, 224; Fiji 401; Taiwan 349–350
anti-foreign sentiment 69
anti-genderism 80
anti-globalization 4, 23–24
anti-government protest 17, 233
anti-imperialism 69
anti-Islam 81, 115, 139, 185, 241, 243, 246, 248–250
anti-partyism 172
anti-pluralism 4
anti-politics 375
anti-science discourse 14–15

Anti-Terrorism Act of 2020 280
anti-Westernism, Pakistan 178–181
Aquino III, B. 152
Arakan Rohingya Salvation Army (ARSA) 260
Ardern, J. 383
Arditi, B. 389, 392
Aris, M. 259
Arroyo, G. M. 277, 278
Asia: conservative moment 89; financial crisis, 1997 322–325; populist leaders in 121; populist movements in 123; religious populism in 124, 128; right-wing populists in 126; secularism and religious populism in 125–126
Asia Pacific 3, 14; communicative aspects of populism in 107; political engagement across 13
Aslanidis, P. 208
Association of Consumers and Taxpayers (ACT) 391, 392, 393n11
Association of Southeast Asian Nations (ASEAN) 283
atheist state 129–130
Atkinson, N. 383
Australia: commercial media logic in 114; disenchantment, populism, and depoliticized neoliberalism 374–377; frame of politics 372–374; media 115; right populism to authoritarianism 377–379
Australian Labor Party (ALP) 372, 374, 377, 378
authoritarian/authoritarianism 92, 140, 195, 198, 199–200, 202, 247, 250, 252, 256, 257, 262, 270, 273, 276, 284, 311,

312, 331, 333, 345, 354; charismatic rule and 92; leadership 89; methods 13; neoliberalism 282–284; peace 281; populism and 89
authoritarian populism 89, 92; Myanmar 258–265; Philippines 270–285; style of politics 124; tendencies 99; *see also* Duterte phenomenon
authority, institutionalized forms of 40
Awami League (AL) 195, 196, 198, 199
awza 259, 266n8
Aziz, S. 176

Bainimarama 13, 396–408
Bamar Buddhists 99–100, 258
Bandaranaike, S. W. R. D. 229
Bangladesh 31; charismatic populism to personalized-authoritarian populism 195–197; clientelism 201–202; corruption 202; cronyism 202; democratic backsliding, entrenched authoritarianism 199–201; independence of 136; militarized-authoritarian fiefdom 198; military leadership to quasi-populism 197–198; QDP 198–199
Bangladesh Nationalist Party (BNP) 197–199
Bangsamoro Autonomous Region, Muslim Mindanao 274
Bangsamoro Organic Law 32
Batto, N. 351
Beautiful Grassland is My Home, The 335, 340n5
Being a Good Soldier for President Xi 336, 341n11
Benson, D. 384
Berman, S. 375
Bharatiya Janata Party (BJP) 4, 77, 81, 93–94, 121, 127, 154–155, 171; discourse of 82; electoral politics 96; PRR discourse 82; transformational logic 96
Bhatia, S. 96, 121–122
Bhutto, B. 136, 176
Bhutto, Z. A. 136, 176–186, 194
Bhutto, Z. I. 29
Big China, A 337, 341n16
Bisaya 275
BN-UMNO 140
bodoh (stupid) 294
Bodu Bala Sena (BBS) 28, 231; ideology 127
bottom-up populism 201
boundary-drawing practice 61
Brexit campaign 65, 66, 107, 108, 168
Broinowski, H. 114, 115–116
Brubaker, R. 22
Buddhism 99, 120, 126, 142, 225–226, 228, 231, 232, 258, 259; socially engaged 98

Buddhists 28, 32, 95, 99, 124, 128, 130, 226–232, 236, 258, 260, 264
Budianto, H. 295
Build, Build, Build (BBB) programme 72, 283
bureaucratic/bureaucracy 91; organization 42; parties 44
Burma Socialist Programme Party (BSPP) 258
Burnham, P. 373

Cadier, D. 53
Canovan, M. 5, 10, 337, 344, 361, 376
Capital Creation Scheme 68
Casanova, J. 125
celeritas 406
Central Reserve Police Force (CRPF) 96
Centre for Study of Society and Secularism (2020) 155
Chadwick, A. 109
Chan-o-cha, P. 69
charismatic/charisma 89; authority 41–42, 45–46, 91–92, 273; default position 92; Duterte, R. 272–273; forms of 91; inherited 259; monks 100; narratives of 96; and plebiscitary leadership 92; rule, qualities of 91; Weber's classical analysis of 90
charismatic leadership 39–41, 45, 123, 192–193; acclamatory politics, and leader democracy 90–93; Aung San Suu Kyi 96–100; description of 89–90; features of 42; Narendra Modi 93–96; studied cases of 43
charismatic-plebiscitary leadership 90, 99; characteristics of 93; fragility of 92
charismatic-plebiscitary rule 92
Chaudhry, F. 176
Cheesman, N. 263
China, China, the Bright Red Sun Never Sets 335, 340n4
China-Pakistan Economic Corridor project. 180
Chinese Communist Party (CCP) 129, 330, 332, 333, 335–339
Chinese politics: CCP 330, 332, 333, 335–339; Chinese nation, perception of 337–338; elites, the 332–333, 336–337; general will 333; patriotic songs 333–335; people, the 332, 334–336; true power 334–335; us vs. themdichotomy 337
Christianity 26, 80, 120, 142
chumocracy 194
Chung-Hee, P. 320, 322, 324, 327
citizenship 125–126
civilisational differences 29
civilisational populism 32
civilizationism 135, 144
civil society organizations 39

Index

clientelism 193
clientelistic parties 44–45
Clinton, B. 378
collective identity 120–121, 124–125, 207, 208–210, 214
collective national identity 28
colonialism/post-colonialism 135, 278, 346, 396, 404
colonization 142, 392
communal difference 84
communicative/communication: form of 110; logic 108; phenomenon 108; populist style of 110–111; strategy 108
Communist Party of Indonesia (PKI) 142
Communist Party of Nepal (Maoist) (CPN(M)) 208, 209, 213, 215, 216
Communist Party of the Philippines (CPP) 273, 274, 277
community: empowerment 71; transmission, denials of 154
comparative evidence 10
comparative politics 49
Comprehensive National Industrial Strategy (CNIS) 72
Congress Forum for Socialist Action (CFSA) 165
contemporary analysis, limitations of 7
contemporary populism 5–8, 90; type of 9–10
contemporary populists 13; repertoire 8, 9–10
Corbett, J. 406–408
corona jihad 155
corrupt elite 110, 114
corruption 194–195, 202
Corruption Perception Index 202
COVID-19 pandemic 186, 235, 251, 256, 270, 274, 335, 363, 387
Crick, B. 172
critical discourse analysis (CDA) 289
crony capitalism 193
cronyism 193–194
cross-regional comparative methodology 53
cross-regional comparison 57
Cross-Strait Service Trade Agreement (CSSTA) 350
cultural/culture: anxiety 50; Christianity 80; differences 24, 29; heritage 129; identity 95; invasion 231; nationalism 11; pluralism 127; protectionism 231; war 231; war, brim of 4
Curato, N. 112, 150, 153

Dae-Jung, K. 321–324
Dakwah movement 28
De Cleen, B. 21
decolonization 135, 317–318; India 317; Philippines 318; South Korea 317–319

Defence of India Rules (DIR) 169
degenerative populism 66, 71–73
de Lima, L. 279
democratic/democracy: antipathetic relationship with 44–45; deterioration in 73; detriment of 73; institutions 112; phases of 134; 'quality' of 3
Democratic Justice Party (DJP) 321
Democratic Labour Party (DLP) 385
democratic pluralism 303
Democratic Progressive Party (DPP) 343, 345, 346, 348–353
democratization 100, 134, 147, 191, 241, 244
dengue fever in the Philippines 150
Dengvaxia inoculation 152
depoliticization 330, 373–375, 378, 379n4
D'Eramo, M. 371
derecognition of the princes, India 165
Descendants of the Dragon, The 338, 341n18
de-secularization, narrative of 128
Deutchman, I. E. 114
developmental populism 66, 67–69
de Vreese, C. 108
Dhan, R. 169
Dharia, M. 169
Dharmapala, A. 226
Dhar, P. N. 165
Diehard Duterte Supporters (DDS) 270, 276, 277
Dietze, G. 80
Digital Security Act 200
Dikshit, U. S. 170
diplomatic bureaucracy 61
discourse: of global governance 53; strategy and 43–44
discursive approach 52
disenchantment, facets of 56
disinformation 156
disposable money machines 152
'distinctive' discourse 21
Divineguma (reawakening) scheme 234
domestic peripheralization 56
Donà, A. 80
Doo-Hwan, C. 320, 327
Dow, G. 371
dramatization 149, 155–156
drug dealers, extra-judicial killing of 72
drug war in Thailand 150–151
dual-representation system 363–365
Dunant, B. 262
Dutertenomics 71–72, 283
Duterte phenomenon: authoritarian neoliberalism and economic populism 282–284; cross-class alliance to centre-right 277–278; electoral victory and popularity 272; exception, biopolitics of

280–281; hegemony 279–280; left- and right-wing populisms 273–274; liberal democracy 275–276; macho populism, Duterte-speak 274–275; peaceful coexistence, authoritarian-populists 281–282; personality cult and charisma 272–273; populist moment and social media 276–277; securitization 278–279
Duterte, R. 4, 10, 11, 13, 32–33, 60, 67, 71, 85, 92, 107, 108, 111–113, 152, 270–285, 345; administration 72, 153; government resources 72; legitimacy 92; policy to combat illegal drugs 72
Duterte-speak 274–275
Dutugamunu (Sinhalese King) 230

Easter Sunday attacks, 2019 231
economics: inequality 8, 12–13, 66; nationalism 68; populism 282–284; stagnation 66
EDSA Republics 272
Eklundh, E. 79–80
elected capitalist absolutism 309
election violence 60
elective affinity 110–111
electocracy 309
electoral democracies 134–135; plebiscitarian elements of 13
elite establishment 152
Ellison, A. 114
Emejulu, A. 211
Emergency period, the 164, 168–171
emotion, religious culture of 14
Engesser, S. 111
Enhanced Defense Cooperation Agreement, 2014 281
Entering into the New Era 336, 341n10
Erdogan, T. 136
Ershad, H. 198–200, 203
Esser, F. 109
Estrada, J. 272, 273, 277, 323
ethnic minorities 24
ethnic nationalism 11, 24
ethnonationalism 22, 212, 282
ethnopopulism 224
ethnos and demos 223–224
European populism 26
European Union 57
Eurosceptic internationalism 58
Euroscepticism 59
Eurozone crisis of 2010 to 2015 57
exclusionary/right-wing populism 163, 164, 171, 257
extraordinary leadership 94

faith-based organizations 129–130
fake news 110

Farris, S. 81
fatwas 201
Fauzee, I. 245
favouritism 193
fear: politics of 14; religious culture of 14
femonationalism 81
Féron, E. 80
Fiji: discourses of governance 404; populist behaviour 405–407; populist description 400–402; Rabuka and Bainimarama, political careers of 397–400
Fiji Sun 402
filter bubble 291
financial crisis 151
first social media election 113
Flyvbjerg, B. 235
foreign policy 49, 52; personalization of 51; politicization of 50; populism in 53
foreign policy analysis (FPA) 51
forging of divisions 149
Freedom Party of Austria (FPÖ) 41
Free Education Policy 230
Freeport Indonesia 70–71
Front National (FN) 41
fundamentalism 125
funding, substantial redistribution of 73

Gaddafi, M. 178
Gandhi, I. 10, 164–171, 173, 192, 224
Gayoom, M. A. 240–245
Gellner, E. 5
gender 14–15, 84–85; collective identity 214; equality 212, 218; extensive scholarship on 79; gender equality 212, 218; gender gap 210; identity construction, Maoist populism 212–215; left populism and feminism 211; nationalism 81; online news media, Indonesia 291–298; peace agreement to gender gains and fragmentation 215–218; and populism 77, 80; PRR and 78; violence 210–211; Yudhoyono, A. 290–300
general will 5, 65
genocide 261
geographical dissemination 4
geopolitical foes 56
Gerbaudo, P. 110
Germani, G. 38
Geun-hye, P. 316, 324, 325
Ghafoor, H. A. 244
Ghar Wapsi (homecoming) 182, 187n5
Ghatak, M. 94
Giorgi, A. 80
Giri, V. V. 165
global dissemination 6

globalization 50; of Islamic religion 231; neoliberal 304
Global North 79, 85
Global South 52, 79; corruption 194; politics in 50; populism in 50
Gokhale, H. R. 170
Golden Land, The 258–259
governance: modes of 125–126; recognizable pattern of 155–156
Grand National Party (GNP) 324–325
gravitas 406
Green, J. E. 92
growth, redistribution, and populism: degenerative populism 71–73; description of 65–67; developmental populism 67–69; pro-business populism 69–71
Gujarat model 94, 95

Habermas, J. 125
habeus corpus 169
Hadj-Abdou, L. 81
Haggard, S. 322
Haider, J. 41
Haksar, P. N. 164
Halliday, M. 292
Hanson, P. 107, 108, 113–116; channels for 115; contemporary social media 116; ideological dimension to 115; media appearances 115
Happy Holiday 335, 340n6
Hashimoto, R. 359
Hashimoto, T 358, 361–363
Hasina, S. 31, 199–202
Hatakka, N. 110, 111
health care policy: developmental capture 69; regulatory _capture 69
health crises, politicization of 156
Hefazat-e-Islam 201
Henderson, G. 321
heterogeneity of populism 10
heuristic attractiveness 42
Hewison, K. 306
Heydarian, R. J. 112, 113
hijabs and burqas, ban on 231
Hindu/Hinduism 30, 120, 124, 126, 142; ideology 82; masculinity 84; nationalism 61; organizations 121–122; revivalism 128; sub-nationalism 94; womanhood 82; women's bodies 84
Hindu-Muslim riots 94
Hindu Rashtra 81
Hindu Swayamsevak Sangh 121
Hindutva 27, 29, 78, 82, 94–96, 121, 127–128; discourse of 82; ecosystem of 96; idea of 95; ideology of 82; political logic of 81

Hirschman, A. 277
Hitler, A. 41
Hlaing, M. A. 256, 265
Hocking, J. 378
Hofstadter, R. 7
Hopster, J. 110–111
Hosokawa, M. 359, 363
humanistic Buddhism 130
human rights violations 150
Hungary 59, 80
Huntington, S. 403
Hussain, A. 248
hybrid media system 109, 111
hyper-capitalism 358

Ibrahim, Q. 247
ideational approach 37
'identikit' populism 22
identity politics 27–28
ideological regional integration 59
illiberalism 44–45
Ilminism 319
immigrants/immigration 22, 44, 50
inclusionary/left-wing populism: bank nationalization 165; checks and balances, erosion of 167–168; dimensions of 257; Emergency period, the 168–171; India 164–167; liberalism and democracy 172–173; popular sovereignty 171; populists 164; princely purses, abolition of 165
income inequality 12, 73, 137
incorporation, notion of 55
incumbent populist 358–360
India 60–61; anti-Modi lobby 154–155; bank nationalization 165; bureaucracy 167; case studies from 90; chauvinism projects in 77; checks and balances, erosion of 167–168; Chief Justice, selection of 167; COVID-19 pandemic in 150; democracy in 94, 96, 171; early elections 166; Emergency period 164, 168–171; family planning 171; foreign policy 61; good governance in 94; Hindu community in 95; inclusionary populism 164–167; leftist policies 167, 168; parliamentary democracy 168; personalization of party, Mrs. Gandhi 168; popular sovereignty 171; post-colonial secular constitution 95; princely purses, abolition of 165; PRR discourse in 80; public health infrastructure 156; vision of 26–27
Indian National Congress party 164
Indonesia/Indonesian 31, 71–72; Constitutional Court 127; corruption 142; drug wars

of 149; elite-non-elite divide 289; finite resources 70; foreign policy 60; Kompas.com 292–298; national ideology of 142; news media, digital era 291–292; politics 31; populism in 69, 143; poverty on foreign forces 144; presidential election, 2014 289–290; socio-political dynamics 142; Yudhoyono, A. 290–298
Indonesian Democratic Party of Struggle (PDI-P) 143
industrialization 38
industrial transformation 72
inequality 66
Information and Communications Technology Act 200
infrastructure flagship projects (IFP) 283
inherited charisma 259
institutional discrimination 140
institutionalized party 37
instrumentalization 136
international change 56
International Convention on the Elimination of All Forms of Racial Discrimination (ICERD) 141
International Criminal Court (ICC) 278
international dimension 55–56
international liberal order 57
international market 67–68
International Monetary Fund (IMF) 23–24, 68, 137, 180–181, 246, 322
international multilateralism 61
international order: ideological engagement with 58; Thailand 58
international politics, importance for 56
international relations 49, 50; concept of 52–53, 56–57; cross-regional perspective 57–61; description of 49–50; distinct discourse of 53; and foreign policy 50–52; international dimension 55–56; phenomenon of 49; populism and 52–55; theory 53; thinking about populism 52–53; Western populism's approach to 57
international-structural dimension 50
international system 55–56; functioning of 56; norms of 56
international technocracy 58–59
intersectional analysis 78
intrusive supranational organizations 56
Ionescu, G. 5
ISIS 144
Islam/Islamic/Islamism 120, 135–136, 142, 144, 177, 182–186, 240, 245; description of 134–135; framing and use of 135; ideas of 140; ideology 240, 251; Indonesia 142–144; Malaysia 139–142; Maldives 240–251; nationalism 241, 245, 247, 249, 251; nationalism, failure of 32; organisations 32; Pakistan 136–139; political 245–247; populist framing 135; populist usage of 135–136; socialism 184, 185; terrorism 96; tradition 80–81
Islamic Defenders Front (IDF) 28
Islamic Foundation of Maldives (IFM) 246
Islamophobia 180, 182, 186
Ismail, G. 182
Ismail, I. 250

Jacob, A. 167
Jacobs, K. 110, 111
Jaffrelot, C. 94, 177
Jagers, J. 108
Jamaat-e-Islami 201
Jamiyathul-Salaf (JS) 246
Janata lockdown 154
Janatha Vimukthi Peramuna (JVP) 229
Japan: dual-representation system 363–365; institutional reforms, 1990s 360–361; Koizumi phenomenon 358–360; LDP 358; local populism, Osaka and Tokyo 361–363; political vacuum 365–366
Jathika Chinthanaya (nationalist thought) 233
Jathika Hela Urumaya (JHU) 228, 229, 231
Jayasinghe, P. 224
Jeffries, S. 179
Jhumhooree Party 247
jihad 134, 144, 247
Jinnah, M. A. 27
Jinping, X. 282, 332, 336
Jintao, H. 334
job insecurity 23–24
Jokowi 60, 67, 69–71; foreign policy 60; government 71; growth strategy 70
Jong-Phil, K. 321, 322
Judaic-Christian heritage 26

Ka Awatea report, 1991 387
Kant, K. 169
Kantola, J. 211
Kapoor, K. 83–84
Kartu Indonesia Pinta _(KIP) 71
Kartu Indonesia Sehat _(KIS) 71
Kenny, P. D. 3, 10, 23, 257, 263
Khan, A. 136, 178, 183
Khan, I. 10, 13, 30, 31, 134, 136, 176–186, 224, 333
Khan, L. A. 182
Khan, Y. 178, 183
Khilafat (Caliphate) Movement 135
Kileygefaanu, I. F. 242
Knott, A. 79–80
knowledge claims, invocation of 149

Index

Koike, Y. 358, 361–363
Koizumi, J. 323, 358–362, 365–367
Koizumi phenomenon 358–360
Kompas.com: delegitimation, authority and trivialization 295–298; discourse strategies 292; elite-public divide, construction of 292–295; excerpt 1 (initial debate, Ani and public) 293; excerpt 2 (unfavourable portrayal, Ani) 294; excerpt 3 (Ani's use of word bodoh) 294–295; excerpt 5 (personal impact, on Erie) 295; excerpt 6 (political communications expert, voice of) 296; excerpt 7 (authoritative voice, use of) 296–297; excerpt 8 (report covering, Ani's attendance at technology fair) 297; excerpt 9 (report covering, Democrat Party rally) 297–298
Krämer, B. 110
Kuala Lumpur Summit 141
Kugelman, M. 180
Kumar, A. 83
Kumaratunga, C. 230
Kuomintang (KMT) 343, 345–353
Kyi, Aung San Suu 10, 89, 90, 96–97; authoritarian and nationalist path 99; as icon of democracy 97; leadership 97; political support 99; relationship of religion 98

Laadheeni 248
Laborde, C. 125
labour market 70
Laclau, E. 52–53, 77–78, 150, 153, 209, 303
Laothamatas, A. 306, 307
Latin America 3, 38; 'pink wave' in 7
leaders/leadership 41–43; analysis, locus classicus of 90; centrality of 13; central role of 23; democracy 91; and followers 89; forms 91; institutional constraints on 45; quality 92–93
Lee, J. A. A. 385
left-wing 7, 24, 50, 57–59, 124, 130, 207, 211, 215, 283
Levitsky, S. 377, 378
liberal democracy 7, 99, 275–276
Liberal Democratic Party (LDP) 358
liberalism 65
liberal regional institutions 60
Liberation Tigers of Tamil Eelam (LTTE) 228–232, 234, 236
Lim, M. 291
Limthongkul, S. 309
L'Internationale 335
Little, G. 388, 389
Lombardo, E. 211

London School of Economics (LSE) 5
Love Jihad 83
Love My Chinese Nation 337, 341n15
Lynch, T. 372

MaBaTha nationalist movement 264
Machidori, S. 366
macho populism 274–275
Macwilliam, S. 404
Madison, J. 172
madrasas (Islamic schools) 201
Magam Ruhunupura Mahinda Rajapaksa Port 234
Mahathir, M. 31, 139–141, 145
Mahavamsa 226, 229
Mahinda Chinthanaya 233
Maiguashca, B. 211
Main, A. 137
Maintenance of Internal Security Act (MISA) 169
Majlis (parliament) 242, 243
majoritarian dictatorship 306
Malaysia 27–28; elections 140; Internal Security Act (ISA) 140; Malay-Muslim population 139; population of 139; pro-Malay policies 140; religion and ethnicity 139; Sharia-driven Islamic state in 141
Malaysian Islamic Party 139
Maldives: democracy, challenges to 249–251; Gayoom, M. A. 242–245; Islamic nationalism 241, 245, 247, 249, 251; political Islam and democratization 245–247; populism and independence 241–242; religious populism 240, 241, 243, 245, 249, 252; Yameen's blood-and-faith nationalism 247–249
Maldivian Democracy Network (MDN) 250
Maldivian Democratic Party (MDP) 241
management studies 39–40
Man Alone (Mulgan) 384
Mann, M. 100
Manucci, L. 109
Maoism 124
Maoist: armed conflict 212–215; ideology 210; populism 212–215
Maori people 383–388, 390–393
Mara, R. K. 397, 398, 400, 405
Marcos, F. 271–273, 276, 277
Marcos, F. Jr. 271
market populism 375
Marxism 7, 55, 95–97, 128
Mattala Rajapaksa International Airport 234
Mauhadu-al Dhiraasaathul Islamiyya 243
Maung, A. 261, 262
Maung, U. K. 259

May Fourth Movement (1919) 333
Mazzoleni, O. 108, 109
McCormick, E. H. 384
measles, resurgence of 153
media and communication: description of 107; logic-populist logic 109–110; mediatization and media populism 109–110; Pauline Hanson 113–116; populism 107, 110–111; Rodrigo Duterte 111–113; study of populist communication 108–109
Media Law No. 12/2014 261
mediatization 107, 109–110
medical populism: concept of 150; COVID-19 pandemic in India 153–155; danger of 156; dengue vaccine controversy in the Philippines 152–153; description of 149; dimensions of 149; drug war in Thailand 150–151; instrument of 151; nature of 156; settings for 155
Medina Constitution 31
Meloni, G. 77
militarized-authoritarian fiefdom 198
military: bureaucracy 198; capitalism 228, 229; coup 10, 27, 89, 97, 99, 177, 256, 258, 303, 305–308, 312, 320–322, 327, 397
Miller-Idriss, C. 22–23
mineral rights, foreign ownership of 70
Ming-teh, S. 350
minimal electoral democracy, necessity of 13
minimal secularism 125
mining contracts, automatic renewal of 70–71
Mining Law 2009 70
Mishra, L. N. 169
modernization, feminent theorist of 39
Modi, N. 4, 10, 11, 29, 30, 60–61, 81, 90, 93–94, 96, 121, 127–128, 150, 153–154, 171, 176, 181, 182, 231; leadership in Gujrat 94; legacy of Islamophobia 155; medical populism of 156; wave 94
Moditva 95
Moffitt, B. 107–108, 111, 112, 115
Mohamad, M. 139, 141
money politicking 309
moneytocracy 309
Morieson, N. 136
Moro Islamic Liberation Front 274
Morrison, S. 4
Mouzelis, N. 38, 39, 41
Mudde, C. 3, 5, 8, 22–23, 172, 256, 263, 371
Muldoon, R. D. 385–387, 392
Müller, J. W. 302, 377–379
multiculturalism 24, 50, 97, 98
Musharraf, P. 136, 178, 179

Muslims 27; communities 124–125; diasporas 134; of secularism and modernity 135; Sri Lanka 227
Mutual Defense Treaty, 1952 281
Myanmar (formerly Burma) 265n1; Bamar majority in 124; case studies from 90; competitive political arena 90; democracy icon/demagogue 263–265; ethnic conflicts 258; free-market system 258; judiciary 262–263; media 261–262; national and racial identity 98–99; NLD 255, 259, 260, 262, 264, 265; political insurgency 258; political party in 96–97; Rohingya crisis 260–261; Suu Kyi, Aung San 258–260; Western version of democracy 98
My Chinese Heart 338, 341n17
Myint, W. 255
My Motherland and I 335, 340n7

Naik, Z. 141, 250
Narain, R. 169
Narayan, J. 168
Naseem, A. 244, 248
Nasheed, M. 240, 241, 245–247, 249–251
Nasir, I. 240–242
Nasser, G. A. 135
National Chengchi University (NCCU) 347
nationalism/national identity 22, 24; analytical approaches 22–23; anti-globalisation 23–24; conflicts 31; enter top-down populism 29–33; ethnos and demos 223–224; exclusionary ethnopopulism 224; nationalist variants 24; new social polarization 229–231; and populism 223, 224; populism and 25; populist nationalism 21–22, 225, 231, 232, 235; religious nationalism 25–26; shifting focus 24–25; in Sri Lanka 225–229; Taiwanese 348–349; unfinished business of 26–29; unfinished business of national identity 26–28; uniform pathology of 24; variants 24
National League for Democracy (NLD) 255, 259, 260, 262, 264, 265
National Task Force to End Local Communist Armed Conflict (NTF-ELCAC) 274
National Thawheed Jamath 227
nationhood, original designs of 26
Nationwide Popular Pro-Democracy Protests 258
nativism 304
Naya Nepal 208, 212, 213
necropolitics 78
necropower 84
negligence, accusations of 152–153

Nehru, J. 95, 123, 164, 167, 224, 318
neoliberal austerity 65
neoliberal crisis of governability 78, 84
neo-liberal market forces 13
neo-mercantilism 68
Nepal: ANWA(R) 213, 214; collective identity 207, 208–210, 214; communist political movement 124; CPN(M) 208, 209, 213, 215, 216; gender and identity construction 212–215; gender, violence and populism 210–212; left populism and feminism 211; peace agreement to gender gains and fragmentation 215–218; People's War 207–208
nepotism 193
New Korean Democratic Party (NKDP) 321
New People's Army (NPA) 274, 277
New Zealand: DLP 385; liberalism 385; Man Alone theme 384; populism 389–391; populist, statesman and kingmaker 386–389; squattocracy 385; wealth redistribution 385
New Zealand Election Study (NZES) 391
New Zealand Literature: A Survey (McCormick) 384
Ngo, T. T. T. 129
Nihon Shintô (Japan New Party) 363
Nkrumah, K. 319
'non-majoritarian' institutions 8
Norocel O. C. 80
Nyunt, M. 262

Obama, B. 112, 282, 304
Official Secrets Act 261
one man one vote 311
One Roh and Three Kims 322
online media 14–15
online news media: delegitimation, authority and trivialization 295–298; digital era, Indonesia 291–292; elite-non-elite divide 289; elite-public divide, construction of 292–295; Kompas.com 292–298
Orbán, V. 93, 264
ordoliberalism 283
Orewa speech 390
'organic' political community 96
Organisation of Islamic Cooperation (OIC) 178, 187n4, 261
Organization of Islamic Cooperation 141
Ostiguy, P. 388
Otake, H. 359
otherness/othering/otherization 29; in Asia 26; process of 140
Our Workers Have the Power 334–336, 340n1
Oxford Handbook of Populism, The 396

Pakistan 121; COVID-19 139; anti-India 181–182; anti-Westernism 178–181; corruption 137; democratization 176; election campaign 137; Imran Khan's government 176, 177; Islam, use of 177, 182–186; military confrontations with India 136; military dictatorships 136; military tutelage 177; no-confidence motion, parliament 176; populist discourses, Bhutto and Khan 178–182; PPP 176, 177, 182, 183; Single National Curriculum 138; terrorism in 138
Pakistan Media Regulatory Authority 138
Pakistan Muslim League (PML) 176
Pakistan Muslim League-Nawaz (PML-N) 137, 177, 181
Pakistan People's Party (PPP) 136, 176, 177, 182–186
Pakistan Tehreek-e-Insaf (PTI) 137, 177, 181, 182
Palaver, W. 122
Palmer, C. 371
Panama Papers 195
Pandora Papers 195
pan-Islamism 135, 178, 186, 241
Panizza, F. 208, 210, 218, 403
Paradise Papers 195
Parashar, S. 218
Parkinson, M. 376
parliamentary democracy 67
partial conceptual evacuation 6
party institutionalization 43
Parvati, C. 213
Pashtun Tahafuz Movement (PTM) 182
patriotic songs, China 333–334
patron-client relationship 13
Pauline Hanson One Nation (PHON) 371
penal populism 271
Pen, M. L. 41
People's Alliance for Democracy (PAD) 308–310
People's Army to Uproot the Thaksin Regime 310
People's Democratic Reform Committee (PDRC) 308, 310–311
People's Liberation Army (PLA) 208–210, 214, 215, 333
People's War (1996G-2006) 207, 208
Pepinsky, T. 257
peripheralization 56
Permanent Court of Arbitration (PCA) 281
personalism 232
personality driven politics 12–13
Peters, W. 383–392
Philippine Development Plan (PDP) 282
Philippine National Police (PNP) 278
Philippines 71; authoritarian peace 281; biopolitics of exception 280–281;

degenerative populism 73; dengue vaccine controversy in 152–153, 156; Dengvaxia controversy in 156; Duterte-speak 274–275; liberal democracy 275–276; macho populism 274–275; mass murder, accusations of 152; mass vaccination program 152; politics 152; populist moment and social media 276–277; securitization 278–279; *see also* Duterte phenomenon

Phillips, J. 384

Piketty, T. 357, 358

pilot cluster 68

Pitidol, T. 309

plebiscitary leader democracy (PLD) 89

plebiscitary leadership 39, 90–92

pluralism 14, 28–29, 98

pluto-populist 306

Poland 59, 80

policy: initiatives, battery of 71–72; values 73; wide-ranging package of 67–68

political Islam 142, 241, 243, 245–247

political/politics: authority 41; communication style 108; community 53, 55; discourses 120, 124; domain in 125; elites 121; expediency 126–127; game 69; identity 95; ideology, spectrum of 73; logic, patterns of 85; mobilization 38; performance 89; phenomenon 149; power 6; realignment 37–38; rule, internationalization of 49; science, margins of 42; strategy 23; style 108; survey of Muslim-majority countries (Indonesia 142–144; Malaysia 139–142; Pakistan 136–139); theory 49; of vortex 321, 323, 328n1

politicians' populism 10–11

poppiewlit 306

popular culture 83–84

popular identity 54

popular movements, incorporation and neutralization of 58

populism: aim of 172; Australia 370–379; Bangladesh 190–203; bi-directional approach 207; charismatic leadership 192–193; Chinese politics 330–340; clientelism 193; and collective identity 208–210; corruption 194–195; cronyism 193–194; definition 240, 256–257, 317; and democracy 172; democracy 303–304; description 172–173; exclusionary 257; exclusionary/right-wing 163, 164, 171; Fiji 396–408; gender and violence 210–212; ideational approach 208; ideational conceptualization 171; inclusionary 257; India 163–173; Indonesia 288–300; Japan 357–367; local, Osaka and Tokyo 361–363; Maldives 240–251; Maoist 212–215; Myanmar 258–265; Nepal 207–219; New Zealand 383–393; Pakistan 176–187; peace agreement to gender gains and fragmentation 215–218; Philippines 271–285; as political framing 344–345; political mobilization 172; as political strategy 256–258; polysemy of 396; populist parties 257; South Korea 316–328; Sri Lanka 223–237; Taiwan 343–354; Thailand 305–312; as thin ideology 163; *see also* inclusionary/left-wing populism

populism/populists 65; in Asia Pacific (ambiguity of nationalism and national identity 11–12; contemporary 5–8; description of 8–10; economic inequalities 12–13; fragility of politicians 10–11; minimal electoral democracy 13; online media, gender, and anti-science discourse 14–15; populist politics 3–4; significance of secularism 14); characteristics of 58; classification of 23; communication, study of 108–109; concept of 3, 54; contemporary academic literature on 5; contemporary debates on 91; contemporary usage 8; cycles of 10; definition of 3, 22, 54, 78–79, 108; distinctive features of 4; dual nature 53; idea of 54; ideational encapsulation of 23; illiberal tendencies of 37; 'inner logic' of 89–90; international perspective of 55–56; international rise of 49; manifestation of 23; nationalism 21, 25, 225, 231, 232, 235; nature of 54; organizations, internal feature of 41; peace 281; precondition of 128; regional contexts as 8; research into 74; sociological roots of 38; strategy 38; theoretical prototypes of 67

populist radical right (PRR) 77, 84–85; conceptualization of women 82; description of 77–78; discourse 80–81; gender: and populist radical right 78–81; ideologies 85; politics 78, 79, 81–82; and religion 81–85

post-colonial cleavages 11–12

post-colonial populism 50

Postel, C. 7

post-secular society 125

poverty: reduction 72; reduction of 66

power: patrimonial forms of 40; sharing 99

pracha-niyom (people-popular) 306

pragmatic/transactional democracy 376
prai (peasants) 307
Prasetyo, E. 294, 295
President Xi's Message 336, 341n12
press freedom 163, 164
Prince Norodom Sihanouk 123
pro-business populism 66, 69–71
procedural authoritarianism 262
programmatic parties 43–45
Progressive Party of Maldives (PPM) 241
Prohibition of Objectionable Matter Act of 1976 169
pro-independence vs. pro-unification 347
pro-people diplomacy 60
Prophet Muhammad 177, 183
pseudopopulist 197
Public Attorney's Office (PAO) 152, 153
public awareness 151
public health: crises 149; institutions 156; policy 153–154; programme 72
public policy 68, 153
public-private partnerships (PPP) 72
public support, degree of 151
Pulse Asia 276
punctuated equilibrium theory 92
Purnama, B. T. 28, 31
Putin, V. 282

Qarase, L. 399–401
Quaid-i-Awam 176
quasi-democratic populism (QDP) 198–199
quasi-populism 197–198
Quezon, M. L. 272
Quijada, J. B. 129

Rabuka, S. 396–407
racialization of religion 84
racialized boundary 81, 83
radicalism 232
radical-right politics 79
radical socio-economic transformation 94
Rahman, S. M. 195–197, 202
Rahman, Z. 197–198
Rajapaksa, G. 4, 10, 32, 122, 224, 227, 231, 233, 234
Rajapaksa, M. 32, 127, 224, 227–229, 232, 233, 235
rapid urbanization 38
Rashtriya Sevika Samiti 82
Rashtriya Swayamsevak Sangh (RSS) 77, 169
Ray, A. N. 167
Razak, N. 140
Realmeter 326, 328n3
redistributive measures 69
redistributive populism 67, 69
Red Shirts 307, 308

Red Songs 333–335
Reform Before Election 310
regional/regionalism 59, 322; cooperation 60; institutions 60; integration 59; structures of 60
Reinemann, C. 108
religio-moral populism 135
religion/religious 84–85, 136; in Asia 121–125; atheist state 129–130; description of 120–121; emotional and moral content of 121; freedom of 28; groups 128; ideology, emotional and moral content of 127; inter-connectedness of 125; minorities 14, 93–94; nationalism 25–26, 29, 32; others 122; pluralism 127, 128; and politics 127; populism and 121, 128, 134–135, 240, 241, 243, 245, 249, 252; role of 123; secularism and 125–126; secular state 128–129; semi-secular state 126–128; and state 126; strategic use of 121
reluctant populist 67
re-politicization 8
Ressa, M. 279
revolutionary force against tradition 90–91
Rhee, S. 318–321, 323, 325, 327, 328
Rice Tariffication Law of 2019 283
right-wing: discourse 81; populism 58
Rikken-minshuto (Constitutional Democratic Party) 363
Rise and Fall of a Young Turk, The (Muldoon) 385
Rizvi, H.-A. 138–139
Roberts, K. M. 172
Rohingya crisis 260–261
Rohingya Muslims 122
Romeo Jihad 83
Roth, J. 80
Routledge Handbook of Global Populism, The 396
Rovira Kaltwasser, C. 256, 263
Royal Air Force (RAF) 242
royal nationalist ideology 307
Roy, S. 94
rule-based party mechanisms 42
ruler-ruled relationship 8
Rural Doctors Society 68

Saffron Revolution 2008 98
Salafi-inspired morality 134
Salary Standardization Law 283
sameness 207, 209, 212, 213, 215
sangha 258
Sangh Parivar 82, 95
sasana 264
Savage, M. J. 385, 386, 392

savvy social media 111
Scandinavia, developments in 85
Schaffer, C. 346
Scott, A. 14, 261
secularism/secularization 28–29, 97, 122, 125, 128–130, 278–279; contentious issue of 125; degree of 121; of government and society 14; ideological practice of 120; significance of 14
secular state 128–129; mechanisms of 129
securitization 53, 122, 278–279, 280
Seddon, R. J. 384–386, 392
Sein, T. 97, 99
self/other dilemma 388
self-sustained oligarchy 69
Selth, A. 263
semi-secular state 126–128
separatism 228
Sereno, M. L. 279
Seymour, D. 391
Shah, A. 177
shalishi (sharia-based arbitration) 201
Sharif, N. M. 137, 182
Shekhar, C. 169
Shia Hazara protestors 138
Shihab, M. R. 143
Shinawatra, T. 44, 59, 67–69, 150, 151, 224, 305–311, 323, 345; drug war 150–151, 156; growth policies 68; model of developmental populism 73; populist regime 67; reluctant populist 67; TRT 67–68; universal health coverage policy 68
Shui-bian, C. 346
Shwe, U. A. 259
Shyu, H. 345, 348
Sinclair, K. 386
Sing a Folk Song to the Party 336, 340n9
Singapore: populists 129; secularism 128
Singh, P. N. 169
Singh, S. 80
single non-transferable vote (SNTV) system 365
Sinhala Buddhist nationalist ideology 224, 228
Sinhala Only Language Act 229
Sinhalese kings in Ceylon 126
Sinpeng, A. 113, 117
Sirisena, M. 233
Sison, J. M. 273, 274
social class 39
social cronyism 194
Social Democratic Party (SDP) 343
social disruption 37–38
socialism 65, 130
socialist populism 130
social media: code of conduct 294, 298; communication 111; elite-non-elite divide 289, 292–299; Instagram 289, 290, 292–296, 298; populism and 110–111; role of 110; and Yudhoyono, A. 290–300
social movements 56
social 'othering' 130
social polarization 96, 128
social transformation 129
social vulnerability 66
Social Weather Station poll in 2016 72
socio-cultural approach 23
socio-economic inequality 12
socio-political contexts 90, 123
socio-political evolution 65
soft populism 224–225; fragility and instability 225; populist nationalism 225
Soga, K. 366
solid economic nationalism 70
Solih, I. M. 240, 241, 249–251
Song of Praise, the 335, 340n3
Soqosoqo Dua ni Lewenivanua (SDL) 399, 400
Soqosoqo ni Vakavulewa ni Taukei (SVT) party 398
South Asia, radical-right populism in 78
Southeast Asian Treaty Organization (SEATO) 178
Southeast Asia, variation of populism in 66
South Korea: and Asian financial crisis 322–325; decolonization 317–318; democratization and regionalism 321–322; governmental party establishment 319–321; ideological division 325–327; political context 327–328
sovereign people 334
sovereignty 52, 59, 60, 66; functioning of 56; in international system 56
Special Powers Act 200
Speight, G. 397
squattocracy 385
Sri Lanka 27–28, 121; ethnicity and language 225–226; leadership and political personalism 232–234; LTTE 228–232, 234, 236; Muslims 227; nationalist politics and populist project investments 234–235; new social polarization 229–231; populist-nationalist shift 228–229; post-colonial 226, 227; pure people 225–227; school system 226; Sinhala Buddhist nationalism in 77; soft populism 224–225
Sri Lanka Freedom Party (SLFP) 229
Sri Lanka Muslim Congress (SLMC) 227
Sri Lanka Podujana Peramuna (SLPP) 231
Srimuang, C. 309
state formation 11, 95–98, 123, 227, 229, 237, 271

State Law and Order Restoration Council (SLORC) 259
State Peace and Development Council (SPDC) 259
state-society relations 60
Stavrakakis, Y. 21
strategic approach to populism: and charismatic leadership 39–41; critics of 38; description of 37; and illiberalism 44–45; leadership 41–43; origins of 37–39; strategy and discourse 43–44
strategic discursive perspective 50
Strömbäck, J. 109
strong social media presence 115
structural crisis 58
structural inequality 373
Subedi, D. B. 14, 224, 261
Subianto, P. 143–144, 288
Sufism 227, 248
Suharto 142
Sui-bien, C. 323
Sukarnoputri, M. 143
Sunflower Movement, 2014 343
Sunni-Islam 138
Susilo Bambang Yudhoyono (SBY) 288–290, 296, 297, 299
Suu Kyi, Aung San 258–260, 263–265
swabhasha (own vernacular) movement 226, 229, 230
Swedish political party 77

Tabloid media 110
Tae-Woo, R. 321, 322
Tahir-ul-Qadri, M. 137
taing-yin-tha 260
Taipei Agricultural Products Marketing Corporation (TAPMC) 351
Taiwan: anti-elitism 349–350; DPP 353; populism as political framing 344–345; presidential campaign, 2019–20 350–353; short-lived populism in 73; Taiwanese identity 346–348; Taiwanese nationalism 348–349
Taliban 137
Tax Reform for Acceleration and Inclusion (TRAIN) 282, 284
technocratic populism 69–70
Tehreek-e-Insaf party 30
Tehreek-e-Labbaik Pakistan (TLP) 139
Telegraph 180
Teng-hui, L. 345
Thablighi Jamaat 227
Thailand 71–72; anti-populism to anti-democracy 308–311; drug addicts in 156; drug war in 149–151; economic development model 58–59; economic growth 67; neoliberal policies 304; populism, allegations of 305–307; populist responses 307–308; royal nationalist ideology 307; traditional elites 59; TRT 305–307; weaponizing populism 305
Thai Rak Thai Party (TRT) 67, 68, 74n1, 305–307, 310, 345
Thaksina-prachaniyom (Anek) 306
Thaksinocracy 306
Thaksinomics, growth strategies in 68
Thaugsuban, S. 310
Thawheed ideology 227
Thawheed Jamaat, the 227
Theravada Buddhism 225, 226, 258, 259
Theravada tradition 98
thin-centred ideology 78, 79
thin ideology 65
Thirty-Eighth Amendment to the Constitution 170
Tin, U. U. 259
Tin, U. W. 259
Toai, D. 365
Tomin-first-no-Kaî (Tokyoites First Party) 363
top-down populism 29–33
trade multilateralism 58
traditional camps, incoherent and chaotic by 65
traditional media 111
Treaty Lunacy and Treaty People 387
Treaty of Waitangi, 1840 384, 387
Triple Talaq Bill 84
Trump, D. 4, 43, 49, 51, 58–59, 65, 107, 108, 110, 112, 176, 224, 282, 304, 332
Tsuji, A. 366
Turkey 136
Tushnet, M. 8

Uchiyama, Y. 359
Uighur Muslims 130
ultra-nationalism 4
Umar, M. 296
ummah 178, 180, 183, 243
ummah ideology 135
Union Solidarity and Development Party (USDP) 259
United Front for Democracy Against Dictatorship (UDD) 307
United Malays National Organization (UMNO) 139
United Nations Human Rights Council 59
United Parents Against Dengvaxia Philippines 153
Universal Access to Quality Tertiary Education Act 283
Universal Health Care Act 283
Unlawful Association Act 261, 262
Urbinati, N. 172
us-vs.-them dichotomy 149
us vs. themrhetoric 209, 211, 215, 249

vaccination programme 155–156
van Dijk, T. A. 291, 292
van Leeuwen, T. 289, 292
Varshney, A. 22, 224
Veenendaal, W. 406–408
Venugopal, R. 228
Village and Urban Revolving Fund 68
violent populism 271
Vishva Hindu Parishad (VHP) 77, 83, 121
Vishwa Keerti Sri Sinhaladhishwara 234
Visiting Forces Agreement, 1999 281
volonté générale (general will) 163

Wahabism 227
Waisbord, S. 108
Walgrave, S. 108
Wall Street Journal 180
war on drugs 270, 276, 278, 307
War on Terror 23
Wazed, S. H. 31
wealth inequality 12
weaponizing populism: anti-populism to anti-democracy 308–311; populism, allegations of 305–307; populist responses 307–308; traditional elites, Thailand 305, 306; TRT 305–307, 310
We Are Marching Along the Wide Road 335, 340n2
Wear, R. 372
Webb, A. 112
Weber, M. 37–40, 42, 91, 92; account of plebiscitary-charismatic leadership 91; forms of authority 39
welfare policies 69
Western Europe, statehood and citizenship in 121
Western imperialism 25–26

Western-influenced view of populism 59
Westminster system, The 196
Weyland, K. 23, 42–43
Wickremasinghe, R. 233
Widodo, J. 4, 69, 288
Wiles, P. 396
Wimalajothi, K. 231
Winichakul, T. 309
Without the Communist Party There Would Be No New China 336, 340n8
Wodak, R. 80
Wojczewski, T. 53
World Economic Forum in January_ 2021 154
world politics, counter-normative discourse of 56
World Trade Organisation (WTO) 23–24, 59, 283

Xiaoping, D. 334

Yameen, A. 240, 241, 247–249
Yassin, M. 141–142
Yilmaz, I. 136
Young-Sam, K. 321–323
Yudhoyono, A. S. 290–300
Yudhoyono, S. B. 70, 288–290, 296, 297, 299
Yuval-Davis, N. 82–83
Yu, V. G. 152

Zardari, A. 179
Zedong, M. 335, 337
Zemin, J. 334
Zia, K. 199–202
Zia-ul-Haq 184
Ziblatt, D. 377, 378
Zulehner, P. 122
Zürn, M. 8